MACROECONOMICS

FOURTEENTH CANADIAN EDITION

MACROECONOMICS

FOURTEENTH CANADIAN EDITION

CHRISTOPHER T.S. RAGAN

McGill University

PEARSON

Toronto

Vice-President, Editorial Director: Gary Bennett
Editor-in-Chief: Nicole Lukach
Acquisitions Editor: Claudine O'Donnell
Marketing Manager: Leigh-Anne Graham
Developmental Editor: Suzanne Schaan
Project Manager: Andrea Falkenberg
Production Editor: Melinda Durham
Project Coordination and Editorial Services: Electronic Publishing Services Inc., NYC
Copy Editor: Linda Jenkins
Proofreader: Megan Smith-Creed
Compositor: Jouve
Photo Researcher: Marta Johnson
Permissions Researcher: Marnie Lamb
Art Director: Julia Hall
Interior Designer: Opushouse Inc./Sonya Thursby
Cover Designer: Miriam Blier
Cover Image: Steve McDonald

---

10 9 8 7 6 5 4 3 2

Library and Archives Canada Cataloguing in Publication

Ragan, Christopher
    Macroeconomics / Christopher T.S. Ragan. — 14th Canadian ed.

Includes index.
ISBN 978-0-321-79488-8

1. Macroeconomics—Textbooks. 2. Macroeconomics—Canada—Textbooks. I. Title.

HB172.5.R35 2013   339   C2012-906729-6

ISBN 978-0-321-79488-8

Brief Contents

Contents

List of Boxes

Applying Economic Concepts

Lessons from History

Extensions in Theory

Additional Topics on MyEconLab (www.myeconlab.com)

Economics is a living discipline, changing and evolving in response to developments in the world economy and in response to the research of many thousands of economists throughout the world. Through fourteen editions, *Macroeconomics* has evolved with the discipline. Our purpose in this edition, as in the previous thirteen, is to provide students with an introduction to the major issues facing the world's economies, to the methods that economists use to study those issues, and to the policy problems that those issues create. Our treatment is everywhere guided by three important principles:

1. Economics is *scientific*, in the sense that it progresses through the systematic confrontation of theory by evidence. Neither theory nor data alone can tell us much about the world, but combined they tell us a great deal.

2. Economics is *useful*, and it should be seen by students to be so. An understanding of economic theory combined with knowledge about the economy produces many important insights about economic policy. Although we stress these insights, we are also careful to point out cases in which too little is known to support strong statements about public policy. Appreciating what is not known is as important as learning what is known.

3. We strive always to be *honest* with our readers. Although we know that economics is not always easy, we do not approve of glossing over difficult bits of analysis without letting readers see what is happening and what has been assumed. We take whatever space is needed to explain why economists draw their conclusions, rather than just asserting the conclusions. We also take pains to avoid simplifying matters so much that students would have to unlearn what they have been taught if they continue their study beyond the introductory course. In short, we have tried to follow Albert Einstein's advice:

Everything should be made as simple as possible, but not simpler.

Current Economic Issues

In writing the fourteenth edition of *Macroeconomics*, we have tried to reflect the major economic issues that we face in the early twenty-first century.

Living Standards and Economic Growth

One of the most fundamental economic issues is the determination of overall living standards. Adam Smith wondered why some countries become wealthy while others remain poor. Though we have learned much about this topic in the past 240 years since Adam Smith's landmark work, economists recognize that there is still much we do not know.

Technological change plays a central role in our discussions of long-run economic growth in Chapters 25 and 26. We explore not only the traditional channels of saving, investment, and population growth, but also the more recent economic theories that emphasize the importance of increasing returns and endogenous growth.

We are convinced that no other introductory economics textbook places as much emphasis on technological change and economic growth as we do in this book. Given the importance of continuing growth in living standards and understanding where that growth comes from, we believe this emphasis is appropriate. We hope you agree.

Financial Crisis, Recession, and Recovery

The collapse of U.S. housing prices in 2007 led to a global financial crisis the likes of which had not been witnessed in a century, and perhaps longer. A deep recession, experienced in many countries, followed quickly on its heels. These dramatic events reawakened many people to two essential facts about economics. First, modern economies *can and do* go into recession. This essential fact had perhaps been forgotten by many who had become complacent after more than two decades of economic prosperity. Second, financial markets are crucial to the operation of modern economies. Like an electricity system, the details of financial markets are a mystery to most people, and the system itself is often ignored when it is functioning properly. But when financial markets cease to work smoothly and interest rates rise while credit flows decline, we are all reminded of their importance. In this sense, the financial crisis of 2007–2008 was like a global power failure for the world economy.

The financial crisis had many macro consequences. It affected the Canadian banking system, discussed in Chapter 27, and led to some aggressive actions by the Bank of Canada, as discussed in Chapter 29. Moreover, as the global financial crisis led to a deep recession worldwide, Canadian fiscal policy was forced to respond, as we review in Chapters 24 and 32. Finally, as has happened several times in history, the recession raised the threat of protectionist policies, as we examine in Chapter 34.

Globalization

Enormous changes have occurred throughout the world over the last few decades. Flows of trade and investment between countries have risen so dramatically that it is now common to speak of the "globalization" of the world economy. Today it is no longer possible to study any economy without taking into account developments in the rest of the world.

Throughout its history, Canada has been a trading nation, and our policies relating to international trade have often been at the centre of political debates. International trade shows up in many parts of this textbook, but it is the exclusive focus of two chapters. Chapter 33 discusses the theory of the gains from trade; Chapter 34 explores trade policy, with an emphasis on NAFTA and the WTO.

With globalization and the international trade of goods and assets come fluctuations in exchange rates. In recent years there have been substantial changes in the Canada–U.S. exchange rate—a 15-percent depreciation followed the Asian economic crisis in 1997–1998, and an even greater appreciation occurred in the 2002–2008 period. Such volatility in exchange rates complicates the conduct of economic policy. In Chapters 28 and 29 we explore how the exchange rate fits into the design and operation of Canada's monetary policy. In Chapter 35 we examine the debate between fixed and flexible exchange rates.

The forces of globalization are with us to stay. In this fourteenth edition of *Macroeconomics*, we have done our best to ensure that students are made aware of the world outside Canada and how events elsewhere in the world affect the Canadian economy.

The Role of Government

Between 1980 and 2008, the political winds shifted in Canada, the United States, and many other countries. Political parties that previously advocated a greater role for government in the economy argued the benefits of limited government. But the political winds shifted again with the arrival of the financial crisis and global recession in 2008, which led governments the world over to take some unprecedented actions. Many soon argued that we were observing the "end of laissez-faire" and witnessing the return of "big government." But was that really true?

Has the *fundamental* role of government changed significantly over the past 35 years? In order to understand the role of government in the economy, students must understand the benefits of free markets as well as the situations that cause markets to fail. They must also understand that governments often intervene in the economy for reasons related more to equity than to efficiency.

In this fourteenth edition of *Macroeconomics*, we continue to incorporate the discussion of government policy as often as possible. Here are but a few of the many examples that we explore:

- fiscal policy (in Chapters 22 and 24)
- policies related to the economy's long-run growth rate (in Chapter 26)
- monetary policy (in Chapters 28, 29, and 30)
- policies that affect the economy's long-run unemployment rate (in Chapter 31)
- the importance of debt and deficits (in Chapter 32)
- trade policies (in Chapter 34)
- policies related to the exchange rate (in Chapter 35)

The Book

Economic growth, financial crisis and recession, globalization, and the role of government are pressing issues of the day. Much of our study of economic principles and the Canadian economy has been shaped by these issues. In addition to specific coverage of growth and internationally oriented topics, growth and globalization appear naturally throughout the book in the treatment of many topics once thought to be entirely "domestic."

Most chapters of *Macroeconomics* contain some discussion of economic policy. We have two main goals in mind when we present these discussions:

1. We aim to give students practice in using economic theory, because applying theory is both a wonderfully effective teaching method and a reliable test of students' grasp of theory.

2. We want to introduce students to the major policy issues of the day and to let them discover that few policy debates are as "black and white" as they often appear in the press.

Both goals reflect our view that students should see economics as useful in helping us to understand and deal with the world around us.

Structure and Coverage

Our treatment of macroeconomics is divided into six parts. We make a clear distinction between the economy in the short run and the economy in the long run, and we get quickly to the material on long-run economic growth. Students are confronted with issues of long-run economic growth *before* they are introduced to issues of money and banking. Given the importance of economic growth in driving overall living standards, we believe that this is an appropriate ordering of the material, but for those who prefer to discuss money before thinking about economic growth, the order can be easily switched without any loss of continuity.

The first macro chapter, Chapter 19, introduces readers to the central macro variables, what they mean, and why they are important. The discussion of national income accounting in Chapter 20 provides a thorough treatment of the distinction between real and nominal GDP, the distinction between GDP and GNP, and a discussion of what measures of national income *do not measure* and whether these omissions really matter.

Part 8 develops the core short-run model of the macro economy, beginning with the fixed-price (Keynesian Cross) model in Chapters 21 and 22 and then moving on to the *AD/AS* model in Chapter 23. Chapter 21 uses a closed economy model with no government to explain the process of national-income determination and the nature of the multiplier. Chapter 22 extends the setting to include international trade and government spending and taxation. Chapter 23 rounds out our discussion of the short run with the *AD/AS* framework, discussing the

importance of both aggregate demand and aggregate supply shocks. We place the Keynesian Cross before the *AD/AS* model to show that there is no mystery about where the *AD* curve comes from and why it is downward sloping; the *AD* curve is derived directly from the Keynesian Cross model. In contrast, books that begin their analysis with the *AD/AS* model are inevitably less clear about where the model comes from. We lament the growing tendency to omit the Keynesian Cross from introductory macroeconomics textbooks; we believe the model has much to offer students in terms of economic insights.

Part 9 begins in Chapter 24 by showing how the short-run model evolves toward the long run through the adjustment of factor prices—what we often call the Phillips curve. We introduce potential output as an "anchor" to which real GDP returns following *AD* or *AS* shocks. This chapter also addresses issues in fiscal policy, including the important distinction between automatic stabilizers and discretionary fiscal stabilization policy. Chapter 25 is a short chapter that contrasts short-run with long-run macroeconomics, emphasizing the different typical causes of output changes over the two time spans. Using Canadian data, we show that long-run changes in GDP have their root causes in changes in factor supplies and productivity, whereas short-run changes in GDP are more closely associated with changes in the factor utilization rate. With this short-run/long-run distinction firmly in place, we are well positioned for the detailed discussion of long-run economic growth that appears in Chapter 26. Our treatment of long-run growth, which we regard as one of the most important issues facing Canada and the world today, goes well beyond the treatment in most introductory texts.

Part 10 focuses on the role of money and financial systems. Chapter 27 discusses the nature of money, various components of the money supply, the commercial banking system, and the Bank of Canada. In Chapter 28 we offer a detailed discussion of the link between the money market and other economic variables such as interest rates, the exchange rate, national income, and the price level. In Chapter 29 we discuss the Bank of Canada's monetary policy, including a detailed discussion of inflation targeting. The chapter ends with a review of Canadian monetary policy over the past 30 years.

Part 11 deals with some of today's most pressing macroeconomic policy issues. It contains separate chapters on inflation, unemployment, and government budget deficits. Chapter 30 on inflation examines the central role of expectations in determining inflation and the importance of credibility on the part of the central bank. Chapter 31 on unemployment examines the determinants of frictional and structural unemployment and discusses likely reasons for increases in the NAIRU over the past few decades. Chapter 32 on budget deficits stresses the effect of deficits on long-term economic growth.

Virtually every macroeconomic chapter contains at least some discussion of international issues. However, the final part of *Macroeconomics* focuses primarily on international economics. Chapter 33 gives the basic treatment of international trade, developing both the traditional theory of static comparative advantage and newer theories based on imperfect competition and dynamic comparative advantage. Chapter 34 discusses both the positive and normative aspects of trade policy, as well as the WTO and NAFTA. Chapter 35 introduces the balance of payments and examines exchange-rate determination. Here we also discuss three important policy issues: the desirability of current-account deficits or surpluses, whether there is a "right" value for the Canadian exchange rate, and the costs and benefits of Canada's adopting a fixed exchange rate.

We hope you find this menu both attractive and challenging; we hope students find the material stimulating and enlightening. Many of the messages of economics are complex—if economic understanding were only a matter of common sense and simple observation, there would be no need for professional economists and no need for textbooks like this one. To understand economics, one must work hard. Working at this book should help readers gain a better understanding of the world around them and of the policy problems faced by all levels of government. Furthermore, in today's globalized world, the return to education is large. We like to think that we have contributed in some small part to the understanding that increased investment in human capital by the next generation is necessary to restore incomes to the rapid growth paths that so benefited our parents and our peers. Perhaps we may even contribute to some income-enhancing accumulation of human capital by some of our readers.

Substantive Changes to This Edition

We have revised and updated the entire text with guidance from an extensive series of formal reviews and other feedback from both users and nonusers of the previous editions of this book. As always, we have striven very hard to improve the teachability and readability of the book. We have focused the discussions so that each major point is emphasized as clearly as possible, without distracting the reader with nonessential points. *Additional Topics*, available on MyEconLab (www.myeconlab.com), address theoretical, empirical, and policy discussions that are interesting but optional. (A complete listing of the *Additional Topics* is provided following the Contents after the List of Boxes.) As in recent editions, we have kept all core material in the main part of the text. Three types of boxes (Applying Economic Concepts, Lessons from History, and Extensions in Theory) are used to show examples or extensions that can be skipped without fear of missing an essential concept. But we think it would be a shame to skip too many of them, as there are many interesting examples and policy discussions in these boxes.

What follows is a brief listing of the main changes that we have made to the textbook.

Microeconomics Introduction

Part 1: What Is Economics?
Chapter 1 has been significantly rewritten and rearranged. We now begin with a brief discussion of six key issues in the Canadian and world economies, and then turn to examine resources and scarcity, coordination in markets, and alternative economic systems. We have added a discussion of the role of economic policy. In Chapter 2, we have improved our discussion of the nature of theories, causation, and predictions, and we have added a new box discussing where economists get jobs and what kinds of work they do.

Part 2: An Introduction to Demand and Supply
In Chapter 3 on the basics of demand and supply, we have added a new box explaining why the model works well for commodities (like apples) but not so well for differentiated products (like iPhones).

Macroeconomics

Part 7: An Introduction to Macroeconomics
We motivate Chapter 19 with a new discussion of the onset and effects of the global financial crisis, as well as the associated debates over the role of government intervention. We have improved our discussion of output gaps and the meaning of full employment. In Chapter 20, we have expanded our discussion of whether and why the omissions from GDP matter.

Part 8: The Economy in the Short Run

In Chapter 21, we have clarified the key assumptions used in the short-run macro model. In Chapter 22, we have sharpened the discussion about fiscal policy in the final section. In Chapter 23, we have streamlined and improved our discussion of the slope of the AS curve, and we have simplified our discussion of how technological changes shift the curve. We have also clarified the existing box on the Keynesian AS curve.

Part 9: The Economy in the Long Run

In Chapter 24, we have clarified what we mean by the short run, the adjustment process, and the long run. We clarify the assumption that AD and AS shocks do not change the value of Y^*, but state that this assumption is debated (and addressed in later chapters). We have improved our discussion of the paradox of thrift and the motivation for fiscal stabilization policy. When examining the connection between fiscal policy and growth, we now address the possibility that fiscal policy may have a direct effect on Y^* and thereby reduce the extent of crowding out. In Chapter 25, we have streamlined the opening discussions about inflation and Japanese growth. We have also added a new box explaining what productivity growth "really looks like" in some easy-to-imagine occupational settings. Chapter 26 on long-run economic growth now has a substantially improved introduction. We have deleted the old boxes on "growth is good" and "growth is bad" but have added a new box outlining the modern and respectable arguments against continued growth in the developed economies. We have shortened the discussion of the opportunity cost of growth, and we have improved our discussion of the limits to growth.

Part 10: Money, Banking, and Monetary Policy

In Chapter 27 we have rewritten and modernized the discussion of deposit money and have streamlined the discussion of commercial banks. In Chapter 28, we have added more on riskiness to our existing discussion of bonds, including reference to some European countries today. We have completely rewritten our section on the neutrality and nonneutrality of money and have added new discussions on hysteresis effects—two reasons why Y^* may be affected by changes in the money supply. We have also added a new box on money neutrality as it applies to monetary reform and a new discussion of the connection between inflation and money growth across countries. In Chapter 29, we have clarified our discussion of how the Bank achieves its target for the overnight rate. We have entirely rewritten our discussion about the motivation for the adoption of inflation targeting, and also about the role of the output gap, although the central messages are unchanged.

Part 11: Macroeconomic Problems and Policies

In Chapter 30, we have streamlined the discussion of accelerating inflation and have substantially shortened the discussion of the three phases of a disinflation. In Chapter 31 on unemployment, we have added a new discussion of discouraged workers and underemployment. We have also entirely rewritten our discussion of competing theories of the labour market—now posed as market-clearing versus non-market-clearing theories. We have deleted the old box on RBC models but have added a new box on additional reasons for wage stickiness. Chapter 32 examines debt and deficits. We have deleted the old box on the algebra of debt dynamics (which now occurs in a math note) and have added a new box that applies the debt-dynamics equation to the situation of Greece in 2011. We have reworked the section on crowding out and make the point that if the fiscal expansion increases the value of Y^* then the extent of crowding out will fall. We have deleted the old box on foreign-held debt and also deleted the repetitive section on the effect of budget surpluses. We have improved the discussion of fiscal rules, especially regarding the emphasis on a relatively stable debt-to-GDP ratio.

Part 12: Canada in the Global Economy

Chapter 33 on the gains from international trade has been updated and revised, but there is no substantial change to its structure or messages. In Chapter 34, we have reworked and clarified our discussion of the case for protection. We have shortened the discussion of countervailing duties but expanded the discussion and examples of national treatment in NAFTA. We have also streamlined our discussion of the ongoing WTO Doha round. Our mention of the new Trans Pacific Partnership now leads us to a new box on the ongoing drive to diversify Canada's trade. In Chapter 35, we have clarified our explanation for why the balance of payments must balance, and we have simplified our discussion of why changes in export prices lead to exchange-rate fluctuations.

* * *

If you are moved to write to us (and we hope that you will be!), please do. You can send any comments or questions regarding the text (or any of the supplementary material, such as the *Instructor's Manual*, the *Study Guide*, the *TestGen*, or the web-based *Additional Topics*) to:

Christopher Ragan
Department of Economics
McGill University
855 Sherbrooke St. West
Montreal, Quebec H3A 2T7
e-mail: christopher.ragan@mcgill.ca

To the Student

Welcome to what is most likely your first book about economics! You are about to encounter what is for most people a new way of thinking, which often causes people to see things differently than they did before. But learning a new way of thinking is not always easy, and you should expect some hard work ahead. We do our best to be as clear and logical as possible and to illustrate our arguments whenever possible with current and interesting examples.

You must develop your own technique for studying, but the following suggestions may prove helpful. Begin by carefully considering the Learning Objectives at the beginning of a chapter. Read the chapter itself relatively quickly in order to get the general idea of the argument. At this first reading, you may want to skip the boxes and any footnotes. Then, after reading the Summary and the Key Concepts (at the end of each chapter), reread the chapter more slowly, making sure that you understand each step of the argument.

With respect to the figures and tables, be sure you understand how the conclusions that are stated in boldface at the beginning of each caption have been reached. You should be prepared to spend time on difficult sections; occasionally, you may spend an hour on only a few pages. Paper and pencil are indispensable equipment in your reading. It is best to follow a difficult argument by building your own diagram while the argument unfolds rather than by relying on the finished diagram as it appears in the book.

The end-of-chapter Study Exercises require you to practise using some of the concepts that you learned in the chapter. These will be excellent preparation for your exams. To provide you with immediate feedback, we have posted Solutions to Selected Study Exercises on MyEconLab (www.myeconlab.Com). We strongly advise that you should seek to understand economics, not to memorize it.

The red numbers in square brackets in the text refer to a series of mathematical notes that are found starting on page M-1 at the end of the book. For those of you who like mathematics or prefer mathematical argument to verbal or geometric exposition, these may prove useful. Others may disregard them.

In this edition of the book, we have incorporated many elements to help you review material and prepare for examinations. A brief description of all the features in this book is given in the separate section that follows.

We encourage you to make use of MyEconLab that accompanies this book (www.myeconlab.com) at the outset of your studies. MyEconLab contains a wealth of valuable resources to help you. MyEconLab provides Solutions to Selected Study Exercises. It also includes many additional practice questions, some of which are modelled on Study Exercises in the book. MyEconLab also contains many *Additional Topics*—these represent material written especially for this textbook and include many interesting theoretical, empirical, and policy discussions. You can also find animations of some of the key figures in the text, marked with the symbol ☼ below the figure number, as well as an electronic version of the textbook. For more details about MyEconLab, please see the description on p. ii.

We strongly suggest you make use of the excellent *Study Guide* written expressly for this text. The *Study Guide* is closely integrated with the book; it offers practice questions and exercises that will test and reinforce your understanding of the concepts and analytical techniques stressed in each chapter of the text and will help you prepare for your examinations. Explanations are provided for the answers to many of the Multiple-Choice Questions to facilitate your independent study. Being able to solve problems and to communicate and interpret your results are important goals in an introductory course in economics. The *Study Guide* can play a crucial role in your acquisition of these skills.

Over the years, the book has benefited greatly from comments and suggestions we have received from students. Please feel free to send your comments to christopher.ragan@mcgill.ca. Good luck, and we hope you enjoy your course in economics!

Features of This Edition

We have made a careful effort with this edition to incorporate features that will facilitate the teaching and learning of economics.

- A set of **Learning Objectives** at the beginning of each chapter, correlated to the **Chapter Outline**, clarifies the skills and knowledge to be learned in each chapter. These same learning objectives are used in the chapter summaries, as well as in the *Study Guide*.

- **Major ideas** are highlighted with a yellow background in the text.

- **Key terms** are boldfaced where they are defined in the body of the text and they are restated with their definitions in the margins. In the index at the back of the book, each key term and the page reference to its definition are boldfaced.

- **Weblinks** to useful Internet addresses are given in the margins. Each weblink presents a URL address, along with a brief description of the material available there. Some links are to government home pages where you can obtain much additional data. Other links are to organizations such as OPEC, the UN, and the WTO.

- The **colour scheme for figures** consistently uses the same colour for each type of curve. For example, all demand curves are blue and all supply curves are red.

- **A caption for each figure and table** summarizes the underlying economic reasoning. Each caption begins with a boldfaced statement of the relevant economic conclusion.

- **Applying Economic Concepts** boxes demonstrate economics in action, providing examples of how theoretical material relates to issues of current interest.

- **Extensions in Theory** boxes provide a deeper treatment of a theoretical topic that is discussed in the text.

- **Lessons from History** boxes contain discussions of a particular policy debate or empirical finding that takes place in a historical context.

- **Photographs with short captions** are interspersed throughout the chapters to illustrate some of the arguments.

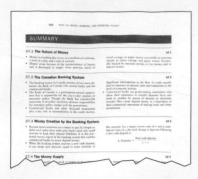

- **Chapter Summaries** are organized using the same numbered heading as found in the body of the chapter. The relevant Learning Objective (LO) numbers are given in red next to each heading in the summary.
- **Key Concepts** are listed near the end of each chapter.

- A set of **Study Exercises** is provided for each chapter. These often quantitative exercises require the student to analyze problems by means of computations, graphs, or explanations.

- A set of **Mathematical Notes** is presented in a separate section near the end of the book. Because mathematical notation and derivations are not necessary to understand the principles of economics but are more helpful in advanced work, this seems to be a sensible arrangement. References in the text to these mathematical notes are given by means of red numbers in square brackets.

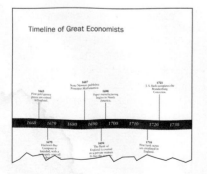

- A **Timeline of Great Economists,** extending from the mid-seventeenth century to the late twentieth century, is presented near the end of the book. Along this timeline we have placed brief descriptions of the life and works of some great economists, most of whom the reader will encounter in the textbook. The timeline also includes some major world events to give readers an appreciation for when these economists did their work.

- For convenience, a list of the **Common Abbreviations Used in the Text** is given on the final page of the text.

Supplements

A comprehensive set of supplements has been carefully prepared to assist students and instructors in using this new edition.

MyEconLab

The moment you know.

Educators know it. Students know it. It's that inspired moment when something that was difficult to understand suddenly makes perfect sense. Our MyLab products have been designed and refined with a single purpose in mind—to help educators create that moment of understanding with their students.

MyEconLab delivers proven results in helping individual students succeed. It provides engaging experiences that personalize, stimulate, and measure learning for each student. And, it comes from a trusted partner with educational expertise and an eye on the future.

MyEconLab can be used by itself or linked to any learning management system. Visit MyEconLab to learn more about how it combines proven learning applications with powerful assessment.

MyEconLab—the moment you know.

MyEconLab provides students with personalized Study Plans and the opportunity for unlimited practice. It also provides instructors with ready-to-use assignments that can be graded electronically. For more information on MyEconLab, please visit www.myeconlab.com.

Pearson eText gives students access to the text whenever and wherever they have access to the Internet. eText pages look exactly like the printed text, offering powerful new functionality for students and instructors. Users can create notes, highlight text in different colours, create bookmarks, zoom, click hyperlinked words and phrases to view definitions, and view in single-page or two-page view. Pearson eText allows for quick navigation to key parts of the eText using a table of contents and provides full-text search. The eText may also offer links to associated media files, enabling users to access videos, animations, or other activities as they read the text.

Study Guide

A robust *Study Guide*, written by Paul T. Dickinson and Gustavo Indart, is available for macroeconomics (978-0-321-82839-2). It is designed for use either in the classroom or by students on their own. The *Study Guide* offers additional study support and reinforcement for each text chapter. It is closely integrated with the textbookoffering relevant practice exercises for each chapter. To facilitate independent study, explanations are provided for about 70 percent of the answers to the Additional Multiple-Choice Questions. For each chapter, the *Study Guide* provides the following helpful material:

- Learning Objectives matching those in the textbook
- Chapter Overview
- Hints and Tips
- Chapter Review consisting of Multiple-Choice Questions, organized into sections matching the numbered sections in the textbook
- Short-Answer Questions
- Exercises
- Extension Exercises
- Additional Multiple-Choice Questions
- Solutions to all of the Questions and Exercises above
- Explanations for the answers to at least 70 percent of the Additional Multiple-Choice Questions

CourseSmart for Students

CourseSmart goes beyond traditional expectations—providing instant, online access to the textbooks and course materials you need at an average savings of 60 percent. With instant access from any computer and the ability to search your text, you'll find the content you need quickly, no matter where you are. And with online tools like highlighting and note-taking, you can save time and study efficiently. See all the benefits at www.coursesmart.com/students.

Instructor's Resource CD-ROM

The *Instructor's Resource CD-ROM* (978-0-321-88969-0) for this new edition contains the following items:

- An Instructor's Manual (in both Word and PDF format) written by Christopher Ragan. It includes full solutions to all the Study Exercises.
- A **Computerized Testbank (Pearson TestGen)** prepared by Ingrid Kristjanson and Christopher Ragan. The testbank consists of 4000 multiple-choice questions, with an emphasis on applied questions (as opposed to recall questions) and quantitative questions (as opposed to qualitative questions). Approximately 60 percent of the questions test applied skills, about 20 percent of the questions are quantitative, and about 20 percent of the questions have a graph or table. All the questions have been carefully checked for accuracy. For each question, the authors have provided the correct answer, identified the relevant section number in the textbook chapter, specified the concept being tested, assigned a level of difficulty (easy, moderate, or challenging), identified the skill tested (recall or applied), noted whether the question is qualitative or quantitative, and noted whether the question involves a graph or table. *TestGen* enables instructors to search for questions according to any of these attributes and to sort questions into any order desired. With *TestGen*, instructors can easily edit existing questions, add questions, generate tests, and print the tests in a variety of formats. *TestGen* also allows instructors to administer tests on a local area network, have the tests graded electronically, and have the results prepared in electronic or printed reports.
- **PowerPoint® Slides**, covering the key concepts of each chapter, that can be adapted for lecture presentations.
- **Clicker Questions,** consisting of more than 600 questions in PowerPoint format, that can be used with any Personal Response System.
- **An Image Library**, consisting of all the figures and tables from the textbook in gif format. These files can easily be imported into PowerPoint slides for class presentation.
- **Additional Topics,** written by Christopher Ragan, offering optional topics on a wide variety of economic subjects. A list of these topics is included in the text; students can access them on MyEconLab (www.myeconlab.com).

These instructor supplements are also available for download from a password protected section of Pearson Education Canada's online catalogue (www.pearsoncanada.ca/highered). Navigate to your book's catalogue page to view a list of those supplements that are available. See your local Pearson representative for details and access.

CourseSmart for Instructors

CourseSmart goes beyond traditional expectations—providing instant, online access to the textbooks and course materials you need at a lower cost for students. And even as students save money, you can save time and hassle with a digital eTextbook that allows you to search for the most relevant content at the very moment you need it. Whether it's evaluating textbooks or creating lecture notes to help students with difficult concepts, CourseSmart can make life a little easier. See how when you visit www.coursesmart.com/instructors.

Technology Specialists

Pearson's **Technology Specialists** work with faculty and campus course designers to ensure that Pearson technology products, assessment tools, and online course materials are tailored to meet your specific needs. This highly qualified team is dedicated to helping students take full advantage of a wide range of educational resources by assisting in the integration of a variety of instructional materials and media formats. Your local Pearson Canada sales representative can provide you with more details about this service program.

Pearson Custom Library

For enrollments of at least 25 students, you can create your own textbook by choosing the chapters that best suit your own course needs. To begin building your custom text, visit www.pearsoncustomlibrary.com. You may also work with a dedicated Pearson Custom editor to create your ideal text—publishing your own original content or mixing and matching Pearson content. Contact your local Pearson representative to get started.

Acknowledgements

It would be impossible to acknowledge here by name all the teachers, colleagues, and students who contributed to the development and improvement of this book over its previous thirteen editions. Hundreds of users have written to us with specific suggestions, and much of the credit for the improvement of the book over the years belongs to them. We can no longer list them individually but we thank them all sincerely.

For the development of this fourteenth edition, we are grateful to the many people who offered informal suggestions. We would also like to thank the following instructors who provided us with formal reviews of the textbook. Their observations and recommendations were extremely helpful.

- Benjamin Atkinson (Mount Royal University)
- Iris Au (University of Toronto Scarborough)
- Lee Bailey (University of Toronto Mississauga)
- Natalya Brown (Nipissing University)
- Marilyn Cottrell (Brock University)
- Ajit Dayanandan (University of Northern British Columbia)
- Paul Dickinson (McGill University)
- Michael Doyle (Memorial University of Newfoundland)
- Byron Eastman (Laurentian University)
- Oliver Franke (Concordia University of Alberta)
- Bruno Fullone (George Brown College)
- David Gray (University of Ottawa)
- Narine Grigoryan (Camosun College)
- Gustavo Indart (University of Toronto)
- Byron Lew (Trent University)
- Junjie Liu (Simon Fraser University)
- M. A. McGregor (Mount Royal University)
- Manish Pandey (University of Winnipeg)
- Amy Peng (Ryerson University)
- Kevin Richter (Douglas College)
- Gary Riser (Memorial University of Newfoundland)
- Rob Scharff (Kwantlen Polytechnic University)
- Jim Sentance (University of PEI)
- Fulton Tom (Langara College)
- and others, who choose to remain anonymous

We would like to express our thanks to the many people at Pearson Canada involved in the development and production of this textbook. We would especially like to thank three individuals with whom we worked closely. Claudine O'Donnell (Acquisitions Editor), Suzanne Schaan (Supervising Developmental Editor) and Leigh-Anne Graham (Senior Marketing Manager) all showed their professionalism, dedication, and enthusiasm in guiding this book through the publication and marketing processes. We would also like to thank the many sales representatives who work to bring this book to professors across the country. These individuals have been a pleasure to work with each step along the way, and we are deeply grateful for their presence and their participation and delighted to consider them friends as well as professional colleagues.

Our thanks also to the many people at Pearson with whom we work less closely but who nonetheless toil behind the scenes to produce this book, including Andrea Falkenberg, Melinda Durham, Julia Hall, Marta Johnson, Sonya Thursby, and Miriam Blier.

Thanks also to Linda Jenkins for copyediting, Kevin Richter for the technical review, and to Megan Smith-Creed for proofreading, all of whom provided an invaluable service with their attention to detail.

In short, we realize that there is a great deal more involved in producing a book than just the writing. Without the efforts of all of these dedicated professionals, this textbook simply would not exist. Our sincere thanks to all of you.

For this fourteenth edition, we enjoyed the help of several students and we would like to thank them all. David Meredith assembled much of the data for the necessary updates in the text; Justine Gagnepain and Katherine Ragan reviewed the solutions to all of the Study Exercises and also helped us to compile a list of websites, and and Hannah Herman closely reviewed all of the questions in the Testbank. We thank all of them for their diligence and hard work.

Finally, Ingrid Kristjanson is deeply involved in the revision of this textbook and has been for several years. Without her participation, the quality and efficiency of this project would suffer greatly. In addition, for the past three editions she has played a leading role in the improvement, rewriting, and expansion of the electronic Testbank. With her active involvement, the lengthy revision of the textbook and its supplements continues to be an enriching and pleasant experience.

Christopher Ragan

About the Author

Chris Ragan received his B.A. in economics from the University of Victoria, his M.A. from Queen's University, and his Ph.D. from the Massachusetts Institute of Technology in Cambridge, Massachusetts in 1990. He then joined the Department of Economics at McGill University in Montreal, where he has taught graduate courses in macroeconomics and international finance and undergraduate courses in macroeconomic theory and policy, current economic issues, and financial crises. Over the years he has taught principles of economics (micro and macro) to thousands of students at McGill and maintains a reputation on campus as being "super-excited" about economics. In 2007, Chris Ragan was awarded the Noel Fieldhouse Teaching Award from McGill for teaching excellence.

Professor Ragan's research focuses mainly on the design and implementation of macroeconomic policy in Canada. He has been privileged to serve the federal government in Ottawa as Special Advisor to the Governor of the Bank of Canada and as the Clifford Clark Visiting Economist at the Department of Finance. He currently serves on the Monetary Policy Council of the C.D. Howe Institute, where he also holds the David Dodge Chair in Monetary Policy.

Chris Ragan used the third edition of this textbook as an undergraduate student in 1981 and joined Richard Lipsey as a co-author in 1997 for the book's ninth edition. For several editions, Lipsey and Ragan worked diligently to maintain the book's reputation as the clearest and most comprehensive introductory economics textbook in Canada. Although Professor Ragan is now the sole listed author, this fourteenth edition of *Economics* still owes much to the dedication of previous authors, including Richard Lipsey, Douglas Purvis, and Gordon Sparks.

About the Cover

The cover image of this edition is an aerial drawing of the bustling port of Collingwood, Ontario, by artist Steve McDonald. Steve is an established Canadian artist and founding member of the acclaimed collective Drawnonward. The collective has been the subject of award-winning documentaries shown on CBC, Bravo, and TVO, profiled for the artists' unique bond with Canada's landscape. For more information, visit www.steviemcd.com.

Economic Issues and Concepts

CHAPTER OUTLINE

1.1 WHAT IS ECONOMICS?

1.2 THE COMPLEXITY OF MODERN ECONOMIES

1.3 IS THERE AN ALTERNATIVE TO THE MARKET ECONOMY?

LEARNING OBJECTIVES (LO)

After studying this chapter you will be able to

1 explain the importance of scarcity, choice, and opportunity cost, and how all three concepts are illustrated by the production possibilities boundary.

2 view the market economy as self-organizing in the sense that order emerges from a large number of decentralized decisions.

3 explain how specialization gives rise to the need for trade, and that trade is greatly facilitated by money.

4 identify the economy's decision makers and see how their actions create a circular flow of income and expenditure.

5 see that all actual economies are mixed economies, having elements of free markets, tradition, and government intervention.

MANY of the challenges we face in Canada and around the world are primarily economic. Some are mostly environmental, social, or political, but with many issues there is also a significant economic dimension. Wars and civil unrest throughout history have often had economic roots, with antagonists competing for control over vital resources; global climate change is a phenomenon that engages the attention of the scientific and environmental communities, but the economic implications of both the problem and its solutions will be tremendous; population aging in Canada and other developed countries will have consequences for the structure of our societies, but it will also have significant economic effects; and the existence of poverty, whether in Canada or in the much poorer nations of the world, most certainly has economic causes and consequences. We begin by discussing several issues that are currently of pressing concern, both inside and outside of Canada.

Productivity Growth Productivity growth lies at the heart of the long-term increase in Canadians' average living standards. Productivity is a measure of how much output (or income) is produced by one hour of work effort, and it has been rising gradually over the past century. In recent years, however, productivity growth has been slowing in Canada, and economists in universities and governments have been examining the cause of the slowdown and also examining what policies, if any, might reverse this trend. If your living standards are to improve over your lifetime as much as your grandparents' did over theirs, Canada's rate of productivity growth will need to increase significantly.

Population Aging The average age of the Canadian population is steadily rising, due both to a long-term decline in fertility and to an increase in average life-expectancy. This population aging has several effects. First, since people eventually retire as they approach their "golden years," there will be a decline in the growth rate of Canada's labour force. As a result, some firms and industries will find it more difficult to find workers, and wages are likely to rise as a result. Second, since our publicly funded health-care system tends to spend much more on seniors than it does on Canadians under the age of 55, there will be a significant increase in public health-care spending as a share of the total size of the economy. This will put new and difficult demands on governments' fiscal positions, and force them either to increase tax rates or reduce spending in order to balance their budgets. This same demographic problem is being encountered in most developed countries.

Climate Change Climate change is a global phenomenon that will have important implications for most nations on Earth. The long-term increase in the emission of greenhouse gases—caused largely from the burning of fossil fuels such as oil, coal, and natural gas—has led to an accumulation of these gases in the atmosphere and is contributing to a long-term increase in Earth's average temperature. The rise in temperature is leading to the melting of polar ice caps, a slow increase in sea level, a creeping expansion of the world's great deserts, and reductions in agricultural productivity. Particularly troubling is that much of the burden of climate change appears to be falling on developing countries that are least able to bear the burden. Global climate change presents a challenge for the design of better economic policy, aimed at reducing greenhouse-gas emissions without unduly slowing the growth of material living standards. It also presents a challenge for global diplomacy, aimed at getting all countries—rich and poor—involved in a collective effort of reducing their emissions.

Global Financial Stability The collapse of the U.S. housing market in 2007–2008 led to the failure of several major financial institutions and caused a global financial crisis. The largest and most synchronized worldwide recession in over 70 years followed in its wake. Many elements came together to cause these events, including new mortgage practices, innovative financial instruments, expansionary monetary policy, regulation in the financial sector, and many others. The crisis led most of the world's major governments to intervene considerably in their economies—by providing assistance to their financial institutions, by directly expanding expenditures on goods and services, and by providing liquidity to their financial markets. By 2010 most of these economies had emerged from recession and were on their way to healthy economic recoveries. However, it was then clear that governments needed to play a role in redesigning their financial systems to reduce the likelihood that similar events would occur in the future. The quest for "financial stability" has become a policy imperative in many countries.

Rising Government Debt The aggressive government response to the global financial crisis led to massive new public spending in an effort to dampen the effects of the recession. These increases in government spending, however, took place when the recession was causing a decline in government tax revenues. As a result, governments' budget deficits increased for several years, and government debt in most countries increased significantly between 2008 and 2012. Even by 2010 it had become clear that government debt in some European countries (especially Greece, Portugal, Ireland, Italy, and Spain) was so high that bondholders were no longer prepared to purchase new government bonds or renew their existing holdings of bonds. The resulting upward spike in interest rates made it almost impossible for these countries to carry out their regular business without special financial assistance from other governments or from the International Monetary Fund. The political tensions created among European governments threatened to spell the end of Europe's common currency, the euro. The European "sovereign debt crisis" is still largely unresolved.

Globalization Canada is a small nation that relies significantly on trade with the rest of the world for its prosperity. We sell our lumber and oil and beef to the world, as we do our engineering and legal and financial services. As consumers we buy a wide variety of products from the rest of the world, including coffee, leather shoes, and fine wine; our firms also buy many inputs from abroad, including machine tools, software, and some specialized raw materials. In short, international trade and the ongoing process of globalization are crucial to Canada's economic prosperity. Yet globalization also presents some challenges. A decision to reduce tariffs on imported goods generates overall benefits for Canada, but it also generates temporary costs for those Canadians who are displaced from their previously protected occupations. And greater competition for Canadian firms from those in developing countries leads to overall increases in domestic living standards, as Canadians now have access to cheaper goods. However, it may also lead to a decline in some middle-level jobs in Canada that get replaced slowly with jobs in expanding sectors.

These six issues are only a small sample of the many economic issues that confront Canada and other countries. To understand any of them it is necessary to have a basic understanding of economics—how markets work, how prices are determined, in what sense markets sometimes fail to work well, and how government policy can be used to improve outcomes. These are the main topics of this book. There is a lot to learn, and not many weeks in your college or university course. So, let's get started at the very beginning.

1.1 What Is Economics?

These issues would not matter much if we lived in an economy of such plenty that there was always enough to fully satisfy everyone's wants. If we could always get all the goods we wanted, it wouldn't be so important to be more productive in our work. Rapid growth in health-care spending would not be such a problem if governments had no limits on what they could spend, or if there were not problems associated with high levels of government debt. And there would be no need to trade with other countries if Canada could easily and cheaply produce coffee, clothing, electronic components, and all those other things that we currently import from foreign lands. But such an economy with unlimited products is impossible. Why?

The short answer is because we live in a world of *scarcity*. Compared with the desires of individuals for products such as better food, clothing, housing, education, holidays, health care, and entertainment, the existing supplies of resources are clearly inadequate. They are sufficient to produce only a small fraction of the goods and services that we desire. This scarcity gives rise to the basic economic problem of choice. If we cannot have everything we want, we must choose what we will and will not have.

One definition of *economics* comes from the great economist Alfred Marshall (1842–1924), who we will encounter at several points in this book: "Economics is a study of mankind in the ordinary business of life." A more informative definition is

> **Economics is the study of the use of scarce resources to satisfy unlimited human wants.**

Scarcity is inevitable and is central to economic problems. What are society's resources? Why is scarcity inevitable? What are the consequences of scarcity?

Resources

A society's resources are often divided into the three broad categories of land, labour, and capital. *Land* includes all natural endowments, such as arable land, forests, lakes, crude oil, and minerals. *Labour* includes all mental and physical human resources, including entrepreneurial capacity and management skills. *Capital* includes all manufactured aids to production, such as tools, machinery, and buildings. Economists call such resources **factors of production** because they are used to produce the things that people desire. We divide what is produced into goods and services. **Goods** are tangible (e.g., cars and shoes), and **services** are intangible (e.g., haircuts and education).

People use goods and services to satisfy many of their wants. The act of making them is called **production**, and the act of using them to satisfy wants is called **consumption**. Goods are valued for the services they provide. For example, a car helps to satisfy its owner's desires for transportation, mobility, and possibly status.

Scarcity and Choice

For almost all of the world's 7 billion people, scarcity is real and ever-present. As we said earlier, relative to our desires, existing resources are inadequate; there are enough to produce only a fraction of the goods and services that we want.

factors of production Resources used to produce goods and services; frequently divided into the basic categories of land, labour, and capital.

goods Tangible commodities, such as cars or shoes.

services Intangible commodities, such as haircuts or medical care.

production The act of making goods or services.

consumption The act of using goods or services to satisfy wants.

But aren't the advanced industrialized nations rich enough that scarcity is nearly banished? After all, they are "affluent" societies. Whatever affluence may mean, however, it does not mean the end of the problem of scarcity. Canadian families that earn $75 000 per year, the average after-tax income for a Canadian family in 2013 but a princely amount by *world* standards, have no trouble spending it on things that seem useful to them, and they would certainly have no trouble convincing you that their resources are scarce relative to their desires.

Because resources are scarce, all societies face the problem of deciding what to produce and how much each person will consume. Societies differ in who makes the choices and how they are made, but the need to choose is common to all. Just as scarcity implies the need for choice, so choice implies the existence of cost. A decision to have more of one thing requires a decision to have less of something else. The less of "something else" can be thought of as the cost of having more of that "one thing."

> Scarcity implies that choices must be made, and making choices implies the existence of costs.

Opportunity Cost To see how choice implies cost, we look first at a trivial example and then at one that affects all of us; both examples involve precisely the same fundamental principles.

Consider the choice David faces when he goes out for pizza and beer with his friends. Suppose that he has only $16 for the night and that each beer costs $4 and each slice of pizza costs $2. Since David is both hungry and thirsty, he would like to have 4 slices of pizza and 3 beers, but this would cost $20 and is therefore unattainable given David's scarce resources of $16. There are several combinations, however, that are attainable: 8 slices of pizza and 0 beers; 6 slices of pizza and 1 beer; 4 slices of pizza and 2 beers; 2 slices of pizza and 3 beers; and 0 slices of pizza and 4 beers.

David's choices are illustrated in Figure 1-1, which graphs the combinations of beers and slices of pizza that David considers buying. The numbers of slices of pizza are shown on the horizontal axis; the numbers of beers are shown on the vertical axis. The downward-sloping line connects the five possible combinations of beer and pizza that use up all of David's resources—$16. This is David's *budget line*. Notice that point A shows a combination—4 slices of pizza and 3 beers—that lies outside the line because its total cost is more than $16. Point A is *unattainable* to David. If David could buy fractions of a beer and of a slice of pizza, *all* points that lie on or inside the line would be *attainable* combinations.

In this setting David can ask himself, "What is the cost of one beer?" One answer is that the cost is $4. An equivalent answer, assuming that he wanted to spend all of this $16 on these two items, is that the cost of one beer is the two slices

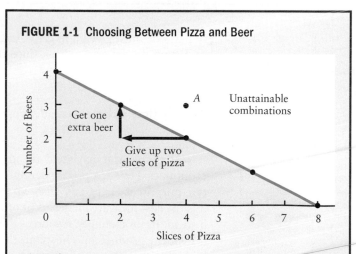

FIGURE 1-1 Choosing Between Pizza and Beer

Limited resources force a choice among competing alternatives. Given a total of $16 to spend on $2 slices of pizza and $4 beers, some choices are unattainable, such as point A. The five points on the green line show *all* combinations that are attainable by spending the $16. If it were possible to buy parts of a beer and parts of a slice of *pizza*, then all combinations on the line and in the green area would be attainable. If the entire $16 is to be spent, the choice between more pizza and more beer involves an opportunity cost. The *slope* of the green line reflects opportunity costs. The opportunity cost of one extra slice of pizza is half of a beer; the opportunity cost of one extra beer is two slices of pizza.

APPLYING ECONOMIC CONCEPTS 1-1

The Opportunity Cost of Your University Degree

The opportunity cost of choosing one thing is what must be given up as the best alternative. Computing the opportunity cost of a college or university education is a good example to illustrate which factors are included in the computation of opportunity cost. You may also be surprised to learn how expensive your university degree really is!*

Suppose that a bachelor's degree requires four years of study and that each year you spend $6000 for tuition fees—approximately the average at Canadian universities in 2013—and a further $1500 per year for books and materials. Does this mean that the cost of a university education is only $30 000? Unfortunately not; the true cost of a university degree to a student is much higher.

The key point is that the opportunity cost of a university education does not include just the out-of-pocket expenses on tuition and books. You must also take into consideration *what you are forced to give up* by choosing to attend university. Of course, if you were not studying you could have done any one of a number of things, but the relevant one is *the one you would have*

chosen instead—your best alternative to attending university.

Suppose that your best alternative to attending university was to get a job. In this case, the opportunity cost of your university degree must include the earnings that you would have received had you taken that job. Suppose that your (after-tax) annual earnings would have been $25 000 per year, for a total of $100 000 if you had stayed at that job for four years. To the direct expenses of $30 000, we must therefore add $100 000 for the earnings that you gave up by not taking a job. This brings the true cost of your university degree—the opportunity cost—up to $130 000!

Notice that the cost of food, lodging, clothing, and other living expenses did not enter the calculation of the opportunity cost in this example. The living expenses must be incurred in either case—whether you attend university or get a job.

If the opportunity cost of a degree is so high, why do students choose to go to university? Maybe students

---

of pizza he must give up to get it. In fact, we say in this case that two slices of pizza is the *opportunity cost* of one beer, since they are the opportunity David must give up to get one extra beer.

> **Every time a choice is made, opportunity costs are incurred.**

opportunity cost The cost of using resources for a certain purpose, measured by the benefit given up by not using them in their best alternative use.

As simple as it may seem, the idea of opportunity cost is one of the central insights of economics. Here is a precise definition: The **opportunity cost** of using resources for a certain purpose is *the benefit given up by not using them in the best alternative way*. That is, it is the cost measured in terms of other goods and services that could have been obtained instead. If, for example, resources that could have produced 20 km of road are best used instead to produce one hospital, the opportunity cost of a hospital is 20 km of road; looked at the other way round, the opportunity cost of 20 km of road is one hospital.

See *Applying Economic Concepts 1-1* for an example of opportunity cost that should seem quite familiar to you: the opportunity cost of getting a university degree.

Production Possibilities Boundary Although David's choice between pizza and beer may seem to be a trivial consumption decision, the nature of the decision is the same whatever the choice being made. Consider, for example, the choice that any country must face between producing military goods (such as ships, tanks, and guns) and civilian goods (such as food, clothing, and housing).

If resources are fully and efficiently employed, it is not possible to have more of both. However, as the government cuts defence expenditures, resources needed to produce civilian goods will be freed up. The opportunity cost of increased civilian goods is therefore

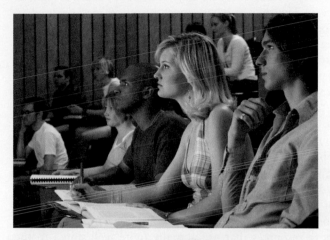

The opportunity cost to an individual completing a university degree in Canada is large. It includes the direct cost of tuition and books as well as the earnings forgone while attending university.

simply enjoy learning and thus are prepared to incur the high cost to be in the university environment. Or maybe they believe that a university degree will significantly increase their future earning potential. In Chapter 14 we will see that this is true. In this case, they are giving up four years of earnings at one salary so that they can invest in building their skills in the hope of enjoying many more years in the future at a considerably higher salary.

Whatever the reason for attending college or university, the recognition that a post-secondary degree is very expensive should convince students to make the best use of their time while they are there. Read on!

---

*This box considers only the cost *to the student* of a university degree. For reasons that will be discussed in detail in Part Six of this book, provincial governments heavily subsidize post-secondary education in Canada. Because of this subsidy, the cost *to society* of a university degree is generally much higher than the cost to an individual student.

the forgone military output. Or, if we were considering an increase in military output, the opportunity cost of increased military output would be the forgone civilian goods.

The choice is illustrated in Figure 1-2. Because resources are scarce, some combinations—those that would require more than the total available supply of resources for their production—cannot be attained. The negatively sloped curve on the graph divides the combinations that can be attained from those that cannot. Points above and to the right of this curve cannot be attained because there are not enough resources, points below and to the left of the curve can be attained without using all of the available resources, and points on the curve can just be attained if all the available resources are used efficiently. The curve is called the **production possibilities boundary**. (Sometimes "boundary" is replaced with "curve" or "frontier.") It has a negative slope because when all resources are being used efficiently, producing more of one good requires producing less of others.

production possibilities boundary
A curve showing which alternative combinations of commodities can just be attained if all available resources are used efficiently; it is the boundary between attainable and unattainable output combinations.

A production possibilities boundary illustrates three concepts: scarcity, choice, and opportunity cost. Scarcity is indicated by the unattainable combinations outside the boundary; choice, by the need to choose among the alternative attainable points along the boundary; and opportunity cost, by the negative slope of the boundary.

The shape of the production possibilities boundary in Figure 1-2 implies that an increasing amount of civilian production must be given up to achieve equal successive increases in military production. This shape, referred to as *concave* to the origin, indicates that the opportunity cost of either good increases as we increase the amount of it that is produced. A straight-line boundary, as in Figure 1-1, indicates that the opportunity cost of one good stays constant, no matter how much of it is produced.

FIGURE 1-2 A Production Possibilities Boundary

Quantity of Military Goods

The negatively sloped boundary shows the combinations that are attainable when all resources are used efficiently. The production possibilities boundary separates the attainable combinations of goods, such as *a, b, c,* and *d,* from unattainable combinations, such as *e* and *f.* Points *a, b,* and *c* represent full and efficient use of society's resources. Point *d* represents either inefficient use of resources or failure to use all the available resources. If production changes from point *a* to point *b,* an opportunity cost is involved. The opportunity cost of producing Δ*x* more military goods is the necessary reduction in the production of civilian goods equal to Δ*y.*

The concave shape in Figure 1-2 is the way economists usually draw a country's production possibilities boundary. The shape occurs because each factor of production is not equally useful in producing all goods. To see why differences among factors of production are so important, suppose we begin at point *c* in Figure 1-2, where most resources are devoted to the production of military goods, and then consider gradually shifting more and more resources toward the production of civilian goods. We might begin by shifting nutrient-rich land that is particularly well suited to growing wheat. This land may not be very useful for making military equipment, but it is very useful for making certain civilian goods (like bread). This shift of resources will therefore lead to a small reduction in military output but a substantial increase in civilian output. Thus, the opportunity cost of producing a few more units of civilian goods, which is equal to the forgone military output, is small. But as we shift more and more resources toward the production of civilian goods, and therefore move along the production possibilities boundary toward point *a,* we must shift more and more resources that are actually quite well suited to the production of military output, like aerospace engineers or the minerals needed to make gunpowder. As we produce more and more civilian goods (by devoting more and more resources to producing them), the amount of military output that must be forgone to produce one *extra* unit of civilian goods rises. That is, the opportunity cost of producing one good rises as more of that good is produced.

Four Key Economic Problems

Modern economies involve millions of complex production and consumption activities. Despite this complexity, however, the basic decisions that must be made are not very different from those that were made in ancient and primitive economies in which people worked with few tools and bartered with their neighbours. Nor is the essence of the decisions in modern, complex economies different from those in current-day developing economies, where many people struggle for their daily survival. In all cases, scarcity, opportunity cost, and the need for choice play crucial roles. Whatever the economic system, whether modern or ancient or complex or primitive, there are four key economic problems.

1. What Is Produced and How? This question concerns the *allocation* of scarce resources among alternative uses. This **resource allocation** determines the quantities of various goods that are produced. Choosing to produce a particular combination of goods means choosing a particular allocation of resources among the industries or regions producing the goods. What determines which goods are produced and which ones are not?

Furthermore, because resources are scarce, it is desirable that they be used efficiently. Hence, it matters which of the available methods of production is used to produce each of the goods. What determines which methods of production get used and which ones do not? Any economy must have some mechanism by which these decisions about resource allocation are made.

resource allocation The allocation of an economy's scarce resources among alternative uses.

Is there some combination of the production of goods that is "better" than others? If so, should governments try to alter the pattern of production in this direction? Could they achieve this if they tried?

2. What Is Consumed and by Whom? Economists seek to understand what determines the distribution of a nation's total output among its people. Who gets a lot, who gets a little, and why? Should governments care about this *distribution* of consumption and, if so, what tools do they have to alter it?

If production takes place on the production possibilities boundary, then how about consumption? Will the economy consume exactly the same goods that it produces? Or will the country's ability to trade with other countries permit the economy to consume a different combination of goods?

3. Why Are Resources Sometimes Idle? Sometimes large numbers of workers who would like to have jobs are unable to find employers to hire them. At the same time, the managers and owners of offices and factories could operate at a higher level of activity—that is, they could produce more goods and services. For some reason, however, these resources—land, labour, and factories—lie idle. Thus, in terms of Figure 1-2, the economy sometimes operates inside its production possibilities boundary.

Why are resources sometimes idle? Should governments worry about such idle resources, or is there some reason to believe that such occasional idleness is necessary for a well-functioning economy? Is there anything governments can do to reduce such idleness?

FIGURE 1-3 The Effect of Economic Growth on the Production Possibilities Boundary

Economic growth shifts the boundary outward and makes it possible to produce more of all products. Before growth in productive capacity, points *a*, *b*, and *c* were on the production possibilities boundary and points *e* and *f* were unattainable. After growth, points *e* and *f* and many other previously unattainable combinations are attainable.

4. Is Productive Capacity Growing? The capacity to produce goods and services grows rapidly in some countries, grows slowly in others, and actually declines in others. Growth in productive capacity can be represented by an outward shift of the production possibilities boundary, as shown in Figure 1-3. If an economy's capacity to produce goods and services is growing, some combinations that are unattainable today will become attainable in the future. What are the determinants of such growth? Are there some undesirable side effects of growth? Can governments do anything to influence economic growth?

Economics and Government Policy

Questions relating to what is produced and how, and what is consumed and by whom, fall within the realm of microeconomics. **Microeconomics** is the study of the causes and consequences of the allocation of resources as it is affected by the workings of the price system and government policies that seek to influence it. Questions relating to the idleness of resources and the growth of the economy's productive capacity fall within the realm of macroeconomics. **Macroeconomics** is the study of the determination of economic aggregates, such as total output, total employment, interest rates, the price level, and the rate of economic growth.

The design and effectiveness of government policy is relevant to discussing all four economic problems. When asking what combination of goods and services is produced in

microeconomics The study of the causes and consequences of the allocation of resources as it is affected by the workings of the price system.

macroeconomics The study of the determination of economic aggregates such as total output, the price level, employment, and growth.

the economy, and whether some combinations might be better than others, government policy enters the discussion. In later chapters we will examine situations called *market failures,* which arise when free markets lead to too much of some goods being produced (like pollution) and too little of others (like national parks). In such situations, government policy could be used to alter the allocation of the economy's resources in such a way as to make society as a whole better off.

When asking who gets to consume the economy's output, it is natural to discuss the *fairness* regarding the distribution of consumption across individuals. Do free markets lead to fair outcomes? Can we even decide objectively what is fair and what is unfair? And if we could, what kind of government policies could be used to improve the distribution? We will see throughout this book that many government policies are designed with fairness in mind. We will also encounter an ongoing debate about how much the government should try to improve the fairness of market outcomes. Some argue that it is reasonable to do so; others argue that attempts to improve fairness often lead to reductions in market efficiency that impose large costs on society.

Government policy is also part of the discussion of why a nation's economic resources are sometimes idle and what can be done to reduce such idleness. For example, when the Canadian economy entered a major global recession in 2009, the federal and provincial governments increased their planned spending significantly in an attempt to dampen the decline in aggregate output and rise in unemployment that was then occurring. Other countries did the same. Some critics argued that such "fiscal stimulus" packages could not increase overall output and income, since the increase in government spending would simply displace private spending. Others argued that recessions are caused largely by a reduction in private spending, and that an increase in government spending can be an effective temporary replacement to help sustain the level of economic activity. Such debates lie at the heart of macroeconomic policy, and we have much to say about them in this book.

1.2 The Complexity of Modern Economies

If you want a litre of milk, you go to your local grocery store and buy it. When the grocer needs more milk, he orders it from the wholesaler, who in turn gets it from the dairy, which in turn gets it from the dairy farmer. The dairy farmer buys cattle feed and electric milking machines, and he gets power to run all his equipment by putting a plug into a wall outlet where the electricity is supplied as he needs it. The milking machines are made from parts manufactured in several different places in Canada, the United States, and overseas. The parts themselves are made from materials mined and smelted in a dozen or more countries.

As it is with the milk you drink, so it is with everything else that you buy. When you go to the appropriate store, what you want is normally on the shelf. Those who make these products find that all the required components and materials are available when they need them—even though these things typically come from many different parts of the world and are made by many people who have no direct dealings with one another.

Your own transactions are only a small part of the remarkably complex set of transactions that takes place every day in a modern economy. Shipments arrive daily at our ports, railway terminals, and airports. These shipments include raw materials, such as iron ore, logs, and oil; parts, such as automobile engines, transistors, and circuit boards; tools, such as screwdrivers, lathes, and digging equipment; perishables, such as fresh flowers, coffee beans, and fruit; and all kinds of manufactured goods, such as washing machines, computers, and cell phones. Railways and trucking lines move these goods among thousands of different destinations within Canada. Some go directly to consumers. Others are used by local firms to manufacture their products—some of which will be sold domestically and others exported to other countries.

The Nature of Market Economies

An *economy* is a system in which scarce resources—such as labour, land, and capital—are allocated among competing uses. Decisions must be made about which goods are produced and which are not; who works where and at what wage; and who consumes which goods at what times. Although each of these individual decisions may seem simple, the entire combination is remarkably complex, especially in modern societies.

Self-Organizing Early in the development of modern economics, thoughtful observers wondered how such a complex set of dealings gets organized. Who coordinates the whole set of efforts? Who makes sure that all the activities fit together, providing jobs to produce the things that people want and delivering those things to where they are wanted? The answer is, surprisingly, no one!

A great insight of early economists was that an economy based on free-market transactions is *self-organizing*.

A market economy is self-organizing in the sense that when individual consumers and producers act independently to pursue their own self-interests, responding to prices determined in open markets, the collective outcome is coordinated—there is a "spontaneous economic order." In that order, literally thousands of millions of transactions and activities fit together to produce the things that people want within the constraints set by the resources that are available to the nation.

The great Scottish economist and political philosopher Adam Smith (1723–1790),[1] who was the first to develop this insight fully, put it this way:

It is not from the benevolence of the butcher, the brewer, or the baker, that we expect our dinner, but from their regard to their own interest. We address ourselves, not to their humanity but to their self-love, and never talk to them of our own necessities but of their advantages.

Smith is not saying that benevolence is unimportant. Indeed, he praises it in many other passages of his book. He is saying, however, that the massive number of economic interactions that characterize

Adam Smith wrote An Inquiry into the Nature and Causes of the Wealth of Nations *in 1776. Now referred to by most people simply as* The Wealth of Nations, *it is considered to be the beginning of modern economics.*

---

[1] Throughout this book, we encounter many great economists from the past whose ideas shaped the discipline of economics. At the back of the book you will find a timeline that begins in the 1600s. It contains brief discussions of many of these thinkers and places them in their historical context.

a modern economy cannot all be motivated by benevolence. Although benevolence does motivate some of our actions, often the very dramatic ones, the vast majority of our everyday actions are motivated by self-interest. Self-interest, not benevolence, is therefore the foundation of economic order.

Efficiency Another great insight, which was hinted at by Smith and fully developed over the next century and a half, was that this spontaneously generated economic order is relatively *efficient*. Loosely speaking, efficiency means that the resources available to the nation are organized so as to produce the various goods and services that people want to purchase and to produce them with the least possible amount of resources.

An economy organized by free markets behaves almost as if it were guided by "an invisible hand," in Smith's now-famous words. This does not literally mean that a supernatural presence runs a market economy. Instead it refers to the relatively efficient order that emerges spontaneously out of the many independent decisions made by those who produce, sell, and buy goods and services. The key to explaining this market behaviour is that these decision makers all respond to the same set of prices, which are determined in markets that respond to overall conditions of national scarcity or plenty. Much of this book is devoted to a detailed elaboration of how this market order is generated and how efficiently that job is done.

That free markets usually generate relatively efficient outcomes does not mean that they are *always* efficient or that everyone views the outcomes as desirable or even *fair*. Free markets sometimes fail to produce efficient outcomes, and these failures often provide a motivation for government intervention. In addition, many market outcomes may be efficient but perceived by many to be quite unfair. For example, we will see that an efficient labour market may nonetheless lead to large differentials in wages, with some individuals receiving low incomes while others receive enormous incomes. So, while a central aspect of economics is the study of how markets allocate resources efficiently, much emphasis is also placed on what happens when markets fail in various ways.

Incentives and Self-Interest Lying at the heart of modern economies are *incentives* and *self-interest*. Individuals generally pursue their own self-interest, buying and selling what seems best for them and their families. They purchase products that they want rather than those they dislike, and they buy them when it makes sense given their time and financial constraints. Similarly, they sell products, including their own labour services, in an attempt to improve their own economic situation. When making such decisions about what to buy or sell and at what prices, people respond to *incentives*. Sellers usually want to sell more when prices are high because by doing so they have command over more resources that can be used to purchase the things they want. Similarly, buyers usually want to buy more when prices are low because by doing so they are better able to use their scarce resources to acquire the many things they desire.

With self-interested buyers and sellers responding to incentives when determining what they want to buy and sell, the overall market prices and quantities are determined by their collective interactions. Changes in their preferences or productive abilities lead to changes in their desired transactions and thus to fluctuations in market prices and quantities.

The millions of market transactions occurring on a daily basis in a modern economy are governed by a set of institutions largely created by government. Most often these institutions are so much a part of the fabric of our society that we barely notice their existence, but their importance should not be ignored. The most important of these institutions are private property, the freedom to enter into contracts, and the rule of law. The natures of private property and contractual obligations are defined by laws passed by legislatures and enforced by the police and the courts.

The Decision Makers and Their Choices

Three broad groups of decision makers operate in any economy. The first group is *consumers*. Sometimes we think of consumers as being individuals and sometimes we think in terms of families or households. Consumers purchase various kinds of goods and services with their income; they usually earn their income by selling their labour services to their employers. Sometimes their income is earned by renting out the land or buildings or machines that they own.

The second group of decision makers is *producers*. Producers may be firms that are interested in earning profits or they may be non-profit or charitable organizations. In any case, producers hire workers, purchase or rent various kinds of material inputs and supplies, and then produce and sell their products. In the cases of charitable organizations, their products are often distributed for free.

The third group of decision makers is *government*. In Canada, this group includes the federal, provincial, territorial, and municipal governments. Like producers, governments hire workers, purchase or rent material and supplies, and produce goods and services. Unlike most producers, however, governments usually provide their goods and services at no direct cost to the final user; their operations are financed not by revenue from the sale of their products but instead by the taxes they collect from individual consumers and producers. In addition to producing and providing many goods and services, governments create and enforce laws, and design and implement regulations that must be followed by consumers and producers.

How Are Decisions Made? How do consumers, producers, and governments make decisions? Thinking about how governments make decisions is not straightforward. Indeed, it is not uncommon to hear Canadians say something like "How could the government possibly do something so stupid?" As we will see in later chapters, however, there is usually a sensible explanation for why a government makes the decisions that it does, though it is often not clear until you think carefully about what the government's objectives really are. We will examine government policies in detail at many points throughout this book.

For now, let's focus on how consumers and producers make their decisions. Economists usually assume that consumers' and producers' decisions are both "maximizing" and "marginal." What does this mean?

Maximizing Decisions. The important assumption that economists usually make about how these two groups make their decisions is that everyone tries to do as well as possible for himself or herself. In the jargon of economics, people are assumed to be *maximizers*. When individuals decide how many factor services to sell to producers and how many products to buy from them, they are assumed to make choices designed to maximize their well-being, or *utility*. When producers decide how many factor services to buy from individuals and how many goods to produce and sell to them, they are assumed to make choices designed to maximize their *profits*. We explore the details of utility and profit maximization in later chapters.

Marginal Decisions. Firms and consumers who are trying to maximize usually need to weigh the costs and benefits of their decisions *at the margin*. For example, when you consider buying an additional pair of shoes, you know the *marginal cost* of the shoes—that is, how much you must pay to get them—and you need to compare that cost to the *marginal benefit* that you will receive—the *extra* satisfaction you get from having those shoes. If you are trying to maximize your utility, you will buy the new pair of shoes only if you think that the benefit to you in terms of extra utility exceeds the marginal cost.

Similarly, a producer attempting to maximize its profits and considering whether to hire an extra worker must determine the *marginal cost* of the worker—the extra wages and benefits that must be paid—and compare it to the *marginal benefit* of the worker—the increase in sales revenues the extra worker will generate. A producer interested in maximizing its profit will hire the extra worker only if the benefit in terms of extra revenue exceeds the cost in terms of extra wages.

> In order to achieve their objectives, maximizing consumers and producers make marginal decisions; they decide whether they will be made better off by buying or selling a little more or a little less of any given product.

Voting in an election is an example in which decisions are *not* made on a marginal basis. When you vote in a Canadian federal election, you have only one vote and you must support one party over the others. When you do, you vote for everything that party stands for, even though you may prefer to pick and choose elements from each party's political platform. You cannot say "I vote for the Liberals on issue A and for the Conservatives on issue B." You must make a total, rather than a marginal, decision.

The Flow of Income and Expenditure Figure 1-4 shows the basic decision makers and the flows of income and expenditure that they set up. Individuals own factors of production. They sell the services of these factors to producers and receive payments in return. These are their incomes. Producers use the factor services that they buy to make goods and services. They sell these to individuals, receiving payments in return. These are the incomes of producers. These basic flows of income and expenditure pass through markets. Individuals sell the services of the factor that they own in what are collectively called *factor markets*. When you get a part-time job during university, you are participating in the factor market. Producers sell their outputs of goods and services in what are collectively called *goods markets*. When you purchase a haircut, an airplane ticket, or a new pair of shoes, for example, you are participating in the goods market.

The prices that are determined in these markets determine the incomes that are earned. People who get high prices for their factor services earn high incomes; those who get low prices earn low incomes. The *distribution of income* refers to how the nation's total income is distributed among its citizens. This is largely determined by the price that each type of factor service receives in factor markets.

FIGURE 1-4 The Circular Flow of Income and Expenditure

The red line shows the flow of goods and services; the blue line shows the payments made to purchase these. Factor services flow from individuals who own the factors (including their own labour) through factor markets to firms that use them to make goods and services. These goods and services then flow through goods markets to those who consume them. Money payments flow from firms to individuals through factor markets. These payments become the income of individuals. When they spend this income buying goods and services, money flows through goods markets back to producers.

Production and Trade

Individual producers decide which goods to produce and how to produce them. Production is a very complex process in any modern economy. For example, a typical car manufacturer assembles a product out of thousands of individual parts. It makes some of these parts itself. Most are subcontracted to parts manufacturers, and many of the major parts manufacturers subcontract some of their work to smaller firms. The same is true for producing consumer electronics, clothing, home appliances, furniture, fashion accessories, cleaning products, restaurant meals, and most other products you can imagine purchasing. Such complex production displays two characteristics noted long ago by Adam Smith—*specialization* and the *division of labour*.

Specialization In ancient hunter–gatherer societies and in modern subsistence economies, most people make most of the things they need for themselves. However, from the time that people first engaged in settled agriculture and some of them began to live in towns, people have specialized in doing particular jobs. Artisan, soldier, priest, and government official were some of the earliest specialized occupations. Economists call this allocation of different jobs to different people the **specialization of labour**. There are two fundamental reasons why specialization is extraordinarily efficient compared with universal self-sufficiency.

> **specialization of labour** The specialization of individual workers in the production of particular goods or services.

First, individual abilities differ, and specialization allows individuals to do what they can do relatively well while leaving everything else to be done by others. Even when people's abilities are unaffected by the act of specializing, the economy's total production is greater when people specialize than when they all try to be self-sufficient. This is true for individuals, but it is also true for entire countries, and it is one of the most fundamental principles in economics: the principle of *comparative advantage*. A much fuller discussion of comparative advantage is found in Chapter 33, where we discuss the gains from international trade.

The second reason why specialization is more efficient than self-sufficiency concerns changes in people's abilities that occur *because* they specialize. A person who concentrates on one activity becomes better at it than could a jack-of-all-trades. This is called *learning by doing,* and it was a factor much stressed by early economists; research shows that it is important in many modern industries.

The Division of Labour Throughout most of history each artisan who specialized in making some product made the whole of that product. But over the last several hundred years, many technical advances have made it efficient to organize production methods into large-scale firms organized around what is called the **division of labour**. This term refers to specialization *within* the production process of a particular product.

> **division of labour** The breaking up of a production process into a series of specialized tasks, each done by a different worker.

Mass Production. In a mass-production factory, work is divided into highly specialized tasks by using specialized machinery. Each individual repeatedly does one or a few small tasks that represent only a small fraction of those necessary to produce any one product.

Flexible Manufacturing. Two recent changes have significantly altered the degree of specialization found in many modern production processes. First, individual artisans have recently reappeared in some lines of production. They are responding to a revival in the demand for individually crafted, rather than mass-produced, products. Second, many manufacturing operations are being reorganized along new lines called *flexible manufacturing,* which was pioneered by Japanese car manufacturers in the mid-1950s. It has led back to a more craft-based form of organization within the factory. In this technique, employees work as a team; each employee is able to do every team member's job rather than only one very specialized task at one point on the assembly line. However, even these workers are practising the division of labour—but the division is not as fine as it is in mass production.

Money and Trade People who specialize in doing only one thing must satisfy most of their wants by consuming things made by other people. In early societies the exchange of goods and services took place by simple mutual agreement among neighbours. In the course of time, however, trading became centred on particular gathering places called markets. For example, the French markets or trade fairs of Champagne were known throughout Europe as early as the eleventh century. Even now, many small towns in Canada have regular market days. Today, however, the term "market" has a much broader meaning, referring to any institutions that allow buyers and sellers to transact with each other, which could be by meeting physically or by trading over the Internet. Also, we use the term "market economy" to refer to a society in which people specialize in productive activities and meet most of their material wants through voluntary market transactions with other people.

> Specialization must be accompanied by trade. People who produce only one thing must trade most of it to obtain all the other things they want.

barter An economic system in which goods and services are traded directly for other goods and services.

Early trading was by means of **barter**, the trading of goods directly for other goods. But barter is costly in terms of time spent searching out satisfactory exchanges. If a farmer has wheat but wants a hammer, he must find someone who has a hammer and wants wheat. A successful barter transaction thus requires what is called a *double coincidence of wants*.

Money eliminates the cumbersome system of barter by separating the transactions involved in the exchange of products. If a farmer has wheat and wants a hammer, she merely has to find someone who wants wheat. The farmer takes money in exchange. Then she finds a person who wants to sell a hammer and gives up the money for the hammer.

> Money greatly facilitates trade, which itself facilitates specialization.

Globalization Market economies constantly change, largely as a result of the development of new technologies and the new patterns of production and trade that result. Many of the recent changes are referred to as *globalization,* a term often used loosely to mean the increased importance of international trade. International trade is, however, a very old phenomenon. The usual pattern over most of the last 200 years was manufactured goods being sent from Europe and North America to the rest of the world, with raw materials and primary products being sent in return. What is new in the last few decades is the globalization of manufacturing. Assembly of a product may take place in the most industrialized countries, but the hundreds of component parts are manufactured in dozens of different countries and delivered to the assembly plant "just in time" for assembly.

Two major causes of globalization are the rapid reduction in transportation costs and the revolution in information technology that have occurred in the past 50 years. The cost of moving products around the world fell greatly over the last half of the twentieth century because of containerization and the increasing size of ships. Our ability to transmit and analyze data increased even more dramatically, while the costs of doing so decreased equally dramatically. For example, today $1000 buys an ultra-slim tablet or laptop computer that has the same computing power as a "mainframe" computer that in 1970 cost $10 million and filled a large room. This revolution in information and communication technology has made it possible to coordinate economic transactions around the world in ways that were difficult and costly 50 years ago and quite impossible 100 years ago.

Globalization is as important for consumers as it is for producers. For example, as some tastes become universal to young people, spread by ever-increasing access to foreign television stations and global social networks, we can see the same clothes and hear the same music in virtually all big cities. McDonald's restaurants are as visible in Moscow or Beijing as in London, New York, Vancouver, or Montreal. Many other brands are also known around the world, such as Louis Vuitton, Hilfiger, Gucci, Rolex, Nike, Coca-Cola, Kellogg's, Heinz, Nestlé, Molson, Toyota, Rolls-Royce, Sony, and Mitsubishi.

The revolution in shipping and in computer technology has drastically reduced communication and transportation costs. This reduction in costs lies at the heart of globalization.

Through the ongoing process of globalization, national economies are ever more linked to the global economy, in which an increasing share of jobs and incomes is created.

Globalization comes with challenges, however. As Canadian firms relocate production facilities to countries where costs are lower, domestic workers are laid off and must search for new jobs, perhaps needing retraining in the process. The location of production facilities in countries with lower environmental or human-rights records raises difficult questions about the standards that should be followed by Canadian-owned firms in foreign lands. And firms often use the threat of relocation in an attempt to extract financial assistance from governments, placing those governments in difficult positions. These concerns have led in recent years to "anti-globalization protests" that have raised awareness of some of the costs associated with the process of globalization. We have more to say about these issues in Chapters 33 and 34.

1.3 Is There an Alternative to the Market Economy?

In this chapter we have discussed the elements of an economy based on free-market transactions—what we call a *market economy*. Are there any alternatives to this type of economy? The answer is no in one sense and yes in another. We answer no because the modern economy has no *practical* alternative to reliance on market determination for many of its transactions. We answer yes because not all transactions take place in free markets even in the most market-oriented society. To go further we need to identify various types of economic systems.

Types of Economic Systems

It is helpful to distinguish three pure types of economies, called *traditional, command,* and *free-market economies*. These economies differ in the way in which economic decisions are coordinated. But no actual economy fits neatly into one of these three categories—all real economies contain some elements of each type.

traditional economy An economy in which behaviour is based mostly on tradition.

Traditional Economies A **traditional economy** is one in which behaviour is based primarily on tradition, custom, and habit. Young men follow their fathers' occupations. Women do what their mothers did. There is little change in the pattern of goods produced from year to year, other than those imposed by the vagaries of nature. The techniques of production also follow traditional patterns, except when the effects of an occasional new invention are felt. Finally, production is allocated among the members according to long-established traditions.

Such a system works best in an unchanging environment. Under such static conditions, a system that does not continually require people to make choices can prove effective in meeting economic and social needs.

Traditional systems were common in earlier times. The feudal system, under which most people in medieval Europe lived, was a largely traditional society. Peasants, artisans, and most others living in villages inherited their positions in that society. They also usually inherited their specific jobs, which they handled in traditional ways.

Some elements of traditional economies persist today. In some cases, the traditional behaviour is natural and probably desirable, as when a child with considerable expertise takes over a successful family business. In other situations, the traditional behaviour is the result of a resistance to change and fear of less familiar and more risky career paths. In these cases, the traditions may clash with the change that is a hallmark of a modern and dynamic economy.

command economy An economy in which most economic decisions are made by a central planning authority.

Command Economies In command economies, economic behaviour is determined by some central authority, usually the government, which makes most of the necessary decisions on what to produce, how to produce it, and who gets to consume which products and in what quantities. Such economies are characterized by the *centralization* of decision making. Because centralized decision makers usually create elaborate and complex plans for the behaviour that they want to impose, the terms **command economy** and *centrally planned economy* are usually used synonymously.

The sheer quantity of data required for the central planning of an entire modern economy is enormous, and the task of analyzing it to produce a fully integrated plan can hardly be exaggerated. Moreover, the plan must be continually modified to take account not only of current data but also of future trends in labour supplies, technological developments, and people's tastes for various goods and services. This is a notoriously difficult exercise, not least because of the unavailability of all essential, accurate, and up-to-date information.

Thirty years ago, more than one-third of the world's population lived in countries that relied heavily on central planning. Today, after the fall of the Berlin Wall and the collapse of the Soviet Union, the number of such countries is small. Even in countries in which central planning is the proclaimed system, as in Cuba, increasing amounts of market determination are gradually being permitted.

free-market economy An economy in which most economic decisions are made by private households and firms.

Free-Market Economies In the third type of economic system, the decisions about resource allocation are made without any central direction. Instead, they result from innumerable independent decisions made by individual producers and consumers. Such a system is known as a **free-market economy** or, more simply, a *market economy*. In such an economy, decisions relating to the basic economic issues are *decentralized*.

Despite the absence of a central plan, these many decentralized decisions are nonetheless coordinated. The main coordinating device is the set of market-determined prices—which is why free-market systems are often called *price systems*.

In a pure market economy, all these decisions are made by buyers and sellers acting through unhindered markets. The government provides the background of defining property rights and protecting citizens against foreign and domestic enemies but, beyond that, markets determine all resource allocation and income distribution.

Mixed Economies Economies that are fully traditional or fully centrally planned or wholly free-market are pure types that are useful for studying basic principles. When we look in detail at any actual economy, however, we discover that its economic behaviour is the result of some mixture of central control and market determination, with a certain amount of traditional behaviour as well.

> In practice, every economy is a mixed economy in the sense that it combines significant elements of all three systems in determining economic behaviour.

mixed economy An economy in which some economic decisions are made by firms and households and some by the government.

Furthermore, within any economy, the degree of the mix varies from sector to sector. For example, in some planned economies, the command principle was used more often to determine behaviour in heavy-goods industries, such as steel, than in agriculture. Farmers were often given substantial freedom to produce and sell what they wanted in response to varying market prices.

When economists speak of a particular economy as being centrally planned, we mean only that the degree of the mix is weighted heavily toward the command principle. When we speak of one as being a market economy, we mean only that the degree of the mix is weighted heavily toward decentralized decision making.

Although no country offers an example of either system working alone, some economies, such as those of Canada, the United States, France, and Hong Kong, rely much more heavily on market decisions than others, such as the economies of China, North Korea, and Cuba. Yet even in Canada, the command principle has some sway. Crown corporations, legislated minimum wages, rules and regulations for environmental protection, quotas on some agricultural outputs, and restrictions on the import of some items are just a few examples.

The Great Debate

As we saw earlier, in 1776 Adam Smith was one of the first people to analyze the operation of markets, and he stressed the relative efficiency of free-market economies. A century later, another great economist and political philosopher, Karl Marx (1818–1883), argued that although free-market economies would indeed be successful in producing high levels of output, they could not be relied on to ensure that this output would be fairly distributed among citizens. He argued the benefits of a centrally planned system in which the government could ensure a more equitable distribution of output.

Beginning with the Soviet Union in the early 1920s, many nations adopted systems in which conscious government central planning

Karl Marx argued that free-market economies could not be relied on to ensure an equitable distribution of income. He advocated a system of central planning in which government owns most of the means of production.

replaced the operation of the free market. For almost a century, a great debate then raged on the relative merits of command economies versus market economies. Along with the Soviet Union, the countries of Eastern Europe and China were command economies for much of the twentieth century. Canada, the United States, and most of the countries of Western Europe were, and still are, primarily market economies. The apparent successes of the Soviet Union and China in the 1950s and 1960s, including the ability to mobilize considerable resources into heavy industries, suggested to many observers that the command principle was at least as good for organizing economic behaviour as the market principle. Over the long run, however, planned economies proved to be a failure of such disastrous proportions that they seriously depressed the living standards of their citizens.

During the last decade of the twentieth century, most of the world's centrally planned economies began the difficult transition back toward freer markets. These transitions occurred at different paces in different countries, but in most cases the initial few years were characterized by significant declines in output and employment. Twenty years later, however, most of the "transition" economies are experiencing growth rates above the ones they had in their final years as centrally planned economies. Living standards are on the rise.

Lessons from History 1-1 discusses in more detail why the centrally planned economies failed. This failure suggests the superiority of decentralized markets over centrally

LESSONS FROM HISTORY 1-1

The Failure of Central Planning

The fall of the Berlin Wall in November 1989 was the beginning of the end of the Soviet system of central planning.

The Bolshevik Revolution in 1917 in Russia brought the world its first example of a large-scale communist society. With the rise to power of Joseph Stalin and the creation of the Soviet Union in 1922, communism and central economic planning began their spread throughout Eastern and Central Europe. This spread of central planning was accelerated by the Soviet Union's role following the Second World War in "liberating" several countries from Nazi domination, thus creating the group of countries that became known as the Eastern Bloc or the Soviet Bloc.

Despite the successful geographic spread of communism, the Soviet system of central economic planning had many difficulties. By 1989, communism had collapsed throughout Central and Eastern Europe, and the economic systems of formerly communist countries began the difficult transition from centrally planned to market economies. Although political issues played an enormous role in these events, the economic changes generally confirmed the superiority of a market-oriented price system over central planning as a method of organizing economic activity. The failure of central planning had many causes, but four were particularly significant.

Failure of Coordination

In the centrally planned economies, a body of planners attempted to coordinate all the economic decisions about production, investment, trade, and consumption that were likely to be made by producers and consumers throughout the country. Without the use of prices to signal relative scarcity and abundance, central planning generally proved impossible to do with any reasonable degree of success. Bottlenecks in production, shortages of some goods, and gluts of others plagued the Soviet economy for decades.

planned ones as mechanisms for allocating an economy's scarce resources. Put another way, it demonstrates the superiority of mixed economies with substantial elements of market determination over fully planned command economies. However, it does *not* demonstrate, as some observers have asserted, the superiority of completely free-market economies over mixed economies.

There is no guarantee that completely free markets will, on their own, handle such urgent matters as controlling pollution, providing public goods (like national defence), or preventing financial crises, such as occurred in 2008–2009 in most of the developed countries. Indeed, as we will see in later chapters, much economic theory is devoted to explaining why free markets often *fail* to do these things. Mixed economies, with significant elements of government intervention, are needed to do these jobs.

Furthermore, acceptance of the free market over central planning does not provide an excuse to ignore a country's pressing social issues. Acceptance of the benefits of the free market still leaves plenty of scope to debate the most appropriate levels and types of government policies directed at achieving specific social goals. It follows that there is still considerable room for disagreement about the degree of the mix of market and government determination in any modern mixed economy—room enough to accommodate such divergent views as could be expressed by conservative, liberal, and modern social democratic parties.

Failure of Quality Control

Central planners could monitor the number of units produced by any factory, reward plants that exceeded their production targets, and punish those that fell short. Factory managers operating under these conditions would meet their quotas by whatever means were available, and once the goods passed out of their factory, what happened to them was someone else's headache.

In market economies, poor quality is punished by low sales, and retailers soon give a signal to factory managers by shifting their purchases to other suppliers. The incentives that obviously flow from such private-sector purchasing discretion were generally absent from centrally planned economies, where purchases and sales were organized by the body of planners, and prices and profits were not used to signal customer satisfaction or dissatisfaction.

Misplaced Incentives

In market economies, relative wages and salaries provide incentives for labour to move from place to place, and the possibility of losing one's job provides an incentive to work diligently. This is a harsh mechanism that punishes job losers with loss of income (although social programs provide floors to the amount of economic punishment that can be suffered). In centrally planned economies, workers usually had complete job security. Industrial unemployment was rare, and even when it did occur, new jobs were usually found for all who lost theirs. Although the high level of security was attractive to many people, it proved impossible to provide sufficient incentives for reasonably hard and efficient work under such conditions.

Environmental Degradation

Fulfilling production plans became the all-embracing goal in centrally planned economies, to the exclusion of most other considerations, including the environment. As a result, environmental degradation occurred in the Soviet Union and the countries of Eastern Europe on a scale unknown in advanced Western nations. A particularly disturbing example (only one of many) occurred in Central Asia, where high quotas for cotton output led to indiscriminate use of pesticides and irrigation. Birth defects became very common, and the vast Aral Sea was more than three-quarters drained, causing major environmental effects.

This failure to protect the environment stemmed from the pressure to fulfill production plans and the absence of a "political marketplace" where citizens could express their preferences for the environment. Imperfect though the system may be in democratic market economies—and in some particular cases it has been quite poor—their record of environmental protection has been vastly better than that of the centrally planned economies.

So, the first answer to the question about the existence of an alternative to the market economy is no: There is no practical alternative to a mixed system with major reliance on markets but some government presence in most aspects of the economy. The second answer is yes: Within the framework of a mixed economy there are substantial alternatives among many different and complex mixes of free-market and government determination of economic life.

Government in the Modern Mixed Economy

Market economies in today's advanced industrial countries are based primarily on voluntary transactions between individual buyers and sellers. Private individuals have the right to buy and sell what they want, to accept or refuse work that is offered to them, and to move where they want when they want.

> Key institutions are private property and freedom of contract, both of which must be maintained by active government policies. The government creates laws of ownership and contract and then provides the institutions, such as police and courts, to enforce these laws.

In modern mixed economies, governments go well beyond these important basic functions. They intervene in market transactions to correct what economists call *market failures*. These are well-defined situations in which free markets do not work well. Some products, called *public goods,* are usually not provided at all by markets because their use cannot usually be restricted to those who pay for them. Defence and police protection are examples of public goods. In other cases, private producers or consumers impose costs called *externalities* on those who have no say in the transaction. This is the case when factories pollute the air and rivers. The public is harmed but plays no part in the transaction. In yet other cases, financial institutions, such as banks, mortgage companies, and investment houses, may indulge in risky activities that threaten the health of the entire economic system. These market failures explain why governments sometimes intervene to alter the allocation of resources.

Also, important issues of *equity* arise from letting free markets determine people's incomes. Some people lose their jobs because firms are reorganizing to become more efficient in the face of new technologies. Others keep their jobs, but the market places so little value on their services that they face economic deprivation. The old and the chronically ill may suffer if their past circumstances did not allow them to save enough to support themselves. For many reasons of this sort, almost everyone accepts some government intervention to redistribute income. Care must be taken, however, not to kill the goose that lays the golden egg. By taking too much from higher-income people, we risk eliminating their incentives to work hard and produce income, some of which is to be redistributed to those in need.

These are some of the reasons that all modern economies are mixed economies. Throughout most of the twentieth century in advanced industrial societies, the mix had been shifting toward more and more government participation in decisions about the allocation of resources and the distribution of income. Starting in the early 1980s, a worldwide movement began to reduce the degree of government participation in economies. With the onset of the global financial crisis of 2008–2009, however, there has been some movement back toward a greater involvement of government in the economy. These shifts in the market/government mix, and the reasons for them, are some of the major issues that will be studied in this book.

SUMMARY

1.1 What Is Economics?   LO 1

- Scarcity is a fundamental problem faced by all economies. Not enough resources are available to produce all the goods and services that people would like to consume.
- Scarcity makes it necessary to choose. All societies must have a mechanism for choosing what goods and services will be produced and in what quantities.
- The concept of opportunity cost emphasizes the problem of scarcity and choice by measuring the cost of obtaining a unit of one product in terms of the number of units of other products that could have been obtained instead.

- A production possibilities boundary shows all the combinations of goods that can be produced by an economy whose resources are fully and efficiently employed. Movement from one point to another along the boundary requires a reallocation of resources.
- Four basic questions must be answered in all economies: What is produced and how? What is consumed and by whom? Why are resources sometimes idle? Is productive capacity growing?
- Issues of government policy enter into discussions of all four questions.

1.2 The Complexity of Modern Economies   LO 2, 3, 4

- A market economy is self-organizing in the sense that when individual consumers and producers act independently to pursue their own self-interest, responding to prices determined in open markets, the collective outcome is coordinated.
- Incentives and self-interest play a central role for all groups of decision makers: consumers, producers, and governments.
- Individual consumers are assumed to make their decisions in an effort to maximize their well-being or utility. Producers' decisions are assumed to be designed to maximize their profits.

- The interaction of consumers and producers through goods and factor markets is illustrated by the circular flow of income and expenditure. Individual consumers sell factor services to producers and thereby earn their income. Similarly, producers earn their income by selling goods and services to individual consumers.
- Modern economies are based on the specialization and division of labour, which necessitate the exchange (trading) of goods and services. Exchange takes place in markets and is facilitated by the use of money.
- Driven by the ongoing revolution in transportation and communications technology, the world economy is rapidly globalizing.

1.3 Is There an Alternative to the Market Economy?   LO 5

- We can distinguish three pure types of economies: traditional, command, and free-market. In practice, all economies are mixed economies in that their economic behaviour responds to mixes of tradition, government command, and price incentives.
- In the late 1980s, events in Eastern Europe and the Soviet Union led to the general acceptance that the system of fully centrally planned economies had failed to produce minimally acceptable living standards for

its citizens. All these countries are now moving toward greater market determination and less state command in their economies.
- Governments play an important role in modern mixed economies. They create and enforce important background institutions such as private property and freedom of contract. They intervene to correct market failures. They also redistribute income in the interests of equity.

KEY CONCEPTS

Resources	Incentives and self-interest	Traditional economies
Scarcity and the need for choice	Specialization	Command economies
Choice and opportunity cost	The division of labour	Free-market economies
Production possibilities boundary	Trade and money	Mixed economies
The self-organizing economy	Globalization	

STUDY EXERCISES

MyEconLab   Make the grade with MyEconLab: Study Exercises marked in red can be found on MyEconLab. You can practise them as often as you want, and most feature step-by-step guided instructions to help you find the right answer.

1. Fill in the blanks to make the following statements correct.

   a. The three general categories of any economy's resources are _____, _____, and _____. Economists refer to these resources as the _____ of production.
   b. When we use any resource, the benefit given up by not using it in its best alternative way is known as the _____ of that resource.
   c. The concepts of scarcity, choice, and opportunity cost can be illustrated by a curve known as the _____.
   d. When looking at a production possibilities boundary, any point that is outside the boundary demonstrates _____. The _____ slope of the production possibilities boundary demonstrates _____.
   e. A straight-line production possibilities boundary (PPB) indicates that the opportunity cost of each good is _____, no matter how much of that good is produced. A PPB that is concave to the origin indicates that a(n) _____ amount of one good must be given up to produce more of the other good.
   f. Consider an economy producing two goods, A and B, with a PPB that is concave to the origin. As the economy produces more of good A and less of good B, its opportunity cost of producing A _____.

2. Explain the three economic concepts illustrated by the production possibilities boundary.

3. Consider an economy that produces only food and clothing. Its production possibilities boundary is shown below.

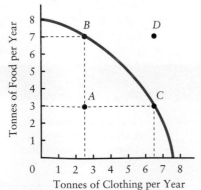

a. If the economy is at point A, how many tonnes of clothing and how many tonnes of food are being produced? At point B? At point C?
b. What do we know about the use of resources when the economy is at point A? At point B? At point C?
c. If the economy is at point B, what is the opportunity cost of producing one more tonne of food? What is the opportunity cost of producing one more tonne of clothing?
d. What do we know about the use of resources at point D? How would it be possible for the economy to produce at point D?

4. Choiceland has 250 workers and produces only two goods, X and Y. Labour is the only factor of production, but some workers are better suited to producing X than Y (and vice versa). The table below shows the maximum levels of output of each good possible from various levels of labour input.

Number of Workers Producing X	Annual Production of X	Number of Workers Producing Y	Annual Production of Y
0	0	250	1300
50	20	200	1200
100	45	150	900
150	60	100	600
200	70	50	350
250	75	0	0

a. Draw the production possibilities boundary for Choiceland on a scale diagram, with the production of X on the horizontal axis and the production of Y on the vertical axis.
b. Compute the opportunity cost of producing an extra 15 units of X if the economy is initially producing 45 units of X and 900 units of Y. How does this compare to the opportunity cost if the economy were initially producing 60 units of X and 600 units of Y?
c. If the economy is producing 40 units of X and 600 units of Y, what is the opportunity cost of producing an extra 20 units of X?
d. Suppose now that the technology associated with producing good Y improves, so that the maximum

level of Y that can be produced from any given level of labour input increases by 10 percent. Explain (or show in a diagram) what happens to the production possibilities curve.

5. Explain why a technological improvement in the production of one good means that a country can now produce more of *other* goods than it did previously. Hint: Draw a country's production possibilities boundary to help answer this question.

6. Consider your decision whether to go skiing for the weekend. Suppose transportation, lift tickets, and accommodation for the weekend cost $300. Suppose also that restaurant food for the weekend will cost $75. Finally, suppose you have a weekend job that you will have to miss if you go skiing, which pays you $120 (after tax) for the one weekend day that you work. What is the opportunity cost of going skiing? Do you need any other information before computing the opportunity cost?

7. Suppose you and a friend are stranded on an island and must gather firewood and catch fish to survive. Through experience, you know that if each of you spends an entire day on either activity, the result is given in the following table:

	Fish	Firewood (bundles)
You	6	3
Your friend	8	2

You and your friend decide that you should each specialize so that one person catches fish while the other gathers firewood. But who should do which task?

a. What is the opportunity cost for you to gather an additional bundle of firewood? What is your friend's opportunity cost of gathering an extra bundle of firewood?

b. Assuming that you and your friend specialize, what allocation of tasks maximizes total output for your one day of joint effort?

c. Suppose you both decide to work for two days according to the allocation in part (b). What is the total amount of output? What would it have been had you chosen the reverse allocation of tasks?

8. In this chapter we used a simple idea of a production possibilities boundary to illustrate the concepts of scarcity, choice, and opportunity cost. We assumed there were only two goods—call them X and Y. But we all know that any economy produces many more than just two goods. Explain why the insights illustrated in Figure 1-2 on page 8 are more general, and why the assumption of only two goods is a useful one.

9. What is the difference between microeconomics and macroeconomics?

10. For each of the following situations, explain how a change in the stated "price" is likely to affect your incentives regarding the stated decision.

a. the price of ski-lift tickets; your decision to purchase a ski-lift ticket

b. the hourly wage for your weekend job; the decision to not work and go skiing on the weekend instead

c. the value of a speeding ticket; your decision to speed on the highway

d. the weight of your course grade attached to an assignment; your decision to work hard on that assignment

e. the level of tuition fees at your college or university; your decision to attend that college or university

11. State and explain two reasons why the specialization of labour is more efficient than universal self-sufficiency.

12. Consider the market for doctors' services. In what way has this market taken advantage of the specialization of labour?

13. List the four main types of economic systems and their main attributes.

14. As we said in the text, the average family income in Canada is about $75 000 per year. Imagine a hypothetical world in which *all* Canadian families had this income.

a. In such a world, would poverty exist in Canada?

b. In such a world, would scarcity exist in Canada?

c. Explain the difference between poverty and scarcity.

15. Comment on the following statement: "One of the mysteries of semantics is why the government-managed economies ever came to be called planned and the market economies unplanned. It is the former that are in chronic chaos, in which buyers stand in line hoping to buy some toilet paper or soap. It is the latter that are in reasonable equilibrium—where if you want a bar of soap or a steak or a shirt or a car, you can go to the store and find that the item is magically there for you to buy. It is the liberal economies that reflect a highly sophisticated planning system, and the government-managed economies that are primitive and unplanned."

A Refresher on Graphing

This appendix is a refresher on the basic graphing techniques you saw in high school mathematics. Economists use graphs to illustrate theories and show data, and you will see many graphs throughout this course. Here, we review the most basic concepts for those who need review.

Displaying Points on a Graph

Coordinate Space A graph begins with two number lines, one horizontal and one vertical. We call the horizontal number line the x axis because we often label the variable displayed along this axis x. We call the vertical number line the y axis because we often label the variable displayed along this axis y. In Figure 1 the x axis displays the number line horizontally from -5 to 5 with intervals of 1. The y axis displays the number line vertically from -3 to 3, also with intervals of 1. We have now created a two-dimensional space that is called a *coordinate space*.

Now look at point A in the figure. Point A represents two numbers: 3 on the horizontal, or x, axis and 2 on the vertical, or y, axis. We write point A as (3, 2)

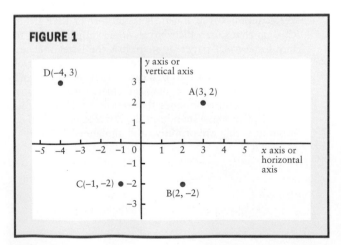

FIGURE 1

and we call the 3 and the 2 the *coordinates* of point A. The usual practice in graphing is to list the x-axis coordinate first and the y-axis coordinate second. In the same way, we can read point B(2, –2), point C(–1, –2), and point D(–4, 3).

Any point on a graph is simply a visual representation of two numbers. For example, point A represents the numbers 3 and 2. For the graph to be meaningful to us, however, the numbers must tell us something. Let's take an example from economics and plot a graph with the information from the table in Figure 2 that shows how much Katie saves at various levels of income (both measured in dollars). Each point on the graph now represents a particular level of income and the associated level of saving, or an income-saving combination. For example, point C shows that at an income of $30 000, Katie saves $5000. It is also easy to see when looking at this graph that when Katie's level of income goes up, her level of saving goes up.

Notice that each increment indicated on the x axis is 10 000 and the increment on the y axis is only 5 000. We adjust the scales on the axes to fit the information we want to graph. In Figure 1 we called each interval 1 on both axes, and in Figure 2 we called each interval on the x axis 10 000 and each interval on the y axis 5 000. Imagine trying to graph Canadian national income, which is in the range of $1.7 trillion, on a graph using intervals of $1 or even $10 000. The resulting graph would have to be enormous, and would not be helpful in displaying the information. Therefore, we choose the scales on each axis to best display the specific data we are considering.

Variables Our graph in Figure 2 now visually represents the relationship between the two variables, income and saving. *Variable* is the word we use to describe the items on the axes to which we are giving numeric values; in this case, income and saving. The *independent* variable, in this case income, is represented on the

FIGURE 2

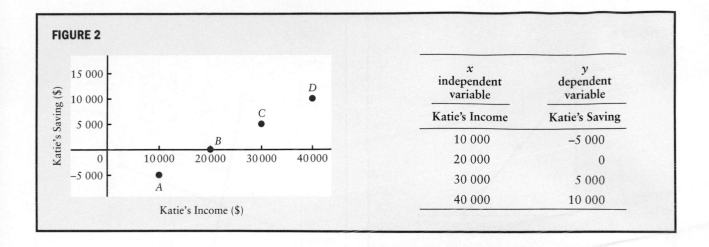

x independent variable	y dependent variable
Katie's Income	Katie's Saving
10 000	–5 000
20 000	0
30 000	5 000
40 000	10 000

horizontal axis (the x axis) and the *dependent* variable, in this case saving, is represented on the vertical axis (the y axis). (Though this is the usual way to draw a graph, you will later see that economists are sometimes accused of doing it backward—see footnote 3 on page 71 in Chapter 3.)

Linear Curves

When two variables move, either in the same or in opposite directions, we can plot the data points on a graph and join their points to form a curve. If joining the points gives us a straight line we call it a linear curve and we say that x and y have a linear *relationship*. A relationship in which the two variables move in the same direction is called a *positive,* or *direct,* relationship—when one variable goes up, the other goes up. A relationship in which the two variables move in opposite directions is called a *negative,* or *inverse,* relationship—when one variable goes up, the other goes down.

A Positive Relationship Figure 3 shows two variables, the number of pizza toppings and the total price of a pizza. A cheese pizza has zero toppings and costs $5; each additional topping costs $1.50. The two variables, number of toppings and price of pizza, move in the same direction—as the number of toppings (the x variable) goes up, the price of the pizza (the y variable) goes up—so this is a positive or direct

FIGURE 3

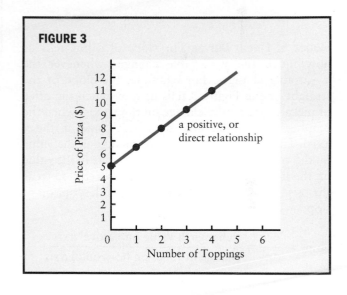

relationship. Joining the points gives us an upward-sloping straight line, so we call this a positive, linear relationship.

A Negative Relationship Figure 4 shows two variables, the price of tickets for a university basketball game and the number of people who choose to purchase tickets and attend the game. (In Chapter 3 we describe such a relationship as a *demand curve* for basketball tickets.) The two variables move in opposite directions—this is a negative, or inverse, relationship. Joining the points gives us a downward-sloping straight line, so we call this a negative linear relationship.

FIGURE 4

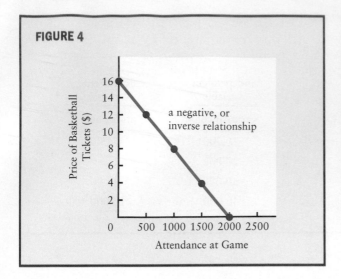

a negative, or inverse relationship

FIGURE 5

Slopes of Linear Curves The slope of a line tells us how much the *y* variable changes whenever the *x* variable changes. For example, the slope of the straight line in Figure 3 tells us how much the price of pizza changes (the change on the *y* axis) when the number of toppings changes (the change on the *x* axis). The slope is defined as the change in the value on the vertical axis divided by the change in the value on the horizontal axis. It is commonly referred to as the "rise over the run." We can write a description of slope in a few ways:

$$\text{Slope} = \frac{\text{rise}}{\text{run}} = \frac{\text{change in value on vertical axis}}{\text{change in value on horizontal axis}}$$

$$= \frac{\Delta y}{\Delta x}$$

The last term uses the Greek letter delta, Δ, which means "the change in." For Figure 3, the slope of the curve is $1.50 per topping, indicating that each extra topping increases the price of the pizza by $1.50.

Figure 5 shows the calculation of slopes for two linear curves. (Work through each of these calculations and then draw various linear curves of your own and practise calculating their slopes. Try using different units and intervals on the axes and see if this affects the slope.) Notice that the upward-sloping curve has a positive slope and the downward-sloping curve has a negative slope. Also notice that the steeper the line, upward- or downward-sloping, the higher the absolute number value of the slope.

A linear curve has the same slope over the entire length of the curve.

Infinite and Zero Slopes Figure 6 shows two extreme cases that we see often in economics. For the horizontal line, we calculate the slope as rise/run = $\Delta y / \Delta x = 0/\infty$. We say that the run, or Δx, is ∞ because the linear curve extends to infinity. Zero divided by infinity is zero. Remember that the flatter is the curve, the smaller is the slope. Here is the extreme case of a flat curve; the slope is zero. For the vertical line, we calculate the slope as rise/run = $\Delta y / \Delta x = \infty/0$. Infinity divided by zero is infinity. Remember that the

FIGURE 6

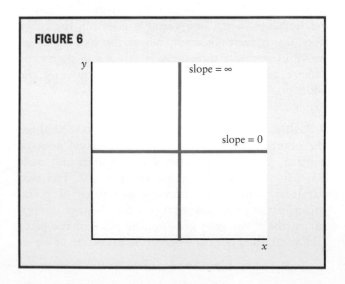

steeper is the curve, the higher is the slope. This is the extreme case of a steep curve; the slope is infinite.

Understanding the concept of the slope of a line is crucial when studying economics. Economists are interested in how much one variable changes in response to a change in another variable, and it is the slope of the curve that tells them this.

Equation of a Linear Curve A linear curve is a visual representation of the linear relationship between two variables. The same relationship can also be described in an equation. The general equation for a linear curve is

$$y = a + bx,$$

where y is the dependent variable and x is the independent variable. The letter a represents the y *intercept,* or the point at which the line intersects the y axis. The letter b represents the slope of the line.

In Figure 7 we plot the linear curve, A, given by the relationship between the x and y variables in Table A of Figure 7. The equation for this linear curve is

$$y = 2 + 0.5x$$

Prove this to yourself by calculating y for any value of x. For example, when $x = 3$, $y = 2 + 0.5(3) = 3.5$. When $x = 7$, $y = 2 + 0.5(7) = 5.5$. The y intercept of this line is 2, and thus the line intersects the y axis at 2.

The slope of the line is 0.5. Verify this by calculating $\Delta y/\Delta x$ between any two points on the line. Between points C and D, for example, the Δy (or the rise) is 1 and the Δx (or the run) is 2. So the slope of the linear curve is $\Delta y/\Delta x = 1/2 = 0.5$.

The equation for a downward-sloping linear curve works the same way. In Figure 7 we plot the linear curve, B, given by the relationship between the x and y variables in Table B of Figure 7. The equation for this linear curve is $y = 8 - 4x$. Once again, prove this to yourself by calculating y for various levels of x. The y intercept for this line is 8 and the slope is –4. Notice, of course, that the slope of the downward-sloping linear curve is negative.

Non-Linear Curves

All the curves we have looked at so far have been straight lines—they have been linear curves. (So they haven't really been "curves" at all!) However, not all relations between two economic variables can be graphed as a straight line. More often, the relation is *non-linear.* In a non-linear relationship between x and y, each unit change in x does not always bring about the same change in the y variable. Figure 8 shows four curves, two with positive slopes and two with negative slopes.

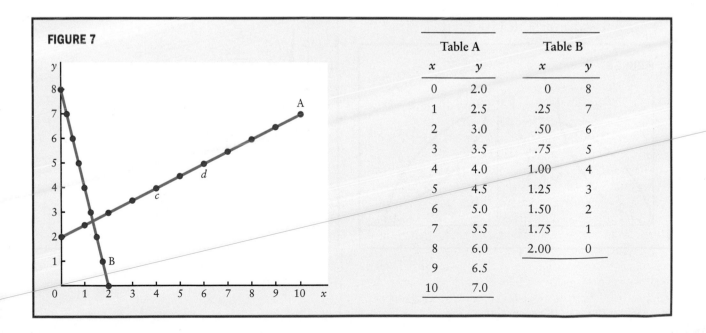

FIGURE 7

Table A		Table B	
x	y	x	y
0	2.0	0	8
1	2.5	.25	7
2	3.0	.50	6
3	3.5	.75	5
4	4.0	1.00	4
5	4.5	1.25	3
6	5.0	1.50	2
7	5.5	1.75	1
8	6.0	2.00	0
9	6.5		
10	7.0		

Curves A and B both show positive relationships between x and y—the slopes are both positive. As x increases, so does y. Curve A, however, becomes flatter as x increases, and curve B becomes steeper as x increases. Similarly, curves C and D both show negative relationships between x and y—both slopes are negative because in each case, as x increases, y decreases. Curve C becomes flatter as x increases and curve D becomes steeper as x increases.

Slopes of Non-Linear Curves Examine curves A, B, C, and D in Figure 8 to see how y changes in response to a one-unit change in x, at various levels of x. You will see that for curves A and C, the change in y becomes smaller as we move along the x axis. We can describe the slopes of curves A and C as starting out steep and becoming flatter as x increases. For curves B and D, however, the change in y becomes larger as we move along the x axis. We can describe the slopes of curves B and D as starting out flat and becoming steeper as x increases. The slopes of these non-linear curves are changing as we move along the curve. How do we measure the slope of a curve when the slope is different at each point along the curve?

Remember that we measured the slope of a straight line by choosing two points on the line and dividing the change in y by the change in x. Doing the same thing to measure the slope of a non-linear curve, however, would give us the slope of the line connecting the two specific points that we chose on the curve but would not give us the slope of the curve itself.

Since the slope of the curve is continuously changing, we must measure the slope *at specific points* along the curve. To do so, we simply draw a straight line *tangent* to the curve at the point at which we want to measure the slope. A line is tangent to a curve if it touches *but does not intersect* the curve at that point. The slope of this tangent line then tells us the slope of the curve *at the point of tangency*. Figure 9 shows the calculation of the slope at three points along a downward-sloping curve like our curve C in Figure 8.

Consider the slope of the curve at point A. The tangent to the curve at point A has a y intercept at 50 and an x intercept at 10. Thus the slope of the tangent line is $\Delta y / \Delta x = -50/10 = -5$. Thus the slope of the curve at point A is –5. Now consider the slope of the curve at point C. The tangent line to point C has an x intercept of 50 and a y intercept of 10. The slope of the tangent line is $\Delta y / \Delta x = -10/50 = -0.2$. Therefore the slope of the curve at point C is –0.2. Thus, although the slope of the curve is always negative, its slope falls (in absolute value) from 5 at point A to 0.2 at point C.

FIGURE 9

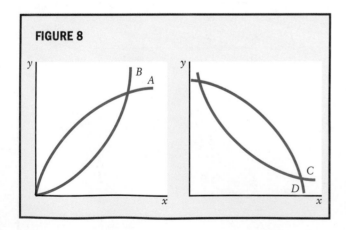

FIGURE 8

We leave it to you to draw more non-linear curves (like curves A, B, and D in Figure 8) and compute the slopes at various points along each curve. For each computation, simply draw a straight line tangent to the curve, and then compute the slope of the tangent line. This will give you the slope of the non-linear curve *at the point of tangency*.

A Final Word

Graphing can be intimidating, but a little practice goes a long way. By working your way carefully through the various parts of this section, plus the graphing questions in the Study Exercises at the end of Chapter 2, you will soon be comfortable with the basics of graphing.

Economic Theories, Data, and Graphs

IF you follow the news, whether online, TV, newspaper, or radio, you are likely to hear the views of economists being discussed—about debt crises, unemployment, attempts to reform the health-care system, environmental policy, changes to corporate income-tax rates, or a myriad of other issues. Where do economists' opinions come from? Are they supported by hard evidence, and if so, why do economists sometimes disagree with each other over important issues?

Economics is a social science, and in this chapter we explore what it means to be "scientific" in the study of economics. Along the way we will learn much about theories, predictions, data, testing, and graphing—economists use all of these tools and techniques in their attempt to understand the economic world. We begin with the important distinction between positive and normative statements.

2.1 Positive and Normative Statements

Economists give two broad types of advice, called *normative* and *positive*. For example, they sometimes advise that the government ought to try harder to reduce unemployment. When they say such things, they are giving normative advice; in this case, they are making judgements about the value of the various things that the government could do with its limited resources and about the costs and benefits of reducing unemployment. Advice that depends on a value judgement is normative—it tells others what they *ought* to do.

Another type of advice is illustrated by the statement "If the government wants to reduce unemployment, reducing unemployment insurance benefits is an effective way of doing so." This is positive advice. It does not rely on a judgement about the value of reducing unemployment. Instead, the expert is saying, "If this is what you want to do, here is a way to do it."

Normative statements depend on value judgements and cannot be evaluated solely by a recourse to facts. In contrast, **positive statements** do not involve value judgements. They are statements about matters of fact, and so disagreements about them are appropriately dealt with by an appeal to evidence. The distinction between positive and normative is fundamental to scientific progress. Much of the success of modern science depends on the ability of scientists to separate their views on *what does happen* in the world from their views on *what they would like to happen*. For example, until the eighteenth century almost everyone believed that Earth was only a few thousand years old. Evidence then began to accumulate that Earth was billions of years old. This evidence was hard for most people to accept, since it ran counter to a literal reading of many religious texts. Many did not want to believe the evidence. Nevertheless, scientists, many of whom were religious, continued their research because they refused to allow their feelings about what they wanted to believe to affect their scientific search for the truth. Eventually, all scientists and most members of the public came to accept that Earth is about 4 billion years old.

normative statement A statement about what ought to be as opposed to what actually is.

positive statement A statement about what actually is (was, or will be), as opposed to what ought to be.

> Distinguishing what is actually true from what we would like to be true requires distinguishing between positive and normative statements.

Examples of both types of statements are given in Table 2-1. All five positive statements in the table are assertions about the nature of the world in which we live. In contrast, the five normative statements involve value judgements. Notice two things about the positive/normative distinction. First, positive statements need not be true. Statement C is almost certainly false, and yet it is positive, not normative. Second, the inclusion of a value judgement in a statement does not necessarily make the statement itself normative. Statement D is a positive statement about the value judgements that people hold. We could conduct a survey to check if people really do prefer low unemployment to low inflation. We could ask them and we could observe how they voted. There is no need for the economist to rely on a value judgement to check the validity of the statement itself.

We leave you to analyze the remaining eight statements to decide precisely why each is either positive or normative. Remember to apply the two tests. First, is the statement only about actual or alleged facts? If so, it is a positive one. Second, are value judgements necessary to assess the truth of the statement? If so, it is normative.

TABLE 2-1   Positive and Normative Statements

Positive	Normative
A Raising interest rates encourages people to save.	F People should be encouraged to save.
B High rates of income tax encourage people to evade paying taxes.	G Governments should arrange taxes so that people cannot avoid paying them.
C Lowering the price of cigarettes leads people to smoke less.	H The government should raise the tax on cigarettes to discourage people from smoking.
D The majority of the population would prefer a policy that reduced unemployment to one that reduced inflation.	I Unemployment is a more important social problem than inflation.
E Government financial assistance to commercial banks is ineffective at preventing job losses.	J Government should not spend taxpayers' money on supporting commercial banks.

Disagreements Among Economists

Economists often disagree with one another in public discussions, frequently because of poor communication. The adversaries fail to define their terms or their points of reference clearly, and so they end up "arguing past" each other, with the only certain result being that the audience is left confused.

Economists often disagree with one another in the media or at conferences, but their debates are more often about normative issues than positive ones.

Another source of disagreement stems from some economists' failure to acknowledge the full state of their ignorance. There are many points on which the evidence is far from conclusive. Informed judgements are required to take a position on even a purely positive question. In such cases, a responsible economist makes clear the extent to which his or her view is based on judgements about the relevant facts.

Many other public disagreements are based on the positive/normative distinction. Different economists have different values, and these normative views play a large part in most discussions of public policy. Many economists stress the importance of individual responsibility and argue, for example, that lower employment insurance benefits would be desirable because people would have a greater incentive to search for a job. Other economists stress the need for a generous "social safety net" and argue that higher employment insurance benefits are desirable because human hardship would be reduced. In such debates, and there are many in economics, it is the responsibility of the economist to state clearly what part of the proffered advice is normative and what part is positive.

Because the world is complex and because no issue can be settled beyond any doubt, economists rarely agree unanimously on an issue. Nevertheless, there is an impressive amount of agreement on many aspects of how the economy works and what happens when governments intervene to alter its workings. A survey published in the *American*

Economic Review, perhaps the most influential economics journal, showed strong agreement among economists on many propositions, including "Rent control leads to a housing shortage" (85 percent yes), "Tariffs usually reduce economic welfare" (93 percent yes), "Large government budget deficits have adverse effects on the economy" (83 percent yes), and "A minimum wage increases unemployment among young workers" (79 percent yes). Notice that all these are positive rather than normative statements. Other examples of these areas of agreement will be found in many places throughout this book.

Whether they agree or disagree with one another, economists are in demand in many sectors of the economy. See *Applying Economic Concepts 2-1* for a discussion of the many organizations that employ economists.

APPLYING ECONOMIC CONCEPTS 2-1

Where Economists Work

This chapter discusses the theoretical and empirical tools that economists use. After reading this material, you might wonder where economists find jobs and what kind of work they actually do. The skills of economists are demanded in many parts of the economy by governments, private and crown corporations, non-profit organizations, and universities.

In Ottawa and the provincial and territorial capitals, economists are hired in most government departments to analyze the effects of government policies and to design ways to improve those policies. At Finance Canada, economists design and analyze the income-tax system and the effects of current spending programs. At Environment Canada, they help design and evaluate policies aimed at reducing water and air pollution. At Industry Canada, they study the sources of productivity growth and design policies to encourage innovation in the private sector. At the Bank of Canada, economists research the link between interest rates, the aggregate demand for goods and services, and the rate of increase in prices. They also monitor developments in the global economy and their effects on the Canadian economy. Statistics Canada employs many economists to design methods of collecting and analyzing data covering all aspects of Canadian society.

The analysis of economic policies also takes place in independent research organizations, often called "think tanks." The C.D. Howe Institute in Toronto is one of Canada's best-known think tanks, and it regularly publishes papers on topics ranging from monetary policy and the state of public pensions to the effects of immigration and the challenges in reforming Canada's policies for foreign development assistance. Other think tanks include the Institute for Research on Public Policy, the Canadian Centre for Policy Alternatives, the Fraser Institute, the Centre for the Study of Living Standards, and the Conference Board of Canada. All of these independent and non-profit organizations hire economists to study economic issues and then write and edit the economic publications that address them.

Private and public (crown) corporations in many sectors of the economy also hire economists in a variety of positions. Economists at Canadian Pacific Railway monitor how changes in world commodity prices will lead to changes in Canadian resource production and thus to changes in the demand for their rail transport services. Economists at Manitoba Hydro study the link between economic growth and electricity demand to help the firm with its long-run investment decisions. Those at Export Development Canada examine how economic and political risks in various countries influence the demand for the products of Canadian exporters. Economists at Bombardier are hired to determine how ongoing negotiations within the World Trade Organization will affect tariff levels in various countries and how these changes will affect the demand for Bombardier jets.

Finally, many economists are hired by universities all over the world to teach students like you and to conduct research on a wide variety of economic topics. Some of this research is theoretical and some is empirical, using data to test economic theories. Other academic economists focus their research on the design and implementation of better economic policy, and often spend considerable time interacting with the economists employed by government departments.

Training in economics provides useful analytical skills that are valuable for learning about the workings of a complex economic world. There is no shortage of demand for people who can think clearly and analytically about economic issues. This course could well be the start of a great career for you. Study hard!

| 2.2 Building and Testing Economic Theories

The economic world is complex. Many things are changing at the same time, and it is difficult to distinguish cause from effect. Economists who are observing the world carefully, however, see regularities in the data—for example, that unemployment tends to rise when national income slows, or that periods of higher inflation often follow periods of very low interest rates. In order to better understand such regularities in the data, and to identify the likely causes and effects, economists develop *theories,* which they sometimes call *models.* Theories are used to both explain events that have already happened and to help predict events that might happen in the future.

What Are Theories?

Theories are constructed to explain things. For example, economists may seek to explain what determines the quantity of eggs bought and sold in a particular month in Manitoba and the price at which they are sold. Or they may seek to explain what determines the quantity of oil bought and sold around the world on a particular day and the price at which it is traded. As part of the answer to such questions, economists have developed theories of demand and supply—theories that we will study in detail in the next three chapters. These and all other theories are distinguished by their *variables, assumptions,* and *predictions.*

variable Any well-defined item, such as the price or quantity of a commodity, that can take on various specific values.

Variables The basic elements of any theory are its variables. A **variable** is a well-defined item, such as a price or a quantity, that can take on different possible values.

In a theory of the egg market, the variable *quantity of eggs* might be defined as the number of cartons of 12 Grade A large eggs. The variable *price of eggs* is the amount of money that must be given up to purchase each carton of eggs. The particular values taken by those two variables might be 20 000 cartons per week at a price of $2.60 in July 2011, 18 000 cartons per week at a price of $2.75 in July 2012, and 19 500 cartons per week at a price of $2.95 in July 2013.

There are two broad categories of variables that are important in any theory. An **endogenous variable** is one whose value is determined within the theory. An **exogenous variable** influences the endogenous variables but is itself determined outside the theory. To illustrate the difference, the price of eggs and the quantity of eggs are endogenous variables in our theory of the egg market—our theory is designed to explain them. The state of the weather, however, is an exogenous variable. It may well affect the number of eggs consumers demand or producers supply, but we can safely assume that the state of the weather is not influenced by the market for eggs.

endogenous variable A variable that is explained within a theory. Sometimes called an *induced variable* or a *dependent variable.*

exogenous variable A variable that is determined outside the theory. Sometimes called an *autonomous variable* or an *independent variable.*

Assumptions A theory's assumptions concern motives, directions of causation, and the conditions under which the theory is meant to apply.

Motives. The theories we study in this book make the fundamental assumption that everyone pursues his or her own self-interest when making economic decisions. Individuals are assumed to strive to maximize their *utility,* while firms are assumed to try to maximize their *profits.* Not only are they assumed to know what they want, but we also assume that they know how to go about getting it within the constraints they face.

Direction Of Causation. When economists assume that one variable is related to another, they are usually assuming some causal link between the two. For example, when the amount of wheat that producers want to supply is assumed to increase when the quality of their fertilizer improves, the causation runs from the quality of fertilizer to the supply of wheat. Producers supply more wheat because they now have access to better fertilizer; they are not assumed to get access to better fertilizers as a result of their increased supply of wheat.

Conditions Of Application. Assumptions are often used to specify the conditions under which a theory is meant to hold. For example, a theory that assumes there is "no government" usually does not mean literally the absence of government but only that the theory is meant to apply when governments are not significantly affecting the situation being studied.

Although assumptions are an essential part of all theories, students are often concerned about those that seem unrealistic. An example will illustrate some of the issues involved. Much of the theory that we are going to study in this book uses the assumption that owners of firms attempt to make as much money as they can—that is, to maximize their profits. The assumption of profit maximization allows economists to make predictions about the behaviour of firms, such as "firms will supply more output if the market price increases."

Profit maximization may seem like a rather crude assumption. Surely, for example, the managers of firms sometimes choose to protect the environment rather than pursue certain highly polluting but profitable opportunities. Does this not discredit the assumption of profit maximization by showing it to be unrealistic?

The answer is no; to make successful predictions, the theory does not require that managers be solely and unwaveringly motivated by the desire to maximize profits at all times. All that is required is that profits be a sufficiently important consideration that a theory based on the assumption of profit maximization will lead to explanations and predictions that are substantially correct. It is not always appropriate to criticize a theory because its assumptions seem unrealistic. A good theory abstracts in a useful way; a poor theory does not. If a theory has ignored some genuinely important factors, its predictions will usually be contradicted by the evidence.

All theory is an abstraction from reality. If it were not, it would merely duplicate the world in all its complexity and would add little to our understanding of it.

Predictions A theory's predictions are the propositions that can be deduced from it. They are often called *hypotheses*. For example, a prediction from a theory of the oil market is that a rise in the world price for oil will lead Canadian oil producers to produce and supply more oil. Another prediction in the same market is that a decision by the members of the OPEC cartel to reduce their annual output of oil will lead to an increase in the world price. The economic logic behind such predictions will be explained in several chapters of this book; for now we can proceed to see how economists *test* such predictions or hypotheses.

Testing Theories

A theory is tested by confronting its predictions with evidence. For example, is an increase in the world price of oil *actually* followed by an increase in oil production by Canadian producers? A theory ceases to be useful when it cannot predict better than an alternative theory. When a theory consistently fails to predict better than an available alternative, it is either modified or replaced.

The old question "Which came first: the chicken or the egg?" is often raised when discussing economic theories. In the first instance, it was observation that preceded economic theories; people were not born with economic theories embedded in their minds. However, once economics was established as a scientific line of inquiry, theories and evidence interacted with each other. It has now become impossible to say that one precedes the other. In some cases, empirical evidence may suggest inadequacies that require the development of better theories. In other cases, an inspired guess may lead to a theory that has little current empirical support but is subsequently found to explain many observations. This interaction between theory and empirical observation is illustrated in Figure 2-1.

FIGURE 2-1 The Interaction Between Theory and Empirical Observation

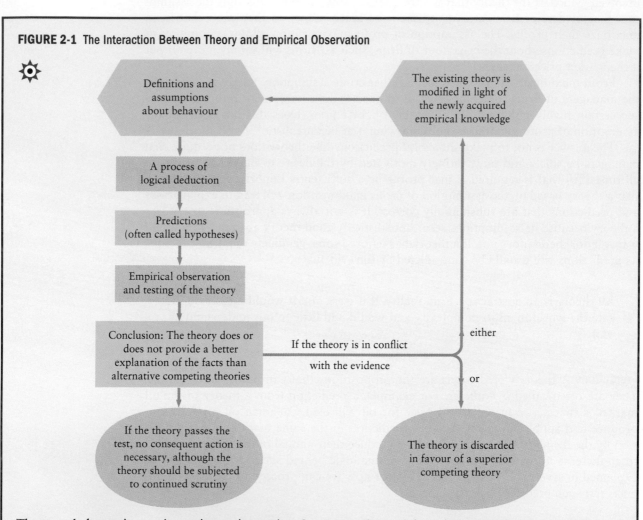

Theory and observation are in continuous interaction. Starting (at the top left) with the assumptions of a theory and the definitions of relevant terms, the theorist deduces by logical analysis everything that is implied by the assumptions. These implications are the predictions or the hypotheses of the theory. The theory is then tested by confronting its predictions with evidence. If the theory is in conflict with facts, it will usually be amended to make it consistent with those facts (thereby making it a better theory), or it will be discarded, to be replaced by a superior theory. The process then begins again: The new or amended theory is subjected first to logical analysis and then to empirical testing.

The scientific approach is central to the study of economics: Empirical observation leads to the construction of theories, theories generate specific predictions, and the predictions are tested by more detailed empirical observation.

Rejection Versus Confirmation An important part of the scientific approach consists of creating a theory that will explain some observation. A theory designed to explain observation X will typically generate a prediction about some other observable variables, Y and Z. The prediction about Y and Z can be tested and may be *rejected* by the data. If the prediction is rejected, the value of the theory is brought into question.

The alternative to this approach is to create a theory and then look for *confirming* evidence. Such an approach is hazardous because the world is sufficiently complex that some confirming evidence can be found for any theory, no matter how unlikely the theory may be. For example, flying saucers, the Loch Ness monster, fortune telling, and astrology all have their devotees who can quote confirming evidence in spite of the failure of many attempts to discover systematic, objective evidence of these things.

Statistical Analysis Most theories generate a prediction of the form "If X increases, then Y will also increase." A specific example is "If national income rises, the level of employment will rise." Statistical analysis can be used to test such predictions and to estimate the numerical values of the function that describes the relationship. In practice, the same data can be used simultaneously to test whether a relationship exists and, if it does exist, to provide an estimate of the magnitude of that relationship.

Because economics is primarily a non-laboratory science, it lacks the controlled experiments central to such sciences as physics and chemistry. Economics must therefore use millions of uncontrolled "experiments" that are going on every day in the marketplace. Households are deciding what to purchase given changing prices and incomes, firms are deciding what to produce and how, and governments are involved in the economy through their various taxes, subsidies, and regulations. Because all these activities can be observed and recorded, a mass of data is continually being produced by the economy.

The variables that interest economists—such as the level of employment, the price of a DVD, and the output of automobiles—are generally influenced by many forces that vary simultaneously. If economists are to test their theories about relations among specific variables, they must use statistical techniques designed for situations in which other things *cannot* be held constant. Fortunately, such techniques exist, although their application is usually neither simple nor straightforward.

Later in this chapter we provide a discussion of some graphical techniques for describing data and displaying some of the more obvious relationships. Further examination of data involves techniques studied in elementary statistics courses. More advanced courses in econometrics deal with the array of techniques designed to test economic hypotheses and to measure economic relations in the complex circumstances in which economic evidence is often generated.

Correlation Versus Causation Suppose you want to test your theory's prediction that "If X increases, Y will also increase." You are looking for a *causal* relationship from X to Y, because a change in X is predicted to *cause* a change in Y. When you look at the data, suppose you find that X and Y are positively correlated—that is, when X rises, Y also tends to rise. Is your theory supported? It might appear that way, but there is a potential problem.

A finding that X and Y are positively correlated means only that X and Y tend to move together. This correlation is *consistent* with the theory that X causes Y, but it is *not* direct evidence of this causal relationship. The causality may be in the opposite direction—from Y to X. Or X and Y may have no direct causal connection; they may instead be jointly caused by some third variable, Z.

Here is an example. Suppose your theory predicts that individuals who get more education will earn higher incomes as a result—the causality in this theory runs from education to income. In the data, suppose we find that education and income are positively correlated (as they are). This should not, however, be taken as direct evidence for the causal prediction. The data are certainly consistent with that theory, but they are also consistent with others. For example, individuals who grow up in higher-income households may "buy" more education, just as they buy more clothes or entertainment. In this case, income causes education, rather than the other way around. Another possibility is that education and income are positively correlated because the personal characteristics that lead people to become more educated—ability and motivation—are the same characteristics that lead to high incomes. In this case, the *causal* relationship runs from personal characteristics to both income and education.

> Most economic predictions involve causality. Economists must take care when testing predictions to distinguish between correlation and causality. Correlation can establish that the data are consistent with the theory; establishing the likelihood of causality usually requires advanced statistical techniques.

2.3 Economic Data

For data on the Canadian economy and many other quantifiable aspects of Canadian life, see Statistics Canada's website: www.statcan.gc.ca

Economists use real-world observations to test their theories. For example, did the amount that people saved last year rise—as the theory predicts it should have—when a large tax cut increased their after-tax incomes? To test this prediction we need reliable data for people's incomes and their savings.

Political scientists, sociologists, anthropologists, and psychologists often collect for themselves the data they use to formulate and test their theories. Economists are unusual among social scientists in mainly using data collected by others, often government statisticians. In economics there is a division of labour between collecting data and using them to test theories. The advantage is that economists do not need to spend much of their scarce research time collecting the data they use. The disadvantage is that they are often not as well informed about the limitations of the data collected by others as they would be if they had collected the data themselves.

After data are collected, they can be displayed in various ways, many of which we will see later in this chapter. They can be laid out in tables. They can be displayed in various types of graphs. And when we are interested in relative movements rather than absolute ones, the data can be expressed in *index numbers*. We begin with a discussion of index numbers.

Index Numbers

Economists frequently look at data on prices or quantities and explore how specific variables change over time. For example, they may be interested in comparing the time paths of output in two industries: steel and newsprint. The problem is that it may be difficult to compare the time paths of the two different variables if we just look at the "raw" data.

Table 2-2 shows some hypothetical data for the volume of output in the steel and newsprint industries. Because the two variables are measured in different units, it is not immediately clear which of the two variables is more volatile or which, if either, has an upward or a downward trend.

It is easier to compare the two paths if we focus on *relative* rather than *absolute* changes. One way to do this is to construct some **index numbers**.

How to Build an Index Number We start by taking the value of the variable at some point in time as the "base" with which the values in other periods will be compared. We call this the *base period*. In the present example, we choose 2004 as the base year for both series. We then take the output in each subsequent year, called the "given year," divide it by the output in the base year, and then multiply the result by 100. This gives us an index number for the output of steel and a separate index number for the output of newsprint. For each index number, the value of output in the base year is equal to 100. The details of the calculations are shown in Table 2-3.

An index number simply expresses the value of some series in any given year as a percentage of its value in the base year. For example, the 2014 index of steel output of 122.5 tells us that steel output in 2014 was 22.5 percent greater than in 2004. In contrast, the 2014 index for newsprint output of 93.8 tells us that newsprint output in 2014 was only 93.8 percent of the output in 2004—that is, output was 6.2 percent

TABLE 2-2   Volume of Steel and Newsprint Output

Year	Volume of Steel (thousands of tonnes)	Volume of Newsprint (thousands of rolls)
2004	200	3200
2005	210	3100
2006	225	3000
2007	215	3200
2008	250	3100
2009	220	3300
2010	265	3100
2011	225	3300
2012	255	3100
2013	230	3200
2014	245	3000

Comparing the time paths of two data series is difficult when absolute numbers are used. Since steel output and newsprint output have quite different absolute numbers, it is difficult to detect which time series is more volatile.

index number A measure of some variable, conventionally expressed relative to a base period, which is assigned the value 100.

TABLE 2-3   Constructing Index Numbers

Year	Steel Procedure	Index	Newsprint Procedure	Index
2004	$(200/200) \times 100 =$	100.0	$(3200/3200) \times 100 =$	100.0
2005	$(210/200) \times 100 =$	105.0	$(3100/3200) \times 100 =$	96.9
2006	$(225/200) \times 100 =$	112.5	$(3000/3200) \times 100 =$	93.8
2007	$(215/200) \times 100 =$	107.5	$(3200/3200) \times 100 =$	100.0
2008	$(250/200) \times 100 =$	125.0	$(3100/3200) \times 100 =$	96.9
2009	$(220/200) \times 100 =$	110.0	$(3300/3200) \times 100 =$	103.1
2010	$(265/200) \times 100 =$	132.5	$(3100/3200) \times 100 =$	96.9
2011	$(225/200) \times 100 =$	112.5	$(3300/3200) \times 100 =$	103.1
2012	$(255/200) \times 100 =$	127.5	$(3100/3200) \times 100 =$	96.9
2013	$(230/200) \times 100 =$	115.0	$(3200/3200) \times 100 =$	100.0
2014	$(245/200) \times 100 =$	122.5	$(3000/3200) \times 100 =$	93.8

Index numbers are calculated by dividing the value in the given year by the value in the base year and multiplying the result by 100. The 2014 index number for steel tells us that steel output in 2014 was 22.5 percent greater than in the base year, 2004. The 2014 index number for newsprint tells us that newsprint output in 2014 was 93.8 percent of the output in the base year, 2004.

lower in 2014 than in 2004. The results in Table 2-3 allow us to compare the relative fluctuations in the two series. It is apparent from the values in the table that the output of steel has shown significantly more percentage variability than has the output of newsprint. This is also clear in Figure 2-2.

The formula of any index number is

$$\text{Value of index in any given period} = \frac{\text{Absolute value in given period}}{\text{Absolute value in base period}} \times 100$$

Care must be taken, however, when using index numbers. The index number always tells you the percentage change compared with the base year, but when comparing an index number across non-base years, the percentage change in the index number is *not* given by the absolute difference in the values of the index number. For example, if you want to know how much steel output changed from 2008 to 2010, we know from Table 2-3 that the index number for steel output increased from 125.0 to 132.5. But this is not an increase of 7.5 percent. The *percentage* increase in steel output is computed as $(132.5 - 125.0)/125.0 = 7.5/125.0 = 0.06$, or 6 percent.

More Complex Index Numbers Perhaps the most famous index number used by economists is the index of average prices—the Consumer Price Index (CPI). This is a price index of the *average* price paid by consumers for the typical basket of goods that they buy. The inclusion of the word "average," however, makes the CPI a more complex index number than the ones we have constructed here.

With what you have just learned, you could construct separate index numbers for the price of beef, the price of coffee, and the price of orange juice. But to get the

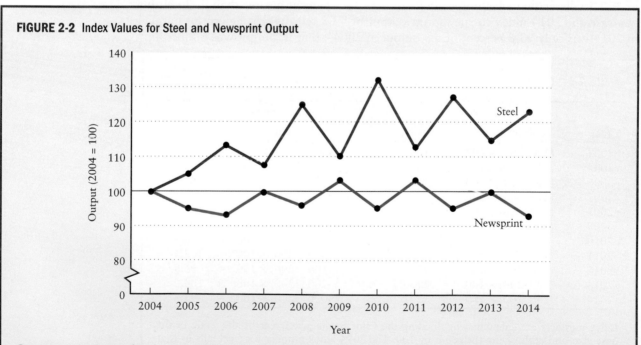

FIGURE 2-2 Index Values for Steel and Newsprint Output

Comparing the time paths of two variables is much easier when index numbers are used. Since both index numbers are equal to 100 in the base year, relative volatility and trends become clear. Steel output is clearly more volatile in percentage terms than newsprint output. Steel output also has an upward trend, whereas newsprint output appears to have little or no trend.

Consumer Price Index, we need to take the *average* of these separate price indexes (plus thousands of others for the goods and services we have ignored here). But it cannot be a simple average. Instead, it must be a *weighted* average, in which the weight assigned to each price index reflects the relative importance of that good in the typical consumer's basket of goods and services. For example, since the typical consumer spends a tiny fraction of income on sardines but a much larger fraction of income on housing, the weight on the "sardines" price index in the CPI is very small and the weight on the "housing" price index is very large. The result is that even huge swings in the price of sardines have negligible effects on the CPI, whereas much more modest changes in the price of housing have noticeable effects on the CPI.

We will spend much more time discussing the Consumer Price Index when we study macroeconomics beginning in Chapter 19. For now, keep in mind the usefulness of the simple index numbers we have constructed here. They allow us to compare the time paths of different variables.

Graphing Economic Data

A single economic variable, such as unemployment, national income, or the average price of a house, can come in two basic forms.

Cross-Sectional and Time-Series Data The first is called **cross-sectional data**, which means a number of different observations on one variable all taken in different places at the same point in time. Figure 2-3 shows an example. The variable in the figure is the average selling price of a house. It is shown for each of the ten Canadian provinces in April 2012.

The second type of data is called **time-series data**. It refers to observations of one variable at successive points in time. The data in Figure 2-4 show the unemployment rate for Canada from 1978 to 2012. (Note that the Canadian unemployment rate is simply a weighted average of the 13 provincial and territorial unemployment rates, where the weight for each region is that region's labour force as a fraction of the total Canadian labour force.) Time-series graphs are quite useful in economics because we often want to know how specific economic numbers are changing over time. As is clear in Figure 2-4, the Canadian unemployment rate is relatively volatile over long periods of time, but in recent years it has been low by historical standards.

Scatter Diagrams Another way data can be presented is in a **scatter diagram**. It is designed to show the relation between two different variables. To plot a scatter

cross-sectional data A set of observations made at the same time across several different units (such as households, firms, or countries).

time-series data A set of observations made at successive periods of time.

scatter diagram A graph showing two variables, one measured on the horizontal and the other on the vertical axis. Each point represents the values of the variables for a particular unit of observation.

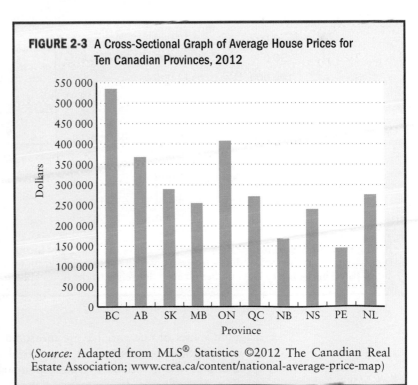

FIGURE 2-3 A Cross-Sectional Graph of Average House Prices for Ten Canadian Provinces, 2012

(*Source:* Adapted from MLS® Statistics ©2012 The Canadian Real Estate Association; www.crea.ca/content/national-average-price-map)

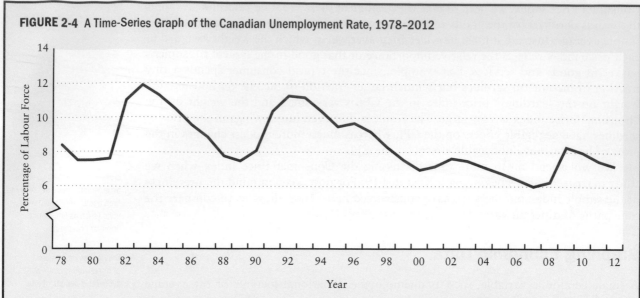

FIGURE 2-4 A Time-Series Graph of the Canadian Unemployment Rate, 1978–2012

Source: Annual average of monthly, seasonally adjusted data from Statistics Canada, CANSIM Table 282-0087; both sexes, 15 years and over)

FIGURE 2-5 A Scatter Diagram of Household Income and Saving

Household	Annual Income	Annual Saving
1	$ 70 000	$10 000
2	30 000	2 500
3	100 000	12 000
4	60 000	3 000
5	80 000	8 000
6	10 000	500
7	20 000	2 000
8	50 000	2 000
9	40 000	4 200
10	90 000	8 000

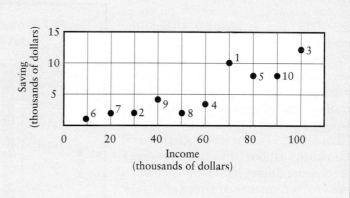

Saving tends to rise as income rises. The table shows the amount of income earned by ten selected households together with the amount they saved during the same year. The scatter diagram plots the income and saving for the ten households listed in the table. The number on each dot refers to the household in the corresponding row of the table.

diagram, values of one variable are measured on the horizontal axis and values of the second variable are measured on the vertical axis. Any point on the diagram relates a specific value of one variable to a corresponding specific value of the other.

The data plotted on a scatter diagram may be either cross-sectional data or time-series data. An example of the former is shown in Figure 2-5. The table in the figure shows data for the income and saving of ten households in one particular year, and these data are plotted on a scatter diagram. Each point in the figure represents one household, showing its income and its saving. The positive relation between the two stands out. The higher the household's income, the higher its saving tends to be.

2.4 Graphing Economic Theories

Theories are built on assumptions about relationships between variables. For example, the quantity of eggs demanded is assumed to fall as the price of eggs rises, and the total amount an individual saves is assumed to rise as his or her income rises. How can such relations be expressed?

Functions

When one variable, X, is related to another variable, Y, in such a way that to every value of X there is only one possible value of Y, we say that Y is a *function* of X. When we write this relation down, we are expressing a *functional relation* between the two variables.

Here is a specific but hypothetical example. Consider the relation between an individual's annual income, which we denote by the symbol Y, and the amount that person spends on goods and services during the year, which we denote by the symbol C (for consumption). Any particular example of the relation between C and Y can be expressed several ways: in words, in a table or schedule, in a mathematical equation, or in a graph.

Verbal Statement. When income is zero, the person will spend $800 a year (either by borrowing the money or by consuming past savings), and for every extra $1 of income the person will increase expenditure by 80 cents.

Schedule. This table shows selected values of the person's income and consumption.

Annual Income	Consumption	Reference Letter
$ 0	$ 800	p
2 500	2 800	q
5 000	4 800	r
7 500	6 800	s
10 000	8 800	t

Mathematical Equation. $C = \$800 + 0.8Y$ is the equation of the relation just described in words and displayed in the table. As a check, you can first see that when Y is zero, C is $800. Further, you can see that every time Y increases by $1, the level of C increases by 0.8($1), which is 80 cents.

Graph. Figure 2-6 shows the points from the preceding schedule and the line representing the equation given in the previous paragraph.

FIGURE 2-6 Income and Consumption

$$C = 800 + 0.8Y$$

Consumption expenditure rises as income rises. The figure graphs the schedule and the equation for the hypothetical functional relation discussed in the text.

FIGURE 2-7 Linear Pollution Reduction

$$\text{Slope} = \frac{\Delta P}{\Delta E} = \frac{-1}{+2} = -0.5$$

Pollution as a linear function of clean-up expenditure. Between points A and B it costs $2000 to reduce pollution by 1000 tonnes. The cost of pollution reduction is the same elsewhere on the line. The slope of the line, -0.5, indicates that any $1 expenditure on pollution clean-up reduces the amount of pollution by 0.5 tonnes.

Comparison of the values on the graph with the values in the schedule, and with the values derived from the equation just stated, shows that these are alternative expressions of the same relation between C and Y. All four of these modes of expression refer to the same relation between the person's consumption expenditure and income.

Graphing Functions

Different functions have different graphs, and we will meet many of these in subsequent chapters. Figure 2-6 is an example of a relation in which the two variables move together. When income goes up, consumption goes up. In such a relation the two variables are *positively related* to each other.

Figure 2-7 gives an example of variables that move in opposite directions. As the amount spent on reducing pollution goes up, the amount of remaining pollution goes down. In such a relation the two variables are *negatively related* to each other.

Both of these graphs are straight lines. In such cases the variables are *linearly related* to each other (either positively or negatively).

The Slope of a Straight Line Slopes are important in economics. They show you how much one variable changes as the other changes. The slope is defined as the amount of change in the variable measured on the vertical axis per unit change in the variable measured on the horizontal axis. In the case of Figure 2-7 it tells us how many tonnes of pollution, symbolized by P, are removed per dollar spent on reducing pollution, symbolized by E. Consider moving from point A to point B in the figure. If we spend $2000 more on clean-up, we reduce pollution by 1000 tonnes. This is 0.5 tonnes per dollar spent. On the graph the extra $2000 is indicated by ΔE, the arrow indicating that E rises by 2000. The 1000 tonnes of pollution reduction is indicated by ΔP, the arrow showing that pollution falls by 1000. (The Greek uppercase letter delta, Δ, stands for "the change in.") To get the amount of pollution reduction per dollar of expenditure, we merely divide one by the other. In symbols this is $\Delta P/\Delta E$.

If we let X stand for whatever variable is measured on the horizontal axis and Y for whatever variable is measured on the vertical axis, the slope of a straight line is $\Delta Y/\Delta X$. [1][1]

---

[1] Red numbers in square brackets indicate mathematical notes that are found in a separate section at the back of the book.

The equation of the line in Figure 2-7 can be computed in two steps. First, note that when $E = 0$, the amount of remaining pollution, P, is equal to 6 (thousand tonnes). Thus, the line meets the vertical axis ($E = 0$) when P equals 6. Second, we have already seen that the slope of the line, $\Delta P/\Delta E$, is equal to -0.5, which means that for every one-unit increase in E, P falls by 0.5 unit. We can thus state the equation of the line as

$$P = 6 - (0.5)E$$

where both P and E are expressed as thousands of units (tonnes and dollars, respectively).

Non-linear Functions Although it is sometimes convenient to simplify a real relation between two variables by assuming them to be linearly related, this is seldom the case over their whole range. Non-linear relations are much more common than linear ones. In the case of reducing pollution, it is usually quite cheap to eliminate the first units of pollution. Then, as the environment gets cleaner and cleaner, the cost of further clean-up tends to increase because more and more sophisticated and expensive methods need to be used. As a result, Figure 2-8 is more realistic than Figure 2-7. Inspection of Figure 2-8 shows that as more and more is spent, the amount of pollution reduction for an additional \$1 of clean-up expenditure gets smaller and smaller. This is shown by the diminishing slope of the curve as we move rightward along it. For example, as we move from point A to point B, an increase in expenditure of \$1000 is required to reduce pollution by 1000 tonnes. Thus, each tonne of pollution reduction costs \$1. But as we move from point C (where we have already reduced pollution considerably) to point D, an extra \$6000 must be spent in order to reduce pollution by 1000 tonnes. Each tonne of pollution reduction therefore costs \$6.

Economists call the change in pollution when a bit more or a bit less is spent on clean-up the *marginal* change. The figure shows that the slope of the curve at each point measures

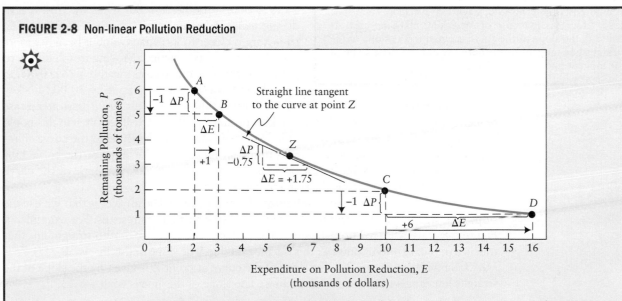

FIGURE 2-8 Non-linear Pollution Reduction

Pollution as a non-linear function of clean-up expenditure. The slope of the curve changes as we move along it. Between points A and B, it costs \$1000 to reduce pollution by 1000 tonnes. Between points C and D, it costs \$6000 to reduce pollution by 1000 tonnes. At point Z, the slope of the curve is equal to the slope of the straight line tangent to the curve at point Z. The slope of the tangent line is $-0.75/1.75 = -0.43$.

FIGURE 2-9 Increasing Production Costs

Production costs increase at an increasing rate as annual output rises. From point *A* to point *B*, an extra annual output of 10 000 hockey sticks increases annual costs by $30 000. Each extra stick costs $3. From point *C* to point *D*, an extra output of 10 000 hockey sticks increases annual costs by $150 000. Each extra hockey stick then costs $15. This is a case of increasing marginal cost. At point *Z*, the slope of the curve is equal to the slope of the straight line tangent to the curve at point *Z*. The slope of the tangent line is 65/8 = 8.13.

this marginal change. It also shows that in the type of curve illustrated, the marginal change per dollar spent is diminishing as we spend more on reducing pollution. There is always a payoff to more expenditure over the range shown in the figure, but the payoff diminishes as more is spent. This relation can be described as *diminishing marginal response*. We will meet such relations many times in what follows, so we emphasize now that diminishing marginal response does not mean that the *total* response is diminishing. In Figure 2-8, the total amount of pollution continues to fall as more and more is spent on clean-up. But diminishing marginal response does mean that the amount of pollution reduced per dollar of expenditure gets less and less as the total expenditure rises.

Figure 2-9 shows a graph in which the marginal response is increasing. The graph shows the relationship between annual production costs and annual output for a firm that makes hockey sticks. Notice that the more sticks produced annually, the higher the firm's costs. This is shown by the positive slope of the line. Notice also that as more and more hockey sticks are produced, the extra amount that the firm must pay to produce each extra stick rises. For example, as the firm moves from point *A* to point *B*, annual costs rise by $30 000 in order to increase its annual output by 10 000 hockey sticks. Each extra stick costs $3 ($30 000/10 000 = $3). But when the firm is producing many more hockey sticks, such as at point *C*, its factory is closer to its capacity and it becomes more costly to increase production. Moving from point *C* to point *D*, the firm's annual costs increase by $150 000 in order to increase its annual output by 10 000 hockey sticks. Each extra stick then costs $15 ($150 000/10 000 = $15). This figure illustrates a case of *increasing marginal cost*, a characteristic of production that we will see often in this book.

Figures 2-8 and 2-9 show that with non-linear functions the slope of the curve changes as we move along the curve. For example, in Figure 2-8, the slope of the curve falls as the expenditure on pollution clean-up increases. In Figure 2-9, the slope of the curve increases as the volume of production increases.

How, exactly, do we measure the slope of a curved line? The answer is that we use the slope of a straight line *tangent to that curve* at the point that interests us. For example, in Figure 2-8, if we want to know the slope of the curve at point *Z*, we draw a straight line that touches the curve *only* at point *Z*; this is a tangent line. The slope of this line is −0.75/1.75 = −0.43. Similarly, in Figure 2-9, the slope of the curve at point *Z* is given by the slope of the straight line tangent to the curve at point *Z*. The slope of this line is 65/8 = 8.13.

For non-linear functions, the slope of the curve changes as *X* changes. Therefore, the marginal response of *Y* to a change in *X* depends on the value of *X*.

Functions with a Minimum or a Maximum So far, all the graphs we have shown have had either a positive or a negative slope over their entire range. But many relations change directions as the independent variable increases. For example, consider a firm that is attempting to maximize its profits and is trying to determine how much output to produce. The firm may find that its unit production costs are lower than the market price of the good, and so it can increase its profit by producing more. But as it increases its level of production, the firm's unit costs may be driven up because the capacity of the factory is being approached. Eventually, the firm may find that extra output will actually cost so much that its profits are *reduced*. This is a relationship that we will study in detail in later chapters, and it is illustrated in Figure 2-10. Notice that when profits are maximized at point *A*, the slope of the curve is zero (because a tangent to the curve at point *A* is horizontal), and so the *marginal response* of profits to output is zero.

Now consider an example of a function with a minimum. You probably know that when you drive a car, the fuel consumption per kilometre depends on your speed. Driving very slowly uses a lot of fuel per kilometre travelled. Driving very fast also uses a lot of fuel per kilometre travelled. The best fuel efficiency—the lowest fuel consumption per kilometre travelled—occurs at a speed of approximately 95 kilometres per hour. The relationship between speed and fuel consumption is shown in Figure 2-11 and illustrates

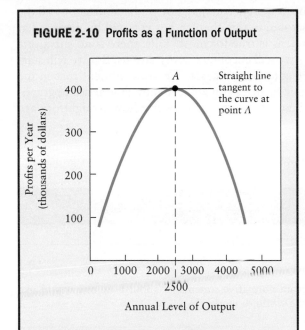

FIGURE 2-10 Profits as a Function of Output

Profits rise and then eventually fall as output rises. When the firm is producing fewer than 2500 units annually, the marginal response of profit to output is positive—that is, an increase in output leads to an increase in profit. Beyond 2500 units annually, the marginal response is negative—an increase in output leads to a reduction in profit. At point *A*, profits are maximized and the marginal response of profit to output is zero. Because the tangent at point *A* is horizontal, the slope of the curve is zero at that point.

FIGURE 2-11 Average Fuel Consumption as a Function of Speed

Average fuel consumption falls and then rises as speed increases. Average fuel consumption in litres per kilometre travelled is minimized at point *A* at a speed of approximately 95 kilometres per hour (km/h). At speeds less than 95 km/h, the marginal response is negative—that is, an increase in speed reduces fuel consumption per kilometre. At speeds above 95 km/h, the marginal response is positive—an increase in speed increases fuel consumption per kilometre. At 95 km/h, the marginal response is zero and fuel consumption per kilometre is minimized.

a function with a minimum. Note that at point A the slope of the curve is zero (because a tangent to the curve at point A is horizontal), and so the *marginal response* of fuel consumption to speed is zero.

> At either a minimum or a maximum of a function, the slope of the curve is zero. Therefore, at the minimum or maximum, the marginal response of Y to a change in X is zero.

A Final Word

We have done much in this chapter. We have discussed why economists develop theories (or models) to help them understand the world. We have also discussed how they test their theories and how there is a continual back-and-forth process between empirical testing of predictions and refining the theory. Finally, we have devoted considerable time and space to exploring the many ways that data can be displayed in graphs and how economists use graphs to illustrate their theories.

Many students find themselves intimidated when they are first confronted with all the details about graphing. But try not to worry. You may not yet be a master of all the graphing techniques that we have discussed in this chapter, but you will be surprised at how quickly it all falls into place. And, as is true for most skills, there is no substitute for practice. In the next three chapters we will encounter many graphs. But we will start simply and then slowly attempt more complicated cases. We are confident that in the process of learning some basic economic theories you will get enough practice in graphing that you will very soon look back at this chapter and realize how straightforward it all is.

SUMMARY

2.1 Positive and Normative Statements

LO 1

- A key to the success of scientific inquiry lies in separating positive statements about the way the world works from normative statements about how one would like the world to work.

2.2 Building and Testing Economic Theories

LO 2, 3

- Theories (sometimes called models) are designed to explain and predict what we see. A theory consists of a set of definitions of the variables to be discussed, a set of assumptions about how things behave, and the conditions under which the theory is meant to apply.
- A theory provides predictions of the type "If one event occurs, then another event will also occur."
- Theories are tested by checking their predictions against evidence. In economics, testing is almost always done using the data produced by the world of ordinary events.

- Economists make use of statistical analysis when testing their theories. They must take care to make the distinction between correlation and causation.
- The progress of any science lies in finding better explanations of events than are now available. Thus, in any developing science, one must expect to discard some existing theories and replace them with demonstrably superior alternatives.

2.3 Economic Data   LO 4

- Index numbers express economic series in relative form. Values in each period are expressed in relation to the value in the base period, which is given a value of 100.
- Economic data can be graphed in three different ways. Cross-sectional graphs show observations taken at the same time. Time-series graphs show observations on one variable taken over time. Scatter diagrams show many points, each of which refers to specific observations on two different variables.

2.4 Graphing Economic Theories   LO 5

- A functional relation can be expressed in words, in a schedule giving specific values, in a mathematical equation, or in a graph.
- A graph of two variables has a positive slope when they both increase or decrease together and a negative slope when they move in opposite directions.
- The marginal response of a variable gives the amount it changes in response to a change in a second variable.
- When the variable is measured on the vertical axis of a diagram, its marginal response at a specific point on the curve is measured by the slope of the line at that point.
- Some functions have a maximum or minimum point. At such points, the marginal response is zero.

KEY CONCEPTS

Positive and normative statements
Endogenous and exogenous variables
Theories and models
Variables, assumptions, and predictions

Correlation versus causation
Functional relations
Positive and negative relations
    between variables

Positively and negatively sloped curves
Marginal responses
Maximum and minimum values

STUDY EXERCISES

MyEconLab   Make the grade with MyEconLab: Study Exercises marked in red can be found on MyEconLab. You can practise them as often as you want, and most feature step-by-step guided instructions to help you find the right answer.

1. Determine whether each of the following statements is positive or normative.

   a. The government should impose stricter regulations on the banking sector to avoid future financial crises.
   b. Financial aid to developing countries has no impact on per capita GDP in those countries.
   c. Tuition fee increases at Canadian universities lead to reduced access for low-income students.
   d. It is unfair that Canadians have universal access to health care but not to dental care.
   e. Canadians currently have too much personal debt.

2. What are some of the positive and normative issues that lie behind the disagreements in the following cases?

   a. Economists disagree on whether the government of Canada should try to stimulate the economy in the next six months.
   b. European and North American negotiators disagree over the desirability of reducing European farm subsidies.
   c. Economists argue about the merits of a voucher system that allows parents to choose the schools their children will attend.

d. Economists debate the use of a two-tier medical system in Canada (whereby health care continues to be publicly provided, but individuals are permitted to be treated by doctors who bill the patient directly—an approach known as "extra billing").

e. Economists debate the costs of global climate change and the relative merits of carbon taxes and other policies to reduce greenhouse gas emissions.

f. Policymakers disagree about the extent to which financial markets need to be regulated.

3. In the following examples, identify the exogenous (or independent) variable and the endogenous (or dependent) variable.

a. The amount of rainfall on the Canadian prairies determines the amount of wheat produced in Canada.

b. When the world price of coffee increases, there is a change in the price of your cup of coffee at Tim Hortons.

c. If student loans were no longer available, there would be fewer students attending university.

d. An increase in the tax on gasoline leads people to drive more fuel-efficient vehicles.

4. Economists sometimes make each of the following assumptions when they construct models. Discuss some situations in which each of these assumptions might be a useful simplification in order to think about some aspect of the real world.

a. Earth is flat.

b. There are no differences between men and women.

c. There is no tomorrow.

d. There are only two periods: this year and next year.

e. A country produces only two types of goods.

f. People are wholly selfish.

5. Fill in the blanks to make the following statements correct.

a. Economists have designed _____ to better explain and predict the behaviour we observe in the world around us.

b. A variable, such as price or quantity, that is determined within a theory is known as a(n) _____ variable. A variable that is determined outside the theory is known as a(n) _____ variable.

c. When, based on a theory, we claim that "If A occurs, then B will follow," we are making a _____ that can then be tested by _____ observation.

d. If we observe that when variable A decreases, variable B also decreases, we can say that the two variables are _____. We cannot necessarily say

that there is a _____ relationship between A and B.

6. Use the appropriate graph—time-series, cross-sectional, or scatter diagram—to illustrate the economic data provided in each part below.

a. The Canadian-dollar price of one U.S. dollar (the "exchange rate") in 2011:

January	0.994
February	0.988
March	0.977
April	0.958
May	0.968
June	0.977
July	0.956
August	0.982
September	1.003
October	1.019
November	1.026
December	1.024

b. A comparison of average household expenditures across provinces in 2010:

British Columbia	$72 486
Alberta	84 087
Saskatchewan	69 237
Manitoba	66 330
Ontario	74 521
Quebec	61 536
New Brunswick	59 943
Nova Scotia	61 907
Prince Edward Island	58 194
Newfoundland and Labrador	60 139

c. Per capita growth rates of real GDP and investment rates for various countries, averaged over the period 1950–2009:

Country	Average Growth Rate (% per year)	Average Investment Rate (% of GDP)
Canada	2.0	18.2
Austria	3.1	22.0
Japan	4.0	26.6
United States	1.9	18.1
United Kingdom	2.0	14.5
Spain	3.4	23.0
Norway	2.8	27.4
South Korea	5.1	27.2
Iceland	2.7	28.0

7. Use the following figure to answer the questions below.

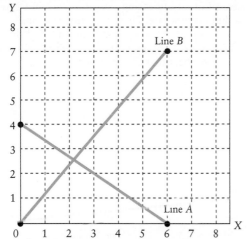

a. Is the slope of Line A positive or negative? Line B?
b. Calculate the slope of Line A. Write the equation describing the line in the form $Y = mX + b$, where m is the slope of the line and b is a constant term.
c. Calculate the slope of Line B. Write the equation describing the line in the form $Y = mX + b$, where m is the slope of the line and b is a constant term.

8. Suppose the relationship between the government's tax revenue (T) and national income (Y) is represented by the following equation: $T = 10 + 0.25Y$. Plot this relationship on a scale diagram, with Y on the horizontal axis and T on the vertical axis. Interpret the equation.

9. Consider the following three specific functions for a functional relation between X and Y:
   i) $Y = 50 + 2X$
   ii) $Y = 50 + 2X + 0.05X^2$
   iii) $Y = 50 + 2X - 0.05X^2$
   a. For the values of X of 0, 10, 20, 30, 40, and 50, plot X and Y on a scale diagram for each specific function. Connect these points with a smooth line.
   b. For each function, state whether the slope of the line is constant, increasing, or decreasing as the value of X increases.
   c. Describe for each function how the marginal change in Y depends on the value of X.

10. Suppose you want to create a price index for the price of a particular physics textbook over ten years in your university bookstore. The price of the book on September 1 of each year is as follows:

Year	Price ($)	Year	Price ($)
2000	85	2006	120
2001	87	2007	125
2002	94	2008	127
2003	104	2009	127
2004	110	2010	130
2005	112		

a. The base year is 2000. Construct a physics textbook price index.
b. What is the percentage increase in the price of the book between the base year and 2005?
c. What is the percentage increase in the price of the book from 2007 to 2010?
d. Are the data listed above time-series or cross-sectional data? Explain why.

11. Suppose you want to create a price index for the price of pizza across several Canadian university campuses, as of March 1, 2013. The data are as follows:

University	Price per Pizza
Dalhousie	$6.50
Laval	5.95
McGill	6.00
Queen's	8.00
Waterloo	7.50
Manitoba	5.50
Saskatchewan	5.75
Calgary	6.25
UBC	7.25
Victoria	7.00

a. Using Calgary as the "base university," construct the Canadian university pizza price index.
b. At which university is pizza the most expensive, and by what percentage is the price higher than in Calgary?
c. At which university is pizza the least expensive, and by what percentage is the price lower than in Calgary?
d. Are the data listed above time-series or cross-sectional data? Explain why.

12. For each of the functional relations listed below, plot the relations on a scale diagram (with X on the horizontal axis and Y on the vertical axis) and compute the slope of the line.
   a. $Y = 10 + 3X$
   b. $Y = 20 + 4X$
   c. $Y = 30 + 5X$
   d. $Y = 10 + 5X$

13. Suppose we divide Canada into three regions: the West, the Centre, and the East. Each region has an unemployment rate, defined as the number of people unemployed, expressed as a fraction of that region's labour force. The table that follows shows each region's unemployment rate and the size of its labour force.

Region	Unemployment Rate	Labour Force
West	5.5%	5.3 million
Centre	7.2%	8.4 million
East	12.5%	3.5 million

a. Compute an unemployment rate for Canada using a simple average of the rates in the three regions. Is this the "right" unemployment rate for Canada as a whole? Explain why or why not.

b. Now compute an unemployment rate for Canada using weights that reflect the size of that region's labour force as a proportion of the overall Canadian labour force. Explain the difference in this unemployment rate from the one in part (a). Is this a "better" measure of Canadian unemployment? Explain why.

14. Draw three graphs in which the dependent variable increases at an increasing rate, at a constant rate, and at a diminishing rate. Then draw three graphs in which it decreases at an increasing, constant, and diminishing rate. State a real relation that each of these graphs might describe, other than the ones given in the text of this chapter.

Demand, Supply, and Price

CHAPTER OUTLINE

LEARNING OBJECTIVES (LO)

After studying this chapter, you will be able to

3.1 DEMAND

1 list the factors that determine the quantity demanded of a good.
2 distinguish between a shift of the demand curve and a movement along the demand curve.

3.2 SUPPLY

3 list the factors that determine the quantity supplied of a good.
4 distinguish between a shift of the supply curve and a movement along the supply curve.

3.3 THE DETERMINATION OF PRICE

5 explain the forces that drive market price to equilibrium, and how equilibrium price is affected by changes in demand and supply.

WE are now ready to study the important question of how markets work. The answer leads us to develop a simple model of supply and demand. And though there is much more to economics than just demand and supply (as many following chapters will illustrate), this is an essential starting point for understanding how a market economy functions.

As a first step, we need to understand what determines the demand for and the supply of particular products. Then we can see how demand and supply together determine the prices of products and the quantities that are bought and sold. Finally, we examine how the price system allows the economy to respond to changes in demand and supply. The concepts of demand and supply help us to understand the price system's successes and failures, and the consequences of many government policies.

This chapter deals with the basic elements of demand, supply, and price. In the next two chapters we use the theory of demand and supply to discuss such issues as cigarette taxes, legislated minimum wages, rent controls, and the burden of payroll taxes.

| 3.1 Demand

What determines the demand for any given product? How have Canadian consumers responded to the recent declines in the prices of smartphones and laptop computers? How will they respond to the next sudden change in the price of gasoline or coffee? We start by developing a theory designed to explain the demand for some typical product.

Quantity Demanded

quantity demanded The amount of a good or service that consumers want to purchase during some time period.

The total amount of any particular good or service that consumers want to purchase in some time period is called the **quantity demanded** of that product. It is important to notice two things about this concept.

First, quantity demanded is a *desired* quantity. It is the amount that consumers want to purchase when faced with a particular price of the product, other products' prices, their incomes, their tastes, and everything else that might matter. It may be different from the amount that consumers actually succeed in purchasing. If sufficient quantities are not available, the amount that consumers want to purchase may exceed the amount that they actually purchase. (For example, think of standing in line to purchase tickets to a show, only to find out that the show is sold out before you get to the head of the line.) To distinguish these two concepts, the term *quantity demanded* is used to refer to desired purchases, and such phrases as *quantity bought* or *quantity exchanged* are used to refer to actual purchases.

Second, quantity demanded refers to a *flow* of purchases, expressed as so much per period of time: 1 million units per day, 7 million per week, or 365 million per year. For example, being told that the quantity of new cars demanded (at current prices) in Canada is 50 000 means nothing unless you are also told the period of time involved. For a country as large as Canada, 50 000 cars demanded per day would be an enormous rate of demand, whereas 50 000 per year would be a very small rate of demand. The important distinction between *stocks* and *flows* is discussed in *Extensions in Theory 3-1*.

The total amount of some product that consumers in the relevant market want to buy in a given time period is influenced by the following important variables: [2]

- Product's own price
- Consumers' income
- Prices of other products
- Tastes
- Population
- Expectations about the future

We will discuss the separate effects of each of these variables later in the chapter. For now, we focus on the effects of changes in the product's own price. But how do we analyze the distinct effect of changes in one variable when all are likely to be changing at once? Since this is difficult to do, we consider the influence of the variables one at a time. To do this, we hold all but one of them constant. Then we let the selected variable

EXTENSIONS IN THEORY 3-1

The Distinction Between Stocks and Flows

An important conceptual issue that arises frequently in economics is the distinction between *stock* and *flow* variables. Economic theories use both, and it takes a little practice to keep them straight.

As noted in the text, a flow variable has a time dimension—it is so much *per unit of time*. For example, the quantity of Grade A large eggs purchased in Edmonton is a flow variable. No useful information is conveyed if we are told that the number purchased was 2000 dozen eggs unless we are also told the period of time over which these purchases occurred. Two thousand dozen eggs per hour would indicate a much more active market in eggs than would 2000 dozen eggs per month.

In contrast, a stock variable is a variable whose value has meaning *at a point in time*. Thus, the number of eggs in the egg producer's warehouse on a particular day—for example, 10 000 dozen eggs on September 3, 2013—is a stock variable. All those eggs are there at one time, and they remain there until something happens to change the stock held in the warehouse. The stock variable is just a number at a point in time, not a rate of flow of so much per unit of time.

The terminology of stocks and flows can be understood using an analogy to a bathtub. At any moment, the tub holds so much water. This is the *stock*, and it can be measured in terms of the volume of water, say, 100 litres. There might also be water flowing into the tub from the tap; this *flow* is measured as so much water per unit time, say, 10 litres per minute.

The distinction between stocks and flows is important. Failure to keep them straight is a common source of confusion and even error. Note, for example, that a stock variable and a flow variable cannot be added together without specifying some time period for which the flow persists. We cannot add the stock of 100 litres of water in the tub to the flow of 10 litres per minute to get 110 litres. The new stock of water will depend on how long the flow persists; if it lasts for 20 minutes, the new stock will be 300 litres; if the flow persists for 60 minutes, the new stock will be 700 litres (or the tub will overflow!).

The amount of income earned is a flow; it is so much per year or per month or per hour. The amount of a consumer's expenditure is also a flow—so much spent per week or per month or per year. The amount of money in a bank account (earned, perhaps, in the past but unspent) is a stock—just so many thousands of dollars. The key test is always whether a time dimension is required to give the variable meaning.

The amount of water behind the dam at any time is the stock of water; the amount moving through the gate is the flow, which is measured per unit of time.

vary and study how its change affects quantity demanded. We can do the same for each of the other variables in turn, and in this way we can come to understand the importance of each variable.

Holding all other variables constant is often described by the expressions "other things being equal," "other things given," or the equivalent Latin phrase, *ceteris paribus*. When economists speak of the influence of the price of gasoline on the quantity of gasoline demanded, *ceteris paribus*, they refer to what a change in the price of gasoline would do to the quantity of gasoline demanded *if all other variables that influence the demand for gasoline did not change*.

Quantity Demanded and Price[1]

We are interested in studying the relationship between the quantity demanded of a product and that product's price. This requires that we hold all other influences constant and ask, "How will the quantity demanded of a product change as its price changes?"

A basic economic hypothesis is that the price of a product and the quantity demanded are related *negatively,* other things being equal. That is, the lower the price, the higher the quantity demanded; the higher the price, the lower the quantity demanded.

The great British economist Alfred Marshall (1842–1924) called this fundamental relation the "law of demand." In Chapter 6, we will derive the law of demand as a prediction that follows from more basic assumptions about the behaviour of individual consumers. For now, let's simply explore why this relationship seems reasonable. Products are used to satisfy desires and needs, and there is almost always more than one product that will satisfy any desire or need. Hunger may be alleviated by eating meat or vegetables; a desire for green vegetables can be satisfied by broccoli or spinach. The desire for a vacation may be satisfied by a trip to the ocean or to the mountains; the need to get there may be satisfied by different airlines, a bus, a car, or a train. For any general desire or need, there are almost always many different products that will satisfy it.

Now consider what happens if income, tastes, population, and the prices of all other products remain constant and the price of only one product changes. As the price goes up, that product becomes an increasingly expensive means of satisfying a desire. Many consumers will decide to switch wholly or partly to other products. Some consumers will stop buying it altogether, others will buy smaller amounts, and still others may continue to buy the same quantity. But the overall effect is that less will be demanded of the product whose price has risen. As meat becomes more expensive, for example, some consumers will switch to meat substitutes; others may forgo meat at some meals and eat less meat at others. Taken together as a group, consumers will want to buy less meat when its price rises.

Conversely, as the price goes down, the product becomes a cheaper way of satisfying a desire. Households will demand more of it. At the same time they will buy less of similar products whose prices have not fallen and as a result have become expensive *relative* to the product in question. For example, when the price of tomatoes falls, many shoppers will switch to tomatoes and cut their purchases of other vegetables that are now relatively more expensive.

Changes in prices lead most consumers to alter their choices. For example, as prices for hotel rooms fall, vacationers may be more likely to take weekend trips.

---

[1] In this chapter we explore a product's demand curve for the market as a whole—what we often call the *market demand curve.* In Chapter 6 we discuss how this market demand curve is derived by adding up, or *aggregating,* the demands of different individuals.

Demand Schedules and Demand Curves

A **demand schedule** is one way of showing the relationship between quantity demanded and the price of a product, other things being equal. It is a table showing the quantity demanded at various prices.

The table in Figure 3-1 shows a hypothetical demand schedule for apples.[2] It lists the quantity of apples that would be demanded at various prices, given the assumption that all other variables are held constant. We should note in particular that average household income is assumed to be $50 000 per year because later we will want to see what happens when income changes. The table gives the quantities demanded for five selected prices, but in fact a separate quantity would be demanded at every possible price.

A second method of showing the relationship between quantity demanded and price is to draw a graph. The five price–quantity combinations shown in the table are plotted in Figure 3-1. Price is plotted on the vertical axis, and the quantity demanded is plotted on the horizontal axis.

The curve drawn through these points is called a **demand curve**. It shows the quantity that consumers would like to buy at each price. The negative slope of the curve indicates that the quantity demanded increases as the price falls. Each point on the demand curve indicates a single price–quantity combination. The demand curve as a whole shows something more.

demand schedule A table showing the relationship between quantity demanded and the price of a commodity, other things being equal.

demand curve The graphical representation of the relationship between quantity demanded and the price of a commodity, other things being equal.

FIGURE 3-1 The Demand for Apples

A Demand Schedule for Apples

Reference Point	Price ($ per bushel)	Quantity Demanded (thousands of bushels per year when average annual income is $50 000)
U	20	110
V	40	85
W	60	65
X	80	50
Y	100	40

A Demand Curve for Apples

Both the table and the graph show the total quantity of apples that would be demanded at various prices, *ceteris paribus*. For example, row *W* indicates that if the price of apples were $60 per bushel, consumers would desire to purchase 65 000 bushels of apples per year, holding constant the values of the other variables that affect quantity demanded. The demand curve, labelled *D*, relates quantity of apples demanded to the price of apples; its negative slope indicates that quantity demanded increases as price falls.

---

[2] We realize that apples are not a very exciting product to discuss, and many students wonder why we do not instead use cell phones, restaurant meals, or cars as our hypothetical example. The model of demand and supply, however, best applies to products that are demanded by many consumers and supplied by many producers, each of which offers for sale a virtually identical ("homogeneous") version of the product. For this reason, we have chosen a simple agricultural product, but we could have illustrated the same principles with beef, wheat, copper, newsprint, oil, and a whole host of what economists call "commodities."

> The demand curve represents the relationship between quantity demanded and price, other things being equal.

When economists speak of demand in a particular market, they are referring not just to the particular quantity being demanded at the moment (i.e., not just to one point on the demand curve) but to the entire demand curve—to the relationship between desired purchases and all the possible prices of the product.

The term **demand** therefore refers to the entire relationship between the quantity demanded of a product and the price of that product. In contrast, a single point on a demand schedule or curve is the quantity demanded at that point. This distinction between "demand" and "quantity demanded" is an extremely important one and we will examine it more closely later in this chapter.

demand The entire relationship between the quantity of a commodity that buyers want to purchase and the price of that commodity, other things being equal.

Shifts in the Demand Curve The demand curve is drawn with the assumption that everything except the product's own price is being held constant. But what if other things change, as they often do? For example, consider an increase in average household income while the price of apples remains constant. If consumers spend some of their extra income on apples, the new quantity demanded cannot be represented by a point on the original demand curve. It must be represented on a new demand curve that is to the right of the old curve. Thus, a rise in income that causes more apples to be demanded *at each price* shifts the demand curve for apples to the right, as shown in Figure 3-2. This shift illustrates the operation of an important general rule.

FIGURE 3-2 An Increase in the Demand for Apples

Demand Schedules

Price ($ per bushel)	Quantity Demanded (thousands of bushels per year when average annual income is $50 000)	Quantity Demanded (thousands of bushels per year when average annual income is $60 000)
p	D_0	D_1
20	110 U	140 U'
40	85 V	115 V'
60	65 W	95 W'
80	50 X	80 X'
100	40 Y	70 Y'

Demand Curves

An increase in annual household income increases the quantity demanded at each price (for all normal goods). This is shown by the rightward shift in the demand curve, from D_0 to D_1. When average income rises from $50 000 to $60 000 per year, quantity demanded at a price of $60 per bushel rises from 65 000 bushels per year to 95 000 bushels per year. A similar rise occurs at every other price.

A demand curve is drawn with the assumption that everything except the product's own price is held constant. A change in any of the variables previously held constant will shift the demand curve to a new position.

A demand curve can shift in two important ways. In the first case, more is desired at each price—the demand curve shifts rightward so that each price corresponds to a higher quantity than it did before. In the second case, less is desired at each price—the demand curve shifts leftward so that each price corresponds to a lower quantity than it did before.

Let's now consider five important causes of shifts in the demand curve.

1. Consumers' Income. If *average* income rises, consumers as a group can be expected to desire more of most products, other things being equal. Goods for which the quantity demanded increases when income rises are called *normal goods*; goods for which the quantity demanded falls when income rises are called *inferior goods*. The term *normal goods* reflects economists' empirical finding that the demand for most goods rises when income rises. We therefore expect that a rise in average consumer income shifts the demand curve for most products to the right, indicating that more will be demanded at any given price. Such a shift is illustrated in Figure 3-2.

A change in the *distribution* of income can also lead to changes in demand. In particular, a change in the distribution of income will cause an increase in the demand for products bought most by consumers whose incomes increase and a decrease in the demand for products bought most by consumers whose incomes decrease. If, for example, the government increases the child tax credit and at the same time raises basic tax rates, income will be transferred from households without children to households with children. Demands for products more heavily bought by persons without children will decline, while demands for products more heavily bought by households with children will increase.

2. Prices of Other Goods. We saw that the negative slope of a product's demand curve occurs because the lower its price, the cheaper the product becomes relative to other products that can satisfy the same needs or desires. These other products are called **substitutes in consumption.** Another way for the same change to come about is that the price of the substitute product rises. For example, apples can become cheap relative to oranges either because the price of apples falls or because the price of oranges rises. Either change will increase the amount of apples that consumers want to buy as some consumers substitute away from oranges and toward apples. Thus, a rise in the price of a substitute for a product shifts the demand curve for the product to the right. More will be demanded at each price.

substitutes in consumption Goods that can be used in place of another good to satisfy similar needs or desires.

Complements in consumption are products that tend to be used jointly. Cars and gasoline are complements; so are golf clubs and golf balls, and airplane flights to Calgary and ski-lift tickets in Banff. Because complements tend to be consumed together, a fall in the price of one will increase the quantity demanded of *both* products. Thus, a fall in the price of a complement for a product will shift that product's demand curve to the right. More will be demanded at each price. For example, a fall in the price of airplane trips to Calgary will lead to a rise in the demand for ski-lift tickets in Banff, even though the price of those lift tickets is unchanged. (The demand curve for ski-lift tickets will shift to the right.)

complements in consumption Goods that tend to be consumed together.

3. Tastes. Tastes have a powerful effect on people's desired purchases. A change in tastes may be long-lasting, such as the shift from typewriters to computers, or it may be a

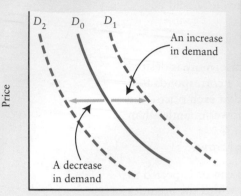

FIGURE 3-3 Shifts in the Demand Curve

Quantity per Period

A rightward shift in the demand curve from D_0 to D_1 indicates an increase in demand; a leftward shift from D_0 to D_2 indicates a decrease in demand. An increase in demand means that more is demanded at each price. Such a rightward shift can be caused by a rise in income, a rise in the price of a substitute, a fall in the price of a complement, a change in tastes that favours that product, an increase in population, or the anticipation of a future event that will increase the price.

A decrease in demand means that less is demanded at each price. Such a leftward shift can be caused by a fall in income, a fall in the price of a substitute, a rise in the price of a complement, a change in tastes that disfavours the product, a decrease in population, or the anticipation of a future event that will decrease the price.

short-lived fad as is common with many electronic games, such as the latest versions of Need for Speed or Just Dance. In either case, a change in tastes in favour of a product shifts the demand curve to the right. More will be demanded at each price. Of course, a change in tastes against some product has the opposite effect and shifts the demand curve to the left.

4. Population. If there is an increase in population with purchasing power, the demands for all the products purchased by the new people will rise. Thus, we expect that an increase in population will shift the demand curves for most products to the right, indicating that more will be demanded at each price.

5. Expectations about the Future. Our discussion has so far focused on how changes in the current value of variables may change demand. But it is also true that changes in people's *expectations about future values* of variables may change demand. For example, suppose you are thinking about buying a vacation property in a small town in Nova Scotia, and you have learned that in the near future a large high-tech firm will be moving its head office and several hundred employees to this same small town. Since their future movement into your town will probably increase the demand for housing and drive up the *future* price of houses, this expectation will lead you (and others like you) to increase your demand *today* so as to make the purchase before the price rises. Thus, the demand curve for houses will shift to the right today in anticipation of a future event.

Figure 3-3 summarizes the changes that cause demand curves to shift.

Movements Along the Curve Versus Shifts of the Whole Curve
Suppose you read in today's newspaper that a sharp increase in the world price of coffee beans has been caused by an increased worldwide demand for coffee. Then tomorrow you read that the rising price of coffee is reducing the typical consumer's purchases of coffee, as shoppers switch to other beverages. The two stories appear to contradict each other. The first associates a rising price with rising demand; the second associates a rising price with declining demand. Can both statements be true? The answer is yes—because the two statements actually refer to different things. The first describes a shift in the demand curve; the second describes a movement along the demand curve in response to a change in price.

Consider first the statement that the increase in the price of coffee has been caused by an increased demand for coffee. This statement refers to a shift in the demand curve for coffee—in this case, a shift to the right, indicating more coffee demanded at each price. This shift, as we will see later in this chapter, will increase the price of coffee.

Now consider the second statement—that less coffee is being bought because of its rise in price. This refers to a movement along the *new* demand curve and reflects a change between two specific quantities demanded, one before the price increased and one afterward.

Possible explanations for the two stories are as follows:

1. A rise in population and income in coffee-drinking countries shifts the demand curve for coffee to the right. This, in turn, raises the price of coffee (for reasons we will soon study in detail). This was the first newspaper story.

2. The rising price of coffee is causing each individual household to cut back on its coffee purchases. The cutback is represented by an upward movement to the left along the new demand curve for coffee. This was the second newspaper story.

To prevent the type of confusion caused by our two newspaper stories, economists use a specialized vocabulary to distinguish between shifts of demand curves and movements along demand curves.

We have seen that "demand" refers to the *entire* demand curve, whereas "quantity demanded" refers to a particular *point* on the demand curve. Economists reserve the term **change in demand** to describe a change in the quantity demanded at *every* price. That is, a change in demand refers to a shift of the entire demand curve. The term **change in quantity demanded** refers to a movement from one point on a demand curve to another point, either on the same demand curve or on a new one.

change in demand A change in the quantity demanded at each possible price of the commodity, represented by a shift in the whole demand curve.

change in quantity demanded A change in the specific quantity of the good demanded, represented by a change from one point on a demand curve to another point, either on the original demand curve or on a new one.

> A change in quantity demanded can result from a shift in the demand curve with the price constant, from a movement along a given demand curve due to a change in the price, or from a combination of the two. [3]

We consider these three possibilities in turn.

An increase in demand means that the whole demand curve shifts to the right; at any given price, an increase in demand causes an increase in quantity demanded. For example, in Figure 3-2 on page 60, the shift in the demand curve for apples from D_0 to D_1 represents an increase in demand, and at a price of $40 per bushel, quantity demanded increases from 85 000 bushels to 115 000 bushels, as indicated by the move from V to V'.

A movement down and to the right along a demand curve represents an increase in quantity demanded. For example, in Figure 3-2, with the demand for apples given by the curve D_1, an increase in price from $40 to $60 per bushel causes a movement along D_1 from V' to W', and quantity demanded decreases from 115 000 bushels to 95 000 bushels.

When there is a change in demand *and* a change in the price, the overall change in quantity demanded is the net effect of the shift in the demand curve and the movement along the new demand curve. Figure 3-4 shows the combined effect of an increase in demand, shown by a rightward shift in the whole demand curve, and an upward movement to the left along the new demand curve caused

FIGURE 3-4 Shifts of and Movements Along the Demand Curve

After price increases to p_2 quantity demanded falls to Q_2

Increase in quantity demanded at initial price of p_0

An increase in demand means that the demand curve shifts to the right, and hence quantity demanded will be higher at each price. A rise in price causes a movement upward and to the left along the demand curve, and hence quantity demanded will fall. The demand curve is originally D_0 and price is p_0, which means that quantity demanded is Q_0. Suppose demand increases to D_1, which means that at any particular price, there is a larger quantity demanded; for example, at p_0, quantity demanded is now Q_1. Now suppose the price rises above p_0. This causes a movement up and to the left along D_1, and quantity demanded falls below Q_1. As the figure is drawn, the quantity demanded at the new price p_2 is less than Q_1 but greater than Q_0. So in this case the combined effect of the increase in demand and the rise in price is an increase in quantity demanded from Q_0 to Q_2.

A rise in the price of wheat, other things being equal, will lead farmers to plant less of other crops and plant more wheat.

by an increase in price. The increase in demand causes an increase in quantity demanded at the initial price, whereas the movement along the new demand curve causes a decrease in the quantity demanded. Whether quantity demanded rises or falls overall depends on the relative magnitudes of these two changes.

| 3.2 Supply

What determines the supply of any given product? Why do Canadian oil producers extract and sell more oil when the price of oil is high? Why do Canadian cattle ranchers raise and sell more beef when the price of cattle-feed falls? We start by developing a theory designed to explain the supply of some typical product.

Quantity Supplied

quantity supplied The amount of a commodity that producers want to sell during some time period.

The amount of some good or service that producers want to sell in some time period is called the **quantity supplied** of that product. Quantity supplied is a flow; it is so much per unit of time. Note also that quantity supplied is the amount that producers are willing to offer for sale; it is not necessarily the amount that they succeed in selling, which is expressed by *quantity sold* or *quantity exchanged*.

As a general rule, any event that makes production of a specific product more profitable will lead firms to supply more of it. The quantity supplied of a product is influenced by the following key variables: [4]

- Product's own price
- Prices of inputs
- Technology
- Some government taxes or subsidies
- Prices of other products
- Number of suppliers

The situation with supply is the same as that with demand: There are several influencing variables, and we will not get far if we try to discover what happens when they all change at the same time. Again, we use the convenient *ceteris paribus* assumption to study the influence of the variables one at a time.

Quantity Supplied and Price

We begin by holding all other influences constant and ask, "How do we expect the total quantity of a product supplied to vary with its own price?"

A basic economic hypothesis is that the price of the product and the quantity supplied are related *positively,* other things being equal. That is, the higher the product's own price, the more its producers will supply; the lower the price, the less its producers will supply.

In later chapters we will derive this hypothesis as a prediction from more basic assumptions about the behaviour of individual profit-maximizing firms. For now we simply note that as the product's price rises, producing and selling this product becomes a more profitable activity. Firms interested in increasing their profit will therefore choose to increase their production.

Supply Schedules and Supply Curves

The general relationship just discussed can be illustrated by a **supply schedule**, which shows the relationship between quantity supplied of a product and the price of the product, other things being equal. The table in Figure 3-5 presents a hypothetical supply schedule for apples.

A **supply curve**, the graphical representation of the supply schedule, is illustrated in Figure 3-5. Each point on the supply curve represents a specific price–quantity combination; however, the whole curve shows something more.

When economists make statements about the conditions of supply, they are not referring just to the particular quantity being supplied at the moment—that is, not to just one point on the supply curve. Instead, they are referring to the entire supply

supply schedule A table showing the relationship between quantity supplied and the price of a commodity, other things being equal.

supply curve The graphical representation of the relationship between quantity supplied and the price of a commodity, other things being equal.

FIGURE 3-5 The Supply of Apples

A Supply Schedule for Apples

Reference Point	Price ($ per bushel)	Quantity Supplied (thousands of bushels per year)
u	20	20
v	40	45
w	60	65
x	80	80
y	100	95

A Supply Curve for Apples

Both the table and the graph show the quantities that producers want to sell at various prices, *ceteris paribus.* For example, row *w* indicates that if the price of apples were $60 per bushel, producers would want to sell 65 000 bushels per year. The supply curve, labelled *S*, relates quantity of apples supplied to the price of apples; its positive slope indicates that quantity supplied increases as price increases.

> The supply curve represents the relationship between quantity supplied and price, other things being equal; its positive slope indicates that quantity supplied increases when price increases.

supply The entire relationship between the quantity of some commodity that producers wish to sell and the price of that commodity, other things being equal.

curve, to the complete relationship between desired sales and all possible prices of the product.

Supply refers to the entire relationship between the quantity supplied of a product and the price of that product, other things being equal. A single point on the supply curve refers to the *quantity supplied* at that price.

Shifts in the Supply Curve A shift in the supply curve means that at each price there is a change in the quantity supplied. An increase in the quantity supplied at each price is shown in Figure 3-6. This change appears as a rightward shift in the supply curve. In contrast, a decrease in the quantity supplied at each price would appear as a leftward shift. For supply, as for demand, there is an important general rule:

> A change in any of the variables (other than the product's own price) that affects the quantity supplied will shift the supply curve to a new position.

Let's now consider the possible causes of shifts in supply curves.

1. Prices of Inputs. All things that a firm uses to produce its outputs, such as materials, labour, and machines, are called the firm's *inputs*. Other things being equal, the higher the price of any input used to make a product, the less profit there will be from making that product. We expect, therefore, that the higher the price of any input used by a firm, the less the firm will produce and offer for sale at any given price of the product. A rise

FIGURE 3-6 An Increase in the Supply of Apples

Supply Schedules

Price ($ per bushel) p	Quantity Supplied (thousands of bushels per year before innovation) S_0	Quantity Supplied (thousands of bushels per year after innovation) S_1
20	20 u	50 u'
40	45 v	75 v'
60	65 w	95 w'
80	80 x	110 x'
100	95 y	125 y'

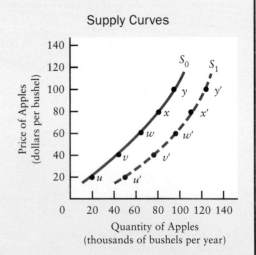

Supply Curves

A cost-saving innovation increases the quantity supplied at each price. This is shown by the rightward shift in the supply curve, from S_0 to S_1. As a result of a cost-saving innovation, the quantity that is supplied at a price of $100 per bushel rises from 95 000 to 125 000 bushels per year. A similar rise occurs at every price.

in the price of inputs therefore shifts the supply curve to the left, indicating that less will be supplied at any given price; a fall in the price of inputs makes production more profitable and therefore shifts the supply curve to the right.

2. Technology. At any time, what is produced and how it is produced depend on what is known. Over time, knowledge changes. The enormous increase in production per worker that has been going on in industrial societies for about 200 years is due largely to improved methods of production. The Industrial Revolution is more than a historical event; it is a present reality. Discoveries in chemistry have led to lower costs of production for well-established products, such as paints, and to a large variety of new products made of plastics and synthetic fibres. Such inventions as silicon chips and fibre optics have radically changed products, such as cell phones, computers, and surgical devices, and the consequent development of smaller computers has revolutionized the production and lowered the costs of countless other non-electronic products.

Any technological innovation that decreases the amount of inputs needed per unit of output reduces production costs and hence increases the profits that can be earned at any given price of the product. Because increased profitability leads to increased willingness to produce, this change shifts the supply curve to the right.

For producers of agricultural products, extreme weather events are similar to a deterioration in technology because they reduce the amount of output that can be produced with a given amount of land, labour, and other inputs. Agricultural production generally depends on specific weather conditions, and extreme deviations from normal can lead to dramatic reductions in output. Droughts, floods, hurricanes, tornados, and early frosts are a few examples of extreme weather events that usually reduce the supply of agricultural products.

3. Government Taxes or Subsidies. We have just seen that anything increasing firms' costs will shift the supply curve to the left, and anything decreasing firms' costs will shift the supply curve to the right. As we will see in later chapters, governments often levy special taxes on the production of specific goods, such as gasoline, cigarettes, and alcohol. These taxes make the production and sale of these goods less profitable. The result is that the supply curve shifts to the left.

For other goods, governments often subsidize producers—that is, they pay producers a specific amount for each unit of the good produced. This often occurs for agricultural products, especially in the United States and the European Union. In such situations, the subsidy increases the profitability of production and shifts the supply curve to the right. For example, environmental concerns have led the U.S. and Canadian governments in recent years to provide subsidies for the production of biofuels. These subsidies have caused the supply curve for biofuels to shift to the right.

4. Prices of Other Products. Changes in the price of one product may lead to changes in the supply of some other product because the two products are either *substitutes* or *complements* in the production process.

A prairie farmer, for example, can plant his field in wheat or oats. If the market price of oats falls, thus making oat production less profitable, the farmer will be more inclined to plant wheat. In this case, wheat and oats are said to be *substitutes* in production—for every extra hectare planted in one crop, one fewer hectare can be planted in the other. In this example, a reduction in the price of oats leads to an increase in the supply of wheat.

An excellent example in which two products are *complements* in production is oil and natural gas, which are often found together below Earth's surface. If the market price of oil rises, producers will do more drilling and increase their production of oil. But as more oil wells are drilled, the usual outcome is that more of *both* natural gas and oil are discovered and then produced. Thus, the rise in the price of oil leads to an increase in the supply of the complementary product—natural gas.

5. Number of Suppliers. For given prices and technology, the total amount of any product supplied depends on the number of firms producing that product and offering it for sale. If profits are being earned by current firms, then more firms will choose to enter this industry and begin producing. The effect of this increase in the number of suppliers is to shift the supply curve to the right. Similarly, if the existing firms are losing money, they will eventually leave the industry; such a reduction in the number of suppliers shifts the supply curve to the left.

Movements Along the Curve Versus Shifts of the Whole Curve As with demand, it is important to distinguish movements along supply curves from shifts of the whole curve. Economists reserve the term **change in supply** to describe a shift of the whole supply curve—that is, a change in the quantity that will be supplied at every price. The term **change in quantity supplied** refers to a movement from one point on a supply curve to another point, either on the same supply curve or on a new one. In other words, an increase in supply means that the whole supply curve has shifted to the right, so that the quantity supplied at any given price has increased; a movement up and to the right along a supply curve indicates an increase in the quantity supplied in response to an increase in the price of the product.

> A change in quantity supplied can result from a change in supply with the price constant, a movement along a given supply curve because of a change in the price, or a combination of the two.

An exercise you might find useful is to construct a diagram similar to Figure 3-4 (see page 63), emphasizing the difference between a shift of the supply curve and a movement along the supply curve.

change in supply A change in the quantity supplied at each possible price of the commodity, represented by a shift in the whole supply curve.

change in quantity supplied A change in the specific quantity supplied, represented by a change from one point on a supply curve to another point, either on the original supply curve or on a new one.

3.3 The Determination of Price

So far we have considered demand and supply separately. We now come to a key question: How do the two forces of demand and supply interact to determine price? Before considering this question, you should know that the demand-and-supply model does *not* apply to all markets. See *Applying Economic Concepts 3-1* for a discussion of why the model in this chapter applies well to apples but not to more interesting products, such as iPhones.

The Concept of a Market

Originally, the term *market* designated a physical place where products were bought and sold. We still use the term this way to describe such places as Granville Island Market in Vancouver, Kensington Market in Toronto, or Jean Talon Market in Montreal.

APPLYING ECONOMIC CONCEPTS 3-1

Why Apples But Not iPhones?

The demand-and-supply model that we have developed in this chapter does *not* apply to the markets for all goods and services, and there is a good reason why our example throughout the chapter has been apples and not, for example, iPhones, cars, brand-name clothing, or even textbooks. Three conditions must be satisfied in order for price determination in a market to be well described by the demand-and-supply model.

1. There must be a large number of consumers of the product, each one small relative to the size of the market.

2. There must be a large number of producers of the product, each one small relative to the size of the market.

3. Producers must be selling identical or "homogeneous" versions of the product.

The first assumption ensures that no single consumer is large enough to influence the market price through their buying actions. This is satisfied in most markets, although there are important exceptions. For example, Canadian provincial governments are dominant purchasers of prescription drugs in Canada, and their *market power* tends to keep prices below what they would otherwise be.

The second assumption ensures that no single producer is large enough to influence the market price through their selling actions. There are many markets in which this is not true. For example, DeBeers controls the sale of a large fraction of the world's rough diamonds, and thus it can alter the market price through its sales restrictions. Hydro Quebec is the sole producer of electricity in the province of Quebec and sets the price that consumers pay. In contrast, most producers of fruits and vegetables are very small relative to the size of the market and have no ability to influence the market price.

The third assumption ensures that there will be a single price in the market because producers have no ability to *differentiate* their product from those of other producers. This condition is satisfied in many markets for commodities—steel, aluminum, copper, wheat, oil, natural gas, lumber, newsprint, beef, pork, etc. But it is *not* satisfied in the markets for many consumer products such as smartphones and other electronic devices, cars and motorcycles, clothing, and fast food and other restaurant meals. In these cases, each producer sells a different version of the product and spends considerable advertising resources trying to convince consumers to purchase their version. In these markets, differentiated products sell at different prices.

When all three conditions are satisfied, economists use the demand-and-supply model to explain the determination of market price and quantity. This model has proven to be very successful in explaining outcomes in markets such as oil, steel, copper, wheat, soybeans, beef, pork, newsprint, lumber, foreign currencies, financial assets like stocks and bonds—and apples!

So be careful when you try to apply the demand-and-supply model. It works very well in describing the events in many markets, but not so well for others. Later chapters in this book will examine the more complex markets for which we need a more advanced model.

Once developed, however, theories of market behaviour were easily extended to cover products, such as wheat or oil, that can be purchased anywhere in the world at a price that tends to be uniform the world over. Today we can also buy and sell items in markets that exist online—consider the auction services provided by eBay or the almost limitless list of products available from Amazon (including a wedding chapel and a UFO detector!). The idea that a *market* must be a single geographic location where consumers can go to buy something became obsolete long ago.

For present purposes, a **market** may be defined as existing in any situation (such as a physical place or an electronic medium) in which buyers and sellers negotiate the exchange of goods or services.

Individual markets differ in the degree of *competition* among the various buyers and sellers. In the next few chapters we will examine markets in which the number of buyers and sellers is sufficiently large that no one of them has any appreciable influence on the market price. This is a rough definition of what economists call *perfectly competitive*

market Any situation in which buyers and sellers can negotiate the exchange of goods or services.

markets. Starting in Chapter 10, we will consider the behaviour of markets in which there are small numbers of either sellers or buyers. But our initial theory of markets, based on the interaction of demand and supply, will be a very good description of the markets for such things as wheat, pork, newsprint, coffee, copper, oil, and many other commodities.

Market Equilibrium

The table in Figure 3-7 brings together the demand and supply schedules from Figures 3-1 and 3-5. The quantities of apples demanded and supplied at each price can now be compared.

There is only one price, $60 per bushel, at which the quantity of apples demanded equals the quantity supplied. At prices less than $60 per bushel, there is a shortage of apples because the quantity demanded exceeds the quantity supplied. This is a situation of **excess demand**. At prices greater than $60 per bushel, there is a surplus of apples because the quantity supplied exceeds the quantity demanded. This is a situation of **excess supply**. This same story can also be told in graphical terms. The quantities demanded and supplied at any price can be read off the two curves; the excess supply or excess demand is shown by the horizontal distance between the curves at each price.

To examine the determination of market price, let's suppose first that the price is $100 per bushel. At this price, 95 000 bushels are offered for sale, but only 40 000 bushels are demanded. There is an excess supply of 55 000 bushels per year. Apple sellers are then likely to cut their prices to get rid of this surplus. And purchasers, observing the stock of unsold apples, will begin to offer less money for the product. In other words, *excess supply causes downward pressure on price.*

Now consider the price of $20 per bushel. At this price, there is excess demand. The 20 000 bushels produced each year are snapped up quickly, and 90 000 bushels of desired purchases cannot be made. Rivalry between would-be purchasers may lead them to offer more than the prevailing price to outbid other purchasers. Also, sellers may begin to ask a higher price for the quantities that they do have to sell. In other words, *excess demand causes upward pressure on price.*

Finally, consider the price of $60. At this price, producers want to sell 65 000 bushels per year, and purchasers want to buy that same quantity. There is neither a shortage nor a surplus of apples. There are no unsatisfied buyers to bid the price up, nor are there unsatisfied sellers to force the price down. Once the price of $60 has been reached, therefore, there will be no tendency for it to change.

Equilibrium implies a state of rest, or balance, between opposing forces. The **equilibrium price** is the one toward which the actual market price will tend. Once established, it will persist until it is disturbed by some change in market conditions that shifts the demand curve, the supply curve, or both.

> The price at which the quantity demanded equals the quantity supplied is called the equilibrium price, or the market-clearing price. [5]

Any price at which the market does not "clear"—that is, quantity demanded does not equal quantity supplied—is called a **disequilibrium price**. Whenever there is either excess demand or excess supply in a market, that market is said to be in a state of **disequilibrium**, and the market price will be changing.

excess demand A situation in which, at the given price, quantity demanded exceeds quantity supplied.

excess supply A situation in which, at the given price, quantity supplied exceeds quantity demanded.

equilibrium price The price at which quantity demanded equals quantity supplied. Also called the *market-clearing price.*

disequilibrium price A price at which quantity demanded does not equal quantity supplied.

disequilibrium A situation in a market in which there is excess demand or excess supply.

FIGURE 3-7 Determination of the Equilibrium Price of Apples

Demand and Supply Schedules

Price ($ per bushel) p	Quantity Demanded (thousands of bushels per year) D	Quantity Supplied (thousands of bushels per year) S	Excess Demand (+) or Excess Supply (−) (tonnes per year) $D - S$
20	110	20	+90
40	85	45	+40
60	65	65	0
80	50	80	−30
100	40	95	−55

Demand and Supply Curves

The equilibrium price corresponds to the intersection of the demand and supply curves. At any price above $60, there is excess supply and thus downward pressure on price. At any price below $60, there is excess demand and thus upward pressure on price. Only at a price of $60 is there no pressure for price to change. Equilibrium occurs at point E, at a price of $60 and quantity exchanged equal to 65 000 bushels.

Figure 3-7 makes it clear that the equilibrium price occurs where the demand and supply curves intersect. Below that price, there is excess demand and hence upward pressure on the existing price. Above that price, there is excess supply and hence downward pressure on the existing price.[3]

Changes in Market Equilibrium

Changes in any of the variables, other than price, that influence quantity demanded or supplied will cause a shift in the demand curve, the supply curve, or both. There are four possible shifts: an increase in demand (a rightward shift in the demand curve), a decrease in demand (a leftward shift in the demand curve), an increase in supply (a rightward shift in the supply curve), and a decrease in supply (a leftward shift in the supply curve).

Commodities & Futures					
	Price (US$)	Chg		Price (US$)	Chg
Crude Oil	96.57	−0.27	Lumber	292.50	−4.40
Natural Gas	2.816	0.041	Cocoa	2400.00	−33.00
Heating Oil	3.1244	−0.0073	Corn	829.25	−2.00
Gold	1642.70	−0.20	Soybeans	1727.50	−5.00
Silver	29.48	−0.034	Oat	393.25	−3.75
Copper	3.4565	−0.0045	Live Cattle	124.775	0.15
Platinum	1524.10	16.30	Wood Pulp	865.00	3.50
Palladium	629.75	5.55	Lean Hogs	75.175	−0.625

Many commodities like those listed here are actively traded in international markets and their equilibrium prices fluctuate daily.

Source: "Commodities & Futures," *TMX Money,* tmx.quote-media.com/futures.php. Accessed August 22, 2012.

---

[3] When economists graph a demand (or supply) curve, they put the variable to be explained (the dependent variable) on the horizontal axis and the explanatory variable (the independent variable) on the vertical axis. This is "backward" to what is usually done in mathematics. The rational explanation of what is now economists' odd practice is buried in the history of economics and dates back to Alfred Marshall's *Principles of Economics* (1890) [6]. For better or worse, Marshall's scheme is now used by all economists, although mathematicians never fail to wonder at this example of the odd ways of economists.

FIGURE 3-8 Shifts in Demand and Supply Curves

(i) The effect of shifts in the demand curve

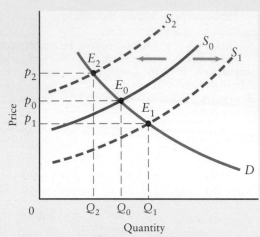

(ii) The effect of shifts in the supply curve

Shifts in either demand or supply curves will generally lead to changes in equilibrium price and quantity. In part (i), suppose the original demand and supply curves are D_0 and S, which intersect to produce equilibrium at E_0, with a price of p_0 and a quantity of Q_0. An increase in demand shifts the demand curve to D_1, taking the new equilibrium to E_1. Price rises to p_1 and quantity rises to Q_1. Starting at E_0, a decrease in demand shifts the demand curve to D_2, taking the new equilibrium to E_2. Price falls to p_2 and quantity falls to Q_2.

In part (ii), the original demand and supply curves are D and S_0, which intersect to produce equilibrium at E_0, with a price of p_0 and a quantity of Q_0. An increase in supply shifts the supply curve to S_1, taking the new equilibrium to E_1. Price falls to p_1 and quantity rises to Q_1. Starting at E_0, a decrease in supply shifts the supply curve from S_0 to S_2, taking the new equilibrium to E_2. Price rises to p_2 and quantity falls to Q_2.

comparative statics The derivation of predictions by analyzing the effect of a change in some exogenous variable on the equilibrium.

To discover the effects of each of the possible curve shifts, we use the method known as **comparative statics**.[4] With this method, we derive predictions about how the *endogenous* variables (equilibrium price and quantity) will change following a change in some *exogenous* variable (the variables whose changes cause shifts in the demand and supply curves). We start from a position of equilibrium and then introduce the change to be studied. We then determine the new equilibrium position and compare it with the original one. The difference between the two positions of equilibrium must result from the change that was introduced, because everything else has been held constant.

The changes caused by each of the four possible curve shifts are shown in Figure 3-8. Study the figure carefully. Previously, we had given the axes specific labels, but because it is now intended to apply to any product, the horizontal axis is simply labelled "Quantity." This means quantity per period in whatever units output is measured. "Price," the vertical axis, means the price measured as dollars per unit of quantity for the same product.

The effects of the four possible curve shifts are as follows:

1. An increase in demand causes an increase in both the equilibrium price and the equilibrium quantity exchanged.

---

[4] The term *static* is used because we are not concerned with the actual path by which the market goes from the first equilibrium position to the second, or with the time taken to reach the second equilibrium. Analysis of these movements would be described as *dynamic analysis*.

2. A decrease in demand causes a decrease in both the equilibrium price and the equilibrium quantity exchanged.

3. An increase in supply causes a decrease in the equilibrium price and an increase in the equilibrium quantity exchanged.

4. A decrease in supply causes an increase in the equilibrium price and a decrease in the equilibrium quantity exchanged.

Demonstrations of these effects are given in the caption to Figure 3-8. The intuitive reasoning behind each is as follows:

1. **An increase in demand (the demand curve shifts to the right).** An increase in demand creates a shortage at the initial equilibrium price, and the unsatisfied buyers bid up the price. This rise in price causes a larger quantity to be supplied, with the result that at the new equilibrium more is exchanged at a higher price.

2. **A decrease in demand (the demand curve shifts to the left).** A decrease in demand creates a surplus at the initial equilibrium price, and the unsuccessful sellers bid the price down. As a result, less of the product is supplied and offered for sale. At the new equilibrium, both price and quantity exchanged are lower than they were originally.

3. **An increase in supply (the supply curve shifts to the right).** An increase in supply creates a surplus at the initial equilibrium price, and the unsuccessful suppliers force the price down. This drop in price increases the quantity demanded, and the new equilibrium is at a lower price and a higher quantity exchanged.

4. **A decrease in supply (the supply curve shifts to the left).** A decrease in supply creates a shortage at the initial equilibrium price that causes the price to be bid up. This rise in price reduces the quantity demanded, and the new equilibrium is at a higher price and a lower quantity exchanged.

By using the tools we have learned in this chapter, we can link many real-world events that cause demand or supply curves to shift and thus lead to changes in market prices and quantities. *Lessons from History 3-1* shows how we can use demand-and-supply analysis to examine the effects of two major weather shocks: Quebec's 1998 ice storm and Hurricane Katrina in 2005.

Our discussion of demand, supply, and market equilibrium has explained why equilibrium price and quantity are found at the intersection of the demand and supply curves. We have shown diagrams (Figures 3-7 and 3-8) illustrating this in the general case. But we have not presented a specific algebraic example of demand and supply and "solved" precisely for the equilibrium price and quantity. See *Extensions in Theory 3-2* for an algebraic solution to a specific model of demand and supply.

Relative Prices and Inflation

The theory we have developed explains how individual prices are determined by the forces of demand and supply. To facilitate matters, we have made *ceteris paribus* assumptions. Specifically, we have assumed the constancy of all prices except the one we are studying. Does this mean that our theory is inapplicable to an inflationary world in which all prices are rising at the same time? Fortunately, the answer is no.

LESSONS FROM HISTORY 3-1

Ice Storms, Hurricanes, and Economics

Here are two simple examples of the demand-and-supply model in action. Both examples show how the weather—something that changes in unpredictable and often dramatic ways—can have significant effects on either the demand or the supply of various products, with obvious implications for the observed market price.

The Weather and a Demand Shock

In January 1998, Quebec, Eastern Ontario, and parts of the northeastern United States were hit by a massive ice storm. So unprecedented was this storm in its magnitude that many electric power systems were devastated. Homes and businesses in the Montreal area went without power for as long as four weeks.

This electric power shortage had many economic effects, including lost factory production, damage to many businesses, the death of farm livestock, and the displacement of thousands of people into shelters. Another effect of the power shortage, as soon as it became clear that it would last for more than just a few hours, was a sudden and substantial increase in the demand for portable gas-powered generators. Within just a few days,

all stores in the greater Montreal area were sold out of such generators, and the prices for newly ordered units increased sharply.

Furthermore, the shortages and price increases for generators were not confined to the area directly hit by the ice storm. As it became clear that there was an excess demand for generators in Quebec, sellers in other parts of the country began to divert their supply toward Quebec. This reduction in supply caused shortages, and thus price increases, in other parts of the country, as far away as Edmonton.

The Weather and a Supply Shock

In late August 2005, Hurricane Katrina emerged from the Caribbean, gathered strength as it crossed the Gulf of Mexico, and unleashed its fury on New Orleans, Louisiana. The damage to New Orleans was massive, especially after the levee holding back Lake Pontchartrain broke and much of the city was flooded. Katrina was then the worst natural disaster in U.S. history; the cost of the damage to buildings, bridges, houses, and other infrastructure was estimated to be close to U.S.$125 billion.

---

absolute price The amount of money that must be spent to acquire one unit of a commodity. Also called *money price*.

relative price The ratio of the money price of one commodity to the money price of another commodity; that is, a ratio of two absolute prices.

The price of a product is the amount of money that must be spent to acquire one unit of that product. This is called the **absolute price** or *money price*. A **relative price** is the ratio of two absolute prices; it expresses the price of one good in terms of (relative to) another.

We have been reminded several times that what matters for demand and supply is the price of the product in question *relative to the prices of other products*; that is, what matters is the relative price. For example, if the price of carrots rises while the prices of other vegetables are constant, we expect consumers to reduce their quantity demanded of carrots as they substitute toward the consumption of other vegetables. In this case, the *relative* price of carrots has increased. But if the prices of carrots and all other vegetables are rising at the same rate, the relative price of carrots is constant. In this case we expect no substitution to take place between carrots and other vegetables.

In an inflationary world, we are often interested in the price of a given product as it relates to the average price of all other products. If, during a period when all prices were increasing by an average of 5 percent, the price of coffee increased by 30 percent, then the price of coffee increased relative to the prices of other goods as a whole. Coffee became *relatively* expensive. However, if coffee had increased in price by

Hurricane Katrina had an instant effect on the world market for oil. Over short periods of time, the world demand curve for oil is relatively steep, reflecting the fact that users of oil initially reduce their purchases only slightly when the price rises.

Hurricane Katrina interrupted the local production and distribution of oil, thereby causing a temporary reduction in world supply. Several large oil rigs in the Gulf of Mexico were damaged and were shut down or operating well below their capacity for several weeks. In addition, the major pipelines that transport this oil from the Gulf ports to the inland refineries were also seriously damaged. For both reasons, the supply curve for oil shifted to the left. And given the relatively steep demand curve, this reduction in supply caused a sharp increase in the equilibrium price. The price per barrel of oil, which had averaged roughly U.S.$40 earlier that year, reached U.S.$70 on August 29, and stayed above U.S.$65 for about a month. As the rigs and pipelines were repaired, and Gulf-area oil production began to approach its pre-Katrina levels, the supply curve shifted back to the right and the price returned to levels between U.S.$55 and U.S.$60 per barrel.

Hurricane Katrina in August 2005 damaged several oil platforms operating in the Gulf of Mexico, causing a temporary reduction in the supply of oil.

30 percent when other prices increased by 40 percent, then the relative price of coffee would have fallen. Although the money price of coffee increased substantially, coffee became *relatively* cheap.

In this chapter we have been assuming that changes in a particular price occur when all other prices are constant. We can easily extend the analysis to an inflationary setting by remembering that any force that raises the price of one product when other prices remain constant will, given general inflation, raise the price of that product faster than the price level is rising. For example, consider a change in tastes in favour of coffee that raises its price by 5 percent when other prices are constant. The same change would raise its price by 8 percent if, at the same time, the general price level were rising by 3 percent. In each case, the price of coffee rises 5 percent *relative to the average of all prices*.

> In microeconomics, whenever we refer to a change in the price of one product, we mean a change in that product's relative price, that is, a change in the price of that product relative to the prices of all other goods.

EXTENSIONS IN THEORY 3-2

The Algebra of Market Equilibrium

This box presents an algebraic model of demand and supply and the method for determining the equilibrium price and quantity. For simplicity, we assume that the demand and supply curves are linear relationships between price and quantity.

Consider the following demand and supply curves:

Demand: $Q^D = a - bp$

Supply: $Q^S = c + dp$

where p is the price, Q^D is quantity demanded, Q^S is quantity supplied, and a, b, c, and d are positive constants. Both relationships are plotted in the accompanying figure.

What is the interpretation of the demand curve and how do we plot it? First, at a price of zero, consumers will buy a units—this is the horizontal intercept of the demand curve. Second, at a price of a/b, consumers will buy zero units, so a/b is the vertical intercept of the demand curve. Finally, the slope of the demand curve is $-1/b$; the quantity demanded increases by b units for every \$1 that price falls.

What is the interpretation of the supply curve, and how do we plot it? First, if the price is zero, suppliers will sell c units—this is the horizontal intercept of the supply curve. Second, for every \$1 increase in price, the quantity supplied increases by d units. Thus, the slope of the supply curve is $1/d$.

Given these demand and supply curves, the market equilibrium can be determined in two ways. The first is to construct a scale diagram and plot the two curves accurately. If you do this carefully, you will be able to read the equilibrium price and quantity off the diagram. But your diagram will have to be very accurate for this to work!

A more precise method is to use algebra to solve for the equilibrium price and quantity. Here is how we do

it. We know that in equilibrium quantity demanded equals quantity supplied, or $Q^D = Q^S$. We call the equilibrium quantity Q^*. But we also know that in equilibrium the price paid by the consumers will equal the price received by the producers—that is, there is only one equilibrium price, which we call p^*. Putting these two facts together, we know that in equilibrium

Demand: $Q^* = a - bp^*$

Supply: $Q^* = c + dp^*$

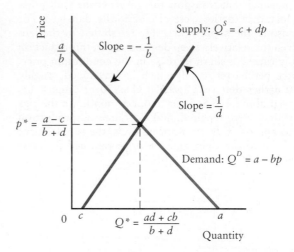

We now have two equations and two unknown variables (p^* and Q^*) and can proceed to solve the system of equations. Since Q^* from the demand curve equals Q^* from the supply curve, it follows that

$$a - bp^* = c + dp^*$$

SUMMARY

3.1 Demand

LO 1, 2

- The amount of a product that consumers want to purchase is called *quantity demanded*. It is a flow expressed as so much per period of time. It is determined by tastes, income, the product's own price, the prices of other products, the size of the population, and expectations about the future.

- The relationship between quantity demanded and price is represented graphically by a demand curve that shows how much will be demanded at each market price. Quantity demanded is assumed to increase as the price of the product falls, other things held constant. Thus, demand curves are negatively sloped.

This implies

$$a - c = (b + d)p^*$$

which can be solved for p^* to get

$$p^* = \frac{a - c}{b + d}$$

This is the solution for the equilibrium market price. By substituting this value of p^* back into *either* the demand curve or the supply curve (it doesn't matter which), we get the solution for Q^*:

$$Q^* = a - bp^* = a - \frac{b(a - c)}{(b + d)}$$

which can be simplified to

$$Q^* = \frac{a(b + d)}{(b + d)} - \frac{b(a - c)}{(b + d)}$$

which can be further simplified to

$$Q^* = \frac{(ad + bc)}{b + d}$$

We now have the precise solutions for the equilibrium price and quantity in this market. Notice that the solutions for p^* and Q^* naturally depend on those (exogenous) variables that shift the demand and supply curves. For example, an increase in demand for the product would be reflected by an increase in a. This would shift the demand curve to the right, increasing both p^* and Q^*. A decrease in supply would have a different effect. It would be reflected by a decrease in c that would shift the supply curve to the left, leading to an increase in p^* and a reduction in Q^*.

Now let's do the same thing but with even more specific demand and supply curves. Suppose we have the following relationships:

$$Q^D = 18 - 3p$$
$$Q^S = 2 + 5p$$

The equilibrium condition is that $Q^D = Q^S = Q^*$. And when quantity is equal to Q^*, price will be equal to p^*. Thus, in equilibrium we will have

$$Q^* = 18 - 3p^*$$
$$Q^* = 2 + 5p^*$$

Since Q^* from the demand curve obviously equals Q^* from the supply curve, we have

$$18 - 3p^* = 2 + 5p^*$$

which can be solved for p^* to get

$$8p^* = 16$$
$$p^* = 2$$

Putting this value of p^* back into the demand curve we get

$$Q^* = 18 - 3(2)$$
$$Q^* = 12$$

We have therefore solved for the equilibrium price and quantity in this specific numerical model of demand and supply.

Mastering the algebra of demand and supply takes a little practice, but is worth the effort. If you would like to practise, try the Study Exercises at the end of the chapter (and Chapters 4 and 5) that deal with the algebra of demand and supply.

- A shift in a demand curve represents a change in the quantity demanded at each price and is referred to as a *change in demand*.
- An increase in demand means the demand curve shifts to the right; a decrease in demand means the demand curve shifts to the left.

- It is important to make the distinction between a movement along a demand curve (caused by a change in the product's price) and a shift of a demand curve (caused by a change in any of the other determinants of demand).

3.2 Supply

- The amount of a good that producers wish to sell is called *quantity supplied*. It is a flow expressed as so much per period of time. It depends on the product's own price, the costs of inputs, the number of suppliers, government taxes or subsidies, the state of technology, and prices of other products.

- The relationship between quantity supplied and price is represented graphically by a supply curve that shows how much will be supplied at each market price. Quantity supplied is assumed to increase as the price of the product increases, other things held constant. Thus, supply curves are positively sloped.
- A shift in the supply curve indicates a change in the quantity supplied at each price and is referred to as a *change in supply.*

- An increase in supply means the supply curve shifts to the right; a decrease in supply means the supply curve shifts to the left.
- It is important to make the distinction between a movement along a supply curve (caused by a change in the product's price) and a shift of a supply curve (caused by a change in any of the other determinants of supply).

3.3 The Determination of Price   LO 5

- The *equilibrium price* is the price at which the quantity demanded equals the quantity supplied. At any price below equilibrium, there will be excess demand; at any price above equilibrium, there will be excess supply. Graphically, equilibrium occurs where the demand and supply curves intersect.
- Price rises when there is excess demand and falls when there is excess supply. Thus, the actual market price will be pushed toward the equilibrium price. When it is reached, there will be neither excess demand nor excess supply, and the price will not change until either the supply curve or the demand curve shifts.
- By using the method of *comparative statics,* we can determine the effects of a shift in either demand or

supply. An increase in demand raises both equilibrium price and equilibrium quantity; a decrease in demand lowers both. An increase in supply raises equilibrium quantity but lowers equilibrium price; a decrease in supply lowers equilibrium quantity but raises equilibrium price.
- The absolute price of a product is its price in terms of money; its relative price is its price in relation to other products. In an inflationary period, a rise in the *relative price* of one product means that its absolute price rises by more than the average of all prices; a fall in its relative price means that its absolute price rises by less than the average of all prices.

KEY CONCEPTS

Stock and flow variables
Ceteris paribus or "other things being equal"
Quantity demanded
Demand schedule and demand curve

Change in quantity demanded versus change in demand
Quantity supplied
Supply schedule and supply curve
Change in quantity supplied versus change in supply

Equilibrium, equilibrium price, and disequilibrium
Comparative statics
Relative price

STUDY EXERCISES

MyEconLab   **Make the grade with MyEconLab: Study Exercises marked in red can be found on MyEconLab. You can practise them as often as you want, and most feature step-by-step guided instructions to help you find the right answer.**

---

1. Fill in the blanks to complete the statements about a supply-and-demand model, as applied in the following situations.

    a. Consider the market for cement in Toronto. If, *ceteris paribus,* half the producers in this market shut down, the _____ curve for cement will shift to the _____, indicating a(n) _____ in _____.

    b. Consider the market for Canadian softwood lumber (a normal good). If, *ceteris paribus,* average incomes in both Canada and the United States rise over several years, the _____ curve for lumber will shift to the _____, indicating a(n) _____ in _____.

c. Consider the market for Quebec artisanal cheeses. If, *ceteris paribus,* the price of imported cheeses from France rises significantly, the _____ curve for Quebec cheeses will shift to the _____, indicating a(n) _____ in _____.

d. Consider the market for milk in the United States. If *ceteris paribus,* the U.S. government decreases subsidies to dairy farmers, the _____ curve for milk will shift to the _____, indicating a(n) _____ in _____.

e. Consider the world market for shipping containers. If, *ceteris paribus,* the price of steel (a major input) rises, the _____ curve for shipping containers will shift to the _____, indicating a(n) _____ in _____.

f. Consider the market for hot dog buns. If, *ceteris paribus,* the price of wieners doubles, the _____ curve for hot dog buns will shift to the _____, indicating a(n) _____ in _____.

2. The following table shows hypothetical demand schedules for sugar for three separate months. To help make the distinction between changes in demand and changes in quantity demanded, choose the wording to make each of the following statements correct.

	Quantity Demanded for Sugar (in kilograms)		
Price/kg	October	November	December
$1.50	11 000	10 500	13 000
1.75	10 000	9 500	12 000
2.00	9 000	8 500	11 000
2.25	8 000	7 500	10 000
2.50	7 000	6 500	9 000
2.75	6 000	5 500	8 000
3.00	5 000	4 500	7 000
3.25	4 000	3 500	6 000
3.50	3 000	2 500	5 000

a. When the price of sugar rises from $2.50 to $3.00 in the month of October there is a(n) (*increase/decrease*) in (*demand for/quantity demanded of*) sugar of 2000 kg.

b. We can say that the demand curve for sugar in December shifted (*to the right/to the left*) of November's demand curve. This represents a(n) (*increase/decrease*) in demand for sugar.

c. An increase in the demand for sugar means that quantity demanded at each price has (*increased/decreased*), while a decrease in demand for sugar means that quantity demanded at each price has (*increased/decreased*).

d. In the month of December, a price change for sugar from $3.50 to $2.75 per kilogram would mean a change in (*demand for/quantity demanded of*) sugar of 3000 kg.

e. Plot the three demand schedules on a graph and label each demand curve to indicate whether it is the demand for October, November, or December.

3. Classify the effect of each of the following as (i) a decrease in the demand for fish or (ii) a decrease in the quantity of fish demanded. Illustrate each diagrammatically.

a. The government of Canada closes the Atlantic cod fishery.

b. People buy less fish because of a rise in fish prices.

c. The Catholic Church relaxes its ban on eating meat on Fridays.

d. The price of beef falls and, as a result, consumers buy more beef and less fish.

e. Fears of mercury poisoning lead locals to shun fish caught in nearby lakes.

f. It is generally alleged that eating fish is better for one's health than eating meat.

4. Are the following two observations inconsistent?

a. Rising demand for housing causes prices of new homes to soar.

b. Many families refuse to buy homes as prices become prohibitive for them.

5. For each of the following statements, determine whether there has been a change in supply or a change in quantity supplied. Draw a demand-and-supply diagram for each situation to show either a movement along the supply curve or a shift of the supply curve.

a. The price of Canadian-grown peaches skyrockets during an unusually cold summer that reduces the size of the peach harvest.

b. An increase in income leads to an increase in the price of family-restaurant meals, and to an increase in their sales.

c. Technological improvements in electronic publishing lead to price reductions for e-books and an increase in e-book sales.

d. A low-carb diet becomes popular and leads to a reduction in the price of bread and less bread being sold.

6. The following diagram describes the hypothetical demand and supply for canned tuna in Canada in 2013.

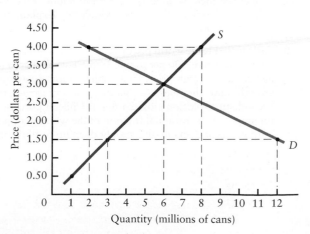

a. Suppose the price of a can of tuna is $4.00. What is the quantity demanded? What is the quantity supplied? At this price, is there a shortage or a surplus? By what amount?

b. Suppose the price of a can of tuna is $1.50. What is the quantity demanded? What is the quantity supplied? At this price, is there a shortage or a surplus? By what amount?

c. What is the equilibrium price and quantity in this market?

7. Consider households' demand for chicken meat. For each of the events listed below, state and explain the likely effect on the demand for chicken. How would each event be illustrated in a diagram?

a. A medical study reports that eating chicken reduces the likelihood of suffering from particular types of heart problems.

b. A widespread bovine disease leads to an increase in the price of beef.

c. Average household income increases.

8. Consider the world market for a particular quality of coffee beans. The following table shows the demand and supply schedules for this market.

Price (per kilogram)	Quantity Demanded	Quantity Supplied
	(millions of kilograms per year)	
$2.00	28	10
$2.40	26	12
$3.10	22	13.5
$3.50	19.5	19.5
$3.90	17	22
$4.30	14.5	23.5

a. Plot the demand and supply schedules on a diagram.

b. Identify the amount of excess demand or supply associated with each price.

c. Identify the equilibrium price in this market.

d. Suppose that a collection of national governments were somehow able to set a minimum price for coffee equal to $3.90 per kilogram. Explain the outcome in the world coffee market.

9. Early in 2011, the world price of copper reached a record high of over $10 000 per tonne. Two events appeared to lie behind this high price. First, China's rapid economic growth and the massive building of infrastructure. Second, an explosion closed a major Chilean port used for shipping a substantial fraction of the world's copper output. Use a demand-and-supply diagram to illustrate

these events in the copper market, and explain how each event shifts either the demand curve or the supply curve.

10. Consider the world market for wheat. Suppose there is a major failure in Russia's wheat crop because of a severe drought. Explain the likely effect on the equilibrium price and quantity in the world wheat market. Also explain why Canadian wheat farmers certainly benefit from Russia's drought. The following diagrams provide a starting point for your analysis.

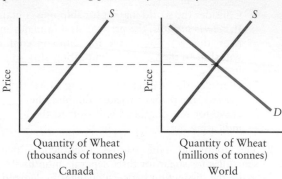

Quantity of Wheat
(thousands of tonnes)
Canada

Quantity of Wheat
(millions of tonnes)
World

11. This question requires you to solve a supply-and-demand model algebraically. Letting p be the price of the product, suppose the demand and supply functions for some product are given by

$$Q^D = 100 - 3p$$
$$Q^S = 10 + 2p$$

a. Plot both the demand curve and the supply curve.

b. What is the condition for equilibrium in this market?

c. By imposing the condition for equilibrium, solve for the equilibrium price.

d. Substitute the equilibrium price into either the demand or the supply function to solve for the equilibrium quantity. Check to make sure you get the same answer whether you use the demand function or the supply function.

e. Now suppose there is an increase in demand so that the new demand function is given by

$$Q^D = 180 - 3p$$

Compute the new equilibrium price and quantity. Is your result consistent with the "law" of demand?

f. Now suppose that with the new demand curve in place, there is an increase in supply so that the new supply function is given by $Q^S = 90 + 2p$. Compute the new equilibrium price and quantity. Is your result consistent with the "law" of supply?

What Macroeconomics Is All About

CHAPTER OUTLINE	LEARNING OBJECTIVES (LO)
	After studying this chapter you will be able to
19.1 KEY MACROECONOMIC VARIABLES	1 define the key macroeconomic variables: national income, unemployment, inflation, interest rates, exchange rates, and net exports.
19.2 GROWTH VERSUS FLUCTUATIONS	2 understand that most macroeconomic issues are about either long-run trends or short-run fluctuations, and that government policy is relevant for both.

DURING the mid-2000s, the economies of Canada, the United States, Europe, and Asia were growing quickly, unemployment was low, and it appeared to many that there was nothing but smooth economic sailing ahead. Then in 2007, house prices in the United States, which had been rising quickly over the previous decade, began to fall—and sharply. Banks and other financial institutions that had invested heavily in mortgage-backed securities were in trouble, and some very large ones in Europe and the United States went bankrupt. The world economy entered its deepest recession in 70 years.

In the fall of 2008, government leaders of the world's largest economies, a group of countries known as the G20, met in Washington, D.C. They discussed large-scale policy interventions to prevent a repeat of the Great Depression, the massive decline in economic activity that occurred between 1929 and 1933 and that had enormous economic, political, and social consequences for years to come. The G20 leaders agreed to take many actions to stave off such an economic disaster, including increasing the level of government spending, reducing interest rates through aggressive central-bank actions, supporting their failing financial institutions, and avoiding the imposition of new tariffs and other protectionist measures.

Why did the U.S. housing collapse lead to serious problems for banks, and why did these problems lead to a global recession? How can various actions by governments help to dampen the scale of recession and what are the side effects of such large-scale policy interventions? These are central questions in macroeconomics, and the events of 2007–2010 show just how important these issues are. The next several chapters are devoted to understanding the essential elements of *macroeconomics*.

macroeconomics The study of the determination of economic aggregates, such as total output, total employment, the price level, and the rate of economic growth.

Macroeconomics is the study of how the economy behaves in broad outline without dwelling on much of the detail that occurs in markets for individual products. Macroeconomics is concerned with the behaviour of economic *aggregates* and *averages*, such as total output, total investment, total exports, and the price level, and with how they may be influenced by government policy. Their behaviour results from activities in many different markets and from the combined behaviour of millions of different decision makers.

An economy producing a lot of wheat and few computers is clearly different from one producing many computers but little wheat. An economy with cheap wheat and expensive computers is also different from one with cheap computers and expensive wheat. When we study aggregates and averages we ignore these important differences in order to focus our attention on some important issues for the economy as a whole.

In return for suppressing some valuable detail, studying macroeconomics allows us to view the big picture. When aggregate output rises, the output of many commodities and the incomes of many people rise with it. When the unemployment rate rises, many workers suffer reductions in their incomes. When significant disruptions occur in the credit markets, interest rates rise and borrowers find it more difficult to finance their desired purchases. Such movements in economic aggregates matter for most individuals because they influence the health of the industries in which they work. These are the reasons why macroeconomic issues get airtime on the evening news, and why we study macroeconomics.

It will become clear as we proceed through this chapter (and later ones) that macroeconomists consider two different aspects of the economy. They think about the *short-run* behaviour of macroeconomic variables, such as output, employment, and inflation, and about how government policy can influence these variables. This concerns, among other things, the study of *business cycles*. They also examine the long-run behaviour of the same variables, especially the long-run path of aggregate output. This is the study of *economic growth* and is concerned with explaining how investment and technological change affect our material living standards over long periods of time.

> A full understanding of macroeconomics requires understanding the nature of short-run fluctuations as well as the nature of long-run economic growth.

Before we examine some key macroeconomic variables, it is worth pointing out that there are two different streams of research in macroeconomics, even though the researchers in the two groups are generally interested in understanding the same macroeconomic phenomena. The first group of researchers takes an approach to macroeconomics that is based explicitly on *microeconomic foundations*. These economists build models of the economy that are populated by workers, consumers, and firms, all of whom are assumed to be *optimizers*—that is, individuals are assumed to maximize their utility and firms are assumed to maximize their profits. Having explicitly modelled these agents' optimization problems, and their resulting choices for work effort, consumption, and investment, the economists proceed to *aggregate* the choices of these agents to arrive at the model's values for aggregate employment, consumption, output, and so on.

The second group of researchers builds macroeconomic models based only implicitly on these same micro foundations. Although they often analyze the behaviour of individuals and firms, they do not formally aggregate their behaviour to derive the aggregate relationships in their models. Instead, these economists construct their models by using aggregate relationships for consumption, investment, and employment, each of which has been subjected to extensive empirical testing and is assumed to represent collectively the behaviour of the many firms and consumers in the economy.

A second difference between these two approaches relates to the assumptions regarding the flexibility of wages and prices. Economists using the first approach usually assume that wages and prices are perfectly flexible and thus adjust quickly to clear their respective markets. In contrast, economists using the second approach usually assume that because of the nature of well-established institutions in both labour and product markets, such as labour unions, long-term employment contracts, or costs associated with changing prices, wages and prices are slow to adjust, and thus markets can be in disequilibrium for longer periods of time.

This textbook follows the second approach to macroeconomic analysis. The macro model we begin building in Chapter 21 is not formally derived from the behaviour of optimizing firms and consumers, although the macro relationships we introduce are well motivated by microeconomic behaviour. Moreover, the model begins in its simplest version by assuming *no* wage and price flexibility. But as we gradually make the model more complicated and also more realistic, we introduce some wage and price flexibility. In later chapters we will see that the degree of wage and price flexibility is crucial in determining how the economy responds to shocks of various kinds, including changes in government policy. We will also see that our macroeconomic model is sufficiently versatile that we can use it to illustrate the case of perfect wage/price flexibility as a special case.

19.1 Key Macroeconomic Variables

In this chapter, we discuss several important macroeconomic variables, with an emphasis on what they mean and why they matter for our well-being. Here and in Chapter 20 we also explain how the key macroeconomic variables are measured. The remainder of this book is about the causes and consequences of changes in each of these variables, the many ways in which they interact, and the effects they have on our well-being.

Output and Income

The most comprehensive measure of a nation's overall level of economic activity is the value of its total production of goods and services, called *national product*, or sometimes just called *output*.

> One of the most important ideas in economics is that the production of goods and services generates income.

As a matter of convention, economists define their terms so that, for the nation as a whole, all of the economic value that is produced ultimately belongs to someone in the form of an income claim on that value. For example, if a firm produces $100 worth of ice cream, that $100 becomes income for the firm's workers, the firm's suppliers of material inputs, and the firm's owners. The value of national product is *by definition* equal to the value of national income.

There are several related measures of a nation's total output and total income. Their various definitions, and the relationships among them, are discussed in detail in the next chapter. In this chapter, we use the generic term *national income* to refer to both the value of total output and the value of the income claims generated by the production of that output.

National Income: Aggregation To measure national income we add up the *values* of the many different goods and services that are produced. We cannot add tonnes of steel to loaves of bread, but we can add the dollar value of steel production to the dollar value of bread production. We begin by multiplying the number of units of each good produced by the price at which each unit is sold. This yields a dollar value of production for each good. We then sum these values across all the different goods produced in the economy to give us the quantity of total output, or national income, *measured in dollars*. This is usually called **nominal national income**.

A change in nominal national income can be caused by a change in either the physical quantities or the prices on which it is based. To determine the extent to which any change is due to quantities or to prices, economists calculate **real national income**. This measures the value of individual outputs, not at current prices, but at a set of prices that prevailed in some base period.

Nominal national income is often referred to as *current-dollar national income*. Real national income is often called *constant-dollar national income*. Real national income tells us the value of current output measured at constant prices—the sum of the quantities valued at prices that prevailed in the base period. Since prices are held constant when computing real national income, changes in real national income from one year to another reflect *only* changes in quantities. Comparing real national incomes of different years therefore provides a measure of the change in real output that has occurred during the intervening period.

National Income: Recent History One of the most commonly used measures of national income is called *gross domestic product* (*GDP*). GDP can be measured in either real or nominal terms; we focus here on real GDP. The details of its calculation will be discussed in Chapter 20.

Part (i) of Figure 19-1 shows real national income produced by the Canadian economy since 1965; part (ii) shows its annual percentage change for the same period. The GDP series in part (i) shows two kinds of movement. The major movement is a positive trend that increased real output by approximately four times since 1965. This is what economists refer to as *long-term economic growth*.

A second feature of the real GDP series is *short-term fluctuations* around the trend. Overall growth so dominates the real GDP series that the fluctuations are hardly visible in part (i) of Figure 19-1. However, as can be seen in part (ii), the growth of GDP has never been smooth. In most years, GDP increases, but in 1982, 1991, and 2009, GDP actually decreased, as shown by the negative rate of growth in the figure. Periods in which real GDP actually falls are called **recessions**.

The **business cycle** refers to this continual ebb and flow of business activity that occurs around the long-term trend. For example, a single cycle will usually include an interval of quickly growing output, followed by an interval of slowly growing or even falling output. The entire cycle may last for several years. No two business cycles are exactly the same—variations occur in duration and magnitude. Some expansions are long and drawn out. Others come to an end before high employment and industrial capacity are reached. Nonetheless, fluctuations are systematic enough that it is useful to identify common factors, as is done in *Applying Economic Concepts 19-1*.

---

nominal national income Total national income measured in current dollars. Also called *current-dollar national income*.

real national income National income measured in constant (base-period) dollars. It changes only when quantities change.

To see the most recent values for most of the macroeconomic variables discussed in this chapter, go to Statistics Canada's website: www.statcan.gc.ca and search for "Latest Indicators."

recession A fall in the level of real GDP. Often defined precisely as two consecutive quarters in which real GDP falls.

business cycle Fluctuations of national income around its trend value that follow a more or less wavelike pattern.

FIGURE 19-1 Growth and Fluctuations in Real GDP, 1965–2011

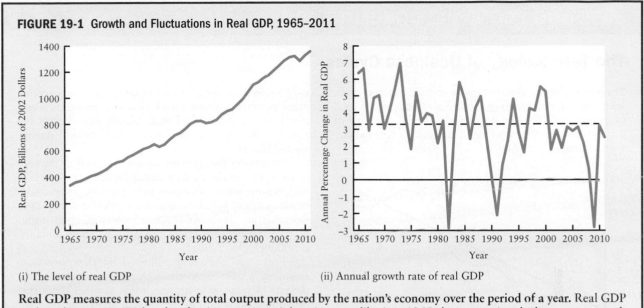

(i) The level of real GDP   (ii) Annual growth rate of real GDP

Real GDP measures the quantity of total output produced by the nation's economy over the period of a year. Real GDP is plotted in part (i). With only a few interruptions, it has risen steadily since 1965, demonstrating the long-term growth of the Canadian economy. Short-term fluctuations are obscured by the long-term trend in part (i) but are highlighted in part (ii). The growth rate fluctuates considerably from year to year. The long-term upward trend in part (i) reflects the positive average growth rate in part (ii), shown by the dashed line.

(*Source:* Adapted from Statistics Canada, CANSIM database, Table 380-0017, Gross Domestic Product. www.statcan. gc.ca. Search for "GDP.")

Potential Output and the Output Gap National output (or income) represents what the economy *actually* produces. An important related concept is the level of output the economy would produce if all resources—land, labour, and capital—were fully employed.[1] This concept is usually called **potential output**. The value of potential output must be estimated using statistical techniques whereas the value of actual output can be measured directly. For this reason, there is often disagreement among researchers regarding the level of potential output, owing to their different estimation approaches. In terms of notation, we use Y to denote the economy's actual output and Y^* to denote potential output.

    The **output gap** measures the difference between potential output and actual output, and is computed as $Y - Y^*$. When actual output is less than potential output $(Y < Y^*)$, the gap measures the market value of goods and services that are not produced because the economy's resources are not fully employed. When Y is less than Y^*, the output gap is called a **recessionary gap**. When actual output exceeds potential output $(Y > Y^*)$, the gap measures the market value of production in excess of what the economy can produce on a sustained basis. Y can exceed Y^* because workers may work longer hours than normal or factories may operate an extra shift. When Y exceeds Y^* there is often upward pressure on prices, and thus we say the output gap is an **inflationary gap**.

potential output (Y^*) The real GDP that the economy would produce if its productive resources were fully employed. Also called *potential GDP*.

output gap Actual output minus potential output, $Y - Y^*$.

recessionary gap A situation in which actual output is less than potential output, $Y < Y^*$.

inflationary gap A situation in which actual output exceeds potential output, $Y > Y^*$.

---

[1] *Full employment* refers to a situation in which the factor markets display neither excess demand nor excess supply. We say more about full employment shortly.

APPLYING ECONOMIC CONCEPTS 19-1

The Terminology of Business Cycles

The accompanying figure shows a stylized business cycle, with real GDP fluctuating around a steadily rising level of potential GDP—the economy's normal capacity to produce output. We begin our discussion of terminology with a trough.

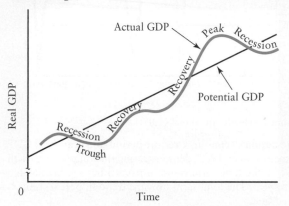

A *trough* is characterized by unemployed resources and a level of output that is low in relation to the economy's capacity to produce. There is a substantial amount of unused productive capacity. Business profits are low; for some individual companies, they are negative. Confidence about economic prospects in the immediate future is lacking, and, as a result, many firms are unwilling to risk making new investments.

The process of *recovery* moves the economy out of a trough. The characteristics of a recovery are many: run-down or obsolete equipment is replaced; employment, income, and consumer spending all begin to rise; and expectations become more favourable. Investments that

once seemed risky may be undertaken as firms become more optimistic about future business prospects. Production can be increased with relative ease merely by re-employing the existing unused capacity and unemployed labour.

Eventually the recovery comes to a *peak* at the top of the cycle. At the peak, existing capacity is used to a high degree; labour shortages may develop, particularly in categories of key skills, and shortages of essential raw materials are likely. As shortages develop, costs begin to rise, but because prices rise also, business remains profitable.

Peaks are eventually followed by slowdowns in economic activity. Sometimes this is just a slowing of the rate of increase in income, while at other times the slowdown turns into a *recession*. A recession, or contraction, is a downturn in economic activity. Common usage defines a recession as a fall in real GDP for two successive quarters. As output falls, so do employment and households' incomes. Profits drop, and some firms encounter financial difficulties. Investments that looked profitable with the expectation of continually rising income now appear unprofitable. It may not even be worth replacing capital goods as they wear out because unused capacity is increasing steadily. In historical discussions, a recession that is deep and long lasting is often called a *depression*, such as the Great Depression in the early 1930s, during which aggregate output fell by 30 percent and the unemployment rate increased to 20 percent!

These terms are non-technical but descriptive: The entire falling half of the business cycle is often called a *slump*, and the entire rising half is often called a *boom*.

Figure 19-2 shows the path of potential GDP since 1985. The upward trend reflects the growth in the productive capacity of the Canadian economy over this period, caused by increases in the labour force, capital stock, and the level of technological knowledge. The figure also shows actual GDP (reproduced from Figure 19-1), which has kept approximately in step with potential GDP. The distance between the two, which is the output gap, is plotted in part (ii) of Figure 19-2. Fluctuations in economic activity are apparent from fluctuations in the size of the output gap.

Why National Income Matters National income is an important measure of economic performance. Short-run movements in the business cycle receive the most attention in politics and in the press, but most economists agree that long-term growth—as reflected by the growth of *potential GDP*—is in many ways the more important of the two.

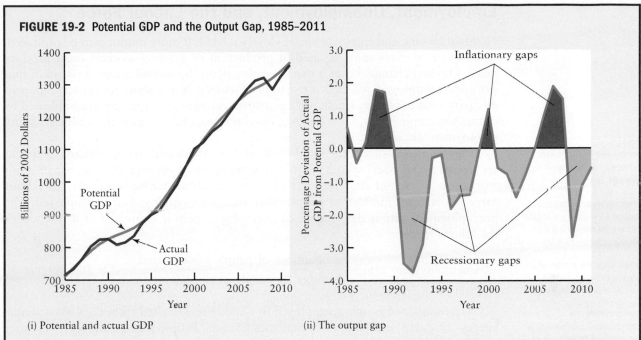

FIGURE 19-2 Potential GDP and the Output Gap, 1985–2011

(i) Potential and actual GDP

(ii) The output gap

Potential and actual GDP both display an upward trend. The output gap measures the difference between an economy's potential output and its actual output; the gap is expressed here as a percentage of potential output. Since 1985, potential and actual GDP have almost doubled. The output gap in part (ii) shows clear fluctuations. Shaded areas show inflationary and recessionary gaps.

(*Source:* Real GDP: Statistics Canada, CANSIM database, Table 380-0017. Output gap: www.bankofcanada.ca. Potential output is based on author's calculations.)

Recessions are associated with unemployment and lost output. When actual GDP is below potential GDP, economic waste and human suffering result from the failure to fully employ the economy's resources. Booms, although associated with high employment and high output, can bring problems of their own. When actual GDP exceeds potential GDP, inflationary pressure usually ensues, causing concern for any government that is committed to keeping the inflation rate low.

The long-run trend in real per capita national income is an important determinant of improvements in a society's overall standard of living. When income per person grows, each generation can expect, on average, to be better off than preceding ones. For example, over the period shown in Figure 19-1, per capita income has grown at an average rate of about 1.5 percent per year. Even at such a modest growth rate, the average person's lifetime income will be about *twice* that of his or her grandparents.

Although economic growth makes people materially better off *on average*, it does not necessarily make *every* individual better off—the benefits of growth are never shared equally by all members of the population. For example, if growth involves significant changes in the structure of the economy, such as a shift away from agriculture and toward manufacturing (as happened in the first part of the twentieth century), or away from manufacturing toward some natural resources (as has been happening in recent years), then these changes will reduce some people's material living standards for extended periods of time.

Employment, Unemployment, and the Labour Force

National income and employment are closely related. If more output is to be produced, either more workers must be used in production or existing workers must produce more. The first change means a rise in employment; the second means a rise in output per person employed, which is a rise in *productivity*. In the short run, changes in productivity tend to be very small; most short-run changes in output are accomplished by changes in employment. Over the long run, however, changes in both productivity and employment are significant.

employment The number of persons 15 years of age or older who have jobs.

Employment denotes the number of adult workers (defined in Canada as workers aged 15 and over) who have jobs. **Unemployment** denotes the number of adult workers who are not employed but who are actively searching for a job. The **labour force** is the total number of people who are either employed or unemployed. The **unemployment rate** is the number of unemployed people expressed as a fraction of the labour force:

unemployment The number of persons 15 years of age or older who are not employed and are actively searching for a job.

$$\text{Unemployment rate} = \frac{\text{Number of people unemployed}}{\text{Number of people in the labour force}} \times 100 \text{ percent}$$

labour force The number of persons employed plus the number of persons unemployed.

unemployment rate Unemployment expressed as a percentage of the labour force.

The number of people unemployed in Canada is estimated from the Labour Force Survey conducted each month by Statistics Canada. People who are currently without a job but who say they have searched actively for one during the sample period are recorded as unemployed.

Frictional, Structural, and Cyclical Unemployment When the economy is at potential GDP, economists say there is *full employment*. But for two reasons there will still be some unemployment even when the economy is at potential GDP.

First, there is a constant turnover of individuals in given jobs and a constant change in job opportunities. New people enter the workforce; some people quit their jobs; others are fired. It may take some time for these people to find jobs. So at any point in time, there is unemployment caused by the normal turnover of labour. Such unemployment is called *frictional unemployment*.

Second, because the economy is constantly adapting to shocks of various kinds, at any moment there will always be some mismatch between the characteristics of the labour force and the characteristics of the available jobs. The mismatch may occur, for example, because labour does not currently have the skills that are in demand or because labour is not in the part of the country where the demand is located. This is a mismatch between the *structure* of the supplies of labour and the *structure* of the demands for labour. Such unemployment is therefore called *structural unemployment*.

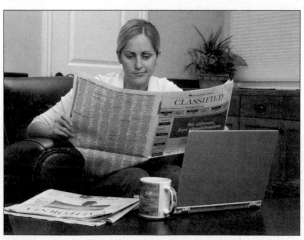

Economists make the distinction between frictional, structural, and cyclical unemployment. This distinction is important for analyzing the economy but it matters little to the individual who has difficulty finding an appropriate job.

Even when the economy is at "full employment," some unemployment exists because of natural turnover in the labour market and mismatch between jobs and workers.

ter 31 we dis-
rend.

is enormous
the least dur-
n people who
d. When only
million work-
et everyone's

individuals.
income does
y a long per-
ime, mental
ployment.
rom friends
t insurance
unemploy-
economic
t insurance
hough dif-

hen the *only* unemployment is frictional and struc-
actual GDP being equal to potential GDP. When
DP, the economy is not at full employment. In these
yclical unemployment. Cyclical unemployment rises
he business cycle. Unemployment also has *seasonal*
nployed in the fishing industry often are unemployed
s may be unemployed in the summer. Because these
regular and therefore easy to predict, Statistics Can-
yment statistics to remove these fluctuations, thereby
nd trend movements in the data. For example, suppose
employment rate increases by 0.3 percentage points in
then adjust the December unemployment rate so that it
ase in the *unadjusted* rate exceeds 0.3 percentage points.
d) December unemployment rate is reported to increase
ore than its normal seasonal increase. All the unemploy-
) data shown in this book are seasonally adjusted.

t: Recent History Figure 19-3 shows the trends in the
unemployment since 1960. Despite booms and slumps,
ly in line with the growth in the labour force. Although
es the employment data, the figure also shows that the
unemployment rate have been substantial. The unemploy-
3.4 percent in 1966 and as high as 12 percent during the
(ii) of Figure 19-3 also shows that there has been a slight

ely stead-
city. This
the level
s from a
on of the
stock of
ut—has
creased

ces per
pital—
easure
labour
umber

r pro-
essed
440.
2002

rked
ness
976
kes

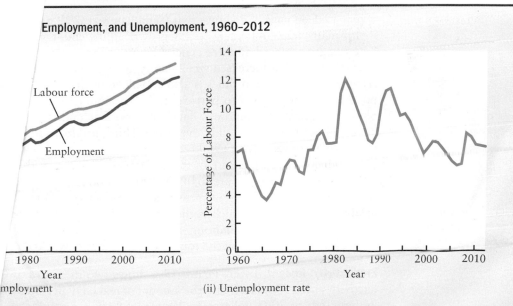

Employment, and Unemployment, 1960–2012

Labour force

Employment

1980   1990   2000   2010
Year
mployment

14
12
10
8
6
4
2
0

Percentage of Labour Force

1960   1970   1980   1990   2000   2010
Year
(ii) Unemployment rate

d employment have grown since 1960 with only a few interruptions. The unemployment rate responds
viour of the economy. The labour force and the level of employment in Canada have both almost tripled
are associated with a low unemployment rate and slumps with a high unemployment rate.

ta are from Statistics Canada's CANSIM database, Table 282-002. Labour force: Series V2062810.
ies V2062811. Unemployment rate is based on author's calculations. Current labour-force statistics
Statistics Canada's website at www.statcan.gc.ca by searching for "unemployment.")

upward trend in the unemployment rate over the past 50 years. In Cha[...]
cuss how some structural changes in the economy can help explain this [...]

Why Unemployment Matters The social significance of unemployment[...]
because it involves economic waste and human suffering. Human effort i[...]
able of economic commodities. If a fully employed economy has 18 milli[...]
are willing to work, their services must either be used this year or waste[...]
16 million people are actually employed, one year's potential output of 2 [...]
ers is lost forever. In an economy in which there is not enough output to m[...]
needs, such a waste of potential output is cause for concern.

The loss of income associated with unemployment is clearly harmful t[...]
In some cases, the loss of income pushes people into poverty. But this lost [...]
not capture the full cost of unemployment. A person's spirit can be broken b[...]
iod of desiring work but being unable to find it. Research has shown that c[...]
illness, and general social unrest tend to be associated with long-term unem[...]

In the not-so-distant past, only personal savings, private charity, or help [...]
and relatives stood between the unemployed and starvation. Today, employme[...]
and social assistance ("welfare") have created a safety net, particularly when [...]
ment is for short periods, as is most often the case in Canada. However, when a[...]
slump lasts long enough, some unfortunate people exhaust their employmen[...]
and lose part of that safety net. Short-term unemployment can be a feasible t[...]
ficult adjustment for many; long-term unemployment can be a disaster.

Productivity

Figure 19-1 on page 477 shows that Canadian real GDP has increased relativ[...]
ily for many years, reflecting steady growth in the country's productive capa[...]
long-run growth has had three general sources. First, as shown in Figure 19-3[...]
of employment has increased significantly. Rising employment generally resul[...]
rising population, but at times is also explained by an increase in the proporti[...]
population that chooses to participate in the labour force. Second, Canada's [...]
physical capital—the buildings, factories, and machines used to produce outp[...]
increased more or less steadily over time. Third, *productivity* in Canada has i[...]
in almost every year since 1960.

Productivity is a measure of the amount of output that the economy produ[...]
unit of input. Since there are many inputs to production—land, labour, and ca[...]
we can have several different measures of productivity. One commonly used n[...]
is **labour productivity**, which is the amount of real GDP produced per unit of [...]
employed. The amount of labour employed can be measured either as the total n[...]
of employed workers or by the total number of hours worked.

labour productivity The level
of real GDP divided by the level
of employment (or total hours
worked).

Productivity: Recent History Figure 19-4 shows two measures of Canadian labou[...]
ductivity since 1976. The first is the amount of real GDP per employed worker (exp[...]
in thousands of 2002 dollars). In 2011, real GDP per employed worker was $78[...]
The second measure shows the amount of real GDP per *hour worked* (expressed in [...]
dollars). In 2011, real GDP per hour worked was $45.50.

The second measure is more accurate because the average number of hours wo[...]
per employed worker changes over time. In addition to fluctuating over the bus[...]
cycle, it has shown a long-term decline, from just over 1850 hours per year in 1[...]
to just under 1700 hours per year in 2011. The second measure of productivity t[...]
account of these changes in hours worked, whereas the first measure does not.

One pattern is immediately apparent for both measures of productivity. There has been a significant increase in labour productivity over the past three decades. Real GDP per employed worker increased by 39.4 percent from 1976 to 2011, an annual average growth rate of 0.95 percent. Real GDP per hour worked increased by 48.5 per cent over the same period, an annual average growth rate of 1.1 percent.

Why Productivity Matters Productivity growth is the single largest cause of rising material living standards over long periods of time. Over periods of a few years, changes in average real incomes have more to do with the ebb and flow of the business cycle than with changes in productivity; increases in employment during an economic recovery and reductions in employment during recessions explain much of the short-run movements in average real incomes. As is clear from Figure 19-1, however, these short-run fluctuations are dwarfed over the long term by the steady upward trend in real GDP—an upward trend that comes in large part from rising productivity.

Why is the real income for an average Canadian this year so much greater than it was for the average Canadian 50 or 100 years ago? Most of the answer lies in the fact that the Canadian worker today is vastly more productive than was his or her counterpart in the distant past. This greater productivity comes partly from the better physical capital with which Canadians now work and partly from their greater skills. The higher productivity for today's workers explains why their *real wages* (the purchasing power of their earnings) are so much higher than for workers in the past.

FIGURE 19-4 Canadian Labour Productivity, 1976–2011

Rising labour productivity is an important contributor to rising material living standards. The figure shows two measures of labour productivity: real GDP per employed worker and real GDP per hour worked. The first is expressed in *thousands* of 2002 dollars per worker and has increased at an average annual rate of 0.95 percent. The second is expressed in 2002 dollars per hour and has grown at the annual rate of 1.1 percent.

(*Source:* All data are based on author's calculations using Statistics Canada's CANSIM database. Real GDP: Table 380-0017. Total weekly hours worked: Table 282-0028. Employment: Table 282-0002.)

The close connection between productivity growth and rising material living standards explains the importance that is now placed on understanding the determinants of productivity growth. It is a very active area of economic research, but there are still many unanswered questions. In Chapter 26 we address the process of long-run growth in real GDP and explore the determinants of productivity growth.

Inflation and the Price Level

Inflation means that prices of goods and services are going up, *on average*. If you are a typical reader of this book, inflation has not been very noticeable during your lifetime. When your parents were your age, however, high inflation was a major economic problem. (Some countries have had their economies almost ruined by very high inflation, called *hyperinflation*. We will say more about this in Chapter 27.)

For studying inflation, there are two related but different concepts that are sometimes confused, and it is important to get them straight. The first is the **price level**, which refers to the average level of all prices in the economy and is given by the symbol *P*. The second is the rate of **inflation**, which is the rate at which the price level is rising.

price level The average level of all prices in the economy, expressed as an index number.

inflation A rise in the average level of all prices (the price level).

To measure the price level, the economic statisticians at Statistics Canada construct a *price index*, which averages the prices of various commodities according to how important they are. The best-known price index in Canada is the **Consumer Price Index (CPI)**, which measures the average price of the goods and services that are bought by the typical Canadian household. *Applying Economic Concepts 19-2* shows how a price index such as the CPI is constructed.

Consumer Price Index (CPI)
An index of the average prices of goods and services commonly bought by households.

APPLYING ECONOMIC CONCEPTS 19-2

How the CPI Is Constructed

Although the details are somewhat more complicated, the basic idea behind the Consumer Price Index is straightforward, as is illustrated by the following hypothetical example.

Suppose we want to discover what has happened to the overall cost of living for typical university students. A survey of student behaviour in 2003 shows that the average university student consumed only three goods—pizza, coffee, and photocopying—and spent a total of $200 a month on these items, as shown in Table 1.

TABLE 1 Expenditure Behaviour in 2003

Product	Price	Quantity per Month	Expenditure per Month
Photocopies	$0.10 per sheet	140 sheets	$14.00
Pizza	8.00 per pizza	15 pizzas	120.00
Coffee	0.75 per cup	88 cups	66.00
Total expenditure			$200.00

By 2013 in this example, the price of photocopying has fallen to 5 cents per copy, the price of pizza has increased to $9.00, and the price of coffee has increased to $1.00. What has happened to the cost of living over this 10-year period? In order to find out, we calculate the cost of purchasing the 2003 bundle of goods at the prices that prevailed in 2013, as shown in Table 2.

The total expenditure required to purchase the bundle of goods that cost $200.00 in 2003 has risen to $230.00. The increase in required expenditure is $30.00, which is a 15 percent increase over the original $200.00.

If we define 2003 as the base year for the "student price index" and assign an index value of 100 to the cost of the average student's expenditure in that year, the value of the index in 2013 is 115. Thus, goods and services that cost $100.00 in the base year cost $115.00 in 2013, exactly what is implied by Table 2.

TABLE 2 2003 Expenditure Behaviour at 2013 Prices

Product	Price	Quantity per Month	Expenditure per Month
Photocopies	$0.05 per sheet	140 sheets	$7.00
Pizza	9.00 per pizza	15 pizzas	135.00
Coffee	1.00 per cup	88 cups	88.00
Total expenditure			$230.00

The Consumer Price Index, as constructed by Statistics Canada, is built on exactly the same principles as the preceding example. In the case of the CPI, many thousands of consumers are surveyed, and the prices of thousands of products are monitored, but the basic method is the same:

1. Survey the consumption behaviour of consumers.

2. Calculate the cost of the goods and services purchased by the average consumer in the year in which the original survey was done. Define this as the base period of the index.

3. Calculate the cost of purchasing the same bundle of goods and services in other years.

4. Divide the result of Step 3 (in each year) by the result of Step 2, and multiply by 100. The result is the value of the CPI for each year.

The CPI is not a perfect measure of the cost of living because it does not automatically account for ongoing quality improvements or for changes in consumers' expenditure patterns. Changes of this type require the underlying survey of consumer expenditure to be updated from time to time to make sure that the expenditure patterns in the survey approximately match consumers' actual expenditure patterns.

As we saw in Chapter 2, a price index is a pure number—it does not have any units. Yet as we all know, prices in Canada are expressed in dollars. When we construct a price index, the units (dollars) are eliminated because the price index shows the price of a basket of goods at some specific time *relative to the price of the same basket of goods in some base period*. Currently, the base year for Statistics Canada's calculation of the CPI is 2002, which means that the price of the basket of goods is set to be 100 in 2002. If the CPI in 2013 is computed to be 123, the meaning is that the price of the basket of goods is 23 percent higher in 2013 than in 2002.

> Since the price level is measured with an index number, its value at any specific time has meaning only when it is compared with its value at some other time.

By allowing us to compare the general price level at different times, a price index, such as the CPI, also allows us to measure the rate of inflation. For example, the value of the CPI in April 2012 was 122.2 and in April 2011 it was 119.8. The *rate of inflation* during that one-year period, expressed in percentage terms, is equal to the change in the price level divided by the initial price level, times 100:

$$\text{Rate of inflation}$$
$$= \frac{122.2 - 119.8}{119.8} \times 100 \text{ percent}$$
$$= 2.0 \text{ percent}$$

Inflation: Recent History The rate of inflation in Canada is currently around 2 percent per year and has been near that level since the early 1990s. But during the 1970s and 1980s inflation in Canada was both high and unpredictable from year to year. It was a serious macroeconomic problem.

Figure 19-5 shows the CPI and the inflation rate (measured by the annual rate of change in the CPI) from 1960 to 2012. What can we learn from this figure? First, we learn that the price level has not fallen at all since 1960 (in fact, the last time it fell was in 1953, and even then it fell only slightly). The cumulative effect of this sequence of repeated increases in the price level is quite dramatic: By 2012, the price level was more than six times as high as it was in 1960. In other words, you now pay more than $6 for what cost $1 in 1960. The second thing we learn is that, although the price level appears in the figure to be smoothly increasing, the rate of inflation is actually quite volatile. The increases in the inflation rate into double-digit levels in 1974 and 1979 were associated with major increases in the world prices of oil and foodstuffs and with loose monetary policy. The declines in inflation in the early 1980s and 1990s were delayed responses to major recessions, which were themselves brought about to a large extent by policy actions designed to reduce the existing inflation. (We will say much more about this in Chapters 29 and 30.)

To compute the rate of inflation from any point in your lifetime to today, check out the "inflation calculator" at the Bank of Canada's website: www.bankofcanada.ca/en/rates/inflation_calc.htm.

Why Inflation Matters Money is the universal yardstick in our economy. This does not mean that we care only about money—it means simply that we measure *economic values* in terms of money, and we use money to conduct our economic affairs. Things as diverse as wages, share values in the stock market, the value of a house, and a university's financial endowment are all stated in terms of money. We value money, however, not for itself but for what we can purchase with it. The terms **purchasing power of money**

purchasing power of money The amount of goods and services that can be purchased with a unit of money.

FIGURE 19-5 The Price Level and the Inflation Rate, 1960–2012

The rate of inflation measures the annual rate of increase in the price level. The trend in the price level has been upward over the past half-century. The rate of inflation has varied from almost 0 to more than 12 percent since 1960.

(*Source:* Based on author's calculations using data from Statistics Canada's CANSIM database: Series V41690973, monthly seasonally adjusted consumer price index. The figures shown are annual averages of the monthly data.)

and *real value of money* refer to the amount of goods and services that can be purchased with a given amount of money. The purchasing power of money is negatively related to the price level. For example, if the price level doubles, a dollar will buy only half as much, whereas if the price level halves, a dollar will buy twice as much. Inflation reduces the real value of anything whose *nominal value* is *fixed* in dollar terms. Thus, the real value of a $20 bill, a savings account, or the balance that is owed on a student loan is reduced by inflation.

> Inflation reduces the purchasing power of money. It also reduces the real value of any sum fixed in nominal (dollar) terms.

When analyzing the effects of inflation, economists usually make the distinction between *anticipated* and *unanticipated* inflation. If households and firms fully anticipate inflation over the coming year, they will be able to adjust many nominal prices and wages so as to maintain their real values. In this case, inflation will have fewer real effects on the economy than if it comes unexpectedly. For example, if both workers and firms expect 2 percent inflation over the coming year, they can agree to increase nominal wages by 2 percent, thus leaving wages constant in real terms.

Unanticipated inflation, on the other hand, generally leads to more changes in the real value of prices and wages. Suppose workers and firms expect 2 percent inflation and they increase nominal wages accordingly. If actual inflation ends up being 5 percent, real wages will be reduced and the quantities of labour demanded by firms and supplied by workers will change. As a result, the economy's allocation of resources will be affected more than when the inflation is anticipated.

> Anticipated inflation has a smaller effect on the economy than unanticipated inflation.

In reality, inflation is rarely fully anticipated or fully unanticipated. Usually there is some inflation that is expected but also some that comes as a surprise. As a result, some adjustments in wages and prices are made by firms, workers, and consumers, but not all the adjustments that would be required to leave the economy's allocation of resources unaffected. We will see later, in our discussions of monetary policy and inflation in Chapters 29 and 30, how the distinction between anticipated and unanticipated inflation helps us to understand the costs associated with *reducing* inflation.

Interest Rates

If a bank lends you money, it will charge you *interest* for the privilege of borrowing the money. If, for example, you borrow $1000 today, repayable in one year's time, you may also be asked to pay $6.67 per month in interest. This makes $80 in interest over the year, which can be expressed as an interest rate of 8 percent per annum.

The **interest rate** is the price that is paid to borrow money for a stated period of time. It is expressed as a percentage amount per year per dollar borrowed. For example, an interest rate of 8 percent per year means that the borrower must pay 8 cents per year for every dollar that is borrowed.

There are many interest rates. A bank will lend money to an industrial customer at a lower rate than it will lend money to you—there is a lower risk of not being repaid. The rate charged on a loan that is not to be repaid for a long time will usually differ from the rate on a loan that is to be repaid quickly.

When economists speak of "the" interest rate, they mean a rate that is typical of all the various interest rates in the economy. Dealing with only one interest rate suppresses much interesting detail. However, because interest rates usually rise and fall together, at least for major changes, following the movement of one rate allows us to consider changes in the general level of interest rates. The *prime interest rate*, the rate that banks charge to their best business customers, is noteworthy because when the prime rate changes, most other rates change in the same direction. Another high-profile interest rate is the *bank rate*, the interest rate that the Bank of Canada (Canada's central bank) charges on short-term loans to commercial banks such as the Royal Bank or the Bank of Montreal. The interest rate that the Canadian government pays on its short-term borrowing is also a rate that garners considerable attention.

Interest Rates and Inflation How does inflation affect interest rates? To begin developing an answer, imagine that your friend lends you $100 and that the loan is repayable in one year. The amount that you pay her for making this loan, measured in dollar terms, is determined by the **nominal interest rate**. If you pay her $108 in one year's time, $100 will be repayment of the amount of the loan (which is called the *principal*) and $8 will be payment of the interest. In this case, the nominal interest rate is 8 percent per year.

How much purchasing power has your friend gained or lost by making this loan? The answer depends on what happens to the price level during the year. The more the price level rises, the worse off your friend will be and the better the transaction will be for you. This result occurs because the more the price level rises, the less valuable are the dollars that you use to repay the loan. The **real interest rate** measures the return on a loan in terms of purchasing power.

If the price level remains constant over the year, the real rate of interest that your friend earns would also be 8 percent, because she can buy 8 percent more goods and services with the $108 that you repay her than with the $100 that she lent you.

interest rate The price paid per dollar borrowed per period of time, expressed either as a proportion (e.g., 0.06) or as a percentage (e.g., 6 percent).

nominal interest rate The price paid per dollar borrowed per period of time.

real interest rate The nominal rate of interest adjusted for the change in the purchasing power of money. Equal to the nominal interest rate minus the rate of inflation.

However, if the price level rises by 8 percent, the real rate of interest would be zero because the $108 that you repay her buys the same quantity of goods as the $100 that she originally gave up. If she is unlucky enough to lend money at 8 percent in a year in which prices rise by 10 percent, the real rate of interest that she earns is –2 percent. The repayment of $108 will purchase 2 percent fewer goods and services than the original loan of $100.

The burden of borrowing depends on the real, not the nominal, rate of interest.

For example, a nominal interest rate of 8 percent combined with a 2 percent rate of inflation (a real rate of 6 percent) is a much greater real burden on borrowers than a nominal rate of 16 percent combined with a 14 percent rate of inflation (a real rate of 2 percent). Figure 19-6 shows the nominal and real interest rates paid on short-term government borrowing since 1965.

Interest Rates and "Credit Flows" A loan represents a flow of credit between lenders and borrowers, with the interest rate representing the price of this credit. Credit is essential to the healthy functioning of a modern economy. Most firms require credit at some point—to finance the construction of a factory, to purchase inventories of intermediate inputs, or to continue paying their workers in a regular fashion even though their revenues may arrive at irregular intervals. Most households also require credit at various times—to finance the purchase of a home or car or to finance a child's university education.

Banks play a crucial role in the economy by *intermediating* between those households and firms that have available funds and those households and firms who require funds. In other words, banks play a key role in "making the credit market"—in channelling the funds from those who have them to those who need them.

During normal times, these credit markets function very smoothly and most of us notice little about them. While there are fluctuations in the price of credit (the interest rate), they tend to be relatively modest. In the fall of 2008, however, credit markets in the United States, Canada, and most other countries were thrown into turmoil by the sudden collapse of several large financial institutions, mainly in the United States and Europe. As a result, many banks became reluctant to lend to any but the safest borrowers, mostly out of fear that the borrowers would go bankrupt before they could repay the loan. The flows of credit slowed sharply and market interest rates spiked upward,

FIGURE 19-6 Real and Nominal Interest Rates, 1965–2012

Inflation over the past five decades has meant that the real interest rate has always been less than the nominal interest rate. The data for the nominal interest rate show the average rate on three-month Treasury bills in each year since 1965. The real interest rate is calculated as the nominal interest rate minus the actual rate of inflation over the same period. Through the early 1970s, the real interest rate was negative, indicating that the inflation rate exceeded the nominal interest rate. The 1980s saw real interest rates rise as high as 8 percent. Since then, real rates have declined again to levels that are closer to the long-term historical average. With the onset of the major global recession in 2008, both real and nominal interest rates fell below their long-term averages.

(*Source:* Nominal interest rate: 3-month Treasury bill rate, Statistics Canada, CANSIM database, Series V122541. Real interest rate is based on author's calculation of CPI inflation, using Series PCPISA from the Bank of Canada, www.bankofcanada.ca.)

reflecting the greater risk premium required by lenders. The reduction in the flow of credit was soon felt by firms who needed credit in order to finance material or labour inputs, and the effect was a reduction in production and employment. This *financial crisis*, by interrupting the vital flows of credit, was an important cause of the recession that enveloped the global economy in late 2008 and through 2009. We will discuss banking and the flow of credit in more detail in Chapter 27.

Why Interest Rates Matter Changes in real interest rates affect the standard of living of savers and borrowers. Many retirees, for example, rely on interest earnings from their stock of accumulated assets to provide much of their household income, and thus benefit when real interest rates rise. In contrast, borrowers are made better off with low real interest rates. This point was dramatically illustrated during the 1970s when homeowners who had long-term fixed-rate mortgages benefited tremendously from several years of high and largely unanticipated inflation, which resulted in *negative* real interest rates (see Figure 19-6).

Interest rates also matter for the economy as a whole. As we will see in Chapter 21, real interest rates are an important determinant of the level of investment by firms. Changes in real interest rates lead to changes in the cost of borrowing and thus to changes in firms' investment plans. Such changes in the level of desired investment have important consequences for the level of economic activity. We will see in Chapters 28 and 29 how the Bank of Canada influences interest rates as part of its objective of controlling inflation.

The International Economy

Two important variables reflecting the importance of the global economy to Canada are the *exchange rate* and *net exports*.

The Exchange Rate If you are going on a holiday to France, you will need euros to pay for your purchases. Many of the larger banks, as well as any foreign-exchange office, will make the necessary exchange of currencies for you; they will sell you euros in return for your Canadian dollars. If you get 0.77 euros for each dollar that you give up, the two currencies are trading at a rate of 1 dollar = 0.77 euros or, expressed another way, 1 euro = 1.30 dollars. This was, in fact, the actual rate of exchange between the Canadian dollar and the euro in June of 2012.

As our example shows, the exchange rate can be defined either as dollars per euro or euros per dollar. In this book we adopt the convention of defining the **exchange rate** between the Canadian dollar and any foreign currency as the number of Canadian dollars required to purchase one unit of foreign currency.

exchange rate The number of units of domestic currency required to purchase one unit of foreign currency.

> The exchange rate is the number of Canadian dollars required to purchase one unit of foreign currency.[2]

---

[2] The media often use a reverse definition of the exchange rate—the number of units of foreign currency that can be purchased with one Canadian dollar. It is up to the student, then, to examine carefully the definition that is being used by a particular writer or speaker. In this book the exchange rate is defined as the number of Canadian dollars required to purchase one unit of foreign currency because this measure emphasizes that foreign currency, like any other good or service, has a price in terms of Canadian dollars. In this case, the price has a special name—the exchange rate.

foreign exchange Foreign currencies that are traded on the foreign-exchange market.

foreign-exchange market The market in which different national currencies are traded.

depreciation A rise in the exchange rate—it takes more units of domestic currency to purchase one unit of foreign currency.

appreciation A fall in the exchange rate—it takes fewer units of domestic currency to purchase one unit of foreign currency.

The term **foreign exchange** refers to foreign currencies or claims on foreign currencies, such as bank deposits, cheques, and promissory notes, that are payable in foreign money. The **foreign-exchange market** is the market in which foreign exchange is traded—at a price expressed by the exchange rate.

Depreciation and Appreciation A rise in the exchange rate means that it takes *more* Canadian dollars to purchase one unit of foreign currency—this is a **depreciation** of the Canadian dollar. Conversely, a fall in the exchange rate means that it takes *fewer* Canadian dollars to purchase one unit of foreign currency—this is an **appreciation** of the dollar.

Figure 19-7 shows the path of the Canadian–U.S. exchange rate since 1970. Since more than 75 percent of Canada's trade is with the United States, this is the exchange rate most often discussed and analyzed in Canada. In countries with trade more evenly spread across several trading partners, more attention is paid to what is called a *trade-weighted exchange rate*—this is a weighted-average exchange rate between the home country and its trading partners, where the weights reflect each partner's share in the home country's total trade. In Canada, the path of such a trade-weighted exchange rate is virtually identical to the Canadian–U.S. exchange rate shown in Figure 19-7, reflecting the very large proportion of total Canadian trade with the United States.

As we will see in later chapters, both domestic policy and external events have important effects on the Canadian exchange rate. For example, most economists believe that the appreciation of the Canadian dollar between 1986 and 1992 was caused in part by the Bank of Canada's efforts to reduce the rate of inflation. The Bank's policy was controversial at the time, not least because of the effect it had on the exchange rate and the many export-oriented firms that were harmed by Canada's strong dollar. We examine the link between monetary policy and exchange rates in detail in Chapters 28 and 29.

The depreciation of the Canadian dollar in the late 1990s is thought by most economists to have resulted from a nearly 30 percent decline in the world prices of commodities, many of which are important Canadian exports. The appreciation of the Canadian dollar during the 2002–2012 period was associated with sharp increases in commodity prices. In both cases, the commodity prices were being driven by changes in global economic growth, illustrating the important point that events in faraway lands can have dramatic effects on the Canadian exchange rate. We examine the link between world commodity prices and the Canadian exchange rate in Chapter 35.

FIGURE 19-7 Canadian–U.S. Dollar Exchange Rate, 1970–2012

The Canadian–U.S. exchange rate has been quite volatile over the past 40 years. The Canadian-dollar price of one U.S. dollar increased from just over $1 in the early 1970s to over $1.55 in 2002, a long-term depreciation of the Canadian dollar. By 2012 the Canadian dollar had appreciated and it again cost about $1 to purchase one U.S. dollar.

(*Source:* Annual average of monthly data, Statistics Canada, CANSIM database, Series V37432.)

Exports and Imports Canada has long been a trading nation, buying many goods and services from other countries— Canada's *imports*—and also selling many goods and services to other countries—Canada's *exports*. Figure 19-8 shows the dollar value of Canada's exports, imports, and *net exports* since 1970. Net exports are the difference between exports and imports and are often called the *trade balance*.

Canadian exports and imports have increased fairly closely in step with each other over the past 40 years. The trade balance has therefore fluctuated mildly over the years, but it has stayed relatively small, especially when viewed as a proportion of total GDP.

Also apparent in Figure 19-8 is that Canadian trade flows (both imports and exports) began to grow more quickly after 1990. The increased importance of international trade is largely due to the Canada–U.S. Free Trade Agreement, which began in 1989, and to the North American Free Trade Agreement (which added Mexico), which began in 1994. Note also the sharp decline in both exports and imports in 2009–2010, a result of the global economic recession that occurred at that time.

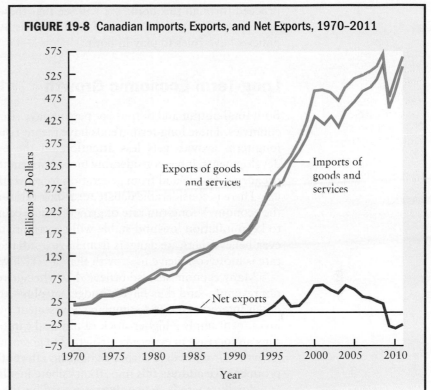

FIGURE 19-8 Canadian Imports, Exports, and Net Exports, 1970–2011

Though imports and exports have increased dramatically over the past 40 years, the trade balance has remained roughly in balance. The nominal values of imports and exports rose steadily over the past few decades because of both price increases and quantity increases. The growth of trade increased sharply after the early 1990s. The trade balance—net exports—is usually close to zero.

(*Source:* Statistics Canada, CANSIM database. Exports: Series V498103. Imports: Series V498106.)

19.2 Growth Versus Fluctuations

This chapter has provided a quick tour through macroeconomics and has introduced you to many important macroeconomic issues. If you take a few moments to flip again through the figures in this chapter, you will notice that most of the macroeconomic variables that we discussed are characterized by *long-run trends* and *short-run fluctuations*.

Figure 19-1 on page 477, which shows the path of real GDP, provides an excellent example of both characteristics. The figure shows that real GDP has increased by over four times since 1965—this is substantial *economic growth*. The figure also shows considerable year-to-year *fluctuations* in the growth rate of GDP.

An important theme in this book is that a full understanding of macroeconomics requires an understanding of both long-run growth and short-run fluctuations. As we proceed through this book, we will see that these two characteristics of modern economies have different sources and explanations. And the government's macroeconomic policies have roles to play in both.

Long-Term Economic Growth

Both total output and output per person have risen for many decades in most industrial countries. These long-term trends have meant rising average living standards. Although long-term growth gets less attention on the evening news than current economic developments, it has considerably more importance for a society's living standards from decade to decade and from generation to generation.

There is considerable debate regarding the ability of government policy to influence the economy's long-run rate of growth. Some economists believe that a policy designed to keep inflation low and stable will contribute to the economy's growth. Some, however, believe there are dangers from having inflation too low—that a moderate inflation rate is more conducive to growth than a very low inflation rate.

Many economists also believe that when governments spend less than they raise in tax revenue—and thus have a budget surplus—the reduced need for borrowing drives down interest rates and stimulates investment by the private sector. Such increases in investment imply a higher stock of physical capital available for future production and thus an increase in economic growth. Do government budget surpluses increase future growth? Or do budget surpluses have no effect at all on the economy's future ability to produce? We address this important debate in Chapter 32.

Finally, there is active debate regarding the appropriate role of the government in developing new technologies. Some economists believe that the private sector, left on its own, can produce a volume of inventions and innovation that will guarantee a satisfactory rate of long-term growth. Others point out that almost all of the major new technologies of the last 75 years were initially supported by public funds: The electronic computer was the creation of governments in the Second World War, miniaturized equipment came from the race to the moon, the Internet came from military communications research, the U.S. software industry was created by the U.S. Department of Defense, much of the early work on biotechnology came out of publicly funded research laboratories in universities and government institutions, and so on. The debate about the place of government in helping to foster inventions and innovations of truly fundamental technologies is an ongoing and highly important one.

Short-Term Fluctuations

Short-run fluctuations in economic activity, like the ones shown in part (ii) of Figure 19-1 (page 477), lead economists to wonder about the causes of *business cycles*. What caused the Great Depression in the 1930s, when almost one-fifth of the Canadian labour force was out of work and massive unemployment plagued all major industrial countries? Why did the Canadian economy begin a significant recession in 1990–1991, from which recovery was initially very gradual? What explains why, by 2007, the Canadian unemployment rate was lower than it had been in more than 30 years? What caused the deep worldwide recession that began in 2008?

Understanding business cycles requires an understanding of monetary policy—the Bank of Canada's policy with respect to the quantity of money that it makes available to the whole economy. Most economists agree that the increase in inflation in the 1970s and early 1980s was related to monetary policy, though they also agree that other events were partly responsible. When the Bank of Canada implemented a policy in the early 1990s designed to reduce inflation, was it merely a coincidence that a significant recession followed? Most economists think not, though they also think that the slowdown in the U.S. economy was an important contributor to Canada's recession. Chapters 28 and 29 focus on how the Bank of Canada uses its policy to influence the level of economic activity.

Government budget deficits and surpluses also enter the discussion of business cycles. Some economists think that, in recessionary years, the government ought to increase spending (and reduce taxes) in an effort to stimulate economic activity. Similarly, they believe that taxes should be raised to slow down a booming economy. Indeed, several government policies, from income taxation to employment insurance, are designed to mitigate the short-term fluctuations in national income. Other economists believe that the government cannot successfully "fine-tune" the economy by making frequent changes in spending and taxing because our knowledge of how the economy works is imperfect and because such policies tend to be imprecise. We address these issues in Chapters 22, 23, and 24.

What Lies Ahead?

There is much work to be done before any of these interesting policy debates can be discussed in more detail. Like firms that invest now to increase their production in the future, the next few chapters of this book will be an investment for you—an investment in understanding basic macro theory. The payoff will come when you are able to use a coherent model of the economy to analyze and debate some of the key macro issues of the day.

We begin in Chapter 20 by discussing the measurement of GDP. National income accounting is not exciting but is essential to a complete understanding of the chapters that follow. We then proceed to build a simple model of the economy to highlight some key macroeconomic relationships. As we proceed through the book, we modify the model, step by step, making it ever more realistic. With each step we take, more of today's controversial policy issues come within the grasp of our understanding. We hope that by the time you get to the end of the book, you will have developed some of the thrill for analyzing macroeconomic issues that we feel. Good luck, and enjoy the journey!

SUMMARY

19.1 Key Macroeconomic Variables   LO 1

- The value of the total production of goods and services in a country is called its national product. Because production of output generates income in the form of claims on that output, the total is also referred to as national income. One of the most commonly used measures of national income is gross domestic product (GDP).
- Potential output is the level of output produced when factors of production are fully employed. The output

gap is the difference between actual and potential output.
- The unemployment rate is the percentage of the labour force not employed and actively searching for a job. The labour force and employment have both grown steadily for the past half-century. The unemployment rate fluctuates considerably from year to year. Unemployment imposes serious costs in the form of economic waste and human suffering.

- Labour productivity is measured as real GDP per employed worker (or per hour of work). It is an important determinant of material living standards.
- The price level is measured by a price index, which measures the cost of purchasing a set of goods in one year relative to the cost of the same goods in a base year. The inflation rate measures the rate of change of the price level. For almost 20 years, the annual inflation rate in Canada has been close to 2 percent.
- The interest rate is the price that is paid to borrow money for a stated period and is expressed as a percentage amount per dollar borrowed. The nominal interest rate is this price expressed in money terms; the real interest rate is this price expressed in terms of purchasing power.
- The flow of credit—borrowing and lending—is very important in a modern economy. Disruptions in the flow of credit can lead to increases in interest rates and reductions in economic activity.
- The exchange rate is the number of Canadian dollars needed to purchase one unit of foreign currency. A rise in the exchange rate is a depreciation of the Canadian dollar; a fall in the exchange rate is an appreciation of the Canadian dollar.

19.2 Growth Versus Fluctuations

LO 2

- Most macroeconomic variables have both long-run trends and short-run fluctuations. The sources of the two types of movements are different.
- Important questions for macroeconomics involve the role of policy in influencing long-run growth as well as short-run fluctuations.

KEY CONCEPTS

National product and national income
Real and nominal national income
Potential and actual output
The output gap
Employment, unemployment, and the labour force
Full employment
Frictional, structural, and cyclical unemployment
Labour productivity
The price level and the rate of inflation
Real and nominal interest rates
Interest rates and credit
The exchange rate
Depreciation and appreciation of the Canadian dollar
Exports, imports, and net exports

STUDY EXERCISES

MyEconLab Make the grade with MyEconLab: Study Exercises marked in red can be found on MyEconLab. You can practise them as often as you want, and most feature step-by-step guided instructions to help you find the right answer.

1. Fill in the blanks to make the following statements correct.

   a. The value of total production of goods and services in Canada is called its _____. National _____ and national _____ are equal because all production generates a claim on its value in the form of income.

   b. In measuring Canada's total output, it would be meaningless to add together all goods and services produced during one year (i.e., 50 000 trucks plus 14 million dozen eggs plus 100 million haircuts, etc.). Instead, total output is measured in _____.

   c. The difference between nominal national income and real national income is that with the latter, _____ are held constant to enable us to see changes in _____.

   d. If all of Canada's resources—its land, labour, and capital—are "fully employed", then we say that Canada is producing its _____.

   e. The output gap measures the difference between _____ and _____. During booms, _____ is greater than _____; during recessions, _____ is less than _____.

2. Fill in the blanks to make the following statements correct.

   a. The labour force includes people who are _____ and people who are _____. The unemployment rate is expressed as the number of people who are _____ as a percentage of people in the _____.

   b. At any point in time, some people are unemployed because of the normal turnover of labour (new entrants to the labour force, job leavers, and job seekers). This unemployment is referred to as _____. Some people are said to be _____ unemployed because their skills do not match the skills necessary for the available jobs.

   c. Suppose 2002 is the base year in which the price of a basket of goods is set to be 100. If the price of the same basket of goods in 2013 is 137, then we can say that the price level is _____ and that the price of the basket of goods has increased by _____ percent between 2002 and 2013.

   d. Suppose Canada's CPI in May 2012 was 122.5 and in May 2013 was 125.1. The rate of inflation during that one-year period was _____ percent.

   e. The price that is paid to borrow money for a stated period of time is known as the _____.

   f. The real interest rate is equal to the nominal interest rate _____ the rate of inflation.

   g. The number of Canadian dollars required to purchase one unit of foreign currency is the _____ between the Canadian dollar and that foreign currency.

   h. A(n) _____ in the exchange rate reflects a depreciation of the Canadian dollar; a(n) _____ in the exchange rate reflects an appreciation of the Canadian dollar.

3. Consider the macroeconomic data shown below for a hypothetical country's economy.

Year	Real GDP Actual (billions of $)	Real GDP Potential (billions of $)	Output Gap (% of potential)	Unemployment Rate (% of labour force)
2005	1168	1188	—	11.1
2006	1184	1196	—	10.2
2007	1197	1205	—	9.1
2008	1211	1215	—	8.3
2009	1225	1225	—	7.6
2010	1240	1236	—	7.3
2011	1253	1247	—	7.1
2012	1262	1258	—	7.3
2013	1270	1270	—	7.6

   a. Compute the output gap for each year.
   b. Explain how GDP can exceed potential GDP.

   c. Does real GDP ever fall in the time period shown? What do economists call such periods?
   d. What is the unemployment rate when this economy is at "full employment"? What kind of unemployment exists at this time?

4. Consider the data shown below for the Canadian Consumer Price Index (CPI), drawn from the Bank of Canada's website.

Year	CPI (2002 = 100)	CPI Inflation (% change from previous year)
2000	95.4	2.7
2001	97.8	—
2002	—	2.3
2003	102.8	2.8
2004	104.7	—
2005	107.0	—
2006	—	2.0
2007	—	2.1
2008	114.1	2.4
2009	114.4	—
2010	—	1.8
2011	119.9	2.9

   a. Compute the missing data in the table.
   b. Do average prices ever fall in the time period shown? In which year do prices come closest to being stable?
   c. Across which two consecutive years is the rate of inflation closest to being stable?
   d. In a diagram with the price level on the vertical axis and time on the horizontal axis, illustrate the difference between a situation in which the price level is stable and a situation in which the rate of inflation is stable.

5. The data below show the nominal interest rate and the inflation rate for several developed economies as reported in The Economist in June 2012.

Country	Nominal Interest Rate (on 10-year government bonds)	Inflation Rate (% change in CPI from previous year)	Real Interest Rate
Australia	3.00	2.2	—
Canada	1.81	2.1	—
Euro area	1.34	2.4	—
Japan	0.87	0.2	—
Switzerland	0.61	−0.3	—
U.K.	1.63	2.8	—
U.S.A.	1.65	2.2	—

a. Compute the real interest rate for each country, assuming that people expected the inflation rate at the time to persist.

b. If you were a lender, in which country would you have wanted to lend in June 2012? Explain.

c. If you were a borrower, in which country would you have wanted to borrow in June 2012? Explain.

6. Consider the following data drawn from *The Economist*. Recall that the Canadian exchange rate is the number of Canadian dollars needed to purchase one unit of some foreign currency.

Currency	Cdn Dollar Exchange Rate	
	June 2012	June 2011
U.S. dollar	1.03	0.98
Japanese yen	0.013	0.012
British pound	1.58	1.61
Swedish krona	0.14	0.16
Euro	1.29	1.44

a. Which currencies appreciated relative to the Canadian dollar from June 2011 to June 2012?

b. Which currencies depreciated relative to the Canadian dollar from June 2011 to June 2012?

c. Using the information provided in the table, can you tell whether the euro depreciated or appreciated *against the U.S. dollar* from June 2011 to June 2012? Explain.

7. As explained in the text, the unemployment rate is defined as:

Unemployment rate =
$$\frac{\text{Number of people unemployed}}{\text{Number of people in the labour force}} \times 100 \text{ percent}$$

a. Explain why people may decide to join the labour force during booms.

b. From part (a), explain why the unemployment rate might rise during a boom, even when the level of employment is also rising.

c. During a recession, suppose unemployed workers leave the labour force because they are discouraged about their inability to find a job. What happens to the unemployment rate?

d. "A declining unemployment rate is a clear positive sign for the economy." Comment.

8. Consider an imaginary 10-year period over which output per worker falls, but GDP increases. How can this happen? Do you think this is likely to be good for the economy?

9. When the Canadian dollar depreciates in foreign-exchange markets, many people view this as "good" for the Canadian economy. Who is likely to be harmed by and who is likely to benefit from a depreciation of the Canadian dollar?

The Measurement of National Income

LEARNING OBJECTIVES (LO)

After studying this chapter you will be able to

1 see how the concept of value added solves the problem of "double counting" when measuring national income.

2 explain the income approach and the expenditure approach to measuring national income.

3 explain the difference between real and nominal GDP and understand the GDP deflator.

4 discuss the many important omissions from official measures of GDP.

5 understand why real per capita GDP is a good measure of average material living standards but an incomplete measure of overall well-being.

THIS chapter provides a detailed look at the measurement of national income. Once we know more precisely what is being measured and how it is measured, we will be ready to build a macroeconomic model to explain the determination of national income. Understanding how national income is measured is an important part of understanding how and why it changes. Indeed, this is a general rule of all economics and all science: Before using any data, it is essential to understand how those data are developed and what they measure.

20.1 National Output and Value Added

The central topic of macroeconomics is the overall level of economic activity—aggregate output and the income that is generated by its production. We start by asking: What do we mean by output?

This question may seem odd. Surely your local bakery knows what it produces. And if Air Canada or Imperial Oil or Bombardier does not know its own output, what does it know? If each firm knows the value of its total output, the national income statisticians simply have to add up each separate output value to get the nation's output—or is it really that simple?

Obtaining a total for the nation's output is not that simple because one firm's output is often another firm's input. The local baker uses flour that is the output of the flour milling company; the flour milling company, in turn, uses wheat that is the farmer's output. What is true for bread is true for most goods and services.

> **Production occurs in stages:** Some firms produce outputs that are used as inputs by other firms, and these other firms, in turn, produce outputs that are used as inputs by yet other firms.

If we merely added up the market values of all outputs of all firms, we would obtain a total greatly in excess of the value of the economy's actual output. Consider the example of wheat, flour, and bread. If we added the total value of the output of the wheat farmer, the flour mill, and the baker, we would be counting the value of the wheat three times, the value of the milled flour twice, and the value of the bread once.

The error that would arise in estimating the nation's output by adding all sales of all firms is called *double counting*. "Multiple counting" would actually be a better term because if we added up the values of all sales, the same output would be counted every time that it was sold by one firm to another. The problem of double counting could in principle be solved by distinguishing between two types of output. **Intermediate goods** are outputs of some firms that are used as inputs by other firms. **Final goods** are products that are not used as inputs by other firms, at least not in the period of time under consideration.

intermediate goods All outputs that are used as inputs by other producers in a further stage of production.

final goods Goods that are not used as inputs by other firms but are produced to be sold for consumption, investment, government, or export during the period under consideration.

If the firms' sales could be easily disaggregated into sales of final goods and sales of intermediate goods, then measuring total output would be straightforward. It would simply be obtained by summing the value of all *final* goods produced by firms. However, when Stelco sells steel to the Ford Motor Company, it does not care, and usually does not know, whether the steel is for final use (say, construction of a warehouse that will not be sold by Ford) or for use as part of an automobile that will be sold again. Even in our earlier example of bread, a bakery cannot be sure that its sales are for final use, for the bread may be further "processed" by a restaurant prior to its final sale to a customer. In general, it is extremely difficult if not impossible to successfully distinguish final from intermediate goods. The problem of double counting must therefore be resolved in some other manner.

value added The value of a firm's output minus the value of the inputs that it purchases from other firms.

To avoid double counting, economists use the concept of **value added**, which is the amount of value that firms and workers add to their products over and above the costs of purchased intermediate goods. An individual firm's value added is

$$\text{Value added} = \text{Sales revenue} - \text{Cost of intermediate goods}$$

Consider an example of a steel mill. A steel mill's value added is the revenue it earns from selling the steel it produces minus the cost of the ore that it buys from the mining company, the cost of the electricity and fuel oil that it uses, and the costs of all other inputs that it buys from other firms.

We have said that a firm's value added equals its sales revenue minus the cost of intermediate goods *purchased from other firms*. Payments made to factors of production, such as the wages paid to workers or the profits paid to owners, are not purchases from other firms and hence are not subtracted from the firm's revenue when computing value added. But since the firm's revenue must be fully exhausted by the cost of intermediate goods *plus* all payments to factors of production, it follows that value added is exactly equal to the sum of these factor payments.[1]

Value added = Payments owed to the firm's factors of production

Value added is the correct measure of each firm's contribution to total output—the amount of market value that is produced by that firm.

The firm's value added is the *net value* of its output. It is this net value that is the firm's contribution to the nation's total output, representing the firm's own efforts that add to the value of what it takes in as inputs. The concept of value added is further illustrated in *Applying Economic Concepts 20-1*. In this simple example, as in all more

APPLYING ECONOMIC CONCEPTS 20-1

Value Added Through Stages of Production

Because the output of one firm often becomes the input of other firms, the total value of goods sold by all firms greatly exceeds the value of the output of final products. This general principle is illustrated by a simple example in which a mining company starts from scratch and produces iron ore valued at $1000; this firm's value added is $1000. The mining company then sells the iron ore to a different firm that produces steel valued at $1500. The steel producer's value added is $500 because the value of the goods is increased by $500 as a result of the firm's activities. Finally, the steel producer sells the steel to a metal fabricator who transforms the steel into folding chairs valued at $1800; the metal fabricator's value added is $300.

We find the value of the final goods, $1800, either by counting only the sales of the last firm or by taking the sum of the values added by each firm. This value is much smaller than the $4300 that we would obtain if we merely added up the market value of the output sold by each firm.

Transactions at Three Different Stages of Production					
	Mining Company	Steel Producer	Metal Fabricator	All Firms	
A. Purchases from other firms	$ 0	$1000	$1500	$2500	Total interfirm sales
B. Payments to factors of production	1000	500	300	1800	Total value added
A + B = value of product	$1000	$1500	$1800	$4300	Total value of all sales

---

[1] We are ignoring here the role of indirect taxes, such as provincial sales taxes or the Goods and Services Tax (GST). Such taxes are included in the market value of a firm's output, but these taxes are remitted to the government and do not represent a payment to factors of production.

complex cases, the value of the nation's total output is obtained by summing all the individual values added.

> The sum of all values added in an economy is a measure of the economy's total output.

20.2 National Income Accounting: The Basics

The measures of national income and national product that are used in Canada derive from an accounting system called the National Income and Expenditure Accounts (NIEA), which are produced by Statistics Canada. These accounts are not simply collections of economic data. They have a logical structure, based on the simple yet important idea of the circular flow of income, which you first saw in Chapter 1 and which is shown again in Figure 20-1. The figure shows the overall flows of national income and expenditure and also how government, the financial system, and foreign countries enter the flows. The key point from the circular flow is as follows:

> The value of domestic output is equal to the value of the expenditure on that output and is also equal to the total income claims generated by producing that output.

The circular flow of income suggests three different ways of measuring national income. The first is simply to add up the value of all goods and services produced in the economy. This requires the concept of value added, which we discussed in the previous section. The remaining two approaches correspond to the two "halves" of the circular flow of income and are the ones most commonly used by Statistics Canada and other countries' national statistical agencies. One approach is to add up the total flow of *expenditure* on final domestic output; the other is to add up the total flow of *income* generated by the flow of domestic production. All three measures yield the same total, which is called **gross domestic product** (**GDP**). When GDP is calculated by adding up total expenditure for each of the main components of final output, the result is called *GDP on the expenditure side*. When GDP is calculated by adding up all the income claims generated by the act of production, it is called *GDP on the income side*.

gross domestic product (GDP) The total value of goods and services produced in the economy during a given period.

The conventions of double-entry bookkeeping require that the value of all production must be accounted for by a claim that someone has to that value. Thus, the two values calculated from the income and the expenditure sides are identical conceptually and differ in practical measurements only because of errors of measurement. Any discrepancy arising from such errors is then reconciled so that one common total is given as *the* measure of GDP. Both calculations are of interest, however, because each gives a different and useful breakdown. Also, having these two independent ways of measuring the same quantity provides a useful check on statistical procedures and on errors in measurement.

FIGURE 20-1 The Circular Flow of Expenditure and Income

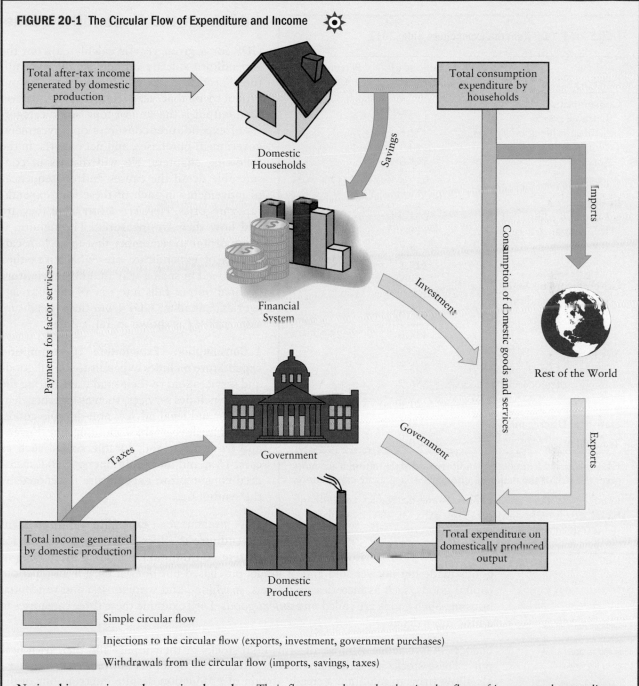

Simple circular flow

Injections to the circular flow (exports, investment, government purchases)

Withdrawals from the circular flow (imports, savings, taxes)

National income is equal to national product. Their flows are shown by the circular flow of income and expenditure. Consider first only the red lines. In this case, the flow would be a simple circle from households to producers and back to households. Now add the blue and green lines. The blue lines represent *injections* to the circular flow (exports, investment, and government purchases), while the green lines represent *withdrawals* from the circular flow (imports, saving, and taxes). Injections and withdrawals complicate the picture but do not change the basic relationship: Domestic production creates an income claim on the value of that production. When all the income claims are correctly added up, they must equal the total value of production.

TABLE 20-1 GDP from the Expenditure Side, 2011

Category	Billions of Dollars	Percent of GDP
Consumption		
Durable goods	113.7	
Semi-durable goods	72.6	
Non-durable goods	240.3	
Services	556.0	
	982.6	57.1
Investment		
Plant and equipment	201.9	
Residential structures	118.5	
Inventories	4.7	
	325.1	18.9
Government Purchases		
Current expenditure	367.6	
Investment	67.0	
	434.6	25.2
Net Exports		
Exports of goods and services	535.7	
Imports of goods and services	−556.7	
	−21.0	−1.2
Statistical Discrepancy	−0.5	0.0
Total GDP	1720.7	100.0

GDP measured from the expenditure side of the national accounts gives the size of the major components of aggregate expenditure.

(*Source:* Statistics Canada, "Gross Domestic Product, Expenditure-based, 2011," CANSIM database, Table 380-0017. Available at www.statcan.gc.ca.)

GDP from the Expenditure Side

GDP for a given year is calculated from the expenditure side by adding up the expenditures needed to purchase the final output produced in that year. Total expenditure on final output is the sum of four broad categories of expenditure: consumption, investment, government purchases, and net exports. In the following chapters, we will discuss in considerable detail the causes and consequences of movements in each of these four expenditure categories. Here we define what they are and how they are measured. Throughout, it is important to remember that these four categories of expenditure are exhaustive—they are *defined* in such a way that all expenditure on final output falls into one of the four categories. Canadian GDP from the expenditure side for 2011 is shown in Table 20-1.

1. Consumption Expenditure Consumption **expenditure** includes expenditure on all goods and services sold to their final users during the year. It includes services, such as haircuts, dental care, and legal advice; non-durable goods, such as fresh vegetables, clothing, cut flowers, and fresh meat; and durable goods, such as cars, TVs, and air conditioners. *Actual* measured consumption expenditure is denoted by the symbol C_a.

2. Investment Expenditure Investment **expenditure** is expenditure on goods not for present consumption, including inventories of goods made but not yet sold and of inputs purchased but not yet used in production; capital goods, such as factories, computers, machines, and warehouses; and residential housing. Such goods are called *investment goods*. Let's examine these three categories in a little more detail.

Changes in Inventories. Almost all firms hold stocks of their inputs and their own outputs. These stocks are called **inventories**. Inventories of inputs and unfinished materials allow firms to maintain a steady stream of production despite interruptions in the deliveries of inputs bought from other firms. Inventories of outputs allow firms to meet orders despite fluctuations in the rate of production.

The accumulation of inventories during any given year counts as positive investment for that year because it represents goods produced but not used for current consumption. These goods are included in the national income accounts at market value, which includes the wages and other costs that the firm incurred in producing them as well as the profit that the firm expects to make when they are sold in the future. The drawing down of inventories, often called *decumulation*, counts as disinvestment (negative

consumption expenditure
Household expenditure on all goods and services. Represented by the symbol *C*.

investment expenditure
Expenditure on the production of goods not for present consumption. Represented by the symbol *I*.

inventories Stocks of raw materials, goods in process, and finished goods held by firms to mitigate the effect of short-term fluctuations in production or sales.

investment) because it represents a reduction in the stock of finished goods that are available to be sold.

New Plant and Equipment. All production uses capital goods, which are manufactured aids to production, such as tools, machines, computers, vehicles, and factory buildings. The economy's total quantity of capital goods is called the **capital stock**. This is often called "plant and equipment," although the term refers to any manufactured aid to production used by firms. Creating new capital goods is an act of investment and is called *business fixed investment,* often shortened to **fixed investment**.

capital stock The aggregate quantity of capital goods.

fixed investment The creation of new plant and equipment.

New Residential Housing. A house or an apartment building is a durable asset that yields its utility over a long period of time. Because such an asset meets the definition of investment that we gave earlier, housing construction—the building of a *new* house—is counted as investment expenditure rather than as consumption expenditure. However, when an individual purchases an existing house from a builder or from another individual, the ownership of an existing asset is simply transferred, and the transaction is not part of national income. Only when a new house is built does it appear as residential investment in the national accounts.

Gross and Net Investment. The total investment that occurs in the economy is called *gross investment*. Gross investment is divided into two parts: replacement investment and net investment. Replacement investment is the amount of investment required to replace that part of the capital stock that loses its value through wear and tear; this loss in value is called **depreciation**. Net investment is equal to gross investment minus depreciation:

depreciation The amount by which the capital stock is depleted through the production process.

$$\text{Net investment} = \text{Gross investment} - \text{Depreciation}$$

When net investment is positive, the economy's capital stock is growing. If net investment is negative—which rarely happens—the economy's capital stock is shrinking.

All investment goods are part of the nation's total current output, and their production creates income whether the goods produced are a part of net investment or are merely replacement investment. Thus, all of gross investment is included in the calculation of national income. *Actual* total investment expenditure is denoted by the symbol I_a.

3. Government Purchases When governments provide goods and services that households want, such as street-cleaning and firefighting, they are adding to the sum total of valuable output in the economy. With other government activities, the case may not seem so clear. Should expenditures by the federal government to send soldiers overseas, or to pay a civil servant to refile papers from a now-defunct department, be regarded as contributions to national income?

government purchases All government expenditure on currently produced goods and services, exclusive of government transfer payments. Represented by the symbol G.

National income statisticians do not speculate about such matters. Instead they include all **government purchases** of goods and services as part of national income (some of which is government expenditure on investment goods). *Actual* government purchases of goods and services are denoted G_a.

Cost Versus Market Value. Government output is typically valued at cost rather than at market value. In many cases, there is really no choice. What, for example, is the market value of the law courts or of police protection or of the economic analysis done by economists at the

Unsold merchandise becomes part of firms' inventories. In national-income accounting, firms' expenditures on inventories are considered one part of investment expenditure.

Department of Finance? No one knows. But since we do know what it costs the government to provide these services, we value them at their cost of production.

Although valuing at cost is the only possible way to measure many government activities, it does have one curious consequence. If, because of an increase in productivity, one civil servant now does what two used to do, and the displaced worker shifts to the private sector, the government's measured contribution to national income will fall (but the private sector's contribution will rise). Conversely, if two workers now do what one worker used to do, the government's contribution will rise. Both changes could occur even though what the government actually produces has not changed. This is an inevitable but curious consequence of measuring the value of the government's output by the cost of producing it.

Government Purchases Versus Government Expenditure. Only government *purchases* of currently produced goods and services are included as part of GDP. As a result, a great deal of government spending does *not* count as part of GDP. For example, when the government makes payments to a retired person through the Canada Pension Plan, there is no market transaction involved as the government is not purchasing any currently produced goods or services from the retiree. The payment itself does not add to total output. The same is true of payments for employment insurance and welfare, and interest on the national debt (which transfers income from taxpayers to holders of government bonds). These are examples of **transfer payments**, which are government expenditures that are not made in return for currently produced goods and services. They are not a part of expenditure on the nation's total output and are therefore not included in GDP. (Of course, the recipients of transfer payments often choose to spend their money on consumption goods. Such expenditure then counts in the same way as any other consumption expenditure.)

4. Net Exports The fourth category of aggregate expenditure arises from foreign trade. How do imports and exports influence national income? **Imports** are domestic expenditure on foreign-produced goods and services, whereas **exports** are foreign expenditure on domestically produced goods and services.

Exports. If Canadian firms sell goods to German households, the goods are part of German consumption expenditure but constitute expenditure *on Canadian output*. Indeed, all goods and services that are produced in Canada and sold to foreigners must be counted as part of Canadian production and income; they are produced in Canada, and they create incomes for the Canadian residents who produce them. They are not purchased by Canadian residents, however, so they are not included as part of C_a, I_a, or G_a. Therefore, to arrive at the total value of expenditure *on Canadian output*, it is necessary to add in the value of Canadian exports of goods and services. The value of actual exports is denoted X_a.

Imports. If you buy a car that was made in Japan, only a small part of that value will represent expenditure on Canadian production. Some of it represents payment for the services of the Canadian dealers and for transportation; the rest is expenditure on Japanese products. If you take your next vacation in Italy, much of your expenditure will be on goods and services produced in Italy and thus will contribute to Italian GDP rather than to Canadian GDP.

Similarly, when a Canadian firm makes an investment expenditure on a machine that was made partly with imported raw materials, only part of the expenditure is on Canadian production; the rest is expenditure on foreign production. The same is true for government expenditure on such things as roads and dams; some of the expenditure is for imported materials, and only part of it is for domestically produced goods and

transfer payments Payments to an individual or institution not made in exchange for a good or service.

imports The value of all domestically produced goods and services purchased from firms, households, or governments in other countries.

exports The value of all goods and services sold to firms, households, and governments in other countries.

services. The same is also true for exports, most of which use some imported inputs in their production process.

Consumption, investment, government purchases, and exports all have an import content. To arrive at total expenditure *on Canadian products*, we need to subtract from total Canadian expenditure the economy's total expenditure on imports. The value of actual imports is given the symbol IM_a.

It is customary to group actual imports and actual exports together as **net exports**. Net exports are defined as total exports minus total imports $(X_a - IM_a)$, which is also denoted NX_a. When the value of Canadian exports exceeds the value of Canadian imports, net exports are positive. When the value of imports exceeds the value of exports, net exports are negative.

net exports The value of total exports minus the value of total imports. Represented by the symbol *NX*.

Total Expenditures Gross domestic product measured from the expenditure side is equal to the sum of the four major expenditure categories that we have just discussed. In terms of a simple equation, we have

$$GDP = C_a + I_a + G_a + (X_a - IM_a)$$

These data are shown in Table 20-1 for Canada in 2011, including some data on the expenditure in the various subcategories.

Measured from the expenditure side, GDP is equal to the total expenditure on domestically produced output. GDP is equal to $C_a + I_a + G_a + NX_a$.

GDP from the Income Side

As we said earlier, the conventions of national income accounting ensure that the production of a nation's output generates income *exactly* equal to the value of that production. Labour must be employed, land must be rented, and capital must be used. The calculation of GDP from the income side involves adding up factor incomes and other claims on the value of output until all of that value is accounted for.

1. Factor Incomes National income accountants distinguish three main components of factor incomes: wages and salaries, interest, and business profits (which includes rent received by property owners).

Wages and Salaries. Wages and salaries are the payment for the services of labour and they include all pre-tax labour earnings: take-home pay, income taxes withheld, employment-insurance contributions, pension-fund contributions, and other employee benefits. In total, wages and salaries represent the part of the value of production that is paid to labour.

Interest. Interest includes interest that is earned on bank deposits, interest that is earned on loans to firms, and miscellaneous other investment income (but excludes interest income earned from loans to Canadian governments).[2]

---

[2] The treatment of interest in the national accounts is a little odd. Interest paid by the government is considered a transfer payment, whereas interest paid by private households or firms is treated as expenditure (and its receipt is counted as a factor payment). This is only one example of arbitrary decisions in national income accounting. Others are discussed in *Extensions in Theory 20-1* on page 508.

Business Profits. Some profits are paid out as *dividends* to owners of firms; the rest are held by firms and are called *retained earnings*. Both dividends and retained earnings are included in the calculation of GDP. For accounting purposes, total profits include corporate profits, incomes of unincorporated businesses (mainly small businesses, farmers, partnerships, and professionals), rent paid on land and buildings, and profits of government business enterprises and Crown corporations (such as Canada Post and Export Development Canada).

Profits and interest together represent the payment for the use of capital—interest for borrowed capital and profits for capital contributed by the owners of firms.

Net Domestic Income. The sum of wages and salaries, interest, and profits is called *net domestic income at factor cost*. It is "net" because it excludes the value of output that is used as replacement investment. It is "domestic income" because it is the income accruing to domestic factors of production. It is "at factor cost" because it represents only that part of the value of final output that accrues to factors in the form of payments due to them for their services. As we will see next, some part of the value of final output does not accrue to the factors at all.

2. Non-factor Payments Every time a consumer spends $10 on some item, less than $10 is generated as income for factors of production. This shortfall is due to the presence of indirect taxes and depreciation.

Indirect Taxes and Subsidies. An important claim on the market value of output arises out of indirect taxes, which are taxes on the production and sale of goods and services. In Canada, the most important indirect taxes are provincial sales taxes, excise taxes on specific products, and the federal Goods and Services Tax (GST).

For example, if a good's market price of $10.00 includes 60 cents in provincial sales taxes and 50 cents in federal GST, only $8.90 is available as income to factors of production. Governments are claiming $1.10 of the $10.00 initial value of the good. Adding up income claims to determine GDP therefore necessitates including the portion of the total market value of output that is the governments' claims exercised through their taxes on goods and services.

Sometimes the government gives subsidies to firms, which act like negative taxes. When these occur, it is necessary to *subtract* their value, since they allow factor incomes to *exceed* the market value of output. Suppose a municipal bus company spends $150 000 providing bus rides and covers its costs by selling $140 000 in fares and obtaining a $10 000 subsidy from the local government. The total income that the company will generate from its production is $150 000, but the total market value of its output is only $140 000, with the difference made up by the subsidy. To get from total factor income to the market value of its total output, we must subtract the amount of the subsidy.

Depreciation. Another claim on the value of final output is depreciation. As we said earlier, depreciation is the loss in the value of physical capital generated by wear and tear during the production process. It is part of gross profits, but because it is needed to compensate for capital used up in the process of production, it is not part of net profits. Hence, depreciation is not income earned by any factor of production.

Total National Income The various components of the income side of the GDP in the Canadian economy in 2011 are shown in Table 20-2. Note that one of the terms in the table is called *statistical discrepancy*, a term that appears with equal magnitude but opposite sign in Table 20-1. This is a "fudge factor" to make sure that the independent measures of income and expenditure come to the same total. Statistical discrepancy is a clear indication that national income accounting is not error-free. Although national income and national expenditure are conceptually identical, in practice both are measured with slight error.

> From the income side, GDP is the sum of factor incomes *plus* indirect taxes (net of subsidies) *plus* depreciation.

We have now seen the two commonly used methods for computing a country's national income. Both are correct and give us the same measure of GDP, but each gives us some different additional information. For some questions, such as what will be the likely future path of the nation's capital stock, it is useful to know the relative importance of consumption and investment. In this case, the expenditure approach for computing GDP provides some of the necessary information (Table 20-1 on page 502). For other questions, such as what is happening to the distribution of income between labour and capital, we need information about the composition of factor incomes. In this case, a useful starting point would be to examine GDP on the income side (Table 20-2).

Measuring national income is not problem-free. As in any accounting exercise, many arbitrary rules must be used. Some of them seem odd, but the important thing is that these rules be used consistently over time. Comparisons of GDP over time will then reflect genuine changes in economic activity, which is what we desire for the measure. *Extensions in Theory 20-1* discusses the issue of arbitrariness in national income accounting.

TABLE 20-2 GDP from the Income Side, 2011

Category	Billions of Dollars	Percent of GDP
Factor Incomes		
Wages, salaries, and supplementary income	889.5	51.7
Interest and miscellaneous investment income	73.8	4.3
Business profits (including rent and net income of farmers and unincorporated businesses)	336.7	19.5
Net Domestic Income at Factor Cost	1300.0	75.5
Non-factor Payments		
Depreciation	240.3	14.0
Indirect taxes less subsidies	178.0	10.5
Statistical Discrepancy	0.5	0.0
Total	1720.7	100.0

GDP measured from the income side of the national accounts gives the sizes of the major components of the income generated by producing the nation's output.

(*Source:* Statistics Canada, "Gross Domestic Product, Income-based, 2011," CANSIM database, Table 380-0001. Available at www.statcan.gc.ca.)

20.3 National Income Accounting: Some Further Issues

Now that we have examined the basics of national income accounting, we are ready to explore some more detailed issues. We discuss the distinction between GDP and the related concept of gross national product (GNP), the difference between real and nominal GDP, the major omissions from measured GDP, and the connection between GDP and "living standards."

EXTENSIONS IN THEORY 20-1

Arbitrary Decisions in National Income Accounting

National income accounting practices contain many arbitrary decisions. For example, goods that are finished and held in inventories are valued at market value, thereby anticipating their sale, even though the actual selling price may not be known. In the case of a Ford in a dealer's showroom, this practice may be justified because the *value* of this Ford is perhaps virtually the same as that of an identical Ford that has just been sold to a customer. However, what is the correct market value of a half-finished house or an unfinished novel? Accountants arbitrarily treat goods in process at cost (rather than at market value) if the goods are being made by firms. They ignore completely the value of the unfinished novel. The arbitrary nature of these decisions is inevitable: Because people must arrive at some practical compromise between consistent definitions and measurable magnitudes, any decision will be somewhat arbitrary.

Such arbitrary decisions surely affect the size of measured GDP. But does it matter? The surprising answer, for many purposes, is no. It is wrong to think that just because a statistical measure is imperfect (as all statistical measures are), it is useless. Simple measures often give estimates that are quite accurate, and substantial improvements in sophistication may make only trivial improvements in these estimates.

In 2011, for example, Canadian GDP was measured as $1720.7 billion. It is certain that the market value of all production in Canada in that year was neither $500 billion nor $2500 billion, but it might well have been $1600 billion or $1800 billion had different measures been defined with different arbitrary decisions built in. Similarly, Canadian per capita GDP is about three times the Mexican per capita GDP and is about 20 percent less than U.S. per capita GDP. Other measures might differ, but it is unlikely that any measure would reveal the Mexican per capita GDP to be higher than Canada's, or Canada's to be significantly above that of the United States.

GDP and GNP

gross national product (GNP) The value of total incomes earned by domestic residents.

A measure of national output closely related to GDP is **gross national product (GNP)**. The difference between GDP and GNP is the difference between *income produced* and *income received*. GDP measures the value of total output *produced in Canada* and the total income generated as a result of that production. GNP measures the total amount of income *received by Canadian residents*, no matter where that income was generated. How can GDP differ from GNP? Let's consider two examples.

For the first example, consider a Toyota factory located in Cambridge, Ontario. Suppose in 2013 that the value added generated by that factory is $100 million. Canadian GDP is therefore higher by $100 million as a result of that production. But suppose $5 million of the profits (part of the value added) generated at that factory is remitted to foreign owners. Since only $95 million of the value added generates income *for Canadian residents*, Canadian GNP is higher by only $95 million.

The second example involves any Canadian-owned business located outside of Canada. The value added produced by that business contributes to the GDP in a foreign country but not in Canada. But if there are profits remitted to the Canadian owners, those profits will be part of the income of Canadian residents and thus part of Canadian GNP.

> GDP measures the value of all production located in Canada, no matter who receives the income from that production. GNP measures the income received by Canadian residents, no matter where the production occurred to generate that income.

The relative sizes of GDP and GNP depend on the balance between income earned by Canadian residents from Canadian investments located abroad, and income paid to foreign residents from foreign-owned investments located in Canada. For most of Canada's history, Canada has been a *net debtor* country. Thus, the value of foreign-located assets owned by Canadian residents has been less than the value of Canadian-located assets owned by foreigners. As a result, the foreign-generated income received by Canadian residents is less than the Canadian-generated income going to foreigners. This makes Canadian GNP less than Canadian GDP. But the difference is small. In most years, GNP is only 3 or 4 percent lower than GDP.

Toyota cars produced in Canada contribute to Canada's GDP. But the portion of profits that returns to foreign shareholders is not part of Canada's GNP.

Which Measure Is Better? Given the difference between GDP and GNP, we are naturally led to ask if one measure is better than the other. The answer depends on what we want to measure.

> GDP is superior to GNP as a measure of domestic economic activity. GNP is superior to GDP as a measure of the income of domestic residents.

If you want to know how easy it will be to find a job, or to determine whether factories are working double shifts or new buildings are going up, look to changes in the GDP. By its definition, it is the GDP that tells us how much is being produced within a nation's borders. To know how much income is available to the residents of a country, however, one should look at the GNP, which counts income earned abroad and subtracts income generated at home that accrues to residents of other nations. Thus, the GNP is a better measure of the income of a country's residents.

Disposable Personal Income Both GDP and GNP are important measures of overall economic activity and of national income. Most important to individual households, however, is **disposable personal income**, the part of national income that is available to households to spend or to save. The easiest way to calculate disposable personal income is to subtract from GNP the parts of the GNP that are not available to households. Hence, we must subtract all taxes (both income and sales taxes), depreciation, retained earnings, and interest paid to institutions. We then need to add in the transfer payments made to households. In recent years, disposable income has represented about 60 percent of GDP.

disposable personal income The part of national income that accrues to households and is available to spend or save.

Real and Nominal GDP

In Chapter 19, we distinguished between real and nominal measures of aggregate output. When we add up dollar values of outputs, expenditures, or incomes, we end up with what are called *nominal values*. Nominal GDP increased by 153.1 percent between 1990 and 2011. If we want to compare *real* GDP in 2011 to that in 1990, we need to determine how much of that nominal increase was due to increases in prices and how

TABLE 20-3 Nominal and Real GDP in Canada: Selected Years (billions of dollars)

Year	Nominal GDP (current prices)	Real GDP (2002 prices)	GDP Deflator
1985	485.7	716.1	67.8
1990	679.9	825.3	82.4
1995	810.4	898.8	90.2
2000	1076.6	1100.5	97.8
2002	1152.9	1152.9	100.0
2005	1373.8	1247.8	110.1
2010	1624.6	1325.0	122.6
2011	1720.7	1356.9	126.8

Nominal GDP tells us about the money value of output; real GDP tells us about the quantity of physical output. Nominal GDP gives the total value of output in any year, valued at the prices of that year. Real GDP gives the total value of output in any year, *valued at prices from some base year*, in this case 2002. The comparison of real and nominal GDP implicitly defines a price index, changes in which reveal changes in the (average) prices of goods produced domestically. Note that in 2002, nominal GDP equals real GDP (measured in 2002 prices), and thus the GDP deflator equals 100.

(*Source:* Statistics Canada, CANSIM database. Real GDP: Series V1992067. Nominal GDP: Series V1997757.)

much was due to increases in quantities produced. Although there are many possible ways of doing this, the underlying principle is always the same: The value of output in each period is computed by using a common set of *base-period prices*. When this is done, economists say that real output is measured in *constant dollars*.

> Total GDP valued at current prices is called *nominal* GDP. GDP valued at base-period prices is called *real* GDP.

Any change in nominal GDP reflects the combined effects of changes in quantities and changes in prices. However, when real income is measured over different periods by using a common set of base-period prices, changes in real income reflect only changes in quantities. Table 20-3 shows real and nominal GDP for selected years in Canada since 1985.

The GDP Deflator If nominal and real GDP change by different amounts over a given time period, then prices must have changed over that period. For example, if nominal GDP has increased by 6 percent and real GDP has increased by only 4 percent over the same period, we know that average prices must have increased by 2 percent. Comparing what has happened to nominal and real GDP over the same period implies the existence of a price index measuring the change in prices over that period—"implies" because no explicit price index is used in calculating either real or nominal GDP. However, an index can be inferred by comparing these two values. The *GDP deflator* is defined as follows:

$$\text{GDP deflator} = \frac{\text{GDP at current prices}}{\text{GDP at base-period prices}} \times 100 = \frac{\text{Nominal GDP}}{\text{Real GDP}} \times 100$$

GDP deflator An index number derived by dividing nominal GDP by real GDP. Its change measures the average change in price of all the items in the GDP.

The **GDP deflator** is the most comprehensive available index of the price level because it includes all the goods and services that are produced by the entire economy. It uses the current year's basket of production to compare the current year's prices with those prevailing in the base period. (Because it uses the current basket of goods and services, it does not run into the CPI's problem of sometimes being based on an out-of-date basket.) The GDP deflator was 26.8 percent higher in 2011 than in the base year 2002 (see Table 20-3). Thus, for those goods and services produced in 2011, their average price increased by 26.8 percent over the previous nine years. *Applying Economic Concepts 20-2* illustrates the calculation of real and nominal GDP and the GDP deflator for a simple hypothetical economy that produces only wheat and steel.

As we have said, a change in nominal GDP can be split into the change of prices and the change of quantities. For example, from the data in Table 20-3 we can calculate that in 2011, Canadian nominal GDP was 153.1 percent higher than in 1990. This increase was due to a 53.9 percent increase in prices (as calculated by the percentage change in the GDP deflator) and a 64.4 percent increase in real GDP.[3]

GDP Deflator Versus the CPI An important point about the GDP deflator is that it does not necessarily change in line with changes in the CPI. The two price indices are measuring different things. Movements in the CPI measure the change in the average price of consumer goods, whereas movements in the GDP deflator reflect the change in the average price of goods produced in Canada. So changes in the world price of coffee, for example, would have a larger effect on the CPI than on the GDP deflator, since Canadians drink a lot of coffee but no coffee is produced here. Conversely, a change in the world price of wheat is likely to have a bigger effect on the GDP deflator than on the CPI, since most of Canada's considerable production of wheat is exported to other countries, thus leaving a relatively small fraction to appear in the Canadian basket of consumer products.

> Changes in the GDP deflator and Consumer Price Index (CPI) similarly reflect overall inflationary trends. But changes in relative prices may lead the two price indices to move in different ways.

Omissions from GDP

National income as measured in the National Income and Expenditure Accounts provides an excellent measure of the flow of economic activity in organized markets in a given year. But much economic activity takes place outside the markets that the national income accountants survey. Although these activities are not typically included in the measure of GDP, they nevertheless use real resources.

Illegal Activities GDP does not measure illegal activities, even though many of them are ordinary business activities that produce goods and services sold in markets and that generate factor incomes. Many forms of illegal gambling, prostitution, and drug trade come into this category. To gain an accurate measure of the total demand for factors of production, of total marketable output, or of total incomes generated, we should include these activities, whether or not they are legal. The omission of illegal activities is no trivial matter: The drug trade alone is a multi-billion-dollar business.

Prostitution and other illegal activities involve genuine market transactions, but they are not included in official measures of national income.

Note that some illegal activities do get included in national income measures, although they are generally misclassified by industry. The income is included because people sometimes report their illegally earned income as part of their earnings from legal activities. They do this to avoid the fate of Al Capone, the famous Chicago gangster in the 1920s and 1930s, who, having avoided conviction on many more serious charges, was finally caught and imprisoned for income-tax evasion.

---

[3] For large percentage changes in price and quantity, the nominal percentage change is not exactly equal to the sum of the price and the quantity changes; generally, the relationship is multiplicative. In this case, prices and quantities are respectively 1.539 and 1.644 times their original values. Thus, nominal GDP is $(1.539) \times (1.644) = 2.531$ times its original value, which is an increase of 153.1 percent. For small percentage changes, the sum is a very good approximation of the multiplicative change. For example, if prices grow by 2 percent and quantities by 3 percent, the nominal change is $(1.02) \times (1.03) = 1.0506$, which is very close to 1.05, an increase of 5 percent.

APPLYING ECONOMIC CONCEPTS 20-2

Calculating Nominal and Real GDP

To see what is involved in calculating nominal GDP, real GDP, and the GDP deflator, an example may be helpful. Consider a simple hypothetical economy that produces only two commodities, wheat and steel.

Table 1 gives the basic data for output and prices in the economy for two years.

TABLE 1 Data for a Hypothetical Economy

| | Quantity Produced | | Prices | |
	Wheat (bushels)	Steel (tonnes)	Wheat ($/bushel)	Steel ($/tonne)
Year 1	100	20	10	50
Year 2	110	16	12	55

Table 2 shows nominal GDP, calculated by adding the dollar values of wheat output and of steel output for each year. In year 1, the values of both wheat and steel production were $1000, so nominal GDP was $2000. In year 2, wheat output rose to $1320, and steel output fell to $880. Since the rise in the value of wheat was greater than the fall in the value of steel, nominal GDP rose by $200.

TABLE 2 Calculation of Nominal GDP

Year 1: $(100 \times \$10) + (20 \times \$50) = \$2000$
Year 2: $(110 \times \$12) + (16 \times \$55) = \$2200$

Table 3 shows real GDP, calculated by valuing output in each year *at year-2 prices*; that is, year 2 is used as the base year. In year 2, wheat output rose, but steel output fell. If we use year-2 prices, the fall in the value of steel output between years 1 and 2 exceeded the rise in the value of wheat output, and so real GDP fell.

TABLE 3 Calculation of Real GDP Using Year-2 Prices

Year 1: $(100 \times \$12) + (20 \times \$55) = \$2300$
Year 2: $(110 \times \$12) + (16 \times \$55) = \$2200$

In Table 4, the ratio of nominal to real GDP is calculated for each year and multiplied by 100. This ratio implicitly measures the change in prices over the period in question and is called the *GDP deflator*. The deflator shows that average prices increased by 15 percent between year 1 and year 2.

TABLE 4 Calculation of the GDP Deflator

Year 1: $(2000/2300) \times 100 = 86.96$
Year 2: $(2200/2200) \times 100 = 100.00$

Throughout this box we have used year 2 as the base year. But we could just as easily have used year 1. The changes we would have computed in real GDP and the deflator would have been very similar—but not identical—to the ones we did compute using year 2 as the base year. The choice of base year matters because of different *relative* prices in the different years (note that the price of steel relative to the price of wheat is lower in year 2 than in year 1). Put simply, with different relative prices in different years, the various output changes are weighted differently depending on which prices we use, and thus the *aggregate* measure of real GDP changes by different amounts. (If you want to understand this point in more detail, try doing Study Exercise #8 on page 517.)

How do we choose the "right" base year? As with many other elements of national income accounting, there is some arbitrariness in the choice. There is no "right" year. The important thing is not which year to use—the important thing is to be clear about which year you are using and then, for a given set of comparisons, to be sure that you are consistent in your choice. In recent years, Statistics Canada has avoided this problem by using "chain weighting," a technique that essentially uses an average over several measures, each one corresponding to a different base year.

The Underground Economy A significant omission from GDP is the so-called underground economy. The transactions that occur in the underground economy are perfectly legal in themselves; the only illegality involved is that such transactions are not reported for tax purposes. Because such transactions go unreported, they are omitted from GDP. One example of this is the carpenter who repairs a leak in your roof and takes payment in cash (and does not report it as income) to avoid taxation.

The growth of the underground economy is facilitated by the rising importance of services in the nation's total output. It is much easier for a carpenter to pass unnoticed by government authorities than it is for a manufacturing establishment. Estimates of the value of income earned in the underground economy run from 2 percent to 15 percent of GDP. In some countries, the figures are even higher. The Italian underground economy, for example, has been estimated at close to 25 percent of that country's GDP.

"Home Production" and Other Non-market Activities If a homeowner hires a firm to do some landscaping, the value of the landscaping enters into GDP (as long as the landscaper records the transaction and thus declares the income); if the homeowner does the landscaping herself, the value of the landscaping is omitted from GDP because there is no recorded market transaction. Such production of goods and services in the home is called *home production* and includes all of the "ordinary" work that is required to keep a household functioning, such as cooking, cleaning, shopping, and doing laundry. Other non-market activities include voluntary work, such as

The extraction, refining, and transportation of oil are all included as goods and services in measures of GDP. But the environmental damage inflicted by an oil spill—an economic "bad"—is not included in any measure of GDP.

canvassing for a political party or coaching a local hockey team. Both home production and volunteer activities clearly add to economic well-being, and both use economic resources. Yet neither is included in official measures of national income since they are non-market activities.

Another extremely important non-market activity is *leisure*. If a lawyer voluntarily chooses to reduce her time at work from 2400 hours to 2200 hours per year, measured national income will fall by the lawyer's wage rate times 200 hours. Yet the value to the lawyer of the 200 hours of new leisure enjoyed outside of the marketplace must exceed the lost wages (otherwise she would not have chosen to reduce her work effort by 200 hours), so total economic well-being has increased even though measured GDP has fallen. Over the years, one of the most important ways in which economic growth has benefited people is by permitting increased amounts of leisure. Because the leisure time is not marketed, its value does not show up in measures of national income.

Economic "Bads" When a coal-burning electric power plant sends sulphur dioxide into the atmosphere, leading to acid rain and environmental damage, the value of the electricity sold is included as part of GDP, but the value of the damage done by the acid rain is not deducted. Similarly, the gasoline that we use in our cars is part of national income when it is produced, but the environmental damage done by burning that gasoline is not deducted. To the extent that economic growth brings with it increases in pollution, congestion, and other disamenities of modern living, measurements of national income will overstate the improvement in living standards. Such measures capture the increased output of goods and services, but they fail to account for the increased output of "bads" that generally accompany economic growth.

Do the Omissions Matter? Should our current measure of GDP be modified to deal with these omissions? Changing the formal GDP measure to include illegal activities and home production would be extremely difficult, if not impossible. Not only would it be very costly to get accurate measurements of the level of these activities, but in the case of home production there are no prices associated with the "transactions."

Including economic "bads" in the measure of GDP would be possible but doing so would fundamentally change the nature of the measurement such that it would no longer give an accurate measure of the level of economic activity. Damage to the environment is certainly important, but addressing that problem does not require including it in a measure of economic activity.

The current approach to measuring GDP continues to be used for three reasons. First, as we have just said, correcting the major omissions in the measure would be difficult if not impossible. Second, even though the *level* of measured GDP in any given year may be inaccurate, the *change* in GDP from one year to the next is a good indication of the *changes* in economic activity (as long as the omissions are themselves not changing a lot from one year to the next).

The third reason is that policymakers need to measure the amount of market output in the economy in order to design policies to control inflation and set tax rates. To do so, they need to know the flow of money payments made to produce and purchase Canadian output. Modified measures that included non-market activities would distort these figures and likely lead to policy errors.

That the conventional measure of GDP continues to be used is not to say that economists and policymakers are not concerned about the imperfections and omissions. Statistics Canada is constantly striving to improve the measurement of GDP, while at the same time there is a recognition that some problems in measurement will probably always exist.

GDP and Living Standards

We have said that GDP does a good job of measuring the flow of economic activity during a given time period. But we have also said that many things are omitted from this measure, some of which represent beneficial economic activity and some of which represent economic "bads." These observations lead to the obvious question: To what extent does GDP provide even a rough measure of our living standards?

The answer depends on what we mean by "living standards." For many people, this term refers to our *purchasing power* or *real income*. When GDP rises, do we experience a rise in our average real incomes? The answer is not necessarily. As we will see in detail in Chapters 25 and 26, real GDP can rise for two general reasons. First, there may be an increase in the amounts of land, labour, and capital used as inputs to production. Second, these inputs may become more productive in the sense that there is an increase in the amount of output *per unit of input*. The *average* level of real income in the economy is best measured by real GDP *per person*, but this does not necessarily rise whenever real GDP rises. If real GDP rises because more people become employed, real GDP per person may not rise. However, if real GDP rises because the existing labour force becomes more productive, then average real incomes will also rise. This explains why most economists believe that productivity growth is such an important determinant of living standards.

To many people, however, the term "living standards" is much broader than simply real per capita income—it includes such important but intangible things as religious and political freedom, the quality of local community life, environmental sustainability, the distribution of income, and our ability to prevent and treat illness and disease. And since measures of real GDP omit many of these intangible things that contribute positively to our overall well-being, it is not even clear that changes in real per capita GDP accurately reflect changes in this broader concept of living standards. For example, greater productivity may lead to an increase in real per capita income and thus to a rise in our average *material* living standards, but if this change also leads to greater environmental damage or greater inequality in the distribution of income, some people may argue that while our material living standards have increased, our overall well-being has declined.

Changes in real per capita income are a good measure of average material living standards. But material living standards are only part of what most people consider their overall well-being.

SUMMARY

20.1 National Output and Value Added   LO 1

- Each firm's contribution to total output is equal to its value added, which is the value of the firm's output minus the values of all intermediate goods and services

that it uses. The sum of all the values added produced in an economy is the economy's total output, which is called gross domestic product (GDP).

20.2 National Income Accounting: The Basics   LO 2

- From the circular flow of income, there are two commonly used ways to compute national income. One is to add up total expenditure on domestic output. The other is to add up the total income generated by domestic production. By standard accounting conventions, these two aggregations define the same total.
- From the expenditure side of the national accounts,

$$GDP = C_a + I_a + G_a + (X_a - IM_a)$$

- C_a comprises consumption expenditures of households. I_a is investment in plant and equipment, residential construction, and inventory accumulation. G_a is government purchases of goods and services. $(X_a - IM_a)$ represents net exports of goods and services.
- GDP measured from the income side adds up all claims to the market value of production. Wages, interest, profits, depreciation, and indirect taxes (net of subsidies) are the major categories.

20.3 National Income Accounting: Some Further Issues   LO 3, 4, 5

- GDP measures the value of all production located in Canada, no matter who receives the income from that production. GNP measures the income received by Canadian residents, no matter where the production occurred to generate that income.
- Real measures of national income reflect changes in real quantities. Nominal measures of national income reflect changes in both prices and quantities. Any change in nominal income can be split into a change in quantities and a change in prices.
- The comparison of nominal and real GDP yields the implicit GDP price deflator, an index of the average price of all goods and services produced in the economy.
- GDP and related measures of national income must be interpreted with their limitations in mind. GDP excludes

production resulting from activities that are illegal, that take place in the underground economy, or that do not pass through markets.
- Notwithstanding its limitations, GDP remains an important measure of the total economic activity that passes through the nation's markets. Recorded *changes* in GDP will generally do an accurate job of measuring *changes* in economic activity.
- Real per capita GDP is a good measure of average material living standards. But because GDP omits many intangible things that contribute positively to our quality of life, GDP-based measures miss important parts of our overall well-being.

KEY CONCEPTS

Intermediate and final goods
Value added
GDP as the sum of all values added
GDP from the expenditure side

GDP from the income side
GNP versus GDP
Disposable personal income
GDP deflator

Omissions from GDP
Per capita GDP and productivity
Living standards and GDP

STUDY EXERCISES

MyEconLab

Make the grade with MyEconLab: Study Exercises marked in red can be found on MyEconLab. You can practise them as often as you want, and most feature step-by-step guided instructions to help you find the right answer.

1. Fill in the blanks to make the following statements correct.

   a. If, when measuring Canada's national output, we add the market values of all firms' outputs in Canada, then we are committing the error of _____. Such an amount would greatly _____ the economy's actual output.

   b. Statisticians use the concept of _____ to avoid double counting in measuring national income. Each firm's _____ is the value of its output minus the costs of _____ that it purchases from other firms.

   c. If we measure GDP from the expenditure side, we are adding four broad categories of expenditure: _____, _____, _____, and _____. As an equation it is written as GDP = _____.

   d. If we measure GDP from the income side, we are adding three main components of factor incomes: _____, _____, and _____. To these items we must add non-factor payments of _____ and _____.

2. Fill in the blanks to make the following statements correct.

   a. Comparing GDP and GNP, if we want the best measure of Canada's domestic economic activity, we should look at _____; if we want the best measure of the income of Canada's residents, then we should look at _____.

   b. If nominal GDP increases by 35 percent over a 10-year period, then it is unclear how much of this increase is due to increases in _____ and how much is due to increases in _____. To overcome this problem, we look at GDP valued at _____

prices and we refer to this measure as _____ national income.

   c. GDP divided by total population gives us a measure of _____.

   d. GDP divided by the number of employed persons in Canada gives us a measure of labour _____.

3. In measuring GDP from the expenditure side (GDP = $C_a + I_a + G_a + NX_a$), which of the following expenditures are included and within which of the four categories?

   a. expenditures on automobiles by consumers
   b. expenditures on automobiles by firms
   c. expenditures on new machinery by Canadian-owned forest companies located in Canada
   d. expenditures on new machinery by Canadian-owned forest companies located in the United States
   e. expenditures on new machinery by U.S.-owned forest companies located in Canada
   f. reductions in business inventories
   g. purchases of second-hand cars and trucks
   h. the hiring of economic consultants by the Manitoba government
   i. the purchase of Canadian-produced software by a firm in Japan

4. The list below provides some national income figures for the country of Econoland. All figures are in millions of dollars.

Wages and salaries	5000
Interest income	200
Personal consumption	3900
Personal saving	1100

Personal income taxes	200
Business profits	465
Indirect taxes	175
Subsidies	30
Government purchases	1000
Exports	350
Imports	390
Net private investment	950
Depreciation	150

a. Using the expenditure approach, what is the value of GDP for Econoland?

b. Using the income approach, what is the value of GDP?

c. What is the value of net domestic income at factor cost?

5. The table below shows data for real and nominal GDP for a hypothetical economy over several years.

Year	Nominal GDP (billions of $)	Real GDP (billions of 2010 $)	GDP Deflator
2008	775.3	798.4	—
2009	814.1	838.6	—
2010	862.9	862.9	—
2011	901.5	882.5	—
2012	951.3	920.6	—
2013	998.8	950.5	—

a. Compute the GDP deflator for each year.

b. Compute the total percentage change in nominal GDP from 2008 to 2013. How much of this change was due to increases in prices and how much was due to changes in quantities?

6. Would inflation, as measured by the rate of change in the GDP deflator, ever be different from inflation as measured by the rate of change in the Consumer Price Index? Would it ever be the same? Explain.

7. For each of the following events, describe the likely effect on real GDP in Canada.

a. A major ice storm in Quebec damages homes and thus increases the demand for building materials.

b. A flood on the Red River destroys the annual barley crop on hundreds of thousands of acres of Manitoba farmland.

c. In a near-perfect growing season in 2012, Saskatchewan's wheat crop increases by 20 percent above normal levels.

d. A 30 percent increase in the world price of oil in 2011 causes Alberta-based oil producers to increase their oil production (measured in barrels) by 5 percent.

e. A large new hospital complex is built in Montreal in 2012.

f. The building of a larger arena in Toronto increases the demand for Maple Leafs tickets by Torontonians.

g. The building of a larger arena in Toronto increases the demand for Maple Leafs tickets by residents of Buffalo, New York.

8. Consider the following data for a hypothetical economy that produces two goods, milk and honey.

	Quantity Produced		Prices	
	Milk (litres)	Honey (kg)	Milk ($/litre)	Honey ($/kg)
Year 1	100	40	2	6
Year 2	120	25	3	6

a. Compute nominal GDP for each year in this economy.

b. Using year 1 as the base year, compute real GDP for each year. What is the percentage change in real GDP from year 1 to year 2?

c. Using year 1 as the base year, compute the GDP deflator for each year. What is the percentage change in the GDP deflator from year 1 to year 2?

d. Now compute the GDP deflator for each year, using year 2 as the base year.

e. Explain why the measures of real GDP growth (and growth in the deflator) depend on the choice of base year.

9. Residents of some Canadian cities have recently become concerned about the growing proportion of their local real estate that is being bought up by foreign residents. What is the effect of this transfer of ownership on Canadian GDP and GNP?

10. In 2011, the United Nations ranked Norway first on the Human Development Index—a ranking of the "quality of life" in many countries. Yet Norway was *not* ranked first in terms of real per capita GDP. Explain how the two rankings can be different.

11. A company's wages and salaries are part of its value added. Suppose, however, that the cleaning and machinery maintenance that its own employees used to do are now contracted out to specialist firms who come in to do the same work more cheaply.

a. What happens to the company's value added when it "contracts out" such work?

b. What happens to value added in the economy as a whole?

12. As we saw in the text, the expenditure approach to measuring GDP shows that

$$GDP = C_a + I_a + G_a + NX_a$$

a. Is this equation a *causal* relationship, suggesting that an increase in any one of the right-hand-side terms *causes* an increase in GDP?

b. It is common to hear commentators suggest that an increase in imports reduces Canadian GDP. Is this true?

The Simplest Short-Run Macro Model

CHAPTER OUTLINE	LEARNING OBJECTIVES (LO)
	After studying this chapter you will be able to
21.1 DESIRED AGGREGATE EXPENDITURE	1 explain the difference between desired and actual expenditure. 2 identify the determinants of desired consumption and desired investment.
21.2 EQUILIBRIUM NATIONAL INCOME	3 understand the meaning of equilibrium national income.
21.3 CHANGES IN EQUILIBRIUM NATIONAL INCOME	4 explain how a change in desired expenditure affects equilibrium income through the "simple multiplier."

IN Chapters 19 and 20, we encountered a number of important macroeconomic variables. We considered how they are measured and how they have behaved over the past several decades. We now turn to a more detailed study of what *causes* these variables to behave as they do. In particular, we study the forces that determine real national income and the price level over short periods of time, say, up to a few years. We call this the *short run*.[1] In particular, in this chapter and the next two, we examine how the level of real GDP is determined and how it fluctuates around the level of potential GDP. For simplicity, we assume that potential GDP is constant; in later chapters we explore the long-run forces that explain the growth of potential GDP.

Real GDP and the price level are determined simultaneously. It is, however, easier to study them one at a time. So, in this chapter and the next, we simplify matters by seeing how real national income is determined *under the assumption that the price level is constant*. The simplified analysis is an important first step toward understanding how prices and GDP are determined together, which is the subject of Chapter 23.

Throughout this and later chapters, we will make many statements about what will happen as a result of some "shock" such as a change in household or firm behaviour or a change in government policy. In all such cases we are describing the predicted result in the model we are developing. Whether this predicted result also happens in reality depends on how well our model predicts real-world behaviour. This suggests two points. First, we would not waste time discussing our model of the economy if there was not ample reason to believe that it does to a significant extent predict the outcome of real-world events. Second, we must constantly keep in mind that our statements only apply formally to our model and that we need to be aware of the possibility that the model's ability to predict real-world behaviour may change over time.

Where do we begin? Our ability to explain the behaviour of real GDP depends on our understanding of what determines the amount that households and firms desire to spend. We therefore begin with an examination of their expenditure decisions.

---

[1] Readers who have studied microeconomics are familiar with a different concept of the short run. In microeconomics, the short run varies industry by industry and corresponds to the period of time for which there are one or more *fixed* factors of production. In macroeconomics, the short run refers to a period of time during which prices and wages have not fully adjusted to various shocks. We say much more about this adjustment process in later chapters.

21.1 Desired Aggregate Expenditure

In Chapter 20, we discussed how national income statisticians divide *actual* GDP into its expenditure components: consumption, investment, government purchases, and net exports. In this chapter and the next, we are concerned with a different concept. It is variously called *desired* or *planned* expenditure. Of course, most people would like to spend virtually unlimited amounts, if only they had the resources. Desired expenditure does not refer, however, to what people would like to do under imaginary circumstances; it refers to what people desire to spend out of the resources that they actually have. Recall from Chapter 20 that the *actual* values of the various categories of expenditure are indicated by C_a, I_a, G_a, and $(X_a - IM_a)$. Economists use the same letters without the subscript "*a*" to indicate the *desired* expenditure in the same categories: C, I, G, and $(X - IM)$.

Everyone makes expenditure decisions. Fortunately, it is unnecessary for our purposes to look at each of the millions of such individual decisions. Instead, it is sufficient to consider four main groups of decision makers: domestic households, firms, governments, and foreign purchasers of domestically produced commodities. The sum of their *desired* expenditures on domestically produced output is called **desired aggregate expenditure** (*AE*):

$$AE = C + I + G + (X - IM)$$

Desired expenditure need not equal actual expenditure, either in total or in any individual category. For example, firms might not plan to invest in inventory accumulation this year but might do so unintentionally if sales are unexpectedly low—the unsold goods that pile up on their shelves are undesired inventory accumulation. In this case, actual investment expenditure, I_a, will exceed desired investment expenditure, I.

National income accounts measure *actual* expenditures in each of the four expenditure categories. Our model of the macro economy also deals with *desired* expenditures in each of these four categories.

You may be wondering why the distinction between desired and actual expenditure is so important. The answer will become clear in the next section, where we discuss the concept of *equilibrium* national income, which involves the relationship between desired and actual expenditure. For now, however, the remainder of this section examines more fully the various components of desired expenditure.

Autonomous Versus Induced Expenditure. In what follows, it will be useful to distinguish between *autonomous* and *induced* expenditure. Components of aggregate expenditure that do *not* depend on national income are called **autonomous expenditures**. Autonomous expenditures can and do change, but such changes do not occur systematically in response to changes in national income. Components of aggregate expenditure that *do* change systematically in response to changes in national income are called **induced expenditures**. As we will see, the induced response of desired aggregate expenditure to a change in national income plays a key role in the determination of equilibrium national income.

desired aggregate expenditure (*AE*) The sum of desired or planned spending on domestic output by households, firms, governments, and foreigners.

autonomous expenditure Elements of expenditure that do not change systematically with national income.

induced expenditure Any component of expenditure that is systematically related to national income.

Important Simplifications. Our goal in this chapter is to develop the simplest possible model of national-income determination. We begin by making three simplifying assumptions:

- there is no trade with other countries—that is, the economy we are studying is a **closed economy**
- there is no government—and hence no taxes
- the price level is constant.

closed economy An economy that has no foreign trade in goods, services, or assets.

These extreme assumptions serve a vital purpose. As we will soon see, the presence of government and foreign trade is *not* essential to understanding the basic principles of national-income determination. By simplifying the model as much as possible, we are better able to understand its structure and therefore how more complex versions of the model work. In following chapters we will complicate our simple macro model by adding a government and international trade and then by removing the assumption of a fixed price level. The result will be a more complete and useful model of the macro economy.

Desired Consumption Expenditure

Recall from Chapter 20 that *disposable income* is the amount of income households receive after deducting what they pay in taxes and adding what they receive in transfers. In our simple model with no government and no taxation, disposable income, Y_D, is equal to national income, Y. We define **saving** as all disposable income that is not spent on consumption.

saving All disposable income that is not spent on consumption.

> By definition, there are only two possible uses of disposable income—consumption and saving. When the household decides how much to put to one use, it has automatically decided how much to put to the other use.

Figure 21-1 shows the time series for real per capita consumption and disposable income in Canada since 1981. It is clear that the two variables tend to move together over time, although the relationship is not exact. The vertical distance between the two lines is the amount of saving done by households, and the figure shows that household saving as a share of disposable income has been declining over this period. In the early 1980s, household saving was roughly 25 percent of disposable income, whereas by 2010 it was about 7 percent. What determines the amount of their disposable income that households decide to consume and the amount they decide to save? The factors that influence this decision are summarized in the *consumption function* and the *saving function*.

The Consumption Function The **consumption function** relates the total desired consumption expenditures of all households to the several factors that determine it. The key factors influencing desired consumption are assumed to be

consumption function The relationship between desired consumption expenditure and all the variables that determine it. In the simplest case, the relationship between desired consumption expenditure and disposable income.

- disposable income
- wealth
- interest rates
- expectations about the future

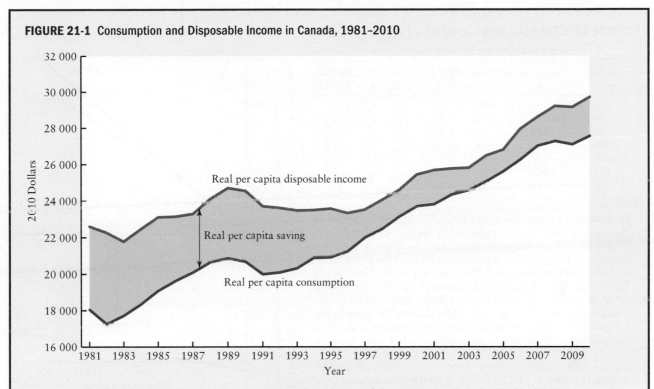

FIGURE 21-1 Consumption and Disposable Income in Canada, 1981–2010

Per capita consumption and disposable income move broadly together over time. The relationship between consumption and disposable income is not exact, but they clearly move broadly together. The vertical distance between the lines is household saving, which as a share of income has been declining since 1981.

(*Source:* Based on author's calculations using data from Statistics Canada, CANSIM database. Disposable income: Series V691566. Consumption expenditure: Series V691578. Population: Series V466668. Conversion from nominal to real values based on CPI: Series V41690973.)

In building our simple macro model, we emphasize the role of disposable income in influencing desired consumption; however, as we will see later, changes in the other variables are also important.

The assumption that desired consumption is related to disposable income is not surprising. As income rises, households naturally want to spend more, both now and in the future. For example, if a household's monthly disposable income permanently increases from $3000 to $3500, its monthly consumption will also increase, but probably by less than the full $500 increase. The remainder will be added to its monthly saving—assets that will accumulate and be available to finance future vacations, education, home purchases, or even retirement.

Holding constant other determinants of desired consumption, an increase in disposable income is assumed to lead to an increase in desired consumption.

The consumption function has an interesting history in economics. *Extensions in Theory 21-1* discusses consumption behaviour in two hypothetical households and

FIGURE 21-2 The Consumption and Saving Functions

Disposable Income (Y_D)	Desired Consumption (C)	Desired Saving (S)	$APC = C/Y_D$	ΔY_D	ΔC	$MPC = \Delta C/\Delta Y_D$
0	30	−30	—			
30	54	−24	1.80	30	24	0.8
150	150	0	1.00	120	96	0.8
300	270	30	0.90	150	120	0.8
450	390	60	0.87	150	120	0.8
525	450	75	0.86	75	60	0.8
600	510	90	0.85	75	60	0.8

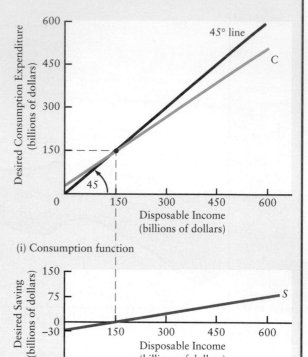

(i) Consumption function

(ii) Saving function

Both desired consumption and desired saving are assumed to rise as disposable income rises. Line C in part (i) of the figure relates desired consumption expenditure to disposable income by plotting the data from the second column of the accompanying table. The consumption function cuts the 45° line at the break-even level of disposable income. Note that the level of autonomous consumption is $30 billion; even with zero disposable income, consumers have this amount of desired consumption. The slope of the consumption function is equal to the marginal propensity to consume, which is shown in the table to be 0.8.

The relationship between desired saving and disposable income is shown in part (ii) by line S, which plots the data from the third column of the table. The vertical distance between C and the 45° line in part (i) is by definition the height of S in part (ii); that is, any given level of disposable income must be either consumed or saved. Note that the level of autonomous saving is −$30 billion.

illustrates a debate regarding the importance of *current* disposable income in determining consumption. As the discussion shows, however, our simple assumption that desired consumption is positively related to current disposable income is a good approximation of the behaviour of the *average* household and therefore is suitable for explaining aggregate behaviour.

Part (i) of Figure 21-2 illustrates a hypothetical consumption function. The first two columns of the table show the value of desired consumption (C) associated with each value of disposable income (Y_D). There is clearly a positive relationship. The figure plots these points and connects them with a smooth line. In this hypothetical economy, the equation of the consumption function is

$$C = 30 + 0.8Y_D$$

In words, this equation says that if disposable income is zero, desired aggregate consumption will be $30 billion, and that for every one-dollar increase in Y_D, desired consumption rises by 80 cents.

The $30 billion is said to be *autonomous* consumption because it is autonomous (or independent) of the level of income. Autonomous consumption is greater than zero because consumers are assumed to have some desired consumption even if there is no disposable income. The $0.8Y_D$ is called *induced* consumption because it is induced

EXTENSIONS IN THEORY 21-1

The Theory of the Consumption Function

Though it may seem natural to assume that a household's current consumption depends largely on its current disposable income, much debate and research has surrounded the issue of how to model consumption behaviour. To see what is involved, consider two quite different households.

The first household is short-sighted and spends everything it receives and puts nothing aside for the future. When some overtime work results in a large paycheque, the members of the household go out and spend it. When it is hard to find work, the household's paycheque is small and its members reduce their expenditures. This household's monthly expenditure is therefore exactly equal to its current monthly disposable income.

The second household is forward-looking. Its members think about the future as much as the present and make plans that stretch over their lifetimes. They put money aside for retirement and for the occasional rainy day when disposable income may fall temporarily. An unexpected windfall of income will be saved. An unexpected shortfall of income will be cushioned by spending some of the accumulated savings that were put aside for just such a rainy day. In short, this household's monthly expenditure will be closely related to the average monthly income it expects over its lifetime—the household's *permanent* income. Fluctuations in its current monthly income will have little effect on its current consumption expenditure. Economists refer to this behaviour as *consumption smoothing*.

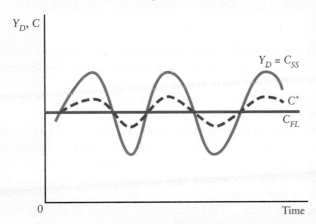

The figure shows the difference between our two sample households, short-sighted and forward-looking, and how their respective consumption expenditure is related to their current disposable income. We assume that disposable income, Y_D, fluctuates over time, as shown by the solid blue line. C_{SS} is the consumption path of the short-sighted household and is the same as the path of

disposable income. C_{FL} is the consumption path for the forward-looking household and is flat.

John Maynard Keynes (1883–1946), the famous English economist who developed much of the basic theory of macroeconomics, populated his theory with households whose current consumption expenditure depended mostly on their current income. But these households are not as extreme as the short-sighted households we just discussed. Keynes did not assume that households *never* saved. He simply assumed that their current level of expenditure and saving depended on their current level of income, as we do in this book. To this day, a consumption function based on this assumption is called a *Keynesian consumption function*.

In the 1950s, two U.S. economists, Franco Modigliani and Milton Friedman, both of whom were subsequently awarded Nobel Prizes in economics, analyzed the behaviour of forward-looking households. Their theories, which Modigliani called the *life-cycle theory* and Friedman called the *permanent-income theory*, explain some observed consumer behaviour that cannot be explained by the Keynesian consumption function.

The differences between the theories of Keynes, on the one hand, and Friedman and Modigliani on the other, are not as great as they might seem at first. To see why this is so, let us return to our two imaginary households.

Even the extremely short-sighted household may be able to do some consumption smoothing in the face of income fluctuations. Most households have some money in the bank and some ability to borrow, even if it is just from friends and relatives. As a result, every change in income need not be matched by an equal change in consumption expenditures.

In contrast, although the forward-looking household wants to smooth its pattern of consumption, it may not have the borrowing capacity to do so. Its bank may not be willing to lend money for consumption when the security consists of nothing more than the *expectation* that the household's income will be higher in later years. As a result, the household's consumption expenditure may fluctuate with its current income more than it would want.

The foregoing discussion suggests that the consumption expenditure of both types of households will fluctuate to some extent with their current disposable incomes and to some extent with their expectations of future disposable income. Moreover, in any economy there will be households of both types, and aggregate consumption will be determined by a mix of the two types. The consumption behaviour for the *average* household in such an economy is shown in the figure as the path C*. Consumption fluctuates in response to changes in disposable income, rising when income rises and falling when income falls.

(or brought about) by a change in income. In part (i) of Figure 21-2, the autonomous part of desired consumption is the vertical intercept of the consumption function. The induced part of consumption occurs as disposable income changes and we move along the consumption function.

We now go on to examine the properties of the consumption function in more detail.

Average and Marginal Propensities to Consume. To discuss the consumption function concisely, economists use two technical expressions.

average propensity to consume (APC) Desired consumption divided by the level of disposable income.

The **average propensity to consume (*APC*)** is the proportion of disposable income that households want to consume. It is equal to desired consumption expenditure divided by disposable income:

$$APC = C/Y_D$$

The fourth column of the table in Figure 21-2 shows the *APC* calculated from the data in the table. Note that with this consumption function the *APC* falls as disposable income rises.

marginal propensity to consume (MPC) The change in desired consumption divided by the change in disposable income that brought it about.

The **marginal propensity to consume (*MPC*)** relates the *change* in desired consumption to the *change* in disposable income that brought it about. *MPC* is the change in desired consumption divided by the change in disposable income:

$$MPC = \Delta C/\Delta Y_D$$

where the Greek letter Δ, delta, means "a change in." The last column of the table in Figure 21-2 shows the *MPC* that corresponds to the data in the table. Note that in this simple example, the *MPC* is constant and equal to 0.8. [28]

The Slope of the Consumption Function. The consumption function shown in Figure 21-2 has a slope of $\Delta C/\Delta Y_D$, which is, by definition, the marginal propensity to consume. The positive slope of the consumption function shows that the *MPC* is positive; increases in disposable income lead to increases in desired consumption expenditure. The *constant* slope of the consumption function shows that the *MPC* is the same at any level of disposable income.

The 45° Line. Figure 21-2(i) contains a line that is constructed by connecting all points where desired consumption (measured on the vertical axis) equals disposable income (measured on the horizontal axis). Because both axes are given in the same units, this line has a positive slope equal to 1; that is, it forms an angle of 45° with the axes. The line is therefore called the *45° line.*

The 45° line is a useful reference line. In part (i) of Figure 21-2, the consumption function cuts the 45° line at what is called the "break-even" level of income—in this example, at $150 billion. When disposable income is less than $150 billion, desired consumption exceeds disposable income. In this case, desired saving must be negative; households are financing their consumption either by spending out of their accumulated saving or by borrowing funds. When disposable income is greater than $150 billion, desired consumption is less than disposable income and so desired saving is positive; households are paying back debt or accumulating assets. At the break-even level of disposable income, desired consumption exactly equals disposable income and so desired saving is zero.

The Saving Function Households decide how much to consume and how much to save. As we have said, this is only a single decision—how to divide disposable income between consumption and saving. Therefore, once we know the relationship between desired consumption and disposable income, we automatically know the relationship between desired saving and disposable income.

There are two saving concepts that are exactly parallel to the consumption concepts of APC and MPC. The **average propensity to save (APS)** is the proportion of disposable income that households want to save, computed by dividing desired saving by disposable income:

$$APS = S/Y_D$$

The **marginal propensity to save (MPS)** relates the change in desired saving to the change in disposable income that brought it about:

$$MPS = \Delta S/\Delta Y_D$$

There is a simple relationship between the saving and the consumption propensities. APC and APS must sum to 1, and MPC and MPS must also sum to 1. Because all disposable income is either spent or saved, it follows that the fractions of income consumed and saved must account for all income (APC + APS = 1). It also follows that the fractions of any *increment* to income consumed and saved must account for all of that increment (MPC + MPS = 1). [29]

Look back at the table in Figure 21-2 and calculate APC and APS for yourself by computing C/Y_D and S/Y_D for each row in the table. You will notice that the sum of APC and APS is *always* 1. Similarly, calculate MPC and MPS by computing $\Delta C/\Delta Y_D$ and $\Delta S/\Delta Y_D$ for each row in the table. You will also notice that MPC and MPS *always* sum to 1.

Part (ii) of Figure 21-2 shows the saving function in our simple model. Notice that it is positively sloped, indicating that increases in disposable income are assumed to lead to an increase in desired saving. Note also that the amount of desired saving is always equal to the vertical distance between the consumption function and the 45° line. When desired consumption exceeds income, desired saving is negative; when desired consumption is less than income, desired saving is positive.

Shifts of the Consumption Function Earlier we said that desired consumption is assumed to depend on four things—disposable income, wealth, interest rates, and households' expectations about the future. In Figure 21-2, we illustrate the most important relationship—between desired consumption and disposable income (when the other determinants are held constant). In this diagram, changes in disposable income lead to *movements along* the consumption function. Changes in the other three factors will lead to *shifts of* the consumption function. Let's see why.

A Change in Household Wealth. Household wealth is the value of all accumulated assets minus accumulated debts. The most common types of household assets are savings accounts, mutual funds, portfolios of stocks or bonds, Registered Retirement Savings Plans (RRSPs), and the ownership of homes and cars. The most common household debts are home mortgages, car loans, and outstanding lines of credit from banks (including credit-card debt).

What happens to desired consumption if household wealth increases even while disposable income is unchanged? Suppose, for example, that a rising stock market (often called a "bull" market) leads to an increase in aggregate household wealth. To the extent that this increase in wealth is expected to persist, less current income needs

average propensity to save (APS) Desired saving divided by disposable income.

marginal propensity to save (MPS) The change in desired saving divided by the change in disposable income that brought it about.

FIGURE 21-3 Shifts in the Consumption Function

(i) The consumption function shifts upward with an increase in wealth, a decrease in interest rates, or an increase in optimism about the future

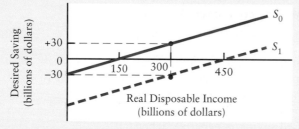

(ii) The saving function shifts downward with an increase in wealth, a decrease in interest rates, or an increase in optimism about the future

Changes in wealth, interest rates, or expectations about the future shift the consumption function. In part (i), line C_0 reproduces the consumption function from part (i) of Figure 21-2. The consumption function then shifts up by $60 billion, so with disposable income of $300 billion, for example, desired consumption rises from $270 billion to $330 billion.

The saving function in part (ii) shifts down by $60 billion, from S_0 to S_1. At a disposable income of $300 billion, for example, desired saving falls from $30 billion to −$30 billion.

to be saved for the future, and households will therefore tend to spend a larger fraction of their current income. The consumption function will shift up, and the saving function down, as shown in Figure 21-3. Current estimates based on research from the International Monetary Fund suggest that an increase in aggregate Canadian wealth of $1 billion leads to an increase in desired aggregate consumption of approximately $50 million.

> An increase in household wealth shifts the consumption function up at any level of disposable income; a decrease in wealth shifts the consumption function down.

A Change in Interest Rates. Household consumption can be divided into consumption of *durable* and *non-durable* goods. Durable goods are goods that deliver benefits for several years, such as cars and household appliances. Non-durable goods are consumption goods that deliver benefits to households for only short periods of time, such as groceries, restaurant meals, and clothing. Since many durable goods are also expensive, many of them are purchased on credit—that is, households borrow in order to finance their purchases.

The cost of borrowing, as we discussed in Chapter 19, is the interest rate. A fall in the interest rate reduces the cost of borrowing and generally leads to an increase in desired consumption expenditure, especially of durable goods. That is, for any given level of disposable income, a fall in the interest rate leads to an increase in desired consumption; the consumption function shifts up and the saving function shifts down, as shown in Figure 21-3.[2]

> A fall in interest rates usually leads to an increase in desired consumption at any level of disposable income; the consumption function shifts up. A rise in interest rates shifts the consumption function down.

A Change in Expectations. Households' expectations about the future are important in determining their desired consumption. Suppose, for example, that large numbers of

---

[2] This is the *substitution* effect of a reduction in the interest rate, which induces all consumers to spend more when the interest rate falls (and less when it rises). The *income* effect of a change in the interest rate works in the opposite direction for creditors and debtors. Since these income effects tend to cancel out in the aggregate economy, they are ignored here.

households become pessimistic about the future state of the economy and about their own employment prospects. In many cases, these fears will lead households to increase their current desired saving in anticipation of rough economic times ahead. But increasing their current saving implies a reduction in current consumption at any given level of disposable income. The result will be a downward shift in the consumption function.

The reverse also tends to be true. Favourable expectations about the future state of the economy will lead many households to increase their current desired consumption and reduce their current desired saving. The result will be an upward shift in the consumption function and a downward shift in the saving function, as shown in Figure 21-3.

Expectations about the future state of the economy often influence desired consumption. Optimism leads to an upward shift in the consumption function; pessimism leads to a downward shift in the consumption function.

Summary It is useful to summarize what we have learned so far about the consumption function. As you will soon see, it will play a crucial role in our simple model of national income determination. The main points are as follows:

1. Desired consumption is assumed to be positively related to disposable income. In a graph, this relationship is shown by the positive slope of the consumption function, which is equal to the marginal propensity to consume (*MPC*).

2. There are both *autonomous* and *induced* components of desired consumption. A movement along the consumption function shows changes in consumption induced by changes in disposable income. A shift of the consumption function shows autonomous changes in consumption.

3. An increase in household wealth, a fall in interest rates, or greater optimism about the future are all assumed to lead to an increase in desired consumption and thus an upward shift of the consumption function.

4. All disposable income is either consumed or saved. Therefore, there is a saving function associated with the consumption function. Any event that causes the consumption function to shift must also cause the saving function to shift by an equal amount in the opposite direction.

Desired Investment Expenditure

Our simple macroeconomic model has only consumption and investment. Having spent considerable time discussing desired consumption expenditure, we are now ready to examine the determinants of desired investment. Recall from Chapter 20 the three categories of investment:

- inventory accumulation
- residential construction
- new plant and equipment

Investment expenditure is the most volatile component of GDP, and changes in investment are strongly associated with aggregate economic fluctuations. As shown in Figure 21-4, total investment in Canada fluctuates around an average of about 20 percent of GDP. In each of the last three recessions (1982, 1991, and 2009), investment as a share of GDP fell by between three and five percentage points. In contrast, consumption, government purchases, and net exports are much smoother over the business cycle, each typically changing by less than one percentage point. An important part of our understanding of business cycles will therefore rely on our understanding of the fluctuations in investment.

What explains such fluctuations in investment? Here we examine three important determinants of aggregate investment expenditure:

- the real interest rate
- changes in the level of sales
- business confidence

Let's now examine these in turn.

Desired Investment and the Real Interest Rate The real interest rate represents the real opportunity cost of using money (either borrowed money or retained earnings) for investment purposes. A rise in the real interest rate therefore reduces the amount of desired investment expenditure. This relationship is most easily understood if we separate investment into its three components: inventories, residential construction, and new plant and equipment.

Inventories. Changes in inventories represent only a small percentage of private investment in a typical year. As shown by the bottom line in Figure 21-4, inventory investment has been between –2 percent and 2 percent of GDP over the past 30 years. (Inventory investment of –2 percent in a year means that inventories *fall* by 2 percent of GDP.) But the average

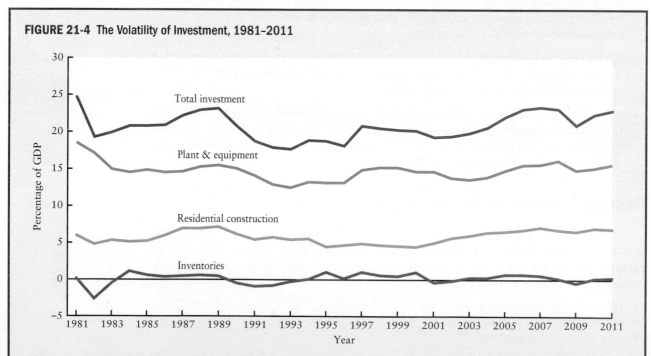

FIGURE 21-4 The Volatility of Investment, 1981–2011

The major components of investment fluctuate considerably as a share of GDP. The recessions of 1982, 1991, and 2009 are evident from the reductions in all components of investment.

(*Source:* Based on author's calculations using data from Statistics Canada's CANSIM database. Plant and Equipment: Table 380-0026. Residential Construction: Table 380-0025. Inventories: Table 380-0028. The measures are shown here as a fraction of current dollar GDP, Table 380-0017.)

amount of inventory investment is not an adequate measure of its importance. Since inventory investment is quite volatile, it has an important influence on fluctuations in investment expenditure.

When a firm ties up funds in inventories, those same funds cannot be used elsewhere to earn income. As an alternative to holding inventories, the firm could lend the money out at the going rate of interest. Hence, the higher the real rate of interest, the higher the opportunity cost of holding an inventory of a given size; the higher the opportunity cost, the smaller the inventories that will be desired.

Residential Construction. Expenditure on newly built residential housing is also volatile. Most houses are purchased with money that is borrowed by means of mortgages. Interest on the borrowed money typically accounts for more than one-half of the purchaser's annual mortgage payments; the remainder is repayment of the original loan, called the *principal*. Because interest payments are such a large part of mortgage payments, variations in interest rates exert a substantial effect on the demand for housing.

New Plant and Equipment. The real interest rate is also a major determinant of firms' investment in factories, equipment, and a whole range of durable capital goods that are used for production. When interest rates are high, it is expensive for firms to borrow funds that can be used to build new plants or purchase new capital equipment. Similarly, firms with cash on hand can earn high returns on interest-earning assets, again making investment in new capital a less attractive alternative. Thus, high real interest rates lead to a reduction in desired investment in capital equipment, whereas low real interest rates increase desired investment.

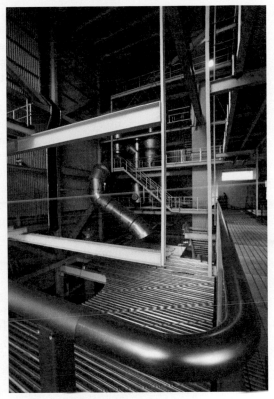

The largest part of investment by firms is in new plants and equipment, such as this expansion of a pulp mill in British Columbia.

> The real interest rate reflects the opportunity cost associated with investment, whether it is investment in inventories, residential construction, or new plant and equipment. The higher the real interest rate, the higher the opportunity cost of investment and thus the lower the amount of desired investment.

Desired Investment and Changes in Sales Firms hold inventories to meet unexpected changes in sales and production, and they usually have a target level of inventories that depends on their normal level of sales. Because the size of inventories is related to the level of sales, the *change* in inventories (which is part of current investment) is related to the *change* in the level of sales.

For example, suppose a firm wants to hold inventories equal to 10 percent of its monthly sales. If normal monthly sales are $100 000, it will want to hold inventories valued at $10 000. If monthly sales increase to $110 000, it will want to increase its inventories to $11 000. Over the period during which its stock of inventories is being increased, there will be a total of $1000 of new inventory investment.

> The higher the level of sales, the larger the desired stock of inventories. Changes in the rate of sales therefore cause temporary bouts of investment (or disinvestment) in inventories.

Changes in sales have similar effects on investment in plant and equipment. For example, if there is a general increase in consumers' demand for products that is expected to persist and that cannot be met by existing capacity, investment in new plant and equipment will be needed. Once the new plants have been built and put into operation, however, the rate of new investment will fall.

Desired Investment and Business Confidence Investment takes time. When a firm invests, it increases its future capacity to produce output. If it can sell the new output profitably, the investment will prove to be a good one. If the new output does not generate profits, the investment will have been a bad one. When it undertakes an investment, the firm does not know if it will turn out well or badly—it is betting on a favourable future that cannot be known with certainty.

When firms expect good times ahead, they will want to invest now so that they have a larger productive capacity in the future ready to satisfy the greater demand. When they expect bad times ahead, they will not invest because they expect no payoff from doing so.

The Conference Board of Canada publishes regular surveys of business and consumer confidence. Visit its website:
www.conferenceboard.ca.

Investment depends on firms' expectations about the future state of the economy. Optimism about the future leads to more desired investment; pessimism leads to less desired investment.

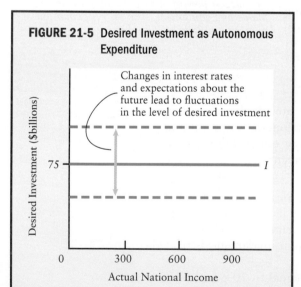

FIGURE 21-5 Desired Investment as Autonomous Expenditure

In this simple macro model, desired investment is assumed to be autonomous with respect to current national income. In this example, the level of desired investment is $75 billion. However, changes in interest rates or business confidence will lead to upward or downward shifts in the investment function.

Desired Investment as Autonomous Expenditure We have seen that desired investment is influenced by many things, and a complete discussion of the determination of national income is not possible without including all of these factors.

For the moment, however, our goal is to build the *simplest* model of the aggregate economy in which we can examine the interaction of actual national income and desired aggregate expenditure. To build this simple model, we begin by treating desired investment as *autonomous*—that is, we assume it to be unaffected by changes in national income. Figure 21-5 shows the investment function as a horizontal line.

It is important not to confuse the assumption that desired investment is *autonomous* with respect to national income (which we are making) with the assumption that it is *constant* (which we are not making). As we have said, investment is the most volatile component of aggregate expenditure, and it will therefore be important in our model that investment be able to change; shocks to firms' investment behaviour (upward or downward shifts in the investment function) will end up being an important explanation for fluctuations in national income. Our assumption that investment is autonomous with respect to national income (and hence the *I* function in Figure 21-5 is horizontal) is mainly a simplifying one. But the assumption does reflect the fact that investment is an act undertaken by firms for *future* benefit, and thus the *current* level of GDP is unlikely to have a significant effect on desired investment.

The Aggregate Expenditure Function

The **aggregate expenditure (AE) function** relates the level of desired aggregate expenditure to the level of actual national income. (In both cases we mean *real* as opposed to *nominal* variables.) In the simplified economy of this chapter without government and international trade, there is no G or $(X - IM)$ in our function. Desired aggregate expenditure is thus equal to desired consumption plus desired investment, $C + I$.

$$AE = C + I$$

aggregate expenditure (AE) function The function that relates desired aggregate expenditure to actual national income.

The table in Figure 21-6 shows how the *AE* function can be calculated, given the consumption function from Figure 21-2 on page 522 and the investment function from Figure 21-5 on page 530. The *AE* function is constructed by vertically summing the *C* function and the *I* function, thus showing desired total spending at each level of national income. In this specific case, all of desired investment expenditure is autonomous, as is the $30 billion of consumption that would be desired if national income were equal to zero. Total autonomous expenditure is therefore $105 billion—induced expenditure is just equal to induced consumption, which is equal to the *MPC* times disposable income ($0.8 \times Y_D$). Furthermore, since our simple model has no government and no taxes, disposable income, Y_D, is equal to national income, Y. Hence, desired aggregate expenditure can be written as

$$AE = \$105 \text{ billion} + (0.8)Y$$

The Marginal Propensity to Spend The fraction of any increment to national income that people spend on purchasing domestic output is called the economy's **marginal propensity to spend**. The marginal propensity to spend is measured by the change in desired aggregate expenditure divided by the change in national income that brings it about, or $\Delta AE/\Delta Y$. This is the slope of the aggregate expenditure function. In this book, the marginal propensity to spend is denoted by the symbol z, which is a number greater than zero and less than 1. For the example given in Figure 21-6, the marginal propensity to spend is 0.8. If national income increases by a dollar, 80 cents will go into increased desired (consumption) expenditure; 20 cents will go into increased desired saving. The marginal propensity to spend should not be confused with the marginal propensity to consume.

marginal propensity to spend The change in desired aggregate expenditure on domestic output divided by the change in national income that brought it about.

The marginal propensity to spend is the amount of extra total expenditure induced when national income rises by $1, whereas the marginal propensity to consume is the amount of extra consumption expenditure induced when households' disposable income rises by $1.

In the simple model of this chapter, however, the marginal propensity to spend is equal to the marginal propensity to consume because consumption is the only kind of expenditure that is assumed to vary with national income. In later chapters, when we add government and international trade to the model, the marginal propensity

FIGURE 21-6 The Aggregate Expenditure Function

National Income (Y)	Desired Consumption Expenditure (C = 30 + 0.8 × Y)	Desired Investment Expenditure (I = 75)	Expenditure (AE = C + I)
30	54	75	129
150	150	75	225
300	270	75	345
450	390	75	465
525	450	75	525
600	510	75	585
900	750	75	825

The aggregate expenditure function relates desired aggregate expenditure to actual national income. The curve AE in the figure plots the data from the first and last columns of the accompanying table. Its intercept, which in this case is $105 billion, shows the sum of autonomous consumption and autonomous investment. The slope of AE is equal to the marginal propensity to spend, which in this simple economy is just the marginal propensity to consume.

to spend will differ from the marginal propensity to consume. Both here and in later chapters, it is the more general measure—the marginal propensity to spend—that is important for determining equilibrium national income.

21.2 Equilibrium National Income

We have constructed an *AE* function that combines the spending plans of households and firms. The function shows, for any given level of *actual* national income, the level of *desired* aggregate spending. We are now ready to see what determines the *equilibrium* level of national income. When something is in equilibrium, there is no tendency for it to change. Any conditions that are required for something to be in equilibrium are called *equilibrium conditions*. We will see that the distinction between desired and actual expenditure is central to understanding the equilibrium conditions for national income.

In this chapter and the next, we make an important assumption that influences the nature of equilibrium. In particular, we assume that firms are able and willing to produce any amount of output that is demanded of them and that changes in their production levels do not require a change in their product prices. In this setting, we say that output is *demand determined*. This is an extreme assumption, and we will relax it in Chapter 23. Until then, however, it is a very useful assumption that allows us to more easily understand how our macro model works.

Table 21-1 illustrates the determination of equilibrium national income for our simple model economy. Suppose firms are producing a final output of $300 billion, and thus *actual* national income is $300 billion. According to the table, at this level of actual national income, *desired* aggregate expenditure is $345 billion. If firms persist in producing a current output of only $300 billion in the face of desired aggregate expenditure of $345 billion, one of two things will happen.

One possibility is that households and firms will be unable to spend the extra $45 billion that they would like to spend, so lines or waiting lists of unsatisfied customers will appear. These shortages will send a signal to firms that they could increase their sales if they increased their production. When the firms do increase their production, actual national income rises. Of course, the individual firms are interested only in their own sales and profits, but their individual actions have as their inevitable consequence an increase in GDP.

A more realistic possibility is that all spenders will spend everything that they wanted to spend and there will be no lineups of unsatisfied customers. Since desired expenditure exceeds the actual amount of output, this is possible only if some sales come from the producers' accumulated inventories. In our example, the fulfillment of plans to purchase $345 billion worth of goods in the face of a current output of only $300 billion will reduce inventories by $45 billion. As long as inventories last, more goods can be sold than are currently being produced. But since firms want to maintain a certain level of inventories, they will eventually increase their production. Once again, the consequence of each individual firm's decision to increase production is an increase in actual national income. Thus, the final response to an excess of desired aggregate expenditure over actual output is a rise in national income.

Actual National Income (Y)	Desired Aggregate Expenditure (AE = C + I)	Effect
30	129 ⎫	Inventories are falling;
150	225 ⎪	firms increase output
300	345 ⎬	
450	465 ⎭	
525	525	Equilibrium income
600	585 ⎫	Inventories are rising;
900	825 ⎭	firms reduce output

TABLE 21-1 Equilibrium National Income

National income is in equilibrium when desired aggregate expenditure equals actual national income. The data are from Figure 21-6.

For any level of national income at which desired aggregate expenditure exceeds actual income, there will be pressure for actual national income to rise.

Next consider the $900 billion level of actual national income in Table 21-1. At this level of output, desired expenditure on domestically produced goods is only $825 billion. If firms persist in producing $900 billion worth of goods, $75 billion worth must remain unsold. Therefore, inventories must rise. However, firms will not allow inventories of unsold goods to rise indefinitely; sooner or later, they will reduce the level of output to the level of sales. When they reduce their level of output, national income will fall.

For any level of income at which desired aggregate expenditure is less than actual income, there will be pressure for national income to fall.

Changes in firms' accumulated inventories often signal changes in desired aggregate expenditure and eventually induce firms to change their production decisions.

Finally, look at the national income level of $525 billion in Table 21-1. At this level, and only at this level, desired aggregate expenditure is equal to actual national income. Purchasers can fulfill their spending plans without causing inventories to change. There is no incentive for firms to alter output. Because everyone wants to purchase an amount equal to what is actually being produced, output and income will remain steady; they are in equilibrium.

> The equilibrium level of national income occurs where desired aggregate expenditure equals actual national income.

In other words, the *equilibrium condition* for our simple model of national income determination is

$$AE = Y$$

As we will now see, the combination of our AE function and this condition will determine the equilibrium level of national income.

Consider Figure 21-7. The line labelled AE graphs the specific aggregate expenditure function that we have been working with throughout this chapter. The 45° line ($AE = Y$) graphs the equilibrium condition that desired aggregate expenditure equals actual national income. Anywhere along the 45° line, the value of desired aggregate expenditure, which is measured on the vertical axis, is equal to the value of actual national income, which is measured on the horizontal axis.

Graphically, equilibrium occurs at the level of income at which the AE line intersects the 45° line. This is the level of income at which desired aggregate expenditure is just equal to actual national income. In Figure 21-7, the equilibrium level of national income (real GDP) is Y_0.

To understand how Figure 21-7 illustrates economic behaviour, consider some level of real GDP below Y_0. At this level of income, the AE curve lies above the 45° line, indicating that desired spending exceeds actual output. The vertical distance between AE and the 45° line reflects the size of this excess demand. As we said earlier, this excess demand will induce firms to increase their production. Conversely, at any level of GDP above Y_0, the AE curve is below the 45° line, indicating that desired spending is less than actual output. The vertical distance between the curves in this case shows the size of the excess supply, which will induce firms to reduce their production. Only when real GDP equals Y_0 is desired spending equal to actual output, thus providing firms with no incentive to change their production.

Now that we have explained the meaning of equilibrium national income, we will go on to examine the various forces that can *change* this equilibrium. We will then be well on our way to understanding some of the sources of short-run fluctuations in real GDP.

FIGURE 21-7 Equilibrium National Income

Equilibrium national income is that level of national income where desired aggregate expenditure equals actual national income. If actual national income is below Y_0, desired aggregate expenditure will exceed national income, and output will rise. If actual national income is above Y_0, desired aggregate expenditure will be less than national income, and production will fall. Only when national income is equal to Y_0 will the economy be in equilibrium, as shown at E_0.

21.3 Changes in Equilibrium National Income

Figure 21-7 shows that the equilibrium level of national income occurs where the AE function intersects the 45° line. Through the adjustment in firms' inventories and production levels, the level of actual national income will adjust until this equilibrium level is achieved. Because the AE function plays a central role in determining equilibrium national income, you should not be surprised to hear that *shifts* in the AE function are central to explaining why the equilibrium level of national income changes.

Shifts of the *AE* Function

The AE function shifts when one of its components shifts—that is, when there is a shift in the consumption function or in the investment function. As we have already mentioned, both the consumption function and the investment function will shift if there is a change in interest rates or expectations of the future state of the economy. A change in household wealth is an additional reason for the consumption function to shift. Let's now consider what happens when there is an upward shift in the AE function.

Upward Shifts in the *AE* Function Suppose households experience an increase in wealth and thus increase their desired consumption spending at each level of disposable income. Or suppose firms' expectations of higher future sales lead them to increase their planned investment. What is the effect of such events on national income?

Because any increase in autonomous expenditure shifts the entire AE function upward, the same analysis applies to each of the changes mentioned. Two types of shifts in AE can occur. First, if the same addition to expenditure occurs at all levels of income, the AE function shifts parallel to itself, as shown in part (i) of Figure 21-8. Second, if there is a change in the marginal propensity to spend, the slope of the AE function changes, as shown in part (ii) of Figure 21-8.

Figure 21-8 shows that an upward shift in the AE function increases equilibrium national income. After the shift in the AE curve, income is no longer in equilibrium at its original level because at that level desired aggregate expenditure exceeds actual national income. Given this excess demand, firms' inventories are being depleted and firms respond by increasing production. Equilibrium national income rises to the higher level indicated by the intersection of the *new* AE curve with the 45° line.

Downward Shifts in the *AE* Function What happens to national income if there is a decrease in the amount of consumption or investment expenditure desired at each level of income? These changes shift the AE function downward, as shown in Figure 21-8 by the movement from the dashed AE curve to the solid AE curve. An equal reduction in desired expenditure at all levels of income shifts AE parallel to itself. A fall in the marginal propensity to spend out of national income reduces the slope of the AE function. In both cases, the equilibrium level of national income decreases; the new equilibrium is found at the intersection of the 45° line and the *new* AE curve.

FIGURE 21-8 Shifts in the Aggregate Expenditure Function

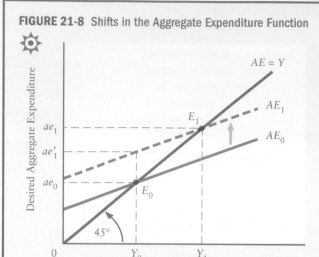

(i) A parallel shift in AE

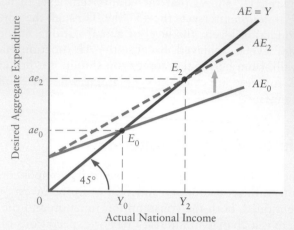

(ii) A change in the slope of AE

Upward shifts in the AE function increase equilibrium income; downward shifts decrease equilibrium income. In parts (i) and (ii), the AE function is initially AE_0 with equilibrium national income equal to Y_0.

In part (i), a parallel upward shift in the AE curve from AE_0 to AE_1 reflects an increase in desired expenditure at each level of national income. For example, at Y_0, desired expenditure rises from ae_0 to ae'_1 and therefore exceeds actual national income. Equilibrium is reached at E_1, where income is Y_1. The increase in desired expenditure from ae'_1 to ae_1, represented by a movement along AE_1, is an induced response to the increase in income from Y_0 to Y_1.

In part (ii), a non-parallel upward shift in the AE curve from AE_0 to AE_2 reflects an increase in the marginal propensity to spend. This leads to an increase in equilibrium national income. Equilibrium is reached at E_2, where national income is equal to Y_2.

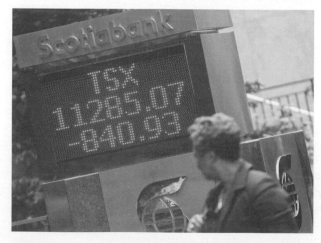

Changes in household wealth, such as those created by large and persistent swings in stock-market values, are predicted to lead to changes in households' desired consumption expenditure, thus changing the equilibrium level of national income.

The Results Restated We have derived two important general propositions from our simple model of national income determination:

1. A rise in the amount of desired aggregate expenditure at each level of national income will shift the AE curve upward and increase equilibrium national income.

2. A fall in the amount of desired aggregate expenditure at each level of national income will shift the AE curve downward and reduce equilibrium national income.

In addition, part (ii) of Figure 21-8 suggests a third general proposition regarding the effect of a change in the *slope* of the AE function:

3. An increase in the marginal propensity to spend, z, steepens the AE curve and increases equilibrium national income. Conversely, a decrease in the marginal propensity to spend flattens the AE curve and decreases equilibrium national income.

The Multiplier

We have learned how specific changes in the *AE* function cause equilibrium national income to rise or fall. We would now like to understand what determines the *size* of these changes. A measure of the magnitude of such changes is provided by the *multiplier*. A change in autonomous expenditure increases equilibrium national income by a *multiple* of the initial change in autonomous expenditure. That is, the change in national income is *larger than* the initial change in desired expenditure.

> The multiplier is the change in equilibrium national income divided by the change in autonomous expenditure that brought it about. In the simple macro model, the multiplier is greater than 1.[3]

To see why the multiplier is greater than 1 in this model, consider a simple example. Imagine what would happen to national income if Kimberley-Clark decided to spend an additional $500 million per year on the construction of new paper mills. Initially, the construction of the paper mills would create $500 million worth of new national income and a corresponding amount of income for households and firms who produce the goods and services on which the initial $500 million is spent. But this is not the end of the story. The increase in national income of $500 million would cause an induced increase in desired consumption.

FIGURE 21-9 The Simple Multiplier

An increase in autonomous aggregate expenditure increases equilibrium national income by a multiple of the initial increase. The initial equilibrium is at E_0, where AE_0 intersects the 45° line. At this point, desired aggregate expenditure, ae_0, is equal to actual national income, Y_0. An increase in autonomous expenditure of ΔA then shifts the AE function upward to AE_1.

Equilibrium occurs when income rises to Y_1. Here desired expenditure, ae_1, equals national income, Y_1. The increase in desired expenditure from ae_1' to ae_1 represents the induced increase in expenditure that occurs as national income rises. Because ΔY is greater than ΔA, the simple multiplier is greater than 1 ($\Delta Y / \Delta A > 1$).

With our theory of the consumption function, electricians, masons, carpenters, and others—who gain new income directly from the building of the paper mills—will spend some of it on food, clothing, entertainment, cars, TVs, and other commodities. When output expands to meet this demand, new incomes will be created for workers and firms in the industries that produce these goods and services. When they, in turn, spend their newly earned incomes, output will rise further. More income will be created, and more expenditure will be induced. Indeed, at this stage, we might wonder whether the increases in income will ever come to an end. To deal with this concern, we need to consider the multiplier in somewhat more precise terms.

Let autonomous expenditure be denoted by *A*. Now consider an increase in autonomous expenditure of ΔA, which in our example is $500 million per year. Remember that ΔA stands for any increase in autonomous expenditure; this could be an increase

---

[3] In this chapter and the next, we assume that firms can readily change their output in response to changes in demand (perhaps because there is some unemployed labour and capital). This assumption of *demand-determined output* is central to the result of a multiplier being greater than 1. We relax this assumption in later chapters.

in investment or in the autonomous component of consumption. The *AE* function shifts upward by ΔA. National income is no longer in equilibrium because desired aggregate expenditure now exceeds actual national income. Equilibrium is restored by a *movement along* the new *AE* curve.

simple multiplier The ratio of the change in equilibrium national income to the change in autonomous expenditure that brought it about, calculated for a constant price level.

The **simple multiplier** measures the change in equilibrium national income that occurs in response to a change in autonomous expenditure when the price level is constant (reflecting the assumption that output is demand determined). We refer to it as "simple" because we have simplified the situation by assuming that the price level is fixed (an assumption we will remove in Chapter 23). Figure 21-9 illustrates the simple multiplier and makes clear that it is greater than 1. *Applying Economic Concepts 21-1* provides a numerical example.

The Size of the Simple Multiplier The size of the simple multiplier depends on the slope of the *AE* function—that is, on the marginal propensity to spend, *z*.

As shown in Figure 21-10, a high marginal propensity to spend means a steep *AE* curve. The expenditure induced by any initial increase in income is large, with the result that the final rise in income is correspondingly large. By contrast, a low marginal propensity to spend means a relatively flat *AE* curve. The expenditure induced by the initial increase in income is small, and the final rise in income is not much larger than the initial rise in autonomous expenditure that brought it about.

APPLYING ECONOMIC CONCEPTS 21-1

The Simple Multiplier: A Numerical Example

Consider an economy that has a marginal propensity to spend out of national income of 0.80. Suppose an increase in business confidence leads many firms to increase their investment in new capital equipment. Specifically, suppose desired investment increases by $1 billion per year. National income initially rises by $1 billion, but that is not the end of it. The factors of production that received the first $1 billion spend $800 million. This second round of spending generates $800 million of new production and income. This new income, in turn, induces $640 million of third-round spending, and so it continues, with each successive round of new production and income generating 80 percent as much in new expenditure. Each additional round of expenditure creates new production and income and yet another round of expenditure.

The table carries the process through 10 rounds. Students with sufficient patience (and no faith in mathematics) may compute as many rounds in the process as they want; they will find that the sum of the rounds of expenditures approaches a limit of $5 billion, which is five times the initial increase in expenditure. [30]

Notice that most of the total change in national income occurs in the first few rounds. Of the total change

of $5 billion, 68 percent ($3.4 billion) occurs after only five rounds of activity. By the end of the tenth round, 89 percent ($4.5 billion) of the total change has taken place.

Round of Spending	Increase in Expenditure	Cumulative Total
	(millions of dollars)	
1 (initial increase)	1000.0	1000.0
2	800.0	1800.0
3	640.0	2440.0
4	512.0	2952.0
5	409.6	3361.6
6	327.7	3689.3
7	262.1	3951.4
8	209.7	4161.1
9	167.8	4328.9
10	134.2	4463.1
11 to 20 combined	479.3	4942.4
All others	57.6	5000.0

FIGURE 21-10 The Size of the Simple Multiplier ☼

(i) Flat *AE*, multiplier equal to 1   (ii) Intermediate case   (iii) Steep *AE*, multiplier large

The larger the marginal propensity to spend out of national income (z), the steeper is the *AE* curve and the larger is the simple multiplier. In each part of the figure, the initial *AE* function is AE_0, equilibrium is at E_0, with income Y_0. The *AE* curve then shifts upward to AE_1 as a result of an increase in autonomous expenditure of ΔA. ΔA is the same in each part. The new equilibrium in each case is at E_1.

In part (i), the *AE* function is horizontal, indicating a marginal propensity to spend of zero ($z = 0$). The change in equilibrium income ΔY is only the increase in autonomous expenditure because there is no induced expenditure by the people who receive the initial increase in income. The simple multiplier is then equal to 1, its minimum possible value.

In part (ii), the *AE* curve slopes upward but is still relatively flat (z is low). The increase in equilibrium national income to Y_2 is only slightly greater than the increase in autonomous expenditure that brought it about. The simple multiplier is slightly greater than 1.

In part (iii), the *AE* function is quite steep (z is high). Now the increase in equilibrium income to Y_3 is much larger than the increase in autonomous expenditure that brought it about. The simple multiplier is much larger than 1.

> **The larger the marginal propensity to spend, the steeper the *AE* function and thus the larger the simple multiplier.**

We can derive the precise value of the simple multiplier by using elementary algebra. (The formal derivation is given in *Extensions in Theory 21-2*.) The result is

$$\text{Simple multiplier} = \frac{\Delta Y}{\Delta A} = \frac{1}{1 - z}$$

For the simple model we have developed in this chapter, $z = 0.8$ and so the simple multiplier $= 1/(1 - 0.8) = 1/0.2 = 5$. In this model, therefore, a \$1 billion increase in autonomous expenditure leads to a \$5 billion increase in equilibrium national income.

Recall that z is the marginal propensity to spend out of national income and is between zero and 1. The smallest simple multiplier occurs when z equals zero. In this case, $(1 - z)$ equals 1 and so the multiplier equals 1. On the other hand, if z is very close to 1, $(1 - z)$ is close to zero and so the multiplier becomes very large. The relationship between the slope of the *AE* function (z) and the size of the multiplier is shown in Figure 21-10.

The Algebra of the Simple Multiplier

Basic algebra is all that is needed to derive the exact expression for the simple multiplier. First, we derive the equation for the *AE* curve. Desired aggregate expenditure comprises autonomous expenditure and induced expenditure. In the simple model of this chapter, autonomous expenditure is equal to investment plus autonomous consumption. Induced expenditure is equal to induced consumption. Hence, we can write

$$AE = zY + A \qquad [1]$$

where *A* is autonomous expenditure and *zY* is induced expenditure, *z* being the marginal propensity to spend out of national income.

Now we write the equation of the 45° line,

$$AE = Y \qquad [2]$$

which states the equilibrium condition that desired aggregate expenditure equals actual national income. Equation 1 and 2 are two equations with two unknowns, *AE* and *Y*. To solve them, we substitute Equation 1 into Equation 2 to obtain

$$Y = zY + A \qquad [3]$$

Equation 3 can be easily solved to get *Y* expressed in terms of *A* and *z*. The solution is

$$Y = \frac{A}{1 - z} \qquad [4]$$

Equation 4 tells us the equilibrium value of *Y* in terms of autonomous expenditures and the marginal propensity to spend out of national income. Now consider a \$1 increase in *A*. The expression $Y = A/(1 - z)$ tells us that if *A* changes by one dollar, the resulting change in *Y* will be $1/(1 - z)$ dollars. Generally, for a change in autonomous spending of *A*, the resulting change in *Y* will be

$$\Delta Y = \frac{\Delta A}{1 - z} \qquad [5]$$

Dividing through by ΔA gives the value of the multiplier:

$$\text{Simple multiplier} = \frac{\Delta Y}{\Delta A} = \frac{1}{1 - z} \qquad [6]$$

Economic Fluctuations as Self-Fulfilling Prophecies

Expectations about the future play an important role in macroeconomics. We said earlier that households' and firms' expectations about the future state of the economy influence desired consumption and desired investment. But as we have just seen, changes in desired aggregate expenditure will, through the multiplier process, lead to changes in national income. This link between expectations and national income suggests that expectations about a healthy economy can actually produce a healthy economy—what economists call a *self-fulfilling prophecy*.

Imagine a situation in which many firms begin to feel optimistic about future economic prospects. This optimism may lead them to increase their desired investment, thus shifting up the economy's *AE* function. As we have seen, however, any upward shift in the *AE* function will lead to an increase in national income. Such "good" economic times will then be seen by firms to have justified their initial optimism. Many firms in such a situation may take pride in their ability to predict the future—but this would be misplaced pride. The truth of the matter is that if enough firms are optimistic and take actions based on that optimism, their actions will *create* the economic situation that they expected.

Now imagine the opposite situation, in which many firms begin to feel pessimistic about future economic conditions. This pessimism may lead them to scale down or cancel planned investment projects. Such a decline in planned investment would shift the *AE* function down and lead to a decrease in national income. The "bad" economic times will then be seen by the firms as justification for their initial pessimism, and many will take pride in their predictive powers. But again their pride would be misplaced; the truth is that sufficient pessimism on the part of firms will tend to *create* the conditions that they expected.

The aggregate consequences of pessimism on the part of both firms and consumers were an important contributing factor to the global recession that started in late 2008. In many countries, including Canada, the events surrounding the financial crisis of 2008–2009 led to a shattering of economic optimism. Measures of business and consumer confidence fell by more than had been observed in decades, and this decline in confidence partly explained the large declines in investment and household consumption that occurred at the time and lasted for more than a year. As we will see in later chapters, governments took actions to replace this drop in private-sector demand with increases in government spending.

SUMMARY

21.1 Desired Aggregate Expenditure

LO 1, 2

- Desired aggregate expenditure (*AE*) is equal to desired consumption plus desired investment plus desired government purchases plus desired net exports. It is the amount that economic agents want to spend on purchasing the national product.

$$AE = C + I + G + (X - IM)$$

- The relationship between disposable income and desired consumption is called the consumption function. The constant term in the consumption function is autonomous expenditure. The part of consumption that responds to income is called induced expenditure.
- A change in disposable income leads to a change in desired consumption and desired saving. The responsiveness of

these changes is measured by the marginal propensity to consume (*MPC*) and the marginal propensity to save (*MPS*), both of which are positive and sum to 1, indicating that all disposable income is either consumed or saved.

- Changes in wealth, interest rates, or expectations about the future lead to a change in autonomous consumption. As a result, the consumption function shifts.
- Firms' desired investment depends, among other things, on real interest rates, changes in sales, and business confidence. In our simplest model of the economy, investment is treated as autonomous with respect to changes in national income.

21.2 Equilibrium National Income

LO 3

- Equilibrium national income is defined as that level of national income at which desired aggregate expenditure equals actual national income. At incomes above equilibrium, desired expenditure is less than national income. In this case, inventories accumulate and firms will eventually reduce output. At incomes below equilibrium, desired expenditure exceeds national income. In

this case, inventories are depleted and firms will eventually increase output.

- Equilibrium national income is represented graphically by the point at which the aggregate expenditure (*AE*) curve cuts the 45° line—that is, where desired aggregate expenditure equals actual national income.

21.3 Changes in Equilibrium National Income LO 4

- Equilibrium national income is increased by a rise in either autonomous consumption or autonomous investment expenditure. Equilibrium national income is reduced by a fall in these desired expenditures.
- The magnitude of the effect on national income of shifts in autonomous expenditure is given by the multiplier. It is defined as $\Delta Y/\Delta A$, where ΔA is the change in autonomous expenditure.
- The simple multiplier is the multiplier when the price level is constant. The simple multiplier $= \Delta Y/\Delta A = 1/(1 - z)$, where z is the marginal propensity to spend

out of national income. The larger is z, the larger is the simple multiplier.
- It is a basic prediction of our simple macro model that the simple multiplier is greater than 1.
- Expectations play an important role in the determination of national income. Optimism can lead households and firms to increase desired expenditure, which, through the multiplier process, leads to increases in national income. Pessimism can similarly lead to decreases in desired expenditure and national income.

KEY CONCEPTS

Desired versus actual expenditure
The consumption function
Average and marginal propensities to consume
Average and marginal propensities to save

The aggregate expenditure (AE) function
Marginal propensity to spend
Equilibrium national income
Effect on national income of shifts in the AE curve

The simple multiplier
The size of the multiplier and slope of the AE curve

STUDY EXERCISES

MyEconLab Make the grade with MyEconLab: Study Exercises marked in red can be found on MyEconLab. You can practise them as often as you want, and most feature step-by-step guided instructions to help you find the right answer.

1. Fill in the blanks to make the following statements correct.
   a. The equation for *actual* national income from the expenditure side is written as GDP = _____.
   b. The equation for *desired* aggregate expenditure is written as AE = _____.
   c. National income accounts measure _____ expenditures in four broad categories. National income theory deals with _____ expenditure in the same four categories.
   d. The equation for a simple consumption function is written as $C = a + bY$. The letter a represents the _____ part of consumption. The letters bY represent the _____ part of consumption. When graphing a consumption function, the vertical intercept is given by the letter _____, and the slope of the function is given by the letter _____.

   e. In the simple macro model of this chapter, all investment is treated as _____ expenditure, meaning that it is unaffected by changes in national income.
   f. The aggregate expenditure function in the simple macro model of this chapter is written as AE = _____ and is graphed with _____ on the vertical axis and _____ on the horizontal axis.
   g. An example of an aggregate expenditure function is $AE = \$47$ billion $+ 0.92Y$. Autonomous expenditure is _____ and the marginal propensity to spend out of national income is _____. In the simple model in this chapter, the marginal propensity to spend is the same as the marginal propensity to consume because _____.

2. Fill in the blanks to make the following statements correct.

   a. If actual national income is $200 billion and desired aggregate expenditure is $180 billion, inventories may begin to _____, firms will _____ the level of output, and national income will _____.

   b. If actual national income is $200 billion and desired aggregate expenditure is $214 billion, inventories may begin to _____, firms will _____ the level of output, and national income will _____.

   c. If households experience an increase in wealth that leads to an increase in desired consumption, the AE curve will shift _____. Equilibrium national income will _____ to the level indicated by the intersection of the AE curve with the _____ line.

   d. When autonomous desired expenditure increases by $10 billion, national income will increase by _____ than $10 billion. The magnitude of the change in national income is measured by the _____.

   e. The larger is the marginal propensity to spend, the _____ is the multiplier. Where z is the marginal propensity to spend, the multiplier is equal to _____.

3. Consider the following table showing aggregate consumption expenditures and disposable income. All values are expressed in billions of constant dollars.

Disposable Income (Y_D)	Desired Consumption (C)	$APC = C/Y_D$	$MPC = \Delta C/\Delta Y_D$
0	150	—	—
100	225	—	—
200	300	—	—
300	375	—	—
400	450	—	—
500	525	—	—
600	600	—	—
700	675	—	—
800	750	—	—

   a. Compute the average propensity to consume for each level of income and fill in the table.

   b. Compute the marginal propensity to consume for each successive change in income and fill in the table.

   c. Plot the consumption function on a scale diagram. What is its slope?

4. This question relates to desired saving, and is based on the table in Question 3.

   a. Compute desired saving at each level of disposable income. Plot the saving function on a scale diagram. What is its slope?

   b. Show that the average propensity to save plus the average propensity to consume must equal 1.

5. Relate the following newspaper headlines to shifts in the C, S, I, and AE functions and to changes in equilibrium national income.

   a. "Revival of consumer confidence leads to increased spending."

   b. "High mortgage rates discourage new house purchases."

   c. "Concern over future leads to a reduction in inventories."

   d. "Accelerated depreciation allowances in the new federal budget set off boom on equipment purchases."

   e. "Consumers spend as stock market soars."

6. In the chapter we explained at length the difference between *desired* expenditures and *actual* expenditures.

   a. Is national income accounting based on desired or actual expenditures? Explain.

   b. Suppose there were a sudden decrease in desired consumption expenditure. Explain why this would likely lead to an equally sudden increase in *actual* investment expenditure. Which type of investment would rise?

   c. Illustrate the event from part (b) in a 45°-line diagram.

7. Consider the following diagram of the AE function and the 45° line.

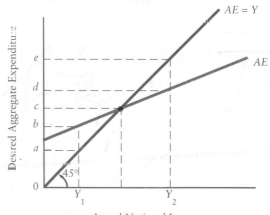

Actual National Income

   a. Suppose the level of actual national income is Y_1. What is the level of desired aggregate expenditure? Is it greater or less than actual output? Are inventories being depleted or accumulated?

   b. If actual income is Y_1, explain the process by which national income changes toward equilibrium.

   c. Suppose the level of actual national income is Y_2. What is the level of desired aggregate expenditure? Is it greater or less than actual output? Are inventories being depleted or accumulated?

   d. If actual income is Y_2, explain the process by which national income changes toward equilibrium.

8. Consider a simple model like the one developed in this chapter. The following equations show the levels of desired consumption and investment:

$$C = 500 + 0.9Y$$
$$I = 100$$

Y	C	I	AE
0	—	—	—
2 000	—	—	—
4 000	—	—	—
6 000	—	—	—
8 000	—	—	—
10 000	—	—	—

  a. Complete the table above.
  b. What is the equilibrium level of national income in this model? Why?

9. Suppose you are given the following information for an economy without government spending, exports, or imports. C is desired consumption, I is desired investment, and Y is income. C and I are given by

$$C = 1400 + 0.8Y$$
$$I = 400$$

  a. What is the equation for the aggregate expenditure (AE) function?
  b. Applying the equilibrium condition that $Y = AE$, determine the level of equilibrium national income.
  c. Using your answer from part (b), determine the values of consumption, saving, and investment when the economy is in equilibrium.

10. For each of the following aggregate expenditure (AE) functions, identify the marginal propensity to spend and calculate the simple multiplier.
  a. $AE = 150 + 0.4Y$
  b. $AE = 900 + 0.62Y$
  c. $AE = 6250 + 0.92Y$
  d. $AE = 457 + 0.57Y$
  e. $AE = 500 + 0.2Y$
  f. $AE = 1000 + 0.35Y$

11. Consider an economy characterized by the following equations:

$$C = 500 + 0.75Y + 0.05W$$
$$I = 150$$

where C is desired consumption, I is desired investment, W is household wealth, and Y is national income.

  a. Suppose wealth is constant at $W = 10\,000$. Draw the aggregate expenditure function on a scale diagram along with the 45° line. What is the equilibrium level of national income?
  b. What is the marginal propensity to spend in this economy?
  c. What is the value of the simple multiplier?
  d. Using your answer from part (c), what would be the change in equilibrium national income if desired investment increased to 250? Show this in your diagram.
  e. Begin with the new equilibrium level of national income from part (d). Now suppose household wealth increases from 10 000 to 15 000. What happens to the AE function and by how much does national income change?

12. The "Paradox of Thrift" is a famous idea in macroeconomics—one that we will discuss in later chapters. The basic idea is that if every household in the economy tries to increase its level of desired saving, the level of national income will fall and they will end up saving no more than they were initially. Use the model and diagrams of this chapter to show how an (autonomous) increase in desired saving would reduce equilibrium income and lead to no change in aggregate saving. (Though it is not essential, you may find it useful to see **Investment, Saving, and Equilibrium GDP** in the *Additional Topics* section of MyEconLab.)

13. In the simple model of this chapter, aggregate investment was assumed to be autonomous with respect to national income. The simple multiplier was $1/(1 - z)$, where z was the marginal propensity to spend. And with autonomous investment, the marginal propensity to spend is simply the marginal propensity to consume.

   But now suppose firms' investment is *not* completely autonomous. That is, suppose that $I = \bar{I} + \beta Y$, where $\bar{I}$ is autonomous investment and β is the "marginal propensity to invest" ($\beta > 0$). Explain how this modification to the simple model changes the simple multiplier, and why.

Adding Government and Trade to the Simple Macro Model

LEARNING OBJECTIVES (LO)

After studying this chapter you will be able to

1 understand how government purchases and tax revenues relate to national income.

2 understand how exports and imports relate to national income.

3 distinguish between the marginal propensity to consume and the marginal propensity to spend.

4 explain why the introduction of government and foreign trade in the macro model reduces the value of the simple multiplier.

5 explain how government can use fiscal policy to influence the level of national income.

6 understand that output is demand determined in our simple macro model.

IN Chapter 21, we developed a simple short-run model of national income determination in a closed economy with fixed prices. In this chapter, we add a government and a foreign sector to that model. In Chapter 23, we will expand the model further to explain the determination of the price level.

Adding government to the model allows us to understand how the government's use of its taxing and spending powers can affect the level of national income. Adding foreign trade allows us to examine some ways in which external events affect the Canadian economy. Fortunately, the key elements of the previous chapter's theory of income determination are unchanged even after government and the foreign sector are incorporated.

22.1 Introducing Government

fiscal policy The use of the government's tax and spending policies to achieve government objectives.

A government's **fiscal policy** is defined by its plans for taxes and spending. Government spending and taxation influence national income in both the short and the long run. Our discussion of fiscal policy begins in this chapter; we go into more detail in Chapter 24 and again in Chapter 32.

Government Purchases

In Chapter 20, we distinguished between government *purchases of goods and services* and government *transfer payments*. The distinction bears repeating here. When the government hires a public servant, buys office supplies, purchases fuel for the Canadian Forces, or commissions a study by consultants, it is adding directly to the demands for the economy's current output of goods and services. Hence, desired government purchases, G, are part of aggregate desired expenditure.

The other part of government spending, transfer payments, also affects desired aggregate expenditure but only indirectly. Consider welfare or employment-insurance benefits, for example. These government expenditures place no direct demand on the nation's production of goods and services since they merely transfer funds to the recipients. The same is true of government transfers to firms, which often take the form of subsidies. However, when individuals or firms spend some of these payments on consumption or investment, their spending is part of aggregate expenditure. Thus, government transfer payments do affect aggregate expenditure but only through the effect these transfers have on households' and firms' spending.

In this chapter we make the simple assumption that the level of government purchases, G, is autonomous with respect to the level of national income. As GDP rises or falls, the level of the government's transfer payments will generally change, but we assume that G does not automatically change just because GDP changes. We then view any change in G as a result of a government policy decision.

Net Tax Revenues

Taxes reduce households' disposable income relative to national income. In contrast, transfer payments raise disposable income relative to national income. For the purpose of calculating the effect of government policy on desired consumption expenditure, it is the net effect of the two that matters.

net tax revenue Total tax revenue minus transfer payments, denoted T.

Net tax revenue is defined as total tax revenue received by the government minus total transfer payments made by the government, and it is denoted T. (For the remainder of this chapter, the term "taxes" means "net taxes" unless stated otherwise.) Because transfer payments are smaller than total tax revenues, net tax revenues are positive. In the model in this chapter, we assume that net tax revenues vary directly with the level of national income. As national income rises, a tax system with given tax rates will yield more revenue (net of transfers). For example, when income rises, people will pay more income tax in total even though the tax *rates* are unchanged. In addition, when income rises, the government generally reduces its transfers to households. We will use the following simple form for government net tax revenues, T:

$$T = tY$$

net tax rate The increase in net tax revenue generated when national income rises by one dollar.

where t is the **net tax rate**—the increase in net tax revenue generated when national income increases by \$1.

It may be tempting to think of t as the income-tax rate, but note that we are representing in a simple way what in reality is a complex tax and transfer structure that includes, in addition to several different types of financial transfers to households, the personal income tax, the corporate income tax, the GST, provincial sales tax, and property taxes. For that reason, t is not the rate on one specific type of tax. It is the amount by which total government tax revenues (less transfers) change when national income changes.

The Budget Balance

The *budget balance* is the difference between total government revenue and total government expenditure; equivalently, it equals net tax revenue minus government purchases, $T - G$. When net revenues exceed purchases, the government has a **budget surplus**. When purchases exceed net revenues, the government has a **budget deficit**. When the two amounts are equal, the government has a *balanced budget*.

When the government runs a budget deficit, it must borrow the excess of spending over revenues. It does this by issuing additional *government debt* (bonds or Treasury bills). When the government runs a surplus, it uses the excess revenue to buy back outstanding government debt. Budget deficits and government debt are the principal topics of Chapter 32.

budget surplus Any excess of current revenue over current expenditure.

budget deficit Any shortfall of current revenue below current expenditure.

Provincial and Municipal Governments

Many people are surprised to learn that the combined activities of the many Canadian provincial and municipal governments account for *more* purchases of goods and services than does the federal government. The federal government raises about the same amount of tax revenue as do the provincial and municipal governments combined, but it transfers a considerable amount of its revenue to the provinces.

> When measuring the overall contribution of government to desired aggregate expenditure, all levels of government must be included.

As we proceed through this chapter discussing the role of government in the determination of national income, think of "the government" as the combination of all levels of government—federal, provincial, territorial, and municipal.

The federal Department of Finance designs and implements Canada's fiscal policy. See its website: www.fin.gc.ca.

Summary

Before introducing foreign trade, let's summarize how the presence of government affects our simple model.

1. All levels of government add directly to desired aggregate expenditure through their purchases of goods and services, G. Later in this chapter when we are constructing the aggregate expenditure (AE) function for our model, we will include G and we will treat it as autonomous expenditure.

2. Governments also collect tax revenue and make transfer payments. Net tax revenues are denoted T and are positively related to national income. Since T does not represent any expenditure on goods and services, it is not included directly in

the *AE* function. *T* will enter the *AE* function *indirectly*, however, through its effect on disposable income (Y_D) and consumption. Recall that $Y_D = Y - T$ and that desired consumption is assumed to depend on Y_D.

22.2 Introducing Foreign Trade

Canada imports all kinds of goods and services, from French wine and Peruvian anchovies to Swiss financial and American architectural services. Canada also exports a variety of goods and services, including timber, nickel, automobiles, engineering services, computer software, flight simulators, and commuter jets. U.S.–Canadian trade is the largest two-way flow of trade between any two countries in the world today.

Of all the goods and services produced in Canada in a given year, roughly 35 percent are exported. A similar value of goods and services is imported into Canada every year. Thus, although *net* exports may contribute only a few percent to Canada's GDP in a typical year, foreign trade is tremendously important to Canada's economy.

Net Exports

Exports depend on spending decisions made by foreign households and firms that purchase Canadian products. Typically, exports will not change as a result of changes in Canadian national income. We therefore treat exports as autonomous expenditure.

Imports, however, depend on the spending decisions of Canadian households and firms. Almost all consumption goods have an import content. Canadian-made cars, for example, use large quantities of imported components in their manufacture. Canadian-made clothes most often use imported cotton or wool. And most restaurant meals contain some imported fruits, vegetables, or meats. Hence, as consumption rises, imports will also increase. Because consumption rises with national income, we also get a positive relationship between imports and national income. In this chapter, we use the following simple form for desired imports:

marginal propensity to import The increase in import expenditures induced by a $1 increase in national income. Denoted by *m*.

$$IM = mY$$

where *m* is the **marginal propensity to import**, the amount that desired imports rise when national income rises by $1.

In our simple model, net exports can be described by the following simple equation:

$$NX = X - mY$$

Since exports are autonomous with respect to Y but imports are positively related to Y, we see that *net exports* are negatively related to national income. This negative relationship is called the *net export function*. Data for a hypothetical economy with autonomous exports and with imports that are 10 percent of national income ($m = 0.1$) are

International trade is very important for the Canadian economy. More than $2.5 billion worth of goods and services flows across the Canada–U.S. border every day, much of it in trucks like these.

illustrated in Figure 22-1. In this example, exports form the autonomous component and imports form the induced component of desired net exports.

Shifts in the Net Export Function

Any given net export function is drawn under the assumption that everything affecting net exports, except domestic national income, remains constant. The two major influences that are held constant when we draw the NX function are foreign national income and international relative prices. If either one changes, the NX function will shift. Notice that anything affecting Canadian exports will shift the NX function parallel to itself, upward if exports increase and downward if exports decrease. Also notice that anything affecting the *proportion of income* that Canadian consumers want to spend on imports will change the *slope* of the NX function. Let's now explore some of these changes in detail.

Changes in Foreign Income An increase in foreign income, other things being equal, will lead to an increase in the quantity of Canadian goods demanded by foreign countries—that is, to an increase in Canadian exports. This change causes the X curve in Figure 22-1 to shift upward and therefore the NX function also to shift upward, parallel to its original position. A fall in foreign income leads to a reduction in Canadian exports and thus to a parallel downward shift in the NX function.

Changes in International Relative Prices Any change in the prices of Canadian goods *relative* to those of foreign goods will cause both imports and exports to change. These changes will shift the NX function.

Consider what happens with a rise in Canadian prices relative to those in foreign countries. The increase in Canadian prices means that foreigners now see Canadian goods as more expensive relative both to goods produced in their own country and to goods imported from countries other than Canada.

FIGURE 22-1 The Net Export Function ☀

Actual National Income (Y)	Exports (X)	Imports ($IM = 0.1Y$)	Net Exports ($NX = X - IM$)
0	72	0	72
300	72	30	42
600	72	60	12
720	72	72	0
900	72	90	−18

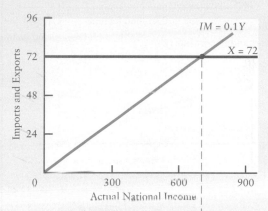

(i) Export and import functions

(ii) Net export function

Net exports fall as national income rises. The data are hypothetical. In part (i), exports are constant at \$72 billion while imports rise with national income; the marginal propensity to import is assumed to be 0.10. Therefore, net exports, shown in part (ii), decline with national income. The slope of the import function in part (i) is equal to the marginal propensity to import. The slope of the net export function in part (ii) is the negative of the marginal propensity to import.

FIGURE 22-2 The Net Export Function and a Change in International Relative Prices

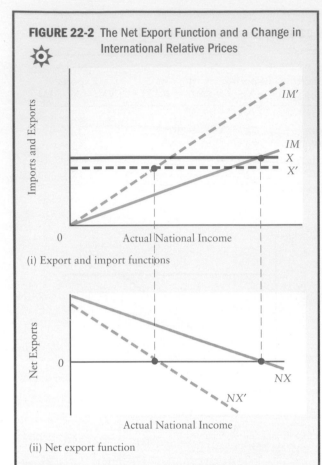

(i) Export and import functions

(ii) Net export function

Changes in international relative prices shift the NX function. A rise in Canadian prices relative to foreign prices lowers exports from X to X' and raises the import function from IM to IM'. This shifts the net export function downward from NX to NX'. A fall in Canadian prices (relative to foreign prices) has the opposite effect.

For lots of interesting information on Canada's international trade, go to the website for the Department of Foreign Affairs and International Trade: www.international.gc.ca.

As a result, the value of Canadian exports will fall.[1] The X curve shifts down in Figure 22-2. Similarly, Canadians will see imports from foreign countries become cheaper relative to the prices of Canadian-made goods. As a result, they will shift their expenditures toward foreign goods and away from Canadian goods. That is, the marginal propensity to import (m) will rise, and so the IM curve will rotate up. The combination of these two effects is that the net export function shifts downward and becomes steeper. A fall in Canadian prices relative to foreign prices would have the opposite effect, shifting the X function up and the IM function down, and thus shifting the NX function up.

> **A rise in Canadian prices relative to those in other countries reduces Canadian net exports at any level of national income. A fall in Canadian prices increases net exports at any level of national income.**

The most important cause of a change in international relative prices is a change in the exchange rate. A *depreciation* of the Canadian dollar means that foreigners must pay less of their money to buy one Canadian dollar, and Canadian residents must pay more Canadian dollars to buy a unit of any foreign currency. As a result, the price of foreign goods in terms of Canadian dollars rises, and the price of Canadian goods in terms of foreign currency falls. This reduction in the relative price of Canadian goods will cause a shift in expenditure away from foreign goods and toward Canadian goods. Canadian residents will import less at each level of Canadian national income, and foreigners will buy more Canadian exports. The net export function thus shifts upward.

An example may help to clarify the argument. Suppose something causes the Canadian dollar to depreciate relative to the euro (the common currency in the European Union). The depreciation of the Canadian dollar leads Canadians to switch away from French wines and German cars, purchasing instead more B.C. wine and Ontario-made cars. This reduction in the marginal propensity to import (m) is shown by a downward rotation of the IM curve. The depreciation of the Canadian dollar relative to the euro also stimulates Canadian exports. Quebec furniture and Maritime vacations now appear cheaper to Europeans than previously, and so their expenditure on such Canadian goods increases. This

---

[1] The rise in Canadian prices leads to a reduction in the quantity of Canadian goods demanded by foreigners. But in order for the *value* of Canadian exports to fall, the price elasticity of demand for Canadian exports must exceed 1 (so that the quantity reduction dominates the price increase). Throughout this book, we make this assumption.

increase in Canadian exports is shown by an upward shift in the X curve. The overall effect is that the net export function shifts up and becomes flatter.

One final word of caution is needed regarding prices, exchange rates, and net exports. It is important to keep in mind that the simple model in this chapter treats prices and exchange rates as *exogenous* variables. That is, though we can discuss what happens if they change, we do not yet *explain* where these changes come from. Of course, in the actual economy the price level and the exchange rate are key macroeconomic variables whose changes we want to understand. In the next chapter, the price level will be *endogenous* in our model and we can therefore consider why it changes. In Chapter 35, we explain in detail what causes the exchange rate to change. For now, however, keep in mind that the price level and the exchange rate are exogenous variables—we can explain what happens in our model *if* they change but we cannot use the current simple version of our model to explain *why* they change.

Summary

How does the presence of foreign trade modify our basic model? Let's summarize.

1. Foreign firms and households purchase Canadian-made goods. Changes in foreign income and international relative prices (including exchange rates) will affect Canadian exports (X), but we assume that X is autonomous with respect to Canadian national income. When we construct the economy's aggregate expenditure (AE) function, we will include X since it represents expenditure on domestically produced goods and services.

2. All components of domestic expenditure (C, I, and G) include some import content. Since C is positively related to national income, imports (IM) are also related positively to national income. When we construct the economy's AE function, which shows the desired aggregate expenditure on *domestic* products, we will *subtract IM* because these expenditures are on foreign products.

22.3 Equilibrium National Income

As in Chapter 21, equilibrium national income is the level of income at which desired aggregate expenditure equals actual national income. The addition of government and net exports changes the calculations that we must make but does not alter the equilibrium concept or the basic workings of the model.

Desired Consumption and National Income

Recall that disposable income is equal to national income minus net taxes, $Y_D = Y - T$. We take several steps to determine the relationship between consumption and national income in the presence of taxes.

1. First, assume that the net tax rate, t, is 10 percent, so that net tax revenues are 10 percent of national income:

$$T = (0.1)Y$$

2. Disposable income must therefore be 90 percent of national income:

$$Y_D = Y - T$$
$$= Y - (0.1)Y$$
$$= (0.9)Y$$

3. The consumption function we used last chapter is given as

$$C = 30 + (0.8)Y_D$$

which tells us that the *MPC* out of disposable income is 0.8.

4. We can now substitute $(0.9)Y$ for Y_D in the consumption function. By doing so, we get

$$C = 30 + (0.8)(0.9)Y$$
$$\Rightarrow C = 30 + (0.72)Y$$

So, we can express desired consumption as a function of Y_D or as a *different* function of Y. In this example, 0.72 is equal to the *MPC* times $(1 - t)$, where t is the net tax rate. Whereas 0.8 is the marginal propensity to consume out of *disposable* income, 0.72 is the marginal propensity to consume out of *national* income.

> In the presence of taxes, the marginal propensity to consume out of national income is less than the marginal propensity to consume out of disposable income.

The *AE* Function

In Chapter 21, the only components of desired aggregate expenditure were consumption and investment. We now add government purchases and net exports. The separate components in their general form are

$C = c + MPC \times Y_D$	consumption
I	autonomous investment
G	autonomous government purchases
$T = tY$	net tax revenues
X	autonomous exports
$IM = mY$	imports

Our first step in constructing the *AE* function is to express desired consumption in terms of national income. By using the four steps from above, we write desired consumption as

$$C = c + MPC(1 - t)Y$$

where c is autonomous consumption and *MPC* is the marginal propensity to consume. Now we sum the four components of desired aggregate expenditure:

$$AE = C + I + G + (X - IM)$$
$$= c + MPC(1 - t)Y + I + G + (X - mY)$$
$$AE = \underbrace{[c + I + G + X]}_{\substack{\text{Autonomous} \\ \text{expenditure}}} + \underbrace{[MPC(1 - t) - m]Y}_{\substack{\text{Induced} \\ \text{expenditure}}}$$

In this last equation, we can see the distinction between autonomous aggregate expenditure and induced aggregate expenditure. The first square bracket brings together all the autonomous parts of expenditure. The second square bracket brings together all the parts of expenditure that change when national income changes—the induced part of consumption and imports. The term in the second square bracket shows how much total desired spending on domestically produced output changes when national income changes by $1—the marginal propensity to spend out of national income.

Figure 22-3 graphs the *AE* function for our hypothetical economy in which we assume that desired investment is $75 billion and the level of government purchases is $51 billion. Notice that the slope of the *AE* function measures the change in desired aggregate expenditure (*AE*) that comes about from a $1 increase in national income (*Y*). This is the marginal propensity to spend out of national income and is equal to $MPC(1 - t) - m$.

Note that, unlike in Chapter 21, the marginal propensity to spend out of national income (*z*) is not simply equal to the marginal propensity to consume (*MPC*). To understand why, suppose the economy produces $1 of extra national income and that the

---

FIGURE 22-3 The Aggregate Expenditure Function

The aggregate expenditure function is the sum of desired consumption, investment, government purchases, and net export expenditures. The autonomous components of desired aggregate expenditure are desired investment, desired government purchases, desired export expenditures, and the autonomous part of desired consumption. These sum to $228 billion in the given example and this sum is the vertical intercept of the *AE* curve. The induced component is $[MPC(1 - t) - m]Y$, which in our example is equal to $(0.8(0.9) - 0.1)Y = 0.62Y$.

The equation for the *AE* function is $AE = 228 + 0.62Y$. The slope of the *AE* function, $\Delta AE/\Delta Y$, is 0.62, indicating that a $1 increase in *Y* leads to a 62-cent increase in desired expenditure. This is the marginal propensity to spend on domestic output. The equilibrium level of national income is $600 billion, the level of *Y* where the *AE* function intersects the 45° line.

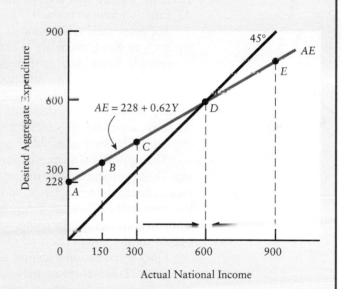

Point	Actual National Income (Y)	Desired Consumption Expenditure (C = 30 + 0.72Y)	Desired Investment Expenditure (I = 75)	Desired Government Expenditure (G = 51)	Desired Net Export Expenditure (X − IM = 72 − 0.1Y)	Desired Aggregate Expenditure (AE = C + I + G + X − IM)
A	0	30	75	51	72	228
B	150	138	75	51	57	321
C	300	246	75	51	42	414
D	600	462	75	51	12	600
E	900	678	75	51	−18	786

response to this is governed by the relationships in Figure 22-3. Because 10 cents is collected by the government as net taxes, 90 cents becomes disposable income, and 80 percent of this amount (72 cents) is spent on consumption. However, 10 cents of all expenditure goes to imports, so expenditure on *domestic* goods rises by only 62 cents (72 − 10). Hence, z, the marginal propensity to spend, is 0.62. In algebraic terms,

$$z = MPC(1 - t) - m$$
$$= (0.8)(1 - 0.1) - 0.1$$
$$= 0.72 - 0.1$$
$$= 0.62$$

Equilibrium National Income

As in Chapter 21, we are assuming (for now) that firms are able and willing to produce whatever level of output is demanded of them at a constant price level. When output is *demand determined* in this way, the equilibrium level of national income is that level of national income where desired aggregate expenditure (along the *AE* function) equals the actual level of national income. As was also true in Chapter 21, the 45° line shows the *equilibrium condition*—the collection of points where $Y = AE$. Thus, the equilibrium level of national income in Figure 22-3 is at point *D*, where the *AE* function intersects the 45° line.

Suppose national income is less than its equilibrium amount. The forces leading back to equilibrium are exactly the same as those described in Chapter 21. When households, firms, foreign demanders, and governments try to spend at their desired amounts, they will try to purchase more goods and services than the economy is currently producing. Hence, some of the desired expenditure must either be frustrated or take the form of purchases of inventories of goods that were produced in the past. As firms see their inventories being depleted, they will increase production, thereby increasing the level of national income.

The opposite sequence of events occurs when national income is greater than its equilibrium amount. Now the total of desired household consumption, business investment, government purchases, and net foreign demand on the economy's production is less than national output. Firms will notice that they are unable to sell all their output. Their inventories will be rising, and sooner or later they will seek to reduce the level of output until it equals the level of sales. When they do, national income will fall.

Only when national income is equal to desired aggregate expenditure ($600 billion in Figure 22-3) is there no pressure for output to change. Desired consumption, investment, government purchases, and net exports just add up to national output.

22.4 Changes in Equilibrium National Income

Changes in any of the components of desired aggregate expenditure will cause changes in equilibrium national income. In Chapter 21, we investigated the consequences of shifts in the consumption function and in the investment function. Here we take a first look at fiscal policy—the effects of changes in government spending and taxation. We also consider shifts in the net export function. First, we explain why the simple multiplier is reduced by the presence of taxes and imports.

The Multiplier with Taxes and Imports

In Chapter 21, we saw that the *simple multiplier*, the amount by which equilibrium real GDP changes when autonomous expenditure changes by $1 was equal to $1/(1 - z)$, where z is the marginal propensity to spend out of national income. In the simple model of Chapter 21, with no government and no international trade, z was simply the marginal propensity to consume out of disposable income. But in the more complex model of this chapter, which contains both government and foreign trade, we have seen that the marginal propensity to spend out of national income is slightly more complicated.

The presence of imports and taxes reduces the marginal propensity to spend out of national income and therefore reduces the value of the simple multiplier.

Let's be more specific. In Chapter 21, the marginal propensity to spend, z, was just equal to the marginal propensity to consume. Let ΔY be the change in equilibrium real GDP brought about by a change in autonomous spending, ΔA. We then have the following relationships:

Without Government and Foreign Trade:

$$z = MPC$$

$$\text{Simple multiplier} = \frac{\Delta Y}{\Delta A} = \frac{1}{1 - z}$$

$$= \frac{1}{1 - MPC}$$

In our example, the MPC was 0.8, and so the simple multiplier was equal to 5.

$$\text{Simple multiplier} = 1/(1 - 0.8) = 1/0.2 = 5$$

In our expanded model with government and foreign trade, the marginal propensity to spend out of national income must take account of the presence of net taxes and imports, both of which reduce the value of z.

With Government and Foreign Trade:

$$z = MPC(1 - t) - m$$

$$\text{Simple multiplier} = \frac{\Delta Y}{\Delta A} = \frac{1}{1 - z}$$

$$= \frac{1}{1 - [MPC(1 - t) - m]}$$

In our example, $MPC = 0.8$, $t = 0.1$, and $m = 0.1$. This makes the simple multiplier equal to 2.63.

$$\text{Simple multiplier} = 1/\{1 - [0.8(1 - 0.1) - 0.1]\} = 1/[1 - (0.72 - 0.1)]$$
$$= 1/(1 - 0.62) = 2.63$$

What is the central point here? When we introduce government and foreign trade to our model, the simple multiplier becomes smaller. Since some of any increase in national income goes to taxes and imports, the induced increase in desired expenditure on domestically produced goods is reduced. (The AE curve is flatter.) The result is that, in response to any change in autonomous expenditure, the overall change in equilibrium GDP is smaller.

The higher is the marginal propensity to import, the lower is the simple multiplier. The higher is the net tax rate, the lower is the simple multiplier.

Applying Economic Concepts 22-1 examines what the size of the simple multiplier is likely to be in the Canadian economy. You may be surprised at the result!

APPLYING ECONOMIC CONCEPTS 22-1

How Large Is Canada's Simple Multiplier?

In our macro model, the "simple multiplier" expresses the overall change in equilibrium national income resulting from an increase in desired autonomous spending. To the extent that increases in output are only possible in the short run by increasing the level of employment, the multiplier can also tell us something about the total change in employment that will result from an initial increase in spending. And this is the way we usually hear about the effects of the multiplier in the popular press.

Imagine you hear a news story about a recent announcement by the government to increase its annual spending by $5 billion on the repairs of highways and bridges. Rather than claiming that the $5 billion increase in spending will lead to an overall increase in national income larger than $5 billion, the official making the announcement is likely to speak in terms of the number of jobs "created" in the economy as a result of the new government spending. For example, the official might claim that this new spending will *directly* create 5000 new jobs and that an additional 10 000 new jobs will be created *indirectly*. With such a claim, the government official appears to believe that the simple multiplier is equal to 3—the total increase in employment (and output) will be three times the direct increase. Is a simple multiplier of 3 a realistic estimate for Canada?

In the simple model we have developed in this chapter, we have used values for key parameters that are simple to work with but not necessarily realistic. In particular, we assumed values of t and m that are well below their actual values. To find a realistic estimate for the multiplier in Canada, we need to use more realistic values for the net tax rate (t) and the marginal propensity to import (m). In Canada a reasonable value for t is 0.25, the approximate share of combined government

net taxation in GDP. Imports into Canada are close to 35 percent of GDP and so $m = 0.35$ is a reasonable value. If we use these more realistic values for t and m, and continue the reasonable assumption that the marginal propensity to consume out of disposable income is 0.8, the implied value of z is

$$z = MPC(1 - t) - m$$
$$= 0.8(1 - 0.25) - 0.35 = 0.25$$

and so the implied value of the simple multiplier is

Simple multiplier $= 1/(1 - z) = 1/0.75 = 1.33$

Two main lessons emerge from this analysis:

1. Net taxes and imports reduce the size of the simple multiplier.

2. Realistic values of t and m in Canada suggest a simple multiplier that is closer to 1 than to 2 and certainly far below the value of 5 that we used in the very simple model of Chapter 21.

So the next time you hear a government official make claims about how new spending plans are likely to have large effects on the level of employment and economic activity, think about what the implied value of the simple multiplier must be in order for the claims to be reasonable. The analysis here suggests that the simple multiplier in Canada is likely to be only moderately greater than 1.*

_____
* In the next two chapters we will see that once we allow for a price level that can adjust to changes in demand, the multiplier gets even smaller.

Net Exports

Earlier in this chapter, we discussed the determinants of net exports and of shifts in the net export function. As with the other elements of desired aggregate expenditure, if the net export function shifts upward, equilibrium national income will rise; if the net export function shifts downward, equilibrium national income will fall.

Generally, exports themselves are autonomous with respect to domestic national income. Foreign demand for Canadian products depends on foreign income, on foreign and Canadian prices, and on the exchange rate, but it does not depend on Canadian income. Export demand could also change because of a change in foreigners' preferences. Suppose foreign consumers develop a preference for Canadian-made furniture and desire to consume $1 billion more per year of these goods than they had in the past. The net export function (and the aggregate expenditure function) will shift up by $1 billion, and equilibrium national income will increase by $1 billion times the simple multiplier.

Fiscal Policy

In Chapter 19 we introduced the concept of potential GDP, the level of GDP that would exist if all factors of production were fully employed. Deviations of actual GDP (Y) from potential GDP (Y^*) usually create problems. When $Y < Y^*$, factor incomes are low and unemployment of factors is high; when $Y > Y^*$, rising costs create inflationary pressures. To reduce these problems, governments often try to *stabilize* the level of real GDP close to Y^*. Any attempt to use government policy in this manner is called **stabilization policy**, and here we focus on stabilization through fiscal policy. In Chapters 24 and 32, we examine some important details about fiscal policy, including why the real-world practice of fiscal policy is more complicated than our simple model suggests.

The basic idea of fiscal stabilization policy follows from what we have already learned. A reduction in net tax rates or an increase in government purchases shifts the *AE* curve upward, setting in motion the multiplier process that tends to increase equilibrium national income. An increase in tax rates or a decrease in government purchases shifts the *AE* curve downward and tends to decrease equilibrium income.

Once we know the direction in which the government wants to change national income, the *directions of the required changes in government* purchases or taxation are easy to determine. But the *timing* and *magnitude* of the changes are more difficult issues. The issue of timing is difficult because it takes an uncertain amount of time before fiscal policies have an effect on real GDP. The issue of magnitude is difficult because the level of potential output can only be estimated imperfectly (and so the gap between actual and potential GDP is uncertain).

Let's now examine these two policy tools in more detail.

stabilization policy Any policy designed to reduce the economy's cyclical fluctuations and thereby stabilize national income.

Changes in Government Purchases Suppose the government decides to reduce its purchases of all economic consulting services, thus eliminating $100 million per year in spending. Planned government purchases (G) would fall by $100 million, shifting *AE* downward by the same amount. How much would equilibrium income change? This amount can be calculated by using the simple multiplier. Government purchases are part of autonomous expenditure, so a *change* in government purchases of ΔG will lead to a *change* in equilibrium national income equal to the simple multiplier times ΔG. In this example, equilibrium income will fall by $100 million times the simple multiplier.

FIGURE 22-4 The Effect of Changing the Net Tax Rate

A change in the net tax rate changes equilibrium income by rotating the *AE* curve. A reduction in the net tax rate rotates the *AE* curve from AE_0 to AE_1. The new curve has a steeper slope because the lower net tax rate withdraws a smaller amount of national income from the desired consumption flow. Equilibrium income rises from Y_0 to Y_1. An increase in the net tax rate has the opposite effect.

Earlier we argued that a realistic value for the simple multiplier in Canada is about 1.3. Using this value in our example, the effect of the $100 million reduction in *G* is to reduce equilibrium national income by $130 million.

Increases in government purchases would have the opposite effect. If the government increases its spending by $1 billion on new highways, equilibrium national income will rise by $1 billion times the simple multiplier.

Changes in Tax Rates Recall that the slope of the *AE* function is *z*, the marginal propensity to spend on domestic output. As we saw earlier,

$$z = MPC(1 - t) - m$$

A change in the net tax rate will change *z*, rotate the *AE* function, and change the equilibrium level of national income.

Consider first a decrease in tax rates. If the government decreases its net tax rate so that it collects 5 cents less out of every dollar of national income, disposable income rises in relation to national income. Hence, desired consumption also rises at every level of national income. This increase in consumption results in an upward *rotation* of the *AE* curve—that is, an increase in the slope of the curve, as shown in Figure 22-4. The result of this shift will be an increase in equilibrium national income.

A rise in tax rates has the opposite effect. A rise in the net tax rate causes a decrease in disposable income, and hence desired consumption expenditure, at each level of national income. This results in a downward rotation of the *AE* curve and decreases the level of equilibrium national income.

Note that when the *AE* function rotates, as happens if anything causes *z* to change, the simple multiplier is *not* used to tell us about the resulting change in equilibrium national income. The simple multiplier is only used to tell us how much equilibrium national income changes in response to a change in *autonomous* desired spending—that is, in response to a *parallel shift* in the *AE* function.

22.5 Demand-Determined Output

In this and the preceding chapter, we have discussed the determination of the four categories of aggregate expenditure and have seen how they simultaneously determine equilibrium national income in the short run. An algebraic exposition of the complete model is presented in the appendix to this chapter.

Our macro model is based on three central concepts, and it is worth reviewing them.

Equilibrium National Income The equilibrium level of national income is that level at which *desired* aggregate expenditure equals *actual* national income ($AE = Y$). If actual national income exceeds desired expenditure, firms will eventually reduce production, causing national income to fall. If actual national income is less than desired expenditure, firms will eventually increase production, causing national income to rise.

The Simple Multiplier The simple multiplier measures the change in equilibrium national income that results from a change in the *autonomous* part of desired aggregate expenditure. The simple multiplier is equal to $1/(1 - z)$, where z is the marginal propensity to spend out of national income. In the model of Chapter 21, in which there is no government and no international trade, z is simply the marginal propensity to consume out of disposable income. In our expanded model that contains both government and foreign trade, z is reduced by the presence of net taxes and imports. To review:

> Simple multiplier $= 1/(1 - z)$
>
> Closed economy with no government: $\quad z = MPC$
>
> Open economy with government: $\quad z = MPC(1 - t) - m$

Demand-Determined Output The model that we have examined is constructed *for a given price level*—that is, the price level is assumed to be constant. This assumption of a given price level is related to another assumption that we have been making. We have been assuming that firms are able and willing to produce any amount of output that is demanded without requiring any change in prices. When this is true, national income depends only on how much is demanded—that is, national income is *demand determined*. Things get more complicated if firms are either unable or unwilling to produce enough to meet all demands without requiring a change in prices. We deal with this possibility in Chapter 23 when we consider *supply-side* influences on national income.

There are two situations in which we might expect national income to be demand determined. First, when there are unemployed resources and firms have excess capacity, firms will often be prepared to provide whatever is demanded from them at unchanged prices. In contrast, if the economy's resources are fully employed and firms have no excess capacity, increases in output may be possible only with higher unit costs, and these cost increases may lead to price increases.

The second situation occurs when firms are *price setters*. Readers who have studied some microeconomics will recognize this term. It means that the firm has the ability to influence the price of its product, either because it is large relative to the market or, more usually, because it sells a product that is *differentiated* to some extent from the products of its competitors. Firms that are price setters often respond to changes in demand by altering their production and sales, at least initially, rather than by adjusting their prices. Only after some time has passed, and the change in demand has persisted, do such firms adjust their prices. This type of behaviour corresponds well to our short-run macro model in which changes in demand lead to changes in output (for a given price level).

> Our simple model of national income determination assumes a constant price level. In this model, national income is demand determined.

In the following chapters, we expand the model by making the price level an *endogenous* variable. In other words, movements in the price level are explained within the model. We do this by considering the *supply side* of the economy—that is, those things that influence the costs at which firms can produce, such as technology and factor prices. When we consider the demand side and the supply side of the economy simultaneously, we will see that changes in desired aggregate expenditure usually cause both prices and real GDP to change.

SUMMARY

22.1 Introducing Government

- Government desired purchases, G, are assumed to be part of autonomous aggregate expenditure. Taxes minus transfer payments are called net taxes and affect aggregate expenditure indirectly through households' disposable income. Taxes reduce disposable income, whereas transfers increase disposable income.

- The budget balance is defined as net tax revenues minus government purchases, $(T - G)$. When $(T - G)$ is positive, there is a budget surplus; when $(T - G)$ is negative, there is a budget deficit.

22.2 Introducing Foreign Trade

- Exports are foreign purchases of Canadian goods, and thus do not depend on Canadian national income. Desired imports are assumed to increase as national income increases. Hence, net exports decrease as national income increases.
- Changes in international relative prices lead to shifts in the net export function. A depreciation of the Canadian

dollar implies that Canadian goods are now cheaper relative to foreign goods. This leads to a rise in exports and a fall in imports, shifting the net export function up. An appreciation of the Canadian dollar has the opposite effect.

22.3 Equilibrium National Income

- As in Chapter 21, national income is in equilibrium when desired aggregate expenditure equals actual national income. The equilibrium condition is

  $Y = AE$, where $AE = C + I + G + (X - IM)$

- The slope of the AE function in the model with government and foreign trade is $z = MPC(1 - t) - m$, where MPC is the marginal propensity to consume out of disposable income, t is the net tax rate, and m is the marginal propensity to import.

22.4 Changes in Equilibrium National Income

- The presence of taxes and net exports reduces the value of the simple multiplier. With taxes and imports, every increase in national income induces less new spending than in a model with no taxes or imports.
- An increase in government purchases shifts up the AE function and thus increases the equilibrium level of national income. A decrease in the net tax rate makes

the AE function rotate upward and increases the equilibrium level of national income.
- An increase in exports can be caused by an increase in foreign demand for Canadian goods, a fall in the Canadian price level, or a depreciation of the Canadian dollar. An increase in exports shifts the AE function up and increases the equilibrium level of national income.

22.5 Demand-Determined Output

- Our simple model of national income determination is constructed for a given price level. That prices are assumed not to change in response to an increase in desired expenditure reflects a related assumption that output is demand determined.

- Output may be demand determined in two situations: if there are unemployed resources, or if firms are price setters.

KEY CONCEPTS

Taxes, transfers, and net taxes
The budget balance
The net export function

Calculation of the simple multiplier in
 an open economy with government
Fiscal policy

Changes in government purchases
Changes in net tax rates
Demand-determined output

STUDY EXERCISES

MyEconLab   Make the grade with MyEconLab: Study Exercises marked in red can be found on MyEconLab. You can practise them as often as you want, and most feature step-by-step guided instructions to help you find the right answer.

1. Consider the following table showing national income and government net tax revenues in billions of dollars. Assume that the level of government purchases is $155 billion.

Actual National Income (Y)	Net Tax Revenues (T)	Budget Balance ($T - G$)
100	45	
200	70	—
300	95	—
400	120	—
500	145	—
600	170	—
700	195	—
800	220	—

a. Compute the government's budget balance for each level of national income and fill in the table.
b. Suppose that net taxes are given by T, where $T = t_0 + t_1 Y$. Using the data in the table, determine the values of t_0 and t_1.
c. What is the interpretation of t_0?
d. What is the interpretation of t_1?
e. Suppose the government decides to increase the level of its purchases of goods and services by $15 billion. What happens to the budget balance for any level of national income?

2. Consider the following table showing national income and imports in billions of dollars. Assume that the level of exports is $300 billion.

Actual National Income (Y)	Imports (IM)	Net Exports ($X - IM$)
100	85	—
200	120	—
300	155	—
400	190	—
500	225	
600	260	—
700	295	—
800	330	—

a. Compute the level of net exports for each level of national income and fill in the table.
b. Plot the net export function on a scale diagram. Explain why it is downward sloping.
c. Suppose desired imports are given by $IM = m_0 + m_1 Y$. Using the data in the table, determine the values of m_0 and m_1.
d. What is the interpretation of m_0?
e. What is the interpretation of m_1?
f. Suppose that a major trading partner experiences a significant recession. Explain how this affects the net export function in your diagram.

3. Each of the following headlines describes an event that will have an effect on desired aggregate expenditure. What will be the effect on equilibrium national income? In each case, describe how the event would be illustrated in the 45°-line diagram.

a. "Minister takes an axe to the armed forces."
b. "Russia agrees to buy more Canadian wheat."

c. "High-tech firms to cut capital outlays."

d. "Finance minister pledges to cut income-tax rates."

e. "U.S. imposes import restrictions on Canadian lumber."

f. "Booming Chinese economy expands market for Canadian coal."

g. "Weak dollar spurs exports from Ontario manufacturers."

h. "Prime minister promises burst of infrastructure spending."

4. The following diagram shows desired aggregate expenditure for the economy of Sunset Island. The *AE* curve assumes a net tax rate (*t*) of 10 percent, autonomous exports of $25 billion, and a marginal propensity to import (*m*) of 15 percent.

a. What is the level of desired investment expenditure (*I*)?

b. What is the level of government purchases (*G*)?

c. What is the autonomous portion of consumption?

d. What is total autonomous expenditure?

e. Starting from equilibrium national income of $250 billion, suppose government purchases decreased by $25 billion. Describe the effect on the *AE* curve and on equilibrium national income.

f. Starting from equilibrium national income of $250 billion, suppose the net tax rate increased from 10 percent to 30 percent of national income. Describe the effect on the *AE* curve and on equilibrium national income.

g. Starting from equilibrium national income of $250 billion, suppose investment increased by $50 billion. Describe the effect on the *AE* curve and on equilibrium national income.

h. Starting from equilibrium national income of $250 billion, suppose the marginal propensity to import fell from 15 percent to 5 percent of national

income. Describe the effect on the *AE* curve and on equilibrium national income.

5. The economy of Sunrise Island has the following features:
   - fixed price level
   - no foreign trade
   - autonomous desired investment (*I*) of $20 billion
   - autonomous government purchases (*G*) of $30 billion
   - autonomous desired consumption (*C*) of $15 billion
   - marginal propensity to consume out of disposable income of 0.75
   - net tax rate of 0.20 of national income

a. Write an equation expressing consumption as a function of disposable income.

b. Write an equation expressing net tax revenues as a function of national income.

c. Write an equation expressing disposable income as a function of national income.

d. Write an equation expressing consumption as a function of national income.

e. What is the marginal propensity to spend out of national income?

f. Calculate the simple multiplier for Sunrise Island.

6. The following table shows alternative hypothetical economies and the relevant values for the marginal propensity to consume out of disposable income (*MPC*), the net tax rate (*t*), and the marginal propensity to import, *m*.

Economy	MPC	t	m	z	Simple Multiplier $1/(1 - z)$
A	0.75	0.2	0.15	—	—
B	0.75	0.2	0.30	—	—
C	0.75	0.4	0.30	—	—
D	0.90	0.4	0.30	—	—

a. Recall that *z*, the marginal propensity to spend out of national income, is given by the simple expression $z = MPC(1 - t) - m$. By using this expression, compute *z* for each of the economies and fill in the table.

b. Compare Economies A and B (they differ only by the value of *m*). Which one has the larger multiplier? Explain why the size of the multiplier depends on *m*.

c. Compare Economies B and C (they differ only by the value of *t*). Which one has the larger multiplier? Explain why the size of the multiplier depends on *t*.

d. Compare Economies C and D (they differ only by the value of *MPC*). Which one has the larger multiplier? Explain why the size of the multiplier depends on *MPC*.

7. This question is based on the *Additional Topic* **The Saving-Investment Approach to Equilibrium in an Open Economy with Government,** which is found on this book's MyEconLab. Consider the diagram below that shows the national saving function and the national asset formation function.

Actual National Income

a. Explain why the national asset formation function is downward sloping. What determines its slope?
b. Explain why the national saving function is upward sloping. What determines its slope?
c. Suppose the government decided to increase its level of purchases. How would this policy change be illustrated in the diagram? What would happen to national income?
d. Suppose domestic firms decided to increase their desired investment. How would this change be illustrated in the diagram? What would happen to national income?
e. Suppose the Canadian government reduced net tax rates. How would this change be illustrated in the diagram? What would happen to national income?

8. This question requires you to solve a macro model algebraically. Reading the appendix to this chapter will help you to answer this question. But, just in case, we lead you through it step by step. The equations for the model are as follows:

i) $C = c + MPC \times Y_D$ consumption
ii) $I = I_0$ investment (autonomous)
iii) $G = G_0$ government purchases (autonomous)
iv) $T = tY$ net tax revenue
v) $X = X_0$ exports (autonomous)
vi) $IM = mY$ imports

a. Step 1: Recall that $Y_D = Y - T$. By using this fact, substitute the tax function into the consumption function and derive the relationship between desired consumption and national income.
b. Step 2: Sum the four components of desired aggregate expenditure (C, I, G, NX). This is the aggregate expenditure (AE) function. Collect the autonomous terms separately from the induced terms.
c. Step 3: Recall the equilibrium condition, $Y = AE$. Form the equation $Y = AE$, where AE is your expression for the AE function from part (b).

d. Step 4: Now collect terms and solve for Y. This is the equilibrium value of national income.
e. Step 5: Suppose the level of autonomous expenditure, which we could call A, rises by ΔA. What is the effect on the level of equilibrium national income?

9. This question repeats the exercise of Question 8, but for specific numerical values. The equations of the model are

$C = 50 + 0.7Y_D$ $T = (0.2)Y$
$I = 75$ $X = 50$
$G = 100$ $IM = (0.15)Y$

a. Compute the AE function and plot it in a diagram. What is total autonomous expenditure?
b. What is the slope of the AE function?
c. Compute the equilibrium level of national income.
d. Suppose X rises from 50 to 100. How does this affect the level of national income?
e. What is the simple multiplier in this model?

10. In the 2009 and 2010 Canadian federal budgets in the midst of a major global recession, the minister of finance presented a plan to stimulate the economy.

a. Describe the basic fiscal tools at his disposal.
b. Using the model from this chapter, explain the effect on GDP from an increase in G by $5 billion.
c. Using the model from this chapter, explain the effect on GDP from a tax rebate equal in value to $5 billion.
d. Can you offer one reason why the minister of finance chose to emphasize increases in government spending rather than tax reductions in his 2009 and 2010 federal budgets?

11. Classify each of the following government activities as either government purchases or transfers.

a. Welfare payments for the poor
b. Payments to teachers in public schools
c. Payments to teachers at a military college
d. Payments on account of hospital and medical care
e. Public vaccination programs

12. In Chapter 20 we examined how national income was *measured*. By using the expenditure approach, we showed that GDP is always equal to the sum of consumption, investment, government purchases, and net exports. In Chapters 21 and 22 we examined the *determination* of national income. We showed that equilibrium national income occurs when actual national income equals the sum of desired consumption, investment, government purchases, and net exports.

a. Does this mean that national income is always at its equilibrium level?
b. Explain the important difference between "actual" and "desired" expenditures.

We start with the definition of desired aggregate expenditure:

$$AE = C + I + G + (X - IM) \qquad [1]$$

For each component of AE, we write down a behavioural function:

$$C = a + bY_D \text{ (consumption function)} \qquad [2]$$

$$I = I_0 \text{ (autonomous investment)} \qquad [3]$$

$$G = G_0 \text{ (autonomous government purchases)} \qquad [4]$$

$$X = X_0 \text{ (autonomous exports)} \qquad [5]$$

$$IM = mY \text{ (imports)} \qquad [6]$$

where a is autonomous consumption spending, b is the marginal propensity to consume, and m is the marginal propensity to import. Obviously, the "behavioural" functions for investment, government purchases, and exports are very simple: These are all assumed to be independent of the level of national income.

Before deriving aggregate expenditure, we need to determine the relationship between national income (Y) and disposable income (Y_D), because it is Y_D that determines desired consumption expenditure. Y_D is defined as income after net taxes. In Chapter 22 we examined a very simple linear tax of the form

$$T = tY \qquad [7]$$

Taxes must be subtracted from national income to obtain disposable income:

$$Y_D = Y - tY = Y(1 - t) \qquad [8]$$

Substituting Equation 8 into the consumption function allows us to write consumption as a function of national income.

$$C = a + b(1 - t)Y \qquad [9]$$

Now we can add up all the components of desired aggregate expenditure, substituting Equations 3, 4, 5, 6, and 7 into Equation 1:

$$AE = a + b(1 - t)Y + I_0 + G_0 + X_0 - mY \qquad [10]$$

Equation 10 is the AE function, which shows desired aggregate expenditure as a function of actual national income.

In equilibrium, desired aggregate expenditure must equal actual national income:

$$AE = Y \qquad [11]$$

Equation 11 is the equilibrium condition for our model. It is the equation of the 45° line in the figures in this chapter.

To solve for the equilibrium level of national income, we want to solve for the level of Y that satisfies both Equation 10 and 11. That is, solve for the level of Y that is determined by the intersection of the AE curve and the 45° line. Substitute Equation 11 into Equation 10:

$$Y = a + b(1 - t)Y + I_0 + G_0 + X_0 - mY \qquad [12]$$

Group all the terms in Y on the right-hand side, and subtract them from both sides:

$$Y = Y[b(1 - t) - m] + a + I_0 + G_0 + X_0 \qquad [13]$$

$$Y - Y[b(1 - t) - m] = a + I_0 + G_0 + X_0 \qquad [14]$$

Notice that $[b(1 - t) - m]$ is exactly the marginal propensity to spend out of national income, defined earlier as z. When national income goes up by one dollar, only $1 - t$ dollars go into disposable income, and only b of that is spent on consumption. Additionally, m is spent on imports, which are not expenditures on domestic national income. Hence $[b(1 - t) - m]$ is spent on domestic output.

Substituting z for $[b(1 - t) - m]$ and solving Equation 14 for equilibrium Y yields

$$Y = \frac{a + I_0 + G_0 + X_0}{1 - z} \qquad [15]$$

Notice that the numerator of Equation 15 is total autonomous expenditure, which we call A. Hence, Equation 15 can be rewritten as

$$Y = \frac{A}{1 - z} \qquad [16]$$

Notice also that if autonomous expenditure rises by some amount ΔA, Y will rise by $\Delta A / (1 - z)$. So, the simple multiplier is $1/(1 - z)$.

The Algebra Illustrated

The numerical example that was carried through Chapters 21 and 22 can be used to illustrate the preceding exposition. In that example, the behavioural equations are:

$$C = 30 + 0.8Y_D \qquad [17]$$

$$I = 75 \qquad [18]$$

$$G = 51 \qquad [19]$$

$$X - IM = 72 - 0.1Y \qquad [20]$$

$$T = 0.1Y \qquad [21]$$

From Equation 8, disposable income is given by $Y(1 - t) = 0.9Y$. Substituting this into Equation 17 yields

$$C = 30 + 0.72Y$$

as in Equation 9.

Now, recalling that in equilibrium $AE = Y$, we add up all the components of AE and set the sum equal to Y, as in Equation 12:

$$Y = 30 + 0.72Y + 75 + 51 + 72 - 0.1Y \quad [22]$$

Collecting terms yields

$$Y = 228 + 0.62Y$$

Subtracting $0.62Y$ from both sides gives

$$0.38Y = 228$$

and dividing through by 0.38, we have

$$Y = \frac{228}{0.38} = 600$$

This can also be derived by using Equation 16. Autonomous expenditure is 228, and z, the marginal propensity to spend out of national income, is 0.62. Thus, from Equation 16, equilibrium income is $228/(1 - 0.62) = 600$, which is exactly the equilibrium we obtained in Figure 22-3 on page 553.

Output and Prices in the Short Run

CHAPTER OUTLINE	LEARNING OBJECTIVES (LO)
	After studying this chapter you will be able to
23.1 THE DEMAND SIDE OF THE ECONOMY	1 explain why an exogenous change in the price level shifts the *AE* curve and changes the equilibrium level of real GDP.
	2 derive the aggregate demand (*AD*) curve and understand what causes it to shift.
23.2 THE SUPPLY SIDE OF THE ECONOMY	3 describe the meaning of the aggregate supply (*AS*) curve and understand why it shifts when technology or factor prices change.
23.3 MACROECONOMIC EQUILIBRIUM	4 explain how *AD* and *AS* shocks affect equilibrium real GDP and the price level.

IN Chapters 21 and 22, we developed a simple model of national income determination. We saw that changes in wealth, interest rates, the government's fiscal policies, or expectations about the future lead to changes in desired aggregate expenditure. Through the multiplier process, such changes in desired expenditure cause equilibrium national income to change.

The simple model in Chapters 21 and 22 had a constant price level. We assumed that firms were prepared to provide more output when it was demanded without requiring an increase in prices. In this sense, we said that output was *demand determined*.

The actual economy, however, does not have a constant price level. Rather than assuming it is constant, we would like to understand what causes it to change. We therefore expand our model to make the price level an *endogenous* variable—one whose changes are explained within the model.

We make the transition to a variable price level in three steps. First, we study the consequences for national income of *exogenous* changes in the price level—changes that happen for reasons that are not explained by our model of the economy. We ask how changes in the price level affect desired aggregate expenditure. That is, we examine the *demand side* of the economy. Second, we examine the *supply side* by exploring the relationship among the price level, the prices of factor inputs, and the level of output producers would like to supply. Finally, we examine the concept of *macroeconomic equilibrium* that combines both the demand and the supply sides to determine the price level and real GDP simultaneously.

23.1 The Demand Side of the Economy

Consider the macro model in Chapter 22 in which the price level is assumed to be constant. What would happen to equilibrium GDP in that model if there were a *different* price level? To find out, we need to understand how an exogenous change in the price level affects desired aggregate expenditure.

Exogenous Changes in the Price Level

The *AE* curve shifts in response to a change in the price level—a change, that is, in *all the economy's prices*. This shift occurs because a change in the price level affects desired consumption expenditures and desired net exports. These are the changes on which we will focus in this chapter. (In later chapters, we will see that changes in the price level will also change interest rates and thus shift the *AE* curve for an additional reason.)

Changes in Consumption You might think it is obvious that a fall in the price level leads to an increase in desired consumption for the simple reason that the demand curves for most individual products are negatively sloped. As we will see in a few pages, however, this logic is incorrect in the context of an aggregate model—our focus here is on the *aggregate* price level rather than on the prices of individual products. The relationship between the price level and desired consumption has to do with how changes in the price level lead to changes in household *wealth* and thus to changes in desired spending.

Much of the private sector's total wealth is held in the form of assets with a fixed nominal value. The most obvious example is money itself. We will discuss money in considerable detail in Chapters 27 and 28, but for now just note that most individuals and businesses hold money in their wallets, in their cash registers, or in their bank accounts. What this money can buy—its real value—depends on the price level. The higher the price level, the fewer goods and services a given amount of money can purchase. For this reason, a rise in the domestic price level lowers the real value of money holdings. Similarly, a reduction in the price level raises the real value of money holdings.

> A rise in the price level lowers the real value of money held by the private sector. A fall in the price level raises the real value of money held by the private sector.

Changes in the price level cause changes in the real value of cash held by households and firms. This change in wealth leads to changes in the amount of desired consumption expenditure.

Other examples of assets that have fixed nominal values include government and corporate bonds. The bondholder has lent money to the issuer of the bond and receives a repayment from the issuer when the bond matures. What happens when there is a change in the price level in the intervening period? A rise in the price level means that the repayment to the bondholder is lower in real value than it otherwise would be. This is a decline in wealth for the bondholder. However, the issuer of the bond, having made a repayment of lower real value because of the increase in the price level, has experienced an increase in wealth. In dollar terms, the bondholder's reduction in wealth is exactly offset by the issuer's increase in wealth.

> Changes in the price level change the wealth of bondholders and bond issuers, but because the changes offset each other, there is no change in aggregate wealth.[1]

In summary, a rise in the price level leads to a reduction in the real value of the private sector's wealth. And as we saw in Chapter 21, a reduction in wealth leads to a decrease in autonomous desired consumption and thus to a downward shift in the *AE* function. A fall in the domestic price level leads to a rise in wealth and desired consumption and thus to an upward shift in the *AE* curve.

Changes in Net Exports When the domestic price level rises (and the exchange rate remains unchanged), Canadian goods become more expensive relative to foreign goods. As we saw in Chapter 22, this change in international relative prices causes Canadian consumers to reduce their purchases of Canadian-made goods, which have now become relatively more expensive, and to increase their purchases of foreign goods, which have now become relatively less expensive. At the same time, consumers in other countries reduce their purchases of the now relatively more expensive Canadian-made goods. We saw in Chapter 22 that these changes cause a downward shift in the net export function.

> A rise in the domestic price level (with a constant exchange rate) shifts the net export function downward, which causes a downward shift in the *AE* curve. A fall in the domestic price level shifts the net export function upward and hence the *AE* curve upward.

Changes in Equilibrium GDP

Because it causes downward shifts in both the net export function and the consumption function, an exogenous rise in the price level causes a downward shift in the *AE* curve, as shown in Figure 23-1. When the *AE* curve shifts downward, the equilibrium level of real GDP falls.

Conversely, with a fall in the price level, Canadian goods become relatively cheaper internationally, so net exports rise. Also, the purchasing power of nominal assets increases, so households spend more. The resulting increase in desired expenditure on Canadian goods causes the *AE* curve to shift upward. The equilibrium level of real GDP therefore rises.

A Change of Labels. In Chapters 21 and 22 the horizontal axis was labelled "Actual National Income" because we wanted to emphasize the important difference between *actual* income and *desired* expenditure. Notice in Figure 23-1, however, that we have labelled the horizontal axis "Real GDP." We use GDP rather than *national income*, but these have the same meaning. It is still *actual*, as opposed to *desired*, but we leave that

---

[1] If bonds are issued by domestic firms or governments but held by foreigners, the changes in domestic wealth caused by a change in the domestic price level will not completely offset each other. In particular, a rise in the domestic price level will lead to a transfer of wealth away from foreign bondholders and toward domestic bond issuers. This is why bondholders who expect future inflation usually demand higher returns in order to hold bonds. In Canada, most corporate and government bonds are held by Canadian firms or individuals and so we ignore this issue; in many other countries, where much debt is held abroad, the issue is of greater importance.

off, also for simplicity. Finally, we add *real* because from this chapter onward the price level will be changing and thus it is necessary to distinguish changes in nominal GDP from changes in real GDP.

The Aggregate Demand Curve

We have just seen, in the simple model from Chapters 21 and 22, that the price level and real equilibrium GDP are negatively related to each other. This negative relationship can be shown in an important new concept, the *aggregate demand curve.*

Recall that the AE curve is drawn with real GDP on the horizontal axis and desired aggregate expenditure on the vertical axis, and that it is plotted for a *given* price level. We are now going to let the price level vary and keep track of the various equilibrium points that occur as the AE function shifts. By doing so we can construct an **aggregate demand (AD) curve** that shows the relationship between the price level and the equilibrium level of real GDP. It will be plotted with the price level on the vertical axis and real GDP on the horizontal axis. Because the horizontal axes of both the AE and the AD curves measure real GDP, the two curves can be placed one above the other so that the levels of GDP on both can be compared directly. This is shown in Figure 23-2.

Now let us derive the AD curve. Given a value of the price level, P_0, equilibrium GDP is determined in part (i) of Figure 23-2 at the point where the AE_0 curve crosses the 45° line. The equilibrium level of real GDP is Y_0. Part (ii) of the figure shows the same equilibrium level of GDP, Y_0, plotted against the price level P_0. The equilibrium point in part (i), E_0, corresponds to point E_0 on the AD curve in part (ii).

As the price level rises to P_1, the AE curve shifts down to AE_1 and the equilibrium level of real GDP falls to Y_1. This determines a second point on the AD curve, E_1. By joining these points, we trace out the AD curve.

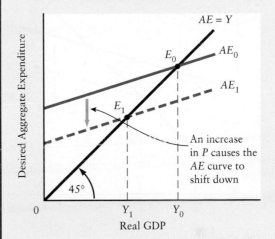

FIGURE 23-1 Desired Aggregate Expenditure and the Price Level

An exogenous change in the price level causes the AE curve to shift and equilibrium GDP to change. At the initial price level, the AE curve is given by AE_0, and hence equilibrium is at E_0 with real GDP equal to Y_0. An increase in the price level causes the AE curve to shift downward to the dashed line, AE_1. As a result, equilibrium changes to E_1 and equilibrium GDP falls to Y_1.

Recall from Chapter 22 that a change in the domestic price level also affects the marginal propensity to import (m) and thus the *slope* of the AE function. For simplicity, that effect is ignored in this chapter.

aggregate demand (AD) curve A curve showing combinations of real GDP and the price level that make desired aggregate expenditure equal to actual national income.

> For any given price level, the AD curve shows the level of real GDP for which desired aggregate expenditure equals actual GDP.

Note that because the AD curve relates equilibrium GDP to the price level, changes in the price level that cause *shifts in* the AE curve are simply *movements along* the AD curve. A movement along the AD curve thus traces out the response of equilibrium GDP to a change in the price level.[2]

---

[2] Our discussion of Figure 23-2 is for an economy open to international trade, and we emphasize the reduction of consumption and net exports that occurs in response to a rise in the domestic price level. In a *closed* economy, however, the second effect is absent, resulting in a steeper AD curve than what is shown in Figure 23-2.

FIGURE 23-2 Derivation of the *AD* Curve

(i) Aggregate expenditure

As the price level rises, the *AE* curve shifts down and the economy moves upward along the *AD* curve

(ii) Aggregate demand

Equilibrium GDP is determined by the *AE* curve for each given price level; the level of equilibrium GDP and its associated price level are then plotted to yield a point on the *AD* curve. When the price level is P_0, the *AE* curve is AE_0, and hence equilibrium GDP is Y_0, as shown in part (i). Plotting Y_0 against P_0 yields the point E_0 on the *AD* curve in part (ii).

An increase in the price level to P_1 causes the *AE* curve to shift downward to AE_1 and causes equilibrium GDP to fall to Y_1. Plotting this new level of GDP against the higher price level yields a second point, E_1, on the *AD* curve. A further increase in the price level to P_2 causes the *AE* curve to shift downward to AE_2, and thus causes equilibrium GDP to fall to Y_2. Plotting P_2 and Y_2 yields a third point, E_2, on the *AD* curve.

A change in the price level causes a shift of the *AE* curve but a movement along the *AD* curve.

The *AD* Curve Is Not a Micro Demand Curve! Figure 23-2 provides us with sufficient information to establish that the *AD* curve is negatively sloped.

1. A rise in the price level causes the *AE* curve to shift downward and hence leads to a movement upward and to the left along the *AD* curve, reflecting a fall in the equilibrium level of GDP.

2. A fall in the price level causes the *AE* curve to shift upward and hence leads to a movement downward and to the right along the *AD* curve, reflecting a rise in the equilibrium level of GDP.

In Chapter 3, we saw that demand curves for individual goods, such as coffee, T-shirts, and automobiles, are negatively sloped. However, the reasons for the negative slope of the *AD* curve are different from the reasons for the negative slope of individual demand curves used in microeconomics. Why is this the case?

A "micro" demand curve describes a situation in which the price of one commodity changes *while the prices of all other commodities and consumers' dollar incomes are constant*. Such an individual demand curve is negatively sloped for two reasons. First, as the price of the commodity falls, the purchasing power of each consumer's income will rise, and this rise in real income will lead to more units of the good being purchased. Second, as the price of the commodity falls, consumers buy more of that commodity and fewer of the now relatively more expensive substitutes.

The first reason does not apply to the *AD* curve because the dollar value of national income is not being held constant as the price level changes and we move along the *AD* curve. The second reason applies to the *AD* curve but only in a limited way. A change in the price level does not change the *relative* prices of domestic goods and thus does not cause consumers to substitute between them. However, a change in the domestic price level (for a given exchange rate) *does* lead to a change in *international* relative prices and thus to some substitution between domestic and foreign products; this is the link between the price level and net exports that we discussed earlier.

To summarize, the *AD* curve is negatively sloped for two reasons:

1. A fall in the price level leads to a rise in private-sector wealth, which increases desired consump-

tion and thus leads to an increase in equilibrium GDP.

2. A fall in the price level (for a given exchange rate) leads to a rise in net exports and thus leads to an increase in equilibrium GDP.

In later chapters, after we have discussed money, banking, and interest rates in detail, we will introduce a third reason for the negative slope of the AD curve.

Shifts in the AD Curve What can cause the AD curve to shift? For a given price level, any event that leads to a change in equilibrium GDP will cause the AD curve to shift. The event could be a change in government policy, such as the level of government purchases or taxation (or, as we will see later, a policy-induced change in interest rates). Or the event could be something beyond the government's control, such as a change in households' consumption expenditure, firms' investment behaviour, or foreigners' demand for Canadian exports.

Figure 23-3 shows a shift in the AD curve. Because the AD curve plots equilibrium GDP as a function of the price level, anything that alters equilibrium GDP *at a given price level* must shift the AD curve. In other words, any change—other than a change in the price level—that causes the AE curve to shift will also cause the AD curve to shift. Such a shift is called an **aggregate demand shock.**

For example, in the 2002–2008 period, strong economic growth in the world economy led to an increase in demand for Canadian-produced raw materials. This increase in demand caused an upward shift in Canada's net export function. This event, taken by itself, would shift Canada's AE function upward and thus would shift Canada's AD curve to the right.

Beginning in the fall of 2008, however, a dramatic slowdown in world economic growth, caused in large part by the collapse of the U.S. housing market and the resulting worldwide financial crisis, led to a reduction in foreign demand for Canadian products. There was also an associated reduction in both investment and consumption expenditure in Canada, driven partly by the pessimism that accompanied the crisis. The overall effect was a downward shift in the AE curve and thus a leftward shift of Canada's AD curve.

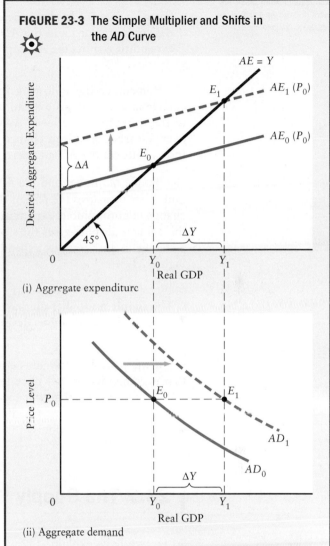

FIGURE 23-3 The Simple Multiplier and Shifts in the *AD* Curve

(i) Aggregate expenditure

(ii) Aggregate demand

A change in autonomous expenditure changes equilibrium GDP for any given price level. The simple multiplier measures the resulting horizontal shift in the AD curve. The original AE curve is AE_0 in part (i). Equilibrium is at E_0, with GDP of Y_0 at price level P_0. This yields point E_0 on the curve AD_0 in part (ii).

The AE curve in part (i) then shifts upward from AE_0 to AE_1 because of an increase in autonomous desired expenditure of ΔA. Equilibrium GDP now rises to Y_1, with the price level still constant at P_0. Thus, the AD curve in part (ii) shifts to the right to point E_1, indicating the higher equilibrium GDP of Y_1 associated with the same price level P_0. The size of the horizontal shift of the AD curve, ΔY, is equal to the simple multiplier times ΔA.

aggregate demand shock Any event that causes a shift in the aggregate demand curve.

> For a given price level, an increase in autonomous aggregate expenditure shifts the *AE* curve upward and the *AD* curve to the right. A fall in autonomous aggregate expenditure shifts the *AE* curve downward and the *AD* curve to the left.

Remember the following important point: In order to shift the *AD* curve, the change in autonomous expenditure must be caused by something *other than* a change in the domestic price level. As we saw earlier in this chapter, a change in aggregate expenditure caused by a change in the domestic price level leads to a movement along (not a shift of) the *AD* curve.

The Simple Multiplier and the *AD* Curve We saw in Chapters 21 and 22 that the simple multiplier measures the size of the change in equilibrium national income caused by a change in autonomous expenditure *when the price level is held constant*. It follows that this same multiplier gives the size of the *horizontal shift* in the *AD* curve in response to a change in autonomous expenditure, as illustrated by the movement from E_0 to E_1 in Figure 23-3.

> The simple multiplier measures the horizontal shift in the *AD* curve in response to a change in autonomous desired expenditure.

If the price level remains constant and producers are willing to supply everything that is demanded at that price level, the simple multiplier will also show the change in equilibrium income that will occur in response to a change in autonomous expenditure. This mention of producers' willingness to supply output brings us to a discussion of the *supply side* of the economy.

23.2 The Supply Side of the Economy

So far, we have explained how the equilibrium level of GDP is determined *when the price level is taken as given* and how that equilibrium changes as the price level is changed exogenously. We are now ready to take the important next step: adding an *explanation* for changes in the price level. To do this, we need to take account of the supply decisions of firms.

The Aggregate Supply Curve

aggregate supply (AS) curve A curve showing the relation between the price level and the quantity of aggregate output supplied, for given technology and factor prices.

Aggregate supply refers to the total output of goods and services that firms would like to produce and sell. The **aggregate supply (*AS*) curve** relates the price level to the quantity of output that firms would like to produce and sell under two assumptions:

- the state of technology is constant
- the prices of all factors of production are constant

What does the *AS* curve look like, and why?

The Positive Slope of the *AS* Curve Suppose firms want to increase their output above current levels. What will this do to their costs per unit of output—usually called their **unit costs?** The aggregate supply curve is drawn under the assumption that technology and the prices of all factors of production remain constant. This does not, however, mean that firms' unit costs will be constant. As output increases, less efficient standby plants may have to be used, and less efficient workers may have to be hired, while existing workers may have to be paid overtime rates for additional work. For these and other similar reasons, unit costs tend to rise as output rises, even when technology and input prices are constant. (Readers who have studied microeconomics will recognize the *law of diminishing returns* as one reason that costs may rise in the short run as firms squeeze more output out of a fixed quantity of capital equipment.)

unit cost Cost per unit of output, equal to total cost divided by total output.

This positive relationship between output and unit costs leads to the positive slope of the *AS* curve, as shown in Figure 23-4. Firms will not be prepared to produce and sell more output unless they are able to charge a higher price sufficient to cover their higher unit costs. This argument applies to *price-taking* firms who sell homogeneous products at market prices beyond their influence. It also applies to *price-setting* firms who sell differentiated products and have some ability to determine the price they charge. In both cases, the fact that unit costs generally rise with output means that firms generally increase their production only if they are able to receive higher prices.

> The actions of both price-taking and price-setting firms cause the price level and the supply of output to be positively related—the aggregate supply (*AS*) curve is positively sloped.

The Increasing Slope of the *AS* Curve In Figure 23-4 we see that at low levels of GDP the *AS* curve is relatively flat, but as GDP rises the *AS* curve gets progressively steeper. What explains this shape?

When output is low, firms typically have excess capacity— some plant and equipment are idle. When firms have excess capacity, only a small increase in the price of their output may be needed to induce them to expand production. Indeed, if firms have enough excess capacity, they may be willing to sell more at their existing prices when the demand for their product increases. In this case, output is truly demand determined up to the level at which costs begin to rise. Once output is pushed above normal capacity, however, unit costs tend to rise quite rapidly. Many higher-cost production methods may have to be adopted—such as standby capacity, overtime, and extra shifts. These higher-cost production methods will not be used unless the selling price of the output has risen enough to cover them. The more output is expanded beyond normal capacity, the more unit costs rise and hence the larger is the rise in price that is necessary to induce firms to increase output.

FIGURE 23-4 The Aggregate Supply Curve

The *AS* curve is positively sloped, indicating that firms will provide more aggregate output only at a higher price level. The *AS* curve is drawn for a given level of technology and factor prices. At price level P_0, firms are prepared to produce and supply output equal to Y_0. An expansion of their output to Y_1 leads to an increase in unit costs, and thus firms are prepared to supply Y_1 only at a higher price level, P_1.

The higher is the level of output, the faster unit costs tend to rise with each extra increment to output. This explains why the *AS* curve becomes steeper as output rises. At low levels of output, firms may have excess capacity and increases in output may not drive up unit costs. In these situations, the *AS* curve would be flat (horizontal).

For many firms, increases in output will drive up their unit costs. As a result, they will be prepared to supply more output only at a higher price. This behaviour gives rise to an upward-sloping AS curve.

aggregate supply shock Any shift in the aggregate supply (*AS*) curve caused by an exogenous force.

As we will see later in this chapter, the shape of the *AS* curve is crucial for determining how the effect of an aggregate demand shock is divided between a change in the price level and a change in real GDP.

Shifts in the *AS* Curve

For a given level of output, anything that changes firms' production costs will cause the *AS* curve to shift. Two sources of such changes are of particular importance: changes in the prices of inputs and changes in firms' production technology. Input prices can, however, change for two different reasons. First, input prices may change because of things that are internal to our model. For example, if a rise in production increases the demand for labour and thus bids up wages, this will shift the *AS* curve upward and to the left. This shift is *endogenous* to our macro model, and we will discuss shifts of this type in Chapter 24. Second, input prices may change because of forces unconnected to our model—*exogenous* forces. For example, the world price of oil may rise and since this will raise the input prices of virtually all firms, it will also shift the *AS* curve upward and to the left. Shifts in the *AS* curve caused by such exogenous forces are called **aggregate supply shocks**. Let's now examine these shocks in more detail.

Changes in Input Prices When factor prices change, the *AS* curve shifts. If factor prices rise, firms will find the profitability of their current production reduced. For any given level of output to be produced, an increase in the price level will be required. If prices do not rise, firms will react by decreasing production. For the economy as a whole, there will be less output supplied at each price level than before the increase in factor prices. Or, to put it another way, there will be a higher price level for each level of output than before the increase in factor prices. Thus, if factor prices rise, the *AS* curve shifts upward (and to the left). This is a decrease in aggregate supply and is shown in Figure 23-5.

Similarly, a fall in factor prices causes the *AS* curve to shift downward (and to the right). There will be more output supplied at each price level. Or, to put the same point differently, the same amount of output will be supplied at a lower price level. This is an increase in aggregate supply. A dramatic example of such a reduction in factor prices occurred in 1998 when the world prices of raw materials fell by an average of 30 percent. In the many countries that use raw materials as inputs in manufacturing, the *AS* curves shifted to the right. The opposite happened in 2002–2008 when energy and other commodity prices increased dramatically, thus shifting the *AS* curves to the left.

Changes in Technology Firms adopt new technologies in order to produce better versions of their products or to produce their existing products at lower costs (or both). For the purposes of our discussion, we define an *improvement* in technology as any change to production methods that reduces unit costs for any given level of output. Improvements in technology reduce unit costs and typically lead to lower prices as competing firms cut prices in attempts to raise their market share. Since the same output can now be sold at lower prices, the *AS* curve shifts downward and to the right. This is an increase in aggregate supply.

A *deterioration* in technology is any change in production methods that raises unit costs for any given level of output. Since firms are unlikely to intentionally adopt new methods that raise their costs, the latter occurrences are rare. However, in industries that rely on specific weather conditions for production—like agriculture—poor weather can be interpreted as a deterioration in technology. A deterioration in technology raises unit costs and causes the *AS* curve to shift upward and to the left, as shown in Figure 23-5.

> A change in either factor prices or technology will shift the *AS* curve, because any given output will be supplied at a different price level than previously. An increase in factor prices or a deterioration in technology shifts the *AS* curve to the left; a decrease in factor prices or an improvement in technology shifts the *AS* curve to the right.

23.3 Macroeconomic Equilibrium

We are now ready to see how both real GDP and the price level are simultaneously determined by the interaction of aggregate demand and aggregate supply. To begin, we assume that input prices and technology are constant.

The equilibrium values of real GDP and the price level occur at the intersection of the *AD* and *AS* curves, as shown by the pair Y_0 and P_0 that arises at point E_0 in Figure 23-6. The combination of real GDP and price level that is on both the *AD* and the *AS* curves is called a *macroeconomic equilibrium*.

To see why E_0 is the only macroeconomic equilibrium, consider what would occur at either a lower or a higher price level. First, consider the price level P_1. At this price level, total desired expenditure is Y_2 but the economy's firms are only prepared to produce and sell an output of Y_1; there is excess demand. Conversely, consider any price level above P_0. At these prices, the amount of output supplied by firms is greater than total desired expenditure; there is excess supply. Only at the price level P_0 is the desired production of output by firms consistent with aggregate expenditure decisions.

> Only at the combination of real GDP and price level given by the intersection of the *AS* and *AD* curves are demand behaviour and supply behaviour consistent.

Macroeconomic equilibrium thus requires that two conditions be satisfied. The first is familiar to us because it comes from Chapters 21 and 22. At the prevailing price level, desired aggregate expenditure must be equal to actual GDP. The *AD* curve is constructed in such a way that this condition holds everywhere along it. The second

FIGURE 23-5 Shifts in the AS Curve

For any given level of output, anything that increases firms' costs will shift the *AS* curve upward (and to the left). Starting from (P_0, Y_0), a rise in input prices or a deterioration in technology would increase firms' unit costs. Firms would be prepared to continue supplying output of Y_0 only at the higher price level P_1. Or, at the initial price level P_0, firms would now be prepared to supply output of only Y_1. In either case, the *AS* curve has shifted up (or to the left) from AS_0 to AS_1. This is called a reduction in aggregate supply.

A fall in input prices or an improvement in technology would cause the *AS* curve to shift down (and to the right). This is an increase in aggregate supply.

FIGURE 23-6 Macroeconomic Equilibrium

Macroeconomic equilibrium occurs at the intersection of the *AD* and *AS* curves and determines the equilibrium values for real GDP and the price level. Given the *AD* and *AS* curves in the figure, macroeconomic equilibrium occurs at E_0.

If the price level were equal to P_1, the desired output of firms would be Y_1. However, at P_1, the level of output that is consistent with expenditure decisions would be Y_2. Hence, when the price level is less than P_0, the desired output of firms will be less than the level of real GDP that is consistent with expenditure decisions. Conversely, for any price level above P_0, the desired output of firms exceeds the level of output that is consistent with expenditure decisions.

The only price level at which the supply decisions of firms are consistent with desired expenditure is P_0. At P_0, firms want to produce Y_0. When they do so, they generate a real GDP of Y_0; when real GDP is Y_0, decision makers want to spend exactly Y_0, thereby purchasing the nation's output. Hence, all decisions are consistent with each other.

requirement for macroeconomic equilibrium is introduced by consideration of aggregate supply. At the prevailing price level, firms must want to produce the prevailing level of GDP, no more and no less. This condition is fulfilled everywhere along the *AS* curve. Only where the two curves intersect are both conditions fulfilled simultaneously.

Changes in the Macroeconomic Equilibrium

The aggregate demand and aggregate supply curves can now be used to understand how various shocks to the economy change both real GDP and the price level.

As indicated earlier, a shift in the *AD* curve is called an aggregate demand shock. A rightward shift in the *AD* curve is an increase in aggregate demand; it means that at all price levels, expenditure decisions will now be consistent with a higher level of real GDP. This is called a *positive* shock. Similarly, a leftward shift in the *AD* curve is a decrease in aggregate demand—that is, at all price levels, expenditure decisions will now be consistent with a lower level of real GDP. This is called a *negative* shock.

Also as indicated earlier, a shift in the *AS* curve caused by an exogenous force is called an aggregate supply shock. A rightward shift in the *AS* curve is an increase in aggregate supply; at any given price level, more real GDP will be supplied. This is a *positive* shock. A leftward shift in the *AS* curve is a decrease in aggregate supply; at any given price level, less real GDP will be supplied. This is a *negative* shock.

> **Aggregate demand and supply shocks are labelled according to their effect on real GDP. Positive shocks increase equilibrium GDP; negative shocks reduce equilibrium GDP.**

Aggregate Demand Shocks

Figure 23-7 shows the effects of an increase in aggregate demand—a positive *AD* shock. This increase could have occurred because of, say, increased investment or government purchases, an increase in foreigners' demand for Canadian goods, or an increase in household consumption resulting from a reduction in personal income taxes or an increase in transfer payments. (Remember that each of these events causes the *AE* curve to shift up, and therefore the *AD* curve to shift to the right.) Whatever the cause, the increase in aggregate demand means that more domestic output is demanded at any given price level. As is shown in the figure, the increase in aggregate demand causes both the price level and real GDP to rise in the new macroeconomic equilibrium. Conversely, a decrease in demand causes both the price level and real GDP to fall.

> Aggregate demand shocks cause the price level and real GDP to change in the same direction; both rise with an increase in aggregate demand, and both fall with a decrease in aggregate demand.

Figure 23-7 shows how the macroeconomic equilibrium changes when there is an aggregate demand shock, but it does not show the complex adjustment going on "behind the scenes." We now examine this adjustment and see how the change in the price level alters the value of the multiplier.

The Multiplier When the Price Level Varies We saw earlier in this chapter that the simple multiplier gives the size of the horizontal shift in the AD curve in response to a change in autonomous expenditure. If the price level remains constant and firms supply all that is demanded at the existing price level (as would be the case with a horizontal AS curve), the simple multiplier gives the increase in equilibrium national income.

But what happens in the more usual case in which the AS curve slopes upward? As can be seen in Figure 23-7, when the AS curve is positively sloped, the change in real GDP caused by a change in autonomous expenditure is no longer equal to the size of the horizontal shift in the AD curve. Part of the expansionary impact of an increase in demand is dissipated by a rise in the price level, and only part is transmitted to a rise in real GDP. Of course, an increase in output does occur; thus, a multiplier may still be calculated, but its value is not the same as that of the *simple multiplier*.

Why is the multiplier smaller when the AS curve is positively sloped? The answer lies in the behaviour that is summarized by the AE curve. To understand this, it is useful to think of the final change in real GDP as occurring in two stages, as shown in Figure 23-8.

First, with a constant price level, an increase in autonomous expenditure shifts the AE curve upward (from AE_0 to AE_1'). This increase in autonomous expenditure is shown in part (ii) by a shift to the right of the AD curve. The movement marked ① is the horizontal shift of the AD curve and is equal to the simple multiplier times the change in autonomous expenditure. This is the end of the first stage, but is not the end of the whole story.

In the second stage we must take account of the rise in the price level that occurs because of the positive slope of the AS curve. As we saw earlier in this chapter, a rise in the price level, via its effect on net exports and desired consumption, leads to a downward shift in the AE curve (from AE_1' to AE_1). This second shift of the AE curve partly counteracts the initial rise in real GDP and so reduces the size of the multiplier. The second stage shows up as a downward shift of the AE curve in part (i)

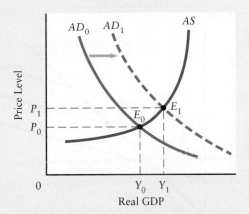

FIGURE 23-7 Aggregate Demand Shocks

Shifts in aggregate demand cause the price level and real GDP to move in the same direction. An increase in aggregate demand shifts the AD curve to the right, from AD_0 to AD_1. Macroeconomic equilibrium moves from E_0 to E_1. The price level rises from P_0 to P_1, and real GDP rises from Y_0 to Y_1, reflecting a movement along the AS curve.

FIGURE 23-8 The Multiplier When the Price Level Varies

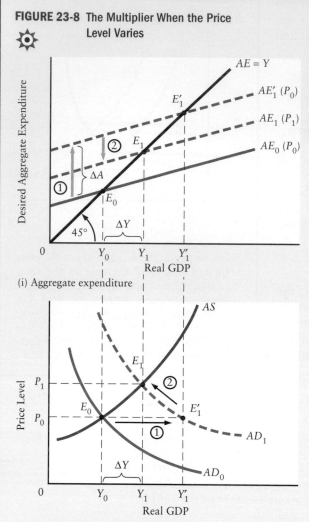

(i) Aggregate expenditure

(ii) Aggregate demand and supply

An increase in autonomous expenditure causes the AE curve to shift upward, but the rise in the price level causes it to shift part of the way down again. Hence, the multiplier is smaller than when the price level is constant. Originally, equilibrium is at point E_0 in both parts (i) and (ii). Desired aggregate expenditure then shifts by ΔA to AE'_1, shifting the AD curve to AD_1. These shifts are shown by arrow ① in both parts. But the adjustment is not yet complete.

The shift in the AD curve raises the price level to P_1 because the AS curve is positively sloped. The rise in the price level shifts the AE curve down to AE_1, as shown by arrow ② in part (i). This is shown as a movement along the new AD curve, as indicated by arrow ② in part (ii). The new equilibrium is thus at E_1. The amount Y_0Y_1 is ΔY, the actual increase in real GDP. The multiplier, adjusted for the effect of the price increase, is the ratio $\Delta Y/\Delta A$.

of Figure 23-8 and a movement upward and to the left along the new AD curve, as shown by arrow ② in part (ii).

> If an aggregate demand shock leads to a change in the price level, the ultimate change in real GDP will be *less than* what is predicted by the simple multiplier. In other words, a variable price level reduces the value of the multiplier.

The Importance of the Shape of the AS Curve We have now seen that the shape of the AS curve has important implications for how the effects of an aggregate demand shock are divided between changes in real GDP and changes in the price level. Figure 23-9 highlights the price level and GDP effects of aggregate demand shocks by considering these shocks in the presence of an AS curve with three distinct ranges.

Over the *flat* range, any change in aggregate demand leads to no change in prices and, as seen earlier, a response of output equal to that predicted by the simple multiplier.

Over the *intermediate* range, along which the AS curve is positively sloped, a shift in the AD curve gives rise to appreciable changes in both real GDP and the price level. Because of the increase in the price level, the multiplier in this case is positive, but smaller than the simple multiplier.

Over the *steep* range, very little more can be produced, no matter how large the increase in demand. This range deals with an economy near its physical capacity constraints. Any change in aggregate demand leads to a sharp change in the price level and to little or no change in real GDP. The multiplier in this case is nearly zero.

> The effect of any given shift in aggregate demand will be divided between a change in real output and a change in the price level, depending on the conditions of aggregate supply. The steeper the AS curve, the greater the price effect and the smaller the output effect.

Extensions in Theory 23-1 deals with the case of a horizontal AS curve—sometimes called a *Keynesian AS* curve. In that case, the aggregate supply curve determines the price level, and the *AD* curve determines real GDP.

Reconciliation with Previous Analysis One of the central points of this chapter is that aggregate demand shocks typically lead to changes in *both* the price level and the level of real GDP. Furthermore, with a vertical *AS* curve, such aggregate demand shocks will result in no change in real GDP, but only a change in the price level. How do we reconcile this possibility with the analysis of Chapters 21 and 22, where shifts in *AE* *always* change real GDP? The answer is that each *AE* curve is drawn on the assumption that there is a constant price level. An upward shift in the *AE* curve shifts the *AD* curve to the right. However, a positively sloped *AS* curve means that the price level rises, and this rise shifts the *AE* curve back down, offsetting some of its initial rise. This process was explained in Figure 23-8.

It is instructive to consider an extreme version of Figure 23-8, one with a vertical *AS* curve. If you draw this diagram for yourself, you will note that an increase in autonomous expenditure shifts the *AE* curve upward, thus raising the amount demanded. However, a vertical *AS* curve means that output cannot be expanded to satisfy the increased demand. Instead, the extra demand merely forces prices up, and as prices rise, the *AE* curve shifts down again. The rise in prices continues until the *AE* curve is back to where it started. Thus, the rise in prices offsets the expansionary effect of the original shift and consequently leaves both real aggregate expenditure and equilibrium real GDP unchanged.

A vertical *AS* curve, however, is quite unrealistic. An *AS* curve shaped something like the one shown in Figure 23-9—that is, relatively flat for low levels of GDP and becoming steeper as GDP rises—is closer to reality.

We now complete our discussion of changes in the macroeconomic equilibrium by discussing supply shocks.

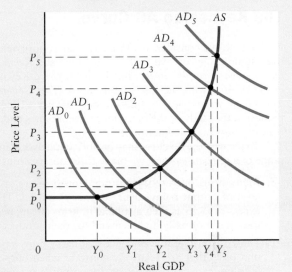

FIGURE 23-9 The Effects of Increases in Aggregate Demand

The effect of increases in aggregate demand is divided between increases in real GDP and increases in the price level, depending on the slope of the *AS* curve. Because of the increasing slope of the *AS* curve, increases in aggregate demand up to AD_0 have virtually no impact on the price level. Successive further increases bring larger price increases and relatively smaller output increases. By the time aggregate demand is at AD_4 or AD_5, virtually all of the effect is on the price level.

Aggregate Supply Shocks

A negative aggregate supply shock, shown by an upward (or leftward) shift in the *AS* curve, means that less real output will be supplied at any given price level. A positive aggregate supply shock, shown by a downward (or rightward) shift in the *AS* curve, means that more real output will be supplied at any given price level.

Figure 23-10 illustrates the effects on the price level and real GDP of a negative aggregate supply shock. This could have occurred because of, say, an increase in the world price of important inputs, such as oil, copper, or iron ore. As can be seen from the figure, following the decrease in aggregate supply, the price level rises and real GDP falls. Conversely, a positive aggregate supply shock leads to an increase in real GDP and a decrease in the price level.

EXTENSIONS IN THEORY 23-1

The Keynesian *AS* Curve

In this box, we consider an *AS* curve that is horizontal over some range of real GDP. It is called the *Keynesian aggregate supply curve*, after John Maynard Keynes (1883–1946), who, in his famous book *The General Theory of Employment, Interest and Money* (1936), pioneered the study of the behaviour of economies under conditions of high unemployment.

To see why the *AS* curve may be horizontal over some range of aggregate output, we make three observations:

1. Many firms operate their production facilities at a level of output below their "capacity" output. The excess capacity is then available to firms during periods of abnormally high demand for their products.

2. There is considerable evidence that many firms have unit costs that are relatively constant when output is below capacity. Once capacity output is reached, however, additional output can be produced only with rising unit costs.

3. For price-setting firms with output below capacity, short-run changes in demand are often met with changes in output but not changes in price. One explanation for this behaviour is that there are costs associated with changing prices.

The behaviour that gives rise to the Keynesian *AS* curve can then be described as follows. When real GDP is below potential GDP (the economy's "capacity" output), individual firms are operating with excess capacity. They then respond to changes in demand by altering output while keeping prices constant. In other words, they will supply whatever they can sell at their existing prices as long as they are producing below their normal capacity.

Under these circumstances, the economy has a horizontal *AS* curve, indicating that any output up to potential output will be supplied at the going price level. The amount that is actually produced is then determined by

John Maynard Keynes was the founder of much of modern macroeconomics, and emphasized the importance of aggregate demand in determining the level of economic activity.

the position of the *AD* curve. Thus, real GDP is said to be *demand determined*. If demand rises enough so that firms are trying to increase their output beyond capacity, their costs will rise and so will their prices. Hence, the horizontal Keynesian *AS* curve applies only to levels of GDP below potential GDP.

The case of a horizontal *AS* curve corresponds to the macro model that we developed in Chapters 21 and 22. Recall that in that simple model we assumed a constant price level. In other words, if the *AS* curve is horizontal, our macro model in this chapter is *exactly the same* as the simple version in Chapters 21 and 22. In this case, a change in autonomous expenditure, ΔA, will lead to increases in equilibrium GDP equal to ΔA times the simple multiplier.

Aggregate supply shocks cause the price level and real GDP to change in opposite directions. With an increase in supply, the price level falls and GDP rises; with a decrease in supply, the price level rises and GDP falls.

Oil-price increases have provided three major examples of negative aggregate supply shocks, the first two during the 1970s and the third between 2002 and 2008. The economy is especially responsive to changes in the price of oil because, in addition to being used to produce energy, oil is an input into plastics, chemicals, fertilizers, and many other materials that are widely used in industry. Massive increases in oil prices occurred during 1973–1974 and 1979–1980, caused by the successful efforts of the OPEC countries to form a cartel and restrict the output of oil. These increases in the price of oil caused leftward shifts in the *AS* curve in most countries. Real GDP fell while the price level rose, a combination commonly referred to as *stagflation*. (We will discuss shortly the more recent oil-price increases that occurred in the 2002–2008 period.)

Commodity prices have provided an important recent example of a positive aggregate supply shock. The Southeast Asian countries of Indonesia, Malaysia, Thailand, and South Korea are all significant users of raw materials. When their economies plunged into a major recession in 1997, the world demand for raw materials fell, and the prices of such goods fell as a result. From 1997 to 1998, the average price of raw materials fell by approximately 30 percent.

Though these were clearly bad economic times for much of Southeast Asia, the reduction in raw materials prices was a *positive* aggregate supply shock for countries that used raw materials as inputs for production. In countries like Canada, the United States, and most of Western Europe, the *AS* curves shifted to the right. The effect was to increase real GDP and reduce the price level.[3]

A Word of Warning

We have discussed the effects of aggregate demand and aggregate supply shocks on the economy's price level and real GDP. Students are sometimes puzzled, however, because some events would appear to be *both* demand and supply shocks. How do we analyze such complicated shocks? For example, when the world price of oil rises, as it did significantly between 2002 and 2008, this is a *negative supply shock* because oil is an important input to production for many firms. But for Canada, which produces and exports oil, doesn't the increase in the world price of oil also imply an increase in export revenue? And doesn't this imply a *positive demand shock*?

The answer to both questions is yes. An increase in world oil prices is indeed a negative aggregate supply shock to any country that uses oil as an input (which means most countries). But for those countries that also produce and

FIGURE 23-10 A Negative Aggregate Supply Shock

(i) Aggregate expenditure

(ii) Aggregate demand and supply

Aggregate supply shocks cause the price level and real GDP to move in opposite directions. The original equilibrium is at E_0, with GDP of Y_0 appearing in both parts of the figure. The price level is P_0 in part (ii), and at that price level, the desired aggregate expenditure curve is AE_0 in part (i).

A negative aggregate supply shock now shifts the *AS* curve in part (ii) to AS_1. At the original price level of P_0, firms are willing to supply only Y_1'. The fall in aggregate supply causes a rise in the price level. The new equilibrium is reached at E_1, where the *AD* curve intersects AS_1. At the new and higher equilibrium price level of P_1, the *AE* curve has shifted down to AE_1, as shown in part (i).

---

[3] Actually, it is more accurate to say that this shock reduced the price level *compared with what it otherwise would have been*. Because of ongoing inflation, the causes of which we will discuss in Chapters 29 and 30, the price level in Canada rarely falls. But we have been assuming throughout this chapter that there is no ongoing inflation, and in that setting a positive *AS* shock like the one described in the text would cause the price level to fall.

LESSONS FROM HISTORY 23-1

The Asian Crisis and the Canadian Economy

In the summer of 1997, the currencies of several countries in Southeast Asia plummeted (relative to the U.S. and Canadian dollars) as their central banks were no longer able to "peg" their exchange rates. In Chapter 35 we will discuss how such pegged exchange rates operate. For now, the important point is that, for various reasons, banks, firms, and households in these countries had accumulated a large stock of debt denominated in foreign currencies, especially U.S. dollars. The sudden depreciations of their currencies—in some cases by 70 percent in just a few days—led to dramatic increases in the amount of domestic income required to pay the interest on this debt. Financial institutions went bankrupt, manufacturing firms were unable to access credit, workers were laid off, and economic output fell sharply. By late in 1997, the economies of Malaysia, Indonesia, Thailand, South Korea, and the Philippines were suffering major recessions.

How did this Asian crisis affect Canada? It had offsetting positive and negative effects on the level of economic activity in Canada. The events in Asia generated both a *negative* aggregate demand shock and a *positive* aggregate supply shock for Canada.

To understand the demand side of the story, we must recognize that these Asian economies are important users of raw materials. When their economies went into recession, their demand for raw materials fell sharply. Indeed, average raw materials prices fell by roughly 30 percent between 1997 and 1998. And raw materials are an important export for Canada. The decline in the world's demand for raw materials implied a reduction in demand for Canadian goods. As a result, Canadian producers of copper, pork, newsprint, lumber, iron ore, and many other raw materials suffered significantly. In terms of our macroeconomic model, the Asian crisis caused a leftward shift of the Canadian AD curve.

The story does not end there. Also important to Canada is the fact that many Canadian firms use raw materials as inputs for their production of car parts, prefabricated houses and trailers, electrical equipment, and so on. A dramatic reduction in the prices of raw materials implies a reduction in costs for these firms. This is a positive aggregate supply shock, and is illustrated by a rightward shift of the Canadian AS curve.

What is the overall effect on the Canadian economy? The effect of each shock taken separately is to reduce the price level—so the overall effect is unambiguously a lower price level.* In contrast, the effect on real GDP would appear to be ambiguous since the AD shock reduces GDP whereas the AS shock increases it. But this is not quite right. Since Canada earns more from its sales of raw materials than it spends on them (that is, Canada is a net exporter of these products), it must experience a decrease in national income when these prices fall. In other words, the net effect of the negative demand shock and the positive supply shock is to reduce Canadian GDP. The figure is therefore drawn with the AD shock being larger than the AS shock and so the new equilibrium level of GDP, Y_1, is lower than in the initial equilibrium, Y_0.

Negative demand shock as demand for Canada's exports (raw materials) falls

Positive supply shock as price of inputs (raw materials) falls

Canada's Real GDP

---

*Recall footnote 3 on page 581. We are assuming in this analysis that there is no ongoing inflation, so a positive AS shock or a negative AD shock reduces the price level. A more accurate description for the Canadian economy in 1998, with some ongoing inflation, is that the price level fell below what it otherwise would have been. This appears as a reduction in the rate of inflation.

export oil—like Canada—a rise in the price of oil generates an increase in income to domestic oil producers and is thus a positive aggregate demand shock. It is no surprise that the economies of the oil-producing regions of Canada, especially Alberta, Saskatchewan, and Newfoundland and Labrador, were booming during the 2002–2008 period, when the price of oil increased from about U.S.$20 per barrel to more than U.S.$80 per barrel (and was very briefly at almost $U.S.150 per barrel during 2008).

A complete analysis of the macroeconomic effect of a rise in world oil prices must consider both a leftward shift of the *AS* curve and, for those countries that produce oil, a rightward shift of the *AD* curve. The equilibrium price level will certainly increase, but the overall effect on real GDP will depend on the relative importance of the demand-side and supply-side effects.

Our discussion here has been about the macroeconomic effects of oil-price increases, but the central message is more general:

For information on OPEC, see its website: www.opec.org.

> Many economic events—especially changes in the world prices of raw materials—cause both aggregate demand and aggregate supply shocks in the same economy. The overall effect on real GDP in that economy depends on the relative importance of the two separate effects.

This general principle should be kept in mind whenever our *AD/AS* macro model is used to analyze the macro economy. *Lessons from History 23-1* uses our model to interpret the effects of the 1997–1998 Asian economic crisis on the Canadian economy. As you will see in that discussion, the Asian crisis generated both *AD* and *AS* shocks for Canada.

SUMMARY

23.1 The Demand Side of the Economy

LO 1, 2

- The *AE* curve shows desired aggregate expenditure for each level of GDP at a particular price level. Its intersection with the 45° line determines equilibrium GDP for that price level. Equilibrium GDP thus occurs where desired aggregate expenditure equals actual GDP. A change in the price level causes a shift in the *AE* curve: upward when the price level falls and downward when the price level rises. This leads to a new equilibrium level of real GDP.
- The *AD* curve plots the equilibrium level of GDP that corresponds to each possible price level. A change in

equilibrium GDP following a change in the price level is shown by a movement along the *AD* curve.

- A rise in the price level lowers exports and lowers autonomous consumption expenditure. Both of these changes reduce equilibrium GDP and cause the *AD* curve to have a negative slope.
- The *AD* curve shifts horizontally when any element of autonomous expenditure changes, and the simple multiplier measures the size of the shift.

23.2 The Supply Side of the Economy

LO 3

- Any aggregate supply (*AS*) curve is drawn for given factor prices and given state of technology.
- The *AS* curve is usually drawn as an upward-sloping curve, reflecting the assumption that firms' unit costs tend to rise when their output rises.
- At levels of output below potential GDP, firms' excess capacity may result in a horizontal *AS* curve.

- An improvement in technology or a decrease in factor prices shifts the *AS* curve to the right. This is an increase in aggregate supply.
- A deterioration in technology or an increase in factor prices shifts the *AS* curve to the left. This is a decrease in aggregate supply.

23.3 Macroeconomic Equilibrium   LO 4

- Macroeconomic equilibrium refers to equilibrium values of real GDP and the price level, as determined by the intersection of the *AD* and *AS* curves. Shifts in the *AD* and *AS* curves, called aggregate demand and aggregate supply shocks, change the equilibrium values of real GDP and the price level.
- When the *AS* curve is positively sloped, an aggregate demand shock causes the price level and real GDP to move in the same direction. When the *AS* curve is flat, shifts in the *AD* curve primarily affect real GDP. When the *AS* curve is steep, shifts in the *AD* curve primarily affect the price level.
- With a positively sloped *AS* curve, a demand shock leads to a change in the price level. As a result, the multiplier is smaller than the simple multiplier in Chapter 22.
- An aggregate supply shock moves equilibrium GDP along the *AD* curve, causing the price level and real GDP to move in opposite directions.
- Some events are both aggregate supply and aggregate demand shocks. Changes in the world prices of raw materials, for example, shift the *AS* curve. If the country (like Canada) is also a producer of such raw materials, there will also be a shift in the *AD* curve. The overall effect then depends on the relative sizes of the separate effects.

KEY CONCEPTS

Effects of an exogenous change in the price level
Relationship between the *AE* and *AD* curves

Negative slope of the *AD* curve
Positive slope of the *AS* curve
Macroeconomic equilibrium
Aggregate demand shocks

The multiplier when the price level varies
Aggregate supply shocks

STUDY EXERCISES

MyEconLab Make the grade with MyEconLab: Study Exercises marked in red can be found on MyEconLab. You can practise them as often as you want, and most feature step-by-step guided instructions to help you find the right answer.

1. Fill in the blanks to make the following statements correct.

   a. In the simple macro model of the previous two chapters, the price level was _____. In the macro model of this chapter, the price level is _____.

   b. A change in the price level shifts the *AE* curve because the price level change affects desired _____ and desired _____.

   c. A rise in the price level causes a(n) _____ in households' wealth, which leads to a(n) _____ in desired consumption, which causes the *AE* curve to shift _____. A fall in the price level causes a(n) _____ in households' wealth, which leads to a(n) _____ in desired consumption, which causes the *AE* curve to shift _____.

   d. A rise in the domestic price level causes net exports to _____, which causes the *AE* curve to shift _____. A fall in the domestic price level causes net exports to _____, which causes the *AE* curve to shift _____.

   e. Equilibrium GDP is determined by the position of the *AE* function for each given price level. An equilibrium point for a particular price level corresponds to one point on the _____ curve.

   f. A rise in the price level causes a downward shift of the _____ curve and a movement upward along the _____ curve.

   g. An increase in autonomous expenditure, with no change in the price level, causes the *AE* curve to _____ and causes the *AD* curve to _____.

2. Fill in the blanks to make the following statements correct.

   a. The _____ curve relates the price level to the quantity of output that firms would like to produce and sell.

   b. Each aggregate supply curve is drawn under the assumption that _____ and _____ remain constant.

   c. The aggregate supply curve is upward sloping because firms will produce more output only if price _____ to offset higher unit costs.

   d. The aggregate supply curve is relatively flat when GDP is below potential output because firms typically have _____ and are able to expand production with little or no increase in unit costs.

   e. The aggregate supply curve is relatively steep when GDP is above potential output because firms are operating above _____ and _____ are rising rapidly.

   f. The aggregate supply curve shifts in response to changes in _____ and changes in _____. These are known as supply _____.

3. Fill in the blanks to make the following statements correct.

   a. Macroeconomic equilibrium occurs at the intersection of _____ and _____, and determines equilibrium levels of _____ and _____.

   b. If the AS curve is upward sloping, a positive AD shock will cause the price level to _____ and real GDP to _____. A negative AD shock will cause the price level to _____ and real GDP to _____.

   c. A positive AS shock will cause the price level to _____ and real GDP to _____. A negative AS shock will cause the price level to _____ and real GDP to _____.

   d. In previous chapters, the simple multiplier measured the change in real GDP in response to a change in autonomous expenditure when the price level was constant. When the price level varies, the multiplier is _____ than the simple multiplier.

   e. An increase in autonomous government spending is a(n) _____ AD shock, which will initially cause a(n) _____ shift of the AE curve and a(n) _____ shift of the AD curve. Given an upward-sloping aggregate supply curve, there will be a(n) _____ in the price level, which leads to a partial _____ shift of the AE curve.

4. Consider the effects of an exogenous increase in the domestic price level. For each of the assets listed, explain how the change in the price level would affect the wealth of the asset holder. Then explain the effect on *aggregate* (private sector) wealth. The footnote on page 568 will help to answer parts (d) and (e) of this question.

   a. Cash holdings
   b. Deposits in a bank account
   c. A household mortgage

   d. A corporate bond that promises to pay the bond-holder $10 000 on January 1, 2015
   e. A government bond that promises to pay the holder $10 000 on January 1, 2015

5. Consider the following simplified AE function:

   $$AE = 350 + 0.8Y + 0.1\,(M/P)$$

   where AE is desired aggregate expenditure, Y is real GDP, M is the private sector's *nominal wealth*, and P is the price level. Suppose that M is constant and equal to 6000.

   a. Fill in the table below:

P	M/P	AE
1	6000	950 + 0.8Y
2	—	—
3	—	—
4	—	—
5	—	—
6	—	—

   b. Plot each of the AE functions—one for each price level—on the same-scale 45°-line diagram.

   c. Compute the level of equilibrium national income (Y) for each of the values of P. For example, when $P = 1$, $AE = 950 + 0.8Y$. Thus the equilibrium level of Y is such that $Y = 950 + 0.8Y$, which implies $Y = 4750$.

   d. Plot the pairs of price level and equilibrium national income on a scale diagram with P on the vertical axis and Y on the horizontal axis. What is this curve you have just constructed?

   e. Explain why the expression for AE above makes sense. Why do M and P enter the AE function?

6. Consider the following diagram showing the AD curves in two different economies. One economy is Autarkland—it does not trade with the rest of the world (*autarky* is a situation in which a country does not trade with other countries). The other economy is Openland—it exports to and imports from the rest of the world.

a. Explain why an increase in the domestic price level (for a given exchange rate) reduces net exports in Openland. How would you illustrate this with the AE curve in the 45°-line diagram?

b. Explain why the AD curve is steeper in Autarkland than in Openland.

c. If there are never any net exports in Autarkland, why isn't the AD curve vertical? Explain what other aspect of the economy generates a downward-sloping AD curve.

7. The economy of Neverland has the following AD and AS schedules. Denote Y_{AD} as the level of real GDP along the AD curve; let Y_{AS} be the level of real GDP along the AS curve. GDP is shown in billions of 2002 dollars.

Price Level	Y_{AD}	Y_{AS}
90	1100	750
100	1000	825
110	900	900
120	800	975
130	700	1050
140	600	1125

a. Plot the AD and AS curves on a scale diagram.

b. What is the price level and level of real GDP in Neverland's macroeconomic equilibrium?

c. Suppose the level of potential output in Neverland is $950 billion. Is the current equilibrium level of real GDP greater than or less than potential? How does one refer to this particular output gap?

8. Each of the following events caused a shift in the AD or AS curve in Canada. Identify which curve was affected and describe the effect on equilibrium real GDP and the price level.

a. OPEC's actions to restrict oil output significantly increased the world price of oil in 1979–1980.

b. World commodity prices increased sharply from 2002 to 2008. Many of these commodities are both produced in Canada and used as important inputs for Canadian firms.

c. The end of the Cold War led to large declines in defence spending in many countries (including Canada).

d. The federal government and (many) provincial governments reduced corporate income-tax rates between 2000 and 2011.

e. The federal government increased its level of government purchases (G) in 2009 and 2010, amidst a global recession.

f. The beginning of a recession in the United States in 2008 led to a large reduction in the demand for many Canadian exports.

9. The following diagrams show the AD and AS curves in two different economies.

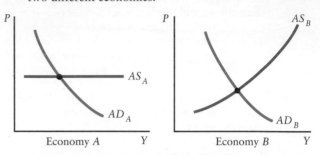

a. Explain what aspect of firms' behaviour might give rise to the horizontal AS curve in Economy A.

b. Explain what aspect of firms' behaviour gives rise to the upward-sloping AS curve in Economy B.

c. In which economy is output purely demand determined? Explain.

d. Consider the effects of an increase in autonomous expenditure. Which economy has the larger multiplier? Explain your reasoning.

10. This question involves algebraically solving the system of two equations given by the AD and AS curves. The equations for the curves are given by

$$AD: Y_{AD} = 710 - 30P + 5G$$

$$AS: Y_{AS} = 10 + 5P - 2P_{OIL}$$

where Y is real GDP, P is the price level, G is the level of government purchases, and P_{OIL} is the world price of oil.

a. Explain the various terms in the AD curve. Explain why G enters positively.

b. What is the value of the simple multiplier? (Hint: Refer back to the caption of Figure 23-3.)

c. Explain the various terms in the AS curve. Explain why the price of oil enters negatively.

d. Solve for the equilibrium value of real GDP and the price level.

e. Using your solution to part (d), what is the effect of a change in G on equilibrium Y and P? Explain.

f. Using your solution to part (d), what is the effect of a change in P_{OIL} on equilibrium Y and P? Explain.

From the Short Run to the Long Run: The Adjustment of Factor Prices

CHAPTER OUTLINE

LEARNING OBJECTIVES (LO)

After studying this chapter you will be able to

24.1 THE ADJUSTMENT PROCESS

1 explain why output gaps cause wages and other factor prices to change.
2 describe how induced changes in factor prices affect firms' costs and shift the *AS* curve.

24.2 AGGREGATE DEMAND AND SUPPLY SHOCKS

3 explain why real GDP gradually returns to potential output following an *AD* or *AS* shock.

24.3 FISCAL STABILIZATION POLICY

4 understand why lags and uncertainty place limitations on the use of fiscal stabilization policy.

IN the previous three chapters, we developed a model of the *short-run* determination of the equilibrium levels of real GDP and the price level. In this chapter, we discuss how this short-run macroeconomic equilibrium evolves, through an adjustment process in which wages and other factor prices change, into a *long-run* equilibrium, in which real GDP is equal to potential output, Y^*. In the next two chapters we examine theories explaining why Y^* increases over many years—what we call *long-run economic growth*. Before we proceed, however, we will define carefully our assumptions regarding the short run, the adjustment process, and the long run.

The Short Run

These are the defining assumptions of the *short run* in our macroeconomic model:

- Factor prices are assumed to be exogenous; they may change, but any change is not explained within the model.
- Technology and factor supplies are assumed to be constant (and therefore Y^* is constant).

With these assumptions, the short-run macroeconomic equilibrium is determined by the intersection of the *AD* and *AS* curves, both of which are subject to shocks of various kinds. These shocks cause the level of real GDP to fluctuate around a *constant* level of potential output, Y^*. This version of our macroeconomic model is convenient to use when analyzing the economy over short periods. Even though factor prices, technology, and factor supplies are rarely constant in reality, even over short periods of time, the simplifying assumption that they are constant in our short-run model allows us to focus on the important role of *AD* or *AS* shocks over this time span.

The Adjustment of Factor Prices

As we will see in detail in this chapter, our theory of the *adjustment process* that takes the economy from the short run to the long run is based on the following assumptions:

- Factor prices are assumed to adjust in response to output gaps.
- Technology and factor supplies are assumed to be constant (and therefore Y^* is constant).

This chapter will explain our model's assumption that deviations of real GDP from potential output cause wages and other factor prices to adjust. It will also explain how this adjustment is central to the economy's evolution from its short-run equilibrium to its long-run equilibrium. Note that, as in the short-run version of the model, the adjustment process is assumed to take place with a constant level of potential output.

Our theory of the macroeconomic adjustment process is useful for examining how the effects of shocks or policies differ in the short and long runs. As we will see, the assumption that potential output is constant leads to the prediction that *AD* or *AS* shocks have no long-run effect on real GDP; output eventually returns to Y^*.

In reality, neither technology nor factor supplies are constant over time; the level of potential output is continually changing. Our assumption throughout much of this chapter of a constant value for Y^* is a simplifying one, allowing us to focus on our theory of the *adjustment process* that brings the level of real GDP back to potential output.

The Long Run

In Chapters 25 and 26 we will examine the defining assumptions of the *long run* in our macro model. They are

- Factor prices are assumed to have fully adjusted to any output gap.
- Technology and factor supplies are assumed to be changing.

The first assumption tells us that, after factor prices have fully adjusted, real GDP will return to the level of potential output. The second assumption implies that the level of potential output is changing (and typically growing). Thus, in the long-run version of our macroeconomic model, our focus is not on the nature of short-run fluctuations in GDP but rather on the nature of *economic growth*—where technological change and the growth of factor supplies play key roles.

TABLE 24-1 **Three Macroeconomic States**

	The Short Run	The Adjustment Process	The Long Run
Key Assumptions	Factor prices are exogenous	Factor prices are flexible/ endogenous	Factor prices are fully adjusted/ endogenous
	Technology and factor supplies (and thus Y^*) are constant/exogenous	Technology and factor supplies (and thus Y^*) are constant/ exogenous	Technology and factor supplies (and thus Y^*) are changing
What Happens	Real GDP (Y) is determined by aggregate demand and aggregate supply	Factor prices adjust to output gaps; real GDP eventually returns to Y^*	Potential GDP (Y^*) grows over the long run
Why We Study This State	To show the effects of AD and AS shocks on real GDP	To see how output gaps cause factor prices to change and why real GDP tends to return to Y^*	To understand the nature of long-run economic growth.

The economy is probably never "in" the long run in the sense that factor prices have fully adjusted to all AD and AS shocks. This is because such shocks are not isolated events but instead events that occur more or less continually. So, before the full adjustment to one shock is complete, another shock occurs and sets the adjustment process in motion again. Nonetheless, the long-run version of our model is very useful for examining some issues. For example, if we want to understand why our children's material standard of living will be significantly greater than our grandparents', we should not focus on short-run AD or AS shocks or the stabilization policies that may follow; the effects of particular shocks will disappear after a few years. Instead, we will gain more understanding if we abstract from short-run issues and focus on why Y^* increases dramatically over periods of several decades.

Summary

The three states of the economy central to macroeconomic analysis are summarized in Table 24-1. Note for each state the assumptions made regarding factor prices and the level of potential output and the causes of changes in real GDP. As we proceed through this chapter and the next two, you may find it useful to refer back to this table.

You already know from Chapter 23 how the short-run version of our macro model works. And now that you have a sketch of what is meant by the adjustment process and the long run, we are ready to fill in the details. In this chapter we will see how this adjustment process takes the economy from its short-run equilibrium to its long-run equilibrium. To repeat, we assume in this chapter that factor prices adjust in response to output gaps and that potential output (Y^*) is constant.

24.1 The Adjustment Process

We develop our theory of the adjustment process by examining the relationship among output gaps, factor markets, and factor prices. We begin by understanding the broad outline of how this process works. We then go on to discuss *how well* it works in greater detail.

Potential Output and the Output Gap

Recall that *potential output* is the total output that can be produced when all productive resources—land, labour, and capital—are fully employed. When a nation's actual output diverges from its potential output, the difference is called the output gap.

Although growth in potential output has powerful effects from one decade to the next, its change from one *year* to the next is small enough that we ignore it when studying the year-to-year behaviour of real GDP and the price level. In this chapter, therefore, we view variations in the output gap as determined solely by variations in *actual* GDP around a constant level of *potential* GDP. (In Chapter 26 we will examine why potential output grows over the long run.)

Figure 24-1 shows real GDP being determined in the short run by the intersection of the *AD* and *AS* curves. Potential output is assumed to be constant, and it is shown by identical vertical lines in the two parts of the figure. In part (i), the *AD* and *AS* curves intersect to produce an equilibrium real GDP less than potential output. The result, as we saw in Chapter 19, is called a *recessionary gap* because recessions are often characterized as having GDP below potential output. In part (ii), the *AD* and *AS* curves intersect to produce an equilibrium real GDP above potential output, resulting in what is called an *inflationary gap*. Why an inflationary output gap puts upward pressure on prices will become clear in the ensuing discussion.

Factor Prices and the Output Gap

We make two key assumptions in our macro model regarding factor prices and the output gap. First, when real GDP is above potential output, there will be pressure on factor prices to rise because of a higher than normal demand for factor inputs. Second,

FIGURE 24-1 Output Gaps in the Short Run

(i) A recessionary gap, $Y < Y^*$

(ii) An inflationary gap, $Y > Y^*$

The output gap is the difference between actual GDP and potential GDP, $Y - Y^*$. Potential output is shown by the vertical line at Y^*. A recessionary gap, shown in part (i), occurs when actual output is less than potential GDP. An inflationary gap, shown in part (ii), occurs when actual output is greater than potential GDP.

when real GDP is below potential output, there will be pressure on factor prices to fall because of a lower than normal demand for factor inputs. These relationships are assumed to hold for the prices of all factors of production, including labour, land, and capital equipment.

Before we examine the detailed relationship between factor prices and output gaps, it is worth noting that even in the absence of an output gap, the presence of ongoing inflation influences factor prices, especially wages. Wage contracts often allow for changes in the price level that are expected to occur during the life of the contract. For the discussion in this chapter, however, we make the simplifying assumption that the price level is expected to be constant (and therefore inflation is expected to be zero); hence changes in nominal wages are also expected to be changes in real wages. We will discuss inflation in detail in Chapters 29 and 30.

Output Above Potential, $Y > Y^*$ Here is the reasoning behind our first assumption. Sometimes the *AD* and *AS* curves intersect where real GDP exceeds potential, as illustrated in part (ii) of Figure 24-1. Because firms are producing beyond their normal capacity output, there is an excess demand for all factor inputs, including labour. Labour shortages will emerge in some industries and among many groups of workers. Firms will try to bid workers away from other firms in order to maintain the high levels of output and sales made possible by the boom conditions.

As a result of this excess demand in factor markets, workers will find that they have considerable bargaining power with their employers, and they will put upward pressure on wages. Firms, recognizing that demand for their goods is strong, will be anxious to maintain a high level of output. To prevent their workers from either striking or quitting and moving to other employers, firms will be willing to accede to some of these upward pressures.

> The boom that is associated with an inflationary gap generates a set of conditions—high profits for firms and an excess demand for labour—that tends to cause wages (and other factor prices) to rise.

This increase in factor prices will increase firms' unit costs. As unit costs increase, firms will require higher prices in order to supply any given level of output, and the *AS* curve will therefore shift up. This shift has the effect of reducing equilibrium real GDP and raising the price level. Real GDP moves back toward potential and the inflationary gap begins to close.

In our model, factor prices are assumed to continue rising as long as some inflationary gap remains. In other words, they will continue rising until the *AS* curve shifts up to the point where the equilibrium level of GDP is equal to potential GDP. At this point, there is no longer an excess demand for factors, no more pressure for factor prices to rise, firms' costs are stable, and the *AS* curve stops shifting.

Output Below Potential, $Y < Y^*$ Here is the reasoning behind our second assumption regarding factor prices. Sometimes the *AD* and *AS* curves intersect where real GDP is less than potential, as illustrated in part (i) of Figure 24-1. Because firms are producing below their normal capacity output, there is an excess supply of all factor inputs, including labour. There will be labour surpluses in some industries and among some groups of workers. Firms will have below-normal sales and not only will resist upward pressures on wages but also may seek reductions in wages.

> The slump that is associated with a recessionary gap generates a set of conditions—low profits for firms and an excess supply of labour—that tends to cause wages (and other factor prices) to fall.[1]

Such a reduction in factor prices will reduce firms' unit costs. As unit costs fall, firms require a lower price in order to supply any given level of output, and the *AS* curve therefore shifts down. This shift has the effect of increasing equilibrium real GDP and reducing the price level. Real GDP moves back toward potential and the recessionary gap begins to close.

In our model, wages and other factor prices are assumed to fall as long as some recessionary gap remains. As factor prices fall, the *AS* curve shifts down, and this process continues until the equilibrium level of GDP is equal to potential output. At this point, there is no longer an excess supply of factors, no more pressure for factor prices to fall, firms' unit costs are stable, and the *AS* curve stops shifting.

Downward Wage Stickiness At this stage, we encounter an important asymmetry in the economy's aggregate supply behaviour. Boom conditions (an inflationary gap), along with labour shortages, cause wages and unit costs to rise. The experience of many developed economies, however, suggests that the downward pressures on wages during slumps (recessionary gaps) often do not operate as strongly or as quickly as the upward pressures during booms. Even when wages do fall, they tend to fall more slowly than they would rise in an equally sized inflationary gap. This *downward wage stickiness* implies that the downward shift in the *AS* curve and the downward pressure on the price level are quite weak.[2]

> Both upward and downward adjustments to wages and unit costs do occur, but there are differences in the speed at which they typically operate. Booms can cause wages to rise rapidly; recessions usually cause wages to fall only slowly.

The Phillips Curve The factor-price adjustment process that we have been discussing was explored many years ago in a famous study of wages and unemployment in the United Kingdom. Using data from the late nineteenth and early twentieth centuries, when wages were more flexible than they are now, A.W. Phillips observed that wages tended to fall in periods of high unemployment and rise in periods of low unemployment. The resulting negative relationship between unemployment and the rate of change in wages has been called the *Phillips* curve ever since. *Extensions in Theory 24-1* discusses the Phillips curve and its relationship to the aggregate supply curve.

---

[1] Because of ongoing inflation and productivity growth, nominal wages rarely fall, even when there is an excess supply of labour. But remember that in this chapter, to allow us to focus on the adjustment process, we are assuming that technology is constant and expected inflation is zero. Thus nominal (and real) wages and other factor prices are assumed to fall when real GDP is below potential output, although perhaps very slowly. With some ongoing inflation in our model, the assumption would be modified so that nominal wages rise less than prices, thus implying a slow reduction in real wages.

[2] This discussion is about the stickiness of aggregate nominal wages in response to cyclical changes in the demand for labour. Another kind of wage adjustment is much quicker, however. When one region or industry experiences an increase in demand, it is usual for nominal wages to rise there, even if nominal wages do not fall in the other regions or industries. The result is that we observe frequent changes in *relative* wages across different parts of the economy. So *relative* wages may be quite flexible even though aggregate nominal wages may be sticky downward.

Inflationary and Recessionary Gaps Now it should be clear why the output gaps are named as they are. When real GDP exceeds potential GDP in our model, there will normally be rising unit costs, and the *AS* curve will be shifting upward. This will in turn push the price level up and create temporary inflation. The larger the excess of real GDP over potential GDP, the greater the inflationary pressure. The term *inflationary gap* emphasizes this salient feature of the economy when $Y > Y^*$.

When actual output is less than potential output, as we have seen, there will be unemployment of labour and other productive resources. Unit costs will tend to fall slowly, leading to a slow downward shift in the *AS* curve. Hence, the price level will be falling only slowly so that *unemployment* will be the output gap's most obvious result. The term *recessionary gap* emphasizes this salient feature that high rates of unemployment occur when $Y < Y^*$.

Potential Output as an "Anchor"

According to our theory, there is pressure on wages and other factor prices to change when output is above or below potential. These changes in factor prices lead to changes in firms' unit costs that shift the *AS* curve and change the equilibrium level of GDP. Moreover, we assumed that this process of factor-price adjustment will continue as long as some output gap remains, coming to a halt only when the equilibrium level of GDP is equal to potential GDP, Y^*. This leads to an important prediction from our macroeconomic model:

> Following an aggregate demand or supply shock, the short-run equilibrium level of output may be different from potential output. Any output gap is assumed to cause wages and other factor prices to adjust, eventually bringing the equilibrium level of output back to potential. In this model, therefore, the level of potential output acts like an "anchor" for the economy.

Potential output acts like an anchor for the level of real GDP. Following aggregate demand or supply shocks that push real GDP below or above potential, the adjustment of factor prices brings real GDP back to potential output.

We now go on to examine our theory of the factor-price adjustment process in greater detail, illustrating it for the cases of positive and negative shocks to aggregate demand and supply. We will also examine this factor-price adjustment process following changes in fiscal policy. The idea that Y^* acts as an "anchor" for the economy will become clear: Shocks of various kinds may cause output to rise above or fall below Y^* in the short run, but the adjustment of factor prices to output gaps ensures that output eventually returns to Y^*.

| 24.2 Aggregate Demand and Supply Shocks

We can now study the consequences of aggregate demand and aggregate supply shocks in our model, distinguishing between the immediate effects of *AD* and *AS* shocks and the longer-term effects, after factor prices have adjusted fully. It is necessary to examine expansionary and contractionary shocks separately because the adjustment of factor prices is not symmetrical for the two cases. Let's begin with demand shocks.

EXTENSIONS IN THEORY 24-1

The Phillips Curve and the Adjustment Process

In the 1950s, Professor A.W. Phillips of the London School of Economics was conducting pioneering research on macroeconomic policy. In his early models, he related the rate of inflation to the difference between actual and potential output. Later he investigated the empirical underpinnings of this equation by studying the relationship between the rate of increase of nominal wages and the level of unemployment. He studied these variables because unemployment data were available as far back as the mid-nineteenth century, whereas very few data on output gaps were available when he did his empirical work. In 1958, he reported that a stable relationship had existed between these two variables for 100 years in the United Kingdom. This relationship came to be known as the **Phillips curve**, which provided an explanation, rooted in empirical observation, of the speed with which wage changes shifted the *AS* curve by changing firms' unit costs.

In the form in which it became famous, the Phillips curve related wage changes to the level of unemployment, as shown in part (i) of the accompanying figure. But we can express the same information in a slightly different way. Note that unemployment and output gaps are negatively related—a recessionary gap is associated with high unemployment, and an inflationary gap is associated with low unemployment. We can therefore create another Phillips curve that plots wage changes against real GDP, as shown in part (ii). Both figures show the same information.

When output equals Y^* the corresponding unemployment rate is sometimes called the natural rate of unemployment, and is denoted U^*. Inflationary gaps (when $Y > Y^*$ and $U < U^*$) are associated with increases in wages. Recessionary gaps (when $Y < Y^*$ and $U > U^*$) are associated with *decreases* in wages.[*] Thus, a Phillips curve that plots wage changes against real GDP is upward sloping, whereas a Phillips curve that plots wage changes against the unemployment rate is downward sloping. When output is at potential, there is neither upward nor downward pressure on wages (or other factor prices) because there is neither an excess demand nor an excess supply of labour. Hence, the Phillips curve cuts the horizontal axis at Y^* (and at U^*). This is how Phillips drew his original curve.

The Phillips curve is *not* the same as the *AS* curve. The *AS* curve has the *price level* on the vertical axis whereas the Phillips curve has the *rate of change of nominal wages* on the vertical axis. How are the two curves related? The economy's location on the Phillips curve indicates how the *AS* curve is shifting as a result of the existing output gap.

Part (iii) of the figure shows how the *AD/AS* diagram relates to the Phillips curve. For example, consider an economy that begins at point *A* in all three diagrams; there is no output gap and wages are stable. Now, suppose a positive aggregate demand shock causes real GDP to increase to Y_1 (and unemployment to fall to U_1) and thus produces an inflationary gap. The excess demand for labour puts upward pressure on wages and the economy moves along the Phillips curve to point *B*, where wages begin rising. The increase in wages increases unit costs and causes the *AS* curve to shift up. Thus, each point on the Phillips curve determines the rate at which the *AS* curve is shifting. To complete the example, note that as the *AS* curve shifts up, the level of GDP will fall back toward Y^* and the inflationary gap will begin to close. The economy moves back

Expansionary *AD* Shocks

Phillips curve Originally, a relationship between the unemployment rate and the rate of change of nominal wages. Now often drawn as a relationship between GDP and the rate of change of nominal wages.

Suppose the economy starts with a stable price level and real GDP equal to potential GDP, as shown by the initial equilibrium in part (i) of Figure 24-2. Now suppose this situation is disturbed by an increase in autonomous expenditure, perhaps caused by an upturn in business confidence and a resulting boom in investment spending. Figure 24-2(i) shows the effects of this aggregate demand shock in raising both the price level and real GDP. The *AD* curve shifts from AD_0 to AD_1, the economy moves along the *AS* curve, and real GDP rises above Y^*. An inflationary gap opens up.

We have assumed that an inflationary gap leads to increases in factor prices, which cause firms' unit costs to rise. The *AS* curve begins to shift up as firms respond by increasing their output prices. As seen in part (ii) of the figure, the upward shift of the *AS* curve causes a further rise in the price level, but this time the price rise is associated with a *fall* in output (along the AD_1 curve).

along the Phillips curve toward point A. Wages continue to rise, but the rate at which they are rising slows. When all adjustment is complete, the new equilibrium will be at point C in part (iii) of the figure, with output equal to Y^* and the price level and nominal wages higher than initially. On the Phillips curve, the economy will be back at point A, where real GDP equals Y^* and wages are stable (but at a higher level than before the demand shock occurred).

Note that the convex shape of the Phillips curve is not accidental—it reflects the adjustment asymmetry we mentioned in the text. The convexity of the Phillips curve implies that an inflationary gap of a given amount will lead to faster wage increases than an equally sized recessionary gap will lead to wage reductions. In other words, an inflationary gap will cause the AS curve to shift up more quickly than a recessionary gap will cause the AS curve to shift down.

Finally, you might be wondering what would happen if the Phillips curve were to shift. And what would cause such a shift? As we will see in Chapter 30 when we discuss the phenomenon of sustained inflation, an important cause of shifts of the Phillips curve is changes in firms' and households' *expectations* of future inflation. In this chapter, however, we have assumed expected inflation to be zero. Whether there is expected inflation or not, the Phillips curve embodies the factor-price adjustment process that is the focus of this chapter.

---

* Recall that we are assuming productivity to be constant so that changes in wages imply changes in unit labour costs. When productivity is growing, however, recessionary output gaps cause unit labour costs to fall. This requires only that wages are growing more slowly than productivity, not actually falling.

(i) Wage changes and unemployment

(ii) Wage changes and real GDP

(iii) Aggregate demand and supply

The increases in unit costs (and the consequent upward shifts of the AS curve) continue until the inflationary gap has been removed—that is, until in part (ii) real GDP returns to Y^*. Only then is there no excess demand for labour and other factors, and only then do factor prices and unit costs, and hence the AS curve, stabilize.

The adjustment in wages and other factor prices eventually eliminates any boom caused by a demand shock; real GDP returns to its potential level.

It is worth remembering here that a key assumption in our macro model is that the level of potential output, Y^*, is unaffected by the AD and AS shocks we are examining. This key assumption lies behind the strong result in our model that the adjustment process, once complete, fully reverses any shock's short-run effects on real GDP.

FIGURE 24-2 The Adjustment Process Following a Positive *AD* Shock

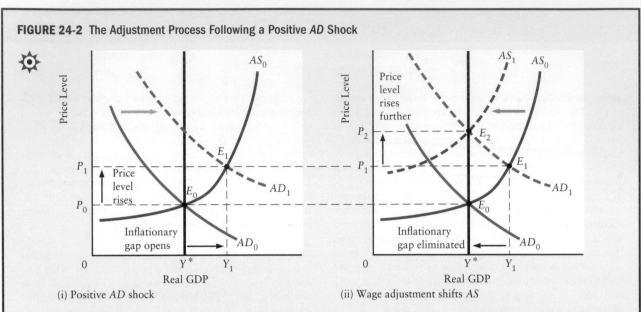

(i) Positive *AD* shock   (ii) Wage adjustment shifts *AS*

A positive *AD* shock first raises prices and output along the *AS* curve. It then induces a shift of the *AS* curve that further raises prices but lowers output along the new *AD* curve. In part (i), the economy is in equilibrium at E_0, at its level of potential output, Y^*, and price level P_0. The *AD* curve then shifts from AD_0 to AD_1. This moves equilibrium to E_1, with income Y_1 and price level P_1, and opens up an inflationary gap.

In part (ii), the inflationary gap results in an increase in wages and other factor prices, which drives up firms' unit costs and shifts the *AS* curve upward. As this happens, output falls and the price level rises along AD_1. Eventually, when the *AS* curve has shifted to AS_1, output is back to Y^* and the inflationary gap has been eliminated. However, the price level has risen to P_2. The eventual effect of the *AD* shock, after all adjustment has occurred, is to raise the price level but leave real GDP unchanged.

Contractionary *AD* Shocks

Suppose again that the economy starts with stable prices and real GDP equal to potential, as shown in part (i) of Figure 24-3. Now assume there is a *decline* in aggregate demand. This negative *AD* shock might be a reduction in investment expenditure, or perhaps a decline in the world demand for Canadian forest products or automobiles.

The first effects of the decline are a fall in output and some downward adjustment of prices, as shown in part (i) of the figure. As real GDP falls below potential, a recessionary gap is created, and unemployment rises. At this point we must analyze two separate cases. The first occurs when wages and other factor prices fall quickly in response to the excess supply of factors. The second occurs when factor prices fall only slowly.

Flexible Wages Suppose wages (and other factor prices) fell quickly in response to the recessionary gap. The *AS* curve would therefore shift quickly downward as the lower wages led to reduced unit costs.

As shown in part (ii) of Figure 24-3, the economy would move along the new *AD* curve, with falling prices and rising output, until real GDP was quickly restored to potential, Y^*. We conclude that if wages were to fall rapidly whenever there was unemployment, the resulting shift in the *AS* curve would quickly eliminate recessionary gaps.

FIGURE 24-3 The Adjustment Process Following a Negative *AD* Shock

(i) Negative *AD* shock   (ii) Wage adjustment shifts *AS*

A negative *AD* shock first lowers the price level and GDP along the *AS* curve and then induces a (possibly slow) shift of the *AS* curve that further lowers prices but raises output along the new *AD* curve. In part (i), the economy is in equilibrium at E_0, at its level of potential output, Y^*, and price level P_0. The *AD* curve then shifts to AD_1, moving equilibrium to E_1, with income Y_1 and price level P_1, and opens up a recessionary gap.

Part (ii) shows the adjustment back to potential output that occurs from the supply side of the economy. The fall in wages and other factor prices shifts the *AS* curve downward. Real GDP rises, and the price level falls further along the new *AD* curve. Unless factor prices are completely rigid, the *AS* curve eventually reaches AS_1, with equilibrium at E_2. The eventual effect of the negative *AD* shock, after all adjustment has occurred, is to reduce the price level but leave real GDP unchanged.

Flexible wages that fall rapidly in the presence of a recessionary gap provide an automatic adjustment process that pushes the economy back quickly toward potential output.

Sticky Wages As we noted earlier, the experience of most economies suggests that wages typically do not fall rapidly in response to even large recessionary gaps. It is sometimes said that wages are "sticky" in the downward direction. This does not mean that wages never fall, only that they tend to fall much more slowly in a recessionary gap than they rise in an equally sized inflationary gap. When wages are sticky, the analysis is the same as when wages are flexible, and thus Figure 24-3 tells the correct story. The significant difference, however, is that the *AS* curve shifts more slowly when wages are sticky and thus the adjustment process may not close the recessionary gap for a long time.

If wages are downwardly sticky, the economy's adjustment process is sluggish and thus will not quickly eliminate a recessionary gap.[3]

---

[3] The causes of downward wage stickiness have been hotly debated among macroeconomists for years. We discuss several possible reasons in Chapter 31 when examining the causes of cyclical unemployment.

The weakness of the adjustment process following a negative demand shock does not mean that recessionary gaps must always be prolonged. Rather, this weakness means that speedy recovery back to potential output must be generated mainly from the demand side. If wages are downwardly sticky and the economy is to avoid a persistent recessionary gap, a quick recovery requires a rightward shift of the *AD* curve. This often happens when private-sector demand revives. But it also raises the possibility that government *stabilization policy* can be used to accomplish such a rightward shift in the *AD* curve. This is an important and contentious issue in macroeconomics, one to which we will return often throughout the remainder of this book.

The difference in the speed of adjustment of wages (and other factor prices) is the important asymmetry in the behaviour of aggregate supply that we noted earlier in this chapter. This asymmetry helps to explain two key facts about the Canadian economy. First, high unemployment can persist for quite long periods without causing decreases in wages of sufficient magnitude to quickly remove the unemployment. For example, during the 1991–1995 and 2009–2012 periods, output was below potential and unemployment remained relatively high. Second, booms, along with labour shortages and production beyond normal capacity, do not persist for long periods without causing increases in wages. The periods 1988–1990, 1999–2000, and 2004–2007 all displayed output above potential and significant increases in wages.

Aggregate Supply Shocks

We have discussed the economy's adjustment process that returns real GDP to Y^* following an aggregate demand shock. The same adjustment process operates following an aggregate supply shock.

Consider an economy that has a stable price level and real GDP at its potential level, as illustrated by point E_0 in part (i) of Figure 24-4. Suppose there is an increase in the world price of an important input, such as oil. An increase in the price of oil increases unit costs for firms and causes the *AS* curve to shift upward. Real GDP falls and the price level increases—a combination often called *stagflation*. The short-run equilibrium is at point E_1. With the opening of a recessionary gap, the economy's adjustment process comes into play, though sticky wages reduce the speed of this adjustment.

In our macro model, the recessionary gap caused by the negative supply shock causes some firms to shut down and some workers to be laid off. The excess supply of labour (and other factors) eventually pushes wages down and begins to reverse the initial increase in unit costs caused by the increase in the price of oil. This adjustment is shown in part (ii) of the figure. As wages fall, the *AS* curve shifts back toward its starting point, and real GDP rises back toward its potential level, Y^*. Since our model assumes that Y^* is constant, the reductions in factor prices eventually bring the economy back to its initial point, E_0. Note, however, that *relative* prices will have changed when the economy returns to E_0. The price level is back to P_0, its starting point, but real wages are lower while the relative price of oil is higher.

We leave it to the reader to analyze the adjustment process following a positive aggregate supply shock. The logic of the analysis is exactly the same as illustrated in Figure 24-4, except that the initial shift in the *AS* curve is to the right, creating an inflationary gap.

> Exogenous changes in input prices cause the *AS* curve to shift, creating an output gap. The adjustment process then reverses the initial *AS* shift and brings the economy back to potential output and the initial price level.

FIGURE 24-4 The Adjustment Process Following a Negative *AS* Shock

(i) Negative *AS* shock

(ii) Wage adjustment returns *AS* to initial position

A negative *AS* shock caused by an increase in input prices causes real GDP to fall and the price level to rise. The economy's adjustment process then reverses the *AS* shift and returns the economy to its starting point. The economy begins at point E_0 in part (i). The increase in the price of oil increases firms' unit costs and causes the *AS* curve to shift up to AS_1. Real GDP falls to Y_1 and the price level rises to P_1. A recessionary gap is created. In part (ii), the excess supply of factors associated with the recessionary gap causes wages and other factor prices to fall, possibly slowly. As factor prices fall, unit costs fall and so the *AS* curve shifts back down to AS_0. The eventual effect of the *AS* shock, after all adjustment has occurred, is to leave the price level and real GDP unchanged.

In this chapter we have emphasized the adjustment of factor prices to output gaps, and how this adjustment process returns real GDP to Y^* following *AD* or *AS* shocks. However, there are *additional* forces in the economy that also help to explain how real GDP changes over the business cycle; these additional forces also explain how recessionary gaps may be closed faster than if the only force at play was the (slow) reduction of factor prices. *Extensions in Theory 24-2* examines the dynamics of the business cycle in more detail.

Long-Run Equilibrium

Following any *AD* or *AS* shocks, we have assumed that the adjustment of factor prices continues until real GDP returns to Y^*. The economy is said to be in a *long-run equilibrium* when this adjustment process is complete, and there is no longer an output gap. In other words, the economy is in its long-run equilibrium when the intersection of the *AD* and *AS* curves occurs at Y^*.

We also assume in our macro model that the value of Y^* depends only on real variables, such as the labour force, capital stock, and the level of technology. We assume, in particular, that Y^* is independent of nominal variables, such as the price level. The level of output that firms will produce in the long run is thus independent of the price level. The vertical line at Y^* that we have seen in our diagrams is sometimes called a *long-run aggregate supply curve*—the relationship between the price level and the amount of output supplied by firms *after all factor prices have adjusted to output gaps.*

EXTENSIONS IN THEORY 24-2

The Business Cycle: Additional Pressures for Adjustment

In Chapter 19 we described the *business cycle* as the ebb and flow of economic activity that alternately tends to create recessionary and inflationary output gaps. In this chapter, we have seen that the factor-price adjustment process tends to eliminate such output gaps whenever they appear. The business cycle itself provides an *additional* set of pressures that reinforces the adjustment of factor prices and helps to return real GDP to Y^*.

During the expansionary phase of the business cycle, real GDP is growing; as the peak of the cycle is reached, real GDP is typically well above Y^* and unemployment is low. Expectations of rising sales and profits created during the economic expansion often lead to gains in stock-market prices that are not justified by current earnings; in addition, firms may undertake capital investments based on the assumption that the economic expansion will continue. As real GDP rises further above Y^*, however, bottlenecks and shortages eventually arise and restrict further expansion, thus slowing the growth rate of real GDP. When growth slows in this way, there is often a drastic revision in firms' expectations. A sell-off of stocks may cause their prices to tumble, thereby reducing consumers' wealth and confidence and hence causing them to curtail their consumption expenditures. The slowdown in growth, combined with the collapse of confidence, can lead firms to reduce their desired investment. These reductions in household consumption and business investment work, through the economy's multiplier process, to reduce real GDP. Thus, even in the absence of wage increases, an economic expansion usually contains the seeds of its own demise; real GDP tends to move back toward Y^*.

Once underway, the economic downturn tends to feed on itself as confidence wanes even further, leading to more cuts in investment and consumer spending. The downturn often overshoots Y^*, creating a recessionary gap. A trough is eventually reached, in which real GDP is well below Y^* and unemployment is high. At this point, the pace of economic activity begins to rise. Stocks of durable consumer goods, such as automobiles and home appliances, that were not replaced during the downturn eventually become depleted or obsolete enough that normal replacement expenditures recover, leading to an increase in the demand for such goods. Similarly, much of firms' replacement investment that has been put off during the economic downturn can be postponed no longer and investment expenditure recovers. The resulting recovery in both household and business spending can cause a revival of favourable expectations concerning the future, leading to further increases in spending. The increases in household consumption and business investment work, through the economy's multiplier process, to increase real GDP. Thus, even in the absence of falling wages, an economic downturn is usually followed by a recovery with real GDP rising back toward Y^*.

In summary, we should note two distinct forces that tend to return real GDP to Y^*. During an inflationary gap, both rising wages (which shift the *AS* curve to the left) and the intrinsic dynamics of the business cycle (which shift the *AD* curve to the left) are powerful forces. During a recessionary gap, however, wages are quite slow to adjust in the downward direction and so the business cycle dynamics typically play a much larger role than the wage-adjustment process in bringing real GDP back to Y^*. In this chapter, we have concentrated on understanding how the wage-adjustment process works. It must be remembered, however, that its strength is asymmetric, strong in removing an inflationary gap but much weaker in removing a recessionary one.

This vertical line is also sometimes called a *Classical aggregate supply curve* because the Classical economists were mainly concerned with the behaviour of the economy in long-run equilibrium.[4]

---

[4] The Classical school of economic thought began with Adam Smith (1723–1790) and was developed through the work of David Ricardo (1772–1823), Thomas Malthus (1766–1834), and John Stuart Mill (1806–1873). These economists emphasized the long-run behaviour of the economy. Beginning in the middle of the nineteenth century, Neoclassical economists devoted much time and effort to studying short-term fluctuations. *The General Theory of Employment, Interest and Money* (1936), written by John Maynard Keynes (1883–1946), was in a long tradition of the study of short-term fluctuations. Where Keynes differed from the Neoclassical economists was in approaching the issues from a macroeconomic perspective that emphasized fluctuations in aggregate expenditure. Each of the economists mentioned in this footnote, along with several others, is discussed in more detail in the timeline at the back of the book.

Figure 24-5 shows an *AD/AS* diagram without the usual upward-sloping *AS* curve. It is useful to omit this curve if our focus is on the state of the economy *after* all factor prices have fully adjusted and output has returned to Y^*. We can use this diagram to examine how shocks affect the economy's long-run equilibrium.

As shown in part (i) of Figure 24-5, any shift in the *AD* curve will cause a change in the price level in the long run but will not affect the level of potential output, Y^*. In our model, the only way that real GDP can change in the long run (*after* factor prices have fully adjusted) is for the level of Y^* to change, as in part (ii) of the figure.

> In the long run, real GDP is determined solely by Y^*; the role of aggregate demand is only to determine the price level.

This strong result—that changes in aggregate demand have no long-run effect on real GDP—follows from the assumption in our macro model that Y^* is independent of the price level and thus unaffected by *AD* shocks.[5]

We will discuss the long-run behaviour of the economy in detail in Chapters 25 and 26. There we develop theories explaining why Y^* grows over extended periods of time and why this growth is important for determining the ongoing increases in our material living standards.

24.3 Fiscal Stabilization Policy

In Chapter 22, we briefly examined fiscal policy in our macro model in which output was demand determined and the price level was assumed to be constant. Now that our model is more complete—and also more realistic—we can examine fiscal policy in more detail. We now consider taxation and government spending as tools of fiscal stabilization policy; in Chapter 32, we return to more advanced aspects of fiscal policy.

Fiscal stabilization policy is fundamentally a short-run policy. In response to various shocks that cause changes in real GDP, the government may use various fiscal tools in an attempt to push real GDP back towards potential output. The alternatives to using fiscal stabilization policy are to wait for the recovery of private-sector demand (a shift in the *AD* curve) or to wait for the economy's adjustment process (a shift in the *AS* curve)

FIGURE 24-5   Changes in Long-Run Equilibrium

(i) A rise in aggregate demand

(ii) A rise in potential output

Potential output determines the long-run equilibrium value of real GDP. Given Y^*, aggregate demand determines the long-run equilibrium value of the price level. In both parts of the figure, the initial long-run equilibrium is at E_0, so the price level is P_0 and real GDP is Y_0^*.

In part (i), a shift in the *AD* curve from AD_0 to AD_1 moves the long-run equilibrium from E_0 to E_1. This raises the price level from P_0 to P_1 but leaves real GDP unchanged at Y_0^* in the long run.

In part (ii), an increase in potential output from Y_0^* to Y_1^* moves the long-run equilibrium from E_0 to E_2. This raises real GDP from Y_0^* to Y_1^* and lowers the price level from P_0 to P_2.

For information on the federal Department of Finance, the ministry in charge of fiscal policy, see www.fin.gc.ca.

---

[5] Whether short-run fluctuations in real GDP have an effect on the value of Y^* is an important area of research in macroeconomics. In Chapters 28 and 31 we discuss reasons why some short-run changes in real GDP may cause Y^* to change in the same direction.

to bring real GDP back to potential. The slower these processes are, the stronger is the justification for government to use its fiscal tools.

There is no doubt that the government can exert a major influence on real GDP. Prime examples are the massive increases in military spending during major wars. Canadian federal expenditure during the Second World War rose from 12.2 percent of GDP in 1939 to 41.8 percent in 1944. At the same time, the unemployment rate fell from 11.4 percent to 1.4 percent. Economists agree that the increase in government spending helped to bring about the rise in output and the associated fall in unemployment. More recently, the Canadian government dramatically increased spending in an effort to dampen the effects of the major global recession that began in late 2008. Most economists agree that this "fiscal stimulus" contributed significantly to real GDP growth in the 2009–2011 period.

In the heyday of "activist" fiscal policy, from about 1945 to about 1970, many economists were convinced that the economy could be stabilized adequately just by varying the size of the government's taxes and expenditures. That day is past. Today, economists are more aware of the many limitations of fiscal stabilization policy.

The Basic Theory of Fiscal Stabilization

In our macroeconomic model, a reduction in tax rates or an increase in government purchases or transfers will shift the AD curve to the right, causing an increase in real GDP. An increase in tax rates or a cut in government purchases or transfers will shift the AD curve to the left, causing a decrease in real GDP.

How Fiscal Stabilization Works A more detailed look at how fiscal stabilization works will help to show some of the complications that arise when implementing fiscal policy.

Closing a Recessionary Gap. A recessionary gap is shown in Figure 24-6; the economy's short-run equilibrium is at point E_0 with real GDP below Y^*. In the absence of a recovery in private-sector demand, such a recessionary gap can be closed in two ways. The first involves the economy's adjustment process. The excess supply of factors at E_0 will eventually cause wages and other factor prices to fall, shifting the AS curve downward and restoring output to Y^*, as shown in part (i) of the figure. However, because of the downward stickiness of wages, this process may take a long time. Policymakers may not be prepared to wait the time necessary for the recessionary gap to correct itself. The second way to close the recessionary gap involves an active policy choice. The government can use expansionary fiscal policy to shift the AD curve to the right. It would do this by reducing tax rates, increasing transfers, or increasing the level of government purchases.

The advantage of using fiscal policy rather than allowing the economy to recover naturally is that it may substantially shorten what might otherwise be a long recession. One disadvantage is that the use of fiscal policy may stimulate the economy just before private-sector spending recovers on its own. As a result, the economy may overshoot its potential output, and an inflationary gap may open up. In this case, fiscal policy that is intended to promote economic stability can actually cause instability.

Closing an Inflationary Gap. An inflationary gap is illustrated in Figure 24-7; the economy's short-run equilibrium is at point E_0, with real GDP above Y^*. In the absence of a downward adjustment of private-sector demand, there are two ways such an inflationary gap may be closed. The first involves the economy's adjustment process. Excess demand for factors will cause wages and other factor prices to rise, shifting the AS curve upward and gradually restoring output to Y^*. Alternatively, the government

FIGURE 24-6 The Closing of a Recessionary Gap

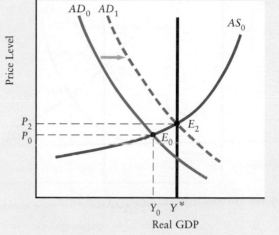

(i) A recessionary gap closed by falling wages and other factor prices

(ii) A recessionary gap closed by fiscal expansion

A recessionary gap may be closed by a (slow) downward shift of the AS curve or an increase in aggregate demand. Initially, equilibrium is at E_0, with real GDP at Y_0 and the price level at P_0. There is a recessionary gap.

As shown in part (i), the gap might be removed by a shift in the AS curve to AS_1, as will eventually happen when wages and other factor prices fall in response to excess supply. The shift in the AS curve causes a movement down and to the right along AD_0 to a new equilibrium at E_1, achieving potential output Y^* and lowering the price level to P_1.

As shown in part (ii), the gap might also be removed by a shift of the AD curve to AD_1, caused by an expansionary fiscal policy (or a recovery of private-sector demand). The shift in the AD curve causes a movement up and to the right along AS_0. This movement shifts the equilibrium to E_2, raising output to Y^* and the price level to P_2.

can use a contractionary fiscal policy to shift the AD curve to the left and close the inflationary gap. The government would do this by increasing tax rates, reducing transfers, or reducing its level of purchases.

The advantage of using a contractionary fiscal policy to close the inflationary gap is that it avoids the inflation that would otherwise occur. One disadvantage is that if private-sector expenditures fall for some unrelated reason, the fiscal contraction may end up being too large and real GDP may be pushed below potential, thus opening up a recessionary gap.

This discussion leads to a key proposition:

When the economy's adjustment process is slow to operate, or produces undesirable side effects such as rising prices, there is a potential stabilization role for fiscal policy.

Fiscal Policy and the Paradox of Thrift Suppose you have a good job but you are sufficiently unsure about your economic future that you decide to increase the fraction of disposable income that you save. Your increased saving today would not influence your current income but these funds would accumulate and be useful in the future if your economic situation changed for the worse. Most people would agree that a decision to increase your saving in these circumstances would be prudent.

FIGURE 24-7 The Closing of an Inflationary Gap

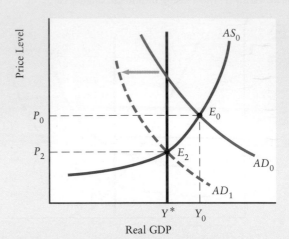

(i) An inflationary gap closed by rising wages and other factor prices

(ii) An inflationary gap closed by contractionary fiscal policy

An inflationary gap may be removed by an upward shift of the AS curve or by a leftward shift of the AD curve. Initially, equilibrium is at E_0, with real GDP at Y_0 and the price level at P_0. There is an inflationary gap.

As shown in part (i), the gap might be removed by a shift in the AS curve to AS_1, as will happen when wages and other factor prices rise in response to the excess demand. The shift in the AS curve causes a movement up and to the left along AD_0. This movement establishes a new equilibrium at E_1, reducing output to its potential level Y^* and raising the price level to P_1.

As shown in part (ii), the gap might also be removed by a shift in the AD curve to AD_1 caused by a contractionary fiscal policy (or by a reduction of private-sector demand). The shift in the AD curve causes a movement down and to the left along AS_0. This movement shifts the equilibrium to E_2, lowering income to Y^* and the price level to P_2.

But what would happen if *many people* did the same thing at the same time? In our macroeconomic model, an increase in the country's total desired saving would shift the AD curve to the left and *reduce* the equilibrium level of real GDP in the short run. Thus, frugality on the part of individuals, which may seem to be prudent behaviour for each individual taken separately, ends up reducing short-run real GDP. This phenomenon is known as the *paradox of thrift*—the paradox being that what may be good for any individual when viewed in isolation ends up being undesirable for the economy as a whole.

The policy implication of this phenomenon is that a major and persistent recession can be battled by encouraging governments, firms, and households to reduce their saving and therefore increase their spending. In times of unemployment and recession, a greater desire to save will only make things worse. This result goes directly against the idea that we should "tighten our belts" when times are tough. The notion that it is not only possible but even *desirable* to spend one's way out of a recession touches a sensitive point with people raised on the belief that success is based on hard work and frugality; as a result, the idea often arouses great hostility.

As is discussed in *Lessons from History 24-1*, the implications of the paradox of thrift were not generally understood during the Great Depression of the 1930s. Most governments, faced with depression-induced reductions in tax revenues, reduced their expenditures to balance their budgets. As a result, many economists argue that the fiscal policies at the time actually made things worse. When Nobel Prize–winning economist Milton Friedman (many years later) said, "We are all Keynesians now," he was referring to the general acceptance of the view that the government's budget is much more than just the revenue and expenditure statement of a very large organization. Whether we like it or not, the sheer size of the government's budget inevitably makes it a powerful tool for influencing the overall level of economic activity.

Knowledge of the fiscal policy mistakes during the Great Depression led most governments to avoid those same mistakes during the global financial crisis of 2008 and the recession that followed. In a decision that was coordinated across governments of the G20 countries, the Canadian government embarked on a program of fiscal stimulus in the 2009–2010 and 2010–2011 fiscal years. Over these two years, spending increased by approximately $40 billion, most of which was directed at public infrastructure projects. The provincial governments acted similarly, and the fiscal stimulus for all governments combined was about $52 billion, an average of 1.7 percent of GDP in each of the two years.

Short Run Versus Long Run The paradox of thrift applies to shifts in aggregate demand that have been caused by changes in saving (and hence spending) behaviour. That is why it applies only in the short run, when the *AD* curve plays an important role in the determination of real GDP.

The paradox of thrift does not apply after factor prices have fully adjusted and the economy has achieved its new long-run equilibrium with real GDP equal to Y^*. Remember from Figure 24-5 that in the long run, aggregate demand does not influence the level of real GDP—output is determined only by the level of potential output, Y^*. In the long run, the more people and government save, the larger is the supply of financial capital available for investment. As we will see in Chapter 26, this increase in the pool of financial capital will reduce interest rates and encourage more investment by firms. The greater rate of investment leads to a higher rate of growth of potential output.

> The paradox of thrift—the idea that an increase in saving reduces the level of real GDP—is true only in the short run. In the long run, the path of real GDP is determined by the path of potential output. The increase in saving has the long-run effect of increasing investment and therefore increasing potential output.

Automatic Fiscal Stabilizers

The fiscal policies that we have been discussing are referred to as *discretionary* because the government uses its discretion in changing its taxation or its spending in an attempt to change the level of real GDP. However, even if the government makes no active decisions regarding changes in spending or taxation, the mere existence of the government's tax-and-transfer system will act as an *automatic stabilizer* for the economy. Let's see how this works.

Consider a shock that shifts the *AD* curve to the right and thus increases the short-run level of real GDP. As real GDP increases, government tax revenues also increase. In addition, since there are fewer low-income households and unemployed persons requiring assistance, governments make fewer transfer payments to individuals. The rise in net tax revenues (taxes minus transfers) dampens the overall increase in real GDP caused by the initial shock. In other words, the tax-and-transfer system reduces the value of the multiplier and thus acts as an **automatic stabilizer** for the economy.

automatic stabilizers Elements of the tax-and-transfer system that reduce the responsiveness of real GDP to changes in autonomous expenditure.

LESSONS FROM HISTORY 24-1

Fiscal Policy in the Great Depression

The Great Depression, which is usually dated as beginning with the massive stock-market crash on October 29, 1929, was one of the most dramatic economic events of the twentieth century. As the accompanying figure shows, Canadian real GDP plummeted by almost 30 percent from its peak in 1929 to its low point in 1933. The price level fell beginning in 1930 and declined by about 20 percent over the next five years. The unemployment rate increased from 3 percent of the labour force in 1929 to an unparalleled 19.3 percent four years later. To put these numbers in perspective, by today's standards a very serious recession (like the most recent one in 2008 and 2009) sees real GDP fall by 2 to 3 percent, the unemployment rate rise to 8 to 10 percent, and prices continue rising but perhaps at a slower rate. The economic events of the 1930s certainly deserve to be called the Great Depression!

The Great Depression was not just a catastrophic event that happened exogenously—its depth and duration were made worse by some fundamental mistakes in policy. Failure to understand the implication of the paradox of thrift led many countries to adopt disastrous fiscal policies during the Great Depression. In addition, failure to understand the role of automatic stabilizers has led many observers to conclude, erroneously, that fiscal expansion was tried in the Great Depression but failed. Let us see how these two misperceptions are related.

The Paradox of Thrift in Action

In 1932, Canadian prime minister R.B. Bennett said, "We are now faced with the real crisis in the history of Canada. To maintain our credit we must practise the most rigid economy and not spend a single cent." His government that year—at the deepest point in the recession—brought down a budget based on the principle of trying to balance revenues and expenditures, and it included *increases* in tax rates.

In the same year, Franklin Roosevelt was elected U.S. president on a platform of fighting the Great Depression with government policies. In his inaugural address he urged, "Our great primary task is to put people to work.... [This task] can be helped by insistence that the federal, state, and local governments act forthwith on the demand that their costs be drastically reduced...."

Across the Atlantic, King George V told the British House of Commons in 1931, "The present condition of the national finances, in the opinion of His Majesty's ministers, calls for the imposition of additional taxation and for the effecting of economies in public expenditure."

As the paradox of thrift predicts, these policies tended to worsen, rather than cure, the Great Depression.

Interpreting the Deficits in the 1930s

In general, governments can have a budget deficit for two different reasons. First, a government might increase its level of purchases without increasing its tax revenues. Such a *deficit-financed* increase in government spending represents an expansion in aggregate demand. Second, a government might leave its purchases unchanged but have lower tax revenues. If the lower tax revenues are caused by a policy decision to reduce *tax rates,* then this policy also represents an expansion in aggregate demand. But if the decline in tax revenues is caused by a fall in real GDP

As we saw in Chapter 22, in the absence of the tax-and-transfer system, the multiplier would be larger and thus any given positive shock would lead to a larger shift in the *AD* curve and thus to a larger increase in real GDP.

The same is true in the presence of a negative *AD* shock. As real GDP declines in response to the shock, the reduction in government net tax revenues dampens the overall decline in real GDP.

> **Even in the absence of discretionary fiscal stabilization policy, the government's tax-and-transfer system provides the economy with an automatic stabilizer.**

At the end of Chapter 22 we argued that realistic Canadian values for our model's key parameters are as follows:

- marginal propensity to consume $(MPC) = 0.8$
- net tax rate $(t) = 0.25$
- marginal propensity to import $(m) = 0.35$

with unchanged tax rates, the existing budget deficit *does not* represent an expansion in aggregate demand. These distinctions are central to interpreting the budget deficits of the 1930s.

Government budget deficits did increase in the 1930s, but they were not the result of an increase in government expenditures or reductions in tax rates. Rather, they were the result of the fall in tax revenues, brought about by the fall in real GDP as the economy sank into depression. The various governments did not advocate programs of massive deficit-financed spending to shift the *AD* curve to the right. Instead, they hoped that a small amount of government spending in addition to numerous policies designed to stabilize prices and to restore confidence would lead to a recovery of private investment expenditure that would substantially shift the *AD* curve. To have expected a massive revival of private investment expenditure as a result of the puny increase in aggregate demand that was instituted by the federal government now seems hopelessly naïve.

When we judge these policies from the viewpoint of modern macro theory, their failure is no mystery. Indeed, Professor E. Cary Brown of MIT, after a careful study for the United States, concluded, "Fiscal policy seems to have been an unsuccessful recovery device in the thirties—not because it did not work, but because it was not tried." Once the massive, war-geared expenditure of the 1940s began, output responded sharply and unemployment all but evaporated. A similar pattern occurred in Canada, as seen clearly in the figure.

The performance of the Canadian and U.S. economies from 1930 to 1945 is well explained by the macroeconomic theory that we have developed in the last few chapters. The governments did not effectively use fiscal policy to stabilize their economies. War brought the Depression to an end because war demands made acceptable a level of government expenditure sufficient to remove the recessionary gap. Had the Canadian and American administrations been able to do the same in the early 1930s, it might have ended the waste of the Great Depression many years sooner.

(*Source:* Urquhart, M.C., and Buckley, K.A.H. (Ed.). (1965). *Historical Statistics of Canada.* Toronto: Macmillan.)

The implied value of z, the marginal propensity to spend on national income, is therefore

$$z = MPC(1-t) - m$$
$$= (0.8)(0.75) - 0.35 = 0.25$$

As a result, a realistic value for the simple multiplier in Canada is

$$\text{Simple multiplier} = 1/(1-z) = 1/0.75 = 1.33$$

The lower is the net tax rate, the larger is the simple multiplier and thus the less stable is real GDP in response to shocks to autonomous spending. For example, if the net tax rate were reduced to 20 percent ($t = 0.20$), the value of z would rise to 0.29 and the simple multiplier would rise to $1/(1 - 0.29) = 1/0.71 = 1.41$. The larger multiplier implies that a shock to autonomous expenditure would result in a larger shift in the *AD* curve and thus a larger total change in GDP—that is, the economy would be less stable. Therefore, whatever benefits might arise from a reduction in the net tax rate (and we will see later that lower rates on some specific taxes may tend to increase the economy's long-run growth rate), one drawback is that the tax reduction would lead to the economy being less stable following shocks to autonomous expenditure.[6]

The great advantage of automatic fiscal stabilizers is that they are "automatic." As long as the tax-and-transfer system is in place (and there is no sign of its imminent disappearance!), some stability is provided without anyone having to make active decisions about fiscal policy. As we see next, the sorts of decisions required for successful *discretionary* fiscal policy are not simple, and some attempts to provide stability through discretionary fiscal policy may actually reduce the stability of the economy.

Practical Limitations of Discretionary Fiscal Policy

According to our earlier discussion of fiscal stabilization policy, returning the economy to potential output would appear to be a simple matter of changing taxes and government spending, in some combination. Why do so many economists believe that such policies would be "as likely to harm as help"? Part of the answer is that the practical use of discretionary fiscal policy is anything but simple.

Decision and Execution Lags To change fiscal policy requires making changes in taxes and government expenditures. The changes must be agreed on by the Cabinet and passed by Parliament. The political stakes in such changes are generally very large; taxes and spending are called "bread-and-butter issues" precisely because they affect the economic well-being of almost everyone. Even if economists agreed that the economy would be helped by, say, a tax cut, politicians would likely spend a good deal of time debating *whose* taxes should be cut and by *how much*. If the assessment by economists was that an increase in government spending was desirable, the lengthy political debate would then be about what *type* of spending should increase and whether it should focus on particular industries or regions. The delay between the initial recognition of a recessionary or inflationary gap and the enactment of legislation to change fiscal policy, which may be several months long, is called a **decision lag**.

Once policy changes are agreed on, there is still an **execution lag**, adding time between the enactment of the legislation and the implementation of the policy action. Furthermore, once the new policies are in place, it will usually take still more time for their economic consequences to be felt. Because of these lags, it is quite possible that by the time a given policy decision has any impact on the economy, circumstances will have changed such that the policy is no longer appropriate.

The decision lag applies more or less equally to both tax and expenditure policies. The execution lag, however, tends to be considerably longer for expenditure than tax policies. Once Parliament agrees to specific tax changes, the effects can be realized quite soon by individual or corporate taxpayers. For an increase in expenditure, however, new programs may need to be created or infrastructure projects planned and designed before the bulk of the new spending can occur. Even for planned reductions in expenditure, it often takes time to scale down or cancel existing spending programs and to identify the public servants who will be laid off.

decision lag The period of time between perceiving some problem and reaching a decision on what to do about it.

execution lag The time that it takes to put policies in place after a decision has been made.

---

[6] We have said that automatic stabilizers reduce the multiplier so that a given change in autonomous expenditures leads to a smaller horizontal shift in the *AD* curve than would otherwise be the case. It is also true that the same automatic stabilizers lead to a *steeper AD* curve; the result is that real GDP is more stable in the presence of *AS* shocks.

Temporary Versus Permanent Tax Changes Changes in taxation that are known to be temporary are generally less effective than measures that are expected to be permanent. For example, if households know that an announced tax cut will last only a year, they may recognize that the effect on their long-run consumption possibilities is small and may choose to save rather than spend their increase in disposable income. If so, the effect of the tax cut on aggregate demand will be nil.

In other cases, however, temporary changes in taxes may be quite effective at changing aggregate demand. If the government temporarily increases employment-insurance (EI) benefits to the long-term unemployed, for example, it is quite likely that they will spend a large fraction of the increased benefits and that aggregate demand will increase as a result.

For most tax changes, the following general principle is a useful guide for policy: The more closely household consumption expenditure is related to *lifetime* income rather than to *current* income, the smaller will be the effects on current consumption of tax changes that are known to be of short duration. Or, to use the language that we used when introducing the consumption function in Chapter 21, the more forward-looking households are, the smaller will be the effects of what are perceived to be temporary changes in taxes.

The Role of Discretionary Fiscal Policy Attempts to use discretionary fiscal policy to "fine tune" the economy are thus fraught with difficulties. **Fine tuning** refers to the use of fiscal (and monetary) policy to offset virtually all fluctuations in private-sector spending so as to keep real GDP at or near its potential level. However, neither economics nor political science has yet advanced far enough to allow policymakers to undo the consequences of every aggregate demand or supply shock. Nevertheless, many economists still argue that when a recessionary gap is large enough and persists for long enough, *gross tuning* may be appropriate. **Gross tuning** refers to the use of fiscal and monetary policy to remove large and persistent output gaps. Other economists believe that fiscal policy should not be used for economic stabilization under any circumstances. Rather, they would argue, tax and spending behaviour should be the outcome of public choices regarding the long-term size and financing of the public sector and should not be altered for short-term considerations. We return to these debates in Chapter 32.

fine tuning The attempt to maintain output at its potential level by means of frequent changes in fiscal or monetary policy.

gross tuning The use of macroeconomic policy to stabilize the economy such that large deviations from potential output do not persist for extended periods of time.

Fiscal Policy and Growth

Fiscal policy has both short run and long-run effects on the economy. Its short-run effects, which we have discussed in this chapter, are reflected by shifts in the *AD* curve and changes in the level of GDP. However, the theory presented in this chapter predicts that the adjustment of factor prices will eventually bring real GDP back to Y^* so that the long-run effects of any given fiscal policy will depend on the policy's effects on Y^*. In both of the following examples, to highlight the difference between the short-run and long-run effects of the policies, we imagine starting in a macroeconomic equilibrium with real GDP equal to Y^*.

Increases in Government Purchases A fiscal expansion created by an increase in government purchases (*G*) will shift the *AD* curve to the right and increase real GDP in the short run. As factor prices rise in response to the inflationary output gap, output will return back to Y^* but at a higher price level. At this point, let's consider two possibilities. In the first, the level of Y^* is unaffected by the increase in *G*; in the second, for reasons that we will see shortly, the increase in *G* causes Y^* to rise.

The Increase in G Leaves Y* Unchanged. As we will see in later chapters, even though the adjustment of factor prices will bring real GDP back to the initial Y^*, the *composition* of output will be altered. From the national-income accounting we saw in Chapter 20, we know that $Y = C_a + I_a + G_a + NX_a$, where the "$a$" subscripts denote the actual components of aggregate expenditure. If real GDP returns to Y^* after factor prices have fully adjusted, then the *rise* in G_a must be equal to the *fall* in $C_a + I_a + NX_a$. In this case we say that the increase in government purchases has "crowded out" private expenditures. Of particular concern is the possibility that private investment in plant and equipment will be reduced. If private investment is crowded out, there will be a slower rate of accumulation of physical capital, and this will likely lead to a reduction in the future growth rate of potential output.[7]

Even if an increase in government purchases leaves the *current level* of potential output unchanged, the crowding out of private investment may reduce the *future growth rate* of potential output.

The Increase in G Causes Y* to Rise. We have assumed throughout this chapter that short-run AD shocks leave Y^* unchanged. Though this is a useful simplifying assumption in our model, it may not be true in the real world. Suppose, in particular, that the increase in G is spent on public infrastructure that increases the productivity of private-sector production. Improved highways, bridges, ports, or public-health networks may all have such an effect. In this case, the rise in G will still cause an inflationary gap and set in place the economy's adjustment process. As factor prices rise, firms' unit costs will increase; the AS curve will shift to the left, thus returning real GDP back toward Y^*. But if Y^* has now increased as a result of the productivity-enhancing increase in G, the extent of crowding out of private expenditures will be less than in the previous case (where Y^* was constant). The result is that the negative effect on the economy's long-run growth rate may be reduced or even eliminated.

If an increase in government purchases leads to an increase in potential output (or its growth rate), the negative effects from the crowding out of private investment will be reduced.

Beginning When Y < Y*. The analysis is slightly different, however, if the fiscal expansion is undertaken when real GDP is initially well below Y^*. In an ideal situation, the increase in government purchases is just enough to increase real GDP back to Y^*; government purchases are then reduced as private consumption and investment recover. In this case, the fiscal policy has put to work resources that would otherwise have been idle and it has no crowding out effect because it is reduced as private expenditure recovers. There is then a short-term gain from raising real GDP above what it would otherwise have been. There may even be some long-term gain to growth if the increased government expenditure was on productive assets, such as infrastructure. Of course, this is an ideal situation. If the government expenditure does not fall as private expenditure recovers, the situation becomes the first case with

---

[7] Since some of the rise in G_a may be government investment in such things as roads or power plants or other productivity-enhancing infrastructure, the overall effect on the path of Y^* depends on the productivity of the new public investment compared with that of the private investment that was crowded out.

an expansionary fiscal policy combined with an economy already at Y^*. In this case, the short-run simulative benefits of the fiscal expansion need to be weighed against the long-run costs.

Reductions in Taxes Now consider a fiscal expansion created by a reduction in tax rates, and suppose that we begin the analysis with real GDP equal to Y^*. The short-run demand-side effects are straightforward. Reductions in the GST rate or in the corporate or personal income-tax rates that are thought to be long-lasting will increase both investment and consumption spending and shift the AD curve to the right. The level of real GDP will rise in the short run. As wages and other factor prices increase, however, the level of output will gradually return to Y^*.

Will the level of Y^* or its growth rate be affected by the reduction in taxes? It depends to a large extent on which taxes are cut, and by how much. Reductions in GST rates and personal income-tax rates may provide an incentive for individuals to increase their work effort, thus increasing overall labour supply and the level of Y^*. Reductions in corporate income-tax rates are likely to increase the economy's rate of investment and, through this channel, increase the future growth rate of Y^*.

> Reductions in tax rates generate a short-run demand stimulus and may also generate a longer-run increase in the level and growth rate of potential output.

Reductions in tax rates *may* lead to increases in the economy's potential growth rate. But this is not a certain outcome. In the event that growth is increased, however, there would appear to be no clear tradeoff between the short run and long-run effects of the fiscal expansion. The economy benefits in the short run from the increase in economic activity and in the long run from the increase in the growth rate. The absence of a tradeoff may, however, be illusory. Even though the growth rate of potential output is higher, the reduced tax revenues lead to fewer resources under the command of government. This means less public spending on many of the things that citizens value, such as national parks, public education, health care, roads, bridges, airports, other infrastructure, and research and development. The essential tradeoff then becomes one between having more resources in the hands of the private sector or more resources in the hands of the public sector. This choice is a crucial one—and often a contentious one—for all economics.

Another extreme possibility is that the reduction in tax rates leads to such a significant increase in potential output that the government's tax revenues actually increase. In this case, the tax reduction unleashes such a flood of investment and work effort that the increase in national income is sufficient to more than offset the reduction in tax rates, thus leaving the government able to fund more worthwhile public spending than before. This idea is central to what is often called "supply side" economics, as popularized during the early 1980s by advisors to U.S. president Ronald Reagan and British prime minister Margaret Thatcher. More recently, the central idea that tax reductions may significantly stimulate economic activity and growth played an important role in the policies of former premiers Ralph Klein of Alberta and Mike Harris of Ontario, as well as in the tax cuts implemented in 2004 by former U.S. president George W. Bush. In these cases, there is ample evidence that the tax cuts helped to generate significant increases in economic activity; there is little or no evidence, however, that they led to *increases* in government tax revenue.

SUMMARY

24.1 The Adjustment Process

- Potential output, Y^*, is the level of real GDP at which all factors of production are fully employed.
- The output gap is the difference between potential output and the actual level of real GDP, the latter determined by the intersection of the AD and AS curves.
- An inflationary gap means that Y is greater than Y^*, and hence there is excess demand in factor markets. As a result, wages and other factor prices rise, causing firms' unit costs to rise. The AS curve shifts upward, and the price level rises.

- A recessionary gap means that Y is less than Y^*, and hence there is excess supply in factor markets. Wages and other factor prices fall but perhaps very slowly. As firms' unit costs fall, the AS curve gradually shifts downward, eventually returning output to potential.
- In our macro model, the level of potential output, Y^*, acts as an "anchor" for the economy. Given the short-run equilibrium as determined by the AD and AS curves, wages and other factor prices will adjust, shifting the AS curve, until output returns to Y^*.

24.2 Aggregate Demand and Supply Shocks

- Beginning from a position of potential output, an expansionary demand shock creates an inflationary gap, causing wages and other factor prices to rise. Firms' unit costs rise, shifting the AS curve upward and bringing output back toward Y^*.
- Beginning from a position of potential output, a contractionary demand shock creates a recessionary gap. Because factor prices tend to be sticky downward, the adjustment process tends to be slow, and a recessionary gap tends to persist for some time.
- Aggregate supply shocks, such as those caused by changes in the prices of inputs, lead the AS curve to shift, changing real GDP and the price level. But the

economy's adjustment process reverses the shift in AS, tending eventually to bring the economy back to its initial level of output and prices.
- In the short run, macroeconomic equilibrium is determined by the intersection of the AD and AS curves. In the long run, the economy is in equilibrium only when real GDP is equal to potential output. In the long run, the price level is determined by the intersection of the AD curve and the vertical Y^* curve.
- Shocks to the AD or AS curves can change real GDP in the short run. For a shock to have long-run effects, the value of Y^* must be altered.

24.3 Fiscal Stabilization Policy

- In our macro model, fiscal policy can be used to stabilize output at Y^*. To remove a recessionary gap, governments can shift AD to the right by cutting taxes or increasing spending. To remove an inflationary gap, governments can adopt the opposite policies.
- In the short run, increases in desired saving on the part of firms, households, and governments lead to reductions in real GDP. This phenomenon is called the paradox of thrift. In the long run, the paradox of thrift does not apply, and increased saving will lead to increased investment and economic growth.
- Because government tax and transfer programs tend to reduce the size of the multiplier, they act as automatic stabilizers.

- Discretionary fiscal policy is subject to decision lags and execution lags that limit its ability to take effect quickly.
- Fiscal policy has different effects in the short and long run. In the short run, a fiscal expansion created by an increase in government purchases (G) will increase real GDP. In the long run, the rise in G may "crowd out" private spending. If private investment is crowded out, the growth rate of potential output may be reduced.
- A fiscal expansion created by a reduction in taxes increases real GDP in the short run. In the long run, if the tax reduction leads to more investment and work effort, there will be a positive effect on the level and growth rate of potential output.

KEY CONCEPTS

The output gap and factor prices
Inflationary and recessionary gaps
Asymmetry of wage adjustment: flexible and sticky wages
The Phillips curve

Potential output as an "anchor" for the economy
Short-run versus long-run effects of *AD* and *AS* shocks
Fiscal stabilization policy

The paradox of thrift
Decision lags and execution lags
Automatic stabilizers
Fine tuning and gross tuning

STUDY EXERCISES

MyEconLab   Make the grade with MyEconLab: Study Exercises marked in red can be found on MyEconLab. You can practise them as often as you want, and most feature step-by-step guided instructions to help you find the right answer.

1. Fill in the blanks to make the following statements correct.

   a. In our short-run macro model, it is assumed that factor prices are _____ and the level of potential output is _____. Changes in real GDP are caused by fluctuations in _____ and _____.

   b. During the adjustment process highlighted in this chapter, the central assumption is that factor prices are _____ and responding to _____. Potential output is assumed to be _____, and acts as a(n) _____ for real GDP following *AD* or *AS* shocks.

2. Fill in the blanks to make the following statements correct.

   a. When actual GDP is higher than potential GDP, we say that there is a(n) _____ gap. When actual GDP is less than potential GDP we say there is a(n) _____ gap.

   b. An inflationary gap leads to excess demand for labour, which causes wages and thus _____ costs to rise. Firms require higher _____ in order to supply any level of output, and so the *AS* curve shifts _____.

   c. A recessionary gap leads to excess supply of labour, which tends to cause wages and thus _____ costs to fall. Firms reduce _____ for any level of output supplied, and so the *AS* curve shifts _____.

   d. The downward adjustment of wages in response to a recessionary gap is much _____ than the upward adjustment of wages in response to a(n)

   _____ gap. Economists refer to this phenomenon as _____.

3. Fill in the blanks to make the following statements correct.

   a. Beginning with output equal to potential, suppose there is a sudden increase in demand for Canadian exports. This is a(n) _____ shock to the Canadian economy, which will result in the _____ curve shifting to the _____ and the opening of a(n) _____ gap. Firms' unit costs will start to _____ and the _____ curve will shift _____. Long-run equilibrium will be restored at _____ output and _____ price level.

   b. Beginning with output equal to potential, suppose there is a drop in business confidence and investment falls. This is a(n) _____ shock to the Canadian economy, which shifts the _____ curve to the left and creates a(n) _____ gap. Unit costs will start to _____ and the _____ curve will shift _____. Long-run equilibrium will (slowly) be restored at _____ output and _____ price level.

   c. Beginning with output equal to potential, suppose there is a large and sudden increase in the price of electricity. This is a(n) _____ shock to the Canadian economy, which will result in the _____ curve shifting _____ and the opening of a(n) _____ gap. If wages are downwardly sticky the economy's _____ process could be very slow and the _____ will persist for a long time.

d. Beginning with output equal to potential, suppose there is a large and sudden decrease in the price of electricity. This is a(n) _____ shock to the Canadian economy, which will result in the _____ curve shifting _____ and the opening of a(n) _____ gap. Unit costs will start to _____ and the _____ curve will shift _____, restoring equilibrium at _____ output and _____ price level.

4. Fill in the blanks to make the following statements correct.

   a. In the long run, total output is determined only by _____. In the long run, aggregate demand determines the _____.

   b. Permanent increases in real GDP are possible only if _____ is increasing.

   c. Suppose illiteracy in Canada were eliminated, and the school dropout rate were reduced to zero. The effect would be a permanent _____ in productivity and a(n) _____ in potential output.

   d. A reduction in corporate income tax is likely to make _____ more attractive and thus shift the _____ curve to the right. The result is a(n) _____ in the short-run level of real GDP. In the long run, the greater rate of _____ by firms will lead to a greater rate of growth of _____.

5. The following diagram shows two economies, A and B. Each are in short-run equilibrium at point E, where the AD and AS curves intersect.

Real GDP
Economy A

Real GDP
Economy B

a. Explain why in Economy A wages and other factor prices will begin to rise, and why this will increase firms' unit costs.

b. Following your answer in part (a), show the effect on the AS curve. Explain what happens to real GDP and the price level.

c. Explain why in Economy B wages and other factor prices will begin to fall, and why this will decrease firms' unit costs.

d. Following your answer in part (c), show the effect on the AS curve. Explain what happens to real GDP and the price level.

6. The table shows several possible situations for the economy in terms of output gaps and the rate of change of wages. Real GDP is measured in billions of dollars. Assume that potential output is $800 billion.

Situation	Real GDP	Output Gap	Rate of Wage Change	Shift of AS Curve
A	775	—	−2.0%	—
B	785	—	−1.2%	—
C	795	—	−0.2%	—
D	800	—	0.0%	—
E	805	—	1.0%	—
F	815	—	2.4%	—
G	825	—	4.0%	—
H	835	—	5.8%	—

a. Compute the output gap $(Y − Y^*)$ for each situation and fill in the table.

b. Explain why wages rise when output is greater than potential but fall when output is less than potential.

c. For each situation, explain whether the economy's AS curve is shifting up, shifting down, or stationary. Fill in the table.

d. Plot the Phillips curve on a scale diagram for this economy, with the rate of change of nominal wages on the vertical axis and the level of GDP on the horizontal axis. (See *Extensions in Theory 24-1* on pages 594–595 for a review of the Phillips curve.)

7. Consider an economy that is in equilibrium with output equal to Y^*. There is then a significant reduction in the world's demand for this country's goods.

   a. Illustrate the initial equilibrium in a diagram.

   b. What kind of shock occurred—aggregate demand or aggregate supply? Show the effects of the shock in your diagram.

   c. Explain the process by which the economy will adjust back toward Y^* in the long run. Show this in your diagram.

   d. Explain why policymakers may want to use a fiscal expansion to restore output back to Y^* rather than wait for the process you described in part (c). What role does downward wage stickiness play in the policymakers' thinking?

8. Consider an economy that is in equilibrium with output equal to Y^*. There is then a significant reduction in the world price of an important raw material, such as iron ore.

   a. Illustrate the initial equilibrium in a diagram.
   b. What kind of shock occurred—aggregate demand or aggregate supply? Show the effects of the shock in your diagram.
   c. Explain the process by which the economy will adjust back toward Y^* in the long run. Show this in your diagram.
   d. Is there a strong case for using a fiscal contraction to return output to Y^*? Explain why or why not.

9. The table below shows hypothetical data for five economies. Real GDP is measured in millions of dollars.

	Real GDP	Potential GDP (Y^*)	Output Gap (% of Y^*)	Rate of Wage Change
Economy 1	10 050	9 100	—	+2.0%
Economy 2	70 000	77 000	—	−0.3%
Economy 3	115 000	130 000	—	−0.5%
Economy 4	4 000	3 700	—	+1.0%
Economy 5	50 000	50 000	—	0.0%

   a. Fill in the missing data. Which economies have an inflationary gap? Which have a recessionary gap?
   b. Which economies likely have the most unused capacity? Explain.
   c. In which economies are labour and other factors of production in excess demand?
   d. Explain why the rate of change of nominal wages is high in Economies 1 and 4, and low in Economies 2 and 3.
   e. Assuming that labour productivity is constant, in which economies are unit costs rising? In which are they falling? Explain.

10. In our discussion of automatic fiscal stabilizers, we argued that income taxes and transfers increased the stability of real GDP in the face of AD and AS shocks. Recall from Chapter 22 that the simple multiplier is given by $1/[1 - MPC(1 - t) - m]$.

   a. Explain how the size of the simple multiplier is related to the *slope* of the AD curve. (You may want to review the relationship between the AE curve and the AD curve, as discussed in Chapter 23.)
   b. Explain how the slope of the AD curve affects the stability of real GDP in the presence of AS shocks.
   c. Now explain how the size of the simple multiplier is related to the size of the *shift* in the AD curve for any given change in autonomous expenditure.
   d. For any given AS curve, show how the size of the AD shift affects the stability of real GDP.
   e. Finally, explain how the economy's automatic stabilizers depend on the sizes of MPC, t, and m.

11. Which of the following would be automatic stabilizers? Explain why.

   a. Employment-insurance payments
   b. Cost-of-living escalators in government contracts and pensions
   c. Income taxes
   d. Free university tuition for unemployed workers after six months of unemployment, provided that they are under 30 years old and have had five or more years of full-time work experience since high school

12. The following diagram shows the AD, AS, and Y^* curves for an economy. Suppose the economy begins at point A. Then the government increases its level of purchases (G).

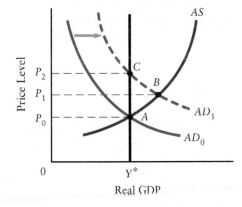

   a. Describe the short-run effects of this fiscal expansion.
   b. Describe the adjustment process, and the new long-run equilibrium for the economy.
   c. Explain how the *composition* of real GDP has changed from the initial to the new long-run equilibrium.
   d. Repeat parts (a), (b), and (c) for a fiscal expansion generated by a reduction in the net tax rate.

13. Between 2006 and 2012, the Canadian government reduced both personal and corporate income taxes. Is this a demand-side or a supply-side policy? Explain.

The Difference Between Short-Run and Long-Run Macroeconomics

LEARNING OBJECTIVES (LO)

After studying this chapter you will be able to

1 see the importance of distinguishing between the short run and the long run when analyzing macroeconomics.

2 understand how any change in real GDP can be decomposed into changes in factor supply, the utilization rate of factors, and productivity.

3 understand that short-run changes in GDP are mostly caused by changes in factor utilization, whereas long-run changes in GDP are mostly caused by changes in factor supplies and productivity.

4 explain why macroeconomic policies will only have a long-run effect on output if they influence the level of potential output.

IN Chapters 21, 22, and 23, we developed a model of the economy in the short run. In Chapter 24, we showed how this model evolves, through a process of factor-price adjustment, from its short-run equilibrium to its long-run equilibrium. There we saw how the level of potential output, Y^*, acts as an "anchor" for the economy. Aggregate demand or supply shocks can lead to short-run deviations of real GDP from Y^*, but the economy's adjustment process tends to bring real GDP back to Y^* in the long run. We are now set to examine why Y^* grows over periods of many years—a process that we call *long-run economic growth*.

In this chapter, we focus on the distinction between the short run and the long run in macroeconomics. This distinction becomes especially important when policy-makers try to evaluate the effects of various policies.

Different economists will sometimes use different time frames for the evaluation of any given policy. For example, one economist may say that a fiscal expansion is desirable because it will provide stimulus to an economy with high unemployment; another economist may claim that it will have negative effects on the economy's long-run growth. Both views might be correct (as we saw at the end of the previous chapter), but the listener is left confused because it is not clear in the debate whether the discussion is about the short-run or the long-run effects of the policy.

In this chapter, we seek to clarify the distinction between short-run GDP fluctuations and long-run GDP growth. With this distinction firmly in place, we will be ready for the detailed discussion of long-run economic growth in the next chapter.

25.1 Two Examples from Recent History

We begin with two examples of the difference between short-run and long-run macro-economic relationships. Though the specific examples date from the 1990s, the principles involved apply more generally.

Inflation and Interest Rates in Canada

In the early 1990s, Canada's central bank (the Bank of Canada) embarked on a policy designed to reduce the rate of inflation. For reasons that we will see in detail in Chapters 29 and 30, the Bank's policy was controversial. The governor of the Bank, however, was committed to explaining the policy to an often-skeptical public. As we will see, the explanation relies crucially on making the distinction between short-run and long-run macroeconomic relationships.

In April 1995, Bank of Canada Governor Gordon Thiessen was interviewed on CBC Radio. Thiessen was asked about the Bank's policy of reducing inflation, from about 6 percent a few years earlier, and maintaining it at a lower rate of about 2 percent. Thiessen argued that the high nominal interest rates of the past were caused mostly by high inflation. The main reason for this connection between inflation and nominal interest rates is that inflation erodes the value of money. Lenders need to be compensated for the inflation-induced fall in the real value of their money between the time they lend it and the time they are repaid. This requires charging a nominal interest rate high enough to cover the effects of inflation and deliver a positive return to the lender. Thus, higher inflation pushes up interest rates; lower inflation pushes them down.

At this point, the interviewer had no problem with Thiessen's line of argument, as he easily recalled the time back in 1981 when inflation was at an all-time high of 12 percent and mortgage rates at Canada's banks were an astounding 20 percent! In contrast, by 1995, the rate of inflation was down to just over 2 percent and mortgage rates were only 8 percent. So periods of high inflation did indeed appear to coincide with periods of high interest rates.

Thiessen then started the next part of his argument. He stated that in order to reduce the rate of inflation the Bank of Canada had to tighten up credit-market conditions and push up interest rates. Understandably confused at this point, the interviewer asked the inevitable question: How can a policy that raises interest rates be a necessary part of a policy designed to *reduce* both inflation and interest rates?

Thiessen understood the apparent contradiction and was ready with his answer. He stressed that the key to answering the question is to understand the different short-run and long-run effects of monetary policy. Thiessen argued that, in the short run, the Bank's policies to raise interest rates will lead firms to reduce their investment and lead households to reduce their spending on big-ticket items. Such reductions in expenditure will lead, through the multiplier process that we have seen in earlier chapters, to a reduction in real GDP. In short, the Bank of Canada's policy shifts the *AD* curve to the left and generates a recession. When we examine the detailed workings of monetary policy in later chapters, we will see that a monetary policy designed to reduce inflation is usually effective precisely because *it creates a temporary recession*.

So much for the short-run effects of the Bank's policy. What happens as wages and other factor prices adjust and the economy therefore starts to approach its new long-run equilibrium? As we saw in Chapter 24, the excess supply of factors that is a key part of the recession puts downward pressure on factor prices. In other words, wages start to increase at a slower rate than before and maybe even begin to fall. As wage growth declines, the pressure on prices to rise also declines. That is, the rate of inflation falls. As inflation falls, nominal interest rates will also fall. In the new long-run equilibrium, both inflation and nominal interest rates will be lower than before the policy was initiated. As Gordon Thiessen said in the interview, "The best way to get low interest rates is to get low inflation."

The details of monetary policy will be discussed in Chapters 28 and 29, and this argument will be repeated in considerable detail. At that time, we will more clearly see the difference between the short-run and long-run effects of monetary policy.

Saving and Growth in Japan

For the entire decade of the 1990s, the Japanese economy showed very little growth. This period is often referred to as Japan's "Lost Decade." Many economists argued that an important part of the solution to Japan's economic malaise was for its firms and consumers to spend more. One problem with Japan, they argued, was that its firms and consumers saved "too much." On the other hand, many of these same economists acknowledged that Japan's remarkable economic success in the 40 years following the Second World War—high growth rates of real GDP and low unemployment—was to a significant extent due to its high saving rate. But if "too much" saving was an important reason for Japan's economic slump during the 1990s, how could high saving also have been a primary reason for its remarkable economic success over four decades? How can both of these views be correct?

Once again, the key to understanding this apparent contradiction is to recognize that the short-run effect of saving is different from its long-run effect. We saw this distinction in Chapter 24 when we discussed the "paradox of thrift," but it is worth repeating. In the short run, with factor prices and technology more or less constant, an increase in households' desire to save, perhaps caused by some uncertainty about future economic events, implies a reduction in expenditure. Uncertainty leads firms to spend less on investment goods; households spend less on all sorts of consumer goods. This reduction in desired expenditure leads, through the usual multiplier process, to a reduction in output. In terms of our macro model, the *AD* curve shifts to the left and real GDP falls. Increased saving in the short run, therefore, can be one reason why an economy, such as Japan's, enters or remains in an economic slump.

If an increase in firms' and households' saving can cause a recession, how can a high saving rate also help to explain Japan's many years of healthy economic growth? The answer is that in the long run, after wages and factor prices adjust to the recessionary gap, greater saving leads to a larger pool of financial capital. This larger pool of available funds drives down the price of credit—the interest rate—and makes firms' investment projects more profitable. More investment in research and development to develop new products as well as more investment in factories, machines, and warehouses leads to a higher level of potential output, and it is to this higher level of potential output that the economy converges in the long run. Once this long-run mechanism is

The high private saving rate in Japan is one reason that the Japanese economic recovery in the 1990s was so slow.

understood, we can see that Japan's high saving rate over many years may indeed be a contributor to its high-growth experience.

This long-run relationship among saving, investment, and growth explains the striking correlation that we will see in the next chapter: over long periods, countries with high saving and investment rates tend to be countries with high rates of per capita GDP growth.

A Need to Think Differently

These two examples from recent history suggest that a complete understanding of macroeconomics requires an understanding of both the short run and the long run. Such an understanding, in turn, requires us to think differently about short-run and long-run behaviour. It is one thing to say that macroeconomic variables behave differently over the short run than over the long run; it is quite another to understand *why* this is the case.

In this chapter, we emphasize the distinction between viewing short-run changes in GDP as deviations of output from potential, and long-run changes in GDP as changes in the level of potential output. We introduce a simple method of GDP accounting that clarifies this distinction and also shows us the various sources of short-run and long-run changes in GDP.[1]

| 25.2 Accounting for Changes in GDP

The simplest illustration of the distinction between short-run and long-run changes in economic activity is the behaviour of real GDP over time, as shown in Figure 25-1. The figure shows the paths of Canadian real GDP and potential GDP, beginning from 1985. Actual GDP is measured by Statistics Canada. Potential GDP is the level of output that the economy produces when all factors of production are "fully employed." But Statistics Canada can't tell us the value of potential GDP because it is not an observed variable—it must be estimated. The value of potential GDP is estimated by combining three pieces of information: the amounts of available factors of production (such as the labour force and the capital stock); an estimate of these factors' rates of utilization when they are fully employed; and an estimate of each factor's productivity.

Figure 25-1 shows two different types of changes in GDP. First, some changes involve departures of actual GDP from potential GDP. For example, notice that actual GDP is equal to potential GDP at point *A* in 1990. As the Canadian economy then entered a major recession, actual GDP dropped below potential GDP to point *B* in 1992. An economic recovery then took place, eventually taking actual GDP back to potential GDP at point *C* in 1999. Real GDP again dropped significantly below potential GDP when a global recession began in 2008; by early in 2013, however, GDP had not yet

---

[1] It is worth emphasizing the different use of the terms "short run" and "long run" in macroeconomics and in microeconomics. In microeconomics, the short run for a firm or industry is the span of time during which the amount of physical capital is constant; the long run is the period of time during which firms are able to adjust their capital stock. In macroeconomics, however, the key distinction relates to whether wages and other factor prices have fully adjusted to excess demand or supply (the output gap) in the aggregate economy. Economists take wages and other factor prices to be given in the short run but fully adjusted to the output gap in the long run.

FIGURE 25-1 Actual and Potential GDP In Canada, 1985–2011

Long-run changes in GDP are reflected by changes in the level of potential GDP. Short-run changes in GDP are shown mostly by changes in the output gap.

(*Source:* Real GDP: Statistics Canada CANSIM database, Table 380-0017. Potential GDP: based on author's calculations using data on the output gap from www.bankofcanada.ca.)

returned to potential. Such changes in GDP are what economists call short-run changes in GDP—they involve primarily the opening and then closing of an output gap.

The second type of change in GDP involves changes in potential GDP, with little or no change in the output gap. For example, the change in actual GDP from point *A* in 1990 to point *D* in 2008 represents entirely a change in potential GDP. We know this because the output gap in both years was zero (that is, in both 1990 and 2008 GDP was equal to potential GDP). Such changes in GDP are what economists call long-run changes in GDP—they involve a change in potential GDP, with little or no change in the output gap.

> When studying long-run trends in GDP, economists focus on the change in potential output. When studying short-run fluctuations, economists focus on the change in the output gap.

Figure 25-1 may make us wonder whether short-run changes in GDP have a different cause than long-run changes. In our macro model this is certainly the case; output is determined in the short run by the *AD* and *AS* curves but in the long run by the level of *Y** (which is usually assumed to be unaffected by the *AD* or *AS* shocks). To explore the different causes of changes in GDP, we turn to a very simple accounting framework that applies to *all* changes in GDP.

GDP Accounting: The Basic Principle

Suppose we could break down any change in GDP into its component parts. By understanding how each component changes, we can then gain some insights into how short-run changes differ from long-run changes. To break up GDP into the parts we want to study, we do the following obvious but useful things. First, we write

$$GDP = GDP$$

This is obviously true! Next, we multiply the right-hand side of the equation by F/F, where F is the economy's total available stock of factors, such as land, labour, and capital. This gives

$$GDP = F \times (GDP/F)$$

Next, we multiply the right-hand side by F_E/F_E, where F_E is the number of the economy's factors that are employed. After reordering the terms, we have

$$GDP = F \times (F_E/F) \times (GDP/F_E) \qquad (25\text{-}1)$$

It may seem like we have done nothing useful since we have simply twice multiplied the right-hand side of an obviously true equation by one. But, in fact, Equation 25-1 is very useful when thinking about the different sources of GDP changes.

First, however, note that Equation 25-1 implies that we have added together units of labour, land, and capital to get a meaningful number for the economy's "available factors," F. This is not actually possible since different factors are measured in different units. For example, we can't add together six workers and five machines and two hectares of land to get a total of 13 factors. In the next section, we will focus on a single factor of production (labour) to avoid this problem. For now, however, our point is simplified by thinking about the economy's total available factors, F, and the number of those factors that are employed, F_E.

To make the discussion less cumbersome, let's name the three components of Equation 25-1.

1. F is the economy's *factor supply*; it is the total amount of all factors of production that the economy currently possesses.

2. F_E/F is the *factor utilization rate*; it is the fraction of the total supply of factors that is actually employed at any time.

3. GDP/F_E is a simple measure of *productivity* because it shows the amount of output (GDP) per unit of input employed (F_E).

Note that Equation 25-1 does nothing more than separate any change in GDP into a change in one or more of the three components, F, F_E/F, or GDP/F_E. For example, Canadian GDP increased dramatically in the 50 years between 1950 and 2000. Also, Canadian GDP increased by only a few percentage points between 2008 and 2012. In both cases, the increase in GDP can be attributed to changes in one or more of the three components—either the factor supply (F) increased, the factor utilization rate (F_E/F) increased, or the level of productivity (GDP/F_E) increased.

> Any change in GDP can be decomposed conceptually into a change in factor supply, a change in factor utilization, and a change in productivity.

The usefulness of this accounting exercise becomes clear when we recognize that two of these components, factor supply and productivity, change mostly over long periods of time, whereas the third component, factor utilization, changes mostly over shorter periods. This points us toward a better understanding of the difference between short-run and long-run changes in GDP. We discuss each component in turn.

The Long Run: Factor Supply Two main factors of production—labour and capital—account for most of the change in the economy's supply of factors.

Labour. The economy's supply of labour can increase for two main reasons. First, population can increase. An increase in population can be caused, in turn, by greater immigration, an increase in birth rates, or a decrease in the mortality rate. The second way to increase the economy's supply of labour is to increase the fraction of the population that chooses to seek employment. This fraction is called the *labour-force participation rate*. In Canada, the labour-force participation rate is currently about 66 percent. It has increased steadily from the 1960s, mostly because of the increase in the participation rate of married women.

No matter how the economy's supply of labour increases, the important point for our purposes is that such changes are mostly *long-run changes*. Population growth, through whatever means, is a very gradual process. Large changes in labour-force participation also tend to take place gradually (although there are some fluctuations over the course of the business cycle as people enter or leave the labour force depending on their assessment of being able to find a job). As a result, the economy's supply of labour does not usually change significantly from year to year. Over a period of many years, however, the increase in the supply of labour can be very substantial.

Capital. The economy's supply of physical capital—computers, machines, factories, and warehouses—increases for one reason. Firms that choose to purchase or build such investment goods today are accumulating physical capital that will be used to produce output in the future. Thus, today's flow of investment expenditure adds to the economy's stock of physical capital.[2]

As is the case for labour, the economy's stock of physical capital changes very gradually. This is not to be confused with the very dramatic swings in investment that are often observed over the course of the business cycle. The difference is that investment is the *flow* that contributes to the *stock* of capital. But the economy's capital stock is so large compared with the annual flow of investment expenditure that even dramatic swings in the annual flow of investment generate almost imperceptible changes in the stock of capital.

> Changes in the economy's supply of labour and capital occur gradually, but over periods of many years their growth is considerable. As a result, changes in factor supply are important for explaining long-run changes in output but relatively unimportant for explaining short-run changes.

The Long Run: Productivity The economy's level of productivity (GDP/F_E) is a measure of the average amount of output that is produced per unit of input. In practice, there are several possible measures of productivity, each one measuring something slightly different. Although there is more than one measure of productivity, Equation 25-1 uses the concept of output per employed factor, GDP/F_E. An increase in productivity is called *productivity growth*. Productivity growth is an important source of long-term increases in per capita income and thus in rising living standards, and we will say much more about it in Chapter 26.

The economy's level of productivity changes only slowly over time. For example, labour productivity in Canada—measured as real GDP per hour of work—has grown at an average rate of 1.3 percent per year since 1975. Such low growth rates do not lead to significant changes in GDP or living standards over short periods of time but can generate huge improvements in living conditions over many years. For example, you would barely notice a 1.3 percent increase in your income from one year to the next, but if this growth were sustained over 55 years your income would double. [31]

---

[2] The part of investment that represents a change in inventories does not add to the economy's capital stock, but this component of investment is typically quite small (though volatile).

The economy's level of productivity grows only gradually from year to year but increases substantially over periods of many years. As a result, productivity growth is very important for explaining long-run changes in output and living standards but less important for explaining short-run changes.

Many people find productivity an abstract concept that is difficult to comprehend, and cannot easily see how productivity grows over time. *Applying Economic Concepts 25-1* provides some examples of productivity-enhancing developments in various occupational settings.

The Short Run: Factor Utilization In Chapters 21, 22, and 23 we examined in detail the behaviour of the economy in the short run. Here we review some of these now-familiar concepts but express them in a way that helps us to understand our central equation decomposing the changes in real GDP.

The factor utilization rate (F_E/F) is the last remaining component from our equation. Recall that it is simply the fraction of the economy's total supply of factors that is employed. An immediate question comes to mind: Why would firms ever use fewer factors than are available to them? The answer has to do with how firms respond to changes in the demand for their product. When a firm's sales start dropping off, it must make a choice. It can continue producing at the current rate and let its inventories build up. Or it can reduce its rate of production. For a firm that is interested in maximizing profits, there is a limit to the amount of costly inventories it will be prepared to accumulate. Eventually, a reduction in demand for its product leads the firm to reduce its output and reduce its employment of factors. Workers are laid off and equipment and other physical capital are used less intensively, thus lowering the value of F_E/F for the economy.

Similarly, a firm that is faced with a sudden increase in demand for its product has two alternatives. It can continue with its previous rate of production and satisfy the increased demand by letting its inventories run down. Or it can increase its rate of production by hiring more available workers and machines. Since profit-maximizing firms do not want to miss an opportunity to make a profitable sale, as would happen if the stockpile of inventories were to get fully depleted, eventually the increase in demand leads them to increase production and hire more factors. Extra workers are hired, existing workers work overtime, and machines and other physical capital are used more intensively, thus increasing F_E/F for the economy.

These responses by firms to changes in demand are only the firms' short-run responses. A low factor utilization rate describes *excess supply* in the factor markets. As we saw in Chapter 24, such a situation of excess supply typically causes some downward pressure on wages and other factor prices. This reduction of factor prices, in turn, reduces firms' costs, shifts the *AS* curve downward, and puts downward pressure on product prices. Similarly, in the case of the increase in demand, the situation of a high factor utilization rate describes *excess demand* in factor markets. Such excess demand causes upward pressure on wages and other factor prices. As factor prices rise, firms' costs increase, the *AS* curve shifts upward, and there is upward pressure on the price level. This process of factor-price adjustment continues in our model until output returns to potential, at which point all factors of production are said to be fully employed.

APPLYING ECONOMIC CONCEPTS 25-1

What Does Productivity Growth Really Look Like?

The most commonly used measure of productivity is *labour productivity*, defined as the amount of output produced per hour of work, and it can be measured for the aggregate economy or for a particular firm or industry. For the aggregate economy, the appropriate measure of output is real GDP, and labour productivity is then measured as real GDP divided by the total number of hours worked. In 2012, Canadian labour productivity was about $46 per hour (expressed in 2002 dollars); it has been rising at an average annual rate of 1.3 percent since the mid-1970s.

How does labour productivity grow over time? Any new production process or technique that raises output proportionally more than it raises labour input will increase labour productivity. Often the introduction of new physical capital or new techniques allow firms to increase output while *reducing* their use of labour. In this case, labour productivity for the firm might increase significantly. Here are some examples from various industries and occupations:

- Accountants who prepare income-tax forms for their clients have experienced an enormous increase in labour productivity with the use of software packages designed specifically for the task. The software allows a given number of accountants to complete more tax returns per hour of work, thus increasing labour productivity.

- Residential landscaping companies move large amounts of soil, sand, and rock. In recent years, the development of small and inexpensive bulldozers has vastly increased the amount of work that can be done with a crew of two or three workers, thus dramatically raising labour productivity.

- In modern, high-tech lumber mills, a computer "reads" each log in three dimensions and then computes how the log can most efficiently be cut into the various regular sizes of cut lumber. Fewer workers are needed to sort the logs and more marketable lumber is produced from a given number of logs because the amount of waste is reduced. Labour productivity rises as a result.

- Doctors who specialize in eye surgery have been greatly aided by the recent development of precise medical lasers. The equipment is expensive, but allows a single doctor to perform more surgical procedures per day than was possible only a decade ago, thus increasing labour productivity.

In each of these examples, the use of new and better capital equipment allows the enterprise in question to produce more output with a given number of workers, or perhaps the same amount of output with a reduced number of workers. Both are an increase in measured labour productivity.

How do we get from these specific micro examples back to macroeconomics and the change in real GDP and aggregate labour productivity? If in each example the amount of work is unchanged but output rises, real GDP and aggregate labour productivity will both be higher as a result. If instead each specific output is unchanged but the amount of work is reduced, then we need to recognize that the workers released from these activities are now available to move to other firms and industries. When they begin working elsewhere in the economy, their new production will constitute an increase in real GDP. In this case, total work effort will be back to its original level but real GDP will be higher—an increase in aggregate labour productivity.

Small digging machines like this have replaced the difficult work of individuals with shovels and have significantly increased labor productivity.

The factor utilization rate fluctuates in response to aggregate demand and aggregate supply shocks. Over time, however, the adjustment of factor prices tends to return the factor-utilization rate to the level consistent with full employment.

When the economy's factors are fully employed (and thus real GDP equals Y^*), the value of F_E/F will be slightly less than one, indicating that some labour is normally unemployed and some capital is normally idle. There is thus some "normal" rate of factor utilization that corresponds to full employment.

What do we mean by a "normal" factor utilization rate? In Chapter 19 we briefly discussed the fact that even when the economy is at potential output, some unemployment still exists because of regular turnover in the labour market and new entrants seeking a first job. The rate of unemployment when real GDP is equal to potential output is often called the *natural rate of unemployment*. This "natural" or "normal" rate of unemployment is the rate of unemployment against which we compare the actual unemployment rate to judge whether the labour market has excess supply or excess demand. That is, if unemployment is above the natural rate, there is an excess supply of labour; if unemployment is below the natural rate, there is an excess demand for labour. For physical capital, the utilization rate is called the *capacity utilization rate* because the amount of physical capital largely determines the productive *capacity* of a given plant or factory. As with labour, so too is there a "natural" or "normal" capacity utilization rate for capital.

> Changes in the factor utilization rate are important for explaining short-run changes in GDP. But after factor prices have fully adjusted, the factor utilization rate returns to its "normal" level. As a result, changes in the factor utilization rate are not important for explaining long-run changes in GDP.

GDP Accounting: An Application

We made some strong statements in the previous section regarding the relative importance of short-run versus long-run changes in productivity, factor supplies, and factor utilization. Are these statements supported by the evidence? In this section, we apply the accounting exercise from Equation 25-1 to Canadian GDP data to illustrate the basic arguments. Unfortunately, we cannot use *exactly* the same equation because, as we noted then, it is not possible to add units of labour together with units of physical capital and units of land. By using exactly the same intuition as earlier, however, we can express the GDP accounting equation in terms of a single factor of production—labour. Letting L be the labour force and E be the number of individuals employed, the new equation is[3]

$$GDP = L \times (E/L) \times (GDP/E) \qquad (25\text{-}2)$$

The basic interpretation of Equation 25-2 is the same as for Equation 25-1, except now the discussion relates only to labour. The labour force (L) is the supply of labour. The employment rate (E/L) is the fraction of the labour force actually employed (which is equal to one minus the unemployment rate). And the measure of productivity—in this case, labour productivity—is GDP/E.[4]

Figure 25-2 shows the behaviour of these three components for Canada beginning in 1960. Each variable is expressed as an index number, with the value in 1960 set

---

[3] We get this equation by beginning with GDP = GDP. We then multiply the right-hand side by E/E and then by L/L.

[4] For reasons of data availability over long periods of time, our denominator for the measure of labour productivity is the number of workers employed rather than total hours worked. This choice makes little difference for the purposes of Figure 25-2.

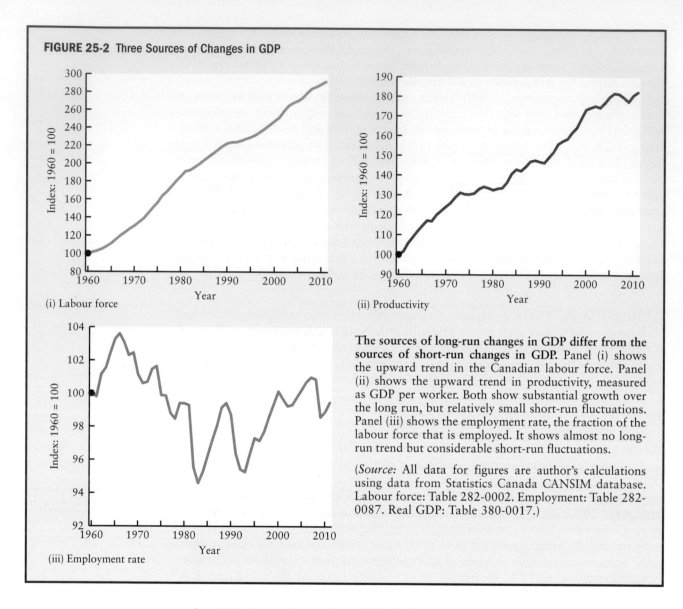

FIGURE 25-2 Three Sources of Changes in GDP

(i) Labour force

(ii) Productivity

(iii) Employment rate

The sources of long-run changes in GDP differ from the sources of short-run changes in GDP. Panel (i) shows the upward trend in the Canadian labour force. Panel (ii) shows the upward trend in productivity, measured as GDP per worker. Both show substantial growth over the long run, but relatively small short-run fluctuations. Panel (iii) shows the employment rate, the fraction of the labour force that is employed. It shows almost no long-run trend but considerable short-run fluctuations.

(*Source:* All data for figures are author's calculations using data from Statistics Canada CANSIM database. Labour force: Table 282-0002. Employment: Table 282-0087. Real GDP: Table 380-0017.)

equal to 100. Expressing each variable in this way makes it easy to see each variable's percentage change over the five decades. Note that the vertical scale is different for each of the three variables. We do this intentionally so that we can see whatever trend and volatility exist for each variable separately. If we used the same vertical scale for graphing employment that we use for graphing the labour force and productivity, we would barely notice the large fluctuations that do exist in employment.

Part (i) of the figure shows the growth of the Canadian labour force. From 1960 to 2011, the index number increased from 100 to 292, an increase of 192 percent. It is clear from the graph that any short-run fluctuations in the Canadian labour force are dwarfed in importance by the long-run upward trend.

Now look at the second panel, showing the growth of Canadian labour productivity. The level of GDP per person employed, expressed as an index number, increases from 100 in 1960 to 182 in 2011, an increase of 82 percent. Like the labour force, the level of labour productivity has its short-run fluctuations, but it is clear that the overriding change—the upward trend—takes place over many years.

Finally, consider part (iii), showing the Canadian employment rate—the utilization rate of labour. Compared with the other two variables graphed in Figure 25-2, the employment rate shows much more short-run volatility and much less long-run change. The employment rate (expressed as an index number) is almost the same in 2011 as it was in 1960. There is very little change over the long run, but considerable changes are occurring over shorter periods of time.

Summing Up

To summarize, we can decompose *any* change in GDP into changes in factor supply, the factor utilization rate, and productivity. But these three components typically contribute to GDP changes over different spans of time. In particular, factor supply and productivity typically change only gradually and hence are important for explaining long-run changes in GDP but are not usually helpful in explaining short-run changes in GDP. In contrast, the factor utilization rate is quite volatile over short periods of time but returns to its normal level over several years. Thus, changes in the factor utilization rate are important for explaining short-run changes in GDP but are not of much importance for explaining long-run changes.

25.3 Policy Implications

Economists think differently about short-run and long-run macroeconomic relationships. When thinking about short-run fluctuations, economists focus on understanding why actual GDP deviates from potential GDP. As we have seen in previous chapters, such changes in real GDP are caused by aggregate demand and aggregate supply shocks. When thinking about long-run growth, however, economists focus on understanding why potential GDP changes over time. As we have said, such long-run growth has its source in the growth of factor supplies and productivity. Thus, in understanding long-run growth, economists focus on what causes factor supplies and productivity to change.

> When studying short-run fluctuations, economists focus on the deviations of actual output from potential output. When studying long-run growth, economists focus on changes in potential output.

Through the development of our macro model in the previous four chapters, we have a better understanding of what causes the *AD* and *AS* curves to shift, and thus a better understanding of the causes of short-run fluctuations in real GDP. Our picture of the short run will be more fully developed after we discuss monetary policy and interest rates in Chapters 27 and 28 and exchange rates and international trade in Chapter 35.

What we have not yet done, however, is discuss in detail why potential output grows substantially over long periods of time, thereby improving average living standards from one generation to the next. In the next chapter we explore the issue of long-run economic growth, focusing on the importance of capital accumulation and technological change.

Before we do that, however, it is worth returning to a point that we raised at the beginning of this chapter—that the distinction between the short run and the long run has an important implication for the role and effectiveness of various macroeconomic policies.

We have discussed in this chapter how shocks to aggregate demand may cause actual GDP to depart from potential GDP. For example, firms may feel optimistic about the future and increase their investment expenditure, thereby increasing the overall level of demand. Or the government may increase its purchases of goods and services, thus adding to demand. Or foreigners may decide to increase their demand for Canadian goods, thus adding to the overall demand for goods produced by Canadian firms. All of these changes would increase the overall level of demand in the economy and, in the short run, would lead actual GDP to rise above potential GDP. Conversely, any decrease in the demand for goods would, in the short run, cause actual GDP to fall below potential GDP.

In the long run, however, the economy has an adjustment process that tends to return the factor utilization rate to its "normal" level. As we saw in Chapter 24, when actual GDP is above potential GDP, there is an excess demand for factors. This causes factor prices to rise and thus the *AS* curve to shift upward, bringing actual GDP back to potential. Conversely, when actual GDP is less than potential GDP, there is an excess supply of factors. This tends to cause factor prices to fall (though perhaps slowly) and thus the *AS* curve to shift downward, thereby bringing actual GDP back to potential.

This adjustment process that brings the economy back to the level of potential output in the long run implies a stark result regarding the effects of macroeconomic policy:

Fiscal and monetary policies affect the short-run level of GDP because they alter the level of demand and thus the position of the *AD* curve. But unless they are able to affect the level of *potential* output, Y^*, they will have no long-run effect on GDP.

As we saw in the previous chapter, fiscal policy can have important effects on the level of potential output—both through changes in government purchases and investment and through changes in personal and corporate taxes. In Chapters 28 and 29 we will explore monetary policy in detail and will see that it has few if any effects on the level of potential output.

Looking Ahead

The discussion in this chapter has focused on one topic—the difference between the short run and the long run in macroeconomics. We have shown that short-run movements in GDP are mostly accounted for by changes in the factor utilization rate. For example, as economic events cause the *AD* or *AS* curves to shift, output will deviate from Y^* and the factor utilization rate will change. In contrast, long-run changes in GDP are mostly accounted for by growth in factor supplies and productivity, which lead to increases in Y^*. This difference forces economists to think differently about macroeconomic relationships that exist over a few months as compared to those that exist over several years.

In the previous four chapters we examined in detail the behaviour of the economy in the short run, and the adjustment process that tends to bring real GDP back to Y^*. We are now ready to take the next step and examine why Y^* increases over time—the process of long-run growth.

SUMMARY

25.1 Two Examples from Recent History

- Macroeconomic variables behave differently over the short run and over the long run. One example: A monetary policy designed to reduce inflation and nominal interest rates in the long run requires an *increase* in interest rates in the short run. Another example: An increase in households' or firms' saving rates will reduce the level of output in the short run, but it will increase output in the long run.
- In the short run, there is some adjustment of output and employment but little adjustment of wages and prices. In the long run, full adjustment of wages and prices is assumed to take place.

25.2 Accounting for Changes in GDP

- Changes in GDP can be accounted for by changes in one or more of the following three variables:
    1. Supply of factors
    2. Factor utilization rates
    3. Factor productivity
- Long-run changes in GDP are caused mostly by changes in factor supplies and factor productivity; the utilization rate of factors does not change significantly over the long run.
- Short-run changes in GDP are caused mostly by changes in the factor utilization rate; factor supplies and productivity have relatively minor short-run fluctuations.

25.3 Policy Implications

- When studying short-run fluctuations, economists focus on changes in the output gap and tend to ignore changes in potential output. When studying long-run growth, economists focus on changes in potential output and ignore changes in the output gap.
- Fiscal and monetary policies affect GDP in the short run because they affect the level of demand, and thus the position of the *AD* curve. Any long-run effect on real GDP must come through their effect on *potential* GDP.

KEY CONCEPTS

Short-run fluctuations
Long-run trends
Changes in the output gap

Changes in potential output
Accounting for changes in GDP
Factor supplies

Factor utilization rates
Productivity

STUDY EXERCISES

MyEconLab   Make the grade with MyEconLab: Study Exercises marked in red can be found on MyEconLab. You can practise them as often as you want, and most feature step-by-step guided instructions to help you find the right answer.

1. Fill in the blanks to make the following statements correct.

    a. Short-run changes in real GDP are caused by _____ and _____ shocks, with little or no change in _____. In the short run, _____ prices and the level of _____ are assumed to be constant.

    b. Long-run trends in GDP involve changes in _____ output. Short-run fluctuations in GDP involve changes in the output gap with little or no change in _____.

c. Any change in GDP is caused by changes in at least one of the following three component parts: _____, _____, and _____.

d. Long-run changes in GDP are caused mainly by changes in _____ and _____. Short-run changes in GDP are caused mainly by changes in _____.

e. The economy's adjustment process returns the _____ rate to its "normal" level in the long run.

f. Fiscal and monetary policies alter the level of output in the short run by causing the _____ curve to shift. There will be a long-run effect on output only if _____ changes.

2. Consider Economies A, B, and C for which you are given data for the factor supply (F), the numbers of factors employed (F_E), and the GDP, for two different time periods.

Economy	Time Period	F	F_E	GDP	F_E/F	GDP/F_E
A	Period 1	1000	800	$100 000	____	____
	Period 2	1300	1040	$155 000	____	____
B	Period 1	2000	1800	$225 000	____	____
	Period 2	2000	1500	$187 500	____	____
C	Period 1	6500	6175	$399 000	____	____
	Period 2	6500	6175	$665 000	____	____

a. For each economy and each period, calculate the factor utilization rate (F_E/F) and a measure of productivity (GDP/F_E). Fill in the table.

b. For each economy and each period, use the numbers from the table to substitute into Equation 25-1 (GDP $= F \times F_E/F \times$ GDP/F_E).

c. For each economy, describe whether you think the economy has experienced a short-run or a long-run change in GDP from Period 1 to Period 2. Explain.

d. Do you detect an important difference between Economies A and C? Explain.

3. Using the basic equation of GDP accounting that we developed in this chapter (GDP $= F \times F_E/F \times$ GDP/F_E), calculate the economy's GDP in each of the following cases.

a. Factor supply is 4 million units, the factor utilization rate is 0.85, and the GDP per unit of input employed is $150.

b. Factor supply is 1.25 million units, the factor utilization rate is 0.9, and the GDP per unit of input employed is $110.

c. Factor supply is 250 million units, the factor utilization rate is 0.92, and the GDP per unit of input employed is $185.

4. Consider the data below for a hypothetical country.

a. Using the definitions in the chapter, compute the employment rate (E/L) and the level of productivity (GDP/E) for each year.

b. For each five-year period, compute the percentage change in the labour force, the employment rate, and the level of productivity.

c. Using Equation 25-2, the percentage change in real GDP for any relatively short period is approximately equal to the sum of the three percentage changes you computed in part (b). Using this approximation, compute the percentage change in real GDP for each five-year period.

Year	Real GDP	L	E	E/L	GDP/E	%ΔL	%Δ(E/L)	%ΔGDP
1960	100	1.5	1.4	—	—			
1965	130	1.6	1.45	—	—	—	—	—
1970	175	1.75	1.55	—	—	—	—	—
1975	250	1.95	1.65	—	—	—	—	—
1980	230	2.15	1.85	—	—	—	—	—
1985	265	2.40	2.0	—	—	—	—	—
1990	300	2.70	2.2	—	—	—	—	—
1995	340	3.0	2.8	—	—	—	—	—
2000	375	3.3	3.05	—	—	—	—	—
2005	410	3.6	3.4	—	—	—	—	—
2010	450	3.95	3.7	—	—	—	—	—

Real GDP: billions of constant dollars
L: labour force (millions of people)
E: employment (millions of people)

d. For each five-year period, what fraction of the percentage change in GDP is accounted for by the change in the employment rate?

e. Now compute the percentage change of real GDP over the entire 50-year period. Do the same for the employment rate. How much of the long-term change in GDP is accounted for by the change in the employment rate? Explain what you find based on the discussion in this chapter.

5. Go to the Bank of Canada's website (www.bankofcanada.ca) and look for data on capacity utilization rates in Canadian industries. The capacity utilization rate is the fraction of the capital stock that is utilized or employed. How has this variable changed over the past several decades? Contrast the short-run versus the long-run movements.

6. At the beginning of the chapter we discussed the short-run and long-run effects of an increase in desired saving (as applied to Japan's economy). Based on what you learned in Chapter 24 regarding the economy's adjustment process, use the *AD/AS* model to do the following:

a. Show the short-run effects of an increase in desired saving (assuming that the economy is initially in a long-run equilibrium with $Y = Y^*$).

b. Describe the adjustment process that brings the economy to its new long-run equilibrium.

c. Compare the initial and the new long-run equilibrium. What is the long-run effect of the increase in desired saving?

7. Figure 25-1 on page 620 shows the path of actual GDP and the path of potential GDP.

a. Describe the economy's adjustment process that brings GDP back to potential, and how it relates to the concept of market-clearing.

b. Suppose that, following the implementation of some policy, actual GDP eventually returns to potential GDP. Does this mean that policy can have no long-run effect on GDP?

c. Based on our discussion of fiscal policy in Chapter 24, explain why an increase in government purchases (*G*) could have a *positive* effect on Y^*.

d. Now provide an example of an increase in *G* that could have a *negative* effect on Y^*.

e. Explain how a politician might sacrifice the long-run behaviour of the economy in order to generate an outcome that is deemed to be desirable in the short run.

Long-Run Economic Growth

ECONOMIC growth is the single most powerful engine for generating long-term increases in living standards. What happens to our material living standards over time depends largely on the growth in real GDP in relation to the growth in population—that is, it depends on the growth of real per capita GDP. Such growth does not necessarily make *everybody* in Canada materially better off in the short term. But it does increase the *average* standard of living over the short term and virtually everyone's in the long term.

What determines the long-run growth rate of per capita GDP in Canada? Is this something that is beyond our control, or are there some government policies that can stimulate economic growth and others that can slow it down? What are the costs and benefits of each type of policy?

In this chapter we examine this important issue of economic growth, beginning with some basic concepts and then moving on to explore the costs and benefits of growth. In the remainder of the chapter we consider various theories of economic growth and then go on to examine the idea that there may be *limits to growth* imposed by resource exhaustion and environmental degradation.

26.1 The Nature of Economic Growth

Economic growth is sought after in the rich, developed economies of Canada, France, and Australia as well as in the much poorer, developing countries of Haiti, South Africa, and Vietnam. Governments in all countries view economic growth as an important objective. While the *urgency* for growth is clearly higher in poorer countries than it is in richer ones, the fundamental nature of growth—its causes and consequences—is strikingly similar across all countries. We begin our discussion by examining some Canadian data.

The Centre for the Study of Living Standards is an Ottawa-based research institute that studies the determinants of economic growth. Visit its website at www.csls.ca.

Figure 26-1 shows the paths of three variables in the Canadian economy since 1960, each of which relates to long-run economic growth. Each variable is expressed as an index number, which takes a value of 100 in 1960. The first is real GDP, which shows an overall growth from 1960 to 2011 of 429 percent, an average annual growth rate of 3.3 percent. Though real GDP is an accepted measure of the amount of annual economic activity that passes through markets, it does not tell us about changes in average material living standards because it does not take into account the growth in the population—more income is not necessarily better if more people have to share it. The second variable shown is the index of real *per capita* GDP. It shows an overall growth of 175 percent between 1960 and 2011, an annual average growth rate of 2.0 percent.

As we will see in this chapter, one of the most important reasons that per capita GDP increases over many years is growth in *productivity*. The third variable provides one measure of productivity; it is an index of real GDP *per employed worker*. Its overall

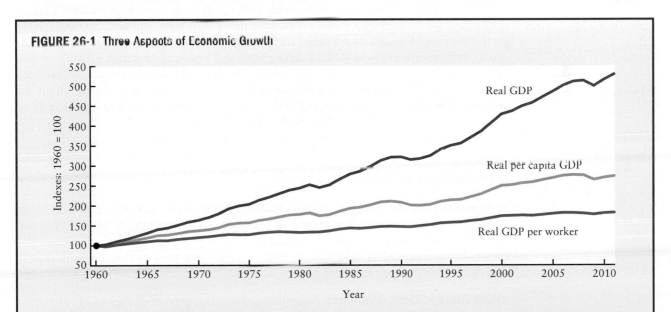

FIGURE 26-1 Three Aspects of Economic Growth

Real GDP, real per capita GDP, and productivity have all grown substantially over the past half-century. Each variable shown is an index number with 1960 = 100. Real GDP has grown faster than real per capita GDP because the population has grown. Real per capita GDP has grown faster than real GDP per worker because the level of employment has grown faster than the population.

(*Source:* All variables are based on author's calculations, using data from Statistics Canada, CANSIM database. Real GDP: Series V1992067. Employment: Series V2091072. Population: Series V2062809.)

TABLE 26-1 The Cumulative Effect of Economic Growth

| | Annual Growth Rate | | | | |
Year	1%	2%	3%	5%	7%
0	100	100	100	100	100
10	111	122	135	165	201
30	135	182	246	448	817
50	165	272	448	1 218	3 312
70	201	406	817	3 312	13 429
100	272	739	2 009	14 841	109 660

Small differences in income growth rates make enormous differences in levels of income over a few decades. Let income be 100 in year 0. At a growth rate of 3 percent per year, it will be 135 in 10 years, 448 after 50 years, and more than 2000 in a century. Notice the difference between 2 percent and 3 percent growth—even small differences in growth rates make big differences in future income levels.

economic growth Sustained, long-run increases in the level of real GDP.

growth from 1960 to 2011 is 83 percent, an average annual growth rate of 1.2 percent; the average Canadian worker produced 83 percent more in 2011 than in 1960.

The three variables in Figure 26-1 show different aspects of **economic growth**, a term that economists usually reserve for describing sustained or long-run increases in real GDP. This chapter will discuss each of these three aspects of economic growth—real GDP, real per capita GDP, and productivity.

The average annual growth rates shown in Figure 26-1 may seem small, especially those for the measure of productivity. It is important to realize, however, that because these growth rates are sustained for many years, they have a profound influence on material living standards from one generation to the next. Table 26-1 illustrates the cumulative effect of what appear to be very small differences in growth rates.

When thinking about the long-run cumulative effect of annual growth rates, it is useful to know the "rule of 72." For any variable that grows at an annual rate of X percent, that variable will double in approximately 72/X years. [31] For example, if your income grows at 2 percent per year, it will double in 36 years; at an annual rate of 3 percent, it will take only 24 years to double. Another application of the rule of 72 is to determine the *gap* in living standards between countries with different growth rates. If one country grows faster than another, the gap in their respective living standards will widen progressively. If, for example, Canada and France start from the same level of income but Canada grows at 3 percent per year while France grows at 2 percent per year, Canada's income will be twice France's in 72 years. The central lesson from Table 26-1 can be summed up as follows: The longer your time horizon is, the more you should care about the economy's long-run growth rate. Small differences in annual growth rates, if sustained for many years, lead to large differences in income levels.

We now examine in more detail the benefits and costs of economic growth.

Benefits of Economic Growth

Economists typically measure average *material* living standards with real per capita GDP.[1] The benefits of long-run growth in per capita GDP may appear obvious. But it is important to distinguish between the increases in average living standards that economic growth brings more or less automatically and the reduction in poverty that economic growth makes possible but that may still require active policy to make a reality.

Rising Average Living Standards Economic growth is a powerful means of improving average material living standards. The average Canadian family today earns about $70 000 per year before taxes. With 2 percent annual growth in its *real* income, that

[1] As we noted in Chapter 20, per capita GDP is a good measure of average *material* living standards because it shows the average person's command over resources. But it is not necessarily a good measure of *well-being*, which is a broader and more subjective measure including such things as income distribution, political and religious freedom, environmental quality, and other things that are not captured by measures of GDP.

same family will earn $85 300 (in constant dollars) in ten years' time, an increase in its purchasing power of almost 22 percent. If the annual growth rate is instead 3 percent, its income will rise to $94 100 in ten years, an increase of over 34 percent.

A family often finds that an increase in its income can lead to changes in the pattern of its consumption—extra money buys important amenities of life and also allows more saving for the future. Similarly, economic growth that raises average income tends to change the whole society's consumption patterns, shifting away from tangible goods such as TVs and furniture and cars and toward services such as vacations, restaurant meals, and financial services. In Canada and other rich, developed countries, services account for roughly 70 percent of aggregate consumption, whereas this ratio is significantly lower in poorer, developing countries.

Another example of how economic growth can improve living standards involves environmental protection. In developing countries, most resources are devoted to providing basic requirements of life, such as food, shelter, and clothing. These countries typically do not have the "luxury" of being concerned about environmental degradation. Some people in richer societies may consider this a short-sighted view, but the fact is that the concerns associated with hunger *today* are much more urgent than the concerns associated with *future* environmental problems. In contrast, richer countries are wealthy enough that they can more easily afford to provide the basic requirements of life *and* devote significant resources to environmental protection. Economic growth provides the higher incomes that often lead to a demand for a cleaner environment, thus leading to higher average living standards that are not directly captured by measures of per capita GDP.

One recent example of this phenomenon can be seen in China, whose government paid almost no attention to environmental protection when the country was very poor. As average income in China has risen in the past 30 years, where it is now well above a subsistence level, concern within China has been growing over the extent of environmental degradation, which in some cases is causing serious human health problems. The Chinese government has been responding with policies to address some of these concerns, and will likely do much more as Chinese prosperity continues to rise.

Addressing Poverty and Income Inequality   Not everyone benefits equally from economic growth, and some may not benefit at all. Many of the poorest members of the population are not in the labour force and do not receive the higher wages and profits that are the primary means by which the gains from growth are distributed. Others, although they *are* in the labour force, may experience wage gains that are far smaller than the average.

In recent years, growing attention has been paid to the fact that the majority of aggregate income growth in many countries, including Canada, has been accruing to the top earners in the income distribution. The result is that, while average per capita incomes have been rising (as shown in Figure 26-1), there has also been a rise in income inequality and also a relative stagnation of incomes for those at or below the middle of the income distribution. Both poverty and income inequality are important challenges for public policy.

A rapid growth rate makes the alleviation of poverty and the reduction of income inequality easier to achieve politically. If existing income is to be redistributed through the government's tax or spending policies, someone's standard of living will actually have to be lowered. However, when there is economic growth and when some of the *increment* in income is redistributed (through active government policy), it is possible to reduce income inequalities while simultaneously allowing all incomes to rise. It is much easier for a rapidly growing economy to be generous toward its less fortunate citizens—or neighbours—than it is for a static economy.

Costs of Economic Growth

Economic growth comes with real costs, some of which may be more obvious than others. For example, the simple act of producing goods and services necessarily uses resources and causes environmental damage. While these effects may be very small for some products, for others they are significant. As a logical matter, we cannot deny that economic production has negative consequences. Indeed, many of those who advocate *against* continued economic growth do so on the grounds that it depletes our natural resources and leads to environmental degradation.

This debate is important, and continues to gain prominence among academic and government economists. *Applying Economic Concepts 26-1* presents a case against continued economic growth, especially in the developed countries. We take up some of these ideas in this chapter's final section where we examine the extent to which there are *limits to growth*. Here, we address two other costs associated with economic growth: the cost of forgone consumption, and the social costs of the disruption that typically accompanies growth.

APPLYING ECONOMIC CONCEPTS 26-1

A Case Against Economic Growth

Economists have long recognized that economic growth comes with real costs. In recent years, however, many economists have been arguing that the benefits of further growth are outweighed by the costs now being imposed on the earth and its inhabitants. While these arguments are not the mainstream view within the profession, they are increasingly receiving serious attention. This box presents some of their main arguments against continued economic growth.[*]

Growth Is Not Sustainable

There is overwhelming evidence that the effects on the biosphere of the world's growing economies and population are not sustainable over the long term. Expanding production and consumption of goods and services is causing biodiversity losses, land degradation, scarcities of fresh water, ocean acidification, climate change, and the disruption of the earth's nutrient cycles. This environmental damage will eventually reduce our capacity to continue producing and consuming at current rates.

In addition, the low-cost supplies of fossil fuels on which economic growth has depended for over a century are rapidly being depleted. As supplies diminish, there is a need to introduce new technologies to obtain resources from less accessible locations. Extraction of oil sands, hydraulic fracturing for natural gas, and deep-sea drilling for oil and gas are examples of new technologies that

bring increased environmental impact and risks. This extraction of less accessible and higher-cost fossil fuels highlights the conflict between the need for new supplies of resources to sustain economic growth and the need to reduce our overall burden on the environment.

The ongoing degradation of the planet in pursuit of economic growth also runs counter to the interests of other species that inhabit Earth. Mainstream economics is not well equipped to address this important ethical issue, but it should not be ignored.

Growth May Not Increase Overall Well-Being

Quite apart from whether current growth rates are sustainable, the benefits from continued growth, especially in developed countries, are questionable. Economists have long understood that GDP is a reasonable measure of the level of economic activity and income but that it is not an accurate measure of overall *well-being*. Other measures that include a range of environmental and social factors suggest that income growth in the developed economies is no longer closely related

---

[*]The author thanks Peter Victor for providing material on which this box is based. For a thorough discussion of the case against economic growth, see Peter Victor, *Managing Without Growth: Slower by Design*, Edward Elgar, 2008.

Forgone Consumption In a world of scarcity, almost nothing is free, including economic growth. As we will soon see, increases in real per capita GDP typically result from investment in capital goods, as well as in such activities as education and scientific research. Often these investments yield no immediate return in terms of goods and services for consumption; thus, they imply that sacrifices are being made by the current generation of consumers.

> Economic growth, which promises more goods and services tomorrow, is achieved by consuming fewer goods today. This sacrifice of current consumption is an important cost of growth.

For example, suppose an economy's annual growth rate could be permanently increased by 1 percentage point if investment as a share of GDP increased permanently by 4 percentage points (and consumption's share fell by 4 percentage points). If such a reallocation of resources were made, consumption would be lower for several years along the new growth path, and the payoff from faster growth—higher future consumption—would not occur for several years. Lower consumption now and in the near future would be the cost of obtaining higher consumption in the more distant future.

with greater well-being. People typically attach far more significance to their income in relation to others' incomes than to its absolute level, and it is simply not possible for economic growth to raise everyone's relative income.

In addition, the growing evidence on income and wealth inequality in the developed economies suggests that over the past few decades the lion's share of total income growth has been captured by the highest income earners. The resulting increase in income and wealth inequality has actually led to rising discontent among large parts of the population. So growth in national income, given its current distribution, may actually be causing a reduction rather than an increase in overall well-being.

The Weakness of the Technological Defence

Economists who argue in favour of further economic growth typically note the possibility of increasing GDP even while reducing resource use and environmental damage. They argue that by producing and consuming fewer goods and more services, employing more efficient and improved technologies, and more compact forms of land use, economic growth can continue indefinitely.

Those who argue against further growth see a serious problem with this argument. While it is true that the amount of resources used per dollar of GDP continues to shrink gradually in the developed countries, it is also true that the absolute resource use and absolute environmental damage continue to grow.

Looking to the future, if the world economy grows at a rate of 3 percent per year, after a century the economy will have increased in size by nearly 20 times. To prevent any absolute increase in resource and energy use would require an ambitious twenty-fold improvement in resource and environmental efficiency—a far greater improvement than we have witnessed over the past century.

So the belief that ongoing technological improvement can be consistent with continued economic growth and a reduced impact on Earth's resources and environment is a belief that must be based on extreme—and probably unrealistic—optimism.

Not So Gloomy

These economists are quick to emphasize that their message is not so gloomy. The good news is that further economic growth in the developed economies isn't necessary for continued prosperity. The benefits of ongoing productivity growth can be taken in the form of reduced work and production, and also by directing effort at reducing our absolute resource use and environmental damage. Making these adjustments will surely require a significant change in most peoples' way of thinking, but there is no reason why they can't be made. Prosperity can continue without economic growth.

Social Costs A growing economy is also a changing economy. Part of growth is accounted for by existing firms expanding and producing more output, hiring more workers, and using more equipment and intermediate goods. But another aspect of growth is that existing firms are overtaken and made obsolete by new firms, old products are made obsolete by new products, and existing skills are made obsolete by new skills.

> The process of economic growth renders some machines obsolete and also leaves the skills of some workers obsolete.

No matter how well trained workers are at age 25, in another 25 years many will find that their skills are at least partly obsolete. A high growth rate usually requires rapid adjustments in the labour force, which can cause much upset and misery to some of the people affected by it.

It is often argued that costs of this kind are a small price to pay for the great benefits that growth can bring. Even if this is true in the aggregate, these personal costs are borne very unevenly. Indeed, many of the people for whom growth is most costly (in terms of lost jobs or lowered incomes) share least in the fruits that growth brings.

Sources of Economic Growth

Four major determinants of growth are

1. *Growth in the labour force.* Growth in population or increases in the fraction of the population that chooses to participate in the labour force cause the labour force to grow.

2. *Growth in human capital.* **Human capital** is the term economists use to refer to the set of skills that workers have; it can increase either through formal education or on-the-job training. Human capital can be thought of as the *quality* of the labour force.

3. *Growth in physical capital.* The stock of physical capital (such as factories, machines, electronic equipment, and transportation and communications facilities) grows only through the process of investment. We include here improvements in the *quality* of the physical capital.

4. *Technological improvement.* This is brought about by innovation that introduces new products, new ways of producing existing products, and new forms of organizing economic activity.

The various theories of economic growth that we explore next emphasize these different sources of economic growth. For example, some theories emphasize the role of increases in physical capital in explaining growth; others emphasize the role of increases in human capital; and still others emphasize the importance of technological improvements.

human capital The set of skills workers acquire through formal education and on-the-job training.

| 26.2 Established Theories of Economic Growth

In this section we discuss some of the theories of economic growth that have been used by economists for many years. These long-established theories remain relevant because they contain important insights about the growth process. Learning them provides a basis for examining the more recent theories in the next section. We begin by studying the relationship among saving, investment, and economic growth. We then examine the precise predictions of what economists call the Neoclassical growth theory. For simplicity, we assume that the economy is closed—there is no trade in goods, services, or assets with the rest of the world.

A Long-Run Analysis

Though our discussion of economic growth will focus on the long-run behaviour of the economy, we can use some of the insights we developed in the short-run version of our macro model. Think back to Chapter 21 when we were building the simplest short-run macro model (with no government or foreign trade). The equilibrium level of real GDP in that model was such that real GDP equals desired consumption plus desired investment:

$$Y = C + I$$

We can rearrange this equilibrium condition to get

$$Y - C = I$$

or

$$S = I$$

which says that at the equilibrium level of real GDP, desired saving equals desired investment. This is just an alternative way to think about exactly the same equilibrium.

Recall also that in Chapter 21 we took the real interest rate as given, or *exogenous*. Taking the interest rate (and several other variables) as exogenous, we then determined the equilibrium level of real GDP. We will now extend that same model to help us consider the long-run behaviour of the economy by making the interest rate an *endogenous* variable—that is, a variable whose value is explained within the model. Fortunately, the equilibrium condition from the simple short-run model also applies in its long-run version. In the long run, with real GDP equal to Y^*, we can use the saving/investment equilibrium condition by turning it "on its head." To do so, we make two assumptions. First, we assume that real GDP is equal to Y^*, which means that all factor-price adjustments discussed in Chapter 24 are complete. Second, we assume that Y^* is constant during the period under consideration (although in reality it is gradually changing through time). With these two assumptions, we take Y^* as given and use the condition that desired saving equals desired investment to determine the equilibrium real interest rate.

> In the short-run macro model, real GDP varies to determine equilibrium, in which desired saving equals desired investment. In the model's long-run version, real GDP is equal to Y^* and the interest rate varies to determine equilibrium.

This long-run perspective of our model will tell us a great deal about the relationship among saving, investment, and economic growth—and the interest rate will play an important role.

A Theory of Investment, Saving, and Growth

We now complicate our model slightly by adding a government sector that purchases goods and services (G) and collects taxes net of transfers (T). National saving is the sum of private saving and public (government) saving. Desired private saving is the difference between disposable income and desired consumption. With real GDP equal to Y^* in the long run, desired private saving is equal to

$$\text{Private saving} = Y^* - T - C$$

Public saving is equal to the combined budget surpluses of the federal, provincial, and municipal governments:

$$\text{Public saving} = T - G$$

National saving is therefore equal to

$$\text{National saving} = NS = (Y^* - T - C) + (T - G)$$
$$\Rightarrow NS = Y^* - C - G$$

For a given level of real GDP in the long run (Y^*), an increase in household consumption or government purchases must imply a reduction in national saving.[2]

Figure 26-2 shows the supply of national saving as a function of the real interest rate. The horizontal axis measures the quantity of national saving, measured in dollars. The real interest rate is shown on the vertical axis. The national saving (NS) curve is upward sloping because, as we first saw in Chapter 21, an increase in the interest rate is assumed to lead households to reduce their current consumption, especially on big-ticket items and durable goods, such as cars, furniture, and appliances, that are often purchased on credit. Note also that the NS curve is quite steep, in keeping with empirical evidence suggesting that household consumption responds only modestly to changes in the real interest rate.

Figure 26-2 also shows a downward-sloping investment demand curve, I. As we first saw in Chapter 21, all components of desired investment (plant and equipment, inventories, and residential investment) are negatively related to the real interest rate because, whether the investment is financed by borrowing or by using the firm's retained earnings, the real interest rate reflects the opportunity cost of using these funds.

The supply curve for national saving (NS) and the investment demand curve (I) make up the economy's market for financial capital. The NS curve shows the

FIGURE 26-2 The Long-Run Connection Between Saving and Investment

In the long run, the condition that desired national saving equals desired investment determines the equilibrium real interest rate. Investment demand by firms is negatively related to the real interest rate. The supply of national (private plus public) saving is positively related to the real interest rate, since increases in the interest rate lead to a decline in desired consumption (C). Since the analysis applies to the long run, we have assumed that real GDP is equal to Y^*. In the long run, the equilibrium real interest rate is i^*. At this real interest rate, the amount of investment is I^*, which equals the amount of national saving, NS^*.

---

[2] It appears in our NS equation that changes in taxes have no effect on the level of national saving, but this is misleading. Changes in T may affect national saving through an *indirect* effect on C. For example, as we saw at the end of Chapter 24, a reduction in taxes is likely to lead to an increase in consumption spending and therefore to a reduction in national saving (for given values of Y^* and G).

supply of financial capital that comes from households and governments. The I curve shows the demand for financial capital derived from firms' desired investment in plant, equipment, and residential construction. The interest rate that clears this market for financial capital determines the amount of investment and saving that occur in the economy's long-run equilibrium, when real GDP is equal to Y^*.[3]

With Figure 26-2 in place, our long-run model of saving and investment is complete. In the short-run model in Chapter 21, the economy is in equilibrium when desired saving equals desired investment. We have now modified that setting in two ways. First, we have added government. Second, because we are holding real GDP constant at Y^*, we let the condition that desired saving equals desired investment determine the equilibrium real interest rate.

> In the long-run version of our macro model, with real GDP equal to Y^*, the equilibrium interest rate is determined where desired national saving equals desired investment.

In Figure 26-2, equilibrium occurs at interest rate i^* where $NS = I$. Imagine what would happen if the real interest rate were above i^* at i_1. At this high interest rate, the amount of desired saving exceeds the amount of desired investment, and this excess supply of financial capital pushes down the price of credit—the real interest rate. Conversely, if the interest rate is below i^* at i_2, the quantity of desired investment exceeds the quantity of desired saving, and this excess demand for financial capital pushes up the real interest rate. Only at point E is the economy in equilibrium, with the real interest rate equal to i^* and desired investment equal to desired saving.

Let's now see how changes in the supply of saving or investment demand lead to changes in the real interest rate and what these changes imply for the economy's long-run economic growth.

An Increase in the Supply of National Saving Suppose the supply of national saving increases, so that the NS curve shifts to the right, as shown in part (i) of Figure 26-3. This increase in the supply of national saving could happen either because household consumption (C) falls or because government purchases (G) fall (or because T rises, which reduces C). A decline in either C or G means that national saving rises at any real interest rate, and so the NS curve shifts to the right.

The increase in the supply of national saving leads to an excess supply of financial capital and thus to a decline in the real interest rate. As the interest rate falls, firms decide to undertake more investment projects and the economy moves from the initial equilibrium E_0 to the new equilibrium E_1. At the new equilibrium, more of the economy's resources are devoted to investment than before, and thus the country's stock of physical capital is rising at a faster rate. The higher rate of investment therefore leads to a higher future growth rate of potential output.

> In the long run, an increase in the supply of national saving reduces the real interest rate and encourages more investment. The higher rate of investment leads to a higher future growth rate of potential output.

---

[3] In Chapters 28 and 29, when we introduce money, banking, and monetary policy, we will see that in the short run, when Y can differ from Y^*, the interest rate is heavily influenced by the policies of the Bank of Canada. In the long-run version of our model, however, this influence is assumed to be negligible.

FIGURE 26-3 Increases in Investment Demand and the Supply of National Saving

(i) Increase in the supply of saving

(ii) Increase in the demand for investment

Changes in the supply of national saving or the demand for investment will change the equilibrium real interest rate and the rate of growth of potential output. In part (i), the increase in the supply of national saving pushes down the real interest rate and encourages more investment. In part (ii), the increase in the demand for investment pushes up the real interest rate and encourages more saving. In both cases, there is an increase in the equilibrium amount of investment (and saving) and the economy moves from E_0 to E_1; this higher rate of capital accumulation leads to an increase in the economy's long-run rate of growth.

An Increase in Investment Demand Now suppose firms' demand for investment increases so that the I curve shifts to the right, as shown in part (ii) of Figure 26-3. The increase in desired investment might be caused by technological improvements that increase the productivity of investment goods or by a government tax incentive aimed at encouraging investment. Whatever its cause, the increase in investment demand creates an excess demand for financial capital and therefore leads to a rise in the real interest rate. The rise in the interest rate encourages households to reduce their current consumption and increase their desired saving. At the new equilibrium, E_1, both the real interest rate and the amount of investment are higher than at the initial equilibrium. The greater investment means faster growth in the economy's capital stock and therefore a higher future rate of growth of potential output.

> In the long run, an increase in the demand for investment pushes up the real interest rate and encourages more saving by households. The higher rate of saving (and investment) leads to a higher future growth rate of potential output.

Summary In our macro model, which we have now extended to enable us to determine the real interest rate in long-run equilibrium, there is a close relationship among saving, investment, and the rate of economic growth. We can see this relationship most clearly when studying the market for financial capital. Let's summarize our results.

1. In long-run equilibrium, with $Y = Y^*$, the condition that desired national saving equals desired investment determines the equilibrium interest rate in the market for financial capital. This equilibrium also determines the economy's flows of investment and saving.

2. An increase in the supply of national saving will lead to a fall in the real interest rate and thus to an increase in the amount of investment. This is a shift of the NS curve and a movement along the I curve.

3. An increase in the demand for investment will lead to a rise in the real interest rate and thus to an increase in the amount of national saving. This is a shift of the I curve and a movement along the NS curve.

4. A shift in either the NS or the I curve will lead to a change in the equilibrium real interest rate and thus to a change in the amount of the economy's resources devoted to investment. An increase in the equilibrium amount of investment implies a greater growth rate of the capital stock and thus a higher future growth rate of potential output.

Investment and Growth in Industrialized Countries Our model predicts that countries with high rates of investment are also countries with high rates of real GDP growth. To provide evidence in support of this prediction, Figure 26-4 shows data from the most industrialized countries between 1950 and 2009. Each point in the figure corresponds to a single country and shows that country's annual average investment rate (as a percentage of GDP) plotted against the annual average growth rate in real per capita GDP. What is clear from the figure is a positive relationship between investment rates and growth rates, as predicted by our model.

Neoclassical Growth Theory

Recall the four sources of economic growth that we discussed at the beginning of this section. Much of the *Neoclassical growth theory* is based on the idea that these four forces of economic growth can be connected by what is called the **aggregate production function**. This is an expression for the relationship between the total amounts of labour (L) and physical capital (K) employed, the quality of labour's human capital (H), the state of technology (T), and the nation's total level of output (GDP). The aggregate production function can be expressed as

$$\text{GDP} = F_T(L, K, H)$$

It is an *aggregate* production function because it relates the economy's *total* output to the *total* amount of the factors that are used to produce that output.[4] (Those who have studied microeconomics will recall that a micro production function, such as is discussed in Chapters 7 and 8, relates the output of *one firm* to the factors of production employed by *that firm*.)

The production function above—indicated by F_T—tells us how much GDP will be produced for given amounts of labour and physical capital employed, given levels of human capital, and a given state of technology. Using the notation F_T is a simple way of indicating that the function relating L, K, and H to GDP depends on the state of

aggregate production function The relationship between the total amount of each factor of production employed in the nation and the nation's total GDP.

---

[4] Natural resources (including land, forests, mineral deposits, etc.) are also important inputs to the production process. We leave them out of this discussion only for simplicity.

FIGURE 26-4 Cross-Country Investment and Growth Rates, 1950–2009

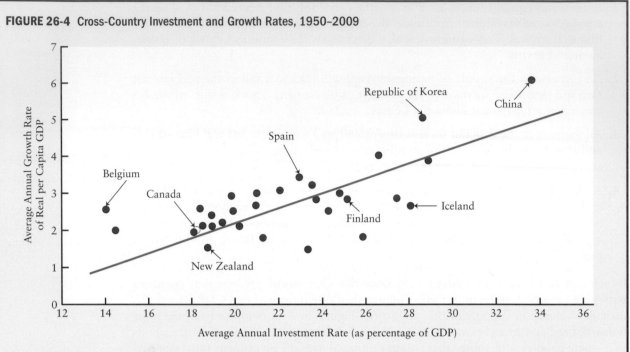

There is a positive relationship between a country's investment rate (as a percentage of GDP) and its growth rate of real per capita GDP. For each of the countries, the annual averages for investment rates and per capita GDP growth rates are computed between 1950 and 2009. Each point represents the average values of these variables for a single country over this 59-year period. The straight line is the "line of best fit" between the growth rates and the investment rates. Countries with high investment rates tend to be countries with high rates of economic growth.

(*Source:* Based on author's calculations by using data from the Penn World Tables 7.0. The data for Greece starts in 1951, China in 1952, South Korea in 1953, Romania in 1960, and Germany, Hungary, and Poland in 1970. Alan Heston, Robert Summers, and Bettina Aten, Penn World Table Version 7.0, Center for International Comparisons of Production, Income and Prices at the University of Pennsylvania, September 2011.)

technology. For a given state of technology (*T*), changes in either *L*, *K*, or *H* will lead to changes in GDP. Similarly, for given values of *L*, *K*, and *H*, changes in *T* will lead to changes in GDP. [32]

Recall that we are assuming throughout this chapter that real GDP is equal to Y^* because we are examining the economy's long-run behaviour. Let's now examine the properties of the aggregate production function and the predictions that follow.

Properties of the Aggregate Production Function The key assumptions of the Neoclassical theory are that the aggregate production function displays diminishing marginal returns when any one of the factors is increased on its own and constant returns to scale when all factors are increased together (and in the same proportion). To explain the meaning of these concepts more clearly, we will assume for simplicity that human capital and physical capital can be combined into a single variable called capital and that technology is held constant; this allows us to focus on the effects of changes in *K* and *L*.

1. Diminishing Marginal Returns. To begin, suppose that the labour force grows while the stock of capital remains constant. More and more people go to work using a fixed quantity of capital. The amount that each new worker adds to total output is called labour's *marginal product*. The **law of diminishing marginal returns** tells us that the employment of additional workers (or hours of work) will eventually add less to total output than the previous worker did. A simple production function is shown in Figure 26-5 and the law of diminishing marginal returns is illustrated.

The law of diminishing returns applies to any factor that is varied while the other factors are held constant. Hence, successive amounts of capital added to a fixed supply of labour will also eventually add less and less to GDP.

law of diminishing marginal returns The hypothesis that if increasing quantities of a variable factor are applied to a given quantity of fixed factors, the marginal product of the variable factor will eventually decrease.

FIGURE 26-5 The Aggregate Production Function and Diminishing Marginal Returns

Units of Labour (1)	Units of Output (GDP) (2)	Average Product of Labour (GDP/L) (3)	Marginal Product of Labour (ΔGDP/ΔL) (4)
1	12.0	12.0	
			5.0
2	17.0	8.5	
			3.8
3	20.8	6.9	
			3.2
4	24.0	6.0	
			2.8
5	26.8	5.4	
			2.6
6	29.4	4.9	
			2.5
7	31.9	4.6	
			2.1
8	34.0	4.2	
			2.0
9	36.0	4.0	
			1.9
10	37.9	3.8	

(i) Total output

(ii) Marginal and average product of labour

With one input held constant, the other input has a declining average and marginal product. We have assumed a hypothetical aggregate production function given by GDP = $4\sqrt{KL}$; we have also assumed that K is constant and equal to 9. Column 2 shows total output as more of the variable factor, labour, is used with a fixed amount of capital. Total output is plotted in part (i) of the figure. Both the average product of labour and the marginal product of labour decline continuously. They are plotted in part (ii) of the figure.

According to the law of diminishing marginal returns, whenever equal increases of one factor of production are combined with a fixed amount of another factor, the *increment* to total production will eventually decline.

constant returns to scale A situation in which output increases in proportion to the change in all inputs as the scale of production is increased.

2. Constant Returns to Scale. The other main assumption concerning the Neoclassical aggregate production function is that it displays **constant returns to scale**. Remember that we are assuming for simplicity that labour and capital are the only two inputs. With constant returns to scale, if L and K both change in an equal proportion, total output will change by that same proportion. For example, if L and K both increase by 10 percent, GDP will also increase by 10 percent. [33]

Economic Growth in the Neoclassical Model To recap: The Neoclassical growth theory assumes that the aggregate production function displays diminishing marginal returns (in both L and K) and also constant returns to scale. What predictions follow from these assumptions? Recall the four major sources of growth:

1. Growth in labour force
2. Growth in human capital
3. Growth in physical capital
4. Technological improvement

What does the Neoclassical theory predict will happen when each of these elements changes? In this section, we focus on the effects of labour-force growth and the accumulation of physical and human capital (combined), holding constant the level of technology. In the next section, we focus on technological change.

1. Labour-Force Growth. Over the long term, we can associate labour-force growth with population growth (although in the short term, the labour force can grow if participation rates rise even though the population remains constant). As more labour is used, more output will be produced. For a given stock of capital, however, the law of diminishing marginal returns tells us that sooner or later, each additional unit of labour employed will cause smaller and smaller additions to GDP. Once both the marginal product and average product of labour are falling (with each additional increment to labour), we get an interesting result. Although economic growth continues in the sense that total output is growing, material living standards are actually *falling* because average GDP *per person* is falling (real GDP is growing more slowly than the population). If we are interested in growth in material living standards, we are concerned with increasing real GDP per person.

In the Neoclassical growth model with diminishing marginal returns, increases in population (with a fixed stock of capital) lead to increases in GDP but an eventual decline in material living standards.

2. Physical and Human Capital Accumulation. Consider the accumulation of both physical and human capital. Growth in physical capital occurs whenever there is positive (net) investment in the economy. For example, if Canadian firms produce $300 billion of capital goods this year, and only $40 billion is for the replacement of old, worn-out equipment, then Canada's capital stock increases by $260 billion.

How does human capital accumulate? Human capital has several aspects. One involves improvements in the health and longevity of the population. Of course, these are desired as ends in themselves, but they also have consequences for both the size and the productivity of the labour force. There is no doubt that improvements in the health of workers tend to increase productivity per worker-hour by cutting down on illness, accidents, and absenteeism. A second aspect of human capital concerns specific training and education—from learning to operate a machine or software program to learning how to be a scientist. Sometimes this increase in human capital occurs through on-the-job training; sometimes it occurs through formal educational programs. Advances in knowledge allow us not only to build more productive physical capital but also to create more effective human capital. Also, the longer a person has been educated, the more adaptable and, hence, the more productive in the long run that person is in the face of new and changing challenges.

Increases in the amount and quality of physical capital lead to improvements in the productivity of labour. These productivity improvements raise material living standards, as measured by real per capita GDP.

The accumulation of capital—either physical or human—affects GDP in a manner similar to population growth. The law of diminishing marginal returns implies that, eventually, each successive unit of capital will add less to total output than each previous unit of capital.

There is, however, a major contrast with the case of labour-force growth because it is output *per person* that determines material living standards, not output per unit of capital. Thus, for a constant population, increases in the stock of physical or human capital *always* lead to increases in living standards because output *per person* increases. However, because the increases in capital are subject to diminishing marginal returns, successive additions to the economy's capital stock bring smaller and smaller increases in per capita output.

In the Neoclassical model, capital accumulation leads to improvements in material living standards, but because of the law of diminishing marginal returns, these improvements become smaller with each additional increment of capital.

3. Balanced Growth with Constant Technology. Now consider what happens if labour and capital (both human and physical capital) grow at the same rate. This is what economists call "balanced" growth. In this case, the Neoclassical assumption of constant returns to scale means that GDP grows in proportion to the increases in inputs. For example, if capital and labour both increase by 2 percent per year, then GDP also increases by 2 percent per year. As a result, per capita output (GDP/*L*) remains constant. Thus, balanced growth in labour and capital leads to growth in total GDP but unchanged per capita GDP.

This balanced growth is not, however, the kind of growth that concerns people interested in explaining rising material living standards. Since increases in living standards are determined by *increases* in per capita output, it is clear that balanced growth is unable to explain *rising* living standards.

If capital and labour grow at the same rate, GDP will increase. But in the Neoclassical growth model with constant returns to scale, such balanced growth will not lead to increases in per capita output and therefore will not generate improvements in material living standards.

New and better microchips enhance the range of capabilities of countless types of physical capital. But such improvements in technology are embodied *in the capital stock, making it difficult to estimate the change in technology independently from the change in the capital stock.*

The Neoclassical growth theory predicts that growth in the labour force alone leads to declining per capita income, while capital accumulation alone leads to positive but ever-diminishing growth rates of per capita income. Increases in labour and capital together cause an increase in real GDP but leave per capita income unchanged. What we observe in many countries around the world, however, is sustained growth in real per capita incomes. How does the Neoclassical theory explain this observation, if not through growth in labour or capital? The answer is technological change, to which we now turn.

The Importance of Technological Change In Neoclassical growth theory, technological change is assumed to be exogenous—that is, it is not explained by the theory itself. This is an important weakness of the theory because it means that the theory is unable to explain what is undoubtedly the most important determinant of long-run improvements in living standards. For now we focus on the importance of technological change itself and on how it might be measured. In the next section we move beyond Neoclassical growth theory and see some more modern theories designed to explain the sources of technological change.

New knowledge and inventions can contribute markedly to the growth of potential output, even without capital accumulation or labour-force growth. To illustrate this point, suppose the proportion of a society's resources devoted to the production of capital goods is just sufficient to replace capital as it wears out. If the old capital is merely replaced in the same form, the capital stock will be constant, and there will be no increase in the capacity to produce. However, if there is a growth of knowledge so that as old equipment wears out it is replaced by more productive equipment, then productive capacity will be growing.

embodied technical change
Technical change that is intrinsic to the particular capital goods in use.

The increase in productive capacity created by installing new and better capital goods is called **embodied technical change**. This term reflects the idea that technological improvements are contained in the new capital goods. Thus, even if the *quantity* of capital may be unchanged, improvements in its *quality* lead to increases in the economy's productive capacity. Embodied technical change has been enormously important through history and continues to be important today. Consider how the invention of propeller and then jet airplanes has revolutionized transportation over the past 50 years, or how the invention of the electronic computer and satellite transmission has revolutionized communications over an even shorter period. Indeed, once you start thinking about embodied technical change, you see many examples of it around you on a daily basis.

Less obvious but nonetheless important are technical changes that are embodied in *human* capital. These are changes that result from a better-educated, more experienced labour force; better management practices and techniques; improved design, marketing, and organization of business activities; and feedback from user experience leading to product improvement.

Many innovations are embodied in either physical or human capital. These innovations cause continual changes in the techniques of production and in the nature of what is produced. Embodied technical change leads to increases in potential output even if the amounts of labour and capital are held constant.

We have been discussing the benefits of technological change in terms of raising overall living standards. Ever since the Industrial Revolution, however, some workers have feared the effects of technological change. After all, changes in technology are often responsible for workers losing their jobs as employers replace less efficient labour with more efficient equipment. *Lessons from History 26-1* examines the relationship between technological progress and changes in employment.

LESSONS FROM HISTORY 26-1

Should Workers Be Afraid of Technological Change?

For centuries people have observed that technological change destroys particular jobs and have worried that it will destroy jobs in general. Should they worry?

Technological change *does* destroy particular jobs. When water wheels were used to automate the production of cloth in twelfth-century Europe, there were riots and protests among the workers who lost their jobs. A century ago, 50 percent of the labour force in North America and Europe was required to produce the required food. Today, less than 5 percent of the labour force is needed in the high-income countries to feed all their citizens. In other words, out of every 100 jobs that existed in 1900, 50 were in agriculture and 45 of those were destroyed by technological progress over the course of the twentieth century.

Individual workers are therefore right to fear that technological changes may destroy particular jobs. This process of job destruction has been going on for centuries and will undoubtedly continue in the future. Those individuals who cannot retrain for jobs in other industries or regions may suffer reduced wages or employment prospects. This concern is especially acute for older workers who may find retraining difficult or who may find it difficult to convince potential new employers to hire them.

What about the overall level of employment? Do workers need to worry that technological changes will cause widespread unemployment? Just as technological change destroys some jobs, it also creates many new jobs. The displaced agricultural workers did not join the ranks of the permanently unemployed—although some of the older ones may have, their children did not. Instead they, and their children, took jobs in the expanding manufacturing and service industries and helped to produce the mass of new goods and services—such as automobiles,

refrigerators, computers, and foreign travel—that have raised living standards over the century.

Worries that technological change will cause general unemployment have been recorded for centuries, but, so far at least, there is no sign that those displaced by technological change (or their children) are being forced into the ranks of the permanently unemployed. Over all of recorded history, technological change has created more jobs than it has destroyed.

How about today? Aren't there good reasons to be more afraid of technological change now than in the past? Modern technologies have two aspects that worry some observers. First, they tend to be *knowledge intensive*. A fairly high degree of literacy and numeracy, as well as familiarity with computers, is needed to work with many of these new technologies. Second, through the process of globalization, unskilled workers in advanced countries have come into competition with unskilled workers everywhere in the world. Both of these forces are decreasing the relative demand for unskilled workers in developed countries and have led to falling relative wages for unskilled workers in countries like Canada. If labour markets are insufficiently flexible, this change in relative demand may also lead to some structural unemployment.

For these reasons, some people blame the high unemployment rates in Europe (and to a lesser extent, in Canada) on the new technologies. This is hard to reconcile, however, with the fact that the lowest unemployment rates in the industrialized countries have (until very recently) been recorded in the United States, the most technologically dynamic of all countries. This suggests that the cause of high European unemployment rates may be not enough technological change and too much inflexibility in labour markets rather than too much technological change.

Can We Measure Technological Change? Technological change is obviously important. You need only look around you at the current products and production methods that did not exist a generation ago, or even a few years ago, to realize how the advance of technology changes our lives. But *how much* does technology change? Unfortunately, technology is not something that is easily measured and so it is very difficult to know just how important it is to the process of economic growth.

In 1957, Robert Solow, an economist at MIT who was awarded the Nobel Prize 30 years later for his research on economic growth, attempted to measure the amount of technical change in the United States. He devised a way to infer from the data (under some assumptions about the aggregate production function) how much of the observed growth in real GDP was due to the growth in labour and capital and how much was due to technical change. His method led to the creation of what is now called the "Solow residual." The Solow residual is the amount of growth in GDP that cannot be accounted for by growth in the labour force or by growth in the capital stock. Since Solow was thinking about changes in GDP as having only three possible sources— changes in capital, changes in labour, and changes in technology—the "residual" was naturally interpreted as a measure of technical change.

Today, economists do not view the Solow residual as a precise estimate of the amount of technical change. One reason is that much technical change is known to be embodied in new physical and human capital, as we discussed earlier. Thus, capital accumulation and technological change are inherently connected. For example, imagine a firm that adds to its stock of capital by purchasing two new computers. These new computers embody the latest technology and are more productive than the firm's existing computers. In this case, there has been an increase in the capital stock but there has also been an increase— though not easily measured—in the level of technology. Solow's method would attribute much of the change in (embodied) technology to the change in the capital stock, even though we know that a technological change has also taken place. Thus, in the presence of embodied technical change that gets measured as increases in capital, the Solow residual is, at best, an underestimate of the true amount of technological change.

Despite these problems, the Solow residual is still used by many economists in universities and government, and it often goes by another name—the rate of growth of *total factor productivity* (TFP).

26.3 Newer Growth Theories

Some newer theories of economic growth go beyond the Neoclassical theory. Economic growth is an active area of research in which there is considerable debate over whether new theories are necessary, or whether the established theories do an adequate job of explaining the process of long-term economic growth.

In this section, we give a brief discussion of two strands of this new research— models that emphasize *endogenous technological change* and models based on *increasing marginal returns*.

Endogenous Technological Change

In Neoclassical growth theory, innovation increases the amount of output producible from a given level of factor inputs. But this innovation is itself unexplained. The Neoclassical model thus views technological change as *exogenous*. It has profound effects on economic variables but it is not itself influenced by economic causes. It just happens.

Yet research by many scholars has established that technological change is responsive to such economic signals as prices and profits; in other words, it is *endogenous* to the economic system. Though much of the earliest work on this issue was done in Europe, the most influential overall single study was by an American, Nathan Rosenberg, whose trailblazing 1982 book *Inside the Black Box: Technology and Economics* argued this case in great detail.

Technological change stems from research and development and from innovating activities that put the results of R&D into practice. These are costly and highly risky activities, undertaken largely by firms and usually in pursuit of profit. It is not surprising, therefore, that these activities respond to economic incentives. If the price of some particular input, such as petroleum or skilled labour, goes up, R&D and innovating activities may be directed to altering the production function to economize on these expensive inputs. This process is not simply a substitution of less expensive inputs for more expensive ones within the confines of known technologies; rather, it is the *development of new technologies* in response to changes in relative prices.

There are several important implications of this new understanding that, to a great extent, growth is achieved through costly, risky, innovative activity that often occurs in response to economic signals.

Learning by Doing The pioneering theorist of innovation, Joseph Schumpeter (1883–1950), developed a model in which innovation flowed in one direction from a pure discovery "upstream," to more applied R&D, then to working machines, and finally to output "downstream."

In contrast, modern research shows that innovation involves a large amount of "learning by doing" at all of its stages. (We discuss this kind of learning in more detail in Chapter 33.) What is learned downstream then modifies what must be done upstream. The best innovation-managing systems encourage such "feedback" from the more applied steps to the purer researchers and from users to designers.

This interaction is illustrated, for example, by the differences that existed for many years between the Japanese automobile manufacturers and their North American competitors in the design and production of new models. North American design was traditionally centralized: design production teams developed the overall design and then instructed their production sections and asked for bids from parts manufacturers to produce according to specified blueprints. As a result, defects in the original design were often not discovered until production was underway, causing many costly delays and rejection of parts already supplied. In contrast, Japanese firms involved their design and production departments and their parts manufacturers in all stages of the design process. Parts manufacturers were not given specific blueprints for production; instead, they were given general specifications and asked to develop their own detailed designs. As they did so, they learned. They then fed information about the problems they were encountering back to the main designers while the general outlines of the new model were not yet finalized. As a result, the Japanese were able to design a new product faster, at less cost, and with far fewer problems than were the North American firms. Since that time, however, the North American automotive firms have adopted many of these Japanese design and production methods.

Knowledge Transfer The diffusion of technological knowledge from those who have it to those who want it is not costless (as it was assumed to be in Schumpeter's model). We often think that once a production process is developed, it can easily be copied by others. In practice, however, the diffusion of new technological knowledge is not so simple. Firms need research capacity just to adopt the technologies developed by others. Some of the knowledge needed to use a new technology can be learned only through experience by plant managers, technicians, and operators.

For example, research has shown that most industrial technologies require technology-specific organizational skills that cannot be "embodied" in the machines themselves, instruction books, or blueprints. The needed knowledge is *tacit* in the sense that it cannot be taught through books and can be acquired only by experience—much like driving a car or playing a video game. Acquiring tacit knowledge requires a deliberate process of building up new skills, work practices, knowledge, and experience.

The fact that diffusion is a costly and time-consuming process explains why new technologies take considerable time to diffuse, first through the economy of the originating country and then through the rest of the world. If diffusion were simple and virtually costless, the puzzle would be why technological knowledge and best industrial practices did not diffuse very quickly. As it is, decades can pass before a new technological process is diffused everywhere that it could be employed.

Market Structure and Innovation Because it is highly risky, innovation is encouraged by strong rivalry among firms and discouraged by monopoly practices. Competition among three or four large firms often produces much innovation, but a single firm, especially if it serves a secure home market protected by trade barriers, often seems much less inclined to innovate. The reduction in trade barriers over the past several decades and the increasing globalization of markets as a result of falling transportation and communication costs have increased international competition. Whereas one firm in a national market might have had substantial monopoly power three or four decades ago, today it is more likely to be in intense competition with firms based in other countries. This greater international competition generally leads to more innovation.

An important implication of this idea is that policies that make firms more competitive—either by lowering protective tariffs or by reducing domestic regulations that hamper competition—are likely to have a positive effect on the amount of innovation and thus on an economy's rate of growth of productivity. This is a central conclusion in William Lewis's *The Power of Productivity*, an influential book published in 2004.

Shocks and Innovation One interesting consequence of endogenous technical change is that shocks that would be unambiguously adverse to an economy operating with fixed technology can sometimes provide a spur to innovation that proves a blessing in disguise. A sharp rise in the price of one input can raise costs and lower the value of output per person for some time. But it may lead to a wave of innovations that reduce the need for this expensive input and, as a side effect, greatly raise productivity. One example is the ongoing development of fuel-efficient jet engines in response to large increases in the world price of oil.

Sometimes individual firms will respond differently to the same economic signal. Sometimes those that respond by altering technology will do better than those that concentrate their efforts on substituting within the confines of known technology. For example, several years ago when the consumer electronics industry was beset with high costs in both Japan and the United States, some U.S. firms moved their operations abroad to avoid high, rigid labour costs. They continued to use their existing technology and went where labour costs were low enough to make that technology pay. Their Japanese competitors, however, stayed at home. They innovated away most of their labour costs and then built factories in the United States to replace the factories of U.S. firms that had gone abroad!

Increasing Marginal Returns

We saw earlier that Neoclassical theories of economic growth assume that investment in capital is subject to diminishing marginal returns. Some research suggests, however, the possibility of *increasing returns* that remain for considerable periods of time: As investment in some new geographic area, new product, or new production technology proceeds through time, new increments of investment are often *more* productive than previous increments. The sources of such increasing returns fall under the two general categories of *market-development costs* and *knowledge*.

Market-Development Costs There are at least three reasons why there may be important costs associated with the initial development of a market. These costs result in increasing marginal returns to investment.

1. Investment in the early stages of development of a country, province, or town may create new skills and attitudes in the workforce that are then available to all subsequent firms, whose costs are therefore lower than those encountered by the initial firms.

2. Each new firm may find the environment more and more favourable to its investment because of the physical infrastructure that has been created by those who came before.

3. The first investment in a new product will encounter countless production problems that, once overcome, cause fewer problems to subsequent investors.

In each of these examples, the returns to later investment are greater than the returns to the same investment made earlier for the simple reason that the economic environment becomes more fully developed over time. Early firms must incur costs in order to develop various aspects of the market, but some benefits of this development are then reaped by later firms that need not incur these costs. As a result, the investment returns for "followers" can be substantially greater than the investment returns for "pioneers."

In short, doing something really new is difficult, whereas making further variations on an accepted and developed new idea becomes progressively easier over time. (For those who have studied microeconomics, the early firms are conferring a positive *externality* on those who follow them, as described in Chapter 16.)

Another important issue concerns the behaviour of customers. When a new product is developed, customers will often resist adopting it, both because they may be conservative and because they know that new products often experience "growing pains." Customers also need time to learn how best to use the new product—they need to do what is called "learning by using." And it may take time and "using experience" before producers get all the bugs out of the design of new products.

The development of the electric car has been expensive for those companies involved at early stages. As a result, there may be significant advantages to other firms who follow the pioneers.

A computer is a private good because if I own it then you cannot also own it. But the knowledge required to build the computer is a public good. And knowledge, unlike traditional factors of production, is not necessarily subject to the law of diminishing returns.

Slow acceptance of new products by customers is not necessarily unreasonable. When a sophisticated new product comes on the market, no one is sure if it will be a success, and the first customers to buy it take the risk that the product may subsequently turn out to be a failure. They also incur the costs of learning how to use it effectively. Many potential users take the reasonable approach of letting others try a new product, following only after the product's success has been demonstrated. This makes the early stages of innovation especially costly and risky.

> Successive increments of investment associated with an innovation often yield a range of increasing marginal returns as costs that are incurred in earlier investment expenditure provide publicly available knowledge and experience and as customer attitudes and abilities become more receptive to new products.

Knowledge Many of the newer growth theories shift the emphasis from the economics of goods to the economics of *ideas*. Physical goods, such as factories and machines, exist in one place at one time. This has two consequences. First, when physical goods are used by someone, they cannot be used by someone else. Second, if a given labour force is provided with more and more physical objects to use in production, sooner or later diminishing marginal returns will be encountered.

Ideas have different characteristics. Once someone develops an idea, it is available for use by everyone. For example, if one firm uses a truck, another firm cannot use it at the same time; but one firm's use of a revolutionary design for a new suspension system on a truck does not prevent other firms from using that design as well. (For those who have studied microeconomics, some knowledge has aspects that make it a *public good*, as we discussed in Chapter 16.)

Ideas are also not necessarily subject to diminishing marginal returns. As our knowledge increases, each increment of new knowledge does not inevitably add less to our productive ability than each previous increment. Indeed, the reverse is often the case: one new idea may spawn several additional ideas that build on or extend it in some ways. For example, the discovery of genes and the subsequent work on gene technology has spawned entire biotechnology industries that are revolutionizing aspects of medicine, agriculture, and environmental control.

Ideas produce what is called *knowledge-driven growth*. New knowledge provides the input that allows investment to produce increasing rather than diminishing marginal returns. Because there are no practical limits to human knowledge, there need be no immediate boundaries to finding new ways to produce more output by using less of all inputs.

> Neoclassical growth theories gave economics the name "the dismal science" by emphasizing diminishing marginal returns under conditions of given technology. Newer growth theories are more optimistic because they emphasize the unlimited potential of knowledge-driven technological change.

Probably the most important contrast between these ideas-based theories and the Neoclassical theory concerns investment and income. In the Neoclassical model, diminishing marginal returns to investment imply a limit to the possible increase of per capita GDP. In the newer theories, investment alone can hold an economy on a "sustained growth path" in which per capita GDP increases without limit, provided that the investment embodies the results of continual advances in technological knowledge.

26.4 Are There Limits to Growth?

Many opponents of growth argue that sustained growth of the world economy is undesirable; some argue that it is impossible. The idea that economic growth is limited by nature is not new. In the early 1970s, a group called the "Club of Rome" published a book entitled *The Limits to Growth*, which focused on the limits to growth arising from the finite supply of natural resources. Extrapolating from the oil shortages and price increases caused by the OPEC cartel, the Club of Rome concluded that industrialized countries faced an imminent absolute limit to growth. Do such limits really exist? We now discuss the two issues of resource exhaustion and environmental degradation.

See the United Nations' website for international data on economic development: www. un.org. Click on "Development" and then go to "Statistics."

Resource Exhaustion

The years since the Second World War have seen a rapid acceleration in the consumption of the world's resources, particularly fossil fuels and basic minerals. World population has increased from fewer than 2.5 billion to more than 7 billion in that period; this increase alone has intensified the demand for the world's resources. Furthermore, as people attain higher incomes, they generally consume more resources. Thus, not only are there more people in the world, but many of those people are consuming increasing quantities of resources.

Most everyone in the world today would like to achieve a standard of living equal to that of the average Canadian family. Unfortunately, the world's current resources and its present capacity to cope with pollution and environmental degradation are insufficient to accomplish this rise in global living standards with present technology.

Most economists, however, agree that absolute limits to growth, based on the assumptions of constant technology and fixed resources, are not relevant. As emphasized by the growth theories we discussed in the previous section, technology changes continually, as do the available stocks of resources. For example, 75 years ago, few would have thought that the world could produce enough food to feed its present population of 7 billion people, let alone the 10 billion at which the population is projected to stabilize sometime later this century. Yet significant advances in agricultural methods make this task now seem feasible. Further, while existing resources are being depleted, new ones are constantly being discovered or developed. One example is the development of the Alberta oil sands. In the early 1970s, this resource appeared to be far too expensive to develop and therefore an unlikely source of economical oil. Four decades later, after considerable technological improvement, the oil sands now rank among the world's largest reserves of economical petroleum.

Another consideration relates to both resource use and technological progress. Along with advances in technological knowledge typically comes an increase in the economy's *resource efficiency*—a reduction in the amount of resources needed to produce one unit of output. In Canada, for example, an average dollar of real GDP is currently produced with nearly 40 percent less energy than was the case in 1978, and if we focus just on petroleum use, the reduction is almost 50 percent. More generally, every dollar's worth of real GDP produced in the world has used steadily fewer resources over the past century. Part of this reduction is due to an improvement in the efficiency with which resources are used; part is due to the gradual shift toward the production of services (and away from the production of goods) in world GDP. Improvements in resource efficiency do not eliminate the concerns about resource exhaustion, but they do underline the importance of recognizing the role of technological change when considering limits to economic growth.

> **Technology is constantly advancing, and many things that seemed impossible a generation ago will be commonplace a generation from now. Such technological advance makes any absolute limits to economic growth less likely.**

Yet there is surely cause for concern. Although many barriers can be overcome by technological advances, such achievements are not instantaneous and are certainly not automatic. There is a critical problem of timing: How soon can we discover and put into practice the knowledge required to solve the problems that are made ever more imminent by the growth in the population, the affluence of the rich nations, and the aspirations of the billions who now live in poverty? There is no guarantee that a whole generation will not be caught in transition between technologies, with enormous social and political consequences.

A final point worth noting is that the extent of resource depletion is not something that "just happens." Since natural resources are typically owned by the public, government policy can be used to influence the rate of resource extraction if that objective is deemed to be appropriate. If we fail to protect some key natural resources, it will not be because we lacked the ability or the technology to do so, only that we lacked the political will to make contentious and difficult decisions—decisions that may nonetheless be in our long-run interests.

The development of the Alberta oil sands has significantly increased Canada's oil-production capacity. At the same time, it has raised concerns regarding environmental degradation, including substantial emissions of greenhouse gases.

Environmental Degradation

A much more important problem associated with economic growth is the generation of pollution and the degradation of our natural environment. Air, water, and soil are polluted by a variety of natural activities, and, for billions of years, the environment has coped with them. The Earth's natural processes had little trouble coping with the pollution generated by its 1 billion inhabitants in 1800. But the 7 billion people who now exist put such extreme demands on Earth's ecosystems that there are now legitimate concerns about environmental sustainability. Smoke, sewage, chemical waste, hydrocarbon and greenhouse-gas emissions, spent nuclear fuel, and a host of other pollutants threaten to overwhelm Earth's natural regenerative processes.

Conscious management of pollution was unnecessary when the world's population was 1 billion people, but such management has now become a pressing matter.

Reducing the extent of environmental degradation, however, is different from advocating an "anti-growth" position. To put it differently, there is nothing inconsistent about an economy displaying *both* high rates of economic growth and active environmental protection. As students of microeconomics will recognize, an important part of a policy designed to reduce the extent of environmental degradation is to get polluters (firms or households) to face the full cost of their polluting activities—especially the external costs that their activities impose on society. This often involves levying some form of tax on polluters for every unit of pollution emitted. Although such policies, if stringently enforced, will lead to output reductions in specific industries, they need not lead to reductions in the *overall* level of economic activity. And long-run economic growth is related to growth in the overall level of economic activity, not to the growth of specific industries.

Furthermore, many technological advances reduce the amount of pollution per unit of output and also reduce the costs of dealing with whatever pollution remains. Rich, advanced economies, such as Canada, the United States, and the European Union, create less pollution per dollar of GDP and find it easier to bear the cost of pollution clean-up than do poorer, less technologically advanced economies.

None of this implies that environmental issues are not serious. It is possible that our management of these issues will be sufficiently inadequate that growth will be impaired and our living standards will suffer by significant amounts. If this happens, it will probably *not* be because we lacked the technology or know-how to solve these problems once they were recognized. If we do create environmental disasters, more likely it will be because we failed to respond quickly enough (if at all) to the growing dangers as they were occurring.

Most climate scientists believe, for example, that we may already be too late to reverse the forces leading to global climate change and that significant increases in sea level are now a virtual certainty over the next few decades. However, most agree that there is still time to take actions that could stabilize Earth's climate over the course of this century. Concerted global actions and considerable political will in many countries must be part of the solution. *Applying Economic Concepts 26-2* explores in more detail the problem of climate change caused by greenhouse-gas emissions associated with the burning of fossil fuels.

Conclusion

The world faces many problems. Starvation and poverty are the common lot of citizens in many countries and are not unknown even in such countries as Canada and the United States, where average living standards are very high. Growth has raised the average citizens of advanced countries from poverty to plenty in the course of two centuries—a short time in terms of human history. Further growth is needed if people in developing countries are to escape material poverty, and further growth would also help advanced countries to deal with many of their pressing economic problems.

Rising population and consumption, however, put pressure on the world's natural ecosystems, especially through the many forms of pollution. Further growth can only occur if it is *sustainable* growth, that is in turn based on knowledge-driven technological change. Past experience suggests that new technologies will use less of all resources per unit of output. But if they are to dramatically reduce the demands placed on the Earth's

APPLYING ECONOMIC CONCEPTS 26-2

Climate Change and Economic Growth

There is no doubt that Earth's average surface temperature has been rising over the past century, and that the increase has been unevenly distributed, from less than 1°C near the equator to over 5°C near the poles. As a result of this global warming, the polar ice caps have been melting significantly, the world's deserts have been gradually increasing in size, and extreme weather events are becoming more frequent and severe. The melting of the Antarctic and Greenland ice caps is predicted to cause a significant increase in sea level, with potentially catastrophic effects for the many highly populated island and coastal regions of Asia and Africa. The creeping desertification and changing rainfall patterns are predicted to cause significant reductions in agricultural productivity, especially in the developing countries. The effects of climate change will be felt by people in many countries, but the most dramatic effects are likely to be experienced in the lowest-income countries least prepared to shoulder the burden.

Although the underlying cause of the rising global temperatures is still debated, the bulk of the scientific evidence points to a clear causal link. The burning of fossil fuels leads to the emission of carbon dioxide and other "greenhouse gases," which accumulate in the atmosphere and remain there for many years. This rising atmospheric concentration of gases acts like a greenhouse to lock in the sun's warmth, thus increasing average global temperature.

The world's annual emissions of greenhouse gases have been increasing steadily, broadly in line with the growth of the world economy. In the absence of policies aimed at reducing these emissions, they are predicted to approximately double between today and 2050. Yet the weight of scientific evidence suggests that in order to stabilize the atmospheric concentration of greenhouse gases (at a level well above today's), and thus to stabilize Earth's average temperature (at a level 1° to 2°C above today's average temperature), annual emissions will need to fall by 80 to 90 percent from *current* levels by 2050. Achieving such reductions will certainly affect the world's economic growth.

What is the connection between global warming and economic growth? First, modern economic growth is a significant cause of global warming. Since energy is an important input to production for most goods and services, and since the burning of fossil fuels is currently one of the most efficient ways to produce energy, it is not surprising that a close relationship exists between the growth of real GDP and the growth of greenhouse-gas emissions. But reducing emissions by reducing world GDP is probably both unrealistic and undesirable. As the world's population continues to grow, and the people of the developing world strive to increase their per capita incomes to levels closer to ours, there will inevitably be a rise in global GDP.

A more realistic way to reduce greenhouse-gas emissions is to reduce our reliance on energy and, in particular, our reliance on those forms of energy that release greenhouse gases into the atmosphere. Most economists argue that the most effective policy to reduce the world's emissions of greenhouse gases involves placing a price on the emission of greenhouse gases, either through a direct tax (such as a "carbon tax") or by directly restricting the amount of total emissions and then allowing the distribution of emissions among firms to be determined through the trading of emissions permits (a "cap-and-trade" system). Either policy approach will increase the cost associated with emitting greenhouse gases and thus will create incentives for firms and households to use non-emitting forms of energy. Incentives will also be created for the further development of non-emitting energy sources such as solar, wind, nuclear, and hydroelectricity.

Since these policies will be effective only by imposing costs on firms and households, their use will highlight a second connection between economic growth and global warming. These higher costs will eventually lead to the adoption of cleaner energy systems and thus a reduction of greenhouse-gas emissions, but they will probably also lead to a reduction in the growth rate of real GDP, at least for several years. Current estimates suggest that reducing Canadian greenhouse-gas emissions by approximately 20 percent from current levels by 2020 would lead to a reduction in real GDP by between 4 and 8 percent from the level that would otherwise exist in 2020. This implies a reduction in the growth rate of real GDP over this period of approximately 0.5 percent per year. Over the long term, however, once the economy adjusts to the new and possibly more efficient fuel sources, it is possible that the rate of economic growth would increase.

Policymakers are thus faced with difficult choices. If their objective was to make such choices sensibly, they would first need to estimate the costs to the economy of taking the "business as usual" approach and thus experiencing the predicted changes in the world climate over the next several decades. Then they would need to estimate the costs associated with taking aggressive policy actions designed to dramatically reduce the emission of greenhouse gases. Finally, they would need to choose a policy approach, appropriately weighing the costs of inaction against the costs of action. These would be very difficult decisions to make, partly because of the uncertainty surrounding the impact of any policies and partly because of the considerable political pressures generated by advocates on both sides of the debate.

ecosystems, price and policy incentives will be needed to direct technological change in more environmentally sustainable ways. Just as present technologies are much less polluting than the technologies of a century ago, the technologies of the future need to be made much less polluting than today's.

There is no guarantee that the world will solve the problems of sustainable growth in the time available, but there is nothing in modern growth theory and existing evidence to suggest that such an achievement is impossible.

SUMMARY

26.1 The Nature of Economic Growth

- Long-term economic growth refers to sustained increases in potential GDP.
- The cumulative effects of even small differences in growth rates become very large over periods of a decade or more.
- The most important benefit of growth lies in its contribution to raising average material living standards.
- Growth also facilitates the redistribution of income among people.

- The opportunity cost of growth is the reduction of consumption as resources are used instead for investment in capital goods.
- An additional cost of growth is the personal losses to those whose skills are made obsolete by the economic disruption caused by growth.
- There are four major determinants of growth: increases in the labour force; increases in physical capital; increases in human capital; and improvements in technology.

26.2 Established Theories of Economic Growth

- The long-run relationship among saving, investment, and economic growth is most easily observed in the market for financial capital, in which the interest rate is determined by the equality of desired investment and desired national saving.
- Increases in the supply of national saving will reduce the interest rate and encourage more investment by firms, thus increasing the rate of growth of potential output.
- Increases in the demand for investment will increase the interest rate and encourage an increase in household saving. The higher saving (and investment) in equilibrium leads to a higher growth rate of potential output.
- Neoclassical growth theory assumes an aggregate production function that displays diminishing marginal returns (when one factor is changed in isolation) and

constant returns to scale (when all factors are changed in equal proportions).
- In a balanced growth path, the quantity of labour, the quantity of capital, and real GDP all increase at a constant rate. But since per capita output is constant, material living standards are not rising.
- Changes in output that cannot be accounted for by changes in the levels of physical and human capital and in the size of the labour force are called growth in total factor productivity (TFP).
- In the Neoclassical growth model, technological change is assumed to be exogenous—unaffected by the size of the labour force, the size of the capital stock, or the level of economic activity.

26.3 Newer Growth Theories

- Unlike the Neoclassical growth theory, newer growth theories emphasize endogenous technological change that responds to market signals, such as prices and profits. In addition, shocks that would be adverse in a setting of fixed technology may provide a spur to innovation and result in technological improvements.
- These growth theories also suggest that investment embodying new technologies may be subject to *increasing* rather than diminishing marginal returns. Investment

that embodies a continuing flow of new technologies can explain ongoing growth in per capita incomes caused by capital accumulation—a phenomenon difficult to explain with the Neoclassical growth model.
- New knowledge is an important input to the growth process and, because it is a public good that can be used simultaneously by many, it is not subject to diminishing marginal returns.

26.4 Are There Limits to Growth?   LO 5

- The critical importance of increasing knowledge and new technology to the goal of sustaining growth is highlighted by the great drain on existing natural resources that has resulted from the explosive growth of population and output in recent decades.
- Without ongoing technological change, world living standards could not be raised to those currently existing in the developed nations.
- Rising population and rising real incomes place pressure on resources. Technological improvements, however, lead to less resource use per unit of output produced and also to the discovery and development of new resources.

- Earth's environment could cope naturally with much of human pollution 200 years ago, but the present population and level of output is so large that pollution has outstripped many of nature's coping mechanisms.
- Although problems associated with environmental degradation have been surmounted in the past, there is no guarantee that the ones now being encountered, such as the effects of global warming, will be effectively addressed by policies before the effects can be reversed.

KEY CONCEPTS

The cumulative nature of growth
Benefits and costs of growth
The market for financial capital and the equilibrium interest rate
Saving, investment, and growth

Neoclassical growth theory
The aggregate production function
Diminishing marginal returns
Constant returns to scale
Balanced growth

Endogenous technical change
Increasing marginal returns to investment
Resource depletion
Environmental degradation

STUDY EXERCISES

MyEconLab Make the grade with MyEconLab: Study Exercises marked in red can be found on MyEconLab. You can practise them as often as you want, and most feature step-by-step guided instructions to help you find the right answer.

1. Fill in the blanks to make the following statements correct.

   a. Long-run, sustained increases in potential output are called _____.
   b. Increases in material living standards occur with increases in real _____.
   c. An important cost of economic growth is the sacrifice of current _____ in exchange for investment that raises future _____.
   d. Four major determinants of growth examined in this chapter are
      - _____
      - _____
      - _____
      - _____

2. In this chapter, we developed a theory of the market for financial capital. Using that theory, fill in the blanks to make the following statements correct.

   a. An increase in the real interest rate leads to a(n) _____ in the amount of national saving as households reduce their _____.
   b. An increase in the interest rate leads firms to _____ their amount of desired investment.
   c. In the long run, with output equal to potential, equilibrium in the market for financial capital determines the interest rate as well as the amount of _____ and _____ in the economy.
   d. Following a shift in either the supply of national saving or the demand for investment, there will be a change in both the equilibrium _____ and the amount of _____ in the economy.

e. An increase in the amount of the economy's resources devoted to _____ leads to an increase in the growth rate of _____.

3. Fill in the blanks to make the following statements correct.

   a. An important aspect of Neoclassical growth theory is that increases in the supply of one factor, all else held constant, imply eventually _____ marginal returns to that factor.

   b. In Neoclassical growth theory, an increase in the labour force alone _____ total output and _____ the level of per capita output.

   c. When a new and better harvesting machine replaces an old harvesting machine on a farm and is more productive than the old one, we say there has been _____ technical change.

   d. Some newer growth theories are based on the assumption that technological change is _____ to the economic system; others are based on the possibility that there are _____ marginal returns to investment.

   e. Neoclassical growth theories are pessimistic because they emphasize _____ returns with a given state of _____. Modern growth theories are more optimistic because they emphasize the unlimited potential of _____.

4. In the text we said that, over many years, small differences in growth rates can have large effects on the level of income. This question will help you understand this important point. Consider an initial value of real GDP equal to Y_0. If real GDP grows at a rate of g percent annually, after N years real GDP will equal $Y_0(1 + g)^N$. Now consider the following table. Let the initial level of GDP in all cases be 100.

Real GDP with Alternative Growth Rates

Year	1% (1)	1.5% (2)	2% (3)	2.5% (4)	3% (5)	3.5% (6)
0	100	100	100	100	100	100
1	—	—	—	—	—	—
3	—	—	—	—	—	—
5	—	—	—	—	—	—
10	—	—	—	—	—	—
20	—	—	—	—	—	—
30	—	—	—	—	—	—
50	—	—	—	—	—	—

   a. By using the formula provided above, compute the level of real GDP in column 1 for each year. For example, in Year 1, real GDP will equal $100(1.01)^1 = 101$. For each year, compute the GDP to two decimal places.

   b. Now do the same for the rest of the columns.

   c. In Year 20, how much larger (in percentage terms) is real GDP in the 3 percent growth case compared with the 1.5 percent growth case?

   d. In Year 50, how much larger (in percentage terms) is real GDP in the 3 percent growth case compared with the 1.5 percent growth case?

5. The diagram below shows two paths for aggregate consumption. One grows at a rate of 3 percent per year; the other grows at 4 percent per year but begins at a lower level.

   a. Suppose the economy jumps from Path 1 to Path 2 in Year 0 because its rate of capital accumulation increases. What is the opportunity cost in this economy for this increase in capital accumulation?

   b. Suppose the economy jumps from Path 1 to Path 2 in Year 0 because its rate of R&D (research and development) expenditures increases. The greater R&D leads to technological improvements that generate the higher growth rate. What is the opportunity cost to this economy for the increase in R&D expenditures?

   c. Given the two paths in the diagram, can you offer a way to identify the "break-even" point for making the jump from Path 1 to Path 2? Explain.

6. Consider an economy in the long run with real GDP equal to the level of potential output, Y^*.

   a. Draw the diagram of the market for financial capital. Explain the slopes of the investment demand curve and the national saving curve.

   b. Suppose the government pursued a fiscal contraction by reducing the level of government purchases. Explain what would happen to the equilibrium interest rate, the amount of investment in the economy, and the long-run growth rate.

   c. Now suppose the fiscal contraction occurs by increasing taxes. Explain what effect this would have on the interest rate, investment, and long-run growth rate. (Hint: An increase in taxes is likely to reduce disposable income and thus reduce aggregate consumption.)

7. The Neoclassical growth theory is based on the existence of an aggregate production function—showing the relationship between labour (L), capital (K), technology (T), and real GDP (Y). The table below shows various values for L, K, and T. In all cases, the aggregate production function is assumed to take the following form:

$$Y = T \times \sqrt{KL}$$

Labour (L)	Capital (K)	Technology (T)	Real GDP (Y)
10	20	1	—
15	20	1	—
20	20	1	—
25	20	1	—
10	20	1	—
15	30	1	—
20	40	1	—
25	50	1	—
20	20	1	—
20	20	3	—
20	20	4	—
20	20	5	—

a. Compute real GDP for each case and complete the table.
b. In the first part of the table, capital is constant but labour is increasing. What property of the production function is displayed? Explain.
c. In the second part of the table, capital and labour are increasing by the same proportion. What property of the production function is displayed? Explain.
d. What type of growth is being shown in the third part of the table?

8. In this chapter we discussed four major determinants of growth in real output: increases in the labour force, increases in the stock of physical capital, increases in human capital, and improvements in technology.

a. For each of the four determinants, give an example of a government policy that is likely to increase growth.
b. Discuss the likely cost associated with each policy.
c. Does one of your proposed policies appear better (in a cost–benefit sense) than the others? Explain.

9. Consider the market for financial capital and the relationship among saving, investment, and the interest rate. In what follows, assume that the economy is in a long-run equilibrium with $Y = Y^*$.

a. Suppose the government wants to encourage national saving. How could it do this, and what would be the effects of such a policy? Illustrate in a diagram.

b. Suppose instead that the government wants to encourage investment. How might this be accomplished, and what would be the effects? Illustrate in a diagram.
c. It is often heard in public debate that "high interest rates are bad for investment and growth." Is this true? Can you come up with a simple rule of thumb to describe the relationship between interest rates, investment, and growth?

10. In the early 1970s the Club of Rome, extrapolating from the rates of resource use at the time, predicted that the supply of natural resources (especially oil) would be used up within a few decades. Subsequent events appear to have proven them wrong.

a. What is predicted to happen to the price of oil (and other natural resources) as population and per capita incomes rise?
b. Given your answer to part (a), what is the likely response by firms and consumers who use such resources?
c. Explain why resource exhaustion should, through the workings of the price system, lead to technological developments that reduce the use of the resource.

11. Dr. David Suzuki, an opponent of further economic growth, has argued that despite the fact that "in the twentieth century the list of scientific and technological achievements has been absolutely dazzling, the costs of such progress are so large that negative economic growth may be right for the future." Policies to achieve this include "rigorous reduction of waste, a questioning and distrustful attitude toward technological progress, and braking demands on the globe's resources." Identify some of the benefits and costs of economic growth, and evaluate Suzuki's position. What government policies would be needed to achieve his ends?

12. This question is based on the MyEconLab *Additional Topic* **Investment and Saving in Globalized Financial Markets.** Consider the market for financial capital and the long-run relationship among saving, investment, and economic growth.

a. For a closed economy, if the government wants a higher long-run growth rate, explain why it can directly promote saving *or* investment.
b. For an open economy, explain why the amount of investment (and growth rate of output) is unlikely to be affected by a policy that encourages national saving.
c. If desired saving need not be equal to desired investment in an open economy, what accounts for the difference?

Money and Banking

CHAPTER OUTLINE

27.1 THE NATURE OF MONEY

27.2 THE CANADIAN BANKING SYSTEM

27.3 MONEY CREATION BY THE BANKING SYSTEM

27.4 THE MONEY SUPPLY

LEARNING OBJECTIVES (LO)

After studying this chapter you will be able to

1 describe the various functions of money, and how money has evolved over time.

2 see that modern banking systems include both privately owned commercial banks and government-owned central banks.

3 explain how commercial banks create money through the process of taking deposits and making loans.

4 describe the various measures of the money supply.

IN the next three chapters, we look at the role of money and monetary policy. The role of money may seem obvious to most readers: money is what people use to buy things. Yet as we will see, increasing the amount of money circulating in Canada may not make the average Canadian better off in the long run. Although money allows those who have it to buy someone else's output, the total amount of goods and services available for everyone to buy depends on the total output produced, and thus may be unaffected by the total amount of money circulating in the economy. In other words, an increase in the quantity of money may not increase the level of potential real GDP. However, most economists agree that changes in the amount of money have important short-run effects on national income. A complete understanding of money's role in the economy requires that we recognize the distinction between the short run and the long run.

We begin by talking in detail about what money is and how it evolved over the centuries to its current form. We then examine the Canadian banking system, which includes a central bank (the Bank of Canada) and many commercial banks. Finally, we explain the process whereby commercial banks "create" money, seemingly out of thin air. This money creation process will play a central role in our discussion of how money influences the level of economic activity, a topic we begin in the next chapter.

| 27.1 The Nature of Money

What exactly is money? In this section, we describe the functions of money and briefly outline its history.

What Is Money?

medium of exchange Anything that is generally accepted in return for goods and services sold.

Money is any generally accepted **medium of exchange**, which means anything widely accepted in a society in exchange for goods and services. Although its medium-of-exchange role is perhaps its most important one, money also acts as a *store of value* and as a *unit of account*. Different kinds of money vary in their abilities to fulfill these functions. As we will see, the *money supply* is measured by using different definitions for different purposes.

barter A system in which goods and services are traded directly for other goods and services.

Money as a Medium of Exchange If there were no money, goods would have to be exchanged by barter. **Barter** is the system whereby goods and services are exchanged directly with each other. The major difficulty with barter is that each transaction requires a *double coincidence of wants*: Anyone who specialized in producing one commodity would have to spend a great deal of time searching for satisfactory transactions. For example, the barber who needs his sink repaired would have to find a plumber who wants a haircut. In a world of many different goods and many different people, the effort required to make all transactions by barter would be extreme. The use of money as a medium of exchange solves this problem. People can sell their output for money and then, in separate transactions, use the money to buy what they want from others.

> The double coincidence of wants is unnecessary when a medium of exchange is used.

By facilitating transactions, money makes possible the benefits of specialization and the division of labour, two concepts we first discussed in Chapter 1. As a result, money greatly contributes to the efficiency of the economic system. Not surprisingly, money has been called one of the great inventions contributing to human freedom and well-being.

To serve as an efficient medium of exchange, money must have a number of characteristics. It must be both easily recognizable and readily acceptable. It must have a high value relative to its weight (otherwise it would be a nuisance to carry around). It must be divisible, because money that comes only in large denominations is useless for transactions having only a small value. It must be reasonably durable (notice that Canadian paper money can easily survive several trips through a washing machine!). Finally, it must be difficult, if not impossible, to counterfeit.

Money as a Store of Value Money is a convenient means of storing purchasing power; goods may be sold today for money and the money may then be stored until it is needed for some future purchase. To be a satisfactory store of value, however, money must have a relatively stable value. Recall from the beginning of Chapter 23 that a rise in the price level causes a decrease in the purchasing power of money. When the price level is stable, the purchasing power of a given sum of money is also stable; when the price level is highly variable, so is the purchasing power of money, and the usefulness of money as a store of value is undermined.

Between the early 1970s and the early 1990s, inflation in Canada was high enough and sufficiently variable to diminish money's usefulness as a store of value. Since 1992, however, inflation has been low and relatively stable, thus increasing money's effectiveness as a store of value. Even Canada's high-inflation experience, however, is very modest compared with that in some other countries, such as Chile in the mid-1970s, Bolivia in the mid-1980s, Argentina, Romania, and Brazil in the early 1990s, and Zimbabwe in the mid-2000s. One of the most infamous experiences of very high inflation—*hyperinflation*—comes from Germany in the early 1920s. This case is discussed in *Lessons from History 27-1*.

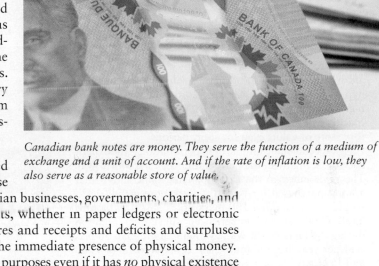

Canadian bank notes are money. They serve the function of a medium of exchange and a unit of account. And if the rate of inflation is low, they also serve as a reasonable store of value.

Money as a Unit of Account Money is also used for accounting, and its use for such purpose does not rely on its physical existence. Canadian businesses, governments, charities, and households all record their financial accounts, whether in paper ledgers or electronic spreadsheets, in terms of dollars. Expenditures and receipts and deficits and surpluses are computed in dollar terms even without the immediate presence of physical money.

Indeed, money can be used for accounting purposes even if it has *no* physical existence whatsoever. For instance, a government store in a communist society might say that everyone was allocated so many "dollars" to use each month. Goods could then be assigned prices and each consumer's purchases recorded, the consumer being allowed to buy until the allocated supply of dollars was exhausted. These dollars need have no existence other than as entries in the store's books, yet they would serve as a perfectly satisfactory unit of account. Whether they could also serve as a medium of exchange between individuals depends on whether the store would agree to transfer dollar credits from one customer to another at the customer's request. Canadian banks transfer dollars credited to deposits in this way each time you make a purchase with your ATM or debit card. Thus, a bank deposit can serve as both a unit of account and a medium of exchange. Notice that the use of *dollars* in this context suggests a further sense in which money is a unit of account. People think about values in terms of the monetary unit with which they are familiar.

The Origins of Money

The origins of money go far back in antiquity. Most primitive societies are known to have made some use of it.

Metallic Money All sorts of commodities have been used as money at one time or another, but gold and silver proved to have great advantages. They were precious because their supplies were relatively limited, and they were in constant demand by the wealthy for ornament and decoration. Further, they were easily recognized, they were divisible into extremely small units, and they did not easily wear out. For these reasons, precious metals came to circulate as money and to be used in many transactions.

Before the invention of coins, it was necessary to carry the metals in bulk. When a purchase was made, the requisite quantity of the metal was carefully weighed on

LESSONS FROM HISTORY 27-1

Hyperinflation and the Value of Money

Hyperinflation is generally defined as inflation that exceeds 50 percent per month. At this rate of inflation, a chocolate bar that costs $1 on January 1 would cost $129.74 by December 31 of the same year. When prices are rising at such rapid rates, is it possible for money to maintain its usefulness as a medium of exchange or as a store of value? Several examples from history have allowed economists to study the role of money during hyperinflation. This historical record is not very reassuring. In a number of instances, prices were rising so quickly that the nation's money ceased to be a satisfactory store of value, even for short periods.

A spectacular example of hyperinflation is the experience of Germany in the period after the First World War. The price index in the accompanying table shows that a good purchased for one 100-mark note in July 1923 would cost *10 million* 100-mark notes only four months later! Germany had experienced substantial inflation during the First World War, averaging more than 30 percent per year, but the immediate postwar years of 1920 and 1921 gave no sign of explosive inflation. By the summer of 1922, however, the rate of inflation was extremely high and by November 1923 the German mark was officially repudiated, its value wholly destroyed. How could such a dramatic increase in prices happen?

The main cause was the German government's inability to finance its rising expenditures with tax revenues and its resort to printing new money on a massive scale. As more and more physical money was being spent to purchase the same volume of real goods and services, the rate of inflation soared.

When inflation becomes so high that people lose confidence in the purchasing power of their currency, they rush to spend it. People who have goods become increasingly reluctant to accept the rapidly depreciating money in exchange. The rush to spend money accelerates the increase in prices until people finally become unwilling to accept money on any terms. What was once money ceases to be money. The price system can then be restored only by repudiation of the old monetary unit and its replacement by a new unit.

About a dozen hyperinflations in world history have been documented, among them the collapse of the continental during the American Revolution in 1776, the ruble during the Russian Revolution in 1917, the drachma during and after the German occupation of Greece in the Second World War, the pengö in Hungary in 1945–1946, the Chinese national currency from 1946 to 1948, the Bolivian peso in 1984–1985, and the Argentinian peso in the early 1990s. Between 2004 and 2009, there was a massive hyperinflation in Zimbabwe—the

During hyperinflation money loses its value so quickly that people cease to accept it as a means of payment. At that point, money may as well be used for wallpaper.

largest in recorded history. At the height of the hyperinflation in 2008, the *annual* inflation rate was estimated at over 230 million percent!

Every one of these hyperinflations was accompanied by great increases in the money supply; new money was printed to give governments purchasing power that they could not or would not obtain by taxation. Further, every hyperinflation occurred in the midst of a major political upheaval in which serious doubts existed about the stability and the future of the government itself.

Is hyperinflation likely in the absence of civil war, revolution, or collapse of the government? Most economists think not. Further, it is clear that high inflation rates over a period of time do not mean the inevitable or even likely onset of hyperinflation.

Date	German Wholesale Price Index (1913 = 1)
January 1913	1
January 1920	13
January 1921	14
January 1922	37
July 1922	101
January 1923	2 785
July 1923	74 800
August 1923	944 000
September 1923	23 900 000
October 1923	7 096 000 000

a scale. The invention of coinage eliminated the need to weigh the metal at each transaction, but it created an important role for an authority, usually a king or queen, who made the coins and affixed his or her seal, guaranteeing the amount of precious metal that the coin contained. This was clearly a great convenience, as long as traders knew that they could accept the coin at its "face value." The face value was nothing more than a statement that a certain weight of the precious metal was contained therein.

However, coins often could not be taken at their face value. The practice of clipping a thin slice off the edge of the coin and keeping the valuable metal became common. This, of course, served to undermine the acceptability of coins, even if they were stamped. To get around this problem, the idea arose of minting the coins with a rough edge. The absence of the rough edge would immediately indicate that the coin had been clipped. This practice, called *milling*, survives on Canadian dimes, quarters, and two-dollar coins as an interesting anachronism to remind us that there were days when the market value of the metal in the coin was equal to the face value of the coin.

Canadian quarters are intentionally produced with rough or bumpy edges. Such milling of coins is now unnecessary, but many decades ago when coins were made from precious metals, it was useful in preventing individuals from clipping the coins.

Not to be outdone by the cunning of their subjects, some rulers were quick to seize the chance of getting something for nothing. The power to mint coins placed rulers in a position to work a very profitable fraud. They often used some suitable occasion—a marriage, an anniversary, an alliance—to remint the coinage. Subjects would be ordered to bring their coins in to the mint to be melted down and coined afresh with a new stamp. Between the melting down and the recoining, however, the rulers had only to toss some further inexpensive base metal in with the melted coins. This *debasing* of the coinage allowed the ruler to earn a handsome profit by minting more new coins than the number of old ones collected and putting the extras in the royal vault. Through debasement, the amount of money in the economy (but not the amount of gold) had increased.

The eventual result of such debasement was inflation. The subjects had the same number of coins as before and hence could demand the same quantity of goods. When rulers paid their bills, however, the recipients of the extra coins could be expected to spend them. This caused a net increase in demand, which in turn bid up prices. Thus, increasing the money supply by debasing the coinage was a common cause of inflation.

Gresham's Law. The early experience of currency debasement led to the observation known as **Gresham's Law**, after Sir Thomas Gresham (1519–1579), an advisor to the Elizabethan court, who coined the phrase "bad money drives out good."

When Queen Elizabeth I came to the throne of England in the middle of the sixteenth century, the coinage had been severely debased. Seeking to help trade, Elizabeth minted new coins that contained their full face value of gold. However, as fast as she fed these new coins into circulation, they disappeared. Why?

Suppose you possessed one of these new coins and one of the old ones, each with the same face value, and had to make a purchase. What would you do? You would use the debased coin to make the purchase and keep the undebased one; you part with less gold that way. Suppose you wanted to obtain a certain amount of gold bullion by melting

Gresham's Law The theory that "bad," or debased, money drives "good," or undebased, money out of circulation.

down the gold coins (as was frequently done). Which coins would you use? You would use new, undebased coins because it would take more of the debased coins than the new coins to get a given amount of gold bullion. The debased coins (bad money) would thus remain in circulation, and the undebased coins (good money) would disappear into peoples' private hoards—the "bad" money would drive out the "good" money.

> Gresham's Law predicts that when two types of money are used side by side, the one with the greater intrinsic value will be driven out of circulation.

Gresham's insights have proven helpful in explaining the experience of a number of modern high-inflation economies. For example, in the 1970s, inflation in Chile raised the value of the metallic content in coins above their face value. Coins quickly disappeared from circulation as the coins were melted down for their metal. Only paper currency remained in circulation and was used even for tiny transactions, such as purchasing a pack of matches. Gresham's law is one reason that modern coins, unlike their historical counterparts, are merely tokens that contain a metallic value that is only a small fraction of their face value.

The development of paper money, such as this bank note issued by The Montreal Bank more than a century ago, was an important step in the evolution of modern, fractional-reserve banking systems. Paper money allowed individuals to avoid the cumbersome transportation of gold when making their daily transactions.

Paper Money The next important step in the history of money was the evolution of paper currency. Artisans who worked with gold required secure safes, and the public began to deposit gold with these goldsmiths for safekeeping. Goldsmiths would give their depositors receipts promising to return the gold on demand. When a depositor wanted to make a large purchase, he could go to his goldsmith, reclaim some of his gold, and pay it to the seller of the goods. If the seller had no immediate need for the gold, he would carry it back to the goldsmith for safekeeping.

If people knew the goldsmith to be reliable, there was no need to go through the cumbersome and risky business of physically transferring the gold. The buyer needed only to transfer the goldsmith's receipt to the seller, who would accept it as long as he was confident that the goldsmith would pay over the gold whenever it was needed. This transferring of paper receipts rather than gold was essentially the invention of paper money.[1]

When it first came into being, paper money represented a promise to pay so much gold on demand. In this case, the promise was made first by goldsmiths and later by banks. Such paper money was *backed* by precious metal and was *convertible on demand* into this metal. In the nineteenth century, private banks commonly issued paper money, called **bank notes**, nominally convertible into gold. As with the goldsmiths, each bank issued its own notes, and these notes were convertible into gold at the issuing bank. Thus, in the nineteenth century, bank notes from many different banks circulated side by side, each of them being backed by gold at the bank that issued them.

bank notes Paper money issued by commercial banks.

---

[1] Paper money dates back as far as the T'ang dynasty in China (A.D. 618–907) but first appeared in Europe much later, in the 1660s in Sweden. For a very readable history of the development of money, see Jack Weatherford, *The History of Money*, Three Rivers Press, 1997.

Fractionally Backed Paper Money. Early on, many goldsmiths and banks discovered that it was not necessary to keep one ounce of gold in the vaults for every claim to one ounce circulating as paper money. At any one time, some of the bank's customers would be withdrawing gold, others would be depositing it, and most would be using the bank's paper notes without any need or desire to convert those notes into gold. As a result, the bank was able to issue more paper money redeemable in gold than the amount of gold that it held in its vaults. This was good business because the extra paper money could be invested profitably in interest-earning loans to households and firms. To this day, banks have many more claims outstanding against them than they actually have in reserves available to pay those claims. We say that such a currency is *fractionally backed* by the reserves.

The major problem with a fractionally backed currency was maintaining its convertibility into the precious metal behind it. The imprudent bank that issued too much paper money would find itself unable to redeem its currency in gold when the demand for gold was even slightly higher than usual. It would then have to suspend payments, and all holders of its notes would suddenly find that the notes were worthless. The prudent bank that kept a reasonable relationship between its note issues and its gold reserves would find that it could meet a normal range of demand for gold without any trouble.

Paper money used to be backed by the value of gold—meaning that it was redeemable for gold. But now money is not redeemable for anything except itself—people hold it because they know that others will accept it as payment for goods and services.

If, for whatever reason, the public lost confidence in the banks and demanded redemption of its currency *en masse*, even the most prudent bank would be unable to honour its promises. The history of nineteenth- and early-twentieth-century banking on both sides of the Atlantic is full of examples of banks that were ruined by "panics," or sudden runs on their gold reserves. When these happened, the banks' depositors and the holders of their notes would find themselves with worthless pieces of paper.

Fiat Money As time went on, currency (notes and coins) issued by private banks became less common, and central banks took control of issuing currency. In time, *only* central banks were permitted by law to issue currency. Originally, the central banks issued currency that was fully convertible into gold. In those days, gold would be brought to the central bank, which would issue currency in the form of "gold certificates" that asserted that the gold was available on demand. The reserves of gold thus set an upper limit on the amount of currency that could circulate in the economy. This practice of backing the currency with gold is known as a **gold standard**.

However, central banks, like private banks before them, could issue more currency than they had in gold because in normal circumstances only a small fraction of the outstanding currency would be presented for payment at any one time. Thus, even though the need to maintain convertibility into gold put some upper limit on note issuance, central banks had substantial discretionary control over the quantity of currency outstanding. For example, if the central bank decided to hold gold reserves equal to at least 20 percent of its outstanding currency, the total amount of currency would be limited to five times the gold reserves. But the central bank would nonetheless have complete discretion in choosing this fraction; the smaller the fraction held in reserves, the larger the supply of paper currency that could be supported with a given stock of gold.

During the period between the First and Second World Wars (1919–1939), almost all the countries of the world abandoned the gold standard; their currencies were thus

gold standard A currency standard whereby a country's currency is convertible into gold at a fixed rate of exchange.

fiat money Paper money or coinage that is neither backed by nor convertible into anything else but is decreed by the government to be legal tender.

no longer convertible into gold. Money that is not convertible by law into anything tangible derives its value from its acceptability in exchange. Such **fiat money** is widely acceptable because it is declared by government order, or *fiat*, to be legal tender. *Legal tender* is anything that by law must be accepted when offered either for the purchase of goods or services or to repay a debt.

Today, no country allows its currency to be converted into gold on demand. Gold backing for Canadian currency was eliminated in 1940, although note issues continued to carry the traditional statement "will pay to the bearer on demand" until 1954. Today's Bank of Canada notes simply say, "This note is legal tender." It is, in other words, fiat money pure and simple.[2]

> If fiat money is generally acceptable, it is a medium of exchange. If its purchasing power remains stable, it is a satisfactory store of value. If both of these things are true, it serves as a satisfactory unit of account. Today, almost all currency is fiat money.

Many people are disturbed to learn that present-day paper money is neither backed by nor convertible into anything more valuable—that it consists of nothing but pieces of paper whose value derives from common acceptance and from confidence that it will continue to be accepted in the future. Many people believe that their money should be more "substantial" than this. Yet money is, in fact, nothing more than generally acceptable pieces of paper.

Modern Money: Deposit Money

Today's bank customers deposit coins and paper money with the banks for safekeeping, just as in former times they deposited gold. Such a deposit is recorded as a credit to the customer's account, and is a liability (a promise to pay) for the commercial bank.

When the customer wants to purchase goods or services, or wants to settle a debt, three options are available. First, the customer can withdraw cash from the bank account and use it to make a transaction. Second, the customer can write a *cheque* to the recipient, who then deposits the cheque in their own bank account. A cheque is simply an order for a *transfer* of funds from the customer's account to the recipient's account, possibly at a different bank. The development of automatic teller machines (ATMs) in the past 30 years has made the cash option more convenient than it was before ATMs existed, and the cheque-writing option was common until quite recently, but is now much less so.

The customer's third option involves an electronic transfer of funds. Like a cheque, although must faster, a purchase using a bank card or debit card leads to a transfer of funds from the bank account of the purchaser to the bank account of the seller. Other electronic transfers of funds are also commonly used, such as direct-deposit payments by employers to employees and online payments that individuals can make from their bank accounts to firms for the provision of various services, such as Internet service, credit cards, and telephone service.

deposit money Money held by the public in the form of deposits with commercial banks.

Deposits contained inside bank accounts can easily be used to facilitate transactions, even though they exist only as electronic entries; they are referred to as **deposit money**.

[2] See *A History of the Canadian Dollar* (written by James Powell and published by the Bank of Canada) for a detailed and very readable discussion of the evolution of Canadian money.

As we will see later in this chapter, the value of deposit money in a modern economy far exceeds the value of coins and paper currency. As in much earlier times, modern banks create more promises to pay (deposit money) than they hold as cash in reserve.

> **Bank deposits are money. Today, just as in the past, banks create money by issuing more promises to pay (deposits) than they have cash reserves available to pay out.**

27.2 The Canadian Banking System

Several types of institutions make up a modern banking system, such as exists in Canada today. The **central bank** is the government-owned and government-operated institution that is the sole money-issuing authority and serves to control the banking system. Through it, the government's monetary policy is conducted. In Canada, the central bank is the Bank of Canada, often called just the Bank.

central bank A bank that acts as banker to the commercial banking system and often to the government as well. Usually a government-owned institution that is the sole money-issuing authority.

Financial intermediaries are privately owned institutions that serve the general public. They are called *intermediaries* because they stand between savers, from whom they accept deposits, and borrowers, to whom they make loans. For many years, government regulations created sharp distinctions among the various types of financial intermediaries by limiting the types of transactions in which each could engage. The past three decades have seen a sweeping deregulation of the financial system so that many of these traditional distinctions no longer apply. In this book, we use the term *commercial banks* to extend to all financial intermediaries that accept deposits and create deposit money, including chartered banks, trust companies, credit unions, and caisses populaires.

The Bank of Canada

Many of the world's early central banks were initially private, profit-making institutions that provided services to ordinary banks. Their importance, however, caused them to develop close ties with government. Central banks soon became instruments of the government, though not all of them were publicly owned. The Bank of England, one of the world's oldest and most famous central banks, began to operate as the central bank of England in the seventeenth century, but it was not formally taken over by the government until 1947.

The similarities in the functions performed and the tools used by the world's central banks are much more important than the differences in their organization. Although we give our attention to the operations of the Bank of Canada, its basic functions are similar to those of the Bank of England, the Federal Reserve System in the United States, or the European Central Bank (the sole issuer of the euro).

Organization of the Bank of Canada The Bank of Canada commenced operations on March 11, 1935. It is a publicly owned corporation; all profits it earns are remitted to the Government of Canada. The responsibility for the Bank's affairs rests with a board of directors composed of the governor, the senior deputy governor, the deputy minister of finance, and 12 directors.

The European Central Bank's website is www.ecb.int.

The Bank of Canada is located on Wellington Street in Ottawa, across the street from the Parliament Buildings.

The governor is appointed by the directors, with the approval of the federal cabinet, for a seven-year term.

For information on the Bank of Canada, see its website: www.bankofcanada.ca.

The organization of the Bank of Canada is designed to keep the operation of monetary policy free from day-to-day political influence. The Bank is not responsible to Parliament for its day-to-day behaviour in the way that the department of finance is for the operation of fiscal policy. In this sense, the Bank of Canada has considerable autonomy in the way it carries out monetary policy. But the Bank is not completely independent. The *ultimate* responsibility for the Bank's actions rests with the government, since it is the government that must answer to Parliament. This system is known as "joint responsibility," and it dates back to 1967.

Under the system of joint responsibility, the governor of the Bank and the minister of finance consult regularly. In the case of fundamental disagreement over monetary policy, the minister of finance has the option of issuing an explicit *directive* to the governor and announcing this decision publicly. In such a case (which has not happened since the inception of joint responsibility), the governor would simply carry out the minister's directive or ignore the directive and resign. In the absence of such a directive, however, responsibility for monetary policy rests with the governor of the Bank.

> The system of joint responsibility keeps the conduct of monetary policy free from day-to-day political influence while ensuring that the government retains ultimate responsibility for monetary policy.[3]

Basic Functions of the Bank of Canada A central bank serves four main functions: as a banker for private banks, as a bank for the government, as the regulator of the nation's money supply, and as a supporter of financial markets. The first three functions are reflected in Table 27-1, which shows the balance sheet of the Bank of Canada as of December 2011.

Banker to the Commercial Banks. The central bank accepts deposits from commercial banks and will, on order, transfer them to the account of another bank. In this way, the central bank provides the commercial banks with the means of settling debts to other banks. The deposits of the commercial banks with the Bank of Canada—part of their *reserves*—appear in Table 27-1. In December 2011 the banks had $107 million on reserve at the Bank of Canada. Notice that the cash reserves of the commercial banks deposited with the central bank are liabilities of the central bank, because it promises to pay them on demand.

Historically, one of the earliest services provided by central banks was that of "lender of last resort" to the banking system. Central banks would lend money to private banks that had sound investments (such as government securities) but were in urgent need of cash. If such banks could not obtain ready cash, they might be forced into insolvency, because they could not meet the demands of their depositors, in spite of

---

[3] This system was motivated by the "Coyne Affair" in 1961, during the Progressive Conservative government of John Diefenbaker. James Coyne, then governor of the Bank of Canada, disagreed with the minister of finance, Donald Fleming, over the conduct of monetary policy and was eventually forced to resign. Louis Rasminsky then accepted the position as governor of the Bank on the condition that the *Bank of Canada Act* be modified to incorporate the idea of joint responsibility. The *Bank of Canada Act* was so amended in 1967. For a discussion of the early history of the Bank of Canada, see George Watts, *The Bank of Canada: Origins and Early History*, Carleton University Press, 1993.

TABLE 27-1 Assets and Liabilities of the Bank of Canada, December 2011 (millions of dollars)

Assets		Liabilities	
Government of Canada securities	62 098.9	Notes in circulation	61 028.8
Advances to commercial banks	81.5	Government of Canada deposits	1 512.5
Net foreign-currency assets	11.7	Deposits of commercial banks (reserves)	106.7
Other assets	2 055.1	Other liabilities and capital	1 599.2
Total	64 247.2	Total	64 247.2

The balance sheet of the Bank of Canada shows that it serves as banker to the commercial banks and to the government of Canada, and as issuer of our currency; it also suggests the Bank's role as regulator of money markets and the money supply. The principal liabilities of the Bank are the basis of the money supply. Bank of Canada notes are currency, and the deposits of the commercial banks give them the reserves they need to create deposit money. The Bank's holdings of Government of Canada securities arise from its operations designed to regulate the money supply and financial markets.

(*Source:* Bank of Canada, *Annual Report 2011*. www.bankofcanada.ca.)

---

their being basically sound. Today's central banks continue to be lenders of last resort. Table 27-1 shows that in December 2011 the Bank of Canada had $81.5 million in outstanding loans to commercial banks.

Banker to the Federal Government. Governments, too, need to hold their funds in an account into which they can make deposits and on which they can write cheques. The Government of Canada keeps some of its chequing deposits at the Bank of Canada. In December 2011, the federal government had $1.5 billion in deposits at the Bank of Canada.

When the government requires more money than it collects in taxes, it needs to borrow, and it does so by issuing government securities (short-term Treasury bills or longer-term bonds). Most are sold directly to financial institutions and large institutional investors, but in most years the Bank of Canada buys some and credits the government's account with a deposit for the amount of the purchase. In December 2011, the Bank of Canada held $62.1 billion in Government of Canada securities. These securities are the Bank of Canada's primary asset, usually representing over 95 percent of the Bank's total assets. It is largely by earning interest on these securities that the Bank of Canada earns a profit every year—a profit that is eventually remitted to the government.

Regulator of the Money Supply. One of the most important functions of a central bank is to regulate the *money supply*. Though we have not yet defined the money supply precisely—and there are several different definitions of the money supply that we will encounter—we will see that most measures of the money supply include currency in circulation plus deposits held at commercial banks. Table 27-1 shows that the vast majority of the Bank of Canada's liabilities (its promises to pay) are the currency in

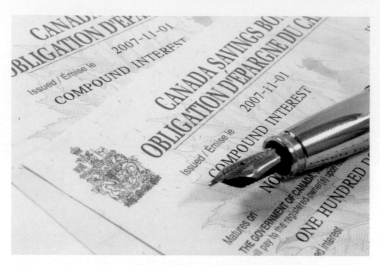

When the Government of Canada borrows money to finance some of its expenditures, it issues bonds like these. The Bank of Canada is the Government's "fiscal agent" and manages its outstanding debt.

circulation (held by the public) or the reserves of the commercial banks.[4] These reserves, in turn, underlie the deposits of households and firms—in exactly the same way that in much earlier times the goldsmith's holdings of gold underlay its issue of notes.

By changing its liabilities (currency plus reserves), the Bank of Canada can change the money supply. The Bank can change the levels of its assets and liabilities in many ways and, as its liabilities rise and fall, so does the money supply. In Chapter 29, we will explore in detail how this happens and how it is related to the Bank's decisions regarding monetary policy. At that point we will see how the Bank's holdings of government securities (its largest asset) are closely related to the value of notes in circulation (its largest liability).

Supporter of Financial Markets. Various institutions—including commercial banks, credit unions, trust companies, and caisses populaires—are in the business of accepting deposits from customers and then using these funds to extend long-term loans to borrowers. Large, unanticipated increases in interest rates tend to squeeze these institutions. The average rate they earn on their portfolio of loans rises only slowly as old contracts mature and new ones are made, but they must either pay higher rates to hold on to their deposits or accept wide-scale withdrawals that could easily bring about insolvency. Such dramatic events are relatively rare in the Canadian banking sector, though Canadian banks have failed in the past and it is possible, though unlikely, that more may fail in the future.

As we have already mentioned, during the global financial crisis of 2008 the Bank of Canada played a much more active role than usual in supporting financial markets. At that time, commercial banks around the world dramatically reduced their interbank lending after the failure of some large U.S. and U.K. financial institutions. The reduction in lending reflected heightened uncertainty regarding the credit-worthiness of *all* commercial banks. In response, the Bank of Canada took unprecedented actions designed to keep credit flowing as normally as possible in Canada, including the significant provision of short-term loans to Canadian financial institutions.

Commercial Banks in Canada

commercial bank A privately owned, profit-seeking institution that provides a variety of financial services, such as accepting deposits from customers and making loans and other investments.

All Canadian banks owned in the private sector are referred to as **commercial banks**. Commercial banks have common attributes: they hold deposits for their customers; they permit certain deposits to be transferred electronically or by cheque from an individual account to other accounts in the same or other banks; they invest in government

---

[4] Currency is a liability for the central bank because holders of currency can take it back to the central bank and redeem it for . . . currency! In the days of the gold standard, currency was redeemable for gold. Today, it is just redeemable for itself.

securities (short-term Treasury bills and longer-term bonds); they make loans to house-holds and firms; and they often divide these loans into small pieces and re-package them into securities, each of which contains a diversified collection of many pieces from the original loans—a process called *securitization*.

Banks are not the only financial institutions in the country. Many other privately owned, profit-seeking institutions, such as trust companies and credit unions, accept deposits and grant loans for specific purposes. Many retail stores and credit-card companies also extend credit so that purchases can be made on a buy-now, pay-later basis.

The Provision of Credit From the perspective of the overall economy, the most important role played by commercial banks and other financial institutions is that of *financial intermediary*. Banks borrow (accept deposits) from households and firms that have money that they do not currently need, and they lend (provide credit) to those households and firms that need credit to achieve their objectives. They therefore act as essential *intermediaries* in the credit market.

Credit can be viewed as the "lifeblood" of a modern economy. Households often require credit to make large purchases, such as home appliances and cars, and they almost always use credit (a mortgage) when they buy a house. Without easy access to credit, most of these household purchases would either be delayed by many years or impossible altogether. Firms require credit to finance several aspects of their operations. For example, payments for workers and for material inputs often must be made well before revenue from the associated production is received. In addition, firms often finance their capital investments—purchases of equipment or the construction of facilities—with the use of borrowed money. Without easy access to credit, many firms would be unable to conduct their normal business operations and, as a result, the level of economic activity would decline.

This crucial function of banks and other financial institutions—the provision of credit—is easy to overlook when credit markets are functioning smoothly. Like the flow of electricity, we usually take it for granted in our daily activities, only to be reminded of its importance when the next power failure occurs. Similarly, when the credit markets cease to function well, as they did during the global financial crisis of 2008, their importance to the economy becomes clear to all. Indeed, the economic recession that began in the United States in 2008 and quickly spread around the world originated in the failure of some large U.S. and U.K. banks, which in turn led to a reduction in the flow of credit and a rise in interest rates (the price of credit) in most countries. The effect on economic activity was quick and significant. A central part of the policy response, in Canada and elsewhere, involved taking actions to ensure that banks and other financial institutions were in a position to extend credit in a normal manner.

Interbank Activities Commercial banks have a number of interbank cooperative relationships. For example, banks often share loans. Even the biggest bank cannot meet all the credit needs of a giant corporation, and often a group of banks will offer a "pool loan," agreeing on common terms and dividing the loan up into manageable segments. Another form of interbank cooperation is the bank credit card. Visa and MasterCard are the two most widely used credit cards, and each is operated by a group of banks.

Probably the most important form of interbank cooperation is cheque clearing and collection, including the clearing of electronic transfers through debit cards and online banking activities. Bank deposits are an effective medium of exchange only because banks accept each other's cheques and allow funds to be transferred electronically when purchases are made with debit cards and other forms of electronic transfer. If a depositor in the Bank of Montreal writes a cheque to someone who deposits it in an account at CIBC, the Bank of Montreal now owes money to CIBC. This creates a need for the banks to present cheques to each other for payment. The same is true for transactions made electronically.

Millions of such transactions take place in the course of a day, and they result in an enormous sorting and bookkeeping job. Multibank systems make use of a **clearing house** where interbank debts are settled. At the end of the day, all the transfers (cheque and electronic) from the Bank of Montreal's customers for deposit to CIBC are totalled and set against the total of all the transfers from CIBC's customers for deposit to the Bank of Montreal. It is necessary only to settle the difference between the two sums. Electronic transfers take place immediately whereas cheques are passed through the clearing house back to the bank on which they were drawn. Both banks are then able to adjust the individual accounts by a set of book entries. An overall transfer between banks is necessary only when there is a net transfer from the customers of one bank to those of another. This is accomplished by a daily transfer of deposits held by the commercial banks with the Bank of Canada.

clearing house An institution in which interbank indebtedness, arising from the transfer of cheques between banks, is computed and offset and net amounts owing are calculated.

Banks as Profit Seekers Banks are private firms that seek to make profits. A commercial bank provides a variety of services to its customers: the convenience of deposits that can be transferred by personal cheque, debit card, or online transaction; a safe and convenient place to earn a modest but guaranteed return on savings; and financial advice and wealth-management services.

Table 27-2 is the combined balance sheet of the chartered banks in Canada. The bulk of any bank's liabilities are deposits owed to its depositors. The principal assets of a bank are the *securities* it owns (including government bonds), which pay interest or dividends, and the interest-earning *loans* it makes to individuals and to businesses, both in Canada and abroad (which may be denominated in foreign currencies). A bank loan is a liability to the borrower (who must pay it back) but an asset to the bank.

Commercial banks attract deposits by paying interest to depositors and by providing them with services, such as clearing cheques, automated teller machines, debit cards, and online banking. Banks earn profits by lending and investing money deposited with them for more than they pay their depositors in terms of interest and other services provided. They also earn profits through the wealth-management and investment services they provide to their customers.

Competition for deposits is active among commercial banks and between banks and other financial institutions. Interest paid on deposits, special high-interest certificates of deposit (CDs), advertising, personal solicitation of accounts, giveaway programs for new deposits to existing accounts, and improved services are all forms of competition for funds.

Commercial Banks' Reserves

Commercial banks keep sufficient cash on hand to be able to meet depositors' day-to-day requirements for cash (plus they keep deposits at the central bank which can be readily converted into cash). However, just as the goldsmiths of long ago discovered that only a fraction of the gold they held was ever withdrawn at any given time, and just as banks of long ago discovered that only a small fraction of convertible bank notes were actually converted, so too do modern bankers know that only a small fraction of their deposits will be withdrawn in cash at any one time.

TABLE 27-2 Consolidated Balance Sheet of the Canadian Chartered Banks, February 2012 (millions of dollars)

Assets		Liabilities	
Reserves (including deposits with Bank of Canada)	9 049	Demand and notice deposits	723 451
Government securities	241 348		
Mortgage and non-mortgage loans	1 606 225	Term deposits	563 401
Canadian corporate securities	186 737	Government deposits	10 667
		Foreign-currency liabilities	1 246 952
Foreign-currency assets	1 193 498	Shareholders' equity	194 626
Other assets	425 870	Other liabilities	923 630
Total	3 662 727	Total	3 662 727

Reserves are only a tiny fraction of deposit liabilities. If all the chartered banks' customers who held demand and notice deposits tried to withdraw them in cash, the banks could not meet this demand without liquidating over $700 billion of other assets. This would be impossible without assistance from the Bank of Canada.

(*Source:* Adapted from Bank of Canada, *Banking and Financial Statistics*, May 2012, Tables C3 and C4.)

The reserves needed to ensure that depositors can withdraw their deposits on demand will normally be quite small.

In abnormal times, however, nothing short of 100 percent would do the job if the commercial banking system had to stand alone. If a major bank were to fail, it would probably cause a general loss of confidence in the ability of other banks to redeem their deposits. The results would then be devastating. Such an event—or even the rumour of it—could lead to a **bank run** as depositors rushed to withdraw their money. Faced with such a panic, banks would have to close until either they had borrowed enough funds or sold enough assets to meet the demand, or the demand subsided. However, banks could not instantly turn their loans into cash because the borrowers would have the money tied up in such things as real estate or business enterprises. Neither could the banks obtain cash by selling their securities to the public because payments would be made by cheques, which would not provide cash to pay off depositors.

bank run A situation in which many depositors rush to withdraw their money, possibly leading to a bank's financial collapse.

The difficulty of providing sufficient reserves to meet abnormal situations is alleviated by the central bank, which can provide all the reserves that are needed to meet any abnormal situation. It can do this in two ways. First, it can lend reserves directly to commercial banks on the security of assets that are sound but not easy to liquidate quickly, such as interest-earning residential or commercial mortgages. Second, it can enter the open market and buy all the government securities that commercial banks need to sell in order to increase their available cash reserves. Once the public finds that deposits can be turned into cash at their request, any panic would usually subside and any further drain of cash out of banks would cease.

The possibility of a bank run in Canada has been all but eliminated by the provision of deposit insurance by the Canada Deposit Insurance Corporation (CDIC), a federal

The late Jimmy Stewart plays George Bailey in It's a Wonderful Life. *In this scene, Bailey, the owner of a small commercial bank, explains to his panicking customers why they can't all take their money out at the same time. It is a great illustration of the workings of a fractional-reserve banking system.*

Crown corporation. The CDIC guarantees that, in the unlikely event of a bank failure, depositors will get their money back, up to a limit of $100 000 per eligible deposit (there are seven different types of deposit that are eligible for CDIC insurance). Most depositors will not rush to withdraw all of their money as long as they are certain they can get it when they need it.

Target and Excess Reserves Canada's banks hold reserves against their deposit liabilities for the simple reason that they want to avoid situations in which they cannot satisfy their depositors' demands for cash, and it is costly for them to borrow from other banks or from the Bank of Canada when they run short of reserves. Look again at Table 27-2. Notice that the chartered banks' reserves of just over $9 billion are less than 1 percent of their *deposit* liabilities of more than $1.25 trillion.

Thus, if the holders of even 1 percent of deposits demanded cash, the banks would be unable to meet the demand without outside help. Reserves can be as low as they are because, first, banks know that it is very unlikely that even 1 percent of their total deposits will be withdrawn at any given time and, second, the banks know that the Bank of Canada will help them out in time of temporary need. The Canadian banking system is thus a **fractional-reserve system**, with commercial banks holding reserves—either as cash or as deposits at the Bank of Canada—of just a small fraction of their total deposits.

A bank's **reserve ratio** is the fraction of its deposits that it *actually* holds as reserves at any point in time, either as cash or as deposits with the Bank of Canada. A bank's **target reserve ratio** is the fraction of its deposits it would *ideally* like to hold as reserves. This target reserve ratio will generally not be constant over time. During holiday seasons, for example, banks may choose to hold more reserves because they know, based on past experience, that there will be heavy demands for cash.

At any given time, any commercial bank will probably not be exactly at its target level of reserves. Reserves may be slightly above or slightly below the target, but the commercial bank will take actions to gradually restore its actual reserves toward its target level. Any reserves in excess of the target level are called **excess reserves**. As we will see next, a bank can expand or contract its portfolio of loans to adjust its actual reserves toward its target level. Understanding this process is the key to understanding the "creation" of deposit money.

fractional-reserve system A banking system in which commercial banks keep only a fraction of their deposits in cash or on deposit with the central bank.

reserve ratio The fraction of its deposits that a commercial bank actually holds as reserves in the form of cash or deposits with the central bank.

target reserve ratio The fraction of its deposits that a commercial bank wants to hold as reserves.

excess reserves Reserves held by a commercial bank in excess of its target reserves.

27.3 Money Creation by the Banking System

We noted before that the *money supply* includes both currency and deposits at commercial banks. The fractional-reserve system provides the means to permit commercial banks to create new deposits and thus to create new money. The process is important, so it is worth examining in some detail.

Some Simplifying Assumptions

To focus on the essential aspects of how banks create money, suppose that banks can invest in only one kind of asset—loans—and they have only one kind of deposit. Two other assumptions are provisional and will be relaxed after we have developed some basic ideas about the creation of money:

1. *Fixed target reserve ratio.* We assume that all banks have the same target reserve ratio, which does not change. In our numerical illustration, we will assume that the target reserve ratio is 20 percent (0.20); that is, for every $5 of deposits, the banks want to hold $1 in reserves, investing the rest in new loans.

2. *No cash drain from the banking system.* We also assume that the public holds a fixed absolute amount of the currency in circulation. In particular, we assume that the amount of currency held by the public is *not* a constant ratio of their bank deposits. (Later on we will assume that the amount of currency held by the public grows as total bank deposits grow. This is called a *cash drain*.)

The Creation of Deposit Money

A hypothetical balance sheet, with assets and liabilities, is shown for TD Bank (TD) in Table 27-3. TD has assets of $200 of reserves, held partly as cash on hand and partly as deposits with the central bank, and $900 of loans outstanding to its customers. Its liabilities are $100 to investors (owners) who contributed financial capital to start the bank and $1000 to current depositors. The bank's ratio of reserves to deposits is 0.20 (200/1000), exactly equal to its target reserve ratio.

What Is a New Deposit? In what follows, we are interested in knowing how the commercial banking system can "create money" when confronted with a new deposit. But what do we mean by a new deposit? By "new," we mean a deposit of cash that is new to the *commercial banking system*. There are three examples.

- First, an individual might immigrate to Canada and bring cash. When that cash is deposited into a commercial bank, it constitutes a new deposit to the Canadian banking system.
- Second, an individual who had some cash stashed under his bed (or in a safety deposit box) has now decided to deposit it into an account at a commercial bank.
- Third is the most interesting but also the most complicated example. If the Bank of Canada were to purchase a government security from an individual or from a firm, it would purchase that asset with a cheque drawn on the Bank of Canada. When the individual or firm deposits the cheque with a commercial bank, it would be a new deposit to the commercial banking system.

The important point to keep in mind here is that the *source* of the new deposit is irrelevant to the process of money creation by the commercial banks. In the

TABLE 27-3 The Initial Balance Sheet of TD

Assets ($)		Liabilities ($)	
Reserves (cash and deposits with the central bank)	200	Deposits	1 000
Loans	900	Capital	100
	1 100		1 100

TD has reserves equal to 20 percent of its deposit liabilities. The commercial bank earns profits by finding profitable investments for much of the money deposited with it. In this balance sheet, loans are its income-earning assets.

TABLE 27-4 TD's Balance Sheet Immediately After a New Deposit of $100

Assets ($)		Liabilities ($)	
Reserves	300	Deposits	1 100
Loans	900	Capital	100
	1 200		1 200

The new deposit raises liabilities and assets by the same amount. Because both reserves and deposits rise by $100, the bank's actual reserve ratio, formerly 0.20, increases to 0.27. The bank now has excess reserves of $80.

TABLE 27-5 TD's Balance Sheet After Making a New Loan of $80

Assets ($)		Liabilities ($)	
Reserves	220	Deposits	1 100
Loans	980	Capital	100
	1 200		1 200

TD converts its excess cash reserves into new loans. The bank keeps $20 as a reserve against the initial new deposit of $100. It lends the remaining $80 to a customer, who writes a cheque to someone who deals with another bank. Comparing Table 27-3 and 27-5 shows that the bank has increased its deposit liabilities by the $100 initially deposited and has increased its assets by $20 of cash reserves and $80 of new loans. It has also restored its target reserve ratio of 0.20.

TABLE 27-6 Changes in the Balance Sheets of Second-Round Banks

Assets ($)		Liabilities ($)	
Reserves	+16	Deposits	+80
Loans	+64		
	+80		+80

Second-round banks receive cash deposits and expand loans. The second-round banks gain new deposits of $80 as a result of the loan granted by TD. These banks keep 20 percent of the cash that they acquire as their reserve against the new deposit, and they can make new loans using the other 80 percent.

discussion that follows, we use the example of the Bank of Canada buying government securities from firms or households as a way of generating a new deposit. But this is not crucial. We use this example because, as we will see in Chapter 29, this is how the Bank of Canada directly alters the level of reserves in the banking system when it chooses to do so. But the general process of money creation we are about to describe applies to *any* new deposit, whatever its source.

The Expansion of Money from a Single New Deposit Suppose the Bank of Canada enters the open market and buys $100 worth of Government of Canada bonds from John Smith. The Bank issues a cheque to Smith, who then deposits the $100 cheque into his account at TD. This $100 is a wholly new deposit for the commercial bank, and it results in a revised balance sheet (Table 27-4). As a result of the new deposit, TD's reserve assets and deposit liabilities have both increased by $100. More important, TD's ratio of reserves to deposits has increased from 0.20 to 0.27 (300/1100). The bank now has $80 in excess reserves; with $1100 in deposits, its target reserves are only $220.

TD can now lend the $80 in excess reserves that it is holding. As it lends the $80, it increases its loan portfolio by $80 but reduces its reserves by the same amount. Table 27-5 shows TD's balance sheet after this new loan is made. Notice that TD has restored its reserve ratio to 20 percent, its target reserve ratio.

So far, of the $100 initial deposited at TD, $20 is held by TD as reserves against the deposit and $80 has been lent out in the system. As a result, other banks have received new deposits of $80 stemming from the loans made by TD; persons receiving payment from those who borrowed the $80 from TD will have deposited those payments in their own banks.

The banks that receive deposits from the proceeds of TD's loan are called second-round banks, third-round banks, and so on. In this case, the second-round banks receive new deposits of $80, and when the cheques clear, they have new reserves of $80. Because they desire to hold only $16 in additional reserves to support the new deposits, they have $64 of excess reserves. They now increase their loans by $64. After this money has been spent by the borrowers and has been deposited in other, third-round banks, the balance sheets of the second-round banks will have changed, as in Table 27-6.

The third-round banks now find themselves with $64 of new deposits. Against these they want to hold only $12.80 as reserves, so they have excess reserves of $51.20 that they can immediately lend out. Thus, there begins a long sequence of new deposits, new loans, new deposits, and new loans. These stages are shown in Table 27-7.

The new deposit of $100 to the banking system has led, through the banks' desire to lend their excess reserves, to the creation of new money. After the completion of the process depicted in Table 27-7, the total change in the combined balance sheets of the entire banking system is shown in Table 27-8.

> If v is the target reserve ratio, a new deposit to the banking system will increase the total amount of deposits by $1/v$ times the new deposit. [34]

In our example, where $v = 0.2$ and the new deposit equals $100, total deposits in the banking system will eventually increase by (1/0.2) times $100—that is, by $500. In our example in which there was an initial new deposit of $100, this $100 was also the amount by which reserves increased in the banking system as a whole. This is because the entire amount of new cash eventually ends up in reserves held against a much larger volume of new deposits. Identifying a new deposit as the change in reserves in the banking system permits us to state our central result slightly differently.

> With no cash drain from the banking system, a banking system with a target reserve ratio of v can change its deposits by $1/v$ times any change in reserves.

Recalling that the Greek letter delta (Δ) means "the change in," we can express this result in a simple equation:

$$\Delta \text{ Deposits} = \frac{\text{New cash deposits}}{v} = \frac{\Delta \text{ Reserves}}{v}$$

The "multiple expansion of deposits" that we have just described applies in reverse to a withdrawal of funds. Deposits of the banking system will fall by $1/v$ times the amount withdrawn from the banking system creating a "multiple contraction of deposits."

Excess Reserves and Cash Drains

The two simplifying assumptions that were made earlier can now be relaxed.

TABLE 27-7 The Sequence of Loans and Deposits After a Single New Deposit of $100

Bank	New Deposits	New Loans	Addition to Reserves
TD	100.00	80.00	20.00
2nd-round bank	80.00	64.00	16.00
3rd-round bank	64.00	51.20	12.80
4th-round bank	51.20	40.96	10.24
5th-round bank	40.96	32.77	8.19
6th-round bank	32.77	26.22	6.55
7th-round bank	26.22	20.98	5.24
8th-round bank	20.98	16.78	4.20
9th-round bank	16.78	13.42	3.36
10th-round bank	13.42	10.74	2.68
Total for first 10 rounds	446.33	357.07	89.26
All remaining rounds	53.67	42.93	10.74
Total for banking system	500.00	400.00	100.00

The banking system as a whole can create deposit money whenever it receives new deposits. The table shows the process of the creation of deposit money on the assumptions that all the loans made by one set of banks end up as deposits in another set of banks (the next-round banks), that the target reserve ratio (v) is 0.20, and that banks always lend out any excess reserves. With no cash drain to the public, the banking system as a whole eventually increases deposits by $1/v$, which, in this example, is five times the amount of any increase in reserves that it obtains.

TABLE 27-8 Change in the Combined Balance Sheets of All the Banks in the System Following the Multiple Expansion of Deposits

Assets ($)		Liabilities ($)	
Reserves	+100	Deposits	+500
Loans	+400		
	+500		+500

The reserve ratio is returned to 0.20. The entire initial deposit of $100 ends up as additional reserves of the banking system. Therefore, deposits rise by (1/0.2) times the initial deposit—that is, by $500.

Excess Reserves If banks do not choose to lend their excess reserves, the multiple expansion that we discussed will not occur. Go back to Table 27-4. If TD had been content to hold 27 percent of its deposits in reserves, it would have done nothing more. Other things being equal, banks will choose to lend their excess reserves because of the profit motive, but there may be times when they believe that the risk is too great. It is one thing to be offered a good rate of interest on a loan, but if the borrower defaults on the payment of interest and principal, the bank will be the loser. Similarly, if the bank expects interest rates to rise in the future, it may hold off making loans now so that it will have reserves available to make more profitable loans after the interest rate has risen.

> Deposit creation does not happen automatically; it depends on the decisions of bankers. If commercial banks do not choose to lend their excess reserves, there will not be a multiple expansion of deposits.

Recall that we have said that the money supply includes both currency and bank deposits. What we have just seen is that the behaviour of commercial banks is crucial to the process of deposit creation. It follows that the money supply is partly determined by the commercial banks—in response, for example, to changes in national income, interest rates, and expectations of future business conditions.

Cash Drain Until now, we have been assuming that the public holds a fixed amount of cash, so that when deposits were multiplying in the economy, there was no change in the amount of cash held by the public. But now suppose that instead of holding a fixed *number* of dollars, people decide to hold an amount of cash equal to a fixed *fraction* of their bank deposits. An extra $100 that now gets injected into the banking system as a new cash deposit will not all stay in the banking system. As the amount of deposits multiplies, some fraction of that $100 will be added to the cash held by the public. In such a situation, any multiple expansion of bank deposits will be accompanied by what is called a *cash drain* to the public. This cash drain will reduce the multiple expansion of bank deposits in exactly the same way that taxes and imports reduced the value of the simple multiplier in Chapter 22.

In the case of a cash drain, the relationship between the eventual change in deposits and a new injection of cash into the banking system is slightly more complicated. If new cash is injected into the system, it will ultimately show up either as reserves or as cash held by the public. If c is the ratio of cash to deposits that people want to maintain, the final change in deposits will be given by

$$\Delta \text{ Deposits} = \frac{\text{New cash deposit}}{c + v}$$

For example, suppose the Bank of Canada were to purchase $100 of government securities from some current bondholders. As the bondholders deposit their $100 into their bank accounts, there is an injection of $100 into the banking system. If commercial banks' target reserve ratio is 20 percent and there is *no* cash drain, the eventual expansion of deposits will be $500 ($\Delta$ Deposits = $100/0.20). But if there is a cash drain of 10 percent, the eventual expansion of deposits will only be $333.33 ($\Delta$ Deposits = $100/(0.10 + 0.20)). [35]

> The larger is the cash drain from the banking system, the smaller will be the total expansion of deposits created by a new cash deposit.

Realistic Expansion of Deposits So far we have explained the expansion of deposits in the banking system by using reserve-deposit and cash-deposit ratios that are easy to work with but unrealistic for Canada. In particular, we have been assuming a reserve-deposit ratio (v) equal to 20 percent, whereas Table 27-2 on page 677 shows that Canadian commercial banks hold reserves equal to *less than 1 percent* of their deposit liabilities. A realistic value for the cash-deposit ratio in Canada is roughly 5 percent—indicating that firms and households hold cash outside the banks equal to 5 percent of the value of their bank deposits. Putting these more realistic values for v and c into our equation, we see that a $100 cash injection (new deposit) to the banking system will eventually lead to a total change in deposits equal to $100/$ $(c + v) = \$100/(0.01 + 0.05) = \$100/(0.06) = \$1666.67$. Therefore, small changes in the amount of cash can lead, through the commercial banks' process of deposit creation, to very large changes in the total level of deposits. Commercial banks really do create a lot of (deposit) money out of thin air!

27.4 The Money Supply

Several times in this chapter we have mentioned the *money supply* without ever defining it precisely. But now that you are familiar with the balance sheets of the Bank of Canada and the commercial banking system, and are comfortable with the idea of deposit creation by the commercial banks, we are ready to be more precise about what we mean by the money supply.

The total stock of money in the economy at any moment is called the **money supply** or the *supply of money*. Economists use several alternative definitions for the money supply. Each definition includes the amount of currency in circulation *plus* some types of deposit liabilities of the financial institutions.

> Money supply = Currency + Bank deposits

The different definitions vary only by which deposit liabilities are included. We begin by looking at the different kinds of deposits.

money supply The total quantity of money in an economy at a point in time. Also called the *supply of money*.

Kinds of Deposits

Over the past 30 years or so, banks have evolved a bewildering array of deposit options. From our point of view, the most important distinction is between deposits that can be readily transferred by cheque, Internet banking, phone, or debit card, and those that cannot be so easily transferred. The first type of deposits are media of exchange; the second type are not.

For many years, the distinction lay between *demand deposits*, which earned little or no interest but were transferable on demand (by cheque), and *savings deposits*, which earned a higher interest return but were not easily transferable. Today, however, it is so easy to transfer funds between almost all accounts that the distinction becomes quite

term deposit An interest-earning bank deposit, subject to notice before withdrawal. Also called a *notice deposit*.

blurred. The deposit that is genuinely tied up for a period of time now takes the form of a **term deposit**, which has a specified withdrawal date a minimum of 30 days into the future, and which pays a much reduced interest rate in the event of early withdrawal. Term and other "notice" deposits pay significantly higher interest rates than do regular demand deposits.

Non-bank financial institutions, such as asset-management firms, now offer *money market mutual funds* and *money market deposit accounts*. These accounts earn higher interest and are chequable, although some are subject to minimum withdrawal restrictions and others to prior notice of withdrawal.

> The long-standing distinction between money and other highly liquid assets used to be that, narrowly defined, money was a medium of exchange that did not earn interest, whereas other liquid assets earned interest but were not media of exchange. Today, this distinction has almost completely disappeared.

Definitions of the Money Supply

M2 Currency plus demand and notice deposits at the chartered banks.

M2+ M2 plus similar deposits at other financial institutions.

Different definitions of the money supply include different types of deposits. Until recently, a common definition of the money supply used by the Bank of Canada was called M1, which included currency in circulation plus demand (chequable) deposits held at the chartered banks. But M1 did not include similar deposits at other financial institutions or any non-chequable term or notice deposits. With the changing nature of deposits, it is now more common to use broader measures of the money supply. Two commonly used measures in Canada today are M2 and M2+. **M2** includes currency in circulation plus demand and notice deposits at the chartered banks; **M2+** includes M2 plus similar deposits at other financial institutions (trust and mortgage-loan companies, credit unions and caisses populaires) and holdings of money-market mutual funds. Table 27-9 shows the composition of M2 and M2+ in Canada as of March 2012.

The Bank of Canada computes other measures of the money supply even broader than M2+. These are referred to as M2++, M3, and so on, where each measure is broader than the previous one, meaning that it includes more types of financial assets. For example, M2++ includes M2+ plus holdings of Canada Savings Bonds and non-money-market funds. In general, the broader the measure of the money supply, the more the concept of money being measured includes assets that do not serve as a direct medium of exchange but do serve the store-of-value function and can be converted into a medium of exchange.

Near Money and Money Substitutes

near money Liquid assets that are easily convertible into money without risk of significant loss of value. They can be used as short-term stores of value but are not themselves media of exchange.

Recall our early discussion of money as a medium of exchange and as a store of value. In arriving at empirical measures of money, we must consider some assets that do not perform one or both of these roles perfectly. This brings us to the concepts of *near money* and *money substitutes*.

Assets that adequately fulfill the store-of-value function and are readily converted into a medium of exchange but are not themselves a medium of exchange are sometimes called **near money**. Term deposits are a good example of near money. When you have a term deposit, you know exactly how much purchasing power you hold (at current prices), and, given modern banking practices, you can turn your deposit into a medium of exchange—cash or a demand deposit—at a moment's notice (though you may pay a penalty in the form of reduced interest if you withdraw the funds before the end of the specified term).

Why then does everybody not keep his or her money in such deposits instead of in demand deposits or currency? The answer is that the inconvenience of continually shifting money back and forth may outweigh the interest that can be earned. One week's interest on $100 (at 5 percent per year) is only about 10 cents, not enough to cover bus fare to the bank, the time spent going to an ATM, or perhaps even the time spent making an online transfer. For money that will be needed soon, it would hardly pay to shift it to a term deposit.

Things that serve as media of exchange but are not a store of value are sometimes called **money substitutes**. Credit cards are a prime example. With a credit card, many transactions can be made without either cash, a debit card, or a cheque. The credit card serves the short-run function of a medium of exchange by allowing you to make purchases, even though you have no cash or bank deposit currently in your possession. But this is only temporary; money remains the final medium of exchange for these transactions when the credit-card bill is paid.

TABLE 27-9 M2 and M2 + in Canada, March 2012 (millions of dollars)	
Currency	58 528
Demand Deposits (chequable)	
Personal	223 494
Non-personal	271 097
Notice Deposits (non-chequable)	
Personal	496 575
Non-personal	25 771
Adjustment	−3 507
M2	**1 071 958**
Deposits at:	
Trust and mortgage-loan companies	28 459
Credit unions and caisses populaires	235 328
Money-market mutual funds	32 819
Other	58 456
M2+	**1 427 020**

M2 and M2+ are two commonly used measures of the money supply in Canada. M2 includes demand (chequable) and notice (non-chequable) deposits at the chartered banks; M2+ adds similar deposits at other financial institutions. These deposits all serve the medium-of-exchange function of money. Still broader measures (like M2++ and M3) include financial assets that best serve the store-of-value function but can readily be converted into a medium of exchange.

(*Source*: Adapted from Bank of Canada, *Weekly Financial Statistics*, June 15, 2012.)

The Role of the Bank of Canada

In this chapter, we have seen that the commercial banking system, when confronted with a new deposit, can create a multiple expansion of bank deposits. This shows how the reserves of the banking system are systematically related to the money supply. In Chapter 29 we will see the details of how the Bank of Canada conducts its monetary policy and how its actions influence the total amount of reserves in the banking system. At that point we will have a more complete picture of the connection among the Bank's monetary policy, reserves in the banking system, and the overall money supply.

Recall that in the previous chapter we examined how in the long run, with real GDP equal to Y^*, the real interest rate was determined by desired saving and desired investment. In the next chapter, we return to the short-run version of our macro model (in which Y is no longer assumed to equal Y^*) but add money to that model explicitly. There we will see how the interaction of money demand and money supply determines the equilibrium interest rate in the short run. We will also see how changes in the money market lead to changes in desired aggregate expenditure and real GDP. In Chapter 29 we examine the details of the Bank of Canada's monetary policy, with an emphasis on its current policy regime of *inflation targeting*.

money substitute Something that serves as a medium of exchange but is not a store of value.

SUMMARY

27.1 The Nature of Money

LO 1

- Money is anything that serves as a medium of exchange, a store of value, and a unit of account.
- Money arose because of the inconvenience of barter, and it developed in stages: from precious metal to metal coinage, to paper money convertible to precious metals, to token coinage and paper money fractionally backed by precious metals, to fiat money, and to deposit money.

27.2 The Canadian Banking System

LO 2

- The banking system in Canada consists of two main elements: the Bank of Canada (the central bank) and the commercial banks.
- The Bank of Canada is a government-owned corporation that is responsible for the day-to-day conduct of monetary policy. Though the Bank has considerable autonomy in its policy decisions, ultimate responsibility for monetary policy resides with the government.
- Commercial banks and other financial institutions play a key role as intermediaries in the credit market.

Significant interruptions in the flow of credit usually lead to increases in interest rates and reductions in the level of economic activity.

- Commercial banks are profit-seeking institutions that allow their customers to transfer deposits from one bank to another by means of cheques or electronic transfer. They create deposit money as a byproduct of their commercial operations of making loans and other investments.

27.3 Money Creation by the Banking System

LO 3

- Because most customers are content to pay by cheque or debit card rather than with cash, banks need only small reserves to back their deposit liabilities. It is this *fractional-reserve aspect* of the banking system that enables commercial banks to create deposit money.
- When the banking system receives a new cash deposit, it can create new deposits equal to some multiple of this amount. For a target reserve ratio of v and a cash-deposit ratio of c, the total change in deposits following a new cash deposit is

$$\Delta \text{ Deposits} = \frac{\text{New cash deposit}}{c + v}$$

27.4 The Money Supply

LO 4

- The money supply—the stock of money in an economy at a specific moment—can be defined in various ways. M2 includes currency plus demand and notice deposits at the chartered banks. M2+ includes M2 plus deposits at non-bank financial institutions and money-market mutual funds.

- Near money includes interest-earning assets that are convertible into money on a dollar-for-dollar basis but that are not currently a medium of exchange. Money substitutes are things such as credit cards that serve as a medium of exchange but are not money.

KEY CONCEPTS

Medium of exchange, store of value, and unit of account
Fully backed, fractionally backed, and fiat money

The banking system and the Bank of Canada
Target reserve ratio and excess reserves

The creation of deposit money
Demand and term deposits
The money supply
Near money and money substitutes

STUDY EXERCISES

MyEconLab   Make the grade with MyEconLab: Study Exercises marked in red can be found on MyEconLab. You can practise them as often as you want, and most feature step-by-step guided instructions to help you find the right answer.

1. Fill in the blanks to make the following statements correct.

   a. Money serves three functions: _____, _____, and _____.

   b. Suppose children at a summer camp are each given a credit of $20 at the snack shop, where purchases are recorded but no cash is exchanged. This is an example of money as a(n) _____ and a(n) _____.

   c. Paper money and coins that are not convertible into anything with intrinsic value, but are declared by the government to be legal tender, are known as _____.

   d. The Bank of Canada has four main functions in the Canadian economy:
      - _____
      - _____
      - _____
      - _____

   e. Canada has a(n) _____ reserve banking system, in which commercial banks keep only a fraction of their total deposits in reserves. A commercial bank has a(n) _____ ratio that governs what it attempts to keep as reserves.

2. Fill in the blanks to make the following statements correct. Answer these questions in the sequence given.

   a. Suppose the Bank of Canada purchases a $1000 bond from Bob's Financial Firm, and Bob's deposits its cheque at the CIBC. This is a(n) _____ deposit to the banking system and will allow the commercial banks to _____.

   b. Continuing on from part (a), if the CIBC has a target reserve ratio of 5 percent, it will keep _____ dollars as reserves and will lend _____ dollars.

   c. Assuming there is no cash drain from the banking system, the ultimate effect is a(n) _____ in deposits in the banking system of _____ × $1000 = _____.

   d. Suppose the Bank of Canada sells a $1000 bond to Bob's Financial Firm, and Bob's pays for that bond with a cheque drawn on its account at the CIBC. This is a(n) _____ of funds from the banking

system and will cause the commercial banks to _____.

   e. If the CIBC pays the $1000 from its reserves, its reserve ratio will then be _____ its target rate of 5 percent. If the CIBC keeps its reserves at the new level, its loans must fall by _____ to restore the 5-percent target reserve ratio.

3. Which of the following items can be considered money in the Canadian economy? Explain your answers by discussing the three functions of money—medium of exchange, store of value, and unit of account.

   a. A Canadian $100 bill
   b. A Visa credit card
   c. A well-known painting by Robert Bateman
   d. The balance in an interest-earning savings account
   e. A US Treasury bill payable in three months
   f. A share of Tim Hortons stock
   g. A $1 bill of Canadian Tire money

4. The table below shows the balance sheet for the Regal Bank, a hypothetical commercial bank. Assume that the Regal Bank has achieved its target reserve ratio.

Balance Sheet: Regal Bank			
Assets		Liabilities	
Reserves	$ 200	Deposits	$4000
Loans	$4200	Capital	$ 400

   a. What is the Regal Bank's target reserve ratio?
   b. What is the value of the owners' investment in the bank?
   c. Suppose someone makes a new deposit to the Regal Bank of $100. Draw a new balance sheet showing the *immediate* effect of the new deposit. What is the Regal Bank's new reserve ratio?
   d. Suppose instead that someone *withdraws* $100 cash from the Regal Bank. Show the new balance sheet and the new reserve ratio.

5. Consider a new deposit to the Canadian banking system of $1000. Suppose that all commercial banks have a target reserve ratio of 10 percent and there is no cash drain. The following table shows how deposits,

reserves, and loans change as the new deposit permits the banks to "create" money.

Round	Δ Deposits	Δ Reserves	Δ Loans
First	$1000	$100	$900
Second	——	——	——
Third	——	——	——
Fourth	——	——	——
Fifth	——	——	——

a. The first round has been completed in the table. Now, recalling that the new loans in the first round become the new deposits in the second round, complete the second round in the table.

b. By using the same approach, complete the entire table.

c. You have now completed the first five rounds of the deposit-creation process. What is the total change in deposits *so far* as a result of the single new deposit of $1000?

d. This deposit-creation process could go on forever, but it would still have a *finite* sum. In the text, we showed that the eventual total change in deposits is equal to $1/v$ times the new deposit, where v is the target reserve ratio. What is the eventual total change in deposits in this case?

e. What is the eventual total change in reserves? What is the eventual change in loans?

6. Consider a withdrawal of $5000 from the Canadian banking system. Suppose all commercial banks have a target reserve ratio of 8 percent and there is no cash drain.

a. Using a table like that shown in the previous question, show the change in deposits, reserves, and loans for the first three "rounds" of activity.

b. Compute the eventual total change in deposits, reserves, and loans.

7. Consider an individual who immigrates to Canada and deposits $3000 in Canadian currency into the Canadian banking system. Suppose all commercial banks have a target reserve ratio of 10 percent and individuals choose to hold cash equal to 10 percent of their bank deposits.

a. In the text, we showed that the eventual total change in deposits is equal to $1/(v + c)$ times the new deposit, where v is the target reserve ratio and c is the ratio of cash to deposits. What is the eventual total change in deposits in this case?

b. What is the eventual total change in reserves?

c. What is the eventual total change in loans?

8. Consider an individual who moves to Canada and brings with him $40 000 in Canadian currency, which he deposits in a Canadian bank. For each of the cases below, compute the overall change in deposits and

reserves in the Canadian banking system as a result of this new deposit.

a. 10 percent target reserve ratio, no cash drain, no excess reserves

b. 10 percent target reserve ratio, 5 percent cash drain, no excess reserves

c. 10 percent target reserve ratio, 5 percent cash drain, 5 percent excess reserves

9. This question is intended to illustrate the similarity between the simple income-expenditure multiplier from Chapters 21 and 22 and the deposit multiplier that we examined in this chapter.

a. Recalling the macro model of Chapters 21 and 22, suppose the marginal propensity to spend out of GDP, z, is 0.6. If autonomous spending increases by $1000, fill in the table below.

Round	Δ AE	Δ Y
First	$1000	$1000
Second	——	——
Third	——	——
Fourth	——	——
Fifth	——	——

b. The sum of the values in the third column should be

$$\Delta Y = \$1000 + z\,\$1000 + z^2\,\$1000 + z^3\,\$1000 + \ldots$$

What is the total change in GDP?

c. Now consider the process of deposit creation from this chapter. Consider a new deposit of $1000 and a target reserve ratio, v, of 0.25 (with no cash drain). Fill in the following table:

Round	Δ Deposits	Δ Reserves	Δ Loans
First	$1000	$250	$750
Second	——	——	——
Third	——	——	——
Fourth	——	——	——
Fifth	——	——	——

d. The sum of the values in the first column should be

$$\Delta \text{Deposits} = \$1000 + (1 - v)\$1000 + (1 - v)^2\,\$1000 + (1 - v)^3\,\$1000 + \ldots$$

What is the total change in deposits?

e. Explain why taxes and imports for the simple multiplier in Chapter 21 are similar to a reserve ratio for the deposit multiplier in this chapter.

10. Suppose that on January 1, 2011, a household had $300 000, which it wanted to hold for use one year later. Calculate, by using resources available online or in your university library, which of the following

would have been the best store of value over that period. Will the best store of value over that period necessarily be the best over the next 24 months?

a. The (Canadian) dollar
b. Stocks whose prices moved with the Toronto Stock Exchange (S&P/TSX) index
c. A Government of Canada 5.75 percent bond coming due in 2029
d. Gold

e. A house whose value changed with the average house price in Canada

11. During the 2008 global financial crisis, the governor of the Bank of Canada expressed concern that the commercial banks were "hoarding" cash rather than extending a more appropriate volume of loans. Why might the banks do this, and what is the implication for the money supply?

Money, Interest Rates, and Economic Activity

IN Chapter 27, we learned how the commercial banking system multiplies a given amount of reserves into deposit money and thus influences the nation's money supply. We also learned that because the Bank of Canada can set the amount of commercial-bank reserves, it too has an influence on the money supply. What we have not yet discussed, however, is *how* the Bank influences the amount of reserves. We will leave that discussion until the next chapter, when we examine Canadian monetary policy. For now, just think of the nation's money supply as being determined jointly by the actions of the Bank of Canada and the commercial banking system.

In this chapter, we develop a theory to explain how money affects the economy. Understanding the role of money, however, requires an understanding of the interaction of money supply and money demand. To examine the nature of money demand, we begin by examining how households decide to divide their total holdings of assets between money and interest-earning assets (which here are called "bonds"). Once that is done, we put money supply and money demand together to examine *monetary equilibrium*. Only then can we ask how changes in the supply of money or in the demand for money affect the economy in the short term—interest rates, real GDP, and the price level. We begin with a discussion of the relationship between bond prices and interest rates.

| 28.1 Understanding Bonds

At any moment, households have a stock of financial wealth that they hold in several forms. Some of it is money in the bank or in the wallet. Some may be in *Treasury bills* and *bonds*, which are IOUs issued by the government or corporations. Some may be in *equity*, meaning ownership shares of a company.

To simplify our discussion, we will group financial wealth into just two categories, which we call "money" and "bonds." By money we mean all assets that serve as a medium of exchange—that is, paper money, coins, and bank deposits that can be transferred on demand by cheque or electronic means. By bonds we mean all other forms of financial wealth; this includes interest-earning financial assets and claims on real capital (equity). This simplification is useful because it emphasizes the important distinction between interest-earning and non–interest-earning assets, a distinction that is central for understanding the demand for money.

Before discussing how individuals decide to divide their assets between money and bonds, we need to make sure we understand what bonds are and how they are priced. This requires an understanding of *present value*.

Economists often simplify the analysis of financial assets by considering only two types of assets— non–interest-bearing "money" and interest-bearing "bonds."

Present Value and the Interest Rate

A bond is a financial asset that promises to make one or more specified payments at specified dates in the future. The **present value** (*PV*) of any asset refers to the value now of the future payments that the asset offers. Present value depends on the market interest rate because when we calculate present value, the interest rate is used to *discount* the value of the future payments to obtain their *present* value. Let's consider two examples to illustrate the concept of present value.

present value (PV) The value now of one or more payments or receipts made in the future, often referred to as *discounted present value*.

A Single Payment One Year Hence We start with the simplest case. What is the value *now* of a bond that will return a single payment of $100 in one year's time?

Suppose the market interest rate is 5 percent. Now ask how much you would have to lend out at that interest rate today in order to have $100 a year from now. If we use *PV* to stand for this unknown amount, we can write $PV \times (1.05) = \$100$. Thus, $PV = \$100/1.05 = \$95.24$.[1] This tells us that the present value of $100 receivable in one year's time is $95.24; if you lend out $95.24 for one year at 5 percent interest you will get back the original $95.24 that you lent (the principal) plus $4.76 in interest, which makes $100.

We can generalize this relationship with a simple equation. If R_1 is the amount we receive one year from now and i is the annual interest rate, the present value of R_1 is

$$PV = \frac{R_1}{1 + i}$$

If the interest rate is 7 percent ($i = 0.07$) and the bond pays $100 in one year ($R_1 = \$100$), the present value of that bond is $PV = \$100/1.07 = \$93.46$. Notice

---

[1] Notice that in this type of formula, the interest rate is expressed as a decimal fraction where, for example, 5 percent is expressed as 0.05, so $1 + i = 1.05$.

that, when compared with the previous numerical example, the higher market interest rate leads to a lower present value. The future payment of $100 gets discounted at a higher rate and so is worth less at the present time.

A Sequence of Future Payments Now consider a more complicated case, but one that is actually more typical. Many bonds promise to make "coupon" payments every year and then return the face value of the bond at the end of the term of the loan. For example, imagine a three-year bond that promises to repay the face value of $1000 in three years, but will also pay a 10 percent coupon payment of $100 at the end of each of the three years that the bond is held. How much is this bond worth now? We can compute the present value of this bond by adding together the present values of each of the payments. If the market interest rate is 7 percent, the present value of this bond is

$$PV = \frac{\$100}{1.07} + \frac{\$100}{(1.07)^2} + \frac{\$1100}{(1.07)^3}$$

The first term is the value today of receiving $100 one year from now. The second term is the value today of receiving the second $100 payment two years from now. Note that we discount this second payment twice—once from Year 2 to Year 1, and once again from Year 1 to now—and thus the denominator shows an interest rate of 7 percent *compounded* for two years. Finally, the third term shows the value today of the $1100 repayment ($1000 of face value plus $100 of coupon payment) three years from now. The present value of this bond is

$$PV = \$93.46 + \$87.34 + \$897.93$$
$$= \$1078.73$$

In general, any asset that promises to make a sequence of payments for T periods into the future of $R_1, R_2, \ldots$, and so on, up to R_T has a present value given by

$$PV = \frac{R_1}{1 + i} + \frac{R_2}{(1 + i)^2} + \cdots + \frac{R_T}{(1 + i)^T}$$

It is useful to try another example. Let's continue with the case in which the bond repays its face value of $1000 three years from now and makes three $100 coupon payments at the end of each year the bond is held. But this time we assume the market interest rate is 9 percent. In this case, the present value of the bond is

$$PV = \frac{\$100}{1.09} + \frac{\$100}{(1.09)^2} + \frac{\$1100}{(1.09)^3}$$
$$= \$91.74 + \$84.17 + \$849.40$$
$$= \$1025.31$$

Notice that when the market interest rate is 9 percent, the present value of the bond is lower than the present value of the same bond when the market interest rate is 7 percent. The higher interest rate implies that any future payments are discounted at a higher rate and thus have a lower present value.

A General Relationship There are many types of bonds. Some make no coupon payments and only a single payment (the "face value") at some point in the future. This is the case for short-term government bonds called *Treasury bills*. Other bonds, typically longer-term government or corporate bonds, make regular coupon payments as well as a final payment of the bond's face value. Though there are many types of bonds, they all have one thing in common: They promise to make some payment or sequence of payments in the future. Because bonds make payments in the future, their present value is negatively related to the market interest rate.

> The present value of any bond that promises a future payment or sequence of future payments is negatively related to the market interest rate.

Present Value and Market Price

Most bonds are bought and sold in financial markets in which there are large numbers of both buyers and sellers. The present value of a bond is important because it establishes the price at which a bond will be exchanged in the financial markets.

> The present value of a bond is the most someone would be willing to pay now to own the bond's future stream of payments.[2]

To understand this concept, let us return to our example of a bond that promises to pay $100 one year from now. When the interest rate is 5 percent, the present value of this bond is $95.24. To see why this is the maximum that anyone would pay for this bond, suppose that some sellers offer to sell the bond at some other price, say, $98. If, instead of paying this amount for the bond, a potential buyer lends $98 out at 5 percent interest, he or she would have at the end of one year more than the $100 that the bond will produce. (At 5 percent interest, $98 yields $4.90 in interest, which when added to the principal makes $102.90.) Clearly, no well-informed individual would pay $98—or, by the same reasoning, any sum in excess of $95.24—for the bond. Thus, at any price above the bond's present value, the lack of demand will cause the price to fall.

Now suppose the bond is offered for sale at a price less than $95.24, say, $90. A potential buyer could borrow $90 to buy the bond and would pay $4.50 in interest on the loan. At the end of the year, the bond yields $100. When this is used to repay the $90 loan and the $4.50 in interest, $5.50 is left as profit. Clearly, it would be worthwhile for someone to buy the bond at the price of $90 or, by the same argument, at any price less than $95.24. Thus, at any price below the bond's present value, the abundance of demand will cause the price to rise.

This discussion should make clear that the present value of an asset determines its equilibrium market price. If the market price of any asset is greater than the present value of its income stream, no one will want to buy it, and the resulting excess supply will push down the market price. If the market price is below its present value, there will be a rush to buy it, and the resulting excess demand will push up the market price. When the bond's market price is exactly equal to its present value, there is no pressure for the price to change.

---

[2] We ignore for now the possibility that the issuer of the bond will *default* and thereby fail to make some or all of the future payments. If such a risk does exist, it will reduce the *expected* present value of the bond and thus reduce the price that buyers will be prepared to pay. We address bond riskiness shortly.

> The equilibrium market price of any bond is the present value of the income stream that it produces.

Interest Rates, Bond Prices, and Bond Yields

We now have two relationships that can be put together to tell us about the link between the market interest rate and bond prices. Let's restate these two relationships.

1. The present value of any given bond is negatively related to the market interest rate.
2. A bond's equilibrium market price will be equal to its present value.

Putting these two relationships together, we come to a key relationship:

> An increase in the market interest rate leads to a fall in the price of any given bond. A decrease in the market interest rate leads to an increase in the price of any given bond.

Remember that a bond is a financial investment for the purchaser. The cost of the investment is the price of the bond, and the return on the investment is the sequence of future payments. Thus, for a given sequence of future payments, a lower bond price implies a higher rate of return on the bond, or a higher *bond yield*.

To illustrate the yield on a bond, consider a simple example of a bond that promises to pay $1000 two years from now. If you purchase this bond for $857.34, your return on your investment will be 8 percent per year because $857.34 compounded for two years at 8 percent will yield $1000 in two years.

$$\$857.34 \times (1.08)^2 = \$1000$$

In other words, your yield on the bond will be 8 percent per year.

Notice that we are making a distinction between the concept of the *yield* on a bond and the *market interest rate*. The bond yield is a function of the sequence of payments and the bond price. The market interest rate is the rate at which you can borrow or lend money in the credit market.

Although they are logically distinct from each other, there is a close relationship between the market interest rate and bond yields. A rise in the market interest rate will lead to a decline in the present value of any bond and thus to a decline in its equilibrium price. As the bond price falls, its yield naturally rises. Thus, we see that market interest rates and bond yields tend to move in the same direction.

> An increase in the market interest rate will reduce bond prices and increase bond yields. A reduction in the market interest rate will increase bond prices and reduce bond yields. Therefore, market interest rates and bond yields tend to move together.

Because of this close relationship between bond yields and market interest rates, economists discussing the role of money in the macroeconomy typically refer to "the" interest rate—or perhaps to "interest rates" in general—rather than to any specific interest rate among the many different rates corresponding to the many different financial assets. Since these rates all tend to rise or fall together, it is a very useful simplification to refer only to "the" interest rate, meaning the rate of return that can be earned by holding interest-earning assets rather than money.

Bond Riskiness

We have been discussing present values and bond prices under the assumption that the bond is *risk free*—that is, that the coupon payments and the repayment of principal are absolutely certain. In reality, however, there is some chance that bond issuers will be unable to make some or all of these payments. In the face of this possibility, purchasers of bonds reduce the price they are prepared to pay by an amount that reflects the likelihood of non-repayment.

Beginning in early 2010, very high levels of Greek government debt led many to expect the government to default on some or all of its bonds. This fear led to a sharp fall in Greek bond prices and thus a sharp increase in bond yields.

It follows that not all changes in bond yields are caused by changes in market interest rates. Sometimes the yields on specific bonds change because of a change in their perceived *riskiness*. For example, if some event increases the likelihood that a specific corporate bond issuer will soon go bankrupt, bond purchasers will revise downward the *expected* present value of the issuer's bonds. As a result, the demand for the bond will fall and its equilibrium price will decline. As the price falls, the bond's yield will rise—the higher bond yield now reflecting the greater riskiness of the bond.

An increase in the riskiness of any bond leads to a decline in its *expected* present value and thus to a decline in the bond's price. The lower bond price implies a higher bond yield.

It is rare in Canada that government bonds are perceived as risky, but in recent years some bonds issued by some southern European countries have been viewed as high-risk assets, and this riskiness has been reflected in high bond yields. In general, however, since governments have the power to collect revenue through taxation, it is unusual for a government bond to be viewed as a risky asset. More usual at any given time is specific corporations that are believed to be in precarious financial situations and thus their bonds are perceived to be risky assets. As a result, there are often very high yields (low bond prices) on specific corporate bonds. *Applying Economic Concepts 28-1* discusses the relationship among bond prices, bond yields, riskiness, and *term to maturity* of government and corporate bonds.

28.2 The Theory of Money Demand

Our discussion of bonds, bond prices, and interest rates leads us to a theory that explains how individuals allocate their current stock of financial wealth between "bonds" and "money." An individual's decision to hold more bonds is at the same time a decision to hold less money, and the decision to hold fewer bonds is a decision to hold more money.

APPLYING ECONOMIC CONCEPTS 28-1

Understanding Bond Prices and Bond Yields

Various kinds of bonds are traded every day, and they differ in terms of the issuer, price, yield, riskiness, and term to maturity. We focus here on how to understand these bond characteristics.

How to Read the Bond Tables

The accompanying table shows seven bond listings just as they appeared on www.globeinvestor.com on June 22, 2012. The five columns are as follows:

1. **Issuer.** This is the issuer of the bond—that is, the borrower of the money. The first five bonds shown are issued by the Government of Canada. The last two are issued by large private-sector firms.

2. **Coupon.** This is the coupon rate—the annual rate of interest that the bond pays before it matures. For example, a 6 percent coupon rate means that the bondholder (the lender) will receive 6 percent of the face value of the bond every year until the bond matures.

3. **Maturity.** This is when the bond matures and the face value is repaid to the bondholder. All debt obligations are then fulfilled.

4. **Price.** This is the market price of the bond (on June 22, 2012), expressed as the price per $100 of face value. For example, a price of $103.93 means that for every $100 of face value, the purchaser must pay $103.93. When the price is greater than $100, we say there is a *premium*; when the price is less than $100, we say the bond is selling at a *discount*.

5. **Yield.** This is the rate of return earned by the bondholder if the bond is bought at the *current* price and held to maturity, earning all regular coupon payments.

Issuer	Coupon (%)	Maturity	Price ($)	Yield (%)
1. Canada	5.25	June 1, 2013	103.93	1.01
2. Canada	2.50	Sept 1, 2013	101.73	1.03
3. Canada	4.00	June 1, 2016	110.62	1.22
4. Canada	9.75	June 1, 2021	167.57	1.60
5. Canada	8.00	June 1, 2027	175.92	2.06
6. Gaz Metro	5.45	July 12, 2021	120.06	2.91
7. Bell Canada	8.88	April 17, 2026	135.52	5.48

Bond Prices and Yields

Three general patterns can be seen in the table. First, for a given issuer and maturity, there is a positive relationship between the bond price and the coupon rate. Rows 1 and 2,

for example, show two bonds, both issued by the Government of Canada and maturing at (almost) the same date in 2013. The common issuer suggests a common risk of non-repayment (in this case a very low risk). The first bond has a 5.25 percent coupon whereas the second has a 2.50 percent coupon. Not surprisingly, the higher coupon payments make the first bond a more attractive asset and thus its market price is higher—$103.93 as compared with $101.73. Note, however, that the implied yield on the two bonds is almost identical. If this weren't the case, demand would shift toward the high-yield (low-price) bond, driving down the yield (increasing the price) until the two yields were the same.

Second, for a given bond issuer, there is a positive relationship between the bond yield and the term to maturity. This is shown in the first five rows, as yields rise from just over 1 percent on bonds maturing in one year's time (from the date of the listing) to 2.06 percent on bonds maturing in 15 years' time. This positive relationship is often referred to as the *yield curve* or the *term structure of interest rates*. The higher yields on longer-term bonds reflect what is often called a *term premium*—the higher yield that bondholders must be paid in order to induce them to have their money tied up for longer periods of time.

Third, for a given term to maturity, there is a positive relationship between the bond yield and the perceived riskiness of the bond issuer. Compare rows 4 and 6, for example. Both bonds have almost identical maturity dates in 2021, but one is issued by the Government of Canada while the other is issued by Gaz Metro Inc. Though it is almost impossible for the Government of Canada to go bankrupt and almost inconceivable that it would default on its debt, it is certainly possible for Gaz Metro to do so. This difference explains the difference in yields. The same is true between rows 5 and 7, where the more than three-percentage-point yield difference is attributable to the higher likelihood of default by Bell Canada than by the Canadian government.

If you run your eyes down the bond tables, you will easily see those corporations viewed by the market as being risky borrowers because the yields on their bonds will be higher—often dramatically so—than the yields on similar-maturity government bonds. For example, in the summer of 2012, when some European banks were experiencing great difficulty, the bonds issued by the Royal Bank of Scotland were selling at such a discount that the implied annual yield was more than 20 percent. Such high yields represent a great investment opportunity only if you are prepared to take the associated risk. Beware!

We can therefore build our theory by considering the desire to hold bonds or by considering the desire to hold money. We follow the tradition among economists by focusing on the desire to hold money. The amount of money that everyone (collectively) wants to hold at any time is called the **demand for money**.

demand for money The total amount of money balances that the public wants to hold for all purposes.

Three Reasons for Holding Money

Why do firms and households hold money? Our theory offers three reasons. First, households and firms hold money in order to carry out transactions. Economists call this the *transactions demand* for money. You carry money in your pocket or keep it in a chequing account in order to have it readily available for your upcoming transactions; it would be very inconvenient to have to sell bonds or withdraw money from your GIC (guaranteed investment certificate) every time you wanted to spend. Similarly, firms are continually making expenditures on intermediate inputs and payments to labour, and they keep money available in their chequing accounts to pay these expenses.

A second and related reason firms and households hold money is that they are uncertain about when some expenditures will be necessary, and they hold money as a precaution to avoid the problems associated with missing a transaction. This is referred to as the *precautionary demand* for money. For example, you might hold some cash because of the possibility that you might need to take an unplanned taxi ride during a rainstorm; a small business may hold cash because of the possibility that it might need the emergency services of a tradesperson, such as a plumber or an electrician. In the days before the invention of ATMs, the precautionary demand for money was quite large, since to be caught on a weekend or away from home without sufficient cash could be a serious matter. Today, this motive for holding money is less important.

The third assumed reason for holding money applies more to large businesses and to professional money managers than to individuals because it involves *speculating* about how interest rates are likely to change in the future. Economists call this the *speculative demand* for money. To understand this reason for holding money, recall what we said earlier about the negative relationship between market interest rates and bond prices. If interest rates are expected to rise in the future, bond prices will be expected to fall. Whenever bond prices fall, bondholders experience a decline in the value of their bond holdings. The expectation of increases in *future* interest rates will therefore lead to the holding of more money (and fewer bonds) *now* as financial managers adjust their portfolios in order to preserve their values.

A related motive for holding money relates to *uncertainty*. Commercial banks that are uncertain about their borrowers' ability to repay loans, or about the riskiness of potential new borrowers, may decide to sacrifice an uncertain rate of return for the safety that comes from holding more cash reserves than normal. Other firms that regularly borrow to finance their operations may choose to hold large cash balances if they are uncertain about whether they will continue to have sufficient access to credit. Both of these reasons for holding large cash balances were evident in the immediate aftermath of the 2008 global financial crisis and recession, and continue today during a slow economic recovery.

The Determinants of Money Demand

We have just seen several reasons why firms and households hold money. We now want to examine which key macroeconomic variables affect the *amount* of money that is demanded in our macro model. We focus on three: the interest rate, the level of real GDP, and the price level.

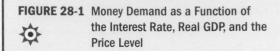

FIGURE 28-1   Money Demand as a Function of the Interest Rate, Real GDP, and the Price Level

The quantity of money demanded is assumed to be negatively related to the interest rate and positively related to real GDP and the price level. The negative slope of the M_D curve comes from the choice between holding money and holding bonds. A fall in the interest rate from i_1 to i_0 reduces the opportunity cost of holding money because the rate of return on bonds declines. Thus, the decision to hold more money (the movement from A to B as the interest rate falls) is the "flip side" of the decision to hold fewer bonds.

We show the initial money demand curve as M_D (Y, P), indicating that the curve is drawn for given values of Y and P. Increases in Y or P shift the M_D curve to the right; decreases in Y or P shift the M_D curve to the left.

The Interest Rate No matter what benefits households or firms receive from holding money, there is also a cost. The cost of holding money is the income that *could have been earned* if that wealth were instead held in the form of interest-earning bonds. This is the *opportunity cost* of holding money. In our macro model, we assume that an increase in the interest rate leads firms and households to reduce their desired money holdings. Conversely, a reduction in the interest rate means that holding money is less costly, and so firms and households are assumed to increase their desired money holdings.

> Other things being equal, the demand for money is assumed to be negatively related to the interest rate.[3]

This negative relationship between interest rates and desired money holdings is shown in Figure 28-1 and is drawn as the money demand (M_D) curve. Remember that the decision to hold money is also the decision *not* to hold bonds, and so movements along the M_D curve imply the substitution of assets between money and bonds. For example, as interest rates decline, bonds become a less attractive asset and money becomes more attractive, so firms and households substitute away from bonds and toward money.

Real GDP As we said earlier, an important reason for holding money is to make transactions. Not surprisingly, the number of transactions that firms and households want to make is positively related to the level of income and production in the economy—that is, to the level of real GDP. This positive relationship between real GDP and desired money holdings is shown in Figure 28-1 by a rightward shift of the M_D curve to M'_D. At any given interest rate, an increase in Y is assumed to generate more transactions and thus greater desired money holdings.

> Other things being equal, the demand for money is assumed to be positively related to real GDP.

The Price Level An increase in the price level leads to an increase in the *dollar* value of transactions even if there is no change in the *real* value of transactions. That is, as P rises, households and firms will need to hold more money in order to carry out an

---

[3] The opportunity cost of holding money is the interest that could have been earned on bonds—this is the *nominal* interest rate. In the presence of expected inflation, we must distinguish between the *nominal* and *real* interest rates. In this chapter we assume, however, that expected inflation is zero, and so we simply speak of "the" interest rate. We discuss inflation in detail in Chapter 30.

unchanged real value of transactions. This positive relationship between the price level and desired money holdings is also shown in Figure 28-1 as a rightward shift of the M_D curve to M'_D.

> **Other things being equal, the demand for money is assumed to be positively related to the price level.**

We can be more precise than just saying that there is a positive relationship between P and desired money holdings. Suppose, for example, that Y and i are constant but that all prices in the economy increase by 10 percent. Since Y is unchanged, the *real* value of desired transactions should also be unchanged. Furthermore, since i is unchanged, the opportunity cost of holding money is constant. Therefore, in order to make the same transactions as before, households and firms must not just hold more money than before—they must hold precisely 10 percent more. In other words, we assume that if real GDP and the interest rate are constant, the demand for money is *proportional* to the price level.

Money Demand: Summing Up

We have discussed the theory of why firms and households hold money, and we have examined the relationship between desired money holding and three macroeconomic variables. Since the demand for money reflects firms' and households' preference to hold wealth in the form of a *liquid* asset (money) rather than a less liquid asset (bonds), economists sometimes refer to the money demand function as a *liquidity preference function*. We can summarize our assumptions regarding money demand with the following algebraic statement:

$$M_D = M_D(\overset{-}{i}, \overset{+}{Y}, \overset{+}{P})$$

This equation says that the amount of money firms and households want to hold at any given time depends on (is a function of) three variables; the sign above each variable indicates whether that variable positively or negatively affects desired money holding. Our central assumptions are as follows:

1. An increase in the interest rate increases the opportunity cost of holding money and leads to a reduction in the quantity of money demanded.

2. An increase in real GDP increases the volume of transactions and leads to an increase in the quantity of money demanded.

3. An increase in the price level increases the dollar value of a given volume of transactions and leads to an increase in the quantity of money demanded.

Remember that money demand is also related to bond demand. Firms and households must decide at any time how to divide their financial assets between money and bonds. Therefore, our statements here about money demand apply in reverse to the demand for bonds. For example, in Figure 28-1, a movement down the M_D curve from point A to point B indicates that firms and households are deciding to hold more money and fewer bonds as the interest rate falls. In other words, the movement from A to B involves a substitution away from holding bonds and toward holding money.

28.3 Monetary Equilibrium and National Income

So far, this chapter has been devoted to understanding bonds and how they relate to the demand for money. In the previous chapter we examined the supply of money. We are now ready to put these two sides of the money market together to develop a theory of how interest rates are determined in the short run. You may recall, however, that we already developed in Chapter 26 a theory of how interest rates are determined. But remember that Chapter 26 was a discussion of long-run economic growth, and real GDP was assumed to be equal to Y^* throughout that discussion. What we do in this chapter and the next is return to the short-run version of our macro model but make it more complete by adding money and interest rates explicitly. We will see how changes in the money market can cause real GDP and interest rates to diverge for short periods of time from their long-run values.

We begin by examining the concept of *monetary equilibrium*—the theory of how interest rates are determined in the short run by the interaction of money demand and money supply. We then explore what economists call the *monetary transmission mechanism*—the chain of events that takes us from changes in the interest rate, through to changes in desired aggregate expenditure, to changes in the level of real GDP and the price level.

Monetary Equilibrium

Figure 28-2 illustrates the money market. The money supply (M_S) curve is vertical, indicating that it is assumed to be independent of the interest rate. The money supply increases (M_S shifts to the right) if the central bank increases reserves in the banking system or if the commercial banks decide to lend out a larger fraction of those reserves. The money supply decreases (M_S shifts to the left) if the central bank decreases reserves in the banking system or if the commercial banks decide to reduce lending. The money demand (M_D) curve is downward sloping, indicating that firms and households decide to hold more money (and fewer bonds) when the interest rate falls.

monetary equilibrium The situation in which the quantity of money demanded equals the quantity of money supplied.

Monetary equilibrium occurs when the quantity of money demanded equals the quantity of money supplied. In Chapter 3, we saw that in a competitive market for some commodity, the price will adjust to establish equilibrium. In the market for money, the interest rate is that "price" that adjusts to bring about equilibrium. Let's see how this equilibrium is achieved.

When a single household or firm finds that it is holding a smaller fraction of its wealth in money than it wants, it can sell some bonds and add the cash proceeds to its money holdings. Such behaviour by an individual firm or a household will have a negligible effect on the economy.

But what happens when *all* the firms and households try to add to their money balances? They all try to sell bonds to obtain the extra money they desire. But what one person can do in this case, all persons cannot do simultaneously. At any moment, the economy's total supply of money and bonds is fixed. Thus, as everyone tries to sell bonds, an excess supply of bonds develops. But since people are simply trying to switch between a given amount of bonds and money, the excess supply of bonds implies an excess demand for money, as shown at interest rate i_1 in Figure 28-2.

What happens when there is an excess supply of bonds? Like any other good or service, an excess supply causes a fall in the market price. As we saw earlier in the chapter, a fall in the price of bonds implies an increase in the interest rate. As the interest rate rises, people economize on money balances because the opportunity cost of holding such balances is rising. Eventually, the interest rate will rise enough that people will no longer be trying to add to their money balances by selling bonds. At that point, there is no longer an excess supply of bonds (or an excess demand for money), and the interest rate will stop rising. The monetary equilibrium will have been achieved, as at point E in Figure 28-2.

Suppose now there is more money than firms and households want to hold. That is, there is an excess supply of money, as at interest rate i_2 in Figure 28-2. The excess supply of money implies an excess demand for bonds—people are trying to "get rid of" their excess money balances by acquiring bonds. But when all households try to buy bonds, they bid up the price of bonds, and the interest rate falls. As the interest rate falls, households and firms become willing to hold larger quantities of money. The interest rate falls until firms and households stop trying to convert bonds into money. In other words, it continues until everyone is content to hold the existing supply of money and bonds, as at point E in Figure 28-2.

> **Monetary equilibrium occurs when the interest rate is such that the quantity of money demanded equals the quantity of money supplied.**

The theory of interest-rate determination depicted in Figure 28-2 is often called the *liquidity preference theory of interest*. This name reflects the fact that when there are only two financial assets, a demand to hold money (rather than bonds) is a demand for the more liquid of the two assets—a preference for liquidity. The theory determines how the interest rate fluctuates in the short term as people seek to achieve *portfolio balance*, given fixed supplies of both money and bonds.

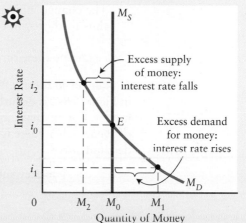

FIGURE 28-2 Monetary Equilibrium

The interest rate rises when there is an excess demand for money and falls when there is an excess supply of money. The fixed quantity of money M_0 is shown by the vertical supply curve M_S. The money supply is determined by the behaviour of the central bank as well as the commercial banks (as we saw in Chapter 27). The demand for money is given by M_D; its negative slope indicates that a fall in the rate of interest causes the quantity of money demanded to increase. Monetary equilibrium is at E, with a rate of interest of i_0.

If the interest rate is i_1, there will be an excess demand for money of M_0M_1. Bonds will be offered for sale in an attempt to increase money holdings. This will force the rate of interest up to i_0 (the price of bonds falls), at which point the quantity of money demanded is equal to the fixed available quantity of M_0. If the interest rate is i_2, there will be an excess supply of money M_2M_0. Bonds will be demanded in return for excess money balances. This will force the rate of interest down to i_0 (the price of bonds rises), at which point the quantity of money demanded is equal to the fixed supply of M_0.

The Monetary Transmission Mechanism

The connection between changes in the demand for and supply of money and the level of aggregate demand is called the **monetary transmission mechanism**. It operates in three stages:

monetary transmission mechanism The channels by which a change in the demand for or supply of money leads to a shift of the aggregate demand curve.

1. Changes in the demand for money or the supply of money cause a change in the equilibrium interest rate in the short run.

2. The change in the interest rate leads to a change in desired investment and consumption expenditure (and net exports in an open economy).

3. The change in desired aggregate expenditure leads to a shift in the *AD* curve and thus to short-run changes in real GDP and the price level.

Let's examine these three stages in more detail.

1. Changes in the Interest Rate The interest rate will change if the equilibrium depicted in Figure 28-2 is disturbed by a change in either the supply of money or the demand for money. For example, as shown in part (i) of Figure 28-3, we see the following sequence of events when there is an increase in the supply of money but no change in the money demand curve:

$\uparrow$ money supply $\Rightarrow$ excess supply of money at initial interest rate

$\Rightarrow$ firms and households buy bonds

$\Rightarrow \uparrow$ bond prices

$\Rightarrow \downarrow$ equilibrium interest rate

Note that the original increase in the supply of money could be caused either by the central bank increasing the reserves in the banking system or by the commercial banks lending out a higher fraction of their existing reserves.

FIGURE 28-3 Changes in the Equilibrium Interest Rate

(i) An increase in the supply of money

(ii) An increase in the demand for money

Changes in the supply of money or in the demand for money cause the equilibrium interest rate to change. In both parts of the figure, the money supply is shown by the vertical curve M_S, and the demand for money is shown by the negatively sloped curve M_D. The initial monetary equilibrium is at E_0, with corresponding interest rate i_0. In part (i), an increase in the money supply causes M_S^0 to shift to M_S^1. The new equilibrium is at E_1, where the equilibrium interest rate has fallen to i_1. In part (ii), an increase in the demand for money shifts M_D^0 to M_D^1. The new monetary equilibrium occurs at E_2, and the equilibrium interest rate increases to i_2.

As shown in part (ii) of Figure 28-3, an increase in the demand for money, with an unchanged supply of money, leads to the following sequence of events:

↑ money demand ⇒ excess demand for money at initial interest rate

⇒ firms and households sell bonds

⇒ ↓ bond prices

⇒ ↑ equilibrium interest rate

The original increase in the demand for money could be caused by an increase in real GDP or by an increase in the price level. It could also be caused by an increased preference to hold money rather than bonds, as would happen if there were an increase in the perceived riskiness of bonds.

> Changes in either the demand for or the supply of money cause changes in the short-run equilibrium interest rate.

2. Changes in Desired Investment and Consumption The second link in the monetary transmission mechanism relates interest rates to desired investment and consumption expenditure. We saw in Chapter 21 that desired investment, which includes expenditure on inventory accumulation, residential construction, and business fixed investment, responds to changes in the interest rate. Other things being equal, a decrease in the interest rate reduces the opportunity cost of borrowing or using retained earnings for investment purposes. As a result, the lower interest rate leads to an increase in desired investment expenditure. We also saw that consumption expenditures, especially on big-ticket durable items such as cars and furniture, which are often purchased on credit, are negatively related to the interest rate. In Figure 28-4, this negative relationship

FIGURE 28-4 The Effects of Changes in the Money Supply on Desired Investment Expenditure

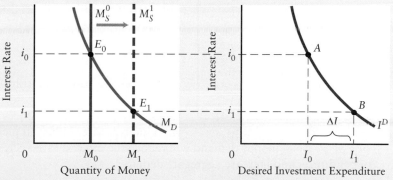

(i) Money demand and supply   (ii) Investment demand

Increases in the money supply reduce the equilibrium interest rate and increase desired investment expenditure. In part (i), monetary equilibrium is at E_0, with a quantity of money of M_0 and an interest rate of i_0. The corresponding level of desired investment is I_0 (point A) in part (ii). An increase in the money supply to M_1 reduces the equilibrium interest rate to i_1 and increases investment expenditure by ΔI to I_1 (point B).

FIGURE 28-5 The Effects of Changes in the Money Supply on Aggregate Demand

(i) A shift in the AE curve

(ii) A shift in the AD curve

Changes in the money supply cause shifts in the AE and AD functions. In Figure 28-4, an increase in the money supply increased desired investment expenditure by ΔI. In part (i) of this figure, the AE function shifts up by ΔI. At any given price level P_0, equilibrium GDP rises from Y_0 to Y_1, as shown by the rightward shift in the AD curve in part (ii).

between desired expenditure and the interest rate is labelled I^D for investment demand, reflecting the fact that investment is the *most* interest-sensitive part of expenditure.

The first two links in the monetary transmission mechanism are shown in Figure 28-4.[4] Although the analysis in Figure 28-4 illustrates a change in the money supply, remember that the transmission mechanism can also be set in motion by a change in the demand for money. In part (i), we see that an increase in the money supply reduces the short-run equilibrium interest rate. In part (ii), we see that a fall in the interest rate leads to an increase in desired investment (and consumption) expenditure.

3. Changes in Aggregate Demand The third link in our theory of the monetary transmission mechanism is from changes in desired expenditure to shifts in the AE function and in the AD curve. This is familiar ground. In Chapter 23, we saw that a shift in the aggregate expenditure curve (caused by something *other than* a change in the price level) leads to a shift in the AD curve. This situation is shown again in Figure 28-5.

An increase in the money supply causes a reduction in the interest rate and an increase in desired investment and other interest-sensitive expenditure; it therefore causes a rightward shift of the AD curve. A decrease in the money supply causes an increase in the interest rate and a decrease in desired investment; it therefore causes a leftward shift of the AD curve.

The entire monetary transmission mechanism is summarized in Figure 28-6 for the case of a shock to the money market that reduces the short-run equilibrium interest rate. Either an increase in money supply or a decrease in money demand will reduce the interest rate, increase desired investment expenditure, and increase aggregate demand.

---

[4] In part (i) of Figure 28-4, it is the *nominal* interest rate—the rate of return on bonds—that affects money demand. In part (ii), however, it is the *real* interest rate that influences desired investment expenditure. It is therefore worth emphasizing that we are continuing with the assumption that inflation is expected to be zero, and thus the nominal and real interest rates are the same. This assumption allows us to use the same vertical axis in the two parts of the figure.

An Open-Economy Modification

So far, the emphasis in our discussion of the monetary transmission mechanism has been on the effect that a change in the interest rate has on desired investment and desired consumption. In an open economy, however, where financial capital flows easily across borders, the monetary transmission mechanism is a little more complex.

Financial capital is very mobile across international boundaries. Bondholders, either in Canada or abroad, are able to substitute among Canadian bonds, U.S. bonds, German bonds, and bonds from almost any country you can think of. Bonds from different countries are generally not *perfect* substitutes for each other because the varying amounts of political and economic instability imply that different levels of *risk* are associated with different bonds. But bonds from similar countries—Canada and the United States, for example—are often viewed as very close substitutes.

The ability of bondholders to substitute easily between bonds from different countries implies that monetary disturbances that cause changes in interest rates often lead to international flows of financial capital, which in turn cause changes in exchange rates and changes in exports and imports.

To understand how capital mobility adds a second channel to the monetary transmission mechanism, consider an example. Suppose the Bank of Canada decides to increase the money supply. As shown in part (i) of Figure 28-4, the increase in money supply reduces the interest rate and increases desired investment expenditure. This is the first channel of the monetary transmission mechanism. But the story does not end there.

The reduction in Canadian interest rates also makes Canadian bonds less attractive relative to foreign bonds. Canadian and foreign investors alike will sell some of their Canadian bonds and buy more of the high-return foreign bonds. But to buy foreign bonds, it is necessary first to exchange Canadian dollars for foreign currency. The desire to sell Canadian dollars and purchase foreign currency causes the Canadian dollar to depreciate relative to other currencies.

> An increase in the Canadian money supply reduces Canadian interest rates and leads to an outflow of financial capital. This capital outflow causes the Canadian dollar to depreciate.

As the Canadian dollar depreciates, however, Canadian goods and services become less expensive relative to those from other countries. As we first saw in Chapter 22, this change in international relative prices causes households and firms—both in Canada and abroad—to substitute away from foreign goods and toward Canadian goods. Imports fall and exports rise.

So the overall effect of the increase in the Canadian money supply is not just a fall in Canadian interest rates and an increase in investment. Because of the international

FIGURE 28-6 Summary of the Monetary Transmission Mechanism

An increase in the supply of money **or** A decrease in the demand for money

↓

Excess supply of money

↓

A fall in the equilibrium interest rate

↓

An increase in desired investment expenditure

↓

An upward shift in the *AE* curve

↓

A rightward shift in the *AD* curve

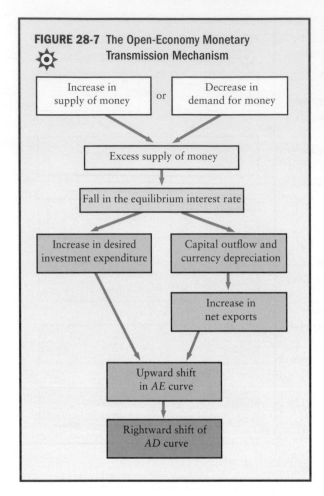

FIGURE 28-7 The Open-Economy Monetary Transmission Mechanism

mobility of financial capital, the low Canadian interest rates also lead to a capital outflow, a depreciation of the Canadian dollar, and an increase in Canadian net exports. This increase in net exports, of course, *strengthens* the positive effect on aggregate demand already coming from the increase in desired investment.

This complete open-economy monetary transmission mechanism is shown in Figure 28-7. This figure is based on Figure 28-6, but simply adds the second channel of the transmission mechanism that works through capital mobility, exchange rates, and net exports.

> In an open economy with capital mobility, an increase in the money supply is predicted to cause an increase in aggregate demand for two reasons. First, the reduction in interest rates causes an increase in investment. Second, the lower interest rate causes a capital outflow, a currency depreciation, and a rise in net exports.

Our example has been that of a monetary expansion. A monetary contraction has the opposite effect, but the logic of the mechanism is the same. A reduction in the Canadian money supply raises Canadian interest rates and reduces desired investment expenditure. The higher Canadian interest rates attract foreign financial capital as bondholders sell low-return foreign bonds and purchase high-return Canadian bonds. This action increases the demand for Canadian dollars in the foreign-exchange market and thus causes the Canadian dollar to appreciate. Finally, the appreciation of the Canadian dollar increases Canadians' imports of foreign goods and reduces Canadian exports to other countries. Canadian net exports fall.

The Slope of the *AD* Curve

We can now use our theory of the monetary transmission mechanism to add to the explanation of the negative slope of the *AD* curve. In Chapter 23, we mentioned two reasons for its negative slope: the change in wealth and the substitution between domestic and foreign goods, both of which occur when the domestic price level changes. A third effect operates through interest rates, and works as follows. A rise in the price level raises the money value of transactions and thus leads to an increase in the demand for money. For a given supply of money (a vertical M_S curve), the increase in money demand means that the M_D curve shifts to the right, raising the equilibrium interest rate. The higher interest rate then leads to a reduction in desired investment expenditure. We therefore have a third reason that the price level and the level of aggregate demand are negatively related. This third reason for the negative slope of the *AD* curve is important because, empirically, the interest rate is the most important link between monetary factors and real expenditure flows.

28.4 The Strength of Monetary Forces

In the previous section we saw that a change in the money supply leads to a change in interest rates. The change in interest rates, in turn, leads to changes in investment and, through international capital flows and changes in the exchange rate, to changes in net exports. A change in the money supply therefore leads to a change in desired aggregate expenditure and to a shift in the AD curve. From our analysis in Chapter 24, we know that a shift in the AD curve will lead to different effects in the short run and in the long run. It is in the long run that factor prices tend to fully adjust to excess demands or excess supplies, and output tends to return to the level of potential output, Y^*. Let's begin by examining the long-run effects of increases in the money supply, and then turn to a long-standing debate about the strength of monetary forces in the short run.

The Neutrality of Money

Starting from a long-run equilibrium in our macro model with real GDP equal to Y^*, any AD or AS shock that creates an output gap sets in place an adjustment process that will eventually close that gap and return real GDP to Y^*. The operation of this adjustment process following an increase in the money supply is illustrated in Figure 28-8. In the figure, the only long-run effect of the shift in the AD curve is a change in the price level; there is no long run effect on real GDP or any other real economic variable. This result is referred to as **long-run money neutrality**. The long-run neutrality of money requires that Y^* be unaffected by changes in the supply of money.

The Classical Dichotomy Many eighteenth- and nineteenth-century economists developed theories of the economy's long-run equilibrium and empha-sized the neutrality of money. They argued that the "monetary side" of the economy was independent from the "real side" in the long run. This belief came to be referred to as the *Classical dichotomy*. In the long run, relative prices, real GDP, employment, investment, and all other real economic variables were assumed to be determined by real factors,

FIGURE 28-8 The Long-Run Neutrality of Money

(i) M_D and M_S

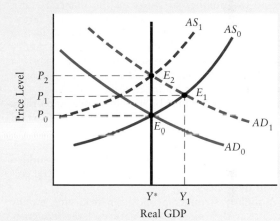

(ii) AD and AS

Money is neutral in the long run if the only long-run effect of an increase in the money supply is a higher price level. The economy begins in long-run equilibrium at E_0 in both diagrams, with real GDP equal to Y^* and the price level equal to P_0. An increase in the money supply from M_S^0 to M_S^1 reduces interest rates immediately to i_1' and stimulates aggregate demand, thus shifting the aggregate demand curve from AD_0 to AD_1. As real GDP and the price level increase, the demand for money increases to M_D^1, thus pushing i_1' up to i_1. The point E_1 in part (i) therefore corresponds to E_1 in part (ii). Since real GDP is now above Y^*, wages and other factor prices start to increase, thus shifting the AS curve upward. The adjustment process continues until Y is back to Y^* and the price level has increased to P_2. In the new long-run equilibrium, the higher price level (with unchanged Y^*) has increased money demand to M_D^2, thus restoring the interest rate to its initial level, i_0.

APPLYING ECONOMIC CONCEPTS 28-2

Monetary Reform and the Neutrality of Money

The least controversial proposition regarding the neutrality of money is that altering the number of zeros on the monetary unit, and on everything else stated in those units, will have no economic consequences. For example, if an extra zero were added to all Bank of Canada notes—so that all $5 bills became $50 bills, all $10 bills became $100 bills, and so on—and the same adjustment was made to all nominal wages, prices, and contracts in the economy, there would be no effects on real GDP, real wages, relative prices, and other real economic variables.*

This proposition has been tested many times since the Second World War, when countries that had suffered major inflations undertook *monetary reform* by reducing the number of zeros on the monetary unit and everything else that was specified in money terms. The evidence is clear that no significant or lasting effects followed from these reforms. That such money neutrality is a testable theory, rather than merely a definitional statement, is shown by the observable possibility that for a short time after the monetary reforms some people may be so ill informed, and others such creatures of habit, that they make mistakes based on assuming that the new money is the same as the old. Although some such behaviour probably occurred, it was not significant enough to show up as a sudden change in any of the economic data that have been collected in these cases.

A slightly stronger proposition regarding money neutrality is that altering the nature of the monetary unit will have no real economic effects. Such a change occurred, for example, in 1971, when the United Kingdom changed from a system in which the basic monetary unit, the pound sterling, was composed of 240 pence to a system in which it contained 100 pence. Another example is Ireland's 1999 conversion from the punt, which contained 240 pence, to the euro, which contained 100 cents. In these cases there were some alterations in real behaviour immediately after the change was made, as many people were confused by the new units. Once again, however, these changes were neither important enough nor long-lasting enough to show up in the macroeconomic data.

These two propositions regarding the neutrality of money are important because they emphasize the nominal nature of money and the important distinction between nominal and real values. It would be unusual indeed if multiplying all nominal values in the economy by the same scalar had any real effect other than some temporary confusion. For this reason, these two propositions are accepted by virtually all economists and central bankers.

The stronger and more controversial proposition regarding money neutrality is the one discussed in the text—that the economy's level of potential output is unaffected by changes in the supply of money. This assumption is common in many macroeconomic models but, as we argue in the text, there are good reasons to think that monetary policy may have effects on Y^* and thus have long-run effects on real GDP.

___

*Of course, there would be *some* real effects from such an adjustment, including the level of inconvenience associated with using paper money with larger denominations (which would be enormous if we added many zeros rather than just one to all existing bills and prices).

---

long-run money neutrality The idea that a change in the supply of money has no long-run effect on any real variables; it affects only the price level.

such as firms' technologies and consumers' preferences. The absolute level of money prices was then determined by the monetary side of the economy, where the quantity of money determined the price level. In macro models that contain this dichotomy, the long-run effect of a change in the money supply is a change in the price level, with no changes to any real economic variables.

The concept of money neutrality is interpreted differently by different people. Our definition above, which emphasizes the independence of Y^* from the country's money supply, is probably the most commonly used definition today, but there are others as well. *Applying Economic Concepts 28-2* examines the concept of money neutrality as it relates to changes in the denominations of a country's paper currency.

> Money is neutral in the long run if a change in the money supply has no long-run effect on real GDP or any other real variables. Much empirical evidence is consistent with long-run money neutrality, although the proposition is often debated.

Hysteresis Effects The proposition of long-run money neutrality is debatable. Though it is a common assumption in many macroeconomic models, there are good reasons to think that changes in a country's money supply may have effects on Y^* and thus have long-run effects on real GDP. Here we examine what is called *hysteresis*—the possibility that the level or growth rate of Y^* may be affected by the short-run path of real GDP.

Investment and Technology. Theories that assume long-run money neutrality typically omit some key economic behaviour that blurs the division between the real and monetary sectors of the economy. Credit plays a key role in linking these two sectors. Most firms use credit to finance aspects of their regular operations as well as their investments in research and development and the expansion of their production facilities. In short, credit can be viewed as an important input to firms' production and investment activities.

Now consider the effects of a change in the country's money supply. As we have seen in this chapter, the likely short-run effects are changes in interest rates and the level of real GDP. But if the change in firms' access to credit—associated with the change in interest rates—also leads firms to alter their capital investment and expenditures on research and development, there may be a permanent effect on the economy's capital stock and state of technology. If so, there will be a permanent effect on the level of potential output.

A dramatic example of the important role of credit occurred with the global financial crisis that began in 2008. As several large U.S. and European banks failed, the flows of credit to non-financial firms dropped sharply in many countries. The reduced access to credit led to reductions in investment, employment, and output, and contributed to the largest global recession in over half a century.

> Long-run money neutrality is called into question by the possibility that a change in the money supply, through its effect on the interest rate, can affect the course of investment and technological change and hence the path of potential output.

Human Capital. Another reason for hysteresis is the effect on human capital that often accompanies prolonged unemployment. Consider a negative shock that reduces real GDP and increases the unemployment rate. If wages and other factor prices are slow to adjust, some individuals will experience long spells of unemployment. Prolonged lack of work for even experienced workers may cause their skills to deteriorate. The effect can be even stronger with first entrants to the labour force. If young people are denied the experience of early jobs that teach them the disciplines and basic skills required of all members of the labour force, it may be difficult or even impossible for them to learn these skills later when jobs do become available. If the recession lasts long enough, both groups may eventually become "unemployable," even after the aggregate economy recovers. In this case, the fall in the level of real GDP, if prolonged, leads through hysteresis effects to a fall in the level of Y^*.

The major global recession that began in 2008 again provides an example to illustrate these effects. Even three years into a slow economic recovery, the amount of long-term unemployment among both experienced and young workers was higher in the United States than at any time in the recent past. In Europe, the situation was even worse, with long-term youth unemployment running from 20 to over 40 percent in the more depressed economies such as Greece and Spain. There is little doubt that the stock of productive human capital that will exist when these countries eventually return to something like full employment will be permanently below what it would have been if the prolonged recession had not occurred.

> If a long period of unemployment associated with a prolonged recessionary gap causes workers to lose human capital, or accumulate less than they otherwise would, both the level and rate of growth of Y^* may be reduced when the recessionary gap is eventually closed.

Money and Inflation

Whether or not money is neutral in the long run, it is certainly closely related to the price level. As we observed in Chapter 27 (in *Applying Economic Concepts 27-1*), there have been many examples throughout history of countries experiencing dramatic increases in the money supply and equally dramatic increases in the price level.

The close connection between money growth and inflation does not hold just in the dramatic examples; it is a connection that applies in the long run to most if not all economies. Figure 28-9 shows a scatter plot of inflation and money growth for a large sample of countries between 1978 and 2010. The vertical axis measures each country's average annual inflation rate. The horizontal axis measures each country's average annual growth rate of the money supply. Each point in the figure represents the rates of inflation and money supply growth for one country averaged over the sample period. As is clear in the figure, there is a strong positive correlation between the growth rate of the money supply and the rate of inflation, as reflected by the tight bunching of points around the upward-sloping line. This line is the statistical "line of best fit" between money supply growth and inflation. Its slope is 0.97, indicating that two countries that differ in their money growth rates by 10 percent will, on average, differ in their inflation rates by 9.7 percent.

> Across many countries over long periods of time, the rate of inflation and the growth rate of the money supply are highly correlated.

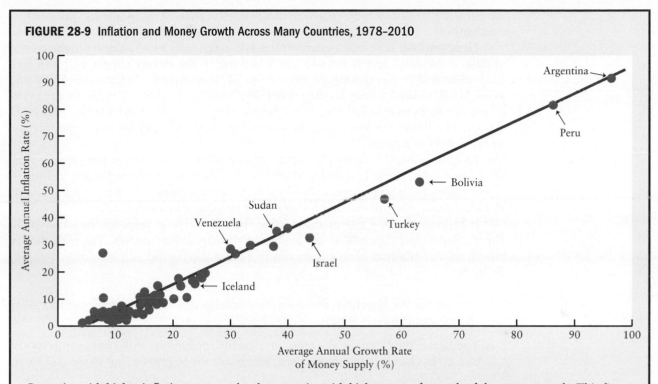

FIGURE 28-9 Inflation and Money Growth Across Many Countries, 1978–2010

Countries with higher inflation rates tend to be countries with higher rates of growth of the money supply. This figure plots long-run data for many countries. Each point shows the average annual inflation rate and the average annual growth rate of the money supply for a specific country for the 1978–2010 period. For all countries, the inflation data refer to the rate of change of the Consumer Price Index; the money supply data refer to the growth rate of M2. The positive relationship between inflation and money supply growth (with a slope of the best-fit line very close to 1) is consistent with the proposition of long-run money neutrality.

(*Source:* Based on author's calculations using data from the World Bank. Go to www.worldbank.org and look for "world development indicators and global development finance.")

The Short-Run Effects of Monetary Shocks

In our macro model, money is clearly not neutral in the short run. We have seen that a change in the money supply shifts the *AD* curve and hence alters the short-run equilibrium level of real GDP. For a given *AS* curve, the short-run effect of a change in the money supply on real GDP and the price level is determined by the extent of the shift of the *AD* curve.

How Effective Is Monetary Policy? How much the *AD* curve shifts in response to an increase in the money supply depends on the amount of investment expenditure that is stimulated. The increase in investment expenditure in turn depends on the strength of two of the linkages that make up the monetary transmission mechanism: the link between money supply and interest rates, and the link between interest rates and investment.[5] Let's look more closely at these separate parts of the monetary transmission mechanism.

First, consider how much interest rates fall in response to an increase in the money supply. If the M_D curve is steep, a given increase in the money supply will lead to a large reduction in the equilibrium interest rate. A steep M_D curve means that firms' and households' desired money holding is not very sensitive to changes in the interest rate, so interest rates have to fall a lot to get people to be content to hold a larger amount of money. The flatter the M_D curve, the less interest rates will fall for any given increase in the supply of money.

Second, consider how much investment expenditure increases in response to a fall in interest rates. If the I^D curve is relatively flat, then any given reduction in interest rates will lead to a large increase in firms' desired investment. The steeper the I^D curve, the less investment will increase for any given reduction in interest rates.

It follows that the size of the shift of the AD curve in response to a change in the money supply depends on the shapes of the M_D and I^D curves. The influence of the shapes of the two curves is shown in Figure 28-10 and can be summarized as follows:

1. The steeper the M_D curve, the more interest rates will change in response to a given change in the money supply.

2. The flatter the I^D curve, the more investment expenditure will change in response to a given change in the interest rate, and hence the larger the shift in the AD curve.

The combination that produces the largest shift in the AD curve for a given change in the money supply is a steep M_D curve and a flat I^D curve. This combination is illustrated in part (i) of Figure 28-10. It makes monetary policy relatively effective as a means of influencing real GDP in the short run. The combination that produces the smallest shift in the AD curve is a flat M_D curve and a steep I^D curve. This combination is illustrated in part (ii) of Figure 28-10. It makes monetary policy relatively ineffective in the short run.

> The effectiveness of monetary policy in inducing short-run changes in real GDP depends on the slopes of the M_D and I^D curves. The steeper is the M_D curve, and the flatter is the I^D curve, the more effective is monetary policy.

Keynesians Versus Monetarists Figure 28-10 illustrates a famous debate among economists that occurred in the three decades following the Second World War. Some economists, following the ideas of John Maynard Keynes, argued that changes in the money supply led to relatively small changes in interest rates, and that investment was relatively insensitive to changes in the interest rate. These *Keynesian* economists concluded that monetary policy was not a very effective method of stimulating aggregate demand—they therefore emphasized the value of using fiscal policy (as Keynes himself had argued during the Great Depression). Another group of economists, led by Milton Friedman, argued that changes in the money supply caused sharp changes

---

[5] As we saw earlier in the chapter, the consumption of durable goods is also sensitive to changes in the interest rate. In this section, however, we simplify by focusing only on the behaviour of desired investment.

FIGURE 28-10 Two Views on the Strength of Monetary Changes

(i) Changes in the money supply are effective

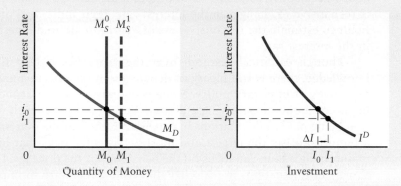

(ii) Changes in the money supply are ineffective

The effect of a change in the money supply on aggregate demand depends on the slopes of the M_D and I^D curves. Initially, in parts (i) and (ii), the money supply is M_S^0, and the economy has an interest rate of i_0 and investment expenditure of I_0. The central bank then expands the money supply from M_S^0 to M_S^1. The rate of interest thus falls from i_0 to i_1, as shown in each of the left panels. This causes an increase in investment expenditure of ΔI, from I_0 to I_1, as shown in each of the right panels.

In part (i), the demand for money is insensitive to the interest rate, so the increase in the money supply leads to a large fall in the interest rate. Further, desired investment expenditure is highly interest sensitive, so the large fall in interest rates also leads to a large increase in investment expenditure. In this case, the change in the money supply will be very effective in stimulating aggregate demand.

In part (ii), the demand for money is more sensitive to the interest rate, so the increase in the money supply leads to only a small fall in the interest rate. Further, desired investment expenditure is much less sensitive to the interest rate, and so the small fall in interest rates leads to only a small increase in investment expenditure. In this case, the change in the money supply will be less effective in stimulating aggregate demand.

in interest rates, which, in turn, led to significant changes in investment expenditure. These *Monetarist* economists concluded that monetary policy was a very effective tool for stimulating aggregate demand.[6]

---

[6] Monetarists argued that monetary policy was very effective for stimulating aggregate demand but they *did not* advocate an "activist" monetary policy. One of their concerns was that monetary forces were so strong that an activist monetary policy would potentially destabilize the economy. We address these issues in Chapter 29.

For brief descriptions of the contributions to economics of the Nobel laureates, go to www.nobel.se/economics/laureates/.

Today, this debate between Keynesians and Monetarists is over. A great deal of empirical research suggests that money demand is relatively insensitive to changes in the interest rate. That is, the M_D curve is quite steep and, as a result, changes in the money supply cause relatively large changes in interest rates (as argued by the Monetarists). The evidence is much less clear, however, on the slope of the I^D curve. Though the evidence confirms that I^D is downward sloping, there is no consensus on whether the curve is steep or flat. Part of the problem facing researchers is that an important determinant of investment is not observable. Firms' expectations about the future—what Keynes famously called firms' "animal spirits"—have a significant effect on their investment decisions (thus shifting the I^D curve), but this variable is not easily measured by researchers. The non-observability of this variable makes it very difficult to estimate precisely the relationship between interest rates and investment. Another problem is that the I^D curve is an aggregation of a number of different investment demands (plant, equipment, inventories, new housing, and durable consumer goods), each subject to different influences. While each type of investment is responsive to changes in the interest rate, their individual differences make it difficult to estimate the responsiveness of *aggregate* desired investment (I^D) to changes in the interest rate.

Though empirical research over the years has largely filled the gaps in our knowledge, there is still plenty of debate about the effectiveness and the appropriate objectives of monetary policy. Some economists argue that monetary policy should be directed only to achieving a desired path of the price level, with little or no attention being paid to fluctuations in real GDP. Others argue that monetary policy should attempt to offset the largest and most persistent shocks that hit the economy, while maintaining a long-run focus on the behaviour of the price level. Yet others argue that short-run fluctuations in real GDP and employment are so important that monetary policy ought to place much less emphasis on the price level and instead be actively engaged in reducing the economy's fluctuations in the face of all but the smallest and most transient shocks.

In the next chapter we examine the details of how monetary policy is conducted in Canada. For several reasons, the real-world practice of monetary policy is more complex than it appears in this chapter. But as we will see, the Bank of Canada's system of *inflation targeting* can be viewed as a means of providing both short-run stabilization and a long-run focus on the behaviour of the price level.

SUMMARY

28.1 Understanding Bonds

LO 1

- The present value of any bond that promises to pay some sequence of payments in the future is negatively related to the market interest rate. A bond's present value determines its market price. Thus, there is a negative relationship between the market interest rate and the price of a bond.
- The yield on a bond is the rate of return the bondholder receives, having bought the bond at its purchase price and then receiving the entire stream of future payments the bond offers. For a given stream of future payments, a lower purchase price implies a higher bond yield.
- An increase in the perceived riskiness of bonds leads to a reduction in bond prices and thus an increase in bond yields.

28.2 The Theory of Money Demand

- In our macro model, households and firms are assumed to divide their financial assets between interest-bearing "bonds" and non–interest-bearing "money." They hold money to facilitate both expected and unexpected transactions, and also to protect against the possibility of a decline in bond prices (a rise in interest rates).
- The opportunity cost of holding money is the interest that would have been earned if bonds had been held instead.
- Households' and firms' desired money holdings are assumed to be influenced by three key macroeconomic variables:

1. Increases in the interest rate reduce desired money holdings.
2. Increases in real GDP increase desired money holdings.
3. Increases in the price level increase desired money holdings.

- These relationships are captured in the M_D curve, which is drawn as a negative relationship between interest rates (i) and desired money holding (M_D). Increases in real GDP (Y) or the price level (P) lead to a rightward shift of this M_D curve.

28.3 Monetary Equilibrium and National Income

- In the short run, the interest rate is determined by the interaction of money supply and money demand. Monetary equilibrium is established when the interest rate is such that the quantity of money supplied is equal to the quantity of money demanded.
- A change in the money supply (coming from the central bank or the commercial banking system) or in the demand for money (coming from a change in Y or P) will lead to a change in the equilibrium interest rate. This is the first stage of the monetary transmission mechanism.

- The second stage of the monetary transmission mechanism is that any change in the interest rate leads to a change in desired investment and consumption expenditure. In an open economy with capital mobility, the change in the interest rate leads to capital flows, changes in the exchange rate, and changes in net exports.
- The third stage of the monetary transmission mechanism is that any change in desired investment, consumption, or net exports leads to a shift in the aggregate demand (AD) curve, and thus to a change in real GDP and the price level.

28.4 The Strength of Monetary Forces

- Changes in the money supply have different effects on the economy in the short run and in the long run.
- Money is said to be neutral in the long run if a change in the money supply leads to no changes in the long-run level of real GDP (or other real variables).
- In the long run, after wages and other factor prices have fully adjusted to any output gaps, real GDP returns to potential output, Y^*. If Y^* is unaffected by the change in the money supply, there will be no long-run effect from the monetary shock.
- If there is *hysteresis*, short-run changes in real GDP will lead to changes in Y^*. In these cases, monetary shocks will have long-run effects on real GDP.

- There is a strong positive correlation between the rate of money growth and the rate of inflation across countries when viewed over the long run.
- In the short run, the effects of a change in the money supply depend on the shape of the M_D and I^D curves in our macro model. The steeper the M_D curve and the flatter the I^D curve, the more effective changes in the money supply will be in causing short-run changes in real GDP.

KEY CONCEPTS

The interest rate and present value
Interest rates, bond prices, and bond yields
Reasons for holding money
The money demand (M_D) function

Monetary equilibrium
The monetary transmission mechanism
The investment demand (I^D) function

Effects of changes in the money supply
Neutrality and non-neutrality of money
Hysteresis

STUDY EXERCISES

MyEconLab   Make the grade with MyEconLab: Study Exercises marked in red can be found on MyEconLab. You can practise them as often as you want, and most feature step-by-step guided instructions to help you find the right answer.

1. Fill in the blanks to make the following statements correctly reflect the theory developed in this chapter.

   a. Monetary equilibrium occurs when the quantity of _____ equals the quantity of _____. Monetary equilibrium determines the _____.

   b. When there is an excess supply of money, households and firms will attempt to _____ bonds. This action will cause the price of bonds to _____ and the interest rate to _____.

   c. When there is an excess demand for money, households and firms will attempt to _____ bonds. This action will cause the price of bonds to _____ and the interest rate to _____.

   d. The _____ _____ _____ refers to the three stages that link the money market to aggregate demand. The first link is between monetary equilibrium and the _____; the second link is between the _____ and desired _____; the third link is between desired _____ and _____.

   e. Suppose the economy is in equilibrium and then the Bank of Canada increases the money supply. The first effect will be an excess _____ of/for money, which will then lead to a(n) _____ in the interest rate, which will in turn lead to a(n) _____ in desired investment.

   f. Suppose the economy is in equilibrium and the Bank of Canada decreases the money supply. The first effect will be an excess _____ of/for money, which will lead to a _____ in the interest rate, which will in turn lead to a(n) _____ in desired investment.

   g. Through the monetary transmission mechanism, a rightward shift of the AD curve can be caused by a(n) _____ in the money supply; a leftward shift of the AD curve can be caused by a(n) _____ in the money supply.

   h. In an open economy with capital mobility, an increase in the money supply causes interest rates to _____, which leads to a capital outflow. This causes a(n) _____ of the Canadian dollar and thus to a(n) _____ in net exports, which leads the AD curve to shift _____.

2. Fill in the blanks to make the following statements correctly reflect the theory developed in this chapter.

   a. If money is neutral in the long run, then changes in the money supply have no effect on _____ in the long run.

   b. If the demand for money is not very sensitive to changes in the interest rate, then the M_D curve will be relatively _____. An increase in the money supply will lead to a(n) _____ reduction in the interest rate.

   c. If the demand for money is very sensitive to changes in the interest rate, then the M_D curve will be relatively _____. An increase in the money supply will lead to a(n) _____ reduction in the interest rate.

   d. A relatively flat investment demand curve means that a change in the interest rate will have a(n) _____ effect on _____, which leads to a relatively large shift in the _____ curve.

   e. A relatively steep investment demand curve means that a change in the interest rate will have a(n) _____ effect on _____, which leads to a relatively small shift in the _____ curve.

   f. Changes in the money supply will have the largest effect on the position of the AD curve when the M_D curve is relatively _____ and the I^D curve is relatively _____.

3. The following table shows the stream of income produced by several different assets. In each case, P_1, P_2, and P_3 are the payments made by the asset in Years 1, 2, and 3.

Asset	Market Interest Rate (i)	P_1	P_2	P_3	Present Value
Treasury Bill	4%	$1000	$0	$0	—
Bond	3%	$0	$0	$5000	—
Bond	5%	$200	$200	$200	—
Stock	6%	$50	$40	$60	—

a. For each asset, compute the asset's present value. (Note that the market interest rate, i, is not the same in each situation.)

b. Explain why the market price for each asset is expected to be the asset's present value.

4. The table below provides information for six different bonds: current market price (P), the face value of the bond (V), and the number of years before the bond matures (N).

Bond Number	Market Price (P)	Face Value (V)	Years to Maturity (N)
1a	$926	$1000	1
1b	$850	$1000	1
2a	$1270	$2000	5
2b	$838	$2000	5
3a	$1760	$5000	10
3b	$684	$5000	10

a. In each case, compute the bond's yield, assuming that you buy the bond at its current market price and hold the bond until it matures. There are no coupons. If x is the bond's yield, then $P(1 + x)^N = V$.

b. Suppose bonds 1a, 2a, and 3a are all issued by the same borrower. Can you offer an explanation for the relationship between the bond yields and the terms to maturity?

c. Suppose bonds 1b, 2b, and 3b are all issued by the same borrower. What can you conclude about the riskiness of the "a" borrower versus that of the "b" borrower? Explain.

d. Notice that the market interest rate is not shown in the table. Explain why knowledge of the market interest rate is unnecessary in order to compute a bond's yield, once you already know the bond's market price. What aspect of the bond does the market interest rate influence, if anything?

5. Consider a bond that promises to make coupon payments of $100 one year from now and $100 two years from now, and to repay the principal of $1000 three years from now. Suppose also that the market interest rate is 8 percent per year, and that no perceived risk is associated with the bond.

a. Compute the present value of this bond.

b. Suppose the bond is being offered for $995. Would you buy the bond at that price? What do you expect to happen to the bond price in the very near future?

c. Suppose the bond is instead being offered at a price of $950. Would you buy the bond at that price? Do you expect the bond price to change in the near future?

d. If the price of the bond is equal to its computed present value from part (a), what is the implied bond yield?

e. Explain why bond yields and the market interest rate tend to move together so that economists can then sensibly speak about "the" interest rate.

6. What motives for holding money—transactions, precautionary, or speculative—do you think explain the following holdings? Explain.

a. Currency in the cash register of the local grocery store at the start of each working day.

b. Money to meet Queen's University's biweekly payroll deposited in the local bank.

c. A household tries to keep a "buffer" of $1000 in its savings account.

d. An investor sells bonds for cash, which she then deposits in a low-return bank account.

e. You carry $20 in your pocket even though you have no planned expenditures.

7. The diagram below shows the demand for money and the supply of money.

a. Explain why the M_D function is downward sloping.

b. Suppose the interest rate is at i_A. Explain how firms and households attempt to satisfy their excess demand for money. What is the effect of their actions?

c. Suppose the interest rate is at i_B. Explain how firms and households attempt to dispose of their excess supply of money. What is the effect of their actions?

d. Now suppose there is an increase in the transactions demand for money (perhaps because of growth in real GDP). Beginning at i^*, explain what happens in the money market. How is this shown in the diagram?

8. The following diagrams show the determination of monetary equilibrium and the demand for investment. The economy begins with money supply M_S, money demand M_D, and investment demand I^D. The interest rate is i_0 and desired investment is I_0.

a. Beginning at the initial equilibrium, suppose the Bank of Canada increases the money supply. What happens in the money market, and what happens to desired investment expenditure?

b. Beginning in the initial equilibrium, suppose there is a reduction in the demand for money (caused, perhaps, by bonds becoming more attractive to firms and households). What happens in the money market, and what happens to desired investment expenditure?

c. Explain why an increase in money supply can have the same effects on desired investment expenditure as a reduction in money demand.

9. In the text we discussed why, in an open economy with international capital mobility, there is a second part to the monetary transmission mechanism. (It may be useful to review Figure 28-7 on page 706 when answering this question.)

a. Explain why an increase in Canada's money supply makes investors shift their portfolios away from Canadian bonds and toward foreign bonds.

b. Explain why this portfolio adjustment leads to a depreciation of the Canadian dollar.

c. Why would such a depreciation of the Canadian dollar lead to an increase in Canada's net exports?

d. Now suppose that the Bank of Canada does not change its policy at all, but the Federal Reserve (the U.S. central bank) increases the U.S. money supply. What is the likely effect on Canada? Explain.

10. In the text we discussed the historical debate between Keynesians and Monetarists regarding the effectiveness of monetary policy in changing real GDP (see Figure 28-10 on page 713 to review). Using the same sort of diagram, discuss two conditions in which a change in the money supply would have *no* short-run effect on real GDP.

11. In 2008, stock markets in Canada and other developed countries experienced very large declines, largely in response to the failure of several large U.S. and European banks and the resulting disruption in global financial markets.

a. Explain how such stock-market declines affect wealth and thus are likely to affect the *AD* curve.

b. If the central banks attempt to keep output close to Y^*, what will they likely do in response? Explain.

c. Did the Bank of Canada act as predicted in part (b)? Explain how you know.

12. Consider the effects of events in the U.S. economy on the Canadian economy and on Canadian monetary policy.

a. If a serious recession begins in the United States, what is the likely effect on Canadian aggregate demand? Explain.

b. If Canadian real GDP was equal to Y^* before the U.S. recession began, what would be the likely response by the Bank of Canada?

c. Given the mobility of financial capital across international boundaries, what is the likely effect on Canadian aggregate demand from a policy by the U.S. Federal Reserve that reduces U.S. interest rates?

d. Given your answer to part (c), explain why Canadian monetary policy might sometimes appear to "mirror" U.S. monetary policy even though the Bank of Canada is wholly independent from the U.S. Federal Reserve.

Monetary Policy in Canada

IN the previous two chapters we encountered many details about money and its importance for the economy. In Chapter 27 we saw how commercial banks, through their activities of accepting deposits and extending loans, create deposit money. These bank deposits, together with the currency in circulation, make up the nation's money supply. In Chapter 28 we examined the variables that influence households' and firms' money demand. We then put money demand together with money supply to examine how interest rates are determined in the short run in monetary equilibrium. Finally, we examined the monetary transmission mechanism—the chain of cause-and-effect events describing how changes in money demand or supply lead to changes in interest rates, aggregate demand, real GDP, and the price level.

Chapters 27 and 28 presented a general view of the role of money in the economy. What is still missing is a detailed account of how the Bank of Canada conducts its monetary policy. We begin this chapter by describing some technical details about how the Bank influences the monetary equilibrium and thereby sets in motion the monetary transmission mechanism. We then discuss the Bank's current system of inflation targeting and how this system helps to stabilize the economy. Finally, we discuss some limitations for monetary policy and some of the Bank's major policy challenges over the past 30 years.

29.1 How the Bank of Canada Implements Monetary Policy

The monetary transmission mechanism describes how changes in the demand for or supply of money cause changes in the interest rate, which then lead to changes in aggregate demand, real GDP, and the price level. But how does the Bank of Canada influence the money market and thereby implement its monetary policy?

As we saw in Chapter 27, the money supply is the sum of currency in circulation and total bank deposits, and commercial banks play a key role in influencing the level of these deposits. As a result, the Bank of Canada cannot directly *set* the money supply. As we will soon see, the Bank of Canada is also unable to directly *set* interest rates. In what follows, therefore, we speak of the Bank "targeting" the money supply or interest rates rather than "setting" them directly.

Money Supply Versus the Interest Rate

In general, any central bank has two alternative approaches for implementing its monetary policy—it can choose to target the money supply or it can choose to target the interest rate. These two approaches are illustrated in Figure 29-1, which shows money demand, money supply, and the equilibrium interest rate. For any given M_D curve, the central bank must choose one approach or the other; it cannot target *both* the money supply and the

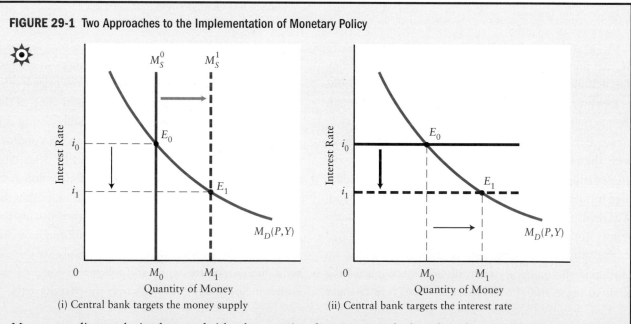

FIGURE 29-1 Two Approaches to the Implementation of Monetary Policy

(i) Central bank targets the money supply

(ii) Central bank targets the interest rate

Monetary policy can be implemented either by targeting the money supply directly or by targeting the interest rate directly—but not both. In part (i), the Bank of Canada could attempt to shift the M_S curve directly and thereby change the equilibrium interest rate. But because the Bank cannot directly control the money supply, and because the slope and position of the M_D curve are uncertain, this is an ineffective way to conduct monetary policy. The Bank's chosen method is illustrated in part (ii), in which it targets the interest rate directly. It then accommodates the resulting change in money demand through its open-market operations.

interest rate independently. If it chooses to target the money supply, monetary equilibrium will determine the interest rate. Alternatively, if the central bank targets the interest rate, the money supply must adjust to accommodate the movement along the M_D curve.

> In principle, monetary policy can be implemented either by targeting the money supply or by targeting the interest rate. But for a given M_D curve, both cannot be targeted independently.

Part (i) of Figure 29-1 shows how the Bank of Canada could attempt to shift the M_S curve directly, by changing the amount of currency in circulation in the economy. It could do this by buying or selling government securities in the financial markets—transactions called *open-market operations*. For example, by using currency to buy $100 000 of government bonds from a willing seller, the Bank of Canada would increase the amount of cash reserves in the banking system by $100 000. As we saw in Chapter 27, commercial banks would then be able to lend out these new reserves and thereby increase the amount of deposit money in the economy. The combined effect of the new reserves and the new deposit money would be an increase in the money supply and thus a shift of the M_S curve to the right. For a given M_D curve, this increase in money supply would lead to a reduction in the equilibrium interest rate and, through the various parts of the transmission mechanism, to an eventual increase in aggregate demand.

The Bank of Canada does not implement its monetary policy in this way, for three reasons. First, while the Bank of Canada *can* control the amount of cash reserves in the banking system (through open-market operations) it *cannot* control the process of deposit expansion carried out by the commercial banks. And since the money supply is the sum of currency and deposits, it follows that the Bank can influence the money supply but cannot *control* it. For example, if the Bank increased the amount of cash reserves in the system, the commercial banks might choose not to expand their lending, and as a result the overall increase in the money supply would be far smaller than the Bank initially intended.

The second reason the Bank does not try to target the money supply directly is the uncertainty regarding the slope of the M_D curve. Even if the Bank had perfect control over the money supply (which it does not), it would be unsure about the change in the interest rate that would result from any given change in the supply of money. Since it is the change in the interest rate that ultimately determines the subsequent changes in aggregate demand, this uncertainty would make the conduct of monetary policy very difficult.

Finally, in addition to being uncertain about the *slope* of the M_D curve, the Bank is also unable to predict accurately the *position* of the M_D curve at any given time. Changes in both real GDP and the price level cause changes in money demand that the Bank can only approximate. Even more difficult to predict are the changes in money demand that occur as a result of innovations in the financial sector. During the late 1970s and early 1980s, for example, the creation of new types of bank deposits led to unprecedented and unpredicted changes in money demand, as people transferred funds between bank accounts of different types. Unpredictable fluctuations in the demand for money make a monetary policy based on the direct control of the money supply difficult to implement.

In summary, the disadvantages of conducting monetary policy by targeting the money supply are as follows:

1. The Bank of Canada cannot control the process of deposit creation.

2. There is uncertainty regarding the slope of the M_D curve.

3. There is uncertainty regarding the position of the M_D curve.

If the Bank of Canada chose to target the money supply, it would have little control over the resulting interest rate. It therefore chooses *not* to implement its monetary policy in this way.

The alternative approach to implementing monetary policy is to target the interest rate directly. This is the approach used by most central banks, including the Bank of Canada. As part (ii) of Figure 29-1 shows, if the Bank can directly change the interest rate, the result will be a change in the quantity of money demanded. In order for this new interest rate to be consistent with monetary equilibrium, the Bank must *accommodate* the change in the amount of money demanded—that is, it must alter the supply of money in order to satisfy the change in desired money holdings by firms and households (we will see shortly how this occurs).

Why does the Bank of Canada choose to implement its monetary policy in this manner? Let's consider the advantages. First, while the Bank cannot control the money supply for the reasons we have just discussed, it *is* able to almost completely control a particular interest rate. (We will see shortly which rate it targets and how it does so.) Second, the Bank's uncertainty about the slope and position of the M_D curve is not a problem when the Bank chooses instead to target the interest rate directly. If the Bank ascertains that a lower interest rate is necessary in order to achieve its policy objectives, it can act directly to reduce the interest rate. Any uncertainty about the M_D curve then implies uncertainty about the ultimate change in the quantity of money, but it is the interest rate that matters, through the transmission mechanism, for determining the level of aggregate demand.

Finally, the Bank can more easily *communicate* its policy actions to the public by targeting the interest rate than by targeting the level of reserves in the banking system. Changes in the interest rate are more meaningful to firms and households than changes in the level of reserves or the money supply. For example, if we hear that the interest rate just decreased by one percentage point, most people can readily assess what this means for their plans to buy a new house financed by a mortgage. In contrast, if we were to hear that the level of reserves in the banking system had just increased by $1 billion, it would not be clear to most people what this means, or that it would have any effect on the interest rate, or by how much. Even the Bank itself might be uncertain about the magnitude of these effects.

In summary, these are the advantages of conducting monetary policy by targeting the interest rate:

1. The Bank of Canada is able to control a particular interest rate.

2. Uncertainty about the slope and position of the M_D curve does not prevent the Bank of Canada from establishing its desired interest rate.

3. The Bank of Canada can easily communicate its interest-rate policy to the public.

The Bank of Canada and the Overnight Interest Rate

We have just explained why the Bank of Canada chooses to implement its monetary policy by targeting the interest rate rather than by targeting the money supply directly. But *how* does the Bank do this, and *which* interest rate (among many) does it target?

As we discussed in Chapter 28, there are many interest rates in the Canadian economy. Commercial banks pay different rates to depositors on each of several different types of bank deposits. They also lend at different rates for different kinds of loans—home mortgages, small business loans, personal lines of credit, and car loans, to name just a few. In addition, government securities trade at different yields (interest rates) depending on the term to maturity. Economists refer to the overall pattern of interest rates corresponding to government securities of different maturities as the *term structure of interest rates*. Since inflation and other risks generally lead bondholders to require a higher rate of return in order to lend their funds for a longer period of time, yields on government securities generally increase as the term to maturity increases. At any given time, the yield on 90-day Treasury bills is usually less than that on 5-year government bonds, which in turn is less than the yield on 30-year bonds. Furthermore, because these various assets are viewed as close substitutes by bondholders, the different interest rates tend to rise and fall together.

The interest rate corresponding to the shortest period of borrowing or lending is called the **overnight interest rate,** which is the interest rate that commercial banks charge one another for overnight loans. Commercial banks that need cash because they have run short of reserves can borrow in the *overnight market* from banks that have excess reserves available. The overnight interest rate is a market-determined interest rate that fluctuates daily as the cash requirements of commercial banks change.

overnight interest rate The interest rate that commercial banks charge one another for overnight loans.

The Bank of Canada exercises enormous influence over the overnight interest rate. As this rate rises or falls, the other interest rates in the economy—from short-term lines of credit to longer-term home mortgages and government securities—tend to rise or fall as well.

> By influencing the overnight interest rate, the Bank of Canada also influences the longer-term interest rates that are more relevant for determining aggregate consumption and investment expenditure.

To see how the Bank of Canada influences the overnight interest rate, we need to make an important distinction between the Bank's target and the instrument that it uses to achieve that target. The Bank establishes a target for the overnight rate and announces this target eight times per year at pre-specified dates called *fixed announcement dates*, or FADs.

The Bank's instrument for achieving its target is its lending and borrowing activities with the commercial banking system. When the Bank announces its target for the overnight rate, it also announces the **bank rate,** an interest rate 0.25 percentage points above the target rate. The Bank promises to lend at this bank rate any amount that commercial banks want to borrow. At the same time, the Bank offers to borrow (accept deposits) in unlimited amounts from commercial banks and pay them an interest rate 0.25 percentage points below the target rate. With these promises by the Bank, the actual overnight interest rate stays within the 0.5-percentage-point range centred around the target rate, and is usually very close to the target rate itself.

bank rate The interest rate the Bank of Canada charges commercial banks for loans.

Consider an example that illustrates the Bank's control over the overnight interest rate. We begin by assuming that the Bank's announced target for the overnight interest rate is 3 percent. The Bank is then willing to lend to commercial banks at the bank rate, 3.25 percent. The Bank is also willing to pay 2.75 percent on any deposits it receives from commercial banks. In this case, what will be the *actual* overnight interest rate? Without knowing more details about commercial banks' demands and supplies for overnight funds, we cannot know exactly what the rate will be, but we can be sure that it will be within the Bank's target range—that is, *between* 2.75 percent and 3.25 percent. It will not be above 3.25 percent because any borrower would rather borrow from the Bank of Canada at 3.25 percent than at a higher rate from any commercial lender. Similarly, it will not be below 2.75 percent because any lender would rather lend to the Bank of Canada at 2.75 percent than accept a lower rate from any commercial borrower. Thus, the Bank can ensure that the actual overnight interest rate remains within its target range.[1]

> The Bank of Canada establishes a target for the overnight interest rate. Its instrument for achieving this target is its borrowing and lending activities with commercial banks. By raising or lowering its target rate, the Bank affects the actual overnight interest rate. Changes in the overnight rate then lead to changes in other, longer-term, interest rates.

Figure 29-2 shows the path of the actual overnight interest rate and the Bank's target rate since 2000. It is almost impossible to tell the difference between the two lines in the figure, which shows the considerable influence that the Bank of Canada's actions have on the actual overnight interest rate.

FIGURE 29-2 The Overnight Interest Rate: Target and Actual

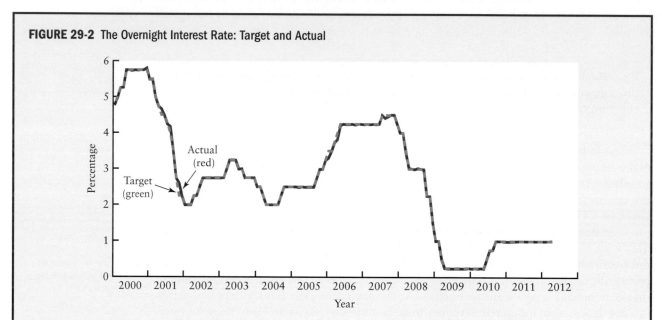

By setting a target for the overnight interest rate, the Bank of Canada exercises considerable influence over the actual overnight interest rate. By establishing an upper lending rate (the bank rate) and a lower borrowing rate, the Bank can ensure that the actual overnight interest rate remains within the Bank's target range. Since 2000, there have been only negligible differences between the actual overnight interest rate, the solid red line, and the Bank's target for the overnight rate, the green dashed line.

(*Source:* All data are from the Bank of Canada: www.bankofcanada.ca. Overnight interest rate: Series V122514. Bank rate: Series V122530. The Bank's target rate is the bank rate minus 0.25 percentage points.)

---

[1] The actual overnight rate is usually indistinguishable from the Bank's target rate, but it occasionally deviates by as much as 10 basis points (0.1 percentage point). When this occurs, typically only a few days per month, the Bank of Canada initiates further temporary lending and borrowing transactions with the commercial banks in order to push the overnight rate back toward the Bank's target rate.

The Money Supply Is Endogenous

When the Bank of Canada changes its target for the overnight rate, the change in the actual overnight rate happens almost instantly. Changes in other market interest rates, from home mortgage rates and the prime interest rate to the yields on short- and long-term government securities, also happen very quickly, usually within a day or two. As these rates adjust, firms and households begin to adjust their borrowing behaviour, but these changes take considerably longer to occur. For example, if the Bank of Canada lowered its target for the overnight rate by 25 basis points (0.25 percentage points), commercial banks might follow immediately by reducing the rate on home mortgages. But individuals will not respond to this rate reduction by immediately increasing their demand for home mortgages. Usually such changes take a while to occur, as borrowers consider how interest-rate changes affect their own economic situations, the affordability of a possible house purchase, or, in the case of firms, the profitability of a potential investment.

As the demand for new loans gradually adjusts to changes in interest rates, commercial banks often find themselves in need of more cash reserves with which to make new loans. When this occurs, banks can sell some of their government securities to the Bank of Canada in exchange for cash (or electronic reserves) and then use this cash to extend new loans. By buying government securities with cash in such an **open-market operation**, the Bank of Canada increases the amount of currency in circulation in the economy. This new currency arrives at the commercial banks as cash reserves, which can then be loaned out to firms or households. As we saw in Chapter 27, this process of making loans results in an expansion in deposit money and thus an expansion of the money supply.

open-market operation The purchase and sale of government securities on the open market by the central bank.

> Through its open-market operations, the Bank of Canada changes the amount of currency in circulation. These operations, however, are not initiated by the Bank; it conducts them to accommodate the changing demand for cash reserves by the commercial banks.

Economists often say that the amount of currency in circulation (and also the money supply) is *endogenous*. It is not directly controlled by the Bank of Canada, but instead is determined by the economic decisions of households, firms, and commercial banks. The Bank of Canada is *passive* in its decisions regarding the money supply; it conducts its open-market operations to accommodate the changing demand for currency coming from the commercial banks. *Applying Economic Concepts 29-1* discusses in more detail how the Bank of Canada conducts open-market operations in response to this changing demand.

Expansionary and Contractionary Monetary Policies

We can now clarify the meaning of a *contractionary* or an *expansionary* monetary policy. As we saw earlier, unpredictable shifts in the money demand curve imply that there is no clear relationship between changes in the interest rate and changes in the quantity of money in circulation. And since what matters for the monetary transmission mechanism is the change in interest rates, economists label a monetary-policy action as being expansionary or contractionary depending on how the policy affects interest rates, rather than on how it affects the overall amount of money.

If the Bank of Canada wants to stimulate aggregate demand, it will reduce its target for the overnight interest rate, and the effect will soon be felt on longer-term market

APPLYING ECONOMIC CONCEPTS 29-1

What Determines the Amount of Currency in Circulation?

The Bank of Canada uses its target for the overnight interest rate to influence the money market and implement its monetary policy. A reduction in the Bank's target for the overnight rate will reduce market interest rates and lead to a greater demand for borrowing and hence spending by firms and households. In contrast, an increase in the Bank's target for the overnight rate will tend to raise market interest rates and reduce the demand for borrowing and spending by firms and households.

In response to these changes in the demand for loans, commercial banks may find themselves either with too few cash reserves with which to make new loans or with too many cash reserves for the amount of loans they want to make. What happens in each case?

If Banks Need More Cash

Suppose that at the current market interest rates and level of economic activity, commercial banks are facing a growing demand for loans. If banks have excess reserves, these loans can be made easily. But once banks reach their target reserve ratio, they will be unable to extend new loans without increasing their cash reserves. Banks can increase their cash reserves by selling some of their government bonds to the Bank of Canada. In this case, the Bank of Canada is *purchasing* government bonds from the commercial banks. This transaction is called an *open-market purchase*.

Suppose a commercial bank wants to sell a $10 000 bond to the Bank of Canada. As the accompanying balance sheets show, this transaction does not change the total assets or liabilities for the commercial bank, although it changes the *form* of its assets. With more cash reserves (and fewer bonds), the commercial bank can now make more loans. For the Bank of Canada, however, there *is* a change in the level of assets and liabilities. Its holdings of bonds (assets) have increased and the amount of currency in circulation (liabilities) has also increased. Open-market purchases by the Bank of Canada are the means by which the amount of currency in the economy increases.

If Banks Have Excess Reserves

Now suppose that at the current market interest rates and level of economic activity the commercial banks cannot find enough suitable borrowers to whom they can lend their excess cash reserves. The commercial banks can reduce their excess cash reserves by using the cash to purchase government bonds from the Bank of Canada. In this case, the Bank of Canada is *selling* government bonds to the commercial banks. This transaction is called an *open-market sale*.

The changes are the opposite of those shown in the accompanying balance sheets. The commercial bank now has less cash and more (interest-earning) bonds, but its total assets and liabilities are unchanged. The Bank of Canada now has fewer bonds and there is also less currency in circulation in the economy.

An Open-Market Purchase of Bonds from a Commercial Bank

Commercial Bank Balance Sheet

Assets		Liabilities
Bonds	− $10 000	No change
Cash Reserves	+ $10 000	

Bank of Canada Balance Sheet

Assets		Liabilities	
Bonds	+ $10 000	Currency in Circulation	+ $10 000

Currency in a Growing Economy

If you look at the Bank of Canada's balance sheets (like the one we showed in Chapter 27) over several years, you will notice that the amount of currency in circulation rarely (if ever) falls. In an economy where real GDP is steadily growing, the demand for loans by firms and households is also usually growing, as is the demand for currency by commercial banks. In some years, the demand for currency is growing very quickly, in which case the Bank of Canada has many open-market purchases. In other years, the demand for currency grows only slowly, in which case the Bank has fewer (or smaller) open-market purchases. In a typical year, however, the amount of currency in circulation increases by about 5 percent, which in 2012 represented about $3 billion. Thus, in a typical week, the Bank of Canada purchases about $55 million of government bonds in the open market.

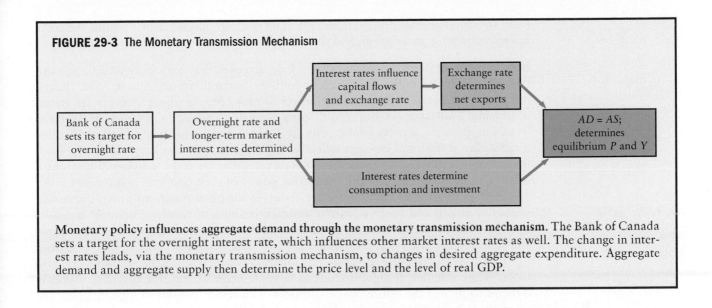

FIGURE 29-3 The Monetary Transmission Mechanism

Monetary policy influences aggregate demand through the monetary transmission mechanism. The Bank of Canada sets a target for the overnight interest rate, which influences other market interest rates as well. The change in interest rates leads, via the monetary transmission mechanism, to changes in desired aggregate expenditure. Aggregate demand and aggregate supply then determine the price level and the level of real GDP.

interest rates. Reducing the interest rate is an *expansionary* monetary policy because it leads to an expansion of aggregate demand. If the Bank instead wants to reduce aggregate demand (or its growth rate), it will increase its target for the overnight interest rate, and longer-term market interest rates will soon rise as a result. Increasing the interest rate is a *contractionary* monetary policy because it leads to a contraction (or a reduction in the growth rate) of aggregate demand.

As the longer-term market interest rates change, the various steps in the monetary transmission mechanism come into play. As we saw in Chapter 28, in an open economy like Canada's there are two separate channels in this transmission mechanism. First, desired investment and consumption expenditure will begin to change. At the same time, international capital flows in response to changes in interest rates will cause the exchange rate to change, which, in turn, causes net exports to change. Taken together, the total changes in aggregate expenditure lead to shifts in the *AD* curve, which then lead to changes in real GDP and the price level. The monetary transmission mechanism is reviewed in Figure 29-3.

29.2 Inflation Targeting

In the previous section we examined the technical details of how the Bank of Canada implements its monetary policy. In this section we examine the Bank's current policy objectives and how it conducts its monetary policy to achieve those objectives. Our emphasis is on the Bank's policy of *inflation targeting*.

Why Target Inflation?

Some people wonder why many central banks have established formal targets for the rate of inflation rather than for other important economic variables such as the rate of growth of real GDP or the unemployment rate. Central banks' focus on inflation comes from two fundamental observations regarding macroeconomic relationships: the costs associated with high inflation, and the ultimate cause of sustained inflation.

High Inflation Is Costly Economists have long accepted that high rates of inflation are damaging to the economy and are costly for firms and individuals. Among other things, inflation reduces the real purchasing power of those people whose incomes are stated in nominal (dollar) terms and insufficiently *indexed* to adjust for changes in the price level. For example, seniors whose pension incomes are not indexed to inflation suffer a reduction in their real incomes whenever inflation occurs. Similarly, those who have made loans or purchased bonds with interest rates that are fixed in nominal terms lose because inflation erodes the real purchasing power of their financial investments.

High inflation also undermines the ability of the price system to provide accurate signals of changes in relative scarcity through changes in relative prices. As a result, both producers and consumers may make mistakes regarding their own production and consumption decisions that they would not have made in the absence of high inflation.

Finally, the *uncertainty* generated by inflation is damaging to the economy in many ways. When inflation is high, it tends to be quite volatile, and this volatility makes it difficult to predict the future course of prices. As a result, periods of high inflation are often characterized as having much *unexpected* inflation. The risk of unexpected inflation makes it difficult for firms to make long-range plans, and such plans are crucial when firms undertake costly investment and R&D activities in order to expand their production facilities or to invent and innovate new products and new production processes. High and volatile inflation is thus likely to be harmful to economic growth.

> High and uncertain inflation leads to arbitrary income redistributions and also hampers the ability of the price system both to allocate resources efficiently and to produce satisfactory rates of economic growth.

Monetary Policy Is the Cause of Sustained Inflation Until recent decades there was uncertainty about the causes of inflation. During the 1970s, many policymakers blamed inflation on the "cost push" exerted on wages by powerful unions and on prices by oligopolistic firms. In response, many governments adopted formal wage-and-price controls in an attempt to contain the inflations that they assumed were being generated from the cost (supply) side of the economy rather than from the demand side.

These attempts to control inflation proved to be costly failures as high inflation continued to plague many Western economies well into the 1980s. As a result of such failures, most economists soon came to adopt the argument that Nobel laureate Milton Friedman had been making for many years, that inflation was mainly a monetary phenomenon. It was already recognized that shocks unrelated to monetary policy cause shifts in the *AD* and *AS* curves and thus cause temporary changes in the rate of inflation as the economy responds to these shocks. The change in view, however, was that *sustained* inflation was not caused by such shocks—instead, sustained inflation appeared to occur only in those situations in which monetary policy was allowing continual and rapid growth in the money supply. In other words, economists came to recognize that sustained inflation must ultimately be caused by monetary policy.

With the acceptance of this view that sustained inflation is ultimately the result of monetary policy, central banks came to be seen as the main actors in the anti-inflation drama. If high and variable inflation rates were harmful to the economy and if central bank validation was a necessary condition for an inflation to be sustained, the central bank could prevent sustained inflation by adopting an appropriate monetary policy. In response to this belief, central banks around most of the developed world were given as their main responsibility the control of the price level and instructed to do this by adopting policies that targeted the rate of inflation.

> Most economists and central bankers accept that monetary policy is the most important determinant of a country's long-run rate of inflation.

The Adoption of Inflation Targeting In 1990, New Zealand became the first country to adopt a formal system of *inflation targeting*. Canada was second, in 1991, followed soon by Israel, the United Kingdom, Australia, Finland, Spain, and Sweden. Since the mid-1990s, the list has grown to include Chile, Brazil, Colombia, Mexico, the Czech Republic, Poland, South Africa, Thailand, and others. The U.S. Federal Reserve has *not* yet adopted a formal inflation target, although its current chairman, Ben Bernanke, has indicated that he would like the Federal Reserve to do so.

When the Bank of Canada first adopted its formal inflation targets in 1991 the annual rate of inflation was almost 6 percent. The targets were expressed as the midpoint of a 2-percentage-point band, in recognition of the fact that it is unrealistic to expect the Bank to keep the inflation rate at a single, precise value in the face of the many shocks that influence it in the short term. Beginning in 1992, the Bank of Canada's target range for inflation was 3 to 5 percent, with the range falling to 2 to 4 percent by 1993 and to 1 to 3 percent by the end of 1995. The Bank's formal inflation targets were renewed every five years between 1991 and 2011, with the current targets in place until 2016. (The Bank now emphasizes its 2 percent inflation target and places much less emphasis on the 1 to 3 percent range.) Figure 29-4 shows quarterly data for Canadian inflation since 1992.

Inflation Targeting and the Output Gap

The control of inflation is the Bank of Canada's stated policy objective. Keeping inflation close to its formal 2 percent target, however, requires the Bank to monitor the output gap and the associated pressures that may be pushing inflation above or below the target.

The Bank recognizes that because monetary policy has the potential to influence real GDP, it simultaneously has the potential to alter the size of the current output gap, from which comes the pressure for inflation to rise or fall. Faced with a persistent recessionary gap ($Y < Y^*$), which eventually tends to reduce inflation below the Bank's 2-percent target, the Bank can pursue an expansionary monetary policy in an attempt to increase real GDP and reduce the recessionary gap. Such a policy would be pursued until the output gap is eliminated and inflationary pressures threaten to move the inflation rate above the 2-percent target. Faced with a persistent inflationary gap ($Y > Y^*$) and the associated tendency for inflation to rise above the 2-percent target, the Bank can pursue a contractionary policy in an attempt to bring real GDP back toward Y^* and the inflation rate closer to 2 percent.

> Persistent output gaps generally create pressure for the rate of inflation to change. To keep the rate of inflation close to the 2-percent target, the Bank of Canada closely monitors real GDP in the short run and designs its policy to keep real GDP close to potential output.

FIGURE 29-4 Canadian CPI and Core Inflation, 1992–2012

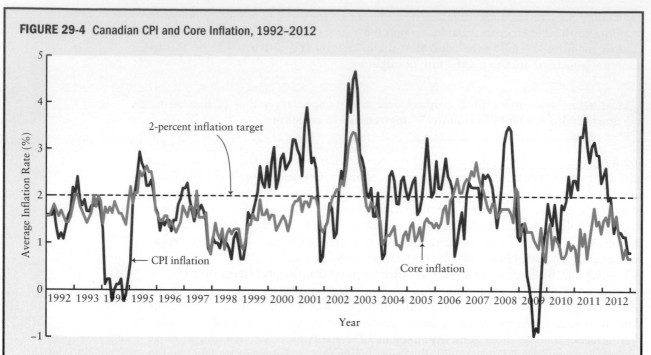

The CPI inflation rate is more volatile than the "core" inflation rate. The core rate of inflation in Canada is the rate of change of a special price index constructed by removing food, energy, and the effects of indirect taxes from the overall Consumer Price Index. For both series shown here, the inflation rate is computed monthly but is the rate of change in the price index from 12 months earlier.

(*Source:* Based on author's calculations using data from Statistics Canada, CANSIM database. CPI: Table 326-0020. Core: Table 176-0003.)

Inflation Targeting as a Stabilizing Policy

If the Bank of Canada is committed to keeping the rate of inflation near 2 percent, positive shocks to the economy that create an inflationary gap and threaten to increase the rate of inflation will be met by a contractionary monetary policy. The Bank will increase interest rates and shift the *AD* curve to the left. This policy will reduce the size of the output gap and push the rate of inflation back toward 2 percent. Similarly, if a negative shock to the economy creates a persistent recessionary gap, the Bank will respond with an expansionary monetary policy, reducing interest rates and shifting the *AD* curve to the right.

The short-run effects of the Bank's actions suggest that its policy of inflation targeting can be seen as an "automatic" stabilizer. But this is an exaggeration, as we can see by recalling our discussion in Chapter 24 of automatic fiscal stabilizers, which are caused by taxes and transfers that vary with the level of national income. Automatic fiscal stabilizers are truly "automatic" in the sense that no group of policymakers has to actively adjust policy—the stabilizers are built right into the tax-and-transfer system. With inflation targeting, however, there must be an active policy decision to keep inflation close to its target rate, and only then will the Bank's policy adjustments work to stabilize the economy in the face of shocks that create inflationary or recessionary output gaps.

Inflation targets are not as "automatic" a stabilizer as the fiscal stabilizers built into the tax-and-transfer system. However, as long as the central bank is committed to achieving its inflation target, its policy adjustments will act to stabilize real GDP.

Complications in Inflation Targeting

So far, our discussion of inflation targeting makes the conduct of monetary policy seem relatively straightforward. But there are several details that complicate the task considerably. In this section we discuss two complications for the conduct of monetary policy, and in the next section we address a more general difficulty.

Volatile Food and Energy Prices Sometimes the rate of inflation increases for reasons unrelated to a change in the output gap. For example, many commodities whose prices are included in the Consumer Price Index (CPI) are internationally traded goods and their prices are determined in world markets. Oil is an obvious example, as are many raw materials and fruits and vegetables. When these prices rise suddenly, perhaps because of political instability in the Middle East (oil) or because of poor crop conditions in tropical countries (fruits and vegetables), the measured rate of inflation of the Canadian CPI also rises. Yet these price increases have little or nothing to do with the size of the output gap in Canada and thus have little implication for what policy should be followed by the Bank of Canada. By focusing exclusively on the rate of inflation of the CPI, the Bank would be misled about the extent of inflationary pressures coming from excess demand in Canada.

For this reason, the Bank of Canada also monitors closely what is called the "core" rate of inflation. This is the rate of growth of a special price index, one that is constructed by extracting food, energy, and the effects of indirect taxes (such as the GST or excise taxes) from the Consumer Price Index. Figure 29-4 shows the paths of core and CPI inflation since 1992. As is clear from the figure, even though the two measures of inflation move broadly together, core inflation is much less volatile than is CPI inflation.

Because the volatility of food and energy prices is often unrelated to the level of the output gap in Canada, the Bank of Canada closely monitors the rate of "core" inflation even though its formal target of 2 percent applies to the rate of CPI inflation. Changes in core inflation are a better indicator of *domestic* inflationary pressures than are changes in CPI inflation.

Note the sharp divergence between the two inflation rates in 1994. At that time, there were substantial decreases in the excise taxes on cigarettes. Since the resulting sharp decline in CPI inflation was caused by a reduction in taxes rather than by domestic excess supply, it would have been inappropriate for the Bank of Canada to respond to this decline in inflation by implementing an expansionary monetary policy. Instead, the Bank focused on the core inflation rate that excludes the effect of changes in indirect taxes. The core inflation rate in 1994 was relatively stable and close to the Bank's 2 percent target, indicating no need for a change in monetary policy.

Note also the volatility of the CPI inflation rate during 2008 and 2009. Energy and commodity prices had been rising for the previous few years, but they increased especially rapidly in the early part of 2008. This helped to push the CPI inflation rate well above 3 percent. But then the worst part of the global financial crisis occurred in the autumn of that year, energy and commodity prices plunged, and the CPI inflation rate fell quickly and was *negative* for a period of a few months in 2009. In contrast, the core rate of inflation was much less volatile during these events and remained much closer to 2 percent.

The Exchange Rate and Monetary Policy Given the large amount of trade that Canadian firms and households do with the rest of the world, it is not surprising that the Bank of Canada pays close attention to movements in the exchange rate, the Canadian-dollar price of one unit of foreign currency. However, because changes in the exchange rate can have several different causes, care must be taken when drawing inferences about the desired change in monetary policy resulting from changes in the exchange rate. As we will see, there is no simple "rule of thumb" for how the Bank should react to a change in the exchange rate.

We consider two illustrative examples. In the first, an appreciation of the Canadian dollar leads the Bank to tighten its monetary policy by raising its target for the overnight interest rate. In the second example, an appreciation of the Canadian dollar leads the Bank to loosen its monetary policy by reducing its target for the overnight interest rate. In both cases, the Bank's actions are consistent with its objective of keeping the inflation rate near the Bank's 2 percent target.

For the first example, suppose that the economies of Canada's trading partners are booming and thus demanding more Canadian exports. Foreigners' heightened demand for Canadian goods creates an increase in demand for the Canadian dollar in foreign-exchange markets. The Canadian dollar therefore appreciates. But the increase in demand for Canadian goods has added directly to Canadian aggregate demand. If this shock persists, it will eventually add to domestic inflationary pressures. In this case, if the Bank notes the appreciation of the dollar (and correctly determines its cause), it can take action to offset the positive demand shock by tightening monetary policy, which it does by raising its target for the overnight interest rate.

The second example involves an increase in demand for Canadian *assets* rather than Canadian goods and has quite different implications from the first example. Suppose that investors, because of events happening elsewhere in the world, decide to liquidate some of their foreign assets and purchase more Canadian assets instead. In this case, the increase in demand for Canadian assets leads to an increase in demand for the Canadian dollar in foreign-exchange markets. This causes an appreciation of the Canadian dollar. As the dollar appreciates, however, Canadian exports become more expensive to foreigners. There will be a reduction in Canadian net exports and thus a reduction in Canadian aggregate demand. If this shock persists, it will eventually create a recessionary gap in Canada. In this case, if the Bank notes the appreciation of the dollar (and correctly determines its cause), it can take action to offset the negative demand shock by loosening monetary policy which it does by reducing its target for the overnight interest rate.

Notice in both examples that the Canadian dollar appreciated as a result of the external shock, but the causes of the appreciation were different. In the first case, there was a positive demand shock to net exports, which then caused the appreciation, which in turn dampened the initial increase in net exports. But the overall effect on the demand for Canadian goods was positive. In the second case, there was a positive shock to the *asset* market, which then caused the appreciation, which in turn reduced the demand for net exports. The overall effect on the demand for Canadian goods was negative. In the first case, the appropriate response for monetary policy was contractionary, whereas in the second case the appropriate response for monetary policy was expansionary.

Changes in the exchange rate can signal the need for changes in the stance of monetary policy. However, the Bank needs to determine the cause of the exchange-rate change before it can design a policy response appropriate for keeping real GDP close to potential and inflation close to the 2 percent target.

29.3 Long and Variable Lags

In Chapter 28 we encountered a debate that was prominent from the 1950s to the early 1980s. *Monetarists* argued that monetary policy was potentially very powerful in the sense that a given change in the money supply would lead to a substantial change in aggregate demand, whereas *Keynesians* argued that monetary policy was much less powerful.

This debate had some of its roots in differing interpretations of the causes of the Great Depression. One interesting part of the debate is why Canada and the United Kingdom had collapses in economic activity similar in magnitude to that in the United States even though they did not suffer the widespread bank failures that featured in the U.S. experience. *Lessons from History 29-1* provides a brief summary of this interesting debate and applies some of the lessons about monetary policy we have learned in the past two chapters.

The debate between Monetarists and Keynesians was about more than just the *effectiveness* of monetary policy. The debate sometimes also focused on the question of whether active use of monetary policy in an attempt to stabilize output and the price level was likely to be successful or whether it would instead lead to an increase in fluctuations in those variables. This debate is as important today as it was then, and at its centre is the role of *lags*.

What Are the Lags in Monetary Policy?

Experience has shown that lags in the operation of policy can sometimes cause stabilization policy to be destabilizing. In Chapter 24, we discussed how decision and implementation lags might limit the extent to which active use of fiscal policy can be relied upon to stabilize the economy. Although both of these sources of lags are less relevant for monetary policy, the full effects of monetary policy nevertheless occur only after quite long time lags. There are two reasons that a change in monetary policy does not affect the economy instantly.

Changes in Expenditure Take Time When the Bank of Canada changes its target for the overnight interest rate, the actual overnight rate changes almost instantly. Other, longer-term interest rates also change quickly, usually within a day or two. However, it takes more time before households and firms adjust their spending and borrowing plans in response to the change in interest rates. Consumers may respond relatively quickly and alter their plans for purchasing durable goods like cars and appliances. But it takes longer for firms to modify their investment plans and then put them into effect.

LESSONS FROM HISTORY 29-1

Two Views on the Role of Money in the Great Depression

In most people's minds, the Great Depression began with the stock market crash of October 1929. In the United States, Canada, and Europe, the decline in economic activity over the next four years was massive. From 1929 to 1933, real output fell by roughly 25 percent, one-quarter of the labour force was unemployed by 1933, the price level fell by more than 25 percent, and businesses failed on a massive scale. In the more than seven decades that have followed, no recession has come close to the Great Depression in terms of reduced economic activity, business failures, or unemployment.

The Great Depression has naturally attracted the attention of economists and, especially in the United States, these few years of experience have served as a kind of "retrospective laboratory" in which they have tried to test their theories.

The Basic Facts

The stock market crash of 1929, and other factors associated with a moderate downswing in business activity during the late 1920s, caused U.S. firms and households to want to hold more cash and fewer demand deposits. The banking system, however, could not meet this increased demand for liquidity (cash) without help from the Federal Reserve System (the U.S. central bank). As we saw in Chapter 27, because of the fractional-reserve banking system, commercial banks are never able to satisfy from their own reserves a large and sudden demand for cash—their reserves are always only a small fraction of total deposits.

The Federal Reserve had been set up to provide just such emergency assistance to commercial banks that were basically sound but were unable to meet sudden demands by depositors to withdraw cash. However, the Federal Reserve refused to extend the necessary help, and successive waves of bank failures followed as a direct result. During each wave, hundreds of banks failed, ruining many depositors, reducing the flow of credit, and worsening an already severe depression. In the second half of 1931, almost 2000 U.S. banks were forced to suspend operations. One consequence of these failures was a sharp drop in the money supply; by 1933, M2 was 33 percent lower than it had been in 1929.

Competing Explanations

After the Great Depression was over, economists were able to examine the data and construct explanations for these dramatic events. To Monetarists, the basic facts seem decisive: to them, the fall in the money supply was clearly the major *cause* of the fall in output and employment that occurred during the Great Depression. Monetarists see the Great Depression as perhaps the single best piece of evidence of the strength of monetary forces and the single best lesson of the importance of monetary policy. In their view, the increased cash drain that led to the massive monetary contraction could have been prevented had the Federal Reserve quickly increased the level of cash reserves in the commercial banking system. In this case, the rise in cash reserves would have offset the increase in the cash drain, so that the money supply (currency plus bank deposits) could be maintained.

Keynesians argued that the fundamental cause of the Great Depression was a reduction in autonomous expenditure. They cite a large decline in housing construction (in response to a glut of housing), a decline in automobile

It may take a year or more before the full increase in investment expenditure occurs in response to a fall in interest rates.

In an open economy such as Canada's, the change in the interest rate also leads to flows of financial capital and a change in the exchange rate. These changes occur very quickly. But the effect on net exports takes more time while purchasers of internationally traded goods and services switch to lower-cost suppliers.

The Multiplier Process Takes Time Changes in consumption, investment, and net export expenditures brought about by a change in monetary policy set off the multiplier process that increases national income. This process, too, takes some time to work through. Furthermore, although the end result is fairly predictable, the speed with which the entire expansionary or contractionary process works itself out can vary in ways that are hard to predict. Thus, though the overall effects of monetary policy might be reasonably straightforward to predict, the timing of those effects is difficult to predict.

purchases (as most first-time buying was done and only replacement demand remained), and a reduction in consumption driven largely by pessimism caused by the stock market crash. Although Keynesians accept the argument that the Federal Reserve's behaviour was perverse and exacerbated an already bad situation, they do not attribute a pivotal role to the Federal Reserve or to the money supply. Instead, they see the fall in the money supply as a *result* of the decline in economic activity (through a reduced demand for loans and thus reduced bank lending) rather than as its cause.

Lessons from Canada's Experience

Canada had broadly the same magnitude of economic collapse as did the United States during the Great Depression, but had *no* bank failures. Unfortunately, Canada's experience is not able to resolve the disagreement—both sides of the debate can offer explanations of the Canadian experience consistent with their central arguments.

Keynesians look to Canada's experience to support their view that money was not central to the cause of the economic collapse in the United States. They point out that since Canada did not escape the Great Depression but *did* escape the banking crisis and the associated collapse in the money supply, money was unlikely to have been the central cause of the U.S. economic collapse.

Monetarists accept the point that Canada did not have a massive reduction in the money supply, but they argue that the economic contraction in the United States (which *was* caused by the collapse in the money supply) spilled over into Canada, largely through a dramatic reduction in demand for Canadian goods. This spillover

implies a large decline in export expenditure for Canada, and thus a decline in Canadian national income. Thus, Monetarists essentially argue that money in the United States was an important contributor to the economic decline in Canada.

During the Great Depression, bank failures were widespread in the United States but did not occur at all in Canada. This difference in experience can be used to test hypotheses regarding the causes of the Great Depression. But considerable disagreement still remains.

For a discussion of these two views, and some attempts to discriminate between them, see Peter Temin, *Did Monetary Forces Cause the Great Depression?*, Norton, 1976.

> Monetary policy is capable of exerting expansionary and contractionary forces on the economy, but it operates with a time lag that is long and difficult to predict.

Economists at the Bank of Canada estimate that it normally takes between 9 and 12 months for a change in monetary policy to have its main effect on real GDP, and a further 9 to 12 months for the policy to have its main effect on the price level (or the rate of inflation).

Destabilizing Policy?

The fact that monetary-policy actions taken today will not affect output and inflation until one to two years in the future means that the Bank of Canada must design its policy for what *is expected* to occur in the future rather than what *has already been observed.* To see why a monetary policy guided only by past and current events may be destabilizing, consider the following simple example. Suppose that on January 1 the Bank observes that real GDP is less than potential output and concludes that an expansionary monetary policy is appropriate. It can reduce its target for the overnight rate at the next fixed announcement date (FAD), typically within a few weeks. By early February, the overnight interest rate will be reduced, as will the longer-term interest rates in the economy. The effects on aggregate demand, however, will not be felt in any significant way until late summer or early fall of that same year.

This policy action may turn out to be destabilizing, however. Some of the cyclical forces in the economy, unrelated to the Bank's actions, may have reversed since January, and by fall there may be an inflationary output gap. However, since the effects of the monetary expansion that was initiated nine months earlier are just beginning to be felt, an expansionary monetary stimulus is adding to the existing inflationary gap.

If the Bank now applies the monetary brakes by raising its target for the overnight interest rate, the output effects of this policy reversal will not be felt for another year or so. By that time, a contraction may have already set in because of the natural cyclical forces of the economy. Thus, the delayed effects of the monetary policy may turn a minor downturn into a major recession.

> **The long time lags in the effectiveness of monetary policy increase the difficulty of stabilizing the economy; monetary policy may have a destabilizing effect.**

The Bank of Canada recognizes the possibility that if it responds to every shock that influences real GDP, the overall effect of its policy may be to destabilize the economy rather than stabilize it. As a result, it is careful to assess the causes of the shocks that buffet the Canadian economy. It tries to avoid situations in which it responds to shocks that are believed to be short-lived and then must reverse its policy in the near future when the shocks disappear. In general, the Bank responds only to those shocks that are significant in magnitude and are expected to persist for several months or more. For example, the global recession that began in 2008 was both large and long-lasting, and the Bank's expansionary policies had ample time to operate in the appropriate direction even after the expected lags in their effectiveness.

Political Difficulties

Long lags in the workings of monetary policy also lead to some political criticism for the central bank.

Figure 29-5 shows a situation in which the current inflation rate is well below the 2 percent target but the expectation of future events suggests that inflation will soon rise and exceed the target. This situation is often faced by the Bank when the economy is in the early stages of an economic recovery, as occurred in late 2012. At that time, monetary policy had been expansionary for over three years in an effort to stimulate the economy and offset the effects of a global economic recession. But as real GDP began to grow and the existing recessionary gap began to narrow, the Bank needed to judge the appropriate time to begin tightening its policy in an attempt to keep inflation from rising above the 2 percent target.

What is the political problem? Remember that because of the time lags involved, any policy change that occurs today has no effect on real GDP for roughly 9 months and the full effect on the price level (or the rate of inflation) does not occur for 18 to 24 months. If the economy is at point *A* in Figure 29-5, and inflation is expected to rise in the near future, then monetary policy must be changed *now* in order to counteract this future inflation. But this action could generate some criticism because the *current* inflation rate is low. In such situations, the Bank finds itself in the awkward position of advocating a tightening of monetary policy, in order to fight the expectation of future inflation, at a time when the *current* inflation rate suggests no need for tightening. But if the goal is to keep inflation close to the 2 percent target, such *pre-emptive* monetary policy is necessary because of the unavoidable time lags.

> Time lags in monetary policy require that decisions regarding a loosening or tightening of monetary policy be forward-looking. This often leads to criticism of monetary policy, especially by those who do not recognize the long time lags.

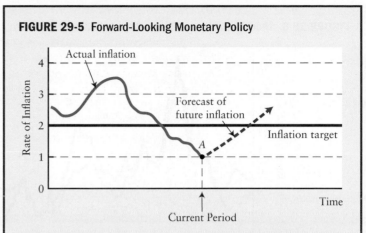

FIGURE 29-5 Forward-Looking Monetary Policy

Since monetary policy works only with a considerable time lag, central-bank actions to keep inflation close to target must be taken in advance of expected future events. Suppose the economy is currently at point *A* with inflation well below the target. If events in the near future are expected to cause inflation to rise and exceed the target, then monetary policy must be tightened, even though *current* inflation is low.

29.4 Thirty Years of Canadian Monetary Policy

This section describes a few key episodes in recent Canadian monetary history. This is not done to teach history for its own sake, but because the lessons of past experience and past policy mistakes, interpreted through the filter of economic theory, provide our best hope for improving our policy performance in the future.

The OPEC oil-price shocks of 1973 and 1979–1980 led to reductions in GDP growth rates and increases in inflation in Canada—what came to be known as *stagflation*. At that time, the role of aggregate-supply shocks and their effect on macroeconomic equilibrium was not as well understood as it is today. The Bank of Canada's policy response involved considerable monetary expansion, and by 1980 the rate of inflation in Canada was more than 12 percent.

The Bank of Canada (and the U.S. Federal Reserve) then embarked on policies designed to reduce the growth rate of the money supply and eventually reduce the inflation rate. Unfortunately, at the same time innovations in the financial sector led to unexpected increases in the demand for money. The result was a much sharper increase in interest rates (see Figure 29-6) than was intended by the Bank of Canada and the most serious recession since the 1930s. But the rate of inflation *did* fall, from more than 12 percent in 1980 to about 4 percent in 1984. This experience taught the Bank two important lessons:

1. Monetary policy can be *very* effective in reducing inflation.

2. Because of unexpected changes in money demand, monetary policy should focus more on interest rates than on the money supply.

As we saw earlier in this chapter, this second lesson is an important reason why the Bank now implements its policy by targeting the interest rate rather than by directly targeting the money supply.

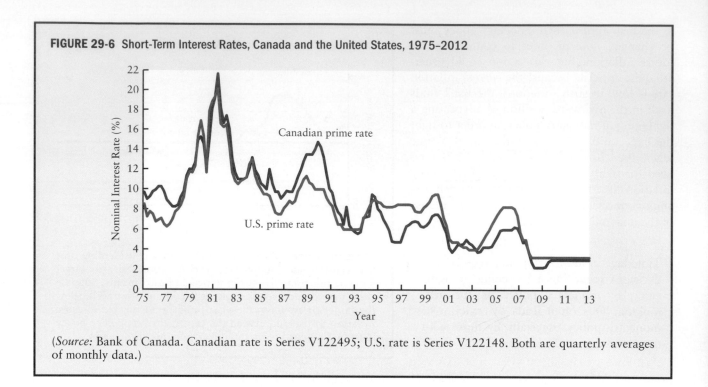

FIGURE 29-6 Short-Term Interest Rates, Canada and the United States, 1975–2012

(*Source:* Bank of Canada. Canadian rate is Series V122495; U.S. rate is Series V122148. Both are quarterly averages of monthly data.)

Economic Recovery: 1983–1987

In early 1983, a sustained recovery began, and by mid-1987, real GDP had moved back toward potential. Much of the growth was centred in the export-oriented manufacturing industries in Ontario and Quebec. The first four years of the recovery saw cumulative real GDP growth of 15.7 percent.

> The main challenge for monetary policy in this period was to create sufficient liquidity to accommodate the recovery without triggering a return to the high inflation rates that prevailed at the start of the decade.

In other words, the Bank of Canada had to increase the money supply to *accommodate* the recovery-induced increase in money demand *without* increasing the money supply so much that it refuelled inflationary pressures.

In spite of much debate and uncertainty, the Bank handled this "re-entry" problem quite well. The Bank allowed a short but rapid burst of growth in the nominal money supply, thus generating the desired increase in real money balances. Once the new level of real balances was achieved, money growth was cut back to a rate consistent with low inflation (and for the underlying rate of growth in real income). The trick with this policy was that to avoid triggering expectations of renewed inflation, the Bank had to generate a one-shot increase in the *level* of the money supply without creating the impression that it was raising the long-term *rate of growth* of the money supply.

In late 1983 and early 1984, when growth in the money supply first started to surge, many voiced the fear that the Bank was being overly expansionary and was risking a return to higher inflation. As the re-entry problem came to be more widely understood and as inflationary pressures failed to re-emerge, these criticisms subsided, and the consensus appeared to be that the Bank had done a commendable job of handling the re-entry problem.

Rising Inflation: 1987–1990

By mid-1987, many observers began to worry that Canadian policymakers were too complacent in accepting the 4 percent range into which Canadian inflation had settled. Further, there was concern that inflationary pressures were starting to build—the money supply was growing quickly, real output growth was strong, unemployment was falling, and an inflationary gap was opening.

> In 1987, many economists argued that if monetary policy was not tightened, Canada would experience gradually increasing inflation until once again a severe monetary restriction would be required to reduce the rate of inflation.

Inflation slowly crept upward. A monetary restriction designed to reduce inflation would obviously impose costs in the form of lower output and higher unemployment. Was the Bank prepared to inflict such costs, especially given that Canada had emerged from a deep recession only five years earlier?

In January 1988, Bank of Canada Governor John Crow announced that monetary policy would henceforth be guided less by short-term stabilization issues and more by the goal of long-term "price stability." Specifically, he said that "monetary policy should be conducted so as to achieve a pace of monetary expansion that promotes stability in the value of money. This means pursuing a policy aimed at achieving and maintaining stable prices."[2]

Disinflation: 1990–1992

This explicit adoption of price stability as the Bank's only target set off a heated debate about the appropriate stance for monetary policy. The debate was fuelled by Crow's decision to give a high profile to his policy by repeatedly articulating and defending it in speeches and public appearances. He believed that this was necessary because expectations of continuing inflation had become entrenched. In his view, until the public believed that the Bank was serious about controlling inflation, whatever the short-term consequences, inflation could not be reduced. Some critics said that price stability was unobtainable. Others said the costs of reaching it would be too large in terms of several years of recessionary gaps. Supporters said that the long-term gains from having a stable price level would exceed the costs of getting there.

John Crow was the governor of the Bank of Canada from 1987 to 1994. In 1988 he announced that "price stability" would thenceforth be the Bank of Canada's objective.

> Despite the Bank's explicit policy of "price stability," the actual inflation rate increased slightly in the years immediately following John Crow's policy announcement, from about 4 percent in 1987 to just over 5 percent in 1990.

---

[2] John W. Crow, "The Work of Canadian Monetary Policy," speech given at the University of Alberta, January 18, 1988; reprinted in *Bank of Canada Review*, February 1988.

The controversy reached new heights when in 1990 the country (and much of the world) entered a sustained recession. Maintaining a tight monetary policy with high interest rates (see Figure 29-6) seemed perverse to many when the economy was already suffering from too little aggregate demand to sustain potential output.

Furthermore, the high Canadian interest rates attracted foreign financial capital. Foreigners who wanted to buy Canadian bonds needed Canadian dollars, and their demands led to an appreciation of the Canadian dollar. This increased the price of Canadian exports while reducing the price of Canadian imports, putting Canadian export and import-competing industries at a competitive disadvantage and further increasing the unemployment that had been generated by the worldwide recession.

Inflation Targeting I: 1991–2000

In spite of heavy political pressure to lower interest rates, and of criticism from some economists who might have supported a move toward price stability in less depressed times, the Bank stood by its tight monetary policy. Indeed, in 1991, it formally announced *inflation-control targets* for the next several years. Beginning in 1992, inflation was to lie within the 3 to 5 percent range, with the range falling to 2 to 4 percent by 1993 and to 1 to 3 percent by the end of 1995.

As a result of the tight monetary policy, the inflation rate fell sharply, from about 5 percent in 1990 to less than 2 percent in 1992. For 1993 and 1994, inflation hovered around 2 percent. Furthermore, short-term nominal interest rates fell from a high of about 13 percent in 1990 to about 6 percent by the end of 1993. Recall that the nominal interest rate is equal to the real interest rate plus the rate of inflation. So this decline in nominal interest rates was the eventual result of the tight monetary policy that reduced inflation.

The Bank had succeeded in coming close to its target of price stability. Controversy continued, however, on two issues. First, was the result worth the price of a deeper, possibly more prolonged recession than might have occurred if the Bank had been willing to accept 3 to 4 percent inflation? Second, would the low inflation rate be sustainable once the recovery took the economy back toward potential output? If the inflation rate were to rise to 4 percent during the post-1993 recovery, then the verdict might well be that the cost of temporarily reducing the rate to below 2 percent was not worth the transitory gains.

Gordon Thiessen became the governor of the Bank of Canada in 1994 after inflation had hovered around 2 percent for about two years.

The debate over the Bank's emphasis on maintaining low inflation became centred on Governor John Crow, especially during the federal election campaign of 1993. Some called for the non-renewal of Crow's term as governor (which was scheduled to end in 1994) and his replacement with someone perceived to care more about the costs of fighting inflation. Others argued that the Bank's policy of "price stability" under Crow's stewardship was the right policy for the times and that the long-run benefits of maintaining low inflation would be worth the costs required to achieve it.

In 1994, the minister of finance appointed Gordon Thiessen, the former senior deputy governor of the Bank, to be the new governor. With some irony, the minister of finance, whose party had been severe critics of Crow's policy while they were in opposition, affirmed the previous monetary policy of the Bank and urged the new governor to maintain the hard-won low inflation rate. The new governor agreed and extended the formal inflation target of 2 percent until 2001.

For the next three years, the rate of inflation continued to hover between 1 and 2 percent. The main challenge for the Bank in the next few years was to keep inflation low while at the same time encouraging the economy to progress through what was viewed as a fragile recovery. Excessive stimulation of the economy would lead to the rise of inflation, which would sacrifice the hard-won gains achieved only a few years earlier. On the other hand, insufficient stimulation would itself be an obstacle to economic recovery.

Beginning in the summer of 1997, the economies of Thailand, Malaysia, Indonesia, and South Korea fell into serious recessions, thus beginning what is now known as the Asian Economic Crisis.[3] Since these countries are major importers of raw materials, their recessions led to a large decline in the world's demand for raw materials. As a result, the world price of raw materials fell by an average of about 30 percent in the subsequent year. Since Canada is a major producer and exporter of raw materials, this decline in the demand for raw materials was a negative aggregate demand shock for Canada. Working in the opposite direction, however, was the expansionary supply-side effect of lower raw materials prices for the many Canadian manufacturing firms that use raw materials as inputs. This positive supply shock was especially important for the United States, a major importer and user of raw materials. The impact of the Asian Crisis on the U.S. economy produced a third effect on Canada as the quickly growing U.S. economy increased its demand for Canadian goods and services.

In the spring of 1997, before the Asian Crisis had begun, the Canadian economy was growing and steadily reducing its recessionary gap. The combination of forces created by the Asian Economic Crisis presented problems for the Bank of Canada and for the appropriate direction for monetary policy. Especially difficult was judging the relative strengths of the three separate effects. As it turned out, Canada's recessionary gap continued to shrink as the economy grew steadily. By 1999, the Asian economies were on their way to a healthy recovery.

Changes in stock-market values also created some challenges for the Bank of Canada in the 1990s. From 1994 through 1999, U.S. and Canadian stocks enjoyed unprecedented bull markets. The Dow Jones Industrial Average (an index of U.S. stock prices) increased from about 3500 in mid-1994 to about 11 000 in late 1999, an average annual increase of 26 percent. The Toronto Stock Exchange Index (now called the S&P/TSX), increased from roughly 4000 to 8000 over the same period, an average annual increase of 14 percent.

The concern for the Bank of Canada during this time was that the increase in wealth generated by these stock-market gains would stimulate consumption expenditures in what was already a steadily growing economy, thus increasing inflationary pressures. In December 1996, the chairman of the U.S. Federal Reserve, Alan Greenspan, warned market participants about their "irrational exuberance," a phrase that is now often quoted. Bank of Canada Governor Gordon Thiessen made similar remarks in Canada. Both central bankers were trying to dampen expectations in the stock market so that the stock-market gains, and thus the increases in wealth-induced spending, would not significantly contribute to inflationary pressures. But they had to be careful not to have their comments create a "crash" in the market that would have even more dramatic effects in the opposite direction.

As it turned out, the crash happened anyway. In both the United States and Canada, the stock markets had reached such levels that many commentators said it was only a matter of time before participants realized that stock prices no longer reflected the

---

[3] An important part of the cause of these recessions was the sudden collapse of their currencies, which were previously pegged in value to the U.S. dollar. We examine fixed and flexible exchange rates in detail in Chapter 35.

David Dodge was the governor of the Bank of Canada from 2001 to early 2008. He needed to steer monetary policy during a time of a strong appreciation of the Canadian dollar, driven partly by rising world commodity prices.

underlying values of the companies, at which point there would be massive selling and an inevitable crash. From the fall of 2000 to the spring of 2001, the major Canadian stock-market indexes fell by roughly 40 percent, driven to a large extent by huge reductions in the stock prices of high-tech firms. This stock-market decline is often referred to as the "dot-com" crash.

Inflation Targeting II: 2001–2007

David Dodge became the new governor of the Bank of Canada in the spring of 2001. During his tenure as governor, the Bank faced several significant policy challenges.

When the terrorist attacks in New York and Washington occurred on September 11, 2001, the stock markets took another dramatic plunge. By late in 2003, stock markets were still far below their pre-crash levels. The main challenge for monetary policy was to provide enough liquidity to the banking systems to prevent the economy from entering a recession. In both Canada and the United States, the central banks dramatically lowered their key interest rates over a period of several months.

From 2002 to 2005, the Bank of Canada's target for the overnight interest rate was 3 percentage points below its level from the summer of 2000. During this period, two external forces on the Canadian economy became apparent and presented a further challenge for the Bank of Canada. First, strong world economic growth, especially in China and India, contributed to a substantial increase in the world prices of oil and other raw materials. Given Canada's position as a major producer and exporter of these products, these price increases represented a significant positive external shock to aggregate demand. They also contributed to a substantial appreciation of the Canadian dollar, by more than 40 percent from 2002 to 2005. Taken by itself, this positive shock to Canadian aggregate demand created a justification for the Bank of Canada to tighten its monetary policy.

Working in the opposite direction was a second external shock, also contributing to an appreciation of the Canadian dollar. During the 2002–2005 period, partly in response to a large and growing U.S. current account deficit, the U.S. dollar was depreciating against the pound sterling and the euro. This "realignment" of the U.S. dollar also involved Canada and explained some part of the Canadian dollar's appreciation during that period. These exchange-rate changes, which were not themselves being caused by changes in the demand for Canadian goods and services, nonetheless tended to reduce Canadian net exports and aggregate demand, thus providing some justification for a loosening of Canadian monetary policy.

The problem for the Bank of Canada during this period was to determine the *relative* strength of these opposing forces and thus the appropriate *overall* direction for monetary policy. During the early part of this period, when Canadian real GDP was below potential, the Bank resisted tightening its policy, choosing instead to allow the commodity-price-driven expansion to close the existing output gap. By the summer of 2005, however, when the output gap appeared to be all but closed, the Bank began a series of increases in the target for the overnight interest rate, and by the summer of 2006 it had increased its target by two percentage points.

Throughout 2006 and 2007, world commodity prices continued their steep ascent and the effect on the Canadian economy was dramatic. Employment grew rapidly, real

GDP grew above the level of potential output, and serious concerns about inflation began to mount. During this period, the Bank of Canada continued to gradually raise its policy interest rate.

A related challenge for the Bank during this period involved regional and sectoral differences in economic performance within Canada. The strong growth in the prices of oil and raw materials naturally led to boom conditions in these sectors, which tend to be located in both Western and Atlantic Canada. However, these price increases harmed the profitability of many central Canadian manufacturing firms who used these products as important inputs. In addition, the appreciation of the Canadian dollar further challenged these firms, as foreign buyers reduced their demand for more expensive Canadian-made products.

Regional and sectoral differences highlight an inherent difficulty with monetary policy in a country as economically diverse as Canada. Because there must be a single monetary policy for the nation as a whole (as long as all parts of Canada continue to use the same currency), policy must be guided by the *average* level of economic activity in order to keep the *average* rate of inflation close to its target. But significant differences in economic activity across regions and/or sectors mean that many people will feel that monetary policy is being conducted inappropriately because economic activity in their specific region or sector is not the same as the national average.

Financial Crisis, Recession, and Recovery: 2007–Present

The next significant phase of Canadian monetary policy was determined largely by events taking place in other countries. From 2002 to 2006, U.S. housing prices had been rising unusually rapidly, but they began to slow their ascent in the middle of 2006. In 2007, these prices reached their peak and then collapsed, falling by more than 30 percent in many parts of the country. On a large scale, U.S. homeowners began "walking away" from their houses, whose market values had fallen below the total amount owing on the associated mortgages. In these situations, the financial institution holding the mortgage no longer receives regular mortgage payments from the homeowner and instead takes ownership of the vacated house.

For the many financial institutions that held the mortgages—or the securities backed by the mortgages—the housing collapse led to a significant decline in the value of their assets. It soon became clear that millions of U.S. mortgages and mortgage-backed securities had been bought by financial institutions all over the world, and thus many large financial institutions in many countries were soon on the edge of insolvency and bankruptcy. What began as a collapse of U.S. housing prices soon became a global financial crisis.

Mark Carney became the new governor of the Bank of Canada in February 2008, just as the financial crisis was entering its most serious phase. With the collapse of major U.S. and U.K. financial institutions only a few months later, panic spread throughout the world's financial sector. It was unclear which institutions held large amounts of these "toxic" mortgage-backed securities and thus which institutions were in danger of going under. In this setting, the widespread fear in financial markets led to a virtual disappearance of short-term interbank

Mark Carney became the Bank of Canada's governor in early 2008, amid a global financial crisis and the beginning of a significant economic recession.

lending. The flow of credit declined, and most lending that did take place was transacted at much higher interest rates. Given the importance of credit in a market economy, restoring the flow of credit was essential to maintaining the level of economic activity.

In Canada, it soon became clear that Canadian banks were far less exposed to these "toxic" mortgage-backed securities than were the banks in the United States and much of Europe. As a result, there was no significant danger of a Canadian bank becoming insolvent during this episode. However, the globalized nature of financial markets implies that short-term credit markets in Canada are highly integrated with those in other countries, with the result that Canada also experienced a decline in interbank lending and a rise in short-term interest rates. The Bank of Canada took two sets of actions during 2007–2008. First, it reduced its target for the overnight rate by more than 3.5 percentage points between the fall of 2007 and the end of 2008. Second, it eased the terms with which it was prepared to make short-term loans to financial institutions. Both sets of actions were designed to restore the flow of credit and reduce interest rates, thus helping to maintain the level of economic activity.

By late in 2008, however, it was clear that Canada would not be shielded from the global recession that was then beginning. The global financial crisis had a dramatic effect on the level of economic activity in the United States, the European Union, and many countries in Asia. With these economies experiencing recessions, there was a sharp decline in demand for Canada's exports. Canadian real GDP slowed sharply in late 2008 and began to fall in early 2009. The Bank of Canada's objective at this time was to provide as much monetary stimulus as was possible, complementing the large fiscal stimulus implemented by the Canadian government in its budget of 2009.

The Canadian economy experienced a significant recession through most of 2009, but returned to positive growth in real GDP in 2010. Despite the fact that the Bank was still holding its target for the overnight rate at historically very low levels, a significant recessionary gap persisted. Two external forces played an important role in dampening the growth of real GDP. First, the U.S. economy, though technically out of recession, was experiencing only a slow and gradual recovery; the low U.S. growth implied low demand for that economy's traditional imports of Canadian goods and services. Second, the global financial crisis of 2008 had eventually led to a "sovereign debt crisis" in Europe, in which government (sovereign) debt had increased dramatically in response to the recession and the provision of financial support to failing banks. By 2011 and 2012, it was unclear whether the high debts, and the unwillingness of bondholders to renew their lending, would force governments to abandon their fiscal policies or even force some governments to exit the European common currency (the euro). The considerable uncertainty in the world's financial markets worked to delay investment activities and dampen already fragile recoveries in many countries.

By early 2013, the Bank of Canada was trying to choose a policy path that balanced the emerging economic strengths and inflationary forces within Canada with the weakness and uncertainty that was originating mostly outside of Canada's borders.

SUMMARY

29.1 How the Bank of Canada Implements Monetary Policy   LO 1

- Monetary policy can be conducted either by setting the money supply or by setting the interest rate. But for a given negatively sloped M_D curve, both cannot be set independently.
- Because of its incomplete control over the money supply, as well as the uncertainty regarding both the slope and the position of the M_D curve, the Bank chooses to implement its policy by setting the interest rate.
- The Bank establishes a target for the overnight interest rate. By offering to lend funds at a rate 25 basis points above this target (the bank rate) and to accept deposits

on which it pays interest at 25 basis points below the target, the Bank of Canada can control the actual overnight interest rate.
- Changes in the Bank's target for the overnight rate lead to changes in the actual overnight rate and also to changes in longer-term interest rates. The various steps in the monetary transmission mechanism then come into play.
- The Bank of Canada conducts an expansionary monetary policy by reducing its target for the overnight interest rate. It conducts a contractionary monetary policy by raising its target for the overnight interest rate.

29.2 Inflation Targeting   LO 2, 3

- It has long been understood that high inflation is damaging to economies and costly for individuals and firms.
- Experience with attempts to control inflation has led to the understanding that sustained inflation is ultimately determined by monetary policy.
- For these two reasons, many central banks now focus their attention on maintaining a low and stable rate of inflation.
- The Bank of Canada's formal inflation target is the rate of CPI inflation. It seeks to keep the annual inflation rate close to 2 percent.

- In the short run, the Bank closely monitors the output gap. By tightening its policy during an inflationary gap (and loosening it during a recessionary gap), the Bank can keep the rate of inflation near 2 percent.
- The policy of inflation targeting helps to stabilize the economy. The Bank responds to positive shocks with a contractionary policy and responds to negative shocks with an expansionary policy.
- Two technical issues complicate the conduct of monetary policy:
  1. Volatile food and energy prices
  2. Changes in the exchange rate

29.3 Long and Variable Lags   LO 4

- Though the Bank of Canada can change interest rates very quickly, it takes time for firms and households to change their expenditure. Even once those new plans are carried out, it takes time for the multiplier process to work its way through the economy, eventually increasing equilibrium national income.

- Long and variable lags in monetary policy lead many economists to argue that the Bank should not try to "fine tune" the economy by responding to economic shocks. Instead, it should respond only to shocks that are significant in size and persistent in duration.

29.4 Thirty Years of Canadian Monetary Policy   LO 5

- In the early 1980s, the Bank of Canada embarked on a policy of tight money to reduce inflation. This policy contributed to the severity of the recession.
- A sustained economic recovery occurred from 1983 to 1987. The main challenge for monetary policy during this time was to create sufficient liquidity to accommodate the recovery without triggering a return to the high inflation rates that prevailed at the start of the decade.
- In 1988, when inflation was between 4 and 5 percent, the Bank of Canada announced that monetary policy

would henceforth be guided by the long-term goal of "price stability." By 1992, the Bank's tight money policy had reduced inflation to below 2 percent.
- Controversy concerned two issues. First, was the cost in terms of lost output and heavy unemployment worth the benefits of lower inflation? Second, could the low inflation rate be sustained?
- This controversy was partly responsible for the 1994 change in the Bank of Canada's governor, from John Crow to Gordon Thiessen. Despite this administrative

change, the stated policy of price stability continued. By 2000, the rate of inflation had been around 2 percent for about seven years.

- Following the stock-market declines in 2000–2001 and the terrorist attacks in the United States in September 2001, the Bank of Canada and the U.S. Federal Reserve dramatically reduced their policy interest rates in an attempt to prevent a recession.
- In the 2002–2005 period, the main challenges for the Bank involved determining the relative strength of the two different forces leading to a substantial appreciation of the Canadian dollar. By summer of 2006, the

Bank had increased its target for the overnight interest rate by two percentage points, to a level still below its previous peak in the summer of 2000.

- The onset of the global financial crisis in 2008 led the Bank of Canada to implement policies designed to restore the flow of credit and also to reduce interest rates.
- By 2012, three years into a modest recovery, the Bank of Canada still had a historically low target for the overnight interest rate. The weakness of the U.S. and European economies at that time were offsetting the stronger economic performance within Canada.

KEY CONCEPTS

Money supply vs. the interest rate
Overnight interest rate
The target overnight interest rate
The bank rate

Endogenous money supply
Open-market operations
Inflation targeting
CPI inflation vs. core inflation

The exchange rate and monetary policy
Lags in the effect of monetary policy

STUDY EXERCISES

MyEconLab   Make the grade with MyEconLab: Study Exercises marked in red can be found on MyEconLab. You can practise them as often as you want, and most feature step-by-step guided instructions to help you find the right answer.

1. Fill in the blanks to make the following statements correct.

   a. In general, there are two approaches to implementing monetary policy. The central bank can attempt to influence _____ directly or to influence _____ directly.

   b. The Bank of Canada chooses to implement its monetary policy by influencing the _____ directly. The Bank then uses _____ to accommodate the resulting change in money demand.

   c. The Bank of Canada does not try to influence the money supply directly because (1) the Bank cannot control the process of _____ carried out by the commercial banks; (2) the Bank is unsure about the change in _____ that would result from a change in the money supply; and (3) the Bank is unsure of the position of the _____ curve at any given time.

2. Fill in the blanks to make the following statements correct.

   a. The interest rate that commercial banks charge each other for overnight loans is called the _____.

   b. The bank rate is _____ points above the target overnight interest rate. At this interest rate, the Bank stands ready to _____ to commercial banks. At a rate _____ points below the target, the Bank stands ready to _____ from commercial banks (and pay that rate as interest).

   c. The Bank of Canada can change the amount of currency in circulation through _____. The Bank conducts these transactions to accommodate the changing demand for _____ by the commercial banks.

   d. An expansionary monetary policy is one where the Bank of Canada _____ its target for the overnight interest rate. A contractionary monetary policy is one in which the Bank _____ its target for the overnight interest rate.

   e. If the Bank of Canada wants to stimulate aggregate demand it can implement a(n) _____ monetary policy by _____ its target for the overnight interest rate. If the Bank wants to dampen aggregate demand it can implement a(n) _____ monetary policy by _____ its target for the overnight interest rate.

3. Fill in the blanks to make the following statements correct.

   a. The long-run policy target for the Bank of Canada is the _____. The current target is to keep the inflation rate at _____ percent.

   b. In the short run, the Bank of Canada closely monitors the _____.

   c. The Bank of Canada conducts its monetary policy by announcing a change in the _____. It then conducts the necessary _____ in order to make this rate an equilibrium in the money market.

   d. The conduct of monetary policy is made more difficult because of lags. Two reasons for these time lags are

      • _____
      • _____

   e. Economists have estimated that a change in monetary policy has an effect on real GDP after a period of _____ months and an effect on the price level after a period of _____ months.

   f. Because of the long time lags involved in the execution of monetary policy, it is very possible that the policy may in fact have a(n) _____ effect on the economy.

4. Read *Applying Economic Concepts 29-1* (page 726), which discusses the Bank of Canada's open-market operations and how these influence the amount of currency in circulation in the Canadian economy. Using simplified balance sheets like the ones shown below, suppose that a commercial bank uses $100 000 of excess cash reserves to purchase a government bond from the Bank of Canada.

   a. What are the immediate effects on assets and liabilities for the commercial bank? Fill in the left-hand table.

   b. What are the changes for the Bank of Canada? Fill in the right-hand table.

   c. Explain what has happened to the amount of currency in circulation.

Commercial Bank		Bank of Canada	
Assets	Liabilities	Assets	Liabilities
Reserves	Deposits	Bonds	Commercial bank deposits
Bonds			
			Currency

5. In the text we stated that the Bank of Canada's long-run policy target is the rate of inflation.

   a. What experiences have led many central banks to choose this long-run policy target?

   b. The Bank of Canada closely monitors the level of real GDP and the output gap in the short run. How does it use this information in pursuit of its long-run policy of targeting the rate of inflation at 2 percent?

6. The diagram below shows the demand for money and the supply of money.

   a. Given the position of the M_D curve, explain why it is not possible for the Bank of Canada to set the money supply and the interest rate at point A or at point B.

   b. In the diagram, draw a new money demand curve, M_D^1, to the right of M_D^0. Suppose the M_D curve is shifting in unpredictable ways between M_D^0 and M_D^1. Why is a monetary policy that sets the interest rate more stable (and therefore preferable) to one that sets the money supply?

   c. The Bank of Canada implements its monetary policy by setting the target for the overnight interest rate. If the Bank reduces its target, explain what happens to the amount of money in the economy. What is the role of open-market operations in the Bank's policy?

7. Milton Friedman was for many years a professor of economics at the University of Chicago and was the most influential Monetarist of his generation. He was known for accusing the Federal Reserve (the U.S. central bank) of following "an unstable monetary policy," arguing that although the Federal Reserve "has given lip service to controlling the quantity of money ... it has given its heart to controlling interest rates."

   a. Explain why if the M_D function were approximately stable, targeting the growth rate in the money supply would produce a "stable" monetary policy. Show this in a diagram.

   b. Explain why if the M_D function moves suddenly and in unpredictable ways, targeting the money supply produces an "unstable" monetary policy. Show this in a diagram.

c. The Bank of Canada conducts its policy by setting short-term interest rates. What is the implication for this policy of an "unstable" M_D function?

8. Suppose it is mid-2007 and the stock market has been growing rapidly for the past five years. Some economists argue that the stock market has become "overvalued" and thus a "crash" is imminent.

    a. How does a rising stock market affect aggregate demand? Show this in an *AD/AS* diagram.

    b. For a central bank that is trying to keep real GDP close to potential, explain what challenges are posed by a rapidly rising stock market.

    c. Suppose the stock market "crashes," falling suddenly by approximately 35 percent as it did in the fall of 2008. How does this affect aggregate demand? Show this in an *AD/AS* diagram.

9. Consider the relationship among exchange-rate changes, aggregate demand, and monetary policy. Assume we begin in a situation with real GDP equal to Y*.

    a. Suppose the world price for raw materials rises because of growing demand for these products. Given that Canada is a net exporter of raw materials, what is the likely effect on Canadian aggregate demand? Show this in an *AD/AS* diagram (assuming no change in the exchange rate).

    b. Suppose instead that there is an increase in the demand by foreigners for Canadian financial assets such as government bonds. What is the direct effect on Canadian aggregate demand? Show this in an *AD/AS* diagram (assuming again no change in the exchange rate).

    c. Both of the shocks described above are likely to cause an appreciation of the Canadian dollar on foreign-exchange markets. As the Canadian dollar appreciates, what are the effects on aggregate demand in part (a) and in part (b)? Show these "secondary" effects in your diagram and explain.

    d. Given your answers to parts (a), (b), and (c), explain why the appropriate monetary policy response to a change in the exchange rate depends crucially on the *cause* of the exchange-rate change. What are the appropriate responses to each of the shocks (assuming they occur separately)?

10. In the last few years, the path of CPI inflation has deviated from the path of core inflation several times (see Figure 29-4 on page 730).

    a. Why is core inflation less volatile than CPI inflation?

    b. Why might the Bank focus more on core inflation during some periods?

11. During the financial crisis of 2007–2008, the Bank of Canada took extraordinary actions to inject liquidity into the banking system. As a result, the amount of reserves in the banking system increased significantly.

    a. Why might the Bank choose to increase reserves in the banking system in such an economic environment?

    b. Despite the large increase in reserves, there was not a large increase in the Canadian money supply. Can you provide an explanation?

    c. Given your answer to part (b), would you predict that the Bank's actions would lead to more inflation? Explain why or why not.

Inflation and Disinflation

IF you are a typical reader of this book, you were born in the mid-1990s. By the time you were old enough to notice some economic developments going on around you, it was the mid-2000s. By that time, the rate of inflation in Canada was about 2 percent per year and had been at that level for over a decade. Thus, unless you are older than the typical student taking a course in introductory economics, or you have come to Canada recently from a high-inflation country, inflation has not been a significant phenomenon in your life. It was not so long ago, however, that inflation was considered to be a serious problem in Canada (and many other countries as well). Even though high inflation in Canada is no longer a "headline" issue, understanding the process of inflation, and how it can be reduced, is central to understanding why the Bank of Canada is so committed to keeping inflation low.

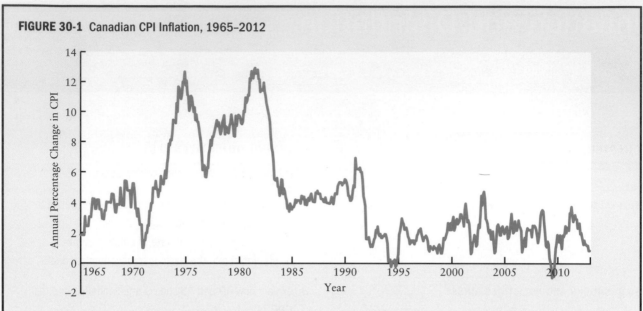

FIGURE 30-1 Canadian CPI Inflation, 1965–2012

(*Source:* Based on author's calculations using data from the Bank of Canada, www.bankofcanada.ca, Series PCPISA. For each month, the inflation rate is computed as the percentage change from the CPI 12 months earlier.)

inflation A rise in the average level of all prices. Usually expressed as the annual percentage change in the Consumer Price Index.

Recall that **inflation** is a rise in the average level of prices—that is, a rise in the price level. Figure 30-1 shows the rate of CPI inflation in Canada since 1965 and shows what is sometimes called the "twin peaks" of inflation. Rising from the mid-1960s, inflation peaked in 1974 at more than 12 percent, fell and then peaked again in 1981 at almost 13 percent, and then started its long but bumpy decline to its current level at around 2 percent, the Bank of Canada's current target rate of inflation.

This bumpy path for the rate of inflation nicely illustrates one of the reasons that inflation is a problem for the economy. As we mentioned in Chapter 19, economists make the distinction between *anticipated* and *unanticipated* inflation, and we showed why unanticipated inflation is the more serious problem. If firms and workers have difficulty predicting what inflation will be, they have problems determining how wages and prices should be set. The result will be unexpected changes in real wages and relative prices as inflation ends up being different from what was expected. These inflation-induced changes in real wages and relative prices cause redistributions of income and may lead to inefficient changes in the economy. As you can imagine by looking at Figure 30-1, many of the changes in inflation between 1965 and 2012 were sudden and thus difficult to predict. To avoid this uncertainty in the economy, the Bank of Canada now strives to keep inflation both *low* and *stable*, near the official target of 2 percent. The result is an environment in which firms, workers, and households can more easily make plans for the future, secure in the knowledge that real wages, real interest rates, and relative prices will not be significantly affected by a volatile inflation rate.

To compute the total inflation since the day of your birth to today, check out the "Inflation Calculator" at the Bank of Canada's website: www.bankofcanada.ca. Click on "Monetary Policy" and then "Inflation."

What causes inflation? How can it be eliminated? And why have policies designed to reduce inflation been so controversial? These are the central topics of this chapter.

30.1 Adding Inflation to the Model

In the previous several chapters we examined the effects of shocks to aggregate demand and aggregate supply. In our macroeconomic model, *AD* and *AS* shocks influenced the values of both real GDP and the price level. Following these shocks, the economy's adjustment process tended to push the economy back toward the potential level of real GDP with a stable price level. In other words, any inflation that we have so far seen in our macroeconomic model was temporary—it existed only while the economy was adjusting toward its long-run equilibrium.

In this chapter we modify our model to explain how a *sustained* and *constant* inflation can exist. After all, even though Canadian inflation is very low by recent historical standards, over the past two decades it has been sustained and relatively stable at an average rate of 2 percent.

As we will soon see, one of the keys to understanding sustained inflation is to understand the role of *inflation expectations*. When combined with excess demand or excess supply, as reflected by the economy's output gap, such expectations give us a more complete explanation of why costs and prices change. Let's begin our analysis by examining in more detail why wages change.

Why Wages Change

Readers who have studied microeconomics will have examined why wages in *particular* firms and industries change relative to wages in other firms and industries. Movements in these *relative* wages are explained by many factors, including the power of industrial labour unions, firms' market power, the nature of work in specific industries, the skills of the workers, and much else. Here we ignore this microeconomic detail and focus instead on the *general* level of wages in the economy. Our emphasis is on the role played by broad macroeconomic forces.

In Chapter 24, when we examined the economy's adjustment process, we saw that increases in wages led to increases in unit costs—because we maintained the assumption that technology (and thus productivity) was held constant. We continue with that assumption in this chapter. Thus, as wages and other factor prices rise, unit costs increase and the *AS* curve shifts up. Conversely, when wages and other factor prices fall, unit costs fall and the *AS* curve shifts down.

What are the macroeconomic forces that cause the overall level of nominal wages to change? The two main forces that we consider are the output gap and expectations of future inflation. Much of what we discuss in the case of the output gap was first seen in Chapter 24, but the points are important enough to bear repeating.

Wages and the Output Gap In Chapter 24, we encountered three propositions about how changes in nominal (or money) wages were influenced by the output gap:

1. The excess demand for labour that is associated with an inflationary gap ($Y > Y^*$) puts upward pressure on nominal wages.

2. The excess supply of labour associated with a recessionary gap ($Y < Y^*$) puts downward pressure on nominal wages, though the adjustment may be quite slow.

3. The absence of either an inflationary or a recessionary gap ($Y = Y^*$) implies that demand forces are not exerting any pressure on nominal wages.

When real GDP is equal to Y^*, the unemployment rate is said to be equal to the NAIRU, which stands for the *non-accelerating inflation rate of unemployment* and is designated by U^*. The use of this particular name will be explained later in this chapter. Another name sometimes used in place of NAIRU is the *natural rate of unemployment*.

The NAIRU is not zero. Instead, even when $Y = Y^*$, there may be a substantial amount of *frictional* and *structural* unemployment caused, for example, by the movement of people between jobs or between regions. When real GDP exceeds potential GDP ($Y > Y^*$), the unemployment rate will be less than the NAIRU ($U < U^*$). When real GDP is less than potential GDP ($Y < Y^*$), the unemployment rate will exceed the NAIRU ($U > U^*$).

We have assumed that nominal wages tend to react to various pressures of demand. These demand pressures can be stated either in terms of the relationship between actual and potential GDP or in terms of the relationship between the actual unemployment rate and the NAIRU. When $Y > Y^*$ (or $U < U^*$), there is an inflationary gap characterized by excess demand for labour, and wages are assumed to rise. Conversely, when $Y < Y^*$ (or $U > U^*$), there is a recessionary gap characterized by excess supply of labour, and wages are assumed to fall.

This assumed relationship between the excess demand or supply of labour and the rate of change of nominal wages is represented by the Phillips curve, which we first discussed in Chapter 24.

Wages and Expected Inflation A second force that can influence nominal wages is *expectations* of future inflation. Suppose both employers and employees expect 2 percent inflation next year. Workers will tend to start negotiations from a base of a 2 percent increase in nominal wages, which would hold their *real wages* constant. Firms will also be inclined to begin bargaining from a base of a 2 percent increase in nominal wages because they expect that the prices at which they sell their products will rise by 2 percent. Starting from that base, workers may attempt to obtain some desired increase in their real wages while firms may attempt to reduce real wages. At this point, such factors as profits and bargaining power become important.

> The expectation of some specific inflation rate creates pressure for nominal wages to rise by that rate.

The key point is that nominal wages can be rising even if no inflationary gap is present. As long as people *expect* prices to rise, their behaviour will put upward pressure on nominal wages. Indeed, in every year since the Second World War, average nominal wages have increased in Canada, even though in some years there were notable recessionary gaps when nominal wages increased by less than prices. The reason is that in every year the price level was expected to increase (and did, in fact, increase). Clarifying the distinction between these two separate forces on nominal wages—excess demand and inflation expectations—is an important objective of this chapter.

The central role for the *expectations* of future inflation suggests the importance of examining how firms and workers *form* their expectations. *Applying Economic Concepts 30-1* discusses the formation of expectations and explains the important difference between *backward-looking* and *forward-looking* expectations.

rational expectations The theory that people understand how the economy works and learn quickly from their mistakes, so that even though random errors may be made, systematic and persistent errors are not.

APPLYING ECONOMIC CONCEPTS 30-1

How Do People Form Their Expectations?

How firms and workers form their expectations about future inflation may have an important effect on that inflation. Generally, we can distinguish two main patterns: One is to look backward at past experience; the other is to look at current circumstances for a clue as to what may happen in the near future.

The first type of expectations are called *backward-looking*. People look at the past in order to predict what will happen in the future. The simplest possible form of such expectations is to expect the past to be repeated in the future. According to this view, if inflation has been 5 percent over the past few years, people will expect it to be 5 percent next year. This expectation, however, is quite naïve. Everyone knows that the inflation rate sometimes changes, and therefore the past cannot be a perfectly accurate guide to the future.

A less naïve version has people revising their expectations in light of the mistakes that they made in estimating inflation in the past. For example, if you thought that this year's inflation rate was going to be 5 percent but it turned out to be only 3 percent, you might revise your estimate of next year's rate down somewhat from 5 percent.

Backward-looking expectations tend to change slowly because some time must pass before a change in the actual rate of inflation provides enough past experience to cause expectations to adjust.

The second main type of expectations are those that look to current economic conditions to estimate what is likely to happen in the future. One version of this type assumes that people look to the government's current macroeconomic policy to form their expectations of future inflation. They are assumed to understand how the economy works, and they form their expectations by predicting the outcome of the policies now being followed. In an obvious sense, such expectations are *forward-looking*.

A strong version of forward-looking expectations is called **rational expectations**. Rational expectations are not necessarily always correct; rather, the *rational expectations hypothesis* assumes that people make the best possible use of all the information available to them. One implication is that they will not continue to make persistent, systematic errors when forming their expectations. Thus, if the economic system about which they are forming expectations remains stable, their expectations

will be correct *on average*. Sometimes next year's inflation rate will turn out to be above what people expected it to be; at other times, it will turn out to be below what people expected it to be. On average over many years, however, the actual rate will not, according to the rational expectations theory, be consistently under- or overestimated.

Forward-looking expectations can adjust quickly to changes in events. Instead of being based on past inflation rates, expected inflation is based on expected economic conditions and government policies.

Assuming that expectations are solely backward-looking seems overly naïve. People do look ahead and assess future possibilities rather than just blindly reacting to what has gone before. Yet the assumption of "fully rational" forward-looking expectations requires workers and firms to have a degree of understanding of the economy that few economists would claim to have. The actual process of wage setting probably combines forward-looking behaviour with expectations based on the experience of the recent past. Depending on the circumstances, expectations will sometimes tend to rely more on past experience and at other times more on present events whose effects are expected to influence the future.

A third type of expectations formation, which combines the other two, fits the current Canadian situation quite well. It assumes that the central bank is committed to maintaining a low and stable inflation rate and has established its credibility by being willing to implement whatever policies are necessary to maintain such a rate. For example, since 1991 the Bank of Canada has taken whatever policy decisions were necessary in the face of various economic shocks to achieve its formal inflation target; since that time, inflation has varied slightly but its annual average over more than 20 years has been almost exactly 2 percent. Once the Bank's credibility is established, expectations will be for the 2 percent rate to continue. Both forward-looking and backward-looking theories would predict that the Bank's target rate would become the expected rate. Even if expectations are formed in some other manner, all that is needed is that the public believes that the Bank is determined and able to maintain its inflation target. This appears to have been the case in Canada since the early 1990s.

Overall Effect on Wages We can now think of changes in average nominal wages as resulting from two different forces:[1]

$$\frac{\text{Change in}}{\text{nominal wages}} = \frac{\text{Output-gap}}{\text{effect}} + \frac{\text{Expectational}}{\text{effect}}$$

What happens to wages is the *net* effect of the two forces. Consider two examples. First, suppose both labour and management expect 2 percent inflation next year and are therefore willing to allow nominal wages to increase by 2 percent. Doing so would leave *real* wages unchanged. Suppose as well that there is a significant inflationary gap with an associated labour shortage and that the excess demand for labour causes wages to rise by an additional 1 percentage point. The final outcome is that nominal wages rise by 3 percent, the net effect of a 2 percent increase caused by expected inflation and a 1 percent increase caused by the excess demand for labour when $Y > Y^*$.

For the second example, assume again that expected inflation is 2 percent, but this time there is a large recessionary gap. The associated high unemployment represents an excess supply of labour that exerts downward pressure on wage bargains. Hence, the output-gap effect now works to dampen wage increases, say, to the extent of 1 percentage point. Nominal wages therefore rise only by 1 percent, the net effect of a 2 percent increase caused by expected inflation and a 1 percent *decrease* caused by the excess supply of labour when $Y < Y^*$.

From Wages to Prices

We saw in Chapters 23 and 24 that shifts in the *AS* curve depend on what happens to wages and other factor prices. We have just seen that output gaps and expectations of future inflation put pressure on wages to change and hence cause the *AS* curve to shift.

> The net effect of the two macro forces acting on wages—output gaps and inflation expectations—determines what happens to the *AS* curve.

If the net effect of the output-gap effect and the expectational effect is to raise wages, then the *AS* curve will shift up. This shift will cause the price level to rise—that is, the forces pushing up wages will be *inflationary*. On the other hand, if the net effect of the output-gap effect and the expectational effect is to reduce wages, the *AS* curve will shift down—the forces reducing wages will be *deflationary*.[2]

Since anything that leads to higher nominal wages will shift the *AS* curve up and lead to higher prices, we can decompose inflation caused by wage increases into two component parts: *output-gap inflation* and *expected inflation*. But because the *AS* curve can also shift for reasons unrelated to changes in wages, we must add a third element. Specifically, we must consider the effect of non-wage supply shocks on the *AS* curve and

---

[1] Average nominal wages may also be affected by things unrelated to output gaps and expected inflation, such as government guidelines and union power. Such factors may be regarded as random shocks and analyzed separately from the two principal macro forces that we examine here.

[2] This is a good time to remind the reader that we are assuming constant productivity throughout this chapter. With ongoing productivity growth, the *AS* curve would shift upward when wages rise *faster than productivity* and shift downward when wages *rise slower than productivity*. But with constant productivity, any increase in nominal wages causes *AS* to shift up and any decrease in nominal wages causes *AS* to shift down.

thus on the price level. The best example of a non-wage supply shock is a change in the prices of imported raw materials. We can then decompose actual inflation into its three systematic components:

$$\begin{array}{ccccc} \text{Actual} \\ \text{inflation} \end{array} = \begin{array}{c} \text{Output-gap} \\ \text{inflation} \end{array} + \begin{array}{c} \text{Expected} \\ \text{inflation} \end{array} + \begin{array}{c} \text{Supply-shock} \\ \text{inflation} \end{array}$$

As an example, consider an economy that begins with real GDP equal to Y^* and expectations of inflation at zero. In this case, the first two terms on the right-hand side are zero. But if an adverse supply shock then occurs, such as a significant increase in the price of imported raw materials, the AS curve shifts up and the price level rises. Actual inflation will be positive. As we will see later in the chapter, such supply shocks are not uncommon, and they generate challenges for the Bank of Canada in its attempt to maintain low inflation.

Having discussed these components of inflation, we are now in a position to see how constant inflation can be included in our macroeconomic model.

Constant Inflation

Suppose the inflation rate is 2 percent per year and has been 2 percent for several years. This is what we mean by a *constant* inflation. In such a setting, people with backward-looking expectations about inflation will expect the actual rate to continue into the future. Furthermore, in the absence of any announcements that the central bank will be altering its monetary policy, people with forward-looking expectations will expect the actual inflation rate to continue. Thus, for the economy as a whole, the expected rate of inflation will equal the actual rate of inflation.

The Conference Board of Canada conducts a regular survey about people's expectations about inflation. See its website at www.conferenceboard.ca.

> If inflation and monetary policy have been constant for several years, the expected rate of inflation will tend to equal the actual rate of inflation.

Suppose there are no supply shocks (we address these later in the chapter). Since actual inflation equals expected inflation, it follows from the equation above that there can be *no* output gap—real GDP must equal its potential level, Y^*.

> In the absence of supply shocks, if expected inflation equals actual inflation, real GDP must be equal to potential GDP.[3]

Figure 30-2 shows a constant inflation in the AD/AS diagram. What is causing this inflation? As we will see, such a constant inflation requires both the *expectations* of inflation (which shift the AS curve) and the continuing expansion of the money supply by the central bank (which shifts the AD curve). Let's see how this works.

Suppose workers and employers expect 2 percent inflation over the coming years and employers are prepared to increase nominal wages by 2 percent per year. As wages rise by 2 percent, the AS curve shifts up by that amount. But in order for 2 percent

---

[3] Another realistic possibility is that real GDP is below Y^* but there is only weak downward pressure on wages, and so relatively constant inflation. Recall our discussion from Chapter 24 that large and persistent recessionary gaps may be necessary to generate even small wage reductions. For simplicity, in this chapter we maintain the assumption that wages *do* fall when $Y < Y^*$, although we recognize that these forces may be both weak and slow.

FIGURE 30-2 Constant Inflation with No Supply Shocks

In the *AD/AS* model with no supply shocks, constant inflation occurs when $Y = Y^*$. Expectations of a constant rate of inflation cause wages and thus the *AS* curve to shift upward at a uniform rate from AS_0 to AS_1 to AS_2. Monetary validation is causing the *AD* curve to shift upward at the same time from AD_0 to AD_1 to AD_2. As a result, real GDP remains at Y^* as the economy moves from equilibrium E_0 to E_1 to E_2 and so on. The constant inflation rate takes the price level from P_0 to P_1 to P_2. Wage costs are rising because of expectations of inflation, and these expectations are being validated by the central bank.

to be the *actual* rate of inflation, the intersection of the *AS* and *AD* curves must be shifting up at the rate of 2 percent. This requires the *AD* curve to be shifting up at the same 2 percent rate—this *AD* shift is caused by the growth of the money supply. So in this case there is no output-gap inflation ($Y = Y^*$), and actual and expected inflation are equal. When the central bank increases the money supply at such a rate that the expectations of inflation end up being correct, it is said to be *validating* the expectations.

> Constant inflation with $Y = Y^*$ occurs when the rate of monetary growth, the rate of wage increase, and the expected rate of inflation are all consistent with the actual inflation rate.

The key point about constant inflation in our macro model is that there is no output-gap effect operating on wages: either there is no output gap at all or whatever gap exists is not large enough to create wage adjustments. As a result, nominal wages rise exactly at the expected rate of inflation. Expansions of the money supply validate those expectations.

Note that in this constant-inflation equilibrium, interest rates are being kept stable by two equal but offsetting forces. The central bank is increasing the money supply, which tends to push interest rates down. But at the same time, rising prices are increasing the demand for money and pushing interest rates up. In equilibrium, the monetary policy is just expansionary enough to accommodate the growing money demand, thus leaving interest rates unchanged. As we will see later in this chapter, in order to *reduce* the rate of inflation, the central bank must implement a contractionary monetary policy—by reducing the growth rate of the money supply sufficiently to raise interest rates.

Figure 30-2 can be used to analyze any constant (and positive) rate of inflation. It could also be used to analyze the case of deflation, a situation in which the price level is falling so that the inflation rate is negative. In this case, the *AD* and *AS* curves would be shifting down at a constant rate, keeping $Y = Y^*$. *Applying Economic Concepts 30-2* discusses deflation, the reasons that some people seem to fear its effect on the economy, and why these fears may be misplaced.

30.2 Shocks and Policy Responses

A constant rate of inflation is a special case in our macroeconomic model because the rising price level is not caused by an inflationary output gap. In many cases of inflation, however, inflationary pressure is initially created by an aggregate demand or aggregate supply shock. In this section we examine the effects of *AS* and *AD* shocks and the subsequent effects of the policy responses chosen by the central bank.

APPLYING ECONOMIC CONCEPTS 30-2

Is Deflation a Problem?

We have discussed how inflation can be incorporated into our basic macroeconomic model. The model can also be used to discuss *deflation*, a situation in which the price level experiences an ongoing decline. For example, a deflation of 2 percent per year means that the price level is falling annually by 2 percent; in other words, deflation means a negative inflation rate.

Sustained deflation is very rare; it has been experienced only a few times in the last century. During the Great Depression, the price level in Canada fell by approximately 25 percent between 1930 and 1933; when the Japanese economy was growing very slowly in the early 2000s, the price level declined by about 1 percent per year.

In recent years, especially during the 2009 recession, it was common to hear media discussion of the dangers of deflation and the need for central banks to take whatever actions were necessary to prevent it. The fear of deflation appears to stem from the belief that deflation causes a decline in economic activity, and this argument is usually based on the evidence drawn from the Great Depression, when real GDP fell by about 30 percent from 1929 to 1933.

How could deflation cause a decline in economic activity? A commonly heard argument is that when prices are falling, firms and consumers delay their spending because they know that prices will be lower in the future. The delay in spending leads to a leftward shift in the *AD* curve and, other things being equal, causes a decline in real GDP.

Economists who reject this line of argument usually make two observations, one about the historical evidence and the other about the proposed link from deflation to recession. First, while it is certainly true that there was significant deflation during the Great Depression, it was probably a *result* rather than a *cause* of the economic events. In this view, a combination of the 1929 stock-market crash, widespread bank failures, inappropriate monetary and fiscal policies, and a significant rise in protectionist trade policies caused a major decline in aggregate demand. This decline, in turn, caused a leftward shift of the *AD* curve, resulting in *both* a decline in real GDP and a decline in the price level (deflation).

The second point relates to the possibility that buyers delay their purchases because of deflation, and that this delay can cause a recession. How important can this effect be? If the rate of deflation were 25 percent per year, it is easy to imagine that many firms and consumers would delay some purchases—after all, a saving of 25 percent provides a significant incentive to wait. But this effect is almost absent when deflation is only 1 or 2 percent per year, as it was in Japan during the early 2000s. And if this effect is absent, there is no fundamental danger associated with a small deflation.

Consider the opposite situation, that of prices rising by 1 or 2 percent annually. In this situation, do we expect firms and consumers to rush to purchase their products before prices rise, thereby pushing real GDP well above the economy's potential? The answer is no. When inflation is low and relatively stable, firms and consumers build it into their expectations, central banks build it into their policy decisions, and the economy can operate with real GDP equal to potential output, as we have shown in this chapter. The same would likely be true of a constant and anticipated deflation of 1 or 2 percent per year.

In this analysis, we make a central assumption in our macro model—that *AD* and *AS* shocks do not influence the level of potential output, *Y**. With this assumption in place, we know that a central prediction of our model is that the long-run effect of *AD* and *AS* shocks involves no change in real GDP because the economy's adjustment process brings real GDP back to (the unchanged) *Y**. As we explained in Chapter 28, however, this assumption is often debated; there are good reasons to believe that *Y** may be influenced by the short-run path of real GDP. For the remainder of this chapter, however, we maintain the strong assumption that *Y** is unaffected by the various *AD* and *AS* shocks that we consider.

Demand Shocks

Any rightward shift in the *AD* curve that creates an inflationary output gap also creates what is called **demand inflation**. The shift in the *AD* curve could have been caused by a reduction in tax rates, by an increase in such autonomous expenditure items as investment, government, and net exports, or by an expansionary monetary policy.

demand inflation Inflation arising from an inflationary output gap caused, in turn, by a positive *AD* shock.

Major demand-shock inflations occurred in Canada during and after the First and Second World Wars. In these cases, large increases in government expenditure without fully offsetting increases in taxes led to general excess demand ($Y > Y^*$). More generally, demand inflation sometimes occurs at the end of a strong upswing, as rising output causes excess demand to develop simultaneously in the markets for labour, intermediate goods, and final output. Demand inflation of this type occurred in Canada in 1989–1990 and to a lesser extent in 2003–2006.

To begin our study of demand inflation, we make some simplifying assumptions. First, we continue to assume that Y^* is constant. Second, we assume that initially there is no ongoing inflation. These two assumptions imply that our starting point is a stable long-run equilibrium, with constant real GDP and price level, rather than the long-run equilibrium with constant inflation as shown in Figure 30-2. We then suppose that this long-run equilibrium is disturbed by a rightward shift in the AD curve. This shift causes the price level and output to rise. It is important next to distinguish between the case in which the Bank of Canada validates the demand shock and the case in which it does not.

No Monetary Validation Because the initial rise in AD takes output above potential, an inflationary gap opens up. The pressure of excess demand soon causes nominal wages to rise, shifting the AS curve upward as shown in Figure 30-3. As long as the Bank of Canada holds the money supply constant, the rise in the price level moves the economy upward and to the left along the new AD curve, reducing the inflationary gap. Eventually, the gap is eliminated, and equilibrium is established at a higher but stable price level, with output at Y^*. In this case, the initial period of inflation is followed by further inflation that lasts only until the new long-run equilibrium is reached.

Monetary Validation Suppose that after the demand shock created an inflationary gap, the Bank of Canada chose to attempt to sustain these "good economic times." It would then validate the demand shock through an expansionary monetary policy. We illustrate this situation in Figure 30-4.

Two forces are now brought into play. Spurred by the inflationary gap, the increase in nominal wages causes the AS curve to shift upward. Fuelled by the expansionary monetary policy, however, the AD curve shifts further to the right. As a result of both of these shifts, the price level rises, but real GDP remains above Y^*. Indeed, if the shift in the AD curve *exactly* offsets the shift in the AS curve, real GDP and the inflationary gap will remain constant.

FIGURE 30-3   A Demand Shock with No Validation

A demand shock that is not validated produces temporary inflation, but the economy's adjustment process eventually restores potential GDP and stable prices. The initial long-run equilibrium is at P_0 and Y^*. A positive demand shock shifts AD_0 to AD_1, generating an inflationary gap. The excess demand puts upward pressure on wages, thus shifting AS_0 to AS_1. There is inflation as the economy moves from E_0 to E_1 to E_2, but at E_2 the price level is again stable.

> Continued validation of a demand shock turns what would have been transitory inflation into sustained inflation fuelled by monetary expansion.

In other words, the Bank of Canada could indeed choose to sustain the "good economic times" characterized by high output and low unemployment. But the result of this choice would be sustained inflation (and as we will soon see, the inflation rate would continually increase).

Supply Shocks

Any leftward shift in the *AS* curve that is *not* caused by excess demand in the markets for factors of production creates what is called **supply inflation**.

An example of a supply shock is a rise in the costs of imported raw materials. Another is a rise in domestic wages not due to excess demand in the labour market. The rise in wages might occur, as we saw earlier, because of generally held expectations of future inflation. If employers and employees expect inflation, nominal wages are likely to rise in anticipation of that inflation. These shocks cause the *AS* curve to shift upward.[1]

The initial effects of any negative supply shock are that the price level rises while output falls, as shown in Figure 30-5. As with the case of a demand shock, what happens next depends on how the Bank of Canada reacts. If the Bank allows the money supply to increase, it validates the supply shock; if it holds the money supply constant, the shock is not validated.

No Monetary Validation The upward shift in the *AS* curve in Figure 30-5 causes the price level to rise and pushes output below Y^*, opening up a recessionary gap. Pressure mounts for nominal wages and other factor prices to fall. As wages and other factor prices fall, unit costs will fall. Consequently, the *AS* curve shifts down, increasing output while reducing the price level. The *AS* curve will continue to shift slowly downward, stopping only when real GDP is returned to Y^* and the price level is returned to its initial value of P_0. Thus, the period of inflation accompanying the original supply shock is eventually reversed until the initial long-run equilibrium is re-established.

A major concern in this case is the speed of wage adjustment. If wages do not fall rapidly in the face of excess supply in the labour market, the adjustment back to potential output can take a long time. For example, suppose the original shock raised firms' costs by 6 percent. To reverse this shock and return real GDP to Y^*, firms' costs must fall by 6 percent. If nominal wages fell by only 1 percent per year, it would take six years to complete the adjustment.[5]

FIGURE 30-4 A Demand Shock with Validation

Monetary validation of a positive demand shock causes the *AD* curve to shift further to the right, offsetting the upward shift in the *AS* curve and thereby leaving an inflationary gap despite the ever-rising price level. An initial demand shock moves the economy along the path of arrow ①, taking output to Y_1 and the price level to P_1. The resulting inflationary gap then causes the *AS* curve to shift upward. This time, however, the Bank of Canada validates the demand shock with a monetary expansion that shifts the *AD* curve to the right. By the time the aggregate supply curve has reached AS_1, the aggregate demand curve has reached AD_2. The new equilibrium is at E_2. Output remains constant at Y_1, leaving the inflationary gap constant while the price level rises to P_2.

The persistent inflationary gap continues to push the *AS* curve upward, while the continued monetary validation continues to push the *AD* curve to the right. As long as this monetary validation continues, the economy moves along the vertical path of arrow ②.

supply inflation Inflation arising from a negative AS shock that is not the result of excess demand in the domestic markets for factors of production.

---

[4] Recall our discussion in Chapter 23 of how some shocks affect *both* the *AD* and the *AS* curves. A rise in the world price of oil is one example. Since Canada both uses and produces oil, a rise in the price of oil causes both the *AD* and *AS* curves to shift upward. In this discussion we confine ourselves to the effect of the *AS* shift.

[5] Nominal wages rarely fall because there is ongoing productivity growth that offsets the effect on wages of excess supply. But in this chapter we are holding productivity (and thus Y^*) constant so we can focus on the causes and consequences of inflation.

FIGURE 30-5 A Supply Shock with and without Validation

Adverse supply shocks initially raise prices while lowering output. An adverse supply shock causes the AS curve to shift upward from AS_0 to AS_1, as shown by arrow ①. Equilibrium is established at E_1. If there is no monetary validation, the reduction in wages and other factor prices makes the AS curve shift slowly back down to AS_0. If there is monetary validation, the AD curve shifts from AD_0 to AD_1, as shown by arrow ②. Equilibrium is re-established at E_2 with output equal to potential output but with a higher price level, P_2.

Whenever wages and other factor prices fall only slowly in the face of excess supply, the recovery to potential output after a non-validated negative supply shock will take a long time.

Concern that such a lengthy adjustment will occur is often the motivation for the Bank of Canada to validate negative supply shocks.

Monetary Validation What happens if the Bank of Canada responds to the negative supply shock by lowering interest rates and so allowing the money supply to increase, thus *validating* the shock? The monetary validation shifts the AD curve to the right and closes the output gap. As the recessionary gap is eliminated, the price level rises further, rather than falling back to its original value as it did when the supply shock was not validated. These effects are also illustrated in Figure 30-5.

Monetary validation of a negative supply shock causes the initial rise in the price level to be followed by a further rise, resulting in a higher price level but a much faster return to potential output than would occur if the recessionary gap were relied on to reduce wages and other factor prices.

The most dramatic example of a supply-shock inflation came in the wake of the first OPEC oil-price shock. In 1974, the member countries of the Organization of the Petroleum Exporting Countries (OPEC) agreed to restrict output. Their action caused a threefold increase in the price of oil and dramatic increases in the prices of many petroleum-related products, such as fertilizer and chemicals. The resulting increase in industrial costs shifted AS curves upward in all industrial countries. At this time, the Bank of Canada validated the supply shock with large increases in the money supply, whereas the Federal Reserve (the U.S. central bank) did not. As the theory predicts, Canada experienced a large increase in its price level but almost no recession, while the United States experienced a much smaller increase in its price level but a deeper recession.

Is Monetary Validation of Supply Shocks Desirable? Suppose the Bank of Canada were to validate a negative supply shock and thus prevent what could otherwise be a protracted recession. Expressed in this way, monetary validation sounds like a good policy. Unfortunately, however, there is also a possible cost associated with this policy. The effect of the monetary validation is to extend the period of inflation. If this inflation leads firms and workers to expect *further* inflation, then point E_2 in Figure 30-5 will not be the end of the story. As expectations for further inflation develop, the AS curve will continue to shift upward. But if the Bank continues its policy of validation, then the AD curve will also continue to shift upward. It may not take long before the economy is in a *wage–price spiral*.

Once started, a wage–price spiral can be halted only if the Bank of Canada stops validating the expectational inflation initially caused by the supply shock. But the longer it waits to do so, the more firmly held will be the *expectations* that it will continue its policy of validating the shocks. These entrenched expectations may cause wages to continue rising even after validation has ceased. Because employers expect prices to rise, they go on granting wage increases. If expectations are entrenched firmly enough, the wage push can continue for quite some time, in spite of whatever downward pressure on wages is caused by the high unemployment associated with the recessionary gap.

Because of this possibility, some economists argue that the wage–price spiral should not be allowed to begin. One way to ensure that it does not begin is to refuse to validate any supply shock and accept whatever recessionary gap the shock creates, as the United States did after the OPEC oil-price shock in the early 1970s. The choice between a deeper recession with less expected inflation and a less severe recession with the possibility of higher entrenched inflation expectations involves an important value judgement and is not a matter that can be settled solely by economic analysis.

For information on OPEC, see its website: www.opec.org.

Accelerating Inflation

Consider a situation in which a demand or supply shock increases real GDP above Y^*. For example, a booming U.S. economy may lead to an increase in demand for Canadian goods, thus shifting Canada's AD curve to the right. Or a reduction in the world price of raw materials may reduce firms' costs and shift the Canadian AS curve downward. In both cases, the effect in Canada would be to increase real GDP above Y^*—unemployment is low and businesses are booming. As we saw in Chapter 29, as real GDP rises above Y^*, the Bank of Canada would normally begin to tighten its monetary policy in order to prevent inflation from rising above its target. Some people, however, might argue that the Bank of Canada should not "spoil the party" and instead should allow these boom conditions to continue. What would be the result if the Bank acted to maintain output above Y^*?

A contract settlement that raises wages for a large number of workers will increase firms' costs and shift the AS curve upward, thus tending to reduce real GDP and raise the price level.

What happens to the rate of inflation is predicted by the **acceleration hypothesis,** which says that when the central bank conducts its policy to hold the inflationary gap constant, the actual inflation rate will *accelerate*. The Bank of Canada may start by validating 2 percent inflation, but soon 2 percent will become expected, and given the demand pressure the inflation rate will rise to 3 percent and, if the Bank insists on validating 3 percent, the rate will become 4 percent, and so on, without limit. The process will end only when the Bank ends its policy of validation. Avoiding this possibility of gradually increasing inflation is one important reason that the Bank has adopted a formal (and unchanging) inflation target of 2 percent.

acceleration hypothesis The hypothesis that when real GDP is held above potential, the persistent inflationary gap will cause inflation to accelerate.

To see the argument in detail, recall our earlier discussion in this chapter about how actual inflation has three separate components: output gaps, expectations, and non-wage supply shocks. It is restated here:

$$\frac{\text{Actual}}{\text{inflation}} = \frac{\text{Output-gap}}{\text{inflation}} + \frac{\text{Expected}}{\text{inflation}} + \frac{\text{Supply-shock}}{\text{inflation}}$$

EXTENSIONS IN THEORY 30-1

The Phillips Curve and Accelerating Inflation

As we first saw in Chapter 24, the Phillips curve describes the relationship between unemployment (or output) and the rate of change of wages. The Phillips curve was born in 1958 when Professor A.W. Phillips from the London School of Economics noted a relationship between unemployment and the rate of change of wages over a period of 100 years in the United Kingdom. Phillips was interested in studying the short-run behaviour of an economy subjected to cyclical fluctuations. In the years following Phillips's study,

however, some economists treated the Phillips curve as establishing a long-term tradeoff between inflation and unemployment.

Suppose the government stabilizes output at Y_1 (and hence the unemployment rate at U_1), as shown by points A in the accompanying figures. To do this, it must validate the ensuing wage inflation, which is indicated by $\dot{W}_1$ in the figures. The government thus *appears* to be able to choose among particular combinations of (wage) inflation and

(i) Wage changes and unemployment

(ii) Wage changes and output

There is no stable tradeoff between inflation and output. To maintain $Y > Y^*$, inflation must be steadily rising.

To illustrate the importance of expectations in accelerating inflation, suppose the inflationary output gap creates sufficient excess demand to push up wages by 2 percent per year. As a result, the *AS* curve will also tend to be shifting upward at 2 percent per year.

When inflation has persisted for some time, however, people will likely come to expect that the inflation will continue. The expectation of 2 percent inflation will tend to push up wages by that amount *in addition to* the demand pressure. As the output-gap effect on wages is augmented by the expectational effect, the *AS* curve will begin to shift upward more rapidly (look back to Figure 30-4). When expectations are for a 2 percent inflation and demand pressure is also pushing wages up by 2 percent, the overall effect will be a 4 percent increase in wages. Sooner or later, however, 4 percent inflation will come to be expected, and the expectational effect will rise to 4 percent. This new expectational component of 4 percent, when added to the output-gap component, will create an inflation rate of 6 percent. And so this cycle will go on. As long as there is excess demand arising from an inflationary output gap, the inflation rate cannot stay constant because expectations will always be revised upward toward the actual inflation rate.

Now we see the reason for the name NAIRU. If real GDP is held above Y^* (and thus the unemployment rate is below the NAIRU), the inflation rate tends to accelerate.

unemployment, in which lower levels of unemployment are attained at the cost of higher rates of inflation.

In the 1960s, Phillips curves were fitted to the data for many countries, and governments made decisions about where they wanted to be on the tradeoff between inflation and unemployment. Then, in the late 1960s, in country after country, the rate of wage and price inflation associated with any given level of unemployment began to rise. Instead of being stable, the Phillips curves began to shift upward. The explanation lay primarily in the rise of inflation expectations.

It was gradually understood that the original Phillips curve concerned only the influence of the output gap and left out inflationary expectations. This was not unreasonable for Phillips's original curve, which was fitted mainly to nineteenth-century data where the price level was relatively constant. But in the inflationary period following the Second World War, this omission proved important and unfortunate. An increase in expected inflation shows up as an upward shift in the original Phillips curve that was drawn in Chapter 24. The importance of expectations can be shown by drawing what is called an **expectations-augmented Phillips curve**, as shown by the dashed Phillips curves here. The height of the Phillips curves above the axis at Y^* and at U^* show the expected inflation rate. These distances represent the amount that wages will rise even when $Y = Y^*$ (or $U = U^*$) and there is neither excess demand nor supply in labour markets. The actual wage

increase is shown by the augmented (dashed) curve, with the increase in wages exceeding expected inflation whenever $Y > Y^*(U < U^*)$ and falling short of expected inflation whenever $Y < Y^*(U > U^*)$.

Now we can see what was wrong with the idea of a stable inflation–unemployment tradeoff. Maintaining a particular output Y_1 or unemployment U_1 in the figures requires some inflation $\dot{W}_1$. And once this rate of inflation comes to be expected, people will demand that much just to hold their own. The Phillips curve will then shift upward to the position shown in the figures and the economy will be at point B. Now there is inflation $\dot{W}_2$ because of the combined effects of expectations and excess demand. However, this higher rate is above the expected rate $\dot{W}_1$. Once this higher rate comes to be expected, the Phillips curve will shift upward once again.

As a result of the combination of output-gap inflation and expectational inflation, the inflation rate associated with any given positive output gap ($Y > Y^*$ or $U < U^*$) rises over time. This is the phenomenon of accelerating inflation that we discussed in the text.

The shifts in the Phillips curve are such that most economists agree that in the long run, when inflationary expectations have fully adjusted to actual inflation, there is no tradeoff between inflation and unemployment. In other words, the long-run Phillips curve is a vertical line above U^* (or Y^*).

The NAIRU is therefore the lowest level of sustained unemployment consistent with a *non-accelerating* rate of inflation.

expectations-augmented Phillips curve The relationship between unemployment and the rate of increase of nominal wages that arises when the output-gap and expectations components of inflation are combined.

> According to the acceleration hypothesis, as long as an inflationary output gap persists, expectations of inflation will be rising, which will lead to increases in the actual rate of inflation.

The tendency for inflation to accelerate is discussed further in *Extensions in Theory 30-1*, which examines how expected inflation affects the position of the Phillips curve.

Inflation as a Monetary Phenomenon

For many years, a debate among economists concerned the extent to which inflation is a monetary phenomenon. Does it have purely monetary causes—changes in the demand or the supply of money? Does it have purely monetary consequences—only the price level is affected? One slogan that states an extreme position on this issue was popularized many years ago by the late Milton Friedman: "Inflation is *everywhere* and *always* a monetary phenomenon." To consider these issues, let us summarize what we have learned already. First, look at the various *causes* of inflation:

- Anything that shifts the *AD* curve to the right will cause the price level to rise (demand inflation).
- Anything that shifts the *AS* curve upward will cause the price level to rise (supply inflation).
- Increases in the price level caused by *AD* and *AS* shocks will eventually come to a halt unless they are continually validated by monetary policy.

The first two points tell us that a temporary burst of inflation need not be a monetary phenomenon. It need not have monetary causes, and it need not be accompanied by monetary expansion. The third point tells us that *sustained* inflation *must* be a monetary phenomenon. If a rise in prices is to continue indefinitely, it *must* be accompanied by a monetary policy that allows the money supply to continually increase. This is true regardless of the cause that set the inflation in motion.

Now, let us summarize the macroeconomic changes that accompany inflation, assuming that real GDP was initially at its potential level.

- In the short run, demand inflation tends to be accompanied by an *increase* in real GDP above its potential level.
- In the short run, supply inflation tends to be accompanied by a *decrease* in real GDP below its potential level.
- When all costs and prices are adjusted *fully* and real GDP has returned to its potential level, the only long-run effect of *AD* or *AS* shocks is a change in the price level.

The first two points tell us that inflation is not, in the short run, a purely monetary phenomenon. The third point tells us that inflation is a monetary phenomenon from the point of view of long-run equilibrium. There is still plenty of room for debate, however, on how long the short run will last. Most economists believe that the short run can be long enough for inflation to have major real effects on important economic variables, such as the distribution of wealth (which partly explains why most economists believe that keeping inflation low is desirable).

We have now reached three important conclusions:

- Without monetary validation, positive demand shocks cause inflationary output gaps and a temporary burst of inflation. The gaps are removed as rising factor prices push the *AS* curve upward, returning real GDP to its potential level but at a higher price level.
- Without monetary validation, negative supply shocks cause recessionary output gaps and a temporary burst of inflation. The gaps are eventually removed when factor prices fall sufficiently to restore real GDP to its potential and the price level to its initial level.
- Only with continuing monetary validation can inflation initiated by either supply or demand shocks continue indefinitely.

To put these conclusions differently, we can modify Friedman's statement slightly to represent the causes of inflation more accurately. While *AD* and *AS* shocks may lead to temporary inflation even in the absence of any actions by the central bank, *sustained* inflation can occur only if there is continual monetary validation by the central bank.

Sustained inflation is everywhere and always caused by sustained monetary expansion.

We have been assuming in our macro model that wages rise when unemployment is less than the NAIRU ($Y > Y^*$) and that wages fall when unemployment exceeds the NAIRU ($Y < Y^*$). This assumption leads to the stark prediction that inflation can only be stable when unemployment exactly equals the NAIRU ($Y = Y^*$). In recent years, however, some economists have come to question this theory, believing instead that the NAIRU is best viewed as a range rather than a unique, precise value. In this case, stable inflation would be consistent with a range of unemployment rates. *Extensions in Theory 30-2* explores this issue in greater detail.

30.3 Reducing Inflation

Suppose an economy has had a sustained and constant rate of inflation for several years. What must the central bank do to reduce the rate of inflation? What are the costs involved in doing so?

The Process of Disinflation

Disinflation means a reduction in the rate of inflation. Canada has had two notable periods of disinflation—in 1981–1982, when inflation fell from more than 12 percent to 4 percent, and in 1990–1992, when inflation fell from 6 percent to less than 2 percent.

disinflation A reduction in the rate of inflation.

The process of reducing sustained inflation can be divided into three phases. In the first phase, the monetary validation is stopped and any inflationary gap is eliminated. In the second phase, the economy still suffers from declining output and rising prices—*stagflation.* In the final phase, the economy experiences both increasing output and increasing prices, but the inflation then comes to an end. We now examine these three phases in detail.

The starting point for our analysis is an economy with an inflationary gap ($Y > Y^*$) and rising inflation.[6]

Phase 1: Removing Monetary Validation The first phase consists of tightening monetary policy by raising interest rates and thus reducing the growth rate of the money supply. This policy action slows the rate at which the *AD* curve is shifting upward. An extreme case of monetary tightening in this setting is one where the Bank of Canada adopts a "cold-turkey approach:" interest rates are increased so much that the growth rate of the money supply is reduced to zero and the upward shift of the *AD* curve is halted abruptly. This extreme case is shown in part (i) of Figure 30-6.

The Bank's tight-money policy stops the *AD* curve from shifting. But under the combined influence of the present inflationary gap and expectations of continued inflation, wages continue to rise. Hence, the *AS* curve continues to shift upward. Eventually, the inflationary gap will be removed, as real GDP falls back toward Y^*.

If the excess demand from the inflationary output gap were the only influence on nominal wages, the story would be ended. At $Y = Y^*$, there would be no upward demand pressure on wages and other factor prices. The *AS* curve would be stabilized, and real GDP would remain at Y^*. But it is usually not so simple.

---

[6] In the simpler case in which the economy begins with $Y = Y^*$ and constant inflation, only the second and third phases are relevant.

EXTENSIONS IN THEORY 30-2

Is the NAIRU Like a Razor's Edge?

We have described the standard theory of inflation in which the only stable position for the economy is one in which unemployment is equal to the NAIRU and real GDP is equal to potential GDP, Y^*. According to this theory, the labour market is poised on a "razor's edge"; wages rise when unemployment is less than the NAIRU and wages fall when unemployment exceeds the NAIRU.

In recent years, however, this view has come under some criticism. For example, Canadian economist Lars Osberg and his colleagues from Dalhousie University were unable to find any unique value for the NAIRU in a careful empirical study of Canada's unemployment and inflation experience. Depending on the precise specification of the empirical model used and the number of years included in the statistical sample, they found that the estimated value for the NAIRU could lie within a range of several percentage points. When unemployment usually varies between a low of 6 percent and a high of 11 percent, a possible range of *several percentage points* indicates a very low degree of precision in the estimated NAIRU.

A glance at the accompanying figure for Canadian inflation and unemployment since 1984 shows no clear tendency for inflation to increase when unemployment is below some critical rate, nor to decrease when unemployment is above such a critical rate. If anything, there appear to be two distinct periods in the data. From 1984 to 1991, the unemployment rate varied between a high of 11.5 percent and a low of 7.5 percent, all while the rate of inflation varied between 4 percent and 6 percent per year. Over the next 20 years, from 1992 until 2012, the unemployment rate fluctuated over a wider range, but inflation was generally less variable around a 2 percent average.

Several possible explanations for these data have been advanced, each of which may contribute something to the full explanation. First, when the public has confidence in the Bank of Canada's commitment to maintaining inflation at some given level, these expectations tend to remain relatively constant as unemployment changes. Thus the influence of inflationary expectations on wages will be relatively insensitive to changes in the unemployment rate. In this case, we say that inflation expectations are "well anchored" because changes in the economic environment do not lead to significant changes in expectations. According to this view, for about a decade starting in 1984 the public had confidence in the Bank of Canada's commitment to keeping inflation in the 4 to 6 percent range. Then from 1992 onward, after the Bank of Canada had adopted its formal inflation target of 2 percent, the public once again believed that the Bank would carry out its stated objective. Thus the influence of inflation expectations on the path of wages was relatively invariant to large variations in the actual level of unemployment and real GDP; as a result, large swings in the unemployment rate were consistent with a relatively stable rate of inflation, as the figure shows.

A second explanation emphasizes the fact that most labour markets are not *auction markets* in which wages continually adjust to equate the demand and supply for labour. If employers have a reduced demand for workers, they usually respond by laying some workers off rather than by driving down wages. Instead of responding quickly to changes in excess demand or supplies in the labour market, wages tend to be set with longer-term conditions in mind. (We will say more about such long-term employment relationships in the next chapter.)

A third explanation is that the willingness of workers to push for higher wages (and in some situations to risk strikes) may depend on the nature of technological change. When technological change is creating good middle-wage jobs faster than it is destroying them, workers may be willing to push for higher wages whenever the labour market becomes relatively tight. This is a good description of the type of technological change that occurred between 1945

Phase 2: Stagflation As we explained earlier, wages depend not only on current excess demand but also on inflation expectations. Once inflation expectations have been established, it is not always easy to get people to revise them downward, even in the face of announced changes in monetary policies. Hence, the *AS* curve continues to shift upward, causing the price level to continue to rise and output to fall. A recessionary gap is created. The combination of increased inflation and a reduction in output (or its growth rate) is called **stagflation**. This is phase 2, shown in part (ii) of Figure 30-6.

stagflation The simultaneous increase in inflation and reduction in output (or its growth rate) that is caused by an upward shift of the *AS* curve.

The ease with which the Bank of Canada can end such an inflation depends on how easy it is to change these expectations of continued inflation. This change is more difficult to the extent that expectations are backward-looking and easier to the extent that expectations are forward-looking.

and the early 1970s, when factory jobs flourished, providing good wages for workers who did not have to be highly skilled. This may explain the appearance during this period of a well-defined Phillips curve with a razor's edge NAIRU. In contrast, the past four decades have seen technological change that destroys middle-wage manufacturing jobs while at the same time creating many high-wage jobs for highly trained and educated persons, as well as many low-wage jobs for the unskilled and uneducated. In this situation, workers who remain in manufacturing jobs may be reluctant to press for wage increases lest they be the next ones to lose their increasingly scarce, good jobs. In such an environment, even tight labour markets may not lead to substantial wage increases and hence there may not be a well-defined Phillips curve with its razor's edge NAIRU.

In summary, the description in our macro model of the wage-adjustment process has a certain compelling and valuable logic: wages tend to rise when labour markets are tight and they tend to fall (although more slowly) when labour markets have excess supply. However, this relationship should be viewed as a general tendency rather than a strict, formulaic rule; there is unlikely to be a unique value of the NAIRU that acts as a "razor's edge" to determine wage adjustments.

Canadian Inflation and Unemployment, 1984–2012

(*Source*: Author's calculations based on data from Statistics Canada. Consumer Price Index: CANSIM V41690973. Unemployment: CANSIM V2062815. The figure uses annual averages of monthly data.)

If most people are backward-looking when forming their expectations, inflation will remain high even well after the Bank of Canada has implemented its tight monetary policy. In this case, the *AS* curve will continue shifting upward and the stagflation will endure. However, if most people are forward-looking, the change in the Bank's policy will be widely acknowledged and expected inflation will fall relatively quickly. In this case, the upward shifts of the *AS* curve will soon come to an end.

How long inflation persists after the inflationary gap has been removed, and the depth of the associated recessionary gap during the stagflationary phase, depend on how quickly inflation expectations are revised downward.

FIGURE 30-6 Eliminating a Sustained Inflation

(i) Phase 1: Removing monetary validation

(ii) Phase 2: Stagflation

(iii) Phase 3: Recovery

(i) Phase 1: The elimination of a sustained inflation begins with a monetary tightening to remove the inflationary gap. The initial position is one where fully validated inflation is taking the economy along the path shown by arrow ①. When the curves reach AS_1 and AD_1, the central bank adopts a tight monetary policy, which halts the growth of the money supply, thus stabilizing aggregate demand at AD_1. Due to the output gap and inflation expectations, wages continue to rise, taking the AS curve leftward. The economy moves along arrow ②, with output falling and the price level rising. When aggregate supply reaches AS_2, the inflationary gap is is removed, output is Y^*, and the price level is P_2.

(ii) Phase 2: Expectations and wage momentum lead to stagflation, with falling output and continuing inflation. The economy moves along the path shown by arrow ③. The driving force is now the AS curve, which continues to shift because inflation expectations cause wages to continue rising. The recessionary gap grows as output falls. Inflation continues, but at a diminishing rate. If wages stop rising when output has reached Y_3 and the price level has reached P_3, the stagflation phase is over, with equilibrium at E_3.

(iii) Phase 3: After expectations are reversed, recovery takes output to Y^* and the price level is stabilized. There are two possible scenarios for recovery. In the first, the recessionary gap causes wages to fall (slowly), taking the AS curve back to AS_2 (slowly), as shown by arrow ④. The economy retraces the path originally followed in part (ii) back to E_2. In the second scenario, the central bank increases the money supply sufficiently to shift the AD curve to AD_2. The economy then moves along the path shown by arrow ⑤. This restores output to potential at the cost of further temporary inflation that takes the price level to P_4. Potential output and a stable price level are now achieved.

The importance of expectations explains why the Bank of Canada and other central banks emphasize their precise objectives in their many public speeches. In 1990–1991, the Bank's governor, John Crow, gave many speeches in an effort to convince the public that the Bank would stick to its newly adopted inflation target. This communications strategy was an attempt to reduce inflationary expectations and thus slow the upward shift of Canada's AS curve. And today, the governor of the Bank of Canada regularly speaks publicly about the Bank's 2 percent inflation target and about the importance of achieving it. Such public communications help to "anchor" inflation expectations at the 2 percent target.

Phase 3: Recovery The final phase is the return to potential output. When the economy comes to rest at the end of the stagflation, the situation is exactly the same as when the economy is hit by a negative supply shock. The move back to potential output can be accomplished in either of two ways. First, the recessionary gap may reduce factor prices, thereby shifting the *AS* curve downward, reducing prices but increasing real GDP. Second, an expansionary monetary policy can shift the *AD* curve upward, increasing both prices and real GDP. These two possibilities are illustrated in part (iii) of Figure 30-6.

Many economists worry about relying on the *AS* curve to shift downward to return the economy to potential output. Their concern is that it will take too long for wages to fall sufficiently to shift the *AS* curve—though output will eventually return to potential, the long adjustment period will be characterized by high unemployment.

Other economists worry about a temporary monetary expansion because they fear that expectations of inflation may be rekindled when the Bank's monetary expansion shifts the *AD* curve to the right. And if inflationary expectations *are* revived, the Bank will then be faced with a tough decision—either it must let another recession develop to break these new inflation expectations or it must validate the inflation to reduce unemployment. In the latter case, the Bank is back where it started, with validated inflation on its hands—and diminished credibility.

The Cost of Disinflation

As the foregoing discussion suggests, disinflation is a classic example of a policy that brings short-term pain for long-term gain. The long-term gain is the reduced costs to individuals and firms associated with the lower rate of inflation; the short-term pain is the temporary loss in economic activity and rise in unemployment that occurs during the process of disinflation.

> The cost of disinflation is the loss of output that is generated in the process.

As we said earlier, the size and duration of the recession depends to a large extent on how quickly inflation expectations are revised downward as the disinflation continues. If expectations are mainly backward-looking and thus slow to adjust to the changes in policy, the recession will be deep and protracted. Conversely, if expectations are mainly forward-looking and thus quick to adjust to changes in policy, the recession may be mild and of short duration.

But *how costly* is the process of disinflation? Economists have derived a simple measure of the cost of disinflation based on the depth and length of the recession and on the amount of disinflation. This measure is called the **sacrifice ratio** and is defined as the cumulative loss of real GDP caused by a given disinflation (expressed as a percentage of potential GDP) divided by the number of percentage points by which inflation has fallen. For example, the 1990–1992 disinflation in Canada reduced inflation by roughly 4 percentage points. Suppose the cumulative loss of real GDP caused by that disinflation was equal to $80 billion and that potential GDP at the time was equal to $800 billion. The cumulative loss of output would then have been 10 percent of potential output. The sacrifice ratio would therefore have been $10/4 = 2.5$. The interpretation of this number is that it "costs" 2.5 percent of real GDP for each percentage point of inflation that is reduced.

The numbers in the previous example are hypothetical, but typical estimates of the sacrifice ratio for many developed countries range between 2 and 4. Figure 30-7

sacrifice ratio The cumulative loss in real GDP, expressed as a percentage of potential output, divided by the percentage-point reduction in the rate of inflation.

FIGURE 30-7 The Cost of Disinflation: The Sacrifice Ratio

The sacrifice ratio is larger the deeper the recession and the longer it takes real GDP to return to potential. In this example, the economy begins with $Y = Y^*$ and inflation of 6 percent. At t_0, a tightening of monetary policy initiates a disinflation. A recessionary gap opens up and inflation falls only slowly. By t_1, real GDP has returned to Y^* and inflation has been reduced by four percentage points. In this figure, the cumulative loss of real GDP is 10 percent of Y^* and inflation has fallen by four percentage points. The sacrifice ratio is therefore $10/4 = 2.5$, indicating that it costs 2.5 percent of GDP to reduce inflation by one percentage point.

illustrates the time paths of real GDP and inflation following a disinflation and shows how to compute the sacrifice ratio. Note an important assumption that is implicit whenever measuring the sacrifice ratio in this way: that all changes in the path of real GDP are *caused by* the disinflation.

Conclusion

Throughout the history of economics, inflation has been recognized as a harmful phenomenon. The high inflation rates that Canada experienced in the 1970s and early 1980s (see Figure 30-1 on page 750) were also experienced in many developed countries. In the past 40 years these countries have learned much about the causes of inflation, the policies required to reduce it, and the costs associated with doing so.

In particular, Canada and several other countries have adopted formal inflation-targeting regimes, which have been successful at keeping inflation low and stable. An important aspect of inflation targeting is to keep the *expectations* of inflation low. As we have seen in this chapter, keeping inflation expectations low is crucial to keeping actual inflation low.

In recent years, some commentators have argued that the dangers of inflation have been eliminated, that inflation is now "dead." Central to these arguments is the view that greater international competition through the process of globalization will keep inflationary pressures at bay. Yet, whatever forces globalization might bring, it remains true that *sustained* inflation is ultimately caused by monetary policy. Unless central banks remain committed to keeping inflation low and stable, damaging inflation could return as a potential threat to the economy.

SUMMARY

30.1 Adding Inflation to the Model

LO 1, 2

- Sustained price inflation will be accompanied by closely related growth in wages and other factor prices such that the AS curve is shifting upward. Factors that influence wages can be divided into two main components: output gaps and expectations.
- Inflationary output gaps tend to cause wages to rise; recessionary output gaps tend to cause wages to fall, but only slowly.
- Expectations of inflation tend to cause wage increases equal to the expected price-level increases. Expectations

can be backward-looking, forward-looking, or some combination of the two.
- With a constant rate of inflation and no supply shocks, expected inflation will eventually come to equal actual inflation. This implies that there is no output-gap effect on inflation.
- With real GDP equal to Y^*, a constant inflation can occur with the AD and AS curves shifting upward at the same rate.

30.2 Shocks and Policy Responses

LO 3, 4

- The initial effects of a single positive demand shock are a rise in the price level and a rise in real GDP. If the shock is unvalidated, output tends to return to its potential level while the price level rises further (as the AS curve shifts upward). Monetary validation allows demand inflation to proceed without reducing the inflationary gap (AD curve continues to shift upward).
- The initial effects of a single negative supply shock are a rise in the price level and a fall in real GDP. If inflation is unvalidated, output will slowly move back to its potential level as the price level slowly falls to its

pre-shock level (AS curve slowly shifts down). Monetary validation allows supply inflation to continue in spite of a persistent recessionary gap (AD curve shifts up with monetary validation).
- If the Bank of Canada tries to keep real GDP constant at some level above Y^*, the actual inflation rate will eventually accelerate.
- Aggregate demand and supply shocks have temporary effects on inflation. But sustained inflation is caused by sustained monetary expansion.

30.3 Reducing Inflation

LO 5, 6

- The process of ending a sustained inflation can be divided into three phases.
  1. Phase 1 consists of ending monetary validation and allowing the upward shift in the AS curve to remove any inflationary gap that does exist.
  2. In Phase 2, a recessionary gap develops as expectations of further inflation cause the AS curve to continue to shift upward even after the inflationary gap is removed.

  3. In Phase 3, the economy returns to potential output, sometimes aided by a one-time monetary expansion that raises the AD curve to the level consistent with potential output.
- The cost of disinflation is the recession (output loss) that is created in the process. The sacrifice ratio is a measure of this cost and is calculated as the cumulative loss in real GDP (expressed as a percentage of Y^*) divided by the reduction in inflation.

KEY CONCEPTS

Temporary and sustained inflation	Expectational, output-gap, and	Expectations-augmented Phillips curve
The NAIRU	supply-shock pressures on inflation	Accelerating inflation
Forward-looking and backward-looking expectations	Monetary validation of demand and supply shocks	Disinflation
		Sacrifice ratio

STUDY EXERCISES

MyEconLab   Make the grade with MyEconLab: Study Exercises marked in red can be found on MyEcon-Lab. You can practise them as often as you want, and most feature step-by-step guided instructions to help you find the right answer. www.myeconlab.com

1. Fill in the blanks to make the following statements correct.

   a. The term NAIRU stands for the _____.
   b. Unemployment is said to be equal to the NAIRU when GDP is equal to _____.

   c. Changes in nominal wages result from two effects: the _____ effect and the _____ effect. Both of these effects cause the _____ curve to shift.
   d. The AS curve shifts up when nominal wages _____ and also shifts up with a negative _____ shock.

e. Actual inflation can come from any of its three component parts. They are _____, _____, and _____.

f. If the rate of inflation is constant at 6 percent and actual GDP equals potential GDP, then we can say that the central bank is _____ inflation expectations. That is, the central bank is permitting a(n) _____ in the money supply such that the expected and actual inflation rates are equal at _____ percent.

2. Fill in the blanks to make the following statements correct.

a. Suppose the economy is initially at potential GDP (Y^*) and then there is a sudden increase in the demand for Canadian exports. The AD curve shifts to the _____ and opens a(n) _____ gap.

b. With an inflationary gap, the economy is operating where GDP is above _____. In an effort to maintain the output gap, the Bank of Canada may choose to validate the inflation by _____ the interest rate and allowing the money supply to _____. The actual inflation rate will _____.

c. The alternative policy response to an inflationary gap is to not validate the inflation. The _____ curve stops shifting upward. The _____ curve shifts upward due to rising wages caused by _____. Real GDP eventually returns to _____ at a higher _____.

d. Sustained inflation can be said to be a(n) _____ phenomenon.

e. Reducing a sustained inflation requires that monetary _____ be stopped. Inflation will persist, however, until _____ of continued inflation are revised downward.

f. The cost of disinflation is the cost of the _____ that is generated in the process.

3. The table below shows several macroeconomic situations, each with a given amount of excess demand (or supply) for labour and a level of inflation expectations. Both are expressed in percentage per year. For example, in Case A excess demand for labour is pushing wages up by 4 percent per year, and expected inflation is pushing wages up by 3 percent per year.

Case	Excess Demand	Inflation Expectations	Total Wage Change	AS Shift
A	+4	+3	___	___
B	+4	0	___	___
C	0	+3	___	___
D	−3	0	___	___
E	−3	+4	___	___

a. For each case, identify whether there is an inflationary or a recessionary output gap.

b. For each case, what is the total effect on nominal wages? Fill in the third column.

c. For each case, in which direction is the AS curve shifting (up or down)? Fill in the last column.

4. This exercise requires you to compute inflationary expectations based on a simple formula, and it will help you to understand why backward-looking expectations adjust slowly to changes in economic events. Suppose that the *actual* inflation rate in year t is denoted Π_t. *Expected* inflation for year $t + 1$ is denoted Π^e_{t+1}. Now, suppose that workers and firms form their expectations according to

$$\Pi^e_{t+1} = \theta\Pi^T + (1 - \theta)\Pi_t \quad (\text{with } 0 < \theta < 1)$$

where Π^T is the central bank's announced *inflation target*. This simple equation says that people's expectations for inflation at $t + 1$ are a weighted average of last year's actual inflation rate and the central bank's currently announced target. We will use this equation to see how the size of θ determines the extent to which expectations are backward-looking. Consider the table below, which shows the data for a reduction in actual inflation from 10 percent to 2 percent.

Year (t)	Π^T	Π_t	$\theta = 0.1$ Π^e_{t+1}	$\theta = 0.9$ Π^e_{t+1}
1	2	10	___	___
2	2	9	___	___
3	2	6	___	___
4	2	3	___	___
5	2	2	___	___
6	2	2	___	___
7	2	2	___	___
8	2	2	___	___

a. Assume that θ is equal to 0.1. Compute expected inflation for each year and fill in the table.

b. On a scale diagram, plot the time path of actual inflation, expected inflation, and the inflation target.

c. Now assume that θ equals 0.9. Repeat parts (a) and (b).

d. Which value of θ corresponds to more backward-looking expectations? Explain.

e. Given the different speed of adjustment of inflationary expectations, predict which disinflation is more costly in terms of lost output—the one with $\theta = 0.1$ or with $\theta = 0.9$. Explain.

5. In the AD/AS diagram here, the economy is in long-run equilibrium with real GDP equal to Y^*; the price level is stable at P_0.

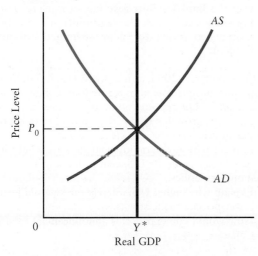

a. Suppose the central bank announces that it will implement an expansionary monetary policy that will shift the AD curve up by 5 percent. Show the likely effect of this announcement on the AS curve.

b. Does the shift of the AS curve in part (a) depend on whether workers and firms believe the central bank's announcement? Explain.

c. In a new AD/AS diagram, show how a sustained and constant inflation of 5 percent is represented (with $Y = Y^*$).

d. In the absence of any supply shocks, explain why a constant inflation is only possible when real GDP is equal to Y^*.

6. Consider the following AD/AS diagram. Suppose the economy experiences a positive aggregate demand shock—say, an increase in the demand for Canada's exports. This increases real GDP to Y_1.

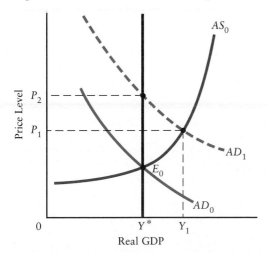

a. Explain what happens if the Bank of Canada does not react to the shock. Show this in the diagram.

b. Now suppose the Bank decides to maintain real GDP at Y_1—that is, it decides to validate the shock. Explain how this is possible, and show it in a diagram.

c. What is the effect on inflation from the policy in part (b)? Is inflation constant or is it rising? Explain.

7. What sources of inflation are suggested by each of the following quotations?

a. A newspaper editorial in Manchester, England: "If American unions were as strong as those in Britain, America's inflationary experience would have been as disastrous as Britain's."

b. An article in *The Economist*: "Oil price collapse will reduce inflation."

c. A Canadian newspaper article in June 2012: "Tensions in Iran fuel an oil-driven inflation."

d. A newspaper headline in October 2008: "Bank's fast growth of money will spur inflation."

e. A newspaper headline in July 2012: "Bumper crops across the West will dampen consumer inflation."

8. Consider the following AD/AS diagram. Suppose the economy experiences a negative aggregate supply shock—say, an increase in wages driven by a major union settlement. This reduces real GDP to Y_1.

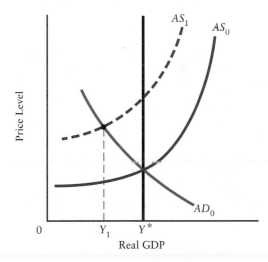

a. Explain what happens if the Bank of Canada does not react to the shock. Show this in the diagram.

b. Now suppose the Bank decides to offset the shock's effect on real GDP—that is, it validates the shock. Explain how this is possible, and show it in a diagram.

c. What danger do many economists see in validating such supply shocks? What is the alternative?

9. The table that follows shows some data on various dis-inflations. In each case, assume that potential GDP is equal to $900 billion.

Case	Inflation Reduction (percentage points)	Cumulative GDP Loss ($ billion)	Sacrifice Ratio
A	5	100	___
B	2	30	___
C	6	60	___
D	8	80	___

a. In each case, compute the sacrifice ratio.
b. Explain why the sacrifice ratio can be expected to be smaller when expectations are more forward-looking.
c. Explain why the sacrifice ratio can be expected to be smaller when central-bank announcements are more credible.

10. What is the relationship between the sacrifice ratio and the central bank's credibility?
a. Explain why a more credible policy of disinflation reduces the costs of disinflation.

b. Explain how you think the Bank of Canada might be able to make its disinflation policy more credible.
c. Can the Bank's policy responses to negative supply shocks influence the credibility it is likely to have when trying to end a sustained inflation? Explain.

11. In the summer of 2006, a time when U.S. inflation was rising and output was above potential, a story in *The Globe and Mail* reported that the release of strong employment-growth data for the United States led to a plunge in prices on the U.S. stock market.
a. Explain why high employment growth would lead people to expect the U.S. central bank to tighten its monetary policy.
b. Explain why higher U.S. interest rates would lead to lower prices of U.S. stocks.
c. How would you expect this announcement to affect Canada?

Unemployment Fluctuations and the NAIRU

LEARNING OBJECTIVES (LO)

After studying this chapter you will be able to

1 compare employment and unemployment changes over the short run and long run.

2 describe the difference between market-clearing and non-market-clearing theories of the labour market.

3 discuss the causes of frictional and structural unemployment

4 explain the various forces that cause the NAIRU to change.

5 discuss policies designed to reduce unemployment.

WHEN the level of economic activity changes, so do the levels of employment and unemployment. When real GDP increases in the short run, employment usually rises and unemployment usually falls. Conversely, when real GDP falls in the short run, employment falls and unemployment rises. Figure 31-1 shows the course of the unemployment rate in Canada over the past few decades. Recall from Chapter 19 that the unemployment rate is the percentage of the labour force that is not working but actively searching for a job. It is clear that the unemployment rate has followed a cyclical path, rising during the recessions of 1981–1982, 1991–1992, and 2009, and falling during the expansions of the late 1980s, late 1990s and mid-2000s. In this chapter we examine theories designed to explain these short-run fluctuations.

In addition to examining short-run fluctuations in the unemployment rate, economists also study the concept of the NAIRU—the rate of unemployment that exists when real GDP is equal to potential output, Y^*. At points A, B, C, and D in Figure 31-1, real GDP was approximately equal to potential output, and thus the unemployment rates then were approximately equal to the NAIRU. We will see in this chapter several reasons why the NAIRU might change over time and thus offer some explanations for the gradual decline in the NAIRU apparent in the figure, from about 8 percent in 1977 (point A) to approximately 6 percent in 2007 (point D).

We begin by examining some basic facts about employment and unemployment.

31.1 Employment and Unemployment

Look back at Figure 19-3 on page 481, which shows the path of employment and the labour force in Canada since 1960. The most striking feature of part (i) of the figure is that both employment and the labour force have tripled over the past half-century, with only relatively minor fluctuations. Also notice in part (ii) of Figure 19-3, and again in Figure 31-1, that the unemployment rate displays considerable short-run fluctuations but no significant long-term trend. These two characteristics of the labour force—long-term growth in employment but short-term fluctuations in the unemployment rate—are common to most developed countries.

> Over the span of many years, increases in the labour force are more or less matched by increases in employment. Over the short term, however, the unemployment rate fluctuates considerably because changes in the labour force are not exactly matched by changes in employment.

Changes in Employment

The amount of employment in Canada has increased dramatically over the past few decades. In 1959, there were approximately 5 million employed Canadians. By 2012, total employment was 17.5 million. The actual amount of employment, of course, is determined both by the demand for labour and by the supply of labour. How have the two "sides" of the Canadian labour market been changing?

On the supply side, the labour force has grown virtually every year since the end of the Second World War. The causes have included a rising population, which boosts entry into the labour force of people born 15 to 25 years previously; increased labour

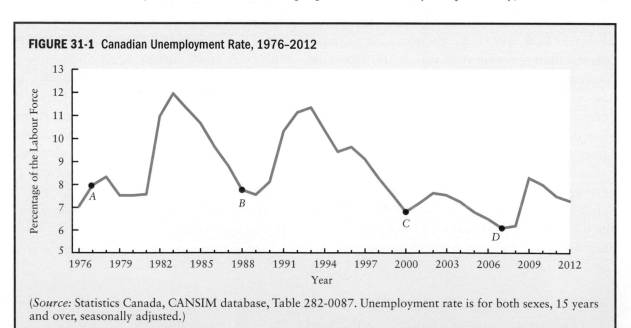

FIGURE 31-1 Canadian Unemployment Rate, 1976–2012

(*Source:* Statistics Canada, CANSIM database, Table 282-0087. Unemployment rate is for both sexes, 15 years and over, seasonally adjusted.)

force participation by various groups, especially women; and net immigration of working-age persons.

On the demand side, many existing jobs are eliminated every year, and many new jobs are created. The technological improvements that drive economic growth often cause great disruptions in an economy. Some sectors of the economy decline while others expand. Jobs are lost in the sectors that are contracting and created in sectors that are expanding. Furthermore, even in relatively stable industries, many firms disappear and many new ones are set up. The net increase in employment is the difference between all the jobs that are created and all those that are lost.

> In most years, enough new jobs are created both to offset the number of jobs that have been eliminated and also to provide jobs for the growing labour force. The result is a net increase in employment in most years.

In 2012, Canadian employment was just over 17.5 million workers. In a typical year employment increases by about 230 000 workers, an annual growth rate of roughly 1.3 percent.

Changes in Unemployment

In the early 1980s, worldwide unemployment rose to high levels. The unemployment rate remained high in many advanced industrial countries and only began to fall, and even then very slowly, during the latter half of the decade. Canadian experience reflected these international developments rather closely. From a high of more than 12 percent in 1983, the Canadian unemployment rate fell to 7.5 percent in 1988, a point that many economists at the time thought was close to the Canadian NAIRU (see point *B* in Figure 31-1).

With the onset of another recession in the early 1990s, the unemployment rate then rose through 1990 and 1991, reaching 11.3 percent by 1992. During the next few years, the unemployment rate fell only slowly as the Canadian recovery was weak; by early 1994 the unemployment rate was still more than 10 percent. But the speed of the Canadian recovery quickened and unemployment began to drop. By early 2000, after five years of steady economic recovery, the unemployment rate was 6.8 percent.

Following the large stock-market decline in late 2000, together with the decline in confidence associated with the 2001 terrorist attacks in New York and Washington, the Canadian and U.S. economies slowed, and unemployment increased. Recovery was rapid, however, and by the summer of 2007 Canadian real GDP was at or above its potential, and the unemployment rate had fallen to just below 6 percent, the lowest it had been in more than 30 years.

With the onset of the 2008 global financial crisis, and the worldwide recession that immediately followed, unemployment increased again. The Canadian economy fared much better than others, however, and unemployment increased only to 8.7 percent at the depth of the recession in mid-2009 (whereas it was considerably higher in the United States and most of Europe). After three years of modest economic recovery, the Canadian unemployment rate was just above 7 percent by early in 2013.

> During periods of rapid economic growth, the unemployment rate usually falls. During recessions or periods of slow growth, the unemployment rate usually rises.

Flows in the Labour Market

For data on current employment and unemployment in Canada, see Statistics Canada's website: www.statcan.gc.ca. Search for "unemployment rate" and follow the suggested links.

As we have just observed, many existing jobs are eliminated every year as existing firms adopt new technologies that require different types of workers, some industries shrink, and some firms disappear altogether. Similarly, new jobs are continually being created, as other industries expand and new firms are born. The public's and the media's focus on the labour market, however, tends to be on the overall level of employment and unemployment rather than on the amount of *job creation* and *job destruction*. This focus can often lead us to the conclusion that few changes are occurring in the labour market when in fact the truth is quite the opposite.

For example, the Canadian unemployment rate was roughly constant at 7.3 percent from 2011 to 2012. Does this mean no jobs were created during the year? Or that the Canadian labour market was stagnant during this period? No. In fact, workers were finding jobs at the rate of roughly 400 000 *per month*. At the same time, however, other workers were leaving jobs or entering the labour force at roughly the same rate. These large flows *out of unemployment* were being approximately matched by the large flows *into unemployment*. The net result was that total unemployment changed only slightly.

> The amount of activity in the labour market is better reflected by the flows into and out of unemployment than by the overall unemployment rate.

By looking at the *gross flows* in the labour market, we are able to see economic activity that is hidden when we look just at changes in the overall amount of employment and unemployment (which is determined by *net* flows). Indeed, the gross flows are typically so large that they dwarf the net flows. See *Applying Economic Concepts 31-1* for more discussion of the gross flows in the Canadian labour market, and how these gross-flows data can be used to compute the average length of unemployment spells.

Measurement Problems

The official labour-market data produced and reported by Statistics Canada understate the full effects of recessions on unemployment. The unemployment data refer to those individuals who are not currently working and who are actively searching for a job. As a recession continues, many workers who have been unable to find a job become discouraged and give up the search. Statistically, these *discouraged workers* are no longer included in the labour force; they are therefore not classified as unemployed, even though they would still accept a job if one were offered. In addition, this pool of discouraged workers becomes larger as the recession continues, which means that the official data become a larger understatement of the amount of "true" unemployment.

A second problem with the official measure of unemployment is that it fails to take account of situations where an individual is *underemployed*. Many workers who have lost their job and are still searching for a suitable replacement may temporarily take a part-time job or a job that requires much lower qualifications than their previous one. These workers prefer a part-time or low-paying job to the alternative of being totally unemployed, and they are appropriately represented in the data as being employed. It is also true, however, that they usually continue to search for a job that is more suited to their experience and qualifications.[1]

Care must therefore be taken when assessing the state of the labour market from the official unemployment data. A fall in the unemployment rate is sometimes caused by discouraged workers giving up the search and leaving the labour force. And just because individuals are recorded as being employed does not mean that they are not still searching for jobs that better match their skills and experience.

Consequences of Unemployment

To most people, unemployment is seen as a social "bad," just as output is seen as a social "good." But this does not mean *all* unemployment is bad, just as we know that not all output—such as noise or air pollution—is good. Indeed, we will see later in this chapter that some unemployment is socially desirable as it reflects the necessary time spent searching to make appropriate matches between firms who are seeking new employees and workers who are seeking new jobs.

We examine two costs of unemployment. The first is the associated loss in output. The second is the harm done to the individuals who are unemployed.

Lost Output Every person counted as unemployed is willing and able to work and is seeking a job but has yet to find one. Hence, unemployed individuals are valuable resources who are currently not producing output. The output that is not produced, but potentially could be, is a loss for society. Once an unemployed person regains employment, however, output rises again and this loss no longer occurs. But nothing makes up for the *past* loss that existed while the person was unemployed. In other words, the loss of output that accompanies unemployment is lost forever. In a world of scarcity with many unsatisfied desires, this loss represents a serious waste of resources.

Personal Costs For the typical Canadian worker, being unemployed for long periods of time is unusual. Most spells of unemployment are short. In 2008, *before* the onset of a major recession, the OECD estimated that only 7.1 percent of Canadian unemployment spells lasted 12 months or longer; this number increased to 12 percent by 2010. In other words, the vast majority of unemployed workers find new jobs in just a few months. Moreover, many workers experiencing temporary unemployment have access to the employment insurance program that provides some income during their spell of unemployment.

This does not mean, however, there are no problems associated with unemployment, especially for those relatively few workers who are unemployed for long periods of time. The effects of long-term unemployment, in terms of the disillusioned who have given up trying to make it within the system and who contribute to social unrest, is a serious social problem. The loss of self-esteem and the dislocation of families that often result from situations of prolonged unemployment are genuine tragedies.

---

[1] The problem of under-employment in Canada is particularly acute among some groups of immigrants, whose foreign credentials for specific, technical occupations are not fully recognized in Canada. This problem is getting increased attention among Canadian policymakers.

APPLYING ECONOMIC CONCEPTS 31-1

Stocks and Flows in the Canadian Labour Market

In most reports about changes in unemployment, both in Canada and abroad, emphasis is typically on the changes in the *stock* of unemployment—that is, on the number of people who are unemployed at a particular point in time. But as we said in the text, the focus on the stock of unemployment can often hide much activity in the labour market, activity that is revealed by looking at *gross flows.*

What Are Labour-Market Flows?

The first figure in this box shows the difference between stocks and flows in the labour market. The blue circles represent the number of individuals at the end of each month (the *stocks*) in each possible "state"—employment (*E*), unemployment (*U*), and *not* in the labour force (*N*). The six red arrows represent the monthly *flows* of individuals among the various states. For example, arrow ① shows the monthly flow of individuals from *E* to *U*. These individuals begin the month in *E*(employed), leave their jobs sometime during the month, and end the month as unemployed individuals, in *U*. Arrow ③ shows the flow from *N* to *U*—these individuals are new entrants to the labour force during the month and begin their labour-force experience as unemployed individuals.

In the second figure, three series of data are shown for Canada from 1976 to 2003—a period that includes the

major recessions of 1981 and 1991. (Unfortunately, Statistics Canada has stopped publishing these data, so more recent data are not available.) The top line is the stock of unemployment—the actual *number* of people unemployed at a specific point in time. During the severe recession of the early 1980s, unemployment peaked at approximately 1.7 million people and then fell during the recovery until 1989. With the onset of the next recession in 1990–1991, unemployment rose again, reaching nearly 1.8 million in 1992.

The two lower lines show *gross flows* in the labour market. (These flows data are not available for 1997 and 1998, which explains the break in the lines at that point.) The orange line shows the monthly flow into unemployment, corresponding to the sum of the flows in arrows ① and ③ in the first figure. This flow into unemployment represents

- workers losing jobs through layoffs or plant closure
- workers quitting jobs to search for different jobs
- new entrants to the labour force searching for jobs

The monthly flow into unemployment varies between approximately 300 000 and 500 000 individuals *per month*.

The green line shows the monthly flow out of unemployment, corresponding to the sum of the flows in arrows ② and ④ in the first figure. This outflow represents

- unemployed individuals finding new jobs
- unemployed individuals becoming discouraged and leaving the labour force

The monthly flow out of unemployment is roughly the same size as the monthly inflow, 300 000 to 500 000 individuals per month.

What is the connection between the flows and the stocks in the labour market? Whenever the flows into unemployment exceed the flows out of unemployment, the stock of unemployment rises. Conversely, whenever the flows out of unemployment exceed the flows into unemployment, the stock of unemployment falls.

Using Flows Data

For two reasons data on flows can be very useful when thinking about the labour market. First, they show the tremendous amount of activity in the labour market even

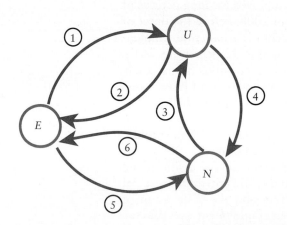

In the United States, as in Canada, the amount of long-term unemployment has historically not been large. For example, in the depths of the recessions of 1982 and 1991, the fraction of total unemployed workers who were unemployed for six months or more was just under 25 percent. In the most recent recession of 2009–2010, however, though the stock of unemployment may not be changing significantly. For example, between 1991 and 1992 the stock of unemployment in Canada varied between 1.4 million and 1.6 million persons. But during that two-year period, roughly 400 000 persons *per month* either became unemployed or ceased being unemployed. This number reflects the massive amount of regular turnover that exists in the Canadian labour market—turnover that is the essence of what economists call *frictional unemployment*.

The second reason flows data are useful is that the relationship between the flows and the stock can tell us something about the amount of time the average unemployed person spends unemployed. If U_s is the stock of unemployment, and U_o is the monthly outflow from unemployment, then one simple estimate of the average length of an unemployment spell is

$$\text{Average duration of unemployment spell} = \frac{U_s}{U_o}$$

Consider the situation in 1999, at the peak of the business cycle (a low point for unemployment). At that time, the stock of unemployment was approximately 1 million people and the outflow from unemployment was approximately 400 000 persons per month. Thus, the average unemployed person in 1999 could expect to leave unemployment in about 2.5 months (1 000 000 people/400 000 people per month = 2.5 months). In contrast, in 1992, at the depth of the previous recession (and thus a high point for unemployment), the expected duration of an unemployment spell was 3.6 months (1 600 000/450 000 = 3.6).

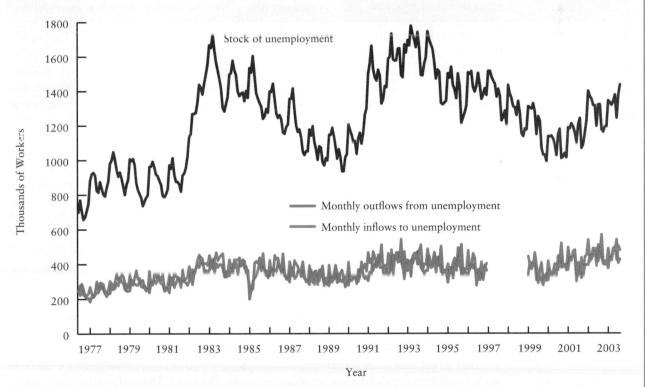

(*Source:* Statistics Canada, Labour Force Survey, available at www.statcan.gc.ca.)

long-term unemployment in the United States became a more serious problem. Even by mid-2012, more than two years into a modest economic recovery, 45 percent of all unemployed U.S. workers had been out of work for over six months. As we will describe later in this chapter, extensive long-term unemployment can be an important force behind increases in the economy's NAIRU. The general case for concern about high unemployment has been eloquently put by Princeton economist Alan Blinder:

> *A high-pressure economy provides opportunities, facilitates structural change, encourages inventiveness and innovation, and opens doors for society's under-dogs. . . . All these promote the social cohesion and economic progress that make democratic mixed capitalism such a wonderful system when it works well. A low-pressure economy slams the doors shut, breeds a bunker mentality that resists change, stifles productivity growth, and fosters both inequality and mean-spirited public policy. All this makes reducing high unemployment a political, economic, and moral challenge of the highest order.*[2]

| 31.2 Unemployment Fluctuations

It is clear from Figure 31-1 on page 776 that the unemployment rate fluctuates considerably over relatively short periods of time. Over the years, economists have debated the sources of these fluctuations, and many different theories have been developed to try to explain them. One set of theories emphasizes the distinction between the unemployment that exists when real GDP is equal to Y^*, and unemployment that is due to deviations of real GDP from Y^*. The former, as we saw in Chapter 19, is called the NAIRU, and is made up of frictional and structural unemployment. The latter is often called **cyclical unemployment,** which falls (or rises) as real GDP rises above (or falls below) Y^*. As we will soon see, this first set of theories suggests that cyclical unemployment exists because real wages do not quickly adjust to clear labour markets in response to shocks of various kinds. We refer to these as "non-market-clearing" theories of the labour market.

The second set of theories contains a very different view of labour markets. In these theories, real wages adjust instantly to clear the labour market after any *AD* or *AS* shock occurs, and as a result real GDP is always equal to Y^*. (As we saw in Chapter 24, if the economy's adjustment process works quickly, real GDP returns to Y^* very soon after any *AD* or *AS* shock.) In this perspective, the unemployment rate still fluctuates, but only due to changes in frictional or structural unemployment. In these "market-clearing" theories, there is no cyclical unemployment whatsoever.

cyclical unemployment Unemployment not due to frictional or structural factors; it is due to deviations of GDP from Y^*.

Market-Clearing Theories

Two major characteristics of modern market-clearing theories of the labour market are that firms and workers continuously optimize and markets continuously clear. In such models, there can be no *involuntary* unemployment. These theories then seek to explain unemployment as the outcome of voluntary decisions made by individuals who are choosing to do what they do, including spending some time out of employment.

Market-clearing theories explain fluctuations in employment and real wages as having one of two causes. First, as shown in part (i) of Figure 31-2, changes in technology that affect the *marginal product* of labour will lead to changes in the demand for labour. If these technological shocks are sometimes positive and sometimes negative,

---

[2] Blinder, A.S., "The challenge of high unemployment," *American Economic Review,* 1988.

they will lead to fluctuations in the level of employment and real wages. Second, as shown in part (ii) of Figure 31-2, changes in the willingness of individuals to work will lead to changes in the supply of labour and thus to fluctuations in the level of employment and real wages. In both cases, however, note that the flexibility of real wages results in a *clearing* of the labour market. In this setting, whatever unemployment exists cannot be involuntary and must be caused by either frictional or structural causes, the two components of the NAIRU.

Market-clearing theories of the labour market assume that real wages always adjust to clear the labour market. People who are not working are assumed to have voluntarily withdrawn from the labour market for one reason or another. There is no involuntary unemployment.

There are two major problems with this theory of labour markets. First, empirical observation is not consistent with the fluctuations in real wages predicted by the theory. In Canada and other developed economies, employment tends to be quite volatile over the business cycle, whereas real wages tend to be relatively stable—they do *not* show the cyclical variation predicted in Figure 31-2. The second problem is that the market-clearing theories predict no involuntary unemployment whatsoever, a prediction that many economists argue is unsupported by empirical observation. In Canada and other countries, a large fraction of unemployed workers are eligible for and collect

FIGURE 31-2 Employment and Wages When Labour Markets Clear

(i) Demand shifts

(ii) Supply shifts

In a market-clearing theory of the labour market, there is no involuntary unemployment. The figure shows a perfectly competitive market for one type of labour. In part (i), the demand curves D_1, D_0, and D_2 are the demands for this market corresponding to low, medium, and high values for the marginal product of labour. As demand rises from D_1 to D_0 to D_2, real wages rise from w_1 to w_0 to w_2, and employment rises from L_1 to L_0 to L_2. In part (ii), changes in workers' willingness to work causes the supply of labour to fluctuate from S_1 to S_0 to S_2, and wages to fluctuate from w_1 to w_0 to w_2. In both parts, the labour market always clears and there is no involuntary unemployment.

employment insurance. In order to collect the insurance benefits, they are required to state that they are actively searching for a job. For those who are truly engaged in an active job search, it is difficult to describe them as *voluntarily* unemployed. We will say more about the distinction between voluntary and involuntary unemployment later in the chapter.

Non-Market-Clearing Theories

The many economists who reject the market-clearing theories of unemployment fluctuations emphasize that labour markets do not operate in the extreme manner shown in Figure 31-2. Just as the prices of TVs, cars, blue jeans, sushi, and cell phones do not change daily, or even monthly, to equate current demand with current supply, so the wages paid to various types of labour, such as factory workers, school-teachers, professors, architects, fast-food workers, train engineers, TV commentators, and product designers, do not change frequently to equate current demands with current supplies. These economists use non-market-clearing theories of the labour market in which "wage stickiness" plays a central role in explaining unemployment fluctuations.

When unemployed workers are looking for jobs during a recession, they do not knock on employers' doors and offer to work at lower wages than are being paid to current workers; instead, they answer help-wanted ads and hope to get the jobs offered but are often disappointed. Nor do employers, seeing an excess of applicants for the few jobs that are available, go to the current workers and reduce their wages until there is no one left looking for a job; instead, they pick and choose until they fill their needs and then hang a sign saying "No Help Wanted."

As a result of this wage stickiness, many people become involuntarily unemployed when the demand for labour falls during a recession. Their unemployment is involuntary in the sense that they would accept an offer of work in jobs for which they are trained, at the going wage rate, if such an offer were made. For example, such involuntary unemployment was evident during the recession that began in 2008 and extended into 2010 (and later in some countries). In the countries hardest hit by the recession, many workers had been unemployed for extended periods and their loss of income caused them to lose their homes and other possessions. In the European Union, where youth unemployment approached 50 percent in some countries, it was obvious that labour markets were not clearing to eliminate involuntary unemployment and that many unemployed workers would have gladly accepted work if it had been available. The cyclical behaviour of involuntary unemployment when wages are sticky is illustrated in Figure 31-3.

FIGURE 31-3 Unemployment and Sticky Wages When Labour Markets Do Not Clear

When the wage rate does not change enough to equate quantity demanded with quantity supplied, there will be unemployment in slumps and labour shortages in booms. When demand is at its normal level D_0, the market is cleared with wage rate w_0, employment is L_0, and there is no involuntary unemployment. In a recession, demand falls to D_1, but the wage falls only to w_1'. As a result, L_1 of labour is demanded and L_1' is supplied. Employment is determined by the quantity demanded at L_1. The remainder of the supply for which there is no demand, L_1L_1', is involuntarily unemployed. In a boom, demand rises to D_2, but the wage rate rises only to w_2'. As a result, the quantity demanded is L_2', whereas only L_2 is supplied. Employment rises to L_2, which is the amount supplied. The rest of the demand cannot be satisfied, making excess demand for labour of L_2L_2'.

The main challenge for these non-market-clearing theories is to explain *why* wages do not quickly adjust to eliminate involuntary unemployment. This issue has been debated among economists for years, and several plausible reasons have been presented.

Long-Term Employment Relationships The most obvious reason for wage stickiness over the business cycle is that many workers and their employers have long-term relationships in which the wages and conditions of work are determined for extended periods of time, often for one or more years. This situation applies to most groups of workers such as schoolteachers, professors, hospital technicians, office workers, supervisors, middle managers, and skilled construction workers. Such long-term relationships between employers and employees are actually the norm in modern, developed economies. The only kind of worker whose wage *does* fluctuate more or less continually with the conditions of current demand and supply are the relatively few casual daily workers who show up at hiring points each day hoping to be offered a job for that day.

Wage stickiness is obvious from even the most casual observation of the conditions under which most people work. The problem for economists is then to explain why such behaviour occurs. Why are the wages of workers not set for short periods of time that could then fluctuate with changes in demand and supply?

To explore this issue, imagine a worker being faced with a choice between two employment arrangements:

1. A high average wage but one that fluctuates over the business cycle, and the chance of job loss during a recession.

2. A somewhat lower wage that is stable over the business cycle, and a reduced chance of job loss during a recession.

Most workers would prefer the second employment arrangement. Most employees value the relative employment (and thus income) security offered by the second arrangement because it allows the individual to make long-term financial

The quick adjustment of wages to excess demands and supplies is not a characteristic of labour markets in which employees and firms have long-term relationships, such as in the health care sector.

plans. The ability to use a mortgage to purchase a home or consumer debt to buy big-ticket items such as cars, furniture, and appliances is more manageable with a relatively secure job and income. The lower wage in the second employment arrangement can be seen as the price the worker pays for greater employment and income security.

Why do employers also prefer such long-term employment arrangements? Employers want to retain workers who have the knowledge required for a particular job—knowledge of the firm's organization, production techniques, operating procedures, and marketing plans. If all workers were identical, an employer would not mind laying off one individual from a particular job during a recession and then hiring a different worker for that job when demand recovers. But, of course, workers are not all the same, even in fairly routine jobs and even among workers having the same formal qualifications. What the worker learns through on-the-job experience is valuable to the firm and makes each individual a unique asset. If a firm laid off one worker and then later hired another worker for the same job, it would lose all the knowledge that the first worker had acquired on the job and would lose efficiency until the new worker acquired similar experience. In today's knowledge-intensive world, this loss can be quite substantial and typically applies for a wide range of workers.

For these and other similar reasons, wages tend to be insensitive to fluctuations in current economic conditions. Wages are often, in effect, regular payments to workers over an extended employment relationship rather than a device for fine-tuning the current supplies of and demands for labour. Employers tend to "smooth" the income of employees by paying a steady wage and letting profits and employment fluctuate to absorb the effects of temporary changes in demand. It is these fluctuations in employment over the business cycle that cause the fluctuations in involuntary unemployment.

A number of labour-market institutions sustain such long-term relationships between employees and employers. For example, many long-term labour contracts provide for a schedule of wages over a period of several years. Similarly, employee benefits, such as pensions and supplementary health insurance, tend to bind workers to particular employers. Salaries or pension benefits that rise with years of service also help to bind the employee to the company, whereas seniority rules for layoffs bind the employer to the long-term worker.

> Long-term relationships between firms and workers are important in most labour markets, and wages in such labour markets do not adjust frequently to eliminate involuntary unemployment.

Economic Climate Versus Economic Weather Two additional observations are important to this discussion. First, despite the fact that wages are *generally* insensitive to short-run changes in labour demand and labour supply, there are exceptional circumstances. For example, wages sometimes fall during a severe recession. Occasionally, management calls the workers together and offers them a stark choice between the firm going out of business or the workers accepting a cut in their wages. The result is some cyclical variation in wages, especially when a recession is deep and long lasting. But the headlines generated by such occurrences speak to their relative infrequency.

The second observation relates to longer-run considerations. As we discussed in Chapter 24, wages do tend to respond to persistent situations of excess demand or excess supply in the labour market. For example, sustained and large recessionary gaps will tend to reduce the rate of growth of wages and, in extreme situations, may even lead to reductions in overall wage levels. Similarly, sustained inflation gaps will tend to cause wages to grow faster than they otherwise would.

The conclusion is that changes in the conditions of labour demand and labour supply, if sustained, are important for determining variations in real wages. But short-run changes in labour-market conditions may cause little or no change in wages because of the widespread long-term relationships between firms and workers.

> Variations in real wages tend to be determined by the long-term economic climate rather than by the short-term economic weather.

We have emphasized the importance of long-term employment relationships as an explanation for wage stickiness and the existence of involuntary unemployment. *Extensions in Theory 31-1* provides some additional explanations.

EXTENSIONS IN THEORY 31-1

Wage Stickiness and Involuntary Unemployment

Economists have developed many labour-market theories in which real wages do not fluctuate continuously to equate labour demand with labour supply. In the text we emphasized the importance of long-term employment relationships. Three additional theories are briefly described here.

Menu Costs

A typical large firm sells dozens of differentiated products and employs many different types of labour. Changing prices and wages in response to every fluctuation in demand is a costly and time-consuming activity. Many firms therefore find it optimal to keep their price lists (*menus*) constant for significant periods of time. Since large firms are often operating in imperfectly competitive markets, they have discretion over the prices of their products. Hence, firms often react to changes in demand by holding prices constant and responding with changes in output and employment.

If firms did alter their prices dramatically over the business cycle, they would be more or less forced to alter wages correspondingly or else suffer losses that could threaten their existence during recessions. As it is, the presence of relatively sticky prices allows firms to keep wages relatively sticky over the cycle for all of the reasons discussed in the text.

Efficiency Wages

Employers may find that they get more output per dollar of wages paid—that is, a more efficient workforce—when they pay labour somewhat more than the minimum amount that would induce people to work for them.

Suppose it is costly for employers to monitor workers' performance on the job so that some workers will be able to shirk duties with a low probability of being caught. Given prevailing labour-market institutions, it is generally impossible for employers to levy fines on employees for shirking on the job since the employees could just leave their jobs rather than pay the fines. So firms may instead choose to pay a wage premium—an *efficiency wage*—to the workers, in excess of the wage that the workers could get elsewhere in the labour market. With such a wage premium, workers will be reluctant to shirk because if they get caught and laid off, they will then lose this high wage.

Such high wages are rational responses of firms to the conditions they face and imply that firms will not alter wages in the face of temporary reductions in demand.

Union Bargaining

In many employment situations, those already working ("insiders") have more say in wage bargaining than those currently not employed ("outsiders"). Employed workers are often represented by a union, which negotiates the wage rate with firms. The union will generally represent the interests of the insiders but will not necessarily reflect the interests of the outsiders. Insiders will naturally want to bid up wages even though to do so will harm the employment prospects of the outsiders. Hence, this theory generates an outcome to the bargaining process between firms and unions in which the wage is set higher than the market-clearing level, just as with efficiency wages.

31.3 What Determines the NAIRU?

When the unemployment rate is equal to the NAIRU, there is only frictional and structural unemployment. Our interest here is in why the NAIRU changes over time and in the extent to which economic policy can affect it.

Frictional Unemployment

As we saw in Chapter 19, **frictional unemployment** results from the normal turnover of labour. One source of frictional unemployment is young people who enter the labour force and look for jobs. Another source is people who leave their jobs. Some may quit because they are dissatisfied with the type of work or their working conditions; others

frictional unemployment Unemployment that results from the turnover in the labour market as workers move between jobs.

may be fired because of incompetence or laid off because their employers go out of business. Yet others may lose their jobs because the jobs themselves are eliminated by the introduction of new technologies. Whatever the reason, they must search for new jobs, which takes time. People who are unemployed while searching for jobs are said to be frictionally unemployed or in *search unemployment*.

> **The normal turnover of labour causes frictional unemployment to persist, even if the economy is at potential output.**

How "voluntary" is frictional unemployment? Some of it is clearly voluntary. For example, a worker may know of an available job but may not accept it so she can search for a better one, or one for which she is more appropriately trained. Some of it is also involuntary, such as when a worker gets laid off and cannot find *any* job offer for a period of weeks, even though he may be actively searching. *Applying Economic Concepts 31-2* shows that the distinction between voluntary and involuntary unemployment is not always as clear as it might at first seem.

Structural Unemployment

structural unemployment
Unemployment caused by a mismatch in skills, industry, or location between available jobs and unemployed workers.

Structural unemployment is defined as a mismatch between the current structure of the labour force—in terms of skills, occupations, industries, or geographical locations—and the current structure of firms' demand for labour. Since changes in the structure of the demand for labour are occurring continually in any modern economy, and since it takes time for workers to adjust, some amount of structural unemployment always exists.

Natural Causes Changes that accompany economic growth shift the structure of the demand for labour. Demand might rise in such expanding areas as British Columbia's Lower Mainland or northern Alberta and might fall in parts of Ontario and Quebec. Demand rises for workers with certain skills, such as computer programming and electronics engineering, and falls for workers with other skills, such as stenography, assembly line work, and middle management. To meet changing demands, the structure of the labour force must change. Some existing workers can retrain and some new entrants can acquire fresh skills, but the transition is often difficult, especially for older workers whose skills become economically obsolete.

Increases in international competition can also cause structural unemployment. As the geographical distribution of world production changes, so does the composition of production and of labour demand in any one country. Labour adapts to such shifts by changing jobs, skills, and locations, but until the transition is complete, structural unemployment exists.

> **Structural unemployment will increase if there is either an increase in the pace at which the structure of the demand for labour is changing or a decrease in the pace at which labour is adapting to these changes.**

Following the Canada–U.S. Free Trade Agreement in 1989 and the North American Free Trade Agreement (NAFTA) in 1994, there were significant shifts of economic activity within Canada. For example, the textiles industry, much of which was located in

APPLYING ECONOMIC CONCEPTS 31-2

Voluntary Versus Involuntary Unemployment

Frictional unemployment is *involuntary* if the job seeker has not yet found a job for which his or her training and experience are suitable, whether or not such jobs exist somewhere in the economy. Frictional unemployment is *voluntary* if the unemployed person is aware of available jobs for which he or she is suited but is searching for better options. But how should we classify an unemployed person who refuses to accept a job at a lower skill level than the one for which she is qualified? What if she turns down a job for which she is trained because she hopes to get a higher wage offer for a similar job from another employer?

In one sense, people in search unemployment are voluntarily unemployed because they could almost always find *some* job, no matter how poorly paid or inappropriate to their training. In another sense, they are involuntarily unemployed because they have not yet succeeded in finding the job that they believe exists and for which they feel they are suited at a rate of pay that they believe is attainable.

Workers do not have perfect knowledge of all available jobs and rates of pay, and they may be able to gain information only by searching the labour market. Facing this uncertainty, they may find it sensible to refuse a first job offer, for the offer may prove to be a poor one in light of further market information. But too much search—for example, holding off while being supported by others in the hope of finding a job better than a job for which one is really suited—is an economic waste. Thus, search unemployment is a grey area: Some of it is useful and some of it is wasteful.

Some search unemployment is desirable because it gives unemployed people time to find an available job that makes the best use of their skills.

How long it pays for people to remain in search unemployment depends on the economic costs of being unemployed. By lowering the costs of being unemployed, employment insurance tends to increase the incentives for more search unemployment. This may or may not increase economic efficiency, depending on whether or not it induces people to search beyond the point at which they acquire new and valuable information about the labour market.

Quebec, contracted; at the same time there was an expansion of the high-tech industry, much of which was located in the Ottawa Valley. The types of workers released from the textiles industry, however, were not exactly what were required in the expanding high-tech industry. This type of mismatch in skills and locations contributed to structural unemployment during the 1990s.

Structural unemployment also increased during the 2002–2008 period in response to the five-fold increase in the world price of oil. The demand for labour increased sharply in the petroleum-producing regions of Alberta, Saskatchewan, and Newfoundland. At the same time, many jobs were lost in the manufacturing heartland of Ontario and Quebec because the rising price of oil significantly increased firms' costs. Some of the displaced workers could find jobs relatively quickly in expanding firms in other regions or sectors, but for most workers this transition was slow. Structural unemployment was the result.

Policy Causes Government policies can influence the speed with which labour markets adapt to changes. Some countries, including Canada, have adopted policies that *discourage* movement among regions, industries, and occupations. These policies (which may be desirable for other reasons) tend to reduce the rate at which unemployed workers are matched with vacant jobs, and thus tend to raise the amount of structural unemployment.

For two related reasons, the employment-insurance (EI) program contributes to structural unemployment. First, the Canadian EI system ties workers' benefits to the regional unemployment rate in such a way that unemployed workers can collect EI benefits for more weeks in regions where unemployment is high than where it is low.

For information on Canada's Employment Insurance program, see the website for Human Resources and Skills Development Canada: www.hrsdc.gc.ca.

Increases in the world price of oil between 2002 and 2008 led to a reduction in manufacturing activity in Central Canada and economic expansions in oil-producing regions of the country, such as the Alberta oil sands shown here. Structural unemployment was created until workers could move from Eastern and Central Canada to Alberta.

The EI system therefore encourages unemployed workers to remain in high-unemployment regions rather than encouraging them to move to regions where employment prospects are more favourable. Second, workers are eligible for employment insurance only if they have worked for a given number of weeks in the previous year—this is known as the *entrance requirement*. In some cases, however, these entrance requirements are very low and thus seasonal workers may be encouraged to work for a few months and then collect employment insurance and wait for the next season, rather than finding other jobs during the off season.[3]

Finally, labour-market policies that make it difficult or costly for firms to fire workers also make employers more reluctant to hire workers in the first place. Such policies, which are very common in the European Union, reduce the amount of turnover in the labour market and are believed to be an important contributor to the amount of long-term unemployment in those countries. In Germany, Italy, and Belgium, for example, the labour laws impose very high costs on firms whenever workers are laid off. In those countries, even when their economies are growing moderately, approximately 50 percent of all unemployment spells last for *longer* than 12 months.

The Frictional–Structural Distinction

As with many distinctions, the one between frictional and structural unemployment is not precise. In a sense, structural unemployment is really long-term frictional unemployment. Consider, for example, what would happen if there were an increase in world demand for Canadian-made car parts but at the same time a decline in world demand for Canadian-assembled cars. This change would require labour to move from one sector (the car-assembly sector) to another (the car-parts manufacturing sector). If the reallocation were to occur quickly, we would call the unemployment *frictional*; if the reallocation were to occur slowly, we would call the unemployment *structural*.

In practice, structural and frictional unemployment cannot be separated. But the two of them, taken together, *can* be separated from cyclical unemployment. Specifically, when real GDP is at its potential level, the *only* unemployment (by definition) is the NAIRU, which comprises frictional and structural unemployment. For example, real GDP in Canada was approximately equal to potential GDP in 2007. (See Figure 31-1.) At that time, the unemployment rate was 6 percent, and thus the NAIRU was approximately 6 percent. In contrast, two years later in 2009, in the midst of the most recent recession, the unemployment rate was about 8.5 percent. If the underlying frictions and structural change in the economy were unaltered over those two years, we could conclude that in 2009, 2.5 percentage points of the actual unemployment rate was due to cyclical factors and the rest was due to frictional and structural factors.

---

[3] That the EI system contributes to the amount of structural unemployment is not to deny the significant benefits from the system. First, EI encourages unemployed workers to search for jobs appropriate to their desires and skills. Second, EI provides a financial cushion that reduces the personal suffering which often accompanies periods of unemployment and low income.

Why Does the NAIRU Change?

In general, the NAIRU can rise for two reasons. First, the economy may be subjected to *more* shocks requiring an adjustment of the labour force between sectors or regions. Second, the *ability* of the labour force to adjust to any given shock may decline. In either case, the amount of frictional or structural unemployment will rise, and the NAIRU will therefore increase. We now examine several specific causes of changes in the NAIRU.

Demographic Shifts Because young people usually try several jobs before settling into one for a longer period of time, young workers have more labour-market turnover and therefore higher unemployment rates than older, more experienced workers. The proportion of young workers in the labour force rose significantly as the baby-boom generation of the 1950s entered the labour force in the 1970s and 1980s. This trend had the effect of increasing the NAIRU during the 1970s and 1980s. But as the baby-boom generation aged, and the fraction of young workers in the labour force declined in the late 1990s and early 2000s, the opposite effect was observed and tended to reduce the NAIRU.

A second demographic trend relates to the labour-force participation of women. During the 1960s and 1970s women tended to have higher unemployment rates than men. Since this was true at all points of the business cycle, the higher unemployment was higher frictional and structural unemployment. Thus, when female labour-force participation rates increased dramatically in the 1960s and 1970s, the NAIRU naturally increased. In recent years, however, female unemployment rates have dropped below the rates for men, and so further increases in female participation will, if anything, tend to decrease the NAIRU.

Young workers have higher unemployment rates than do older workers. As the share of younger workers in the labour force changes, so will the economy's NAIRU.

> Greater labour-force participation by groups with high unemployment rates increases the NAIRU.

See Figure 31-4 for Canadian unemployment rates for various demographic groups in 2012. Notice especially the significantly higher unemployment rates for youth of both sexes. These data form the basis for the often-heard view that while overall unemployment may be at acceptable levels, high youth unemployment may be a serious problem.

Hysteresis We saw in Chapter 28 that short-run changes in real GDP sometimes cause changes in the level of potential output, Y^*. One possible reason that we examined was due to the operation of labour markets, whereby the NAIRU can be influenced by the current rate of unemployment. Such models get their name from the Greek word *hysteresis*, meaning "lagged effect."

One mechanism that can lead to hysteresis arises from the importance of experience and on-the-job training. Suppose a recession causes a significant group of new entrants to the labour force to encounter unusual difficulty obtaining their first jobs. As a result, this unlucky group will be slow to acquire the important skills that workers generally learn in their first jobs. When demand increases again, this group of workers will be at a disadvantage relative to workers with normal histories of experience, and

FIGURE 31-4 Canadian Unemployment Rates by Demographic Groups, 2012

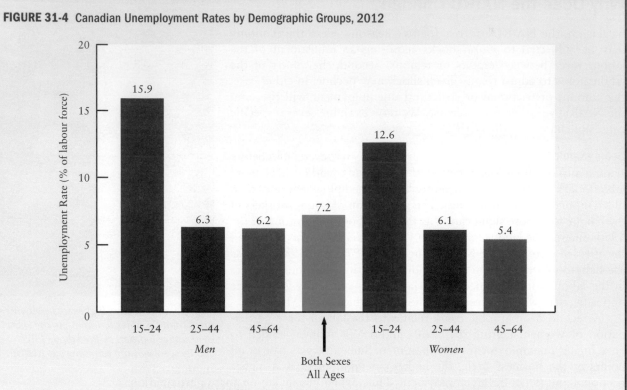

Unemployment is unevenly spread among different groups in the labour force. In 2012, when the overall unemployment rate was 7.2 percent, the unemployment rates for youths (of both sexes) were considerably higher.

(*Source:* These data are available on Statistics Canada's website, www.statcan.gc.ca, by searching for "Labour force" and then "Labour force characteristics by age and sex.")

the unlucky group may take longer to find jobs and thus have unemployment rates that will be higher than average. Hence, the NAIRU will be higher than it would have been had there been no recession.

Another force that can cause hysteresis is emphasized by commentators in the European Union, which has a more heavily unionized labour force than does either Canada or the United States. In times of high unemployment, people who are currently employed ("insiders") may use their bargaining power to ensure that their own status is maintained and prevent new entrants to the labour force ("outsiders") from competing effectively. For this reason, high unemployment—whatever its initial cause—will tend to become "locked in." If outsiders are denied access to the labour market, their unemployment will fail to exert downward pressure on wages, and the NAIRU will tend to rise.

Globalization and Structural Change The ongoing process of globalization, especially since the mid-1970s, has increased the rate at which labour is being reallocated across regions and sectors in the Canadian economy.[4] While most economists argue that the

---

[4] Recall from Chapter 1 that we use the term *globalization* to refer to the significant declines in transportation and communication costs that have been taking place over the past two centuries (especially rapidly over the past 40 years) and which have led to an increased volume of world trade in goods, services, and assets.

growing integration of Canada in the global economy generates net benefits for Canada, they also recognize a downside. One unfortunate consequence is that Canadian labour markets are increasingly affected by changes in demand and supply conditions else-where in the world. As Canadian labour markets require more frequent and larger adjustments to economic events occurring in other parts of the world, the NAIRU will tend to increase.

Policy and Labour-Market Flexibility We mentioned earlier how policies such as employment insurance can increase structural unemployment and thereby increase the NAIRU. This is one example of a policy reducing the *flexibility* of the labour market.

Such inflexibility is an important cause of unemployment. If wages are inflexible, shocks to labour demand or supply can cause unemployment. If workers are unable or unwilling to move between regions or between industries, changes in the structure of the economy can cause unemployment. If it is costly for firms to hire workers, firms will find other ways of increasing output (such as switching to more capital-intensive methods of production). In general, since the economy is always being buffeted by shocks of one sort or another, the less flexible is the labour market, the higher structural unemployment will be.

> Any government policy that reduces labour-market flexibility is likely to increase the NAIRU.

Another example of a policy that reduces labour-market flexibility is mandated job security for workers. In most Western European countries, firms cannot lay off workers without showing cause, which can lead to costly delays and even litigation. When firms do lay workers off, they are required either to give several months' notice before doing so or, in lieu of such notice, are required to make severance payments equal to several months' worth of pay. In Italy, for example, a worker who has been with the firm for 10 years is guaranteed either 20 months' notice before termination or a severance payment equal to 20 months' worth of pay.

Such job-security provisions greatly reduce the flexibility of firms. But this inflexibility on the part of the firms is passed on to workers. Any policy that forces the firm to incur large costs for laying off workers is likely to lead the same firm to be very hesitant about hiring workers in the first place. Given this reduction in labour-market flexibility, such policies are likely to increase the NAIRU.

Such mandated job security is relatively rare in Canada and the United States. Its rarity contributes to the general belief among economists that North American labour markets are much more flexible than those in Europe. Many economists see this as the most important explanation for why unemployment rates in Canada and the United States are below the unemployment rates in Europe and have been for more than two decades.

31.4 Reducing Unemployment

In the remainder of this chapter we briefly examine what can be done to reduce unemployment. Other things being equal, all governments would like to reduce unemployment. The questions are "Can it be done?" and "If so, at what cost?"

Cyclical Unemployment

We do not need to say much more about cyclical unemployment because its control is the subject of stabilization policy, which we have studied in several earlier chapters. A major recession that occurs because of negative *AD* or *AS* shocks can be countered by monetary and fiscal policies to reduce cyclical unemployment.

There is room for debate, however, about *how much* the government can and should do in this respect. Advocates of stabilization policy call for expansionary fiscal and monetary policies to reduce cyclical unemployment (and increase output) during recessionary gaps, at least when they last for sustained periods of time. Advocates of a hands-off approach say that normal market adjustments can be relied on to remove recessionary gaps and that government policy, no matter how well intentioned, will only make things worse. They call for setting simple rules for monetary and fiscal policy that would make discretionary stabilization policy impossible.

Whatever may be argued in principle, however, policymakers have not yet agreed to abandon stabilization measures in practice. In the recession that began in most countries in 2008, for example, governments were quite aggressive in their implementation of expansionary fiscal and monetary policies in an attempt to dampen the recession's effects on falling output and rising unemployment. Today, most economists look back to these decisions and agree that governments' aggressive policy actions helped to reduce what would have otherwise been a much deeper recession.

Frictional Unemployment

The turnover in the labour market that causes frictional unemployment is an inevitable part of the functioning of the economy. Some frictional unemployment is a natural part of the learning process for young workers. As we observed earlier, new entrants to the labour force (many of whom are young) have to try several jobs to see which is most suitable, and this leads to a high turnover rate among the young and hence high frictional unemployment.

Employment insurance is one method of helping people cope with unemployment. It has reduced significantly the human costs of the bouts with unemployment that are inevitable in a changing society. Nothing, however, is without cost. Although employment insurance alleviates the suffering caused by some kinds of unemployment, it also contributes to search unemployment, as we have already observed. As with any policy, a rational assessment of the value of employment insurance requires an evaluation of its costs and benefits. Many Canadians believe that when this calculation is made, the benefits greatly exceed the costs, although many also recognize the scope for reform of certain aspects of the program.

For two of the most widely used job-match websites, go to www.monster.ca or www.workopolis.ca.

Many provisions have been added over the years to the employment insurance scheme to focus it more on people in general need and to reduce its effect of raising the unemployment rate. For example, workers must be actively seeking employment in order to be eligible for EI. Also, workers who voluntarily quit their jobs (without cause) are not eligible to collect EI. In recent years, the benefits received by eligible unemployed workers have been reduced, thus decreasing the likelihood that job seekers will reject early job offers. These changes have contributed to a decline in the amount of frictional unemployment.

Structural Unemployment

The reallocation of labour among occupations, industries, skill categories, and regions that gives rise to structural unemployment is an inevitable part of a market economy. Much of this required reallocation is driven by technological change, which occurs in different ways and at different paces in various parts of the economy. Ever since the beginning of the Industrial Revolution in the late eighteenth century, workers have resisted the introduction of new techniques that replace the older techniques at which they were skilled. Such resistance is understandable. New techniques often destroy the value of the knowledge and experience of workers skilled in the displaced techniques. Older workers may not even get a chance to start over with the new technique. Employers may prefer to hire younger persons who will learn the new skills faster than older workers who are set in their ways of thinking. From society's point of view, new techniques are beneficial because they are a major source of economic growth. From the point of view of the workers they displace, however, new techniques can be an unmitigated disaster.

There are two basic approaches to reducing structural unemployment: try to resist the changes that the economy experiences or accept the changes and try to assist the necessary adjustments. Throughout history, both approaches have been tried.

Resisting Change Over the long term, policies aimed at maintaining employment levels in declining industries run into increasing difficulties. Agreements to hire unneeded workers raise costs and can hasten the decline of an industry threatened by competitive products. An industry that is declining because of economic change becomes an increasingly large burden on the public purse as economic forces become less and less favourable to its success. Sooner or later, public support is withdrawn, and it is followed by a precipitous decline.

As we assess these remedies for structural unemployment, it is important to realize that although they are not viable in the long run for the entire economy, they may be the best alternatives for the affected workers during their lifetimes.

There is often a genuine conflict between the private interest of workers threatened by structural unemployment, whose interests lie in preserving existing jobs, and the social interest served by reallocating resources to where they are most valuable.

Assisting Adjustment A second general approach to dealing with structural change is to accept the decline of specific industries and the loss of specific jobs that go with them and to try to reduce the cost of adjustment for the workers affected. A number of policies have been introduced in Canada to ease the adjustment to changing economic conditions.

One such policy is publicly subsidized education and retraining schemes. The public involvement is motivated partly by positive externalities to education and partly by imperfections in capital markets that make it difficult for workers to borrow funds for education, training, or retraining. A major component of labour-market policies is a system of loans and subsidies for higher education.

Another policy is motivated by the difficulty in obtaining good information about current and future job prospects. In recent years, the development of the Internet has greatly improved the flow of this type of information. Human Resources and Skills

To learn more about the national Job Bank, go to Service Canada's website: www.jobbank.gc.ca.

Development Canada (HRSDC), for example, operates an Internet-based service to speed up and improve the quality of matches between firms and workers. This national Job Bank allows firms (or workers) to specify certain characteristics and skills and then match these characteristics with workers (or firms) on the "other side" of the labour market.

> **Policies to increase retraining and to improve the flow of labour-market information will tend to reduce the amount of structural unemployment.**

The choice between designing policies to "resist change" or "assist adjustment" was apparent early in 2009 when the Canadian, Ontario, and U.S. governments were faced with the probable collapse of Chrysler and General Motors. The desperate financial position of these storied auto companies was partly due to the deep global recession, but it was also partly due to business practices that over several decades had proven to be unsuccessful. If the governments did nothing to help the auto companies, their collapse would likely lead to thousands of job losses in the auto and auto-parts sectors. If instead the governments decided to provide financial assistance to the troubled companies, there was a real possibility that the assistance would only delay the companies' inevitable collapse, but at great cost to taxpayers.

In the end, the three governments coordinated their actions and made large financial contributions to the firms in exchange for partial ownership. In addition, both companies were required to restructure their businesses and provide credible plans for how their firms would compete effectively against their domestic and foreign rivals. By 2013, both companies were doing well amid a modestly growing world economy.

Conclusion

Over the years, unemployment has been regarded in many different ways. Harsh critics see it as proof that the market system is badly flawed. Moderates regard it as a necessary evil of the market system and a suitable object for government policy to reduce its incidence and its harmful effects. More extreme observers see it as overblown in importance and believe that it does not reflect any real inability of workers to obtain jobs if they really want to work.

Most government policy follows a middle route. Fiscal and monetary policies generally seek to reduce at least the most persistent of recessionary gaps, and a host of labour-market policies are designed to reduce frictional and structural unemployment. Such social policies as employment insurance seek to reduce the sting of unemployment for the many who suffer from it for reasons beyond their control.

As global economic competition becomes more intense and as new knowledge-driven methods of production spread, the ability to adjust to economic change will become increasingly important. Countries that succeed in the global marketplace, while also managing to maintain humane social welfare systems, will be those that best learn how to deal with changes in the economic landscape. This will mean avoiding economic policies that inhibit change while adopting social policies that reduce the human cost of adjusting to change. This is an enormous challenge for future Canadian economic and social policies.

SUMMARY

31.1 Employment and Unemployment

- Canadian employment and the Canadian labour force increased along a strong upward trend throughout the twentieth century. The unemployment rate fluctuates significantly over the course of the business cycle.
- Looking only at the level of employment or unemployment misses a tremendous amount of activity in the labour market as individuals flow from unemployment to employment or from employment to unemployment. Such gross flows reflect the turnover that is a normal part of any labour market.
- It is useful to distinguish among several types of unemployment: cyclical unemployment, which is associated with output gaps; frictional unemployment, which is a result of normal labour-market turnover; and structural unemployment, which is caused by the need to reallocate resources among occupations, regions, and industries as the structure of demand and supply changes.
- Together, frictional unemployment and structural unemployment make up the NAIRU. The actual unemployment rate is equal to the NAIRU when real GDP is equal to Y^*.

31.2 Unemployment Fluctuations

- There is a long-standing debate among economists regarding the causes of unemployment fluctuations.
- Market-clearing theories look to explanations that allow the labour market to be cleared continuously by perfectly flexible wages and prices. Such theories can explain cyclical variations in employment but predict no involuntary unemployment.
- Empirical evidence suggests that wages are relatively stable over the business cycle, in contrast to what is predicted by market-clearing theories of the labour market.
- Non-market-clearing theories of the labour market provide an explanation for involuntary unemployment based on wage stickiness; real wages do not adjust frequently in response to all shocks to labour demand and supply.
- To explain wage stickiness, non-market-clearing theories have focused on the long-term nature of employer–worker relationships in which wages tend to respond only a little, and employment tends to respond a lot, to changes in the demand and supply of labour.

31.3 What Determines the NAIRU?

- The NAIRU will always be positive because it takes time for labour to move between jobs both in normal turnover (frictional unemployment) and in response to changes in the structure of the demand for labour (structural unemployment).
- Because different workers have different sets of skills and because different firms require workers with different sets of skills, some unemployment—resulting from workers searching for appropriate job matches with employers—is socially desirable.
- Anything that increases the rate of turnover in the labour market, or the pace of structural change in the economy, will likely increase the NAIRU.
- Employment insurance also increases the NAIRU by encouraging workers to continue searching for an appropriate job. Policies that mandate job security increase the costs to firms of laying off workers. This makes them reluctant to hire workers in the first place and may increase the NAIRU.

31.4 Reducing Unemployment

- Cyclical unemployment can be reduced by using monetary or fiscal policies to close recessionary gaps.
- Frictional and structural unemployment can be reduced by making it easier to move between jobs and by raising the cost of staying unemployed (e.g., by reducing employment insurance benefits).
- In a growing, changing economy populated by people who want to change jobs for many reasons, it is neither possible nor desirable to reduce unemployment to zero.
- Policies that assist workers in retraining and in moving between jobs, regions, or industries may be the most effective way to deal with the various shocks that buffet the economy.

KEY CONCEPTS

Gross flows in the labour market
Cyclical, frictional, and structural unemployment
Market-clearing theories of the labour market

Non-market-clearing theories of the labour market
Long-term employment relationships
Frictional and structural unemployment

Determinants of the NAIRU
Hysteresis
Policies to reduce the NAIRU
Labour-market flexibility

STUDY EXERCISES

MyEconLab   Make the grade with MyEconLab: Study Exercises marked in red can be found on MyEconLab. You can practise them as often as you want, and most feature step-by-step guided instructions to help you find the right answer.

1. Fill in the blanks to make the following statements correct.

   a. The overall unemployment rate in Canada is not a good indicator of the level of *activity* in the labour market because _____.

   b. *Gross* flows in the labour market are much _____ than net flows in the labour market.

   c. In a typical month in Canada, _____ workers flow in each direction between unemployment and employment.

   d. Cyclical unemployment exists when real GDP is _____ than potential GDP. When real GDP is equal to potential GDP, then all unemployment is either _____ or _____.

   e. Market-clearing theories assume that the labour market always _____ with flexible _____ and that any unemployment that does exist is _____.

   f. Non-market-clearing theories assume that wages do not instantly _____ to clear the market. A recessionary gap can persist and result in unemployment that is _____.

2. Fill in the blanks to make the following statements correct.

   a. The NAIRU is composed of _____ unemployment and _____ unemployment. The NAIRU is always _____ than zero.

   b. If there are 1000 loggers in British Columbia who are unemployed, and 1000 vacant positions for call-centre operators in New Brunswick, we say that this unemployment is _____.

   c. Suppose the NAIRU in June 2009 was 6.0 percent. If the actual unemployment rate was 8.2 percent,

   we can conclude that _____ percentage points are due to _____ factors and the remaining _____ percentage points are due to _____ and _____ factors.

   d. Suppose the government increased the number of weeks that an unemployed worker can collect EI benefits from 12 weeks to 16 weeks. The NAIRU is likely to _____ because of an increase in the amount of _____ unemployment.

   e. Countries with greater labour-market flexibility are likely to have _____ unemployment rates than countries in which policies inhibit flexibility.

   f. Cyclical unemployment can be reduced by closing a(n) _____ gap by using _____ and _____ policies.

3. The following table shows the pattern of real GDP, potential GDP, and the unemployment rate for several years in Cycleland.

Year	Real GDP (billions of $)	Potential GDP (billions of $)	Unemployment Rate (%)
2006	790	740	6.3
2007	800	760	6.5
2008	780	780	6.8
2009	750	800	8.2
2010	765	810	8.4
2011	790	830	8.4
2012	815	850	8.0
2013	845	870	7.5
2014	875	890	7.2
2015	900	900	6.8
2016	930	920	6.7

a. On a scale diagram, draw the path of real GDP and potential GDP (with time on the horizontal axis).

b. On a separate diagram (below the first one) show the path of the unemployment rate.

c. For which years is it possible to determine the value of the NAIRU?

d. Does the NAIRU change over the 10-year period? Provide one reason that the NAIRU could increase.

4. Interpret the following statements from newspapers in terms of types of unemployment.

a. "Recession hits local factory; 1800 workers laid off."

b. "Of course, I could take a job as a dishwasher, but I'm trying to find something that makes use of my high school education," says a local teenager in our survey of the unemployed.

c. "Retraining is the best reaction to the increased use of robots."

d. "Uneven growth: Alberta booms while Ontario sputters."

5. The diagram below shows a simple AD/AS diagram. The economy begins in long-run equilibrium at E_0 with real GDP equal to Y^*.

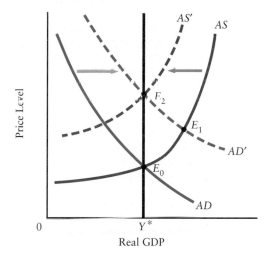

a. At E_0, the unemployment rate is 8 percent. What type of unemployment is this?

b. A positive aggregate demand shock now shifts the AD curve to AD'. At E_1 the unemployment rate is only 6.5 percent. Is there cyclical unemployment at E_1?

c. Describe the economy's adjustment process to E_2.

d. What is the unemployment rate at E_2? What kind of unemployment exists at E_2?

6. The diagram below shows a simple AD/AS diagram. The economy begins in long-run equilibrium at E_0 with real GDP equal to Y^*.

a. At E_0, the unemployment rate is 6 percent. What type of unemployment is this?

b. A negative aggregate supply shock now shifts the AS curve to AS'. At E_1 the unemployment rate is 7.5 percent. Is there cyclical unemployment at E_1? How much?

c. If monetary and fiscal policy do not react to the shock, describe the economy's adjustment process to its new long-run equilibrium.

d. What is the unemployment rate at the economy's new long-run equilibrium? What kind of unemployment exists there? Explain.

7. The diagram below shows a perfectly competitive labour market. The initial equilibrium is with wage w^* and employment L^*.

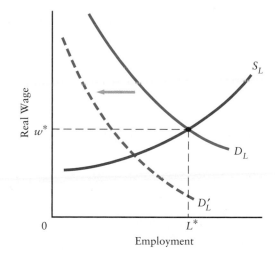

a. Suppose the demand for labour decreases to D_L'. If wages are perfectly flexible, what is the effect on wages and employment? Show this in the diagram.

b. Is there any involuntary unemployment in part (a) after the shock?

c. Now suppose wages can only adjust half as much as in part (a)—that is, wages are sticky. What is the effect on wages and employment in this case? Show this in the diagram.

d. Is there any involuntary unemployment in part (c) after the shock? How much?

8. Consider two hypothetical countries. In Country A, 20 percent of the labour force is unemployed for half the year and employed for the other half; the remaining 80 percent of the labour force is never unemployed. In Country B, 100 percent of the labour force is unemployed for 10 percent of the year and employed for the other 90 percent of the year. Note that both countries have an overall unemployment rate of 10 percent. Which of these countries seems to have the more serious unemployment problem, and why?

9. In 2012, the Canadian government announced its plan to modify the employment insurance (EI) program, and this generated a great deal of debate over the appropriate level of generosity for EI.

a. Explain what problem can be caused by having an EI system that is too generous.

b. Explain what problem can be caused by having an EI system that is not generous enough.

c. If EI generosity were reduced and the NAIRU declined as a result, is this necessarily a desirable outcome?

10. Consider an economy that begins with real GDP equal to potential. There is then a sudden increase in the prices of raw materials, which shifts the AS curve upward.

a. Draw the initial long-run equilibrium in an AD/AS diagram.

b. Now show the immediate effect of the supply shock in your diagram.

c. Suppose wages and prices in this economy adjust instantly to shocks. Describe what happens to unemployment in this economy. Explain.

d. If wages and prices adjust only slowly to shocks, what happens to unemployment? Explain.

11. The table below shows the percentage of the labour force accounted for by youths (15 to 24 years old) and older workers (25 years and older) over several years. Suppose that because of their lower skills and greater turnover, youths have a higher unemployment rate than older workers (see Figure 31-4 on page 792).

| | Percentage of Labour Force | |
Year	Youths	Older Workers
1	20	80
2	21	79
3	22	78
4	23	77
5	25	75
6	27	73
7	29	71
8	31	69

a. Suppose that in Year 1 real GDP is equal to potential GDP, and the unemployment rate among older workers is 6 percent but is 14 percent among youths. What is the economy's NAIRU?

b. Now suppose that for the next eight years real GDP remains equal to potential and that the unemployment rates for each group remain the same. Compute the value of the NAIRU for each year.

c. Explain why the NAIRU rises even though output is always equal to potential.

12. In its 2009 and 2010 budgets, the Canadian government significantly increased its planned spending on infrastructure projects in order to fight the existing recession and protect jobs.

a. Explain why such a policy may "create" jobs.

b. Is such a policy equally likely to create jobs during a recession as when the economy is already operating at potential output? Explain.

Government Debt and Deficits

UNTIL the mid-1990s, no single measure associated with the Canadian federal government was the focus of more attention and controversy than the size of the government's annual budget deficit and its accumulated level of debt. Some people argued that the debt was an economic time bomb, waiting to explode and cause serious harm to our living standards. Others argued that the only real danger posed by debt was from the dramatic policy changes proposed to reduce it.

By 2002, after two decades of debate about debt and deficits, the focus shifted to what the governments—federal and provincial—should do with their actual and projected budget surpluses. Just as earlier debates raged over the harmful effects of high government budget deficits, debates raged then about whether governments facing budget surpluses should increase spending, reduce taxes, or use the surpluses to reduce the outstanding stock of government debt.

By 2009, with the onset of a global economic recession, the federal government then announced a return to significant budget deficits, in part caused by the recession-induced decline in tax revenues and in part caused by an intentional increase in spending designed to stimulate the struggling economy. Debate then turned to the most appropriate set of fiscal policies for the government to implement.

The global recession of 2008–2009 drove up government debt in many countries. As this book went to press in early 2013, news stories around the world were describing the very high government debts in Greece, Spain, Ireland, and other European countries. There was active debate about whether these countries should implement "fiscal austerity" in order to reduce existing debt, or whether they needed "fiscal stimulus" in order to prevent a return to recession.

In this chapter, we examine various issues surrounding government debt, deficits, and surpluses. We begin by considering the simple arithmetic of government budgets. This tells us how the deficit or surplus in any given year is related to the outstanding stock of debt. We then explore why deficits and debt matter for the performance of the economy—as well as what changes we can expect over the near future if Canadian governments are successful in returning to either balanced budgets or budget surpluses.

32.1 Facts and Definitions

There is a simple relationship between the government's expenditures, its tax revenues, and its borrowing. This relationship is summarized in what economists call the government's *budget constraint.*

The Government's Budget Constraint

As is true for any individual's expenditures, government expenditures must be financed either by income or by borrowing. The difference between individuals and governments, however, is that governments typically do not earn income by selling products or labour services; instead, they earn income by levying taxes. Thus, all government expenditure must be financed either by tax revenues or by borrowing. This point is illustrated by the following simple equation, which is called the government's *budget constraint*:

$$\text{Government expenditure} = \text{Tax revenue} + \text{Borrowing}$$

We divide government expenditure into two categories. The first is purchases of goods and services, G. The second is the interest payments on the outstanding stock of debt; this is referred to as **debt-service payments** and is denoted $i \times D$, where i is the interest rate and D is the stock of government debt (which has accumulated over time from the government's past borrowing). A third category of government spending is *transfers* to individuals and firms (such as employment-insurance benefits, public pensions, and industrial subsidies) but, as we did in earlier chapters, we include transfers as part of T, which is the government's *net tax revenue* (tax revenue minus transfers). The government's budget constraint can therefore be rewritten as

$$G + i \times D = T + \text{Borrowing}$$

or, subtracting T from both sides,

$$(G + i \times D) - T = \text{Borrowing}$$

This equation simply says that any excess of total government spending over net tax revenues must be financed by government borrowing.[1]

debt-service payments
Payments that represent the interest owed on a current stock of debt.

budget deficit Any shortfall of current revenue below current expenditure.

government debt The outstanding stock of financial liabilities for the government, equal to the accumulation of past budget deficits.

Debt and Deficits The government's annual **budget deficit** is the excess of government expenditure over tax revenues in a given year. From the budget constraint just given, this annual deficit is exactly the same as the amount borrowed by the government during the year. Since the government borrows by issuing bonds and selling them to lenders, borrowing by the government increases the stock of **government debt**. Since D is the outstanding stock of government debt, ΔD is the *change* in the stock of debt during the course of the year. The budget deficit can therefore be written as

$$\text{Budget deficit} = \Delta D = (G + i \times D) - T$$

[1] A small amount of the Canadian government's annual borrowing (roughly $1 to $3 billion) represents bonds sold to the Bank of Canada as part of its regular operations of increasing the money supply. This process is called *monetizing the debt* and we will discuss it later in the chapter. Our emphasis here is on the vast majority of government borrowing, which is from individuals and private institutions in Canada and elsewhere.

The government's annual budget deficit is the excess of expenditure over tax revenues in a given year. It is also equal to the change in the stock of government debt during the year.

Notice two points about budget deficits. First, a change in the size of the deficit requires a change in expenditures *relative* to tax revenues. For given tax revenues, a smaller deficit can come about only through a reduction in government expenditures; conversely, for given expenditures, a smaller deficit requires an increase in tax revenues. Second, since the budget deficit is equal to the amount of new government borrowing, the stock of government debt will rise whenever the budget deficit is positive. Even a drastic reduction in the size of the annual budget deficit is therefore not sufficient to reduce the outstanding stock of government debt; the stock of debt will fall only if the budget deficit becomes *negative*. In this case, there is said to be a **budget surplus**.

budget surplus Any excess of current revenue over current expenditure.

A budget deficit increases the stock of government debt; a budget surplus reduces it.

The Primary Budget Deficit One component of government expenditure is debt-service payments ($i \times D$). Since at any point in time the outstanding stock of government debt—determined by *past* government borrowing—cannot be influenced by current government policy, the debt-service component of total expenditures is beyond the immediate control of the government. In contrast, the other components of the government's budget (G and T) are determined by the current set of spending programs and tax policies, all of which can be adjusted if the government chooses to do so. To capture the part of the budget deficit that is attributable to current spending and tax policies, we can compute the **primary budget deficit**, defined to be the difference between government purchases and net tax revenues:

primary budget deficit The difference between the government's overall budget deficit and its debt-service payments.

$$\text{Primary budget deficit} = G - T$$

The government's primary budget deficit shows the extent to which current tax revenues are sufficient to finance expenditure on current government programs.

Because of the need to make debt-service payments, there are often large differences between the government's overall budget deficit (or surplus) and its primary budget deficit (or surplus). In the 2005–2006 fiscal year, for example, the Canadian government had an overall budget surplus of $8 billion. Since the debt-service payments in that year were $34 billion, we see that the government actually had a primary surplus that year of $42 billion. In other words, total tax revenues in 2005–2006 were $42 billion more than the *program* spending, but only $8 billion more than *total* spending.

By the 2009–2010 fiscal year, however, the onset of the global recession had changed the budget situation considerably. Tax revenues dropped sharply and program spending increased, and the overall budget deficit was then $56 billion. Debt-service payments that year were $31 billion, so the government's primary deficit was $25 billion. In other words, tax revenues were $25 billion below program spending in 2009–2010, and fully $56 billion below total spending.

For the most recent federal budget forecasts, see the website for the Department of Finance: www.fin.gc.ca.

The primary budget surplus or deficit shows the extent to which current tax revenues can cover the government's current program spending; it is equal to the overall budget deficit minus debt-service payments.

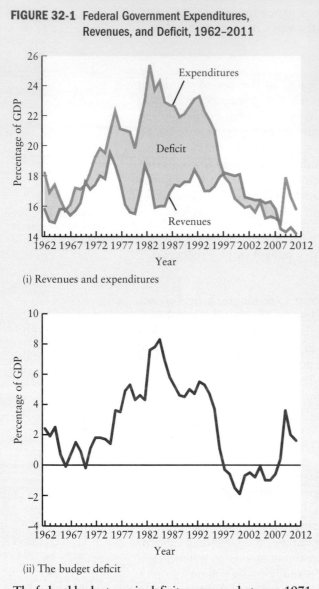

FIGURE 32-1 Federal Government Expenditures, Revenues, and Deficit, 1962–2011

(i) Revenues and expenditures

(ii) The budget deficit

The federal budget was in deficit every year between 1971 and 1997. From 1998 to 2008 there were budget surpluses. The budget returned to deficit in 2009 but is forecast to be back in balance by about 2016. Part (i) shows revenues and expenditures as a percentage of GDP. Part (ii) shows the budget deficit (or surplus) as a percentage of GDP.

(*Source:* Based on data from the Department of Finance, *Fiscal Reference Tables*, October 2012, Tables 4 and 8.)

Deficits and Debt in Canada

In a growing economy, many macroeconomic variables, such as the levels of government expenditure and tax revenue, also tend to grow. As a result, rather than looking at the absolute size of the government deficit or debt, economists focus on government debt and deficits in relation to the overall size of the economy. Some budget deficits that would be unmanageable in a small country like New Zealand might be quite acceptable for a larger country like Canada, and trivial for a huge economy like the United States. Similarly, a government budget deficit that seemed crushing in Canada in 1913 might appear trivial in 2013 because the size of the Canadian economy is many times larger now than it was then.

Federal Government The path of federal budget deficits since 1962 is shown in Figure 32-1. The top panel shows total federal spending and total federal tax revenues as percentages of GDP.[2] The bottom panel shows the total federal budget deficit as a percentage of GDP. Large and persistent budget deficits began in the mid-1970s. Throughout the 1980s and early 1990s, the average budget deficit was over 5 percent of GDP. In the mid-1990s, the federal government embarked on a successful policy of deficit reduction and by 1998 reported its first budget surplus in almost 20 years. The federal budget was then continually in surplus until the 2008–2009 fiscal year, at which point the budget returned to a deficit for several years, mostly as a result of a major recession.

As we saw in the previous section, a deficit implies that the stock of government debt is rising. Thus, the persistent deficits that began in the 1970s have their counterpart in a steadily rising stock of government debt. Figure 32-2 shows the path of Canadian federal government debt since 1940. At the beginning of the Second World War, the stock of federal debt was equal to about 45 percent of GDP. The enormous increase in the debt-to-GDP ratio over the next five years reflects wartime borrowing used to finance military expenditures. From 1946 to 1974, however, there was a continual decline in the debt-to-GDP ratio. The economy was growing quickly during this period, but equally important was that the federal government in the post-war

---

[2] In Figure 32-1 government expenditures include purchases, transfer payments, and debt-service payments. Tax revenues are not net of transfers.

years typically ran significant budget surpluses. These two factors explain the dramatic decline in the debt-to-GDP ratio between 1946 and 1974.

By 1974 the federal debt was only 14 percent of GDP. The large and persistent budget deficits beginning in the mid-1970s, however, along with a general slowdown in the rate of economic growth, led to a significant upward trend in the debt-to-GDP ratio. The ratio climbed steadily from 1979 to 1996, when it peaked at more than 69 percent of GDP. Then, with the significant reductions in the budget deficit beginning in 1996, the debt-to-GDP ratio began to fall. By 2008, the federal government's net debt was just above 30 percent of GDP, the lowest it had been since the early 1980s. The debt ratio then increased during the 2008–2009 recession, but by 2012 was again on a downward path and was forecast to be about 30 percent by 2015.

Provincial Governments Canadian provincial governments are responsible for a significant fraction of total government revenues and expenditures. In many countries, sizable regional governments either do not exist, as in the United Kingdom and New Zealand, or are often legally required to run balanced budgets, as is the case for about two-thirds of the 50 states in the United States. In contrast, the size of Canadian provincial governments—measured by their spending and taxing powers relative to that of the federal government—means that an examination of government debt and deficits in Canada would not be complete without paying attention to the provincial governments' fiscal positions.

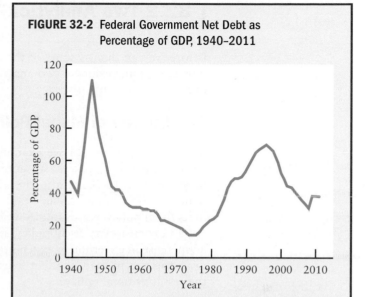

FIGURE 32-2 Federal Government Net Debt as Percentage of GDP, 1940–2011

The federal government's debt-to-GDP ratio fell dramatically after the Second World War and continued falling until 1975. It then increased markedly for the next two decades. In the late 1990s when government deficits were reduced and the economy was in a healthy recovery, the debt-to-GDP ratio began to fall.

(*Source:* Based on author's calculations using data from Statistics Canada, CANSIM database. Nominal GDP; Table 380-0017. Net financial debt; Series V151548. Most recent data from the Department of Finance's *Fiscal Reference Tables 2012.*)

> When examining the size and effects of budget deficits or surpluses, it is important to consider all levels of government—federal, provincial, territorial, and municipal.

During the 1970s, the provincial governments were running budget deficits and so the stock of provincial government debt was increasing. But the deficits were small enough for the debt not to be growing relative to GDP. During the 1980s and early 1990s, however, provincial deficits grew dramatically. Total provincial debt grew from roughly 4 percent of GDP in 1980 to 25 percent in 1998. In the subsequent decade, most provincial governments eliminated their deficits and some had budget surpluses. By 2009, however, economic recession had driven them back into deficit. The total provincial and territorial debt at that time was about 15 percent of GDP and rising.

The Canadian government ran very large budget deficits to finance Canada's participation in the Second World War. As a result, Canadian federal debt increased to 110 percent of GDP by 1946.

| 32.2 Two Analytical Issues

Before we can discuss some of the macroeconomic effects of budget deficits and surpluses, we must examine two analytical issues: the stance of fiscal policy and changes in the debt-to-GDP ratio.

The Stance of Fiscal Policy

For macroeconomic data that are comparable across countries, see the OECD's website: www.oecd.org.

In Chapters 22 and 24 we examined *fiscal policy*, which is the use of government spending and tax policies. We noted there that changes in expenditure and taxation normally lead to changes in the government's budget deficit or surplus. Thus, it is tempting to view any change in the government's budget deficit as reflecting a change in its fiscal policy. For example, we could interpret an increase in the deficit as indicating an expansionary fiscal policy, since the rise in the deficit is associated with either an increase in government expenditures or a decrease in tax revenue (or both). Was the dramatic rise in the Canadian federal budget deficit between 2008 and 2010 *purely* the result of fiscal policy?

No. In general, only some changes in the budget deficit are due to changes in the government's policies regarding expenditure or taxation. Other changes have nothing to do with explicit changes in policy, but instead are the result of changes in the level of economic activity which nonetheless have an impact on the budget. If our goal is to judge the stance of fiscal policy, however, it is only the changes in the deficit *caused by changes in policy* that are relevant.

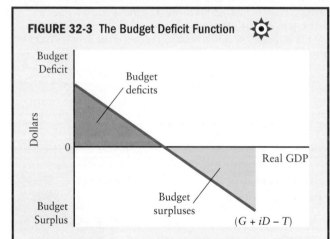

FIGURE 32-3 The Budget Deficit Function

For given government purchases and debt-service payments, there is a negative relationship between real GDP and the government budget deficit. G and iD are assumed to be independent of the level of real GDP. In contrast, a rise in real GDP leads to higher tax revenues and lower transfers, and thus to higher net tax revenue, T. Thus, the budget deficit falls as real GDP increases. Therefore, even with unchanged fiscal policies, changes in real GDP will lead to changes in the budget deficit.

A more expansionary fiscal policy implies an increase in spending or a reduction in net taxes at *any level of real GDP* and thus an upward shift of the budget deficit function. A more contractionary fiscal policy shifts the budget deficit function down.

The Budget Deficit Function To see why the budget deficit can rise or fall even when there is no change in fiscal policy, recall the equation defining the government's budget deficit.

$$\text{Budget deficit} = (G + i \times D) - T$$

As we first discussed in Chapter 22, the level of net tax revenues typically depends on the level of national income, even with unchanged policy. For example, as national income rises the level of tax revenues also rises. In addition, as income rises there are typically fewer transfers (such as welfare or employment insurance) made to the private sector. Thus, net tax revenues, T, increase when national income increases. In contrast, the level of government purchases and debt-service payments can be viewed as more or less independent of the level of national income, at least over short periods of time. Thus, with no changes in the government's fiscal policies, the budget deficit will tend to increase in recessions and fall in booms. That is, there is a negative relationship between real GDP and the government's budget deficit.

> **For a given set of expenditure and taxation policies, the budget deficit rises as real GDP falls, and falls as real GDP rises.**

Figure 32-3 plots this basic relationship, which is called the **budget deficit function**. When the government determines its expenditure and taxation polices, it determines the *position* of the budget deficit function. A more expansionary fiscal policy shifts the budget deficit function up. A more contractionary fiscal policy shifts the budget deficit function down. In contrast, a change in the level of real GDP in the absence of any policy change will represent a *movement along* the budget deficit function. Thus, for a given set of fiscal policies, the budget deficit will decrease when Y rises and increase when Y falls.

budget deficit function A relationship that plots, for a given fiscal policy, the government's budget deficit as a function of the level of real GDP.

cyclically adjusted deficit (CAD) An estimate of what the government budget deficit would be if real GDP were equal to Y*; sometimes called a *structural deficit*.

> **Fiscal policy determines the position of the budget deficit function. Changes in real GDP lead to movements along a given budget deficit function.**

The Cyclically Adjusted Deficit We have said that a more expansionary fiscal policy will shift the budget deficit function up, whereas a more contractionary policy will shift it down. Therefore, *if we could hold real GDP constant*, an increase in the observed budget deficit would reveal a fiscal expansion, whereas a decrease in the deficit would reveal a fiscal contraction. While we cannot actually hold GDP constant in practice, we can accomplish the same thing by estimating what the budget deficit would be at a specific level of GDP. The **cyclically adjusted deficit (CAD)** does just this; it estimates the deficit as if real GDP were equal to Y*. Changes in the CAD then reveal changes in the stance of fiscal policy, as illustrated in Figure 32-4. The cyclically adjusted deficit is sometimes called the *structural deficit* because its emphasis is on the *structure* of fiscal policy, separate from the current *cyclical* position of the economy.

> **An expansionary change in fiscal policy increases the cyclically adjusted deficit; a contractionary change in fiscal policy reduces the cyclically adjusted deficit.**

FIGURE 32-4 The Cyclically Adjusted Deficit and Changes in Fiscal Policy

A more expansionary fiscal policy shifts up the budget deficit function and increases the CAD

A more expansionary fiscal policy increases the cyclically adjusted deficit; a more contractionary fiscal policy reduces it. Initially, fiscal policy gives rise to the budget deficit function B_0. The actual budget deficit will depend on the actual level of real GDP, which is not shown in the figure. The CAD is the deficit that would exist if real GDP were equal to Y*. With the budget deficit function B_0, the cyclically adjusted deficit is CAD_0.

Now suppose that fiscal policy becomes more expansionary because of greater spending or a reduction in tax rates. The budget deficit function shifts upward to B_1 and the cyclically adjusted deficit rises to CAD_1. The increase in the CAD reveals the expansionary change in fiscal policy. Conversely, a more contractionary fiscal policy would shift the budget deficit function down and reduce the CAD.

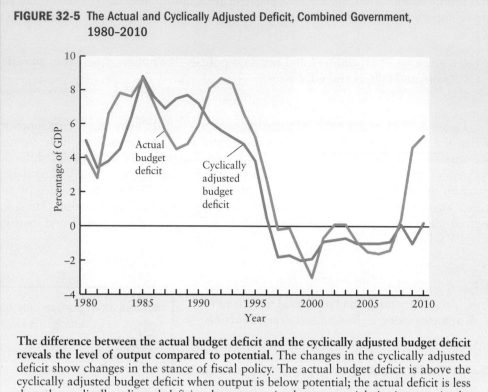

FIGURE 32-5 The Actual and Cyclically Adjusted Deficit, Combined Government, 1980–2010

The difference between the actual budget deficit and the cyclically adjusted budget deficit reveals the level of output compared to potential. The changes in the cyclically adjusted deficit show changes in the stance of fiscal policy. The actual budget deficit is above the cyclically adjusted budget deficit when output is below potential; the actual deficit is less than the cyclically adjusted deficit when output is above potential. An increase in the cyclically adjusted deficit reveals a fiscal expansion; a decrease reveals a fiscal contraction.

(*Source:* Based on data from the Department of Finance, *Fiscal Reference Tables*, September 2011, p. 51.)

Figure 32-5 shows the cyclically adjusted deficit in Canada and plots it together with the actual budget deficit. Both are expressed as percentages of GDP and represent the combined budget deficits of all levels of government. Unlike the actual budget deficit, which can be precisely measured, the cyclically adjusted deficit can only be estimated. The reason is that its value depends on the value of potential GDP, Y^*, which itself is not directly observable and hence must be estimated. Note from Figure 32-5 that the actual deficit is larger than the cyclically adjusted deficit during times of recessionary gaps, such as 1981–1985, 1991–1995, and 2009–2011. This relationship reflects the fact that during these periods actual GDP is less than potential GDP, and thus actual tax revenues are less than they would be if output were equal to potential. Conversely, the actual budget deficit is less than the cyclically adjusted deficit during periods of inflationary gaps, such as 1986–1990, 2000, and 2004–2007, reflecting the fact that during these periods actual GDP is greater than potential and thus tax revenues are greater than they would be if output were equal to potential. In years where the actual deficit is approximately equal to the cyclically adjusted deficit, such as 1985, 1990, and 1999, real GDP is approximately equal to potential.

Changes in the expansionary or contractionary stance of fiscal policy are shown by the *changes* in the cyclically adjusted deficit. For example, the dramatic rise in Canada's cyclically adjusted deficit from 1982 to 1986 reveals a considerable fiscal expansion; the more gradual decline from 1986 to 1996 reveals a moderate fiscal contraction. From 1996 to 2000, the substantial fiscal contraction, at both federal and provincial levels, led to the sharp decline in the cyclically adjusted deficit. Between 2000 and 2008, the combined government sector had an actual and a cyclically adjusted budget surplus of about 1 percent of GDP, and the stance of fiscal policy did not change markedly. Beginning in 2009, there is then a substantial increase in the actual budget deficit to approximately 5 percent of GDP. Most of this rise in the deficit resulted from a decline in real GDP as the economy went into recession. But Canadian governments also increased their spending and reduced some taxes so that the cyclically adjusted deficit also increased but only by about 1 percentage point of GDP.

Debt Dynamics

As we have already observed, in order to gauge the importance of government deficits and debt, they should be considered relative to the size of the economy. This is why economists often discuss the federal government's debt-to-GDP ratio rather than the absolute amount of government debt. Here we examine the link between the overall budget deficit, the primary budget deficit, and changes in the debt-to-GDP ratio.

With a little algebra, it is possible to write a simple expression that relates the government's primary budget deficit to the change in the debt-to-GDP ratio. Economists often use this relationship for analyzing the dynamics of government debt. The equation is

$$\Delta d = x + (r - g) \times d$$

where d is the debt-to-GDP ratio, x is the government's primary budget deficit as a percentage of GDP, r is the real interest rate on government bonds, g is the growth rate of real GDP, and Δd is the *change* in the debt-to-GDP ratio. We will not spend the time necessary to derive this equation here, but readers who are interested in doing so can refer to the math note. [36]

This simple equation shows two separate forces, each of which tends to increase the debt-to-GDP ratio. First, if the real interest rate exceeds the growth rate of real GDP (if r exceeds g), the debt-to-GDP ratio will rise for the simple reason that the debt accumulates at a faster rate than GDP grows. Second, if the government has a *primary budget deficit* (if x is positive), the debt-to-GDP ratio will rise because the government is incurring new debt to finance its program spending.

Let's use some recent numbers for Canada to illustrate the use of this equation. The global financial crisis that began in 2008 was followed immediately by a worldwide recession and, like most of the G20 countries, Canada embarked on a major fiscal expansion to offset its effects. At the beginning of 2009, the federal debt-to-GDP ratio was 29 percent ($d = 0.29$). During that year, revenues fell sharply, expenditures increased, and the government ran a primary budget deficit of 1.7 percent of GDP ($x = 0.017$). The average real interest rate on government bonds in 2009 was 5.3 percent ($r = 0.053$) while real GDP *fell* in that year by 2.8 percent ($g = -0.028$).

Using all of these data, our equation for the change in the federal debt-to-GDP ratio over the course of 2009 becomes:

$$\Delta d = 0.017 + (0.053 - (-0.028)) \times (0.29)$$
$$= 0.017 + (0.081) \times (0.29)$$
$$= 0.017 + 0.023$$
$$= 0.04$$

which means that the government's debt-to-GDP ratio increased during 2009 by four percentage points, from 29 percent to 33 percent. Note also that the *decline* in real GDP during 2009 ($g = -0.028$) substantially contributed to the increase in the debt ratio. In a typical year in which real GDP grows by 2 percent or more, a primary budget deficit of 1.7 percent of GDP would not generate such a large increase in the debt-to-GDP ratio.

Since 2011, the Canadian government has announced its goal of further reducing the debt-to-GDP ratio. What will be necessary for this objective to be met? First, primary budget surpluses will be helpful. Second, a real interest rate that is less than the growth rate of real GDP will be helpful. If both of these occur, the debt ratio will definitely fall; if only one of these two occurs, the overall effect on the debt ratio will depend on the relative size of the two effects. By early 2013, the federal government had a primary surplus and the gap between r and g had fallen. As a result, the debt-to-GDP ratio was on a downward path and was forecast to fall below 30 percent by 2015.

> If the real interest rate on government debt is approximately equal to the growth rate of real GDP, reductions in the debt-to-GDP ratio require the government to run primary budget surpluses.

APPLYING ECONOMIC CONCEPTS 32-1

The Continuing Greek Tragedy of Debt Dynamics

By 2011, the Greek economy had been in recession for three years, the unemployment rate was over 20 percent, and the government was implementing deep cuts in its spending programs in an effort to reduce its overall budget deficit of 9.2 percent of GDP. This toxic mixture of deep recession and large cutbacks in public services brought hundreds of thousands of Greek citizens into the streets—protesting the government's policies and demanding improvements in their country's economic situation.

Why was the Greek government cutting spending if the economy was in a deep recession? And how were these cuts related to the existing level of Greek government debt? We can use the debt-dynamics equation discussed in the text to shed light on these issues. Specifically, we can use the equation to determine how much fiscal adjustment would have been necessary to *stabilize* Greece's debt-to-GDP ratio at its 2011 level.*

Stabilizing the Debt-to-GDP Ratio

Consider the data for Greece as published by the International Monetary Fund (IMF). At the beginning of 2011, Greece's public debt was 143 percent of its GDP ($d = 1.43$). The average nominal interest rate on its government debt was 4.3 percent and inflation was 3.1 percent; the real interest rate, r, was therefore 1.2 percent ($r = 0.012$). The Greek economy was then in its fourth continuous year of recession, and real GDP growth in 2011 was *negative* 6.9 percent ($g = -0.069$).

Using these data, we can compute the value of the primary budget balance that would have been necessary to stabilize the Greek debt-to-GDP ratio during 2011. Recall the equation that describes the change in the debt-to GDP ratio:

$$\Delta d = x + (r - g)d$$

If d is to be held constant ($\Delta d = 0$), the necessary value for x, which we call x^*, is

$$x^* = -(r - g)d$$

Using the data for Greece in 2011 we see that x^* is

$$
\begin{aligned}
x^* &= -(0.012 - (-0.069)) \times (1.43) \\
&= -(0.081) \times (1.43) \\
&= -0.116
\end{aligned}
$$

The interpretation of this number is that Greece would have needed a primary budget *surplus* of 11.6 percent of GDP in 2011 in order to stabilize its debt-to-GDP ratio that year. Its actual primary balance that year was a *deficit* of 2.3 percent. Thus, to stabilize d would have required a reduction in government expenditures and/or an increase in tax revenues of roughly 14 percent of GDP—an enormous fiscal adjustment for any government to make over several years, let alone in a single year.

An Impending Default?

By late in 2011 it was clear to most holders of Greek government bonds that any realistic fiscal adjustment by the Greek government would be insufficient to stabilize the debt-to-GDP ratio in the near future. Instead, the debt ratio would almost certainly continue to rise

As a result of the 2008 global financial crisis and the recession that followed, many highly indebted European governments experienced significant further increases in their public debts. Some of this new debt was incurred as governments provided assistance to failing financial institutions; some was incurred through more conventional fiscal stabilization policies such as those we examined in Chapter 24. By 2011, the public debts in Greece, Portugal, Spain, and some other countries were so high that bondholders came to believe that these governments were effectively bankrupt and would be unable to repay or even service their existing debts. Fear of *debt defaults* by these governments led to massive increases in bond yields and created great uncertainty within the European Union. By early 2013, what became known as Europe's "sovereign debt crisis" had not yet been resolved. *Applying Economic Concepts 32-1* examines how our simple debt-dynamics equation can be used to understand Greece's extremely difficult fiscal situation in 2011.

for several years. Bondholders then wondered how the Greek government would ever repay the existing bonds. Once these concerns became entrenched, the demand for Greek bonds plummeted and the bond yields increased sharply to reflect the risk of default by the Greek government. In 2011, the yields on Greek 10-year bonds were 34 percent—as compared to approximately 2 percent on 10-year bonds issued by the German government.

The increase in yields on Greek bonds exacerbated the fiscal situation of the Greek government and threatened the creation of a vicious cycle. The high bond yields made it more costly to finance its large overall budget deficit (9.2 percent of GDP in 2011) and also more costly to finance the regular "rollover" of existing bonds that occurs regularly in any modern economy. These greater financing costs increased the need for fiscal contraction as a means of reducing the existing budget deficit, but fiscal contraction would reduce aggregate demand and reduce real GDP growth even further. In addition, any further decline in real GDP growth would, as is clear from the debt-dynamics equation, cause an even larger increase in the debt-to-GDP ratio and thus cause further fears of default, thus driving up bond yields even further.

To break this vicious cycle, the Greek government turned to the IMF and other members of the European Union for substantial loans that would permit Greece to finance its budget deficit and bond rollovers at reasonable rates for a few years while Greece implemented its necessary fiscal adjustments and tried to restore its fiscal credibility in the eyes of global bondholders.

Resolution

By early in 2013, the Greek fiscal situation had yet to be resolved. Even after a partial debt default equal to roughly 70 percent of the value of its outstanding debt, and large loans from both the IMF and other members of the European Union, the Greek government could not agree on a set of fiscal policies that would satisfy Greek voters and at the same time satisfy the conditions set forth by the European countries that had become Greece's most important creditors.

A further complication is that Greece shares a currency (the euro) with 16 other members of the European Union. As Greece's fiscal situation worsened, and its resolution was appearing less and less likely, the possibility of Greece leaving the euro zone and re-introducing its own currency became more likely. As this book went to press in January 2013, it was extremely difficult to predict the most likely outcome.

---

*The economic situation in Greece was determined by a complex set of factors, including various problems encountered within a group of countries using a common currency. In this box, we focus only on the *fiscal* situation in Greece. Readers interested in a thorough discussion of the various aspects of the European debt crisis are referred to "The future of the euro: An economic perspective on the Eurozone crisis," McKinsey and Company, January 2012.

| 32.3 The Effects of Government Debt and Deficits

Let's now examine why we should care about the size of the government deficit (or surplus) and its debt. We begin with the important idea that deficits may *crowd out* private-sector activity and thereby may harm future generations by reducing the economy's long-run growth rate. The opposite idea is equally important—that budget surpluses may *crowd in* private-sector activity and be beneficial to future generations by increasing the economy's long-run growth rate.

Before beginning our analysis, we must be clear about one of our assumptions in the macro model that we have developed in previous chapters. As we saw earlier in this chapter, when the government increases its budget deficit, it necessarily increases its borrowing. This increase in borrowing is a reduction in the government's saving. In our model, we make the assumption that any reduction in the government's saving has only small effects on the amount of saving by the private sector—with the result that *national* saving falls along with government saving. Thus, we assume in our model that an increase in the government's budget deficit leads to a reduction in national saving. We make this assumption because it is consistent with the bulk of empirical evidence on this issue.

> In our macro model, we assume that an increase in the government's budget deficit leads to a decrease in national saving.

Do Deficits Crowd Out Private Activity?

It is useful to make the distinction between an economy that is *closed* to international trade in goods, service, and assets and one that is *open* to such trade. We consider the two cases separately.

Investment in Closed Economies Recall from Chapter 26 the close long-run relationship between desired investment and desired national saving in a closed economy. In the long-run version of our macro model, with real GDP equal to Y^*, the real interest rate is determined by the equality of desired investment and desired national saving. What is the effect in this model of an increase in the government's budget deficit, caused either by an increase in government spending or a reduction in taxes? An increase in the budget deficit is assumed to cause a reduction in the supply of national saving. As we saw in Chapter 26, a reduction in the supply of national saving will increase the equilibrium real interest rate and reduce the amount of investment in the economy. This **crowding out** of investment by the expansionary fiscal policy is shown in Figure 32-6.

Note in the figure the different short-run and long-run effects of the fiscal expansion. In the short run, the fiscal expansion shifts the *AD* curve to the right and increases real GDP. In the long run, however, after wages and other factor prices have fully adjusted to the output gap, real GDP returns to Y^* at an increased equilibrium real interest rate. So the amount of investment in the new long-run equilibrium is less than it was prior to the increase in the budget deficit.

> The long-run effect of a fiscal expansion in our macro model is to drive up the real interest rate and crowd out private investment.

crowding out The offsetting reduction in private expenditure caused by the rise in interest rates that follows an expansionary fiscal policy.

Net Exports in Open Economies There is a second effect in an open economy when financial capital is internationally mobile. Consider once again the possibility that the Canadian government increases its budget deficit either by increasing spending or by reducing taxes. What is the effect of the reduction in national saving in an open economy, like Canada's?

As real interest rates rise in Canada, foreigners are attracted to the higher-yield Canadian assets and thus foreign financial capital flows into Canada. But since Canadian dollars are required in order to buy Canadian interest-earning assets, this capital inflow increases the demand for Canadian dollars in the foreign-exchange market and leads to an appreciation of the Canadian dollar. If the currency appreciation is sustained over several months or longer, it will cause a reduction in Canada's exports and an increase in Canada's imports; Canadian net exports, *NX*, will fall.

> In an open economy, the government budget deficit attracts foreign financial capital and appreciates the domestic currency. The long-run result is a crowding out of net exports.

How Much Crowding Out? We have argued that the long-run effect of an increase in the government's budget deficit is to crowd out private investment and net exports. We have said nothing, however, about *how much* crowding out takes place. For example, does a $10 billion increase in the budget deficit reduce private expenditure by the full $10 billion, or by less, or by more?

To examine this issue, recall an equation of national income accounting from Chapter 20:

$$Y = C_a + I_a + G_a + NX_a$$

where the *a* subscripts denote actual (as opposed to desired) quantities. By definition, the sum of the four expenditure components is always exactly equal to real GDP. Now think about the change in these expenditure components as we follow the effects of a fiscal expansion in Figure 32-6. Suppose that we begin in a long-run equilibrium with $Y = Y^*$ and then the government increases its purchases of goods and services. In the short run in our macro model, this fiscal expansion leads to an increase in Y above Y^* and also causes an increase in consumption (which rises as Y rises). In the long run, however, after Y has returned

FIGURE 32-6 The Crowding Out of Investment

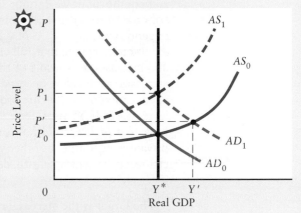

(i) Aggregate demand and supply

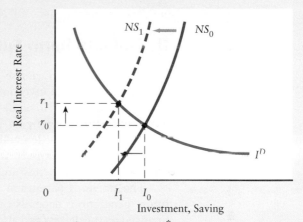

(ii) Saving and investment ($Y = Y^*$)

For a closed economy, the long-run effects of an increase in the budget deficit will be a higher real interest rate and a reduction in private investment. Consider a closed economy that is in long-run equilibrium at Y^* and P_0 in part (i). Suppose the government increases its spending or reduces its taxes, thus increasing the budget deficit. Either policy raises aggregate demand and shifts AD_0 to AD_1. The new short-run equilibrium is at Y' and P', but the adjustment process will then cause factor prices to rise, shifting the AS curve from AS_0 to AS_1. The new long-run equilibrium will be at Y^* and P_1.

The long-run effect of this change on saving and investment can be seen in part (ii), which shows the market for financial capital in the long run, with real GDP equal to Y^*. The increase in the government's budget deficit reduces national saving and shifts NS_0 to NS_1. The equilibrium real interest rate rises and the amount of investment falls from I_0 to I_1.

to Y^*, the higher-than-initial value of government purchases implies that the sum of the three private expenditure components must be lower than it was at the initial long-run equilibrium. We cannot say precisely how the reduction in private spending is distributed across the three components, but in the long run in our model total private expenditure ($C_a + I_a + NX_a$) has been *fully* crowded out by the fiscal expansion.

Note, however, that full crowding out does *not* occur if the level of potential output, Y^*, increases as a result of the fiscal expansion. For example, suppose the government increases its spending on productivity-enhancing infrastructure projects or improvements in education or health-care programs. These kinds of expenditures are likely to increase the level of Y^*. If Y^* rises, then the long-run adjustment in Figure 32-6 brings the economy back to a *higher* level of Y^*, in which case the fiscal expansion does *not* fully crowd out private expenditure. In other words, the extent of crowding out depends crucially on the change in Y^* which, in turn, depends on the nature of the increased government spending.

> The larger is the increase in potential output caused by a fiscal expansion, the less private expenditure will be crowded out.

Do Deficits Harm Future Generations?

In a closed economy, a rise in the government deficit pushes up interest rates and crowds out domestic investment. In an open economy, a rise in the government deficit also appreciates the currency and crowds out net exports. In both cases, there may be a cost to future generations. Economists call this cost the *long-term burden of government debt*. Such a burden will be present if the private expenditure that is crowded out would have added more to the economy's productive capacity than what is added by the government's expenditure financed by the budget deficit.

The previous paragraph suggests that whether government budget deficits harm future generations depends on the nature of the government goods and services being financed by the deficit (and also on the nature of the private expenditure that gets crowded out). At one extreme, the government borrowing may finance a project that generates a substantial return to future generations, and thus the future generations may be made better off by today's budget deficit. An example might be the government's financing of long-term medical research projects that generate a return in the distant future. Another example is the government's financing of a new highway that reduces transport times for people and products for many years. At the other extreme, the government deficit may finance some government program that benefits mainly the current generation. An example might be the government's financing of cultural or sporting events that benefit the current generation but produce little or no benefits for future generations.

The concern that budget deficits may be inappropriately placing a burden on future generations has led some economists to advocate the idea of *capital budgeting* by the government. Under this scheme, the government would essentially classify each of its expenditures as either consumption or investment; the former would be spending that mostly benefits the current generation while the latter would be spending that mostly benefits future generations.

With capital budgeting, government deficits could be used to minimize the undesirable redistributions of income between generations. For example, the government might be committed to borrowing no more in any given year than the expenditures classified as investments. In this way, future generations would receive benefits from current government spending that are at least equal to the future taxes they will pay.

Government budget deficits represent taxes that must be paid by future generations. Whether these future generations are harmed by the current budget deficit depends to a large extent on the nature of the government spending financed by the deficit.

Does Government Debt Hamper Economic Policy?

The costs imposed on future generations by government debt are real, though they are often ignored because they occur in the very distant future. But other problems associated with the presence of government debt are more immediately apparent. In particular, high levels of government debt may make the conduct of monetary and fiscal policy more difficult.

Monetary Policy To see how a large stock of government debt can hamper the conduct of monetary policy, consider a country that has a high debt-to-GDP ratio and that has a real interest rate above the growth rate of GDP. As we saw previously, the debt-to-GDP ratio will continue to grow in this situation unless the government starts running significant primary budget *surpluses*. But such primary surpluses require either increases in taxation or reductions in program spending, both of which may be politically unpopular. If such primary surpluses look unlikely to be achieved in the near future, both foreign and domestic bondholders may come to expect the government to put pressure on the central bank to purchase—or *monetize*—an increasing portion of its deficit. Such monetization means that the money supply is increasing and will eventually cause inflation. Any ensuing inflation would erode the real value of the bonds held by creditors.

Budget deficits used to finance investment projects may not harm future generations because the future generations will benefit from the investment.

Fears of future debt monetization will likely lead to expectations of future inflation and put upward pressure on nominal interest rates and on some prices and wages. Thus, even in the absence of any *current* actions by the central bank to increase the rate of growth of the money supply, a large government debt may lead to the *expectation* of future inflation, thus hampering the task of the central bank in keeping inflation and inflationary expectations low.

Fiscal Policy In Chapter 22 we saw that fiscal policy could potentially be used to stabilize aggregate demand and thereby stabilize real GDP. For example, in a booming economy, the government might reduce spending or increase tax rates to reduce inflationary pressures. Or during a recession, the government might reduce tax rates and increase spending in an attempt to stimulate aggregate demand, as it did in 2009 and 2010 during a major global recession. Having cyclically adjusted budget deficits during recessions and cyclically adjusted budget surpluses during booms is one way of implementing *counter-cyclical fiscal policy*.

How does the presence of government debt affect the government's ability to conduct such counter-cyclical fiscal policy? Perhaps the easiest way to answer this question is to recall the equation that describes the change in the debt-to-GDP ratio:

$$\Delta d = x + (r - g) \times d$$

This equation shows that the *change* in the debt-to-GDP ratio (Δd) depends on the *level* of the debt-to-GDP ratio (d). For example, if the real interest rate exceeds the growth rate of real GDP, so that $r - g$ is positive, the increase in the debt-to-GDP ratio (Δd) will be higher if d is already high than if it is low (for any given value of x). We examine the case where $r - g$ is positive because this is the typical situation in a developed economy such as Canada's.

With this relationship in mind, consider the problem faced during a recession by a government that is considering an expansionary fiscal policy. Such a policy would increase the primary budget deficit and therefore increase x. On the one hand, there would be short-run benefits from the higher level of real GDP; on the other hand, the government may be wary of taking actions that lead to large increases in the debt-to-GDP ratio.

If the stock of outstanding government debt is small relative to the size of the economy, the government has a great deal of flexibility in conducting counter-cyclical fiscal policy. The small value of d implies that d will be rising only slowly in the absence of a primary deficit. Thus, the government may be able to increase the primary deficit—either by increasing program spending or by reducing tax rates—without generating a large increase in the debt-to-GDP ratio. But the government has significantly less flexibility if the stock of outstanding government debt is already very large. In this case, and with our assumption that r is greater than g, the high value of d means that even in the absence of a primary budget deficit, d will be increasing quickly. Thus, any increase in the primary deficit brought about by the counter-cyclical fiscal policy runs the danger of generating increases in the debt-to-GDP ratio that may be viewed by creditors as unsustainable. Such perceptions of unsustainability may lead to an increase in the real interest rate on government debt, which exacerbates the problem by driving d up even faster.

The idea that a large and rising stock of government debt could "tie the hands" of the government in times when it would otherwise want to conduct counter-cyclical fiscal policy was brought to the fore of Canadian economic policy by the late Douglas Purvis of Queen's University (and a co-author of this textbook for many years). Purvis argued in the mid-1980s that Canadian government deficits must be brought under control quickly so that the debt would not accumulate to the point where the government would have no room left for fiscal stabilization policy. These warnings were not heeded. By the onset of the next recession in 1991, the federal government had added roughly $200 billion to the stock of debt and the debt-to-GDP ratio was just less than 70 percent. Predictably, the government felt unable to use discretionary fiscal policy to reduce some of the effects of the recession.

However, by 2008, the federal debt-to-GDP ratio had fallen to less than 30 percent as a result of more than a decade of fiscal restraint and rapid economic growth. When the Canadian economy entered recession late in 2008, the Conservative government recognized that Canada's past fiscal prudence gave it the needed flexibility to design an aggressively counter-cyclical fiscal policy. The federal budgets of 2009 and 2010 announced large spending increases and tax reductions that were predicted to result in budget deficits that would increase the debt-to-GDP ratio by roughly 4 percentage points over the next two years. The government was careful, however, to indicate clearly its intentions of

With the arrival of the global economic recession in 2008, Finance Minister Jim Flaherty implemented a significant fiscal expansion that contributed to a large increase in the federal budget deficit. The federal budget is now projected to return to balance by about 2016.

returning the debt-to-GDP ratio to its previously announced target of 25 percent. The need for short-term fiscal stimulus was tempered by the recognition of the importance of long-term fiscal prudence.

32.4 Formal Fiscal Rules

After more than two decades of persistent budget deficits in Canada, and then several years of budget surpluses, the nature of political debate about fiscal policy shifted considerably. Whereas during the mid-1980s there was active political debate about whether deficits were a problem, and what costs would be involved in reducing them, by 2007 all major political parties in Canada stressed the importance of avoiding budget deficits. But the onset of the global recession in 2008 changed the debate again. As the severity of the recession became clearer, all political parties argued the need for fiscal measures to stimulate the economy, but at the same time accepted the goal of returning to a balanced budget (or surplus) as soon as the economy showed signs of a solid recovery.

In some quarters, there is support for the idea that legislation should be amended to impose restrictions on the size of budget deficits. Would such legislation be desirable? We examine three different proposals.

Annually Balanced Budgets

It would be extremely difficult to balance the budget on an annual basis. The reason is that a significant portion of the government budget is beyond its short-term control, and a further large amount is hard to change quickly. For example, the entire debt-service component of government expenditures is determined by past borrowing and thus cannot be altered by the current government. Also, many spending programs such as equalization and public pensions are set in current legislation and cannot be changed without the lengthy process of legislative reform. In addition, as we saw in our discussion of the cyclically adjusted deficit, changes in real GDP that are beyond the control of the government lead to significant changes in tax revenues (and transfer payments) and thus generate significant changes in the budget deficit or surplus.

Even if it were possible for the government to control its spending and revenues perfectly on a year-to-year basis, it would probably be *undesirable* to balance the budget every year. Recall that tax revenues rise in booms and fall in recessions; and many expenditures on transfers fall in booms and rise in recessions. As we first saw in Chapter 22, this property of the tax-and-transfer system implies that fiscal policy contains a built-in stabilizer. In recessions, the increase in the budget deficit stimulates aggregate demand whereas in booms the budget surplus reduces aggregate demand.

But things would be very different with an annually balanced budget. With a balanced budget, government expenditures would be *forced* to adjust to the changing level of tax revenues. In a recession, when tax revenues naturally decline, a balanced budget would require either a *reduction* in government expenditures or an *increase* in tax rates, thus generating a major *destabilizing* force on real GDP. Similarly, as tax revenues naturally rise in an economic boom, a balanced budget would require either an increase in government expenditures or a reduction in taxes, thus stimulating aggregate demand when an inflationary gap may already exist.

For some forecasts and analysis of the government's fiscal options, see the Royal Bank's website: www.rbc.com. Go to "economics."

An annually balanced budget would eliminate the automatic fiscal stabilizers and accentuate the swings in real GDP.

Cyclically Balanced Budgets

One alternative to the extreme policy of requiring an annually balanced budget is to require that the government budget be balanced over the course of a full economic cycle. Budget deficits would be permitted in recessions as long as they were matched by surpluses in booms. In this way, the built-in stabilizers could still perform their important role, but there would be no persistent build-up of government debt. In principle, this is a desirable treatment of the tradeoff between the short-run benefits of deficits and the long-run costs of debt.

Despite its appeal, the idea of cyclically balanced budgets has its problems as well. Perhaps the most important problem with a cyclically balanced budget is an operational one. In order to have a law that requires the budget to be balanced over the business cycle, it is necessary to be able to *define* the cycle precisely. But there will always be disagreement about what stage of the cycle the economy is currently in, and thus there will be disagreement as to whether the current government should be increasing or reducing its deficit. Compounding this problem is the fact that politicians will have a stake in the identification of the cycle. Those who favour increased deficits will argue that this year is an unusually bad year and thus an increase in the deficit is justified; deficit "hawks," in contrast, will always tend to find this year to be unusually good and thus a time to run budget surpluses.

A second problem is largely political. Suppose one government runs large deficits for a few years during a recession and then gets replaced in an election. Would the succeeding government then be bound to run budget surpluses after the recovery? What one government commits itself to in one year does not necessarily restrict what it (or its successor) does in the next year.

Balancing the budget over the course of the business cycle is in principle a desirable means of reconciling short-term stabilization with long-term fiscal prudence. The difficulty in precisely defining the business cycle, however, suggests that governments could best follow this as an approximate guide rather than as a formal rule.

Maintaining a Prudent Debt-to-GDP Ratio

A further problem with any policy that requires a balanced budget—whether over one year or over the business cycle—is that the emphasis is naturally on the overall budget deficit. But, as we saw earlier in this chapter, what determines the change in the debt-to-GDP ratio is the growth of the debt *relative* to the growth of the economy. With a growing economy, it is possible to have positive overall budget deficits—and thus a growing debt—and still have a falling debt-to-GDP ratio. Thus, to the extent that the debt-to-GDP ratio is the relevant gauge of a country's debt problem, focus should be placed on the debt-to-GDP ratio rather than on the budget deficit itself.

Some economists view a low and relatively stable debt-to-GDP ratio as the appropriate indicator of fiscal prudence. Their view permits a budget deficit such that the stock of debt grows no faster than GDP.

This view recognizes that not all government debt represents a problem. As we argued earlier in this chapter, government expenditure on items that deliver benefits for many years can sensibly be financed by borrowing so that the future generations who benefit from the spending also bear some the burden of repayment. However, admitting that some government debt may be appropriate is not to deny that genuine problems do exist when the government's debt-to-GDP ratio is very high. The challenge is then to permit government budget deficits necessary to finance worthwhile public investment while at the same time ensuring that the debt-to-GDP ratio does not become excessive. Such an approach to fiscal policy would be considered prudent by many economists.

By this standard, the Canadian federal budgets of the last several years have been prudent because they have led to a growth rate in the stock of debt smaller than the growth rate of real GDP, and thus a reduction in the debt-to-GDP ratio. For example, in 1996, the debt-to-GDP ratio reached its recent maximum of 70 percent. Significant fiscal contractions, combined with strong economic growth, led to a decline in the debt-to-GDP ratio to 50 percent by 2001, less than 40 percent by 2005, and less than 30 percent by 2008. The arrival of the 2008 global recession then led to substantial federal (and provincial) budget deficits, partly because of the recession-induced decline in net tax revenues and partly because of policy actions taken to stimulate the economy. The federal debt-to-GDP ratio increased to 38 percent by 2010. By 2012, however, after two years of modest recovery, the federal budget deficit was declining and the debt-to-GDP ratio was projected to fall below 30 percent by 2015.

SUMMARY

32.1 Facts and Definitions

LO 1

- The government's budget deficit is equal to total government expenditure minus total government revenue. Since the government must borrow to finance any shortfall in its revenues, the annual deficit is equal to the annual increase in the stock of government debt. Whenever the deficit is positive, the stock of government debt is growing.
- The primary budget deficit is equal to the excess of the government's program spending over total tax revenues.

- Large and persistent budget deficits beginning in the 1970s increased the stock of debt so that by 1996 the federal government net debt was equal to 70 percent of GDP. By 2008, after several years of fiscal contraction, the federal debt-to-GDP ratio was approximately 30 percent.
- The 2008–2009 recession increased the federal debt-to-GDP ratio to 38 percent, but it was projected to fall back down to 30 percent by 2015.

32.2 Two Analytical Issues

LO 2

- Since tax revenues tend to rise when real GDP rises, the overall budget deficit tends to rise during recessions and fall during booms. This tendency makes the budget deficit a poor measure of the stance of fiscal policy.
- The cyclically adjusted deficit is the budget deficit that would exist with the current set of fiscal policies if real GDP were equal to potential GDP. Changes in the cyclically adjusted deficit reflect changes in the stance of fiscal policy.

- The change in the debt-to-GDP ratio from one year to the next is given by

$$\Delta d = x + (r - g) \times d$$

where d is the debt-to-GDP ratio, x is the primary deficit as a percentage of GDP, r is the real interest rate on government bonds, and g is the growth rate of real GDP.

32.2 The Effects of Government Debt and Deficits   LO 3, 4

- In a closed economy, the long-run effect of an increase in the budget deficit is to reduce national saving and increase real interest rates. This increase in interest rates reduces the amount of investment.
- In an open economy, the long-run effect of an increase in the budget deficit is to push up interest rates and attract foreign financial capital. This leads to a currency appreciation and a reduction in net exports.
- Unless government debt is incurred to finance worthwhile public investments, the long-term burden of the debt is a redistribution of resources away from future generations and toward current generations.
- A large debt-to-GDP ratio may lead creditors to expect increases in inflation, as the government attempts to finance deficits through the creation of money. Such increases in inflationary expectations hamper the conduct of monetary policy.
- The higher is the debt-to-GDP ratio, the more constrained is the government in conducting counter-cyclical fiscal policy.

32.4 Formal Fiscal Rules   LO 5

- Since tax revenues (net of transfers) naturally rise as real GDP increases, legislation requiring an annually balanced budget forces either expenditures to rise or tax rates to fall during booms. This produces destabilizing fiscal policy.
- Cyclically balanced budgets, in principle, permit the short-run benefits of deficits to be realized without incurring the long-run costs of debt accumulation. Implementation of this policy is difficult, however, since the precise identification of the business cycle is controversial.
- Budget deficits need not lead to increases in the debt-to-GDP ratio if the economy is growing.
- Prudent fiscal policy can permit budget deficits during recessions and allow the financing of worthwhile public investments, while ensuring that the debt-to-GDP ratio does not become excessive.

KEY CONCEPTS

Government's budget constraint
Primary budget deficit
The relationship between deficits and the national debt

Debt-service payments
Debt-to-GDP ratio
Crowding out of investment
Crowding out of net exports

Long-term burden of the debt
Annually balanced budget
Cyclically balanced budget

STUDY EXERCISES

MyEconLab   Make the grade with MyEconLab: Study Exercises marked in red can be found on MyEconLab. You can practise them as often as you want, and most feature step-by-step guided instructions to help you find the right answer.

1. Fill in the blanks to make the following statements correct.

   a. The government's budget constraint shows that government expenditures must be equal to the sum of _____ and _____.

   b. The government's annual budget deficit is the excess of total _____ over total _____ in a given year.

   c. If the government's total budget deficit is $20 billion and its debt-service payments are $18 billion, then its _____ is $2 billion. If the total budget deficit is $20 billion and its debt-service payments are $26 billion, then its _____ is $6 billion.

2. Fill in the blanks to make the following statements correct.

   a. When there is no change in the government's fiscal policy it is still possible for the budget deficit to fall because _____.

b. For a given set of fiscal policies, the budget deficit _____ as real GDP rises and _____ as real GDP falls.

c. The cyclically adjusted deficit is the budget deficit that would exist if real GDP equalled _____ and the government's _____ were at their current levels.

d. Suppose the real interest rate is 2 percent and the growth rate of real GDP is 1.5 percent. If the government wants to stabilize the debt-to-GDP ratio, then it is necessary to have a(n) _____.

3. Fill in the blanks to make the following statements correct.

a. In a closed economy, when the government borrows to finance the deficit, interest rates will _____ and some private investment will be _____.

b. In an open economy, when the government borrows to finance the deficit, interest rates will _____, the Canadian dollar will _____, and net exports will _____.

c. Suppose a law was passed that required the government to balance its budget each year. Fiscal policy would then have a(n) _____ effect.

d. A cyclically balanced budget is difficult to implement because it is difficult to identify the _____.

4. The table below shows government spending data over eight years in Debtland. All figures are in billions of dollars. The symbols used are as defined in the text.

Year	G (1)	T (2)	iD (3)	Budget Deficit (4)	Primary Budget Deficit (5)	Stock of Debt (6)
2006	175	175	25	—	—	—
2007	180	180	26	—	—	—
2008	185	185	27	—	—	—
2009	188	190	26	—	—	—
2010	185	195	25	—	—	—
2011	185	200	24	—	—	—
2012	180	205	23	—	—	—
2013	175	210	22	—	—	—

a. Compute Debtland's budget deficit in each year and complete column 4 in the table. (Since we are computing the deficit, a negative number indicates a surplus.)

b. Compute Debtland's primary budget deficit in each year and complete column 5 in the table.

c. Suppose the initial stock of debt (in 2005) was $400 billion. Noting that the deficit in 2006 adds to the existing stock of debt, what is the stock of debt by the end of 2006?

d. Compute the stock of debt for each year and complete column 6 in the table.

e. Suppose you know that Debtland's debt-to-GDP ratio was the same in 2013 as in 2005. By what percentage did GDP grow between 2005 and 2013?

5. The figure below shows the budget deficit function for a country.

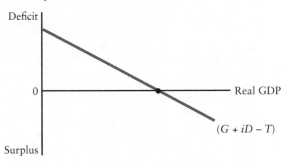

a. Explain why the budget deficit function is downward sloping.

b. If the government increases its level of purchases (G), what happens to the budget deficit at any level of real GDP? Show this in the diagram.

c. If the government increases the net tax rate, what happens to the deficit at any level of real GDP? Show this in the diagram.

d. Explain why a rise in the actual budget deficit does not necessarily reflect a change in fiscal policy.

e. How would a fiscal expansion appear in the diagram? A fiscal contraction?

6. In the late 1990s, the U.S. government was slightly ahead of the Canadian government in reducing its budget deficit. The following table shows the actual budget deficit and the cyclically adjusted deficit (both as a percentage of GDP) for the United States from 1989 to 1997.

Year	Actual Deficit	CAD
1989	2.8	2.9
1990	3.9	3.2
1991	4.6	3.4
1992	4.7	3.7
1993	3.9	3.7
1994	3.0	2.8
1995	2.3	2.6
1996	1.4	1.6
1997	0.3	1.0

a. On a scale diagram (with the year on the horizontal axis), graph the actual deficit and the cyclically adjusted deficit.

b. From 1990 to 1994, the actual budget deficit is above the CAD. Explain why.

c. From 1995 to 1997, the actual budget deficit is below the CAD. Explain why.

d. Identify the periods when U.S. fiscal policy was expansionary.

e. Identify the periods when U.S. fiscal policy was contractionary.

f. Look back at Figure 32-5 on page 808. How does the stance of U.S. fiscal policy over this period compare with Canada's?

7. The following table shows hypothetical data from 2007 to 2013 that can be used to compute the change in the debt-to-GDP ratio. The symbols used are as defined in the text.

Year	x (1)	r (2)	g (3)	d (4)	Δd (5)
2007	0.03	0.045	0.025	0.70	___
2008	0.02	0.04	0.025	___	___
2009	0.01	0.035	0.025	___	___
2010	0.00	0.035	0.025	___	___
2011	−0.01	0.03	0.025	___	___
2012	−0.02	0.03	0.025	___	___
2013	−0.03	0.025	0.025	___	___

a. Remember from the text that the change in the debt-to-GDP ratio (Δd) during a year is given by $\Delta d = x + (r - g)d$. Compute Δd for 2007.

b. Note that d at the beginning of 2008 is equal to d at the beginning of 2007 plus Δd during 2007. Compute d in 2008.

c. Using the same method, compute d and Δd for each year, and complete columns 4 and 5.

d. Plot d in a scale diagram with the year on the horizontal axis. What discretionary variable was most responsible for the observed decline in d?

e. Note that as the primary deficit (x) falls between 2007 and 2013, there is also a downward trend in the real interest rate. Can you offer an explanation for this?

8. The diagram below shows an AD/AS diagram. The economy begins at E_0 with output equal to Y^*. Suppose the government in this closed economy increases G and finances it by running a deficit (borrowing). The AD curve shifts to the right.

a. How does the interest rate at E_1 compare with that at E_0? Explain.

b. Given your answer to part (a), how does investment at E_1 compare with investment at E_0?

c. Explain the economy's adjustment toward E_2. What happens to the interest rate and investment?

d. What is the likely long-run effect for the economy from the fiscal expansion? Explain.

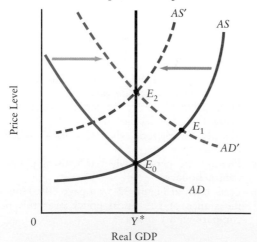

9. The diagram below shows an AD/AS diagram. The economy begins at E_0 with output equal to Y^*. Suppose the government in this closed economy decreases its budget deficit by increasing T (and keeping G unchanged), thus causing the AD curve to shift to the left.

a. How does the interest rate at E_1 compare with that at E_0? Explain.

b. Given your answer to part (a), how does investment at E_1 compare with investment at E_0?

c. Explain the economy's adjustment toward E_2. What happens to the interest rate and investment?

d. What is the long-run effect of the government deficit on the growth rate of Y^*?

e. Comparing the short-run and the long-run effects of this policy, what dilemma does the government face in reducing its deficit?

10. A Member of Parliament recently exclaimed, "The prime minister's policies are working! Lower interest rates combined with staunch fiscal policy have reduced the deficit significantly." What do interest rates have to do with government spending and taxes when it comes to deficit management?

11. The Canadian federal budget moved from a surplus of $9.6 billion in the 2007–2008 fiscal year to a deficit of $5.8 billion the next year, and a large deficit of $55.6 billion in 2009–2010.

a. Suppose real GDP was at potential in each of the first two years. What can you conclude about the cause of the change in the budget deficit? Show this change in a diagram of the budget deficit function.

b. Suppose from 2008–2009 to 2009–2010, two things happened: real GDP fell and the government implemented an expansionary fiscal policy. Show these two separate events in a diagram of the budget deficit function.

The Gains from International Trade

LEARNING OBJECTIVES (LO)

After studying this chapter you will be able to

1 explain why the gains from trade depend on the pattern of comparative advantage.
2 understand how factor endowments and climate can influence a country's comparative advantage.
3 describe the law of one price.
4 explain why countries export some goods and import others.

TRADE between peoples and nations has been going on throughout human history, and humans have gone to great lengths and endured severe hardship in order to reap the benefits of trade. Centuries ago, for example, the inhabitants of remote islands in Southeast Polynesia travelled the open ocean in canoes for days at a time to trade oyster shells, volcanic glass, basalt, and food items with inhabitants of other, distant islands.

Today, the required activities for trade may be far less demanding, but the transactions themselves are no less important. Canadian consumers buy cars from Germany, Germans take holidays in Italy, Italians buy spices from Africa, Africans import oil from Kuwait, Kuwaitis buy Japanese cameras, and the Japanese buy Canadian lumber. *International trade* refers to the exchange of goods and services that takes place across international boundaries.

The founders of modern economics were concerned with foreign trade problems. The great eighteenth-century British philosopher and economist David Hume (1711–1776), one of the first to work out the theory of the price system, developed his concepts mainly in terms of prices in foreign trade. Adam Smith (1723–1790), in *The Wealth of Nations*, attacked government restriction of international trade. David Ricardo (1772–1823) developed the basic theory of the gains from trade that is studied in this chapter. The 1846 repeal of the Corn Laws—tariffs on the importation of corn and other grains into the United Kingdom—and the transformation of that country during the nineteenth century from a country of high tariffs to one of complete free trade were to some extent the result of arguments by economists whose theories of the gains from international trade led them to condemn tariffs.

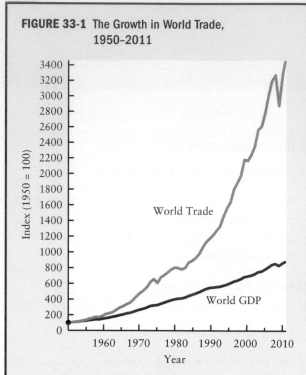

FIGURE 33-1 The Growth in World Trade, 1950–2011

The volume of world trade has grown much faster than world GDP over the past six decades. The figure shows the growth of real GDP and the volume of trade since 1950. Both are expressed as index numbers, set equal to 100 in 1950. Real world GDP has increased more than seven times since 1950; world trade volume has increased by over 33 times. The major global recession in 2009 is clearly evident with the sharp decline in the flow of trade in that year.

(*Source:* World Trade Organization, *International Trade Statistics 2012*, Table A1. www.wto.org.)

For information on world trade, see the World Trade Organization's website: www.wto.org.

International trade is becoming increasingly important, not just for Canada but for the world as a whole. As Figure 33-1 shows, the volume of world trade has grown much faster than world real GDP over the past six decades. Since 1950, the world's real GDP has increased by more than seven times, an average annual growth rate of 3.7 percent. Over the same period, however, the volume of world trade has increased by more than 30 times, an average annual growth rate of 6.1 percent.

Figure 33-2 shows some data for Canadian trade in 2011. The figure shows the value of Canadian exports and imports of goods in several broad industry groupings. There are three important points to note from the figure. First, international trade is very important for Canada. In 2011, Canada exported $458 billion and imported $456 billion in goods—if we added trade in services, each of these values would be higher by about $80 billion; each flow (exports and imports) amounts to about 32 percent of GDP. Second, exports and imports are roughly the same size, so that the *volume* of trade is much larger than the *balance* of trade—the value of exports minus the value of imports. Third, in most of the industry groupings there are significant amounts of both imports and exports. Such *intra-industry trade* will be discussed later in the chapter. Canada does not just export resource products and import manufactured goods; it also imports many resource products and exports many manufactured goods.

In this chapter, we examine the increases in living standards that result from international trade. We find that the source of the gains from trade lies in differing cost conditions among geographical regions. World income would be vastly lower if countries did not specialize in the products in which they have the lowest opportunity costs of production. These costs are partly determined by natural endowments (geographical and climatic conditions), partly by public policy, and partly by historical accident.

33.1 The Gains from Trade

open economy An economy that engages in international trade.

closed economy An economy that has no foreign trade.

An economy that engages in international trade is called an **open economy**; one that does not is called a **closed economy**. A situation in which a country does no foreign trade is called one of *autarky*.

Although politicians often regard foreign trade differently from domestic trade, economists from Adam Smith on have argued that the causes and consequences of international trade are simply an extension of the principles governing trade between domestic firms and individuals. What are the benefits of trade among individuals, among groups, among regions, or among countries?

Interpersonal, Interregional, and International Trade

To begin, consider trade among individuals. Without trade, each person would have to be self-sufficient: Each would have to produce all the food, clothing, shelter, medical services, entertainment, and luxuries that he or she consumed. Because no individual could effectively produce such a large range of products, a world of individual self-sufficiency would be a world with extremely low living standards: individuals would work very hard but not be able to produce or consume very much.

Trade among individuals allows people to specialize in activities they can do well and to buy from others the goods and services they cannot easily produce. A good doctor who is a bad carpenter can provide medical services not only for her own family but also for a good carpenter without the training or the ability to practise medicine. Trade and specialization are intimately connected.

> Without trade, everyone must be self-sufficient; with trade, people can specialize in what they do well and satisfy other needs by trading.

The same principle applies to regions. Without interregional trade, each region would be forced to be self-sufficient. With trade, each region can specialize in producing products for which it has some natural or acquired advantage. Prairie regions can specialize in growing grain, mountain regions in mining and forest products, and regions with abundant power can specialize in manufacturing. Cool regions can produce wheat and other crops that thrive in temperate climates, and hot regions can grow such tropical crops as bananas, sugarcane, and coffee. The living standards of the inhabitants of all regions will be higher when each region specializes in products in which it has some natural or acquired advantage and obtains other products by trade than when all regions seek to be self-sufficient.

This same principle also applies to countries. A national boundary is a political invention and rarely delimits an area that is naturally self-sufficient. Countries, like regions and individuals, can gain from specialization. More of some goods are produced domestically than residents want to consume, while residents would like to consume larger quantities of other goods than are produced domestically. International trade is necessary to achieve the gains that international specialization makes possible.

> With trade, each individual, region, or country is able to concentrate on producing goods and services that it produces efficiently while trading to obtain goods and services that it does not produce efficiently.

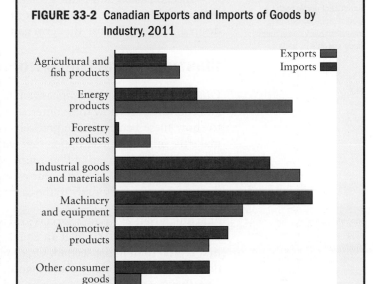

FIGURE 33-2 Canadian Exports and Imports of Goods by Industry, 2011

Billions of Current Dollars

Canada exports and imports large volumes of goods in most industries. The data show the value of goods exported and imported by industry in 2011 (trade in services is not shown). The total value of goods exported was $458 billion; the total value of goods imported was $456 billion.

(*Source:* These data are available on Statistics Canada's website: www.statcan.gc.ca. Search for "International trade" and then "Canada's merchandise exports.")

gains from trade The increased output attributable to the specialization according to comparative advantage that is made possible by trade.

Specialization and trade go hand in hand because there is no incentive to achieve the gains from specialization without being able to trade the goods produced for goods desired. Economists use the term **gains from trade** to embrace the results of both.

Illustrating the Gains from Trade

Our discussion so far has emphasized the *differences* that exist between individuals, regions, and countries, and how these differences lie behind the benefits derived from trade. In order to show these benefits more precisely, we will focus on trade between two countries. We make the important assumption that within each country the average cost of production of any good is independent of *how much* of that good is produced. That is, we are making the assumption of *constant costs*. Our example involves two countries and two products, but the general principles apply to the case of many countries and many products.

absolute advantage The situation that exists when one country can produce some commodity at lower absolute cost than another country.

Absolute Advantage One region is said to have an **absolute advantage** over another in the production of good X when an equal quantity of resources can produce more X in the first region than in the second. Or, to put it differently, if it takes fewer resources to produce one unit of good X there than in another country. Table 33-1 shows an example. The two "countries" are Canada and the European Union (EU), and the two goods are wheat and cloth. The table shows the *absolute cost* of producing one unit of wheat and one unit of cloth in each country. The absolute cost is the dollar cost of the labour, capital, and other resources required to produce the goods. Thus, the country that can produce a specific good with fewer resources can produce it at a lower absolute cost.

In Table 33-1, the absolute cost for both wheat and cloth is less in Canada than in the EU. Canada is therefore said to have an *absolute advantage* over the EU in the production of both wheat and cloth because it is a more efficient producer—it takes less labour and other resources to produce the goods in Canada than in the EU.

The situation in Table 33-1 is hypothetical, but it is encountered often in the real world. Some countries, because they have access to cheap natural resources or better-trained workers or more sophisticated capital equipment, are low-cost producers for a wide range of products. Does this mean that high-cost countries stand no chance of being successful producers in a globalized world of international trade? Will the low-cost countries produce everything, leaving nothing to be done by high-cost countries? The answer is no. As we will see immediately, the gains from international trade do *not* depend on the pattern of absolute advantage.

comparative advantage The situation that exists when a country can produce a good with less forgone output of other goods than can another country.

Comparative Advantage The great English economist David Ricardo (1772–1823) was the first to provide an explanation of the pattern of international trade in a world in which countries had different costs. His theory of *comparative advantage* is still accepted by economists as a valid statement of one of the major sources of the gains from international trade. A country is said to have a **comparative advantage** in the production of good X if the cost of producing X *in terms of forgone output of other goods* is lower in that country than in another. Thus, the pattern of comparative advantage is based on *opportunity costs* rather than absolute costs. Table 33-2 illustrates the pattern of comparative advantage in the Canada–EU example. The opportunity cost in Canada for one kilogram of wheat is computed by determining how much

TABLE 33-1 Absolute Costs and Absolute Advantage

	Wheat (kilograms)	Cloth (metres)
Canada	$1 per kilogram	$5 per metre
EU	$3 per kilogram	$6 per metre

Absolute advantage reflects the differences in absolute costs of producing goods between countries. The numbers show the dollar cost of the total amount of resources necessary for producing wheat and cloth in Canada and the EU. Note that Canada is a lower-cost producer than the EU for both wheat and cloth. Canada is therefore said to have an absolute advantage in the production of both goods.

cloth must be given up in Canada in order to produce an additional kilogram of wheat. From Table 33-1, the absolute costs of wheat and cloth were $1 per kilogram and $5 per metre, respectively. Thus, in order to produce one extra kilogram of wheat, Canada must use resources that could have produced one-fifth of a metre of cloth. So the opportunity cost of one kilogram of wheat is 0.2 metres of cloth. By exactly the same reasoning, the opportunity cost of one metre of cloth in Canada is 5.0 kilograms of wheat. These opportunity costs are shown in Table 33-2.

Even though a country may have an absolute advantage in all goods (as Canada does in Table 33-1), it *cannot* have a comparative advantage in all goods. Similarly, even though a country may be inefficient in absolute terms and thus have an absolute disadvantage in all goods (as is the case for the EU in Table 33-1) it *cannot* have a comparative disadvantage in all goods. In Table 33-2, Canada has a comparative advantage in the production of wheat because Canada must give up less cloth to produce one kilogram of wheat than must be given up in the EU. Similarly, the EU has a comparative advantage in the production of cloth because the EU must give up less wheat in order to produce one metre of cloth than must be given up in Canada.

> The gains from specialization and trade depend on the pattern of comparative, not absolute, advantage.

In our example, total world wheat production can be increased if Canada devotes more resources to the production of wheat and fewer resources to the production of cloth. Similarly, total world cloth production can be increased if the EU devotes more resources to the production of cloth and fewer to wheat. In the extreme case, Canada could *specialize* by producing *only* wheat and the EU could specialize by producing only cloth. Such reallocations of resources increase total world output because each country is specializing in the production of the good in which it has the lowest opportunity cost. The gains from specialization along the lines of comparative advantage are shown in Table 33-3.

> World output increases if countries specialize in the production of the goods in which they have a comparative advantage.

Not *every possible* pattern of specialization, however, is beneficial for the world. In our example, if Canada were to specialize in cloth and the EU in wheat, total world output would *fall*. To see this, note that in order to produce one extra metre of cloth in Canada,

---

TABLE 33-2 Opportunity Costs and Comparative Advantage

Canada:	opportunity cost of 1 kg of wheat = 0.2 m cloth
EU:	opportunity cost of 1 kg of wheat = 0.5 m cloth
Canada:	opportunity cost of 1 m of cloth = 5 kg wheat
EU:	opportunity cost of 1 m of cloth = 2 kg wheat

Comparative advantages reflect opportunity costs that differ between countries. The opportunity costs are computed using the data provided in Table 33-1. For example, for Canada to produce one additional kilogram of wheat, it must use resources that could have been used to produce 0.2 metres of cloth; the opportunity cost of 1 kg of wheat in Canada is therefore 0.2 metres of cloth. The comparative advantages for each country are shown by the shaded rows. Canada has a comparative advantage in wheat production because it has a lower opportunity cost for wheat than does the EU. The EU has a comparative advantage in cloth because its opportunity cost for cloth is lower than that in Canada.

TABLE 33-3 The Gains from Specialization

Changes from each country producing more units of the product in which it has the lower opportunity cost

	Wheat (kilograms)	Cloth (metres)
Canada	+5.0	−1.0
EU	−4.0	+2.0
Total	+1.0	+1.0

Whenever opportunity costs differ between countries, specialization can increase the world's production of both products. These calculations show that there are gains from specialization given the opportunity costs of Table 33-2. To produce five more kilograms of wheat, Canada must sacrifice 1.0 m of cloth. To produce two more metres of cloth, the EU must sacrifice 4.0 kg of wheat. This combination of changes increases world production of both wheat and cloth.

five kilograms of wheat must be sacrificed (see Table 33-2). Similarly, in order to produce four extra kilograms of wheat in the EU, two metres of cloth must be sacrificed. Thus, if each country produced these additional units of the "wrong" good, total world output of wheat would fall by one kilogram and total output of cloth would fall by one metre.

> **Specialization of production *against* the pattern of comparative advantage leads to a decline in total world output.**

We have discussed comparative advantage in terms of opportunity costs. We can also illustrate it by considering the two countries' production possibilities boundaries. Recall from Chapter 1 the connection between a country's production possibilities boundary and the opportunity costs of production. The slope of the production possibilities boundary indicates the opportunity costs. The existence of different opportunity costs across countries implies comparative advantages that can lead to gains from trade. Figure 33-3 illustrates how two countries can both gain from trade when they have different

FIGURE 33-3 The Gains from Trade with Constant Opportunity Costs

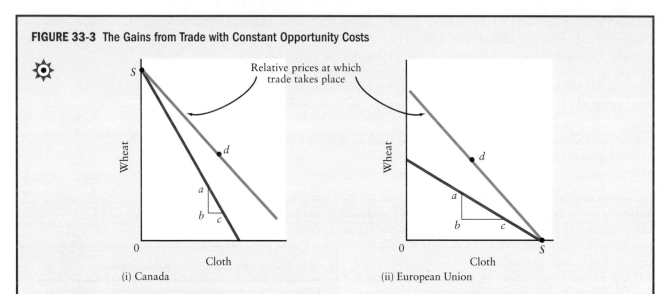

(i) Canada

(ii) European Union

International trade leads to specialization in production and increased consumption possibilities. The purple lines in parts (i) and (ii) represent the production possibilities boundaries for Canada and the EU, respectively. In the absence of any international trade, these also represent each country's consumption possibilities.

The difference in the slopes of the production possibilities boundaries reflects differences in comparative advantage, as shown in Table 33-2. In each part the opportunity cost of increasing production of wheat by the same amount (measured by the distance *ba*) is the amount by which the production of cloth must be reduced (measured by the distance *bc*). The relatively steep production possibilities boundary for Canada thus indicates that the opportunity cost of producing wheat in Canada is less than that in the EU.

If trade is possible at some relative prices between the two countries' opportunity costs of production, each country will specialize in the production of the good in which it has a comparative advantage. In each part of the figure, the slope of the green line shows the relative prices at which trade takes place. Production occurs in each country at point *S* (for specialization); Canada produces only wheat, and the EU produces only cloth.

Consumption possibilities for each country are now given by the green line that passes through point *S*. Consumption possibilities are increased in both countries; consumption may occur at some point, such as *d*, that involves a combination of wheat and cloth that was not attainable in the absence of trade.

opportunity costs in production and those opportunity costs are independent of the level of production. An alternative diagrammatic illustration of the gains from trade appears in *Extensions in Theory 33-1*, where the production possibilities boundary is concave (which means that the opportunity cost for each good is higher when more of that good is being produced).

The conclusions about the gains from trade arising from international differences in opportunity costs are summarized below.

1. The opportunity cost of producing X is the amount of output of other products that must be sacrificed in order to increase the output of X by one unit.

2. Country A has a comparative advantage over Country B in producing a product when the opportunity cost of production in Country A is lower. This implies, however, that it has a comparative *dis*advantage in some other product(s).

3. When opportunity costs for all products are the same in all countries, there is no comparative advantage and there is no possibility of gains from specialization and trade.

4. When opportunity costs differ in any two countries and both countries are producing both products, it is always possible to increase production of both products by a suitable reallocation of resources within each country.

Though the concepts of comparative advantage and specialization are relatively straightforward, it is helpful to work through numerical examples to solidify your understanding. *Applying Economic Concepts 33-1* provides two examples and works through the computations of absolute and comparative advantage.

The Gains from Trade with Variable Costs

So far, we have assumed that opportunity costs are the same whatever the scale of output, and we have seen that there are gains from specialization and trade as long as there are differences in opportunity costs across countries. If costs vary with the level of output, or as experience is acquired via specialization, *additional* gains are possible.

Economies of Scale In many industries, production costs fall as the scale of output increases. The larger the scale of operations, the more efficiently large-scale machinery can be used and the more a detailed division of tasks among workers is possible. Small countries (such as Switzerland, Belgium, and Israel) whose domestic markets are not large enough to exploit economies of scale would find it prohibitively expensive to become self-sufficient by producing a little bit of everything at very high cost.

One of the important lessons learned from patterns of world trade since the Second World War has concerned imperfect competition and product differentiation. Virtually all of today's manufactured consumer goods are produced in a vast array of differentiated product lines. In some industries, many firms produce different items in this array; in others, only a few firms produce the entire array. In either case, they may not exhaust all available economies of scale. Thus, an increase in the size of the market, even in a large economy, may allow the exploitation of some previously unexploited scale economies in individual product lines.

These possibilities were first dramatically illustrated when the European Common Market (now known as the European Union) was set up in the late 1950s.

EXTENSIONS IN THEORY 33-1

The Gains from Trade More Generally

Examining the gains from trade is relatively easy in the case where each country's production possibilities boundary is a straight line. What happens in the more realistic case where the production possibilities boundary is concave? As this box shows, the same basic principles of the gains from trade apply to this more complex case.

International trade leads to an expansion of the set of goods that can be consumed in the economy in two ways:

1. By allowing the bundle of goods consumed to differ from the bundle produced
2. By permitting a profitable change in the pattern of production

Without international trade, the bundle of goods produced must be the same as the bundle consumed. With international trade, the consumption and production bundles can be altered independently to reflect the relative values placed on goods by international markets.

Fixed Production

In each part of the figure, the purple curve is the economy's production possibilities boundary. In the absence of international trade, the economy must consume the same bundle of goods that it produces. Thus, the production possibilities boundary is also the consumption possibilities boundary. Suppose the economy produces and consumes at point a, with x_1 of good X and y_1 of good Y, as in part (i) of the figure.

Next suppose that production remains at point a but we now allow good Y to be traded for good X internationally. The consumption possibilities are now shown by the line tt drawn through point a. The slope of tt indicates the quantity of Y that exchanges for a unit of X on the international market—that is, the relative price of X in terms of Y.

Although production is fixed at point a, consumption can now be anywhere on the line tt. For example, the

consumption point could be at b. This could be achieved by exporting y_2y_1 units of Y and importing x_1x_2 units of X. Because point b (and all others on line tt to the right of a) lies outside the production possibilities boundary, there are potential gains from trade. Consumers are no longer limited by their own country's production possibilities. Let us suppose that they prefer point b to point a. They have achieved a gain from trade by being allowed to exchange some of their production of good Y for some quantity of good X and thus to consume more of good X than is produced at home.

Variable Production

In general, however, openness to trade with other countries will change the pattern of domestic production, and this will create *further* gains from trade. The country can now produce the bundle of goods that is most valuable in world markets. That is represented by the bundle d in part (ii). The consumption possibilities boundary is shifted to the line $t't'$ by changing production from a to d and thereby increasing the country's degree of specialization in good Y. For every point on the original consumption possibilities boundary tt, there are points on the new boundary $t't'$ that allow more consumption of both goods—for example, compare points b and f. Notice also that, except at the zero-trade point d, the new consumption possibilities boundary lies *everywhere above the production possibilities boundary*.

The benefits of moving from a no-trade position, such as point a, to a trading position, such as points b or f, are the *gains from trade* to the country. When the production of good Y is increased and the production of good X decreased, the country is able to move to a point, such as f, by producing more of good Y, in which the country has a comparative advantage, and trading the additional production for good X.

(i) Fixed production

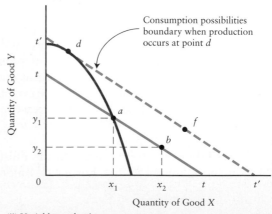

(ii) Variable production

APPLYING ECONOMIC CONCEPTS 33-1

Two Examples of Absolute and Comparative Advantage

Example #1

Argentina and Brazil can both produce fish and leather. The table shows the total resource cost, in dollars, of producing one kilogram of each good in both countries.

	Fish (kg)	Leather (kg)
Argentina	$2	$5
Brazil	$3	$4

Absolute Advantage Argentina is the more efficient producer of fish since its total resource cost ($2) is less than Brazil's ($3), and so it has the absolute advantage in producing fish. Brazil has the absolute advantage in producing leather.

Comparative Advantage To know the pattern of comparative advantage, we must compute the *opportunity costs of production*. In Argentina, producing one more kilogram of leather requires using $5 of resources—the amount that could have been used to produce 2.5 kg of fish. Thus, producing 1 kg of leather involves giving up 2.5 kg of fish. In Brazil, however, one extra kilogram of leather only requires a sacrifice of 1.33 kg of fish. Since Brazil has the lower opportunity cost for leather (it gives up the least fish), it has the comparative advantage in leather production.

The opportunity cost for fish production *must* be the inverse of that for leather. In Argentina, one extra kilogram of fish "costs" 0.4 kg of leather. In Brazil, one extra kilogram of fish "costs" 0.75 kg of leather. Since Argentina has the lower opportunity cost of fish, it has the comparative advantage in fish production.

Specialization If Argentina and Brazil were to trade with each other, total production would be increased if each country specialized in the production of the good in which it has the comparative advantage. Argentina should produce fish and buy its leather from Brazil; Brazil should produce leather and buy its fish from Argentina.

Example #2

Switzerland and Austria can both produce glass and chocolate. Each country has 1000 units of identical resources, which we will call "labour." The table shows the maximum amount of each good that each country could produce if it devoted all of its labour to the production of that good.

	Glass (tonnes)	Chocolate (kg)
Austria	5 000	400 000
Switzerland	4 000	200 000

Absolute Advantage Each unit of labour in Austria can produce 5 tonnes of glass or 400 kg of chocolate. The identical unit of labour in Switzerland can produce only 4 tonnes of glass or 200 kg of chocolate. Switzerland is less efficient than Austria in the production of both goods; Austria therefore has the absolute advantage in *both* goods.

Comparative Advantage Once again, we need to know the opportunity costs of production. In Austria, producing one extra tonne of glass requires giving up 80 kg ($= 400\,000/5000$) of chocolate. In Switzerland, producing one extra tonne of glass "costs" 50 kg ($= 200\,000/4000$) of chocolate. Switzerland has the lower opportunity cost for glass and thus has the comparative advantage in glass production. It follows that Austria *must* have the comparative advantage in the production of chocolate. Austria's opportunity cost of 1 kg of chocolate is 1/80 tonne of glass, whereas Switzerland's opportunity cost of 1 kg of chocolate is 1/50 tonne of glass.

Specialization If the two countries engaged in international trade, total output would be maximized if Austria specialized in the production of chocolate and Switzerland specialized in the production of glass.

Economists had expected that specialization would occur according to the theory of comparative advantage, with one country specializing in cars, another in refrigerators, another in fashion and clothing, another in shoes, and so on. This is not the way it worked out. Instead, much of the vast growth of trade was in *intra-industry* trade—that is, trade of goods or services within the same broad industry. Today, one can buy French, English, Italian, and German fashion goods, cars, shoes, appliances, and a host of other products in Paris, London, Rome, and Berlin. Ships loaded with Swedish furniture bound for London pass ships loaded with English furniture bound for Stockholm, and so on.

Wine is a good example of an industry in which there is much intra-industry trade. Canada, for example, imports wine from many countries but also exports Canadian-made wine to the same countries.

The same increase in intra-industry happened with Canada–U.S. trade over successive rounds of tariff cuts that were negotiated after the Second World War, the most recent being those associated with the 1989 Canada–U.S. Free Trade Agreement, and its 1994 expansion into the North American Free Trade Agreement (NAFTA), which included Mexico. In several broad industrial groups, including automotive products, machinery, textiles, and forestry products, both imports and exports increased in each country. What free trade in Europe and North America did was to allow a proliferation of differentiated products, with different countries each specializing in different subproduct lines. Consumers have shown by their expenditures that they value this enormous increase in the range of choice among differentiated products, and producers have gained economies by being able to operate at a larger scale.

In industries with significant scale economies, small countries that do not trade will have low levels of output and therefore high costs. With international trade, however, small countries can produce for the large global market and thus produce at lower costs. International trade therefore allows small countries to reap the benefits of scale economies.

Learning by Doing The discussion so far has assumed that costs vary with the *level* of output. But they may also vary with the *accumulated experience* in producing a product over time.

learning by doing The reduction in unit costs that often results as workers learn through repeatedly performing the same tasks. It causes a downward shift in the average cost curve.

Early economists placed great importance on a concept that is now called **learning by doing.** They believed that as countries gained experience in particular tasks, workers and managers would become more efficient in performing them. As people acquire expertise, costs tend to fall. There is substantial evidence that such learning by doing does occur. It is particularly important in many of today's knowledge-intensive high-tech industries. The distinction between this phenomenon and economies of scale is illustrated in Figure 33-4. It is one more example of the difference between a movement along a curve and a shift of the curve.

The opportunity for learning by doing has an important implication: Policymakers need not accept current comparative advantages as given. Through such means as education and tax incentives, they can seek to develop new comparative advantages. Moreover, countries cannot complacently assume that their existing comparative advantages will persist. Misguided education policies, the wrong tax incentives, or policies that discourage risk taking can lead to the rapid erosion of a country's comparative advantage in particular products and industries.

Sources of Comparative Advantage

David Ricardo's analysis taught us that the gains from trade arise from the pattern of comparative advantage. However, his analysis did not explain the *sources* of a country's comparative advantage. Why do comparative advantages exist? Since a country's comparative advantage depends on its opportunity costs, we could also ask: Why do different countries have different opportunity costs?

Different Factor Endowments One answer to this question was offered early in the twentieth century by two Swedish economists, Eli Heckscher and Bertil Ohlin. Ohlin was subsequently awarded the Nobel Prize in economics for his work in the theory of international trade. According to their theory, the international cost differences that form the basis for comparative advantage arise because factor endowments differ across countries. This is often called the *factor endowment theory of comparative advantage.*

To see how this theory works, consider the prices for various types of goods in countries *in the absence of trade.* A country that is well endowed with fertile land but has a small population will find that land is cheap but labour is expensive. It will therefore produce land-intensive agricultural goods cheaply and labour-intensive goods, such as machine tools, only at high cost. The reverse will be true for a second country that is small in size but possesses abundant and efficient labour. As a result, the first country will have a comparative advantage in agricultural production and the second in goods that use much labour and little land.

> According to the Heckscher-Ohlin theory, countries have comparative advantages in the production of goods that use intensively the factors of production with which they are abundantly endowed.

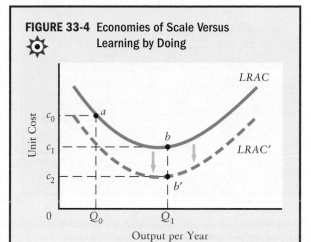

FIGURE 33-4 Economies of Scale Versus Learning by Doing

Specialization may lead to gains from trade through scale economies, learning by doing, or both. Consider a country that wants to consume the quantity Q_0. Suppose it can produce that quantity at an average cost per unit of c_0. Suppose further that the country has a comparative advantage in producing this product and can export the quantity Q_0Q_1 if it produces Q_1. This may lead to cost savings in two ways.

First, the increased level of production of Q_1 compared with Q_0 permits it to move along its long-run cost curve from a to b, thereby reducing costs per unit to c_1. This is an economy of scale.

Second, as workers and management become more experienced, they may be able to produce at lower costs. This is learning by doing and it shifts the cost curve from $LRAC$ to $LRAC'$. At output Q_1, costs per unit fall to c_2. The movement from a to b' incorporates both economies of scale and learning by doing.

For example, Canada is abundantly endowed with forests relative to most other countries. According to the Heckscher-Ohlin theory, Canada has a comparative advantage in goods that use forest products intensively, such as paper, framing materials, raw lumber, and wooden furniture. In contrast, relative to most other countries, Canada is sparsely endowed with labour. Thus, Canada has a comparative disadvantage in goods that use labour intensively, such as cotton or many other textile products.

Different Climates The factor endowment theory provides only part of the entire explanation for the sources of comparative advantage. Another important influence comes from all those natural factors that can be called *climate* in the broadest sense. If you combine land, labour, and capital in the same way in Nicaragua and in Iceland, you will not get the same output of most agricultural goods. Sunshine, rainfall, and average temperature also matter. You can, of course, artificially create any climate you want in a greenhouse, but it costs money to create what is freely provided elsewhere.

> A country's comparative advantage is influenced by various aspects of its climate.

Canada is extremely well endowed with forests. It is no surprise, therefore, that it has a comparative advantage in a whole range of forestry products.

Of course, if we consider "warm weather" a factor of production, then we could simply say that countries like Nicaragua are better endowed with that factor than countries like Iceland. In this sense, explanations of comparative advantage based on different climates are really just a special case of explanations based on factor endowments.

Human Capital Acquired skills, what economists call *human capital*, matter greatly in determining comparative advantage. Beginning in the late nineteenth century, Germany had an excellent set of trade schools that were attended by virtually every male who did not go on to higher academic education. As a result, Germany developed, and still maintains, a strong comparative advantage in many consumer goods that require significant skills to produce, such as electric razors, cake mixers, and blenders. The people of Persia (now Iran) produced carpets of high quality over the centuries, and from childhood their workers developed skills in carpet making that few others could match. So they had a comparative advantage in high-quality carpets and some related commodities.

Early on, Americans developed the skills necessary to mass-produce goods of reasonable quality made from standardized parts. So the United States developed a comparative advantage in many products made with mass-production techniques. One early set of products made in this way was firearms. Rifles and pistols were mass-produced and assembled from standardized parts. This allowed U.S. firms to produce their firearms at much lower costs than in other countries where similar weapons were made one at a time by craftsmen. One of these, the Colt six-shooter, blazed its way into fame in the nineteenth century in the American "Wild West."

Acquired Comparative Advantage The example of human capital makes it clear that many comparative advantages are *acquired*. Further, they can change. Thus, comparative advantage should be viewed as being *dynamic* rather than static. Many of today's industries depend more on human capital than on fixed physical capital or natural resources. The skills of a computer designer, a video game programmer, or a sound mix technician are acquired by education and on-the-job training. Natural endowments of energy and raw materials cannot account for Silicon Valley's leadership in computer technology, for Canada's prominence in communications technology, for Taiwan's excellence in electronics, or for Switzerland's prominence in private banking.

If comparative advantage can be acquired, it can also be *lost*. If firms within one country fail to innovate and adopt the latest technologies available in their industry, but competing firms in other countries are aggressively innovating and reducing their production costs, the first country will eventually lose whatever comparative advantage it once had in that industry. In recent years, for example, pulp and paper mills in Canada have been closing, driven out of the industry by Scandinavian firms that more aggressively pursue improvements in productivity.

With today's growing international competition and rapidly changing technologies, no country's comparative advantages are secure unless its firms innovate and keep up with their foreign competitors and its education system produces workers, managers, and innovators with the requisite skills.

Contrasting Views? The view that a country's comparative advantages change over time and can be influenced by education, innovation, and government policy is a relatively modern one. It contrasts sharply with the traditional view that a country's natural endowments of land, labour, and natural resources are the prime determinants of its comparative advantage. The traditional view suggested that a government interested in maximizing its citizens' material standard of living should encourage specialization of production in goods for which it *currently* had a comparative advantage. If all countries followed this advice, each would have been specialized in a relatively narrow range of distinct products. The British would have produced engineering products, Canadians would have produced resource-based primary products, Americans would have been farmers and factory workers, Central Americans would have been banana and coffee growers, the Chinese would have produced rice and cheap toys, and so on.

There are surely elements of truth in both views. It would be unwise to neglect resource endowments, climate, culture, social patterns, and institutional arrangements. But it would also be unwise to assume that all advantages are innate and immutable.

33.2 The Determination of Trade Patterns

Comparative advantage has been the central concept in our discussion about the gains from trade. If Canada has a comparative advantage in lumber and Italy has a comparative advantage in shoes, then the total output of lumber and shoes can be increased if Canada specializes in the production of lumber and Italy specializes in the production of shoes. With such patterns of specialization, Canada will naturally export lumber to Italy and Italy will export shoes to Canada.

It is one thing to discuss the *potential* gains from trade if countries specialized in the production of particular goods and exported these to other countries. But do *actual* trade patterns occur along the lines of comparative advantage? In this section of the chapter we use a simple demand-and-supply model to examine why Canada exports some products and imports others. We will see that comparative advantage, whether natural or acquired, plays a central role in determining actual trade patterns.

There are some products, such as coffee and mangoes, that Canada does not produce (and will probably never produce). Any domestic consumption of these products must therefore be satisfied by imports from other countries. At the other extreme, there are some products, such as nickel and potash, of which Canada is one of the world's major suppliers, and demand in the rest of the world must be satisfied partly by exports from Canada. Finally, there are some products, such as houses and crushed stone, that are so expensive to transport that every country produces approximately what it consumes.

Our interest in this section is with the vast number of intermediate cases in which Canada is only one of many producers of an internationally traded product, as with beef, oil, copper, wheat, lumber, and newsprint. Will Canada be an exporter or an importer of such products? And what is the role played by comparative advantage?

For data on Canadian trade by industry and by country, go to Statistics Canada's website at www.statcan.gc.ca and search for "trade."

The Law of One Price

Whether Canada imports or exports a product for which it is only one of many producers depends to a great extent on the product's price. This brings us to what economists call the *law of one price*.

The law of one price states that when a product is traded throughout the entire world, the prices in various countries (net of any specific taxes or tariffs) will differ by no more than the cost of transporting the product between countries. Aside from differences caused by these transport costs, there is a single world price.

Many basic products—such as copper wire, steel pipe, iron ore, and computer RAM chips—fall within this category. The world price for each good is the price that equates the quantity demanded worldwide with the quantity supplied worldwide. The world price of an internationally traded product may be influenced greatly, or only slightly, by the demand and supply coming from any one country. The extent of one country's influence will depend on how important its quantities demanded and supplied are in relation to the worldwide totals.

The simplest case for us to study arises when the country, which we will take to be Canada, accounts for only a small part of the total worldwide demand and supply. In this case, Canada does not itself produce enough to influence the world price significantly. Similarly, Canadian purchases are too small a proportion of worldwide demand to affect the world price in any significant way. Producers and consumers in Canada thus face a world price that they cannot influence by their own actions.

In this case, the price that rules in the Canadian market must be the world price (adjusted for the exchange rate between the Canadian dollar and the foreign currency). The law of one price says that this must be so. What would happen if the Canadian domestic price diverged from the world price? If the Canadian price were below the world price, no supplier would sell in the Canadian market because higher profits could be made by selling abroad. The absence of supply to the Canadian market would thus drive up the Canadian price. Conversely, if the Canadian domestic price were above the worldwide price, no buyer would buy from a Canadian seller because lower prices are available by buying abroad. The absence of demand on the Canadian market would thus drive down the Canadian price.

The Pattern of Foreign Trade

Let us now see what determines the pattern of international trade in such circumstances.

An Exported Product To determine the pattern of Canadian trade, we first show the Canadian domestic demand and supply curves for some product, say, lumber. This is done in Figure 33-5. The intersection of these two curves tells us what the price and quantity would be in Canada *if there were no foreign trade*. Now compare this no-trade price with the world price of that product.[1] If the world price is higher, the actual price in Canada will exceed the no-trade

FIGURE 33-5 An Exported Good

Exports occur whenever there is excess supply domestically at the world price. The domestic demand and supply curves are D and S, respectively. The domestic price in the absence of foreign trade is p_d, with Q_d produced and consumed domestically. The world price of p_w is higher than p_d. At p_w, Q_1 is demanded while Q_2 is supplied domestically. The excess of the domestic supply over the domestic demand is exported.

---

[1] If the world price is stated in terms of some foreign currency (as it often is), the price must be converted into Canadian dollars by using the current exchange rate between the foreign currency and Canadian dollars.

price. In this situation there will be an excess of Canadian supply over Canadian demand. Domestic producers want to sell Q_2 units of lumber but domestic consumers want to buy only Q_1 units. If Canada were a closed economy, such excess supply would drive the price down to p_d. But in an open economy with a world price of p_w, this excess supply is exported to Canada's trading partners.

What is the role of comparative advantage in this analysis? We have said that Canada will export lumber if the world price exceeds Canada's no-trade price. Note that in a competitive market the price of the product reflects the product's marginal cost, which in turn reflects the opportunity cost of producing the product. That Canada's no-trade price for lumber is lower than the world price reflects the fact that the opportunity cost of producing lumber in Canada is less than the opportunity cost of producing it in the rest of the world. Thus, by exporting goods that have a low no-trade price, Canada is exporting the goods for which it has a comparative advantage.

> Countries export the goods for which they are low-cost producers. That is, they export goods for which they have a comparative advantage.

An Imported Product Now consider some other product—for example, computer RAM chips. Once again, look first at the domestic demand and supply curves, shown this time in Figure 33-6. The intersection of these curves determines the price that would exist in Canada if there were no foreign trade. The world price of RAM chips is below the Canadian no-trade price so that, at the price ruling in Canada, domestic demand is larger and domestic supply is smaller than if the no-trade price had ruled. The excess of domestic demand over domestic supply is met by imports.

Again, this analysis can be restated in terms of comparative advantage. The high Canadian no-trade price of RAM chips reflects the fact that the production of RAM chips has a higher opportunity cost in Canada than elsewhere in the world. This high cost means that Canada has a comparative disadvantage in RAM chips. So Canada imports goods for which it has a comparative disadvantage.

> Countries import the goods for which they are high-cost producers. That is, they import goods for which they have a comparative disadvantage.

Is Comparative Advantage Obsolete?

It is sometimes said that the theory of comparative advantage is nearly 200 years old, and things have changed so much since then that the theory must surely be obsolete.

Contrary to such assertions, comparative advantage remains an important economic concept. At any one time—because comparative advantage is reflected in international relative prices, and these relative prices determine what goods a country will import

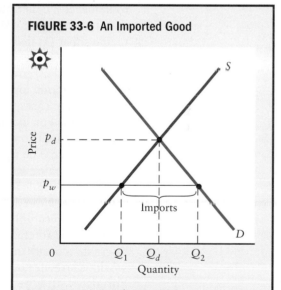

FIGURE 33-6 An Imported Good

Imports occur whenever there is excess demand domestically at the world price. The domestic demand and supply curves are D and S, respectively. The domestic price in the absence of foreign trade is p_d, with Q_d produced and consumed domestically. The world price of p_w is less than p_d. At the world price Q_2 is demanded, whereas Q_1 is supplied domestically. The excess of domestic demand over domestic supply is satisfied through imports.

and what it will export—the operation of the price system will result in trade that follows the current pattern of comparative advantage. For example, if Canadian costs of producing steel are particularly low relative to other Canadian costs, Canada will export steel at international prices (which it does). If Canada's costs of producing textiles are particularly high relative to other Canadian costs, Canada will import textiles at international prices (which it does). Thus, there is no reason to change the view that David Ricardo long ago expounded: *Current comparative advantage is a major determinant of trade under free-market conditions.*

What has changed, however, is economists' views about the *determinants* of comparative advantage. It is now clear that current comparative advantage is more open to change by private entrepreneurial activities and by government policy than used to be thought. Thus, what is obsolete is the belief that a country's current pattern of comparative advantage, and hence its current pattern of imports and exports, must be accepted as given and unchangeable.

> The theory that comparative advantage is a major influence on trade flows is not obsolete, but the theory that comparative advantage is completely determined by forces beyond the reach of decisions made by private firms and by public policy has been discredited.

One caveat should be noted. It is one thing to observe that it is *possible* for governments to influence a country's pattern of comparative advantage. It is quite another to conclude that it is *advisable* for them to try. The case in support of a specific government intervention requires that (1) there is scope for governments to improve on the results achieved by the free market, (2) the costs of the intervention be less than the value of the improvement to be achieved, and (3) governments will actually be able to carry out the required interventionist policies (without, for example, being sidetracked by considerations of electoral advantage).

In many cases, governments have succeeded in creating important comparative advantages. For example, the Taiwanese government virtually created that nation's electronics industry and then passed it over to private hands in which it became a world leader. The government of Singapore created a computer-parts industry that became a major world supplier. However, there are also many examples in which governments failed in their attempts to create comparative advantage. The government of the United Kingdom tried to create a comparative advantage in computers and failed miserably, wasting much public money in the process. The government of Ireland tried to create a comparative advantage in automobile production and failed to create more than a modest, unprofitable industry that eventually disappeared. The world is strewn not only with spectacular successes, which show that it can be done, but also with abject failures, which show that the attempt to do so is fraught with many dangers.

One other comment needs to be made regarding the relevance of the concept of comparative advantage. For understanding international trade in copper wire, lumber, oil, bananas, coffee, textiles, and many other relatively simple products, the concept of comparative advantage is very useful. In some manufacturing industries, however, where products have dozens or perhaps hundreds of components, the determinants of trade flows are more complex than the theory of comparative advantage suggests. For example, it is difficult to see why Canada might have a comparative advantage in the production of automobile transmissions but not in automobile brake systems or air-conditioning systems. Yet, the automobile sector is perhaps the best example of an industry in which a firm's "supply chain" includes products made by several other firms in several countries. *Applying Economic Concepts 33-2* discusses how the forces of globalization and economies of scale have led to the development of complex global supply chains.

The Terms of Trade

We have seen that world production can be increased when countries specialize in the production of the goods for which they have a comparative advantage and then trade with one another. We now ask: How will these gains from specialization and trade be shared among countries? The division of the gain depends on what is called the **terms of trade**, which relate to the quantity of imported goods that can be obtained per unit of goods exported. The terms of trade are measured by the ratio of the price of exports to the price of imports.

A rise in the price of imported goods, with the price of exports unchanged, indicates a *fall in the terms of trade*; it will now take more exports to buy the same quantity of imports. Similarly, a rise in the price of exported goods, with the price of imports unchanged, indicates a *rise in the terms of trade*; it will now take fewer exports to buy the same quantity of imports. Thus, the ratio of these prices measures the amount of imports that can be obtained per unit of goods exported.

The terms of trade can be illustrated with a country's production possibilities boundary, as shown in Figure 33-7. The figure shows the hypothetical case in which Canada can produce only wheat and cloth. As we saw earlier, the slope of Canada's production possibilities boundary shows the relative opportunity costs of producing the two goods in Canada. A steep production possibilities boundary indicates that only a small amount of cloth must be given up to get more wheat; thus cloth is relatively costly and wheat is relatively cheap. A flatter production possibilities boundary indicates that a larger amount of cloth must be given up to get more wheat; thus cloth is relatively cheap and wheat is relatively expensive. Thus, the slope of the production possibilities boundary in Figure 33-7 shows the relative price of cloth (in terms of wheat) that Canada faces in the absence of international trade.

If, through international trade, Canada has access to different relative prices, Canada will be led to specialize in the production of one good or the other. In Figure 33-7, we show a case in which the world relative price of cloth is lower than the relative price Canada would have if it did not trade. (This lower *world* relative price of cloth reflects the fact that other countries can produce cloth more cheaply than Canada.) Faced with a lower relative price of cloth, Canada ends up specializing in the production of the relatively high-priced product (wheat), and importing the relatively low-priced product (cloth). This point of specialization is point *S* in Figure 33-7.

terms of trade The ratio of the average price of a country's exports to the average price of its imports.

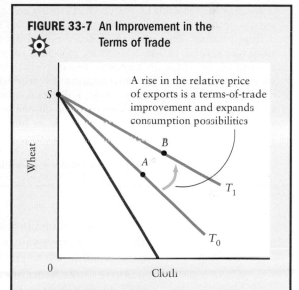

FIGURE 33-7 An Improvement in the Terms of Trade

A rise in the relative price of exports is a terms-of-trade improvement and expands consumption possibilities

Changes in the terms of trade lead to changes in a country's consumption possibilities. The hypothetical production possibilities boundary is shown for Canada. With international trade at relative prices T_0, Canada specializes in the production of wheat, producing at point *S*, but is able to consume at a point like *A*. It pays for its imports of cloth with its exports of wheat.

If the price of wheat rises relative to the price of cloth, production remains at *S* but the line T_1 shows Canada's new consumption possibilities. Consumption can now take place at a point like *B* where consumption of both wheat and cloth has increased. The increase in the terms of trade makes Canada better off because of the increase in consumption possibilities.

APPLYING ECONOMIC CONCEPTS 33-2

Comparative Advantage and Global Supply Chains

The discussion of comparative advantage developed in this chapter applies easily to many products with one or even a few components. One can sensibly speak of national comparative advantages for whole products, such as Costa Rica for bananas, Canada for sawn logs, Chile for copper, Korea for steel, and Saudi Arabia for oil.

For many manufactured products, however, and even for some resource-based products and service industries, production is carried out in complex and integrated "global supply chains," with a product's several different components being produced in different countries and often by different firms. In this world of "integrative trade," it is no longer clear where some products are "made," even though one could easily determine where each of the product's many components is produced and where they are all assembled into a final product. This method of decentralized production has several causes. First, the existence of scale economies provides an incentive for individual firms to reduce their costs by concentrating the production of each individual component in a different specialized large factory. Second, differences in national wage rates for various types of labour provide an incentive for these production facilities to be located in different countries. Third, the current very low costs of communication and transportation make it possible to

coordinate supply chains globally and ship parts and final products anywhere at low cost. (If fuel becomes expensive enough to make transport costs a significant part of total costs, it will become economic to do much more production closer to final markets than it has been over the last several decades.)

Consider three examples. The famous iPod sold by Apple clearly says "Made in China" on the box, but most of the value from its design occurs in the United States, many electronic components come from Korea and Japan, and only the iPod's final assembly occurs in China. Apple chooses to locate assembly in China, using components manufactured elsewhere, because by doing so it can maximize its product quality and minimize costs.

Bombardier jet aircraft designed and assembled in Canada also involve global supply chains. Fuselage parts come from Japan, the wings are produced in Northern Ireland, engines are imported from the United States, and the avionics are engineered in the United States but sourced from Asian suppliers. Bombardier adopts this business model because costs can be reduced and quality maximized by using specialty suppliers at each link in the global supply chain.

Such global supply chains even exist for some products that appear to have few "components," such as fish. For example, a Canadian firm may hire a Chilean trawler to fish in the Indian Ocean, land its catch in Malaysia where it is

---

The *green* lines in the figure show alternative values of the world relative prices—that is, alternative values for Canada's terms of trade. A rise in the terms of trade indicates a fall in the relative price of cloth (or a rise in the relative price of wheat). This increase in the terms of trade is shown as an upward rotation of the green line from T_0 to T_1. A reduction in the terms of trade is shown as a downward rotation in the green line, from T_1 to T_0.

It should be clear from Figure 33-7 why changes in the terms of trade are important. Suppose the international relative prices are initially given by T_0. Canada specializes in the production of wheat (point S) but consumes at some point like A, where it finances its imports of cloth with exports of wheat. Now suppose there is a shift in world demand toward wheat and away from cloth, and this leads to an increase in the relative price of wheat. The terms of trade increase to T_1 and, with unchanged production at point S, Canada can now afford to consume at a point like B where consumption of both wheat and cloth has increased.

A rise in a country's terms of trade is beneficial because it expands the country's consumption possibilities.

frozen, and then send it to China for further processing before it is finally sold to Japanese wholesalers. This supply chain can operate in two different ways. First, the Canadian firm can manage the entire process but leave ownership to the individual firms at each stage of the supply chain. In this case, the Canadian firm is providing management expertise and earns a return that in the data appears as a Canadian export of services. Alternatively, the Canadian firm can own the product but merely hire the services of the required firms at each stage of the supply chain. In this case, the return to the Canadian firm will be significantly higher because of the need to manage the various risks involved in production, such as unexpected swings in prices, natural disasters, and human error.

There are three implications for how we think about international trade in the presence of integrated global supply chains. First, we should not view countries as having comparative advantages in entire products but rather in the specific productive activities that take place along the global supply chain. China may not have a comparative advantage in "producing" consumer electronics but may have one in assembling them. Canada may not have a comparative advantage in "producing" jet aircraft but may have one in designing them.

Second, these comparative advantages may not be long-lasting because they are sensitive to changes in the economic environment and in technology. For example, significant changes in national corporate tax rates, exchange rates, and wages for factory workers will generally change the optimal location for the production of a product's various components. Also, newly developed technologies for producing existing products and creating new ones can alter the patterns of comparative advantage significantly and quickly.

Third, traditional data on international trade does not capture the extent of integration in global supply chains. The iPod assembled in China and exported to the United States appears simply as a Chinese export; but the significant value generated by the U.S.-based design team may appear in no trade statistics whatsoever. It follows that the measured flow of a country's exports of some products does not necessarily correspond closely with the level of local economic activity (production and employment) actually generated by those products. Even in Canada's resource sector, the domestic content of exports is not 100 percent, although it is typically more than 75 percent, meaning that up to one-quarter of the value of the final exported product comes from imported inputs. In most manufacturing industries, however, the domestic content of exports is 50 percent or lower, and in the automobile industry it is only 35 percent.

The presence of such highly integrated global supply chains indicates the importance of two-way trade in the Canadian economy: Access to low-price and high-quality imports is as crucial to the Canadian economy as is our access to world markets where we can sell our intermediate and final products.

Conversely, a reduction in the price of a country's exports (relative to the price of its imports) is harmful for a country. In Figure 33-7, this is shown as a change of the terms of trade from T_1 to T_0. Even though production may remain unchanged, the range of goods available to be consumed falls, and this reduction in consumption possibilities leads to an overall loss of welfare.

How do we measure the terms of trade in real economies? Because international trade involves many countries and many products, we cannot use the simple ratio of the prices of two goods as in Figure 33-7. The basic principle, however, is the same. A country's terms of trade are computed as an index number:

$$\text{Terms of trade} = \frac{\text{Index of export prices}}{\text{Index of import prices}} \times 100$$

A rise in the index is referred to as a *favourable* change in a country's terms of trade (sometimes called a terms of trade *improvement*). A decrease in the index of the terms of trade is called an *unfavourable* change (or a terms of trade *deterioration*). For example, the sharp rise in oil prices in the 1970s led to large unfavourable shifts in the terms of trade of oil-importing countries. When oil prices fell sharply in the mid-1980s, the terms of trade of oil-importing countries changed favourably. The converse was true for oil-exporting countries.

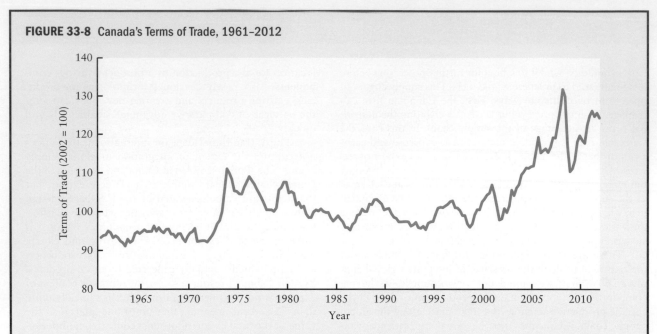

FIGURE 33-8 Canada's Terms of Trade, 1961–2012

Canada's terms of trade have been quite variable over the past 50 years. The data shown are Canada's terms of trade—the ratio of an index of Canadian export prices to an index of Canadian import prices. As the relative prices of lumber, oil, wheat, electronic equipment, textiles, fruit, and other products change, the terms of trade naturally change.

(*Source:* Author's calculations using data from Statistics Canada, CANSIM database, Table 380-0003.)

Canada's terms of trade since 1961 are shown in Figure 33-8. As is clear, the terms of trade are quite variable, reflecting frequent changes in the relative prices of different products. Note the dramatic increase (improvement) in Canada's terms of trade in the early 1970s, reflecting the large increase in oil prices caused by OPEC's output restrictions. Since Canada is a net exporter of oil, its terms of trade improve when the price of oil increases. An even larger increase occurred in the 2002–2008 period, when the world prices of most commodities, especially energy-related commodities, increased sharply.

SUMMARY

33.1 The Gains from Trade

- Country A has an *absolute* advantage over Country B in the production of a specific product when the absolute cost of the product is less in Country A than in Country B.
- Country A has a *comparative* advantage over Country B in the production of a specific good if the forgone output of other goods is less in Country A than in Country B.
- Comparative advantage occurs whenever countries have different opportunity costs of producing particular goods. World production of all products can be increased if each country transfers resources into the production of the products for which it has a comparative advantage.
- Trade allows all countries to obtain the goods for which they do not have a comparative advantage at a lower

opportunity cost than they would face if they were to produce all products for themselves; specialization and trade therefore allow all countries to have more of all products than they could have if they tried to be self-sufficient.
- A nation that engages in trade and specialization may also realize the benefits of economies of large-scale production and of learning by doing.
- Traditional theories regarded comparative advantage as largely determined by natural resource endowments that are difficult to change. Economists now know that some comparative advantages can be acquired and consequently can be changed. A country may, in this view, influence its role in world production and trade.

33.2 The Determination of Trade Patterns

- The law of one price says that the national prices of tradable goods (net of taxes and tariffs) must differ by no more than the costs of transporting these goods between countries. After accounting for these transport costs, there is a single world price.
- Countries will export a good when the world price exceeds the price that would exist in the country if there were no trade. The low no-trade price reflects a low opportunity cost and thus a comparative advantage in that good. Thus, countries export goods for which they have a comparative advantage.
- Countries will import a good when the world price is less than the price that would exist in the country if

there were no trade. The high no-trade price reflects a high opportunity cost and thus a comparative disadvantage in that good. Thus, countries import goods for which they have a comparative disadvantage.
- The terms of trade refer to the ratio of the prices of goods exported to the prices of those imported. The terms of trade determine the quantity of imports that can be obtained per unit of exports.
- A favourable change in the terms of trade—a rise in export prices relative to import prices—is beneficial for a country because it expands its consumption possibilities.

KEY CONCEPTS

Interpersonal, interregional, and international specialization
Absolute advantage and comparative advantage
Opportunity cost and comparative advantage

The gains from trade: specialization, scale economies, and learning by doing
The sources of comparative advantage
Factor endowments

Acquired comparative advantage
The law of one price
The terms of trade

STUDY EXERCISES

MyEconLab   Make the grade with MyEconLab: Study Exercises marked in red can be found on MyEconLab. You can practise them as often as you want, and most feature step-by-step guided instructions to help you find the right answer.

1. Fill in the blanks to make the following statements correct.

   a. The "gains from trade" refers to the increased _____ caused by specialization and trade.

   b. Suppose Argentina can produce one kilogram of beef for $2.50 and Brazil can produce one kilogram of beef for $2.90. Argentina is said to have a(n) _____ in beef production over Brazil. The gains from trade do *not* depend on _____.

   c. Comparative advantage is based on _____ rather than absolute costs.

   d. It is possible for a country to have a comparative advantage in some good and a(n) _____ in none.

   e. If all countries specialize in the production of goods for which they have a comparative advantage, then world output will _____.

   f. If opportunity costs are the same in all countries, there is no _____ and no possibility of _____.

2. Fill in the blanks to make the following statements correct.

   a. Such a product as coffee beans is cheaply transported and is traded around the world. The law of _____ tells us that it will tend to have _____ worldwide price.

   b. If the domestic price of copper wire in Canada (in the absence of trade) is $20 per unit and the world price is $24 per unit, then Canada will have an excess _____, which it will then _____. The opportunity cost of producing copper wire in Canada is _____ than the opportunity cost of producing it in the rest of the world.

   c. Canada will import goods for which it has an excess _____ at the world price. In the absence of trade, the _____ price of these goods would be less than the _____ price.

   d. A rise in Canada's terms of trade means that the average price of Canada's _____ has risen compared with the average price of Canada's _____. This change is referred to as a terms of trade _____.

   e. The terms of trade determine the quantity of _____ that can be obtained per unit of _____.

3. The following diagram shows the production possibilities boundary for Arcticland, a country that produces only two goods, ice and fish. Labour is the only factor of production. Recall that a linear production possibilities boundary reflects *constant* opportunity costs for both products.

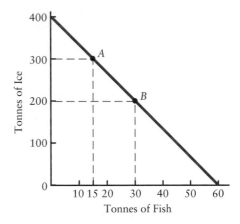

   a. Beginning at any point on Arcticland's production possibilities boundary, what is the opportunity cost of producing 10 more tonnes of fish?

   b. Beginning at any point on Arcticland's production possibilities boundary, what is the opportunity cost of producing 100 more tonnes of ice?

4. The following table shows the production of wheat and corn in Brazil and Mexico. Assume that both countries have one million acres of arable land.

	Brazil	Mexico
Wheat	90 bushels per acre	50 bushels per acre
Corn	30 bushels per acre	20 bushels per acre

   a. Which country has the absolute advantage in wheat? In corn? Explain.

   b. What is the opportunity cost of producing an extra bushel of wheat in Brazil? In Mexico? Which country has the comparative advantage in wheat production? Explain.

c. Which country has the comparative advantage in corn production? Explain.

d. Explain why one country can have an absolute advantage in both goods but cannot have a comparative advantage in both goods.

e. On a scale diagram with wheat on the horizontal axis and corn on the vertical axis, draw each country's production possibilities boundary.

f. What is shown by the slope of each country's production possibilities boundary? Be as precise as possible.

5. The following diagrams show the production possibilities boundaries for Canada and France, both of which produce only two goods, wine and lumber.

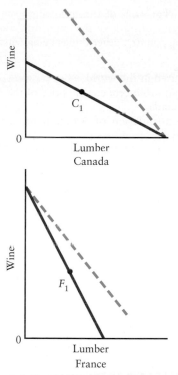

a. Which country has the comparative advantage in lumber? Explain.

b. Which country has the comparative advantage in wine? Explain.

c. Suppose Canada and France are initially not trading with each other and are producing at points C_1 and F_1, respectively. Suppose when trade is introduced, the free-trade relative prices are shown by the slope of the dashed line. Show in the diagrams which combination of goods each country will now produce.

d. In this case, what will be the pattern of trade for each country?

6. The following diagrams show the Canadian markets for newsprint and machinery, which we assume to be competitive.

a. Suppose there is no international trade. What would be the equilibrium price and quantity in the Canadian newsprint and machinery markets?

b. Now suppose Canada is open to trade with the rest of the world and the world price of newsprint is higher than the price of newsprint from part (a). Show in the diagram the quantities of domestic consumption and production and the quantity of newsprint that is either exported or imported.

c. Similarly, suppose the world price of machinery is lower than the price of machinery from part (a). Show in the diagram the quantity of domestic consumption and production and the quantity of machinery that is either exported or imported.

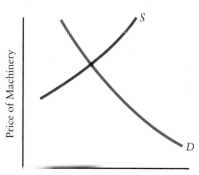

7. The table below shows indexes for the prices of imports and exports over several years for a hypothetical country.

Year	Import Prices	Export Prices	Terms of Trade
2008	90	110	____
2009	95	87	____
2010	98	83	____
2011	100	100	____
2012	102	105	____
2013	100	112	____
2014	103	118	____

a. Compute the terms of trade in each year for this country and fill in the table.

b. In which years do the terms of trade improve?

c. In which years do the terms of trade deteriorate?

d. Explain why a terms of trade "improvement" is good for the country.

8. For each of the following events, explain the likely effect on Canada's terms of trade. Your existing knowledge of Canada's imports and exports should be adequate to answer this question.

a. A hurricane damages much of Brazil's coffee crop.

b. OPEC countries succeed in significantly restricting the world supply of oil.

c. Several new large copper mines come into production in Chile.

d. A major recession in Southeast Asia reduces the world demand for pork.

e. Russia, a large producer of wheat, experiences a massive drought that reduces its wheat crop by more than 30 percent.

f. Three major potash-producing firms form a cartel and restrict the world's output of potash.

9. When the North American Free Trade Agreement (NAFTA) was being negotiated in the early 1990s, there was a great deal of debate. One critic argued that "it can't be in our interest to sign this deal; Mexico gains too much from it." What does the theory of the gains from trade have to say about that criticism?

10. Adam Smith saw a close connection between a nation's wealth and its ability and willingness "freely to engage" in trade with other countries.

a. Based on what you have learned in this chapter, what is the connection?

b. Explain why trading with countries that are "most different" from our own is likely to generate the most benefits. Which differences are of central importance?

c. Under what circumstances are there *no* benefits from a country specializing and trading with other countries?

d. Illustrate the argument from part (c) in a simple diagram of a country's production possibilities boundary.

11. Predict what each of the following events would do to the terms of trade of the importing country and the exporting country, other things being equal.

a. A blight destroys a large part of the coffee beans produced in the world.

b. Korean producers cut the price of the steel they sell to Canada.

c. General inflation of 4 percent occurs around the world.

d. Violation of OPEC output quotas leads to a sharp fall in the price of oil.

Trade Policy

CONDUCTING business in a foreign country is not always easy. Differences in language, in local laws and customs, and in currency often complicate transactions. Our concern in this chapter, however, is not with these complications but with government policy toward international trade, which is called *trade policy*. At one extreme is a policy of free trade—that is, an absence of any form of government interference with the free flow of international trade. Any departure from free trade designed to protect domestic industries from foreign competition is called *protectionism*.

We begin by briefly restating the case for free trade and then go on to examine various valid and invalid arguments that are commonly advanced for some degree of protection. We then explore some of the methods commonly used to restrict trade, such as tariffs and quotas. Finally, we examine the many modern institutions designed to foster freer trade on either a global or a regional basis. In particular, we discuss the North American Free Trade Agreement (NAFTA) and the World Trade Organization (WTO).

34.1 Free Trade or Protection?

Today, most governments accept the proposition that a relatively free flow of international trade is desirable for the health of their individual economies. But heated debates still occur over trade policy. Should a country permit the *completely* free flow of international trade, or should it use policies to restrict the flow of trade and thereby protect its local producers from foreign competition? If some protection is desired, should it be achieved by tariffs or by non-tariff barriers? **Tariffs** are taxes designed to raise the price of imported goods. **Non-tariff barriers (NTBs)** are policies other than tariffs designed to reduce the flow of imports; examples are import quotas and customs procedures that are deliberately more cumbersome than necessary.

tariff A tax applied on imports of goods or services.

non-tariff barriers (NTBs) Restrictions other than tariffs designed to reduce imports.

The Case for Free Trade

The gains from trade were presented in Chapter 33. Comparative advantages arise whenever countries have different opportunity costs. Free trade encourages all countries to specialize in producing products in which they have a comparative advantage. This pattern of specialization maximizes world production and hence maximizes average world living standards (as measured by the world's per capita GDP).

However, free trade does not necessarily make *everyone* better off than they would be in its absence. For example, reducing an existing tariff often results in individual groups receiving a smaller share of a larger world output so that they lose even though the average person gains. If we ask whether it is *possible* for free trade to improve everyone's living standards, the answer is yes because the larger total value of output that free trade generates could, at least in principle, be divided up in such a way that every individual is better off. If we ask whether free trade always does so in practice, however, the answer is, not necessarily.

> Free trade makes the country as a whole better off, even though it may not make every individual in the country better off.

In today's world, a country's products must stand up to international competition if they are to survive. Over even as short a period as a few years, firms that do not develop new products and new production methods fall seriously behind their foreign competitors. If one country protects its domestic firms by imposing a tariff, those firms are likely to become complacent about the need to adopt new technologies, and over time they will become less competitive in international markets. As the technology gap between domestic and foreign firms widens, the tariff wall will provide less and less protection. Eventually, the domestic firms will succumb to foreign competition. Meanwhile, domestic living standards will fall relative to foreign ones.

Given that any country can be better off by specializing in those goods in which it has a comparative advantage, one might wonder why most countries of the world continue in some way to restrict the flow of trade. Why do tariffs and other barriers to trade continue to exist two centuries after Adam Smith and David Ricardo argued the case for free trade? Is there a valid case for some protection?

The Case for Protection

A country engages in trade **protection** whenever it uses policies that restrict the flow of trade in a way that favours domestic firms over their foreign competitors. There are several valid arguments for protection, including

- promoting diversification
- protecting specific groups
- improving the terms of trade
- protecting infant industries
- earning economic profits in foreign markets

We will discuss each of these arguments briefly. Note that the first two arguments generally involve achieving some worthy objective at the cost of a *reduction* in national income. The last three arguments are reasons for protection as a means of *increasing* a country's national income.

Countries whose economies are based on the production of only a few goods face risks from fluctuations in world prices. For this reason, protection to promote diversification may be viewed as desirable.

Promoting Diversification For a very small country, specializing in the production of only a few products—though dictated by comparative advantage—might involve risks that the country does not want to take. One such risk is that technological advances may render its basic product obsolete. Another risk, especially for countries specialized in producing a small range of agricultural products, is that swings in world prices lead to large swings in national income. By using protectionist policies, the government can encourage the creation of some domestic industries that may otherwise not exist. The cost is the loss of national income associated with devoting resources to production in industries in which there is no domestic comparative advantage. The benefit is that overall national income and employment become less volatile.

protection Any government policy that interferes with free trade in order to protect domestic firms and workers from foreign competition.

Protecting Specific Groups Although specialization according to comparative advantage will maximize *average* per capita GDP, some specific groups may have higher incomes under protection than under free trade. Of particular interest in Canada and the United States has been the effect that greater international trade has on the incomes of unskilled workers.

Consider the ratio of skilled workers to unskilled workers. There are plenty of both types throughout the world. Compared with much of the rest of the world, however, Canada has more skilled and fewer unskilled people. When trade is expanded because of a reduction in tariffs, Canada will tend to export goods made by its abundant skilled workers and import goods made by unskilled workers. (This is the basic prediction of the *factor endowment theory* of comparative advantage that we discussed in Chapter 33.) Because Canada is now exporting more goods made by skilled labour, the domestic demand for such labour rises. Because Canada is now importing more goods made by unskilled labour, the domestic demand for such labour falls. This specialization according to comparative advantage raises average Canadian living standards, but it will also tend to raise the wages and employment prospects of skilled Canadian workers relative to the wages of unskilled Canadian workers.

If increasing trade has these effects, then reducing trade by erecting protectionist trade barriers can have the opposite effects. Protectionist policies may raise the incomes of unskilled Canadian workers, giving them a larger share of a smaller total GDP. The conclusion is that trade restrictions can improve the earnings of one group whenever the restrictions increase the demand for that group's services. This is done, however, at the expense of a reduction in *overall* national income and hence the country's average living standards.

This analysis is important because it reveals both the grain of truth and the dangers that lie behind the resistance to policies that promote free trade on the part of some labour groups and some organizations whose main concern is with the poor.

> Social and distributional concerns may lead to the rational adoption of protection-ist policies. But the cost of such protection is a reduction in the country's *average* living standards.

Improving the Terms of Trade Tariffs can be used to change the terms of trade in favour of a country that makes up a large fraction of the world demand for some product that it imports. By restricting its demand for that product through a tariff, it can force down the price that foreign exporters receive for that product. The price paid by domestic consumers will probably rise but as long as the increase is less than the tariff, foreign suppliers will receive less per unit. For example, a 20 percent U.S. tariff on the import of Canadian softwood lumber might raise the price paid by U.S. consumers by 12 percent and lower the price received by Canadian suppliers by 8 percent (the difference between the two prices being received by the U.S. Treasury). This reduction in the price received by the Canadian suppliers of a U.S. import is a terms-of-trade improvement for the United States (and a terms-of-trade deterioration for Canada).

Note that not all countries can improve their terms of trade by levying tariffs on imported goods. A *necessary* condition is that the importing country has *market power*—in other words, that its imports represent a large proportion of total world demand for the good in question, so that its restrictive trade policies lead to a decline in the world price of its imports. Small countries, like Canada, are not large enough importers of any good to have a significant effect on world prices. For small countries, therefore, tariffs cannot improve their terms of trade.

> Large countries can sometimes improve their terms of trade (and thus increase their national income) by levying tariffs on some imported goods; small countries cannot.

Protecting Infant Industries The oldest valid arguments for protection as a means of raising living standards concern economies of scale or learning by doing. It is usually called the **infant industry argument**. An infant industry is nothing more than a new, small industry. If such an industry has large economies of scale or the scope for learning by doing, costs will be high when the industry is small but will fall as the industry grows. In such industries, the country that first enters the field has a tremendous advantage. A developing country may find that in the early stages of development, its industries are unable to compete with established foreign rivals. A trade restriction may protect these industries from foreign competition while they "grow up." When they are large enough, they will be able to produce as cheaply as their larger foreign rivals and thus be able to compete without protection.

Most of the now industrialized countries developed their industries initially under quite heavy tariff protection. (In Canada's case, the National Policy of 1876 established

infant industry argument The argument that new domestic industries with potential for economies of scale or learning by doing need to be protected from competition from established, low-cost foreign producers so that they can grow large enough to achieve costs as low as those of foreign producers.

a high tariff wall behind which many Canadian industries developed and thrived for many years.) Once the industrial sector was well developed, these countries reduced their levels of protection, thus moving a long way toward free trade. Electronics in Taiwan, automobiles in Japan, commercial aircraft in Europe (specifically the consortium of European governments that created Airbus), and shipbuilding in South Korea are all examples in which protection of infant industries was successful. In each case, the national industry, protected by its home government, developed into a major player in the global marketplace.

One practical problem with this argument for protection is that some infants "never grow up." Once the young firm gets used to operating in a protected environment, it may resist having that protection disappear, even though all economies of scale may have been achieved. This is as much a political problem as an economic one. Political leaders must therefore be careful before offering protection to infant industries because they must recognize the political difficulties involved in removing that protection in the future. The countries that were most successful in having their protected industries eventually grow up and succeed in fierce international competition were those, such as Taiwan and South Korea, that ruthlessly withdrew support from unsuccessful infants within a specified time period.

Earning Economic Profits in Foreign Markets Another argument for protectionist policies is to help create an advantage in producing or marketing some product that is expected to generate economic profits through its sales to foreign consumers. If protection of the domestic market, which might include subsidizing domestic firms, can increase the chance that one of the domestic firms will become established and thus earn high profits, the protection may pay off. The economic profits earned in foreign markets may exceed the cost to domestic taxpayers of the protection. This is the general idea of *strategic trade policy.*

Opponents of strategic trade policy argue that it is nothing more than a modern version of age-old and faulty justifications for tariff protection. Once all countries try to be strategic, they will all waste vast sums trying to break into industries in which there is no room for most of them. Domestic consumers would benefit most, they say, if their governments let other countries engage in this game. Consumers could then buy the cheap, subsidized foreign products and export traditional non-subsidized products in return. The opponents of strategic trade policy also argue that democratic governments that enter the game of picking and backing winners are likely to make more bad choices than good ones. One bad choice, with all of its massive development costs written off, would require that many good choices also be made in order to make the equivalent in profits that would allow taxpayers to break even overall.

An ongoing dispute between Canada and Brazil illustrates how strategic trade policy is often difficult to distinguish from pure protection. The world's two major producers of regional jets are Bombardier, based in Montreal, and Embraer SA, based in Brazil. For several years, each company has accused its competitor's government of using illegal subsidies to help the domestic company sell jets in world markets. Brazil's Pro-Ex program provides Embraer's customers with low-interest loans with which to purchase Embraer's jets. Export Development Canada (EDC)

For many years, Canada and Brazil have been in a trade dispute centred on each country's alleged support of aerospace manufacturers. Canada's Bombardier and Brazil's Embraer both receive considerable financial assistance from their respective federal governments. Taxpayers in each country foot the bill.

provides similar loans to Bombardier's customers. In addition, the Canadian government's Technology Partnerships program (which recently expired) subsidized research and development activities in high-tech aerospace and defence companies. As the leading Canadian aerospace company, Bombardier benefited significantly from this program.

Between 1996 and 2002 there were several complaints brought to the World Trade Organization (WTO) by both the Canadian and Brazilian governments. In various rulings the WTO determined that both governments were using illegal subsidy programs to support their aerospace firms. Both countries, however, naturally view their respective programs as necessary responses to the other country's subsidization. Many economists believe that an agreement to eliminate both programs would leave a "level playing field," while saving Brazilian and Canadian taxpayers a considerable amount of money. As of 2012, however, both countries continue to support their respective aerospace firms and both sets of taxpayers continue to foot the bill.

For a list and discussion of many ongoing trade disputes, see the WTO's website: www.wto.org.

> A country can potentially increase its national income by protecting infant industries and by subsidizing "strategic" firms. Unless carefully applied, however, such policies can end up being redistributions from consumers and taxpayers to domestic firms, without any benefit to overall living standards.

Invalid Arguments for Protection

We have seen that free trade is generally beneficial for a country overall even though it does not necessarily make every person better off. We have also seen that there are some situations in which there are valid arguments for restricting trade. For every valid argument, however, there are many invalid arguments—many of these are based, directly or indirectly, on the misconception that in every transaction there is a winner and a loser. Here we review a few arguments that are frequently heard in political debates concerning international trade.

Keep the Money at Home This argument says that if I buy a foreign good, I have the good and the foreigner has the money, whereas if I buy the same good locally, I have the good and our country has the money, too. This argument is based on a common misconception. It assumes that domestic money actually goes abroad physically when imports are purchased and that trade flows only in one direction. But when Canadian importers purchase Japanese goods, they do not send dollars abroad. They (or their financial agents) buy Japanese yen and use them to pay the Japanese manufacturers. They purchase the yen on the foreign-exchange market by giving up dollars to someone who wants to use them for expenditure in Canada. Even if the money did go abroad physically—that is, if a Japanese firm accepted a bunch of Canadian $100 bills—it would be because that firm (or someone to whom it could sell the dollars) wanted them to spend in the only country where they are legal tender—Canada.

Canadian currency ultimately does no one any good except as purchasing power in Canada. It would be miraculous if Canadian money could be exported in return for real goods. After all, the Bank of Canada has the power to create as much new Canadian money as it wants (at almost zero direct cost). It is only because Canadian money can buy Canadian products and Canadian assets that others want it.

Protect Against Low-Wage Foreign Labour This argument says that the products of low-wage countries will drive Canadian products from the market, and the high Canadian standard of living will be dragged down to that of its poorer trading partners. For example, if Canada imports cotton shirts from India, higher-cost Canadian textile firms may go out of business and Canadian workers may be laid off. This argument says that Canada is worse off *overall* by trading with India. Is this really true?

As a prelude to considering this argument, think what the argument would imply if taken out of the context of countries and applied instead to individuals, where the same principles govern the gains from trade. Is it impossible for a rich person to gain by trading with a poor person? Would Bill Gates and Warren Buffett really be better off if they did all their own typing, gardening, cooking and cleaning? No one believes that a rich person gains nothing by trading with those who are less rich.

Why, then, must a rich group of people lose when they trade with a poor group? "Well," some may say, "the poor group will price its goods too cheaply." Consumers gain, however, when they can buy the same goods at a lower price. If Chinese, Mexican, or Indian workers earn low wages and the goods they produce are sold at low prices, Canadians will gain by obtaining imports at a low cost in terms of the goods that must be exported in return. The cheaper our imports are, the better off we are in terms of the goods and services available for domestic consumption.

As we said earlier in this chapter, *some* Canadians may be better off if Canada places high tariffs on the import of goods from China or India or other developing nations. In particular, if the goods produced in these countries compete with goods made by unskilled Canadian workers, then those unskilled workers will be better off if a Canadian tariff protects their firms and thus their jobs. But Canadian income overall—that is, average per capita real income—will be higher when there is free trade.

Exports Are Good; Imports Are Bad Exports create domestic income; imports create income for foreigners. Surely, then, it is desirable to encourage exports by subsidizing them and to discourage imports by taxing them. This is an appealing argument, but it is incorrect.

Exports raise GDP by adding to the value of domestic output and income, but they do not add to the value of domestic consumption. The standard of living in a country depends on the level of consumption, not on the level of income. In other words, income is not of much use except that it provides the means for consumption.

If exports really were "good" and imports really were "bad," then a fully employed economy that managed to increase exports without a corresponding increase in imports ought to be better off. Such a change, however, would result in a reduction in current standards of living because when more goods are sent abroad but no more are brought in from abroad, the total goods available for domestic consumption must fall.

The living standards of a country depend on the goods and services consumed in that country. The importance of exports is that they provide the resources required to purchase imports, either now or in the future.

Create Domestic Jobs It is sometimes said that an economy with substantial unemployment, such as Canada during and immediately after the 2009 recession, provides an exception to the case for freer trade. Suppose tariffs or import quotas reduce the imports of Japanese cars, Indian textiles, German kitchen equipment, and Polish vodka. Surely, the argument goes, these polices will create more employment in Canadian industries producing similar products. This may be true but it will also *reduce* employment in other industries.

The Japanese, Indians, Germans, and Poles can buy products from Canada only if they earn Canadian dollars by selling their domestically produced goods and services to

LESSONS FROM HISTORY 34-1

Trade Protection and Recession

With the onset of the Great Depression in 1929, governments in many countries responded to internal political pressures to protect domestic jobs. In the United States, Congress passed the Smoot-Hawley Tariff Act in June 1930, legislation that raised tariffs on hundreds of different imported products. At the time, a petition against the legislation was signed by 1028 economists who argued that such tariffs would be costly for America and would initiate a "tariff war" between the United States and its trading partners, thereby worsening the economic situation.

In retrospect, the economists were clearly correct. Dozens of countries protested the increase in U.S. tariffs but then retaliated by increasing their own tariffs. Here in Canada, Liberal Prime Minister Mackenzie King raised tariffs on imported U.S. products and lowered them on imports from the rest of the British Empire. Confident that he would earn the public's support for his aggressive actions, he promptly called a federal election. But the Conservatives under R.B. Bennett argued that the Liberal actions were far too timid, and the voters apparently agreed. The Liberals were soundly defeated, Bennett

became prime minister, and Canadian tariffs on U.S. products were raised even further.

Economists today agree that the widespread increase in tariffs in the 1930s contributed significantly to a reduction in global trade and made the economic situation worse. In January of 1929, before the onset of the Depression, the volume of world trade was $5.3 billion. Four years later, at the depth of the Depression, world trade had collapsed to $1.8 billion, a reduction of 66 percent. The net effect, instead of increasing employment in any country, was to shift jobs from efficient export industries to inefficient domestic industries, supplying local markets in place of imports.

When the most recent worldwide recession began in the wake of the 2008 global financial crisis, world leaders were mindful of this important lesson from the Great Depression. When meeting in Washington, D.C., to coordinate their policy responses, the leaders of the world's largest developed and developing countries (the G20 group of countries) publicly committed to not raising any tariffs for at least one year.

Despite this commitment, however, protectionist measures soon emerged. In the United States, the fiscal stimulus package passed by Congress included a "buy American"

Canada (or by borrowing dollars from Canada).[1] The decline in their sales of cars, textiles, kitchen equipment, and vodka will decrease their purchases of Canadian lumber, software, banking services, and holidays. Jobs will be lost in Canadian export industries and gained in industries that formerly faced competition from imports. The major long-term effect is that the same amount of total employment in Canada will merely be redistributed among industries. In the process, average living standards will be reduced because employment expands in inefficient import-competing industries and contracts in efficient exporting industries.

A country that imposes tariffs in an attempt to create domestic jobs risks starting a "tariff war" with its trading partners. Such a trade war can easily leave every country worse off, as world output (and thus income) falls significantly. An income-reducing trade war followed the onset of the Great Depression in 1929 as many countries increased tariffs to protect their domestic industries in an attempt to stimulate domestic production and employment. Most economists agree that this trade war made the Great Depression worse than it otherwise would have been. *Lessons from History 34-1* discusses this relationship between tariffs and recession and how it resurfaced during the major recession that followed the 2008 global financial crisis.

---

[1] They can also get dollars by selling to other countries and then using their currencies to buy Canadian dollars. But this intermediate step only complicates the transaction; it does not change its fundamental nature. Other countries must have earned the dollars by selling goods to Canada or borrowing from Canada.

clause requiring that any funds from the package not be spent on imported construction materials. Similar kinds of protection were built in to the fiscal stimulus packages in China and some European countries. Canada and other major trading nations were understandably concerned by these actions and soon began threatening their own retaliatory measures. The Canadian government went to great lengths to argue that U.S. trade protection would not only hurt Canada but would also hurt the United States by raising prices for American consumers, thus making economic recovery more difficult.

While the lessons from history were being forgotten by some political leaders, a few prominent voices were arguing the dangers of increased trade protection. The World Bank issued a report in March 2009 indicating that in the previous four months world leaders had proposed or implemented 78 different protectionist measures. The president of the World Bank urged leaders to rethink these policies: "Leaders must not heed the siren-song of protectionist fixes, whether for trade, stimulus packages or bailouts. . . . Economic isolationism can lead to a negative spiral of events such as those we saw in the 1930s, which made a bad situation much, much worse."

Canadian Prime Ministers Bennett (left) and Mackenzie King (right) both learned in the 1930s that protectionist policies often make better politics than economics.

34.2 Methods of Protection

We now go on to explore the effects of two specific protectionist policies. Both cause the price of the imported good to rise and the quantity demanded by domestic consumers to fall. They differ, however, in how they achieve these results.

Tariffs

A tariff, also called an *import duty*, is a tax on imported goods. For example, consider a Canadian firm that wants to import cotton T-shirts from India at $5 per shirt. If the Canadian government levies a 20 percent tariff on imported cotton shirts, the Canadian firm pays $5 to the Indian exporter *plus* $1 (20 percent of $5) in import duties to the Canada Revenue Agency. The immediate effect of a tariff is therefore to increase the domestic price of the T-shirt to $6. This price increase has important implications for domestic consumers as well as domestic producers. The effect of a tariff is shown in Figure 34-1.

The initial effect of the tariff is to raise the domestic price of the imported product above its world price by the amount of the tariff. Imports fall. The price received on domestically produced units rises, as does the quantity produced domestically. On both counts, domestic producers earn more. However, the cost of producing the extra production at

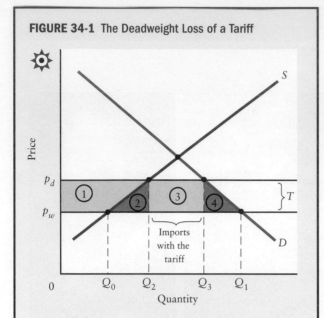

FIGURE 34-1 The Deadweight Loss of a Tariff

A tariff imposes a deadweight loss for the importing country. Before the tariff, the price in the domestic economy is the world price, p_w. Imports are Q_0Q_1. With a tariff of $\$T$ per unit, the domestic price rises to p_d. Domestic consumption falls to Q_3, and consumer surplus falls by areas ① + ② + ③ + ④. Domestic production rises to Q_2 and producer surplus increases by area ①. Imports fall to Q_2Q_3, and the government collects tariff revenue equal to area ③. The sum of areas ② and ④ represents the deadweight loss of the tariff.

home exceeds the price at which it could be purchased on the world market. Thus, the benefit to domestic producers comes at the expense of domestic consumers. Indeed, domestic consumers lose on two counts: First, they consume less of the product because its price rises, and second, they pay a higher price for the amount that they do consume. This extra spending ends up in two places: The extra that is paid on all units produced at home goes to domestic producers, and the extra that is paid on units still imported goes to the government as tariff revenue.

The overall loss to the domestic economy from levying a tariff is best seen in terms of the changes in consumer and producer surplus. Before the tariff, consumer surplus was equal to the entire area below the demand curve and above the price line at p_w.

After the tariff, the price increase leads to less consumption and less consumer surplus. The loss of consumer surplus is the sum of the areas ①, ②, ③, and ④ in Figure 34-1. As domestic producers respond to the higher domestic price by increasing their production and sales, they earn more producer surplus, equal to area ①. Finally, the taxpayers gain the tariff revenue equal to area ③. This is simply a redistribution of surplus away from consumers toward taxpayers. In summary:

Loss of consumer surplus	= ① + ② + ③ + ④
Gain of producer surplus	= ①
Gain of tariff revenue	= ③
Net loss in surplus	= ② + ④

The overall effect of the tariff is therefore to create a deadweight loss to the domestic economy equal to areas ② plus ④. Domestic consumers are worse off, while domestic firms and taxpayers are better off. But the net effect is a loss of surplus for the economy as a whole. This is the overall cost of levying a tariff.

> A tariff imposes costs on domestic consumers, generates benefits for domestic producers, and generates revenue for the government. But the overall net effect is negative; a tariff generates a deadweight loss for the economy.

Quotas and Voluntary Export Restrictions (VERs)

import quota A limit set on the quantity of a foreign commodity that may be imported in a given time period.

voluntary export restriction (VER) An agreement by an exporting country to limit the amount of a good exported to another country.

The second type of protectionist policy directly restricts the quantity of imports of a specific product. A common example is the **import quota**, by which the importing country sets a maximum quantity of some product that may be imported each year. Another measure is the **voluntary export restriction** (VER), an agreement by an exporting country to limit the amount of a product that it sells to the importing country.

Figure 34-2 shows that a quantity restriction and a tariff have similar effects on domestic consumers and producers—they both raise domestic prices, increase domestic production, and reduce domestic consumption. But a direct quantity restriction is actually *worse* than a tariff for the importing country because the effect of the quantity restriction is to raise the price received by the foreign suppliers of the good. In contrast, a tariff leaves the foreign suppliers' price unchanged and instead generates tariff revenue for the government of the importing country.

> Import quotas and voluntary export restrictions (VERs) impose larger deadweight losses on the importing country than do tariffs that lead to the same level of imports.

Canada, the United States, and the European Union have used VERs extensively, and the EU makes frequent use of import quotas. Japan has been pressured into negotiating several VERs with Canada, the United States, and the EU in order to limit sales of some of the Japanese goods that have had the most success in international competition. For example, in 1983, the United States and Canada negotiated VERs whereby the Japanese government agreed to restrict total sales of Japanese cars to these two countries for three years. When the agreements ran out in 1986, the Japanese continued to restrict their automobile sales by unilateral voluntary action. Japan's readiness to restrict its exports to North America reflects the high profits that Japanese automobile producers were making under the system of VERs, as explained in Figure 34-2. In recent years, such VERs have become less important because Japan's major automobile producers have established manufacturing plants in Canada.

Tariffs Versus Quotas: An Application

The dispute that raged for several years between Canada and the United States over the exports of Canadian softwood lumber (spruce, pine, fir, cedar) exports illustrates an important distinction between tariffs and quotas. The United States protected its softwood lumber industry in two ways:

- by imposing tariffs on U.S. imports of Canadian softwood lumber
- by pressuring Canadian governments to place quotas on Canadian exports to the United States

Analysis of Figure 34-1 and 34-2 reveals that the choice between tariffs and quotas matters greatly for Canadian producers.

In the case of a U.S. tariff on imported Canadian softwood lumber, Figure 34-1 illustrates the U.S. market. An import tariff raises the domestic price for U.S. lumber users and also increases the profits of U.S. lumber producers. Canadian lumber producers are harmed because there is less demand for their product at the unchanged world

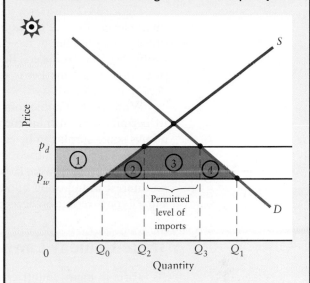

FIGURE 34-2 The Deadweight Loss of an Import Quota

An import quota drives up the domestic price and imposes a deadweight loss on the importing country. With free trade, the domestic price is the world price, p_w. Imports are Q_0Q_1. If imports are restricted to only Q_2Q_3 (through either quotas or VERs), the domestic price must rise to the point where the restricted level of imports just satisfies the domestic excess demand—this occurs only at P_d. The rise in price and reduction in consumption reduces consumer surplus by areas ① + ② + ③ + ④. Domestic producers increase their output as the domestic price rises, and producer surplus increases by area ①. Area ③ does not accrue to the domestic economy; instead this area represents extra producer surplus for the foreign firms that export their product to this country. The net effect of the quota or VER is a deadweight loss for the importing country of areas ② + ③ + ④. Import quotas are therefore worse than tariffs for the importing country.

price. Area ③ in the figure represents U.S. tariff revenue collected on the imports of Canadian lumber—revenue that accrues to the United States government.

Figure 34-2 illustrates the U.S. market for softwood lumber when a quota is placed on the level of Canadian exports (U.S. imports). As with the tariff, the restricted supply of Canadian lumber to the U.S. market drives up the price to U.S. users and also raises profits for U.S. producers. But with a quota there is an important difference: The higher price in the U.S. market is received by the Canadian lumber producers, as shown by area ③ in the figure.

While a tariff and quota may lead to the same reduced volume of exports, the tariff permits some surplus to be captured by the importing country, whereas the quota allows some surplus to be captured by the exporting country (area ③ in both cases). In the U.S.–Canadian softwood lumber dispute, both tariffs and quotas were used. And while both systems were to be preferred *overall* by a system of free trade, Canada had an interest in imposing quotas on Canadian lumber exporters rather than having the same export reduction accomplished by a U.S. tariff.

Trade-Remedy Laws and Non-tariff Barriers

As tariffs in many countries were lowered over the years since the Second World War, countries that wanted to protect domestic industries began using, and often abusing, a series of trade restrictions that came to be known as *non-tariff barriers* (NTBs). The original purpose of some of these barriers was to remedy certain legitimate problems that arise in international trade and, for this reason, they are often called *trade-remedy laws*. All too often, however, such laws are misused and over time become powerful means of simple protection.

Dumping Selling a product in a foreign country at a lower price than in the domestic market is known as **dumping**. For example, if U.S.-made cars were sold for less in Canada than in the United States, the U.S. automobile firms would be said to be *dumping*. Dumping is a form of price discrimination studied in the theory of monopoly (see Chapter 10). Most governments have antidumping duties designed to protect their own industries against what is viewed as unfair foreign pricing practices.

dumping The practice of selling a commodity at a lower price in the export market than in the domestic market for reasons unrelated to differences in costs of servicing the two markets.

> Dumping, if it lasts indefinitely, can be a gift to the receiving country. Its consumers get goods from abroad at lower prices than they otherwise would.

Dumping is more often a temporary measure, designed to get rid of unwanted surpluses, or a predatory attempt to drive competitors out of business. In either case, domestic producers complain about unfair foreign competition. In both cases, it is accepted international practice to levy *antidumping duties* on foreign imports. These duties are designed to eliminate the discriminatory elements in their prices.

Unfortunately, antidumping laws have been evolving over the past three decades in ways that allow antidumping duties to become barriers to trade and competition rather than to provide redress for genuinely unfair trading practices.

Several features of the antidumping system that is now in place in many countries make it highly protectionist. First, any price discrimination between national markets is classified as dumping and is subject to penalties. Thus, prices in the producer's domestic market become, in effect, minimum prices below which no sales can be made in foreign markets, whatever the nature of demand in the domestic and foreign markets. Second, many countries' laws calculate the "margin of dumping" as the difference between the price that is charged in that country's market and the foreign producer's average cost. Thus, when there is a global slump in some industry so that the profit-maximizing price for all producers is below average cost, foreign producers can be convicted of dumping. This gives domestic producers enormous protection whenever the market price falls temporarily below average cost. Third, law in the United States (but not in all other countries) places the onus of proof on the accused. Facing a charge of dumping, a foreign producer must prove that the charge is unfounded. Fourth, U.S. antidumping duties are imposed with no time limit, so they often persist long after foreign firms have altered the prices that gave rise to them.

> Antidumping laws were first designed to permit countries to respond to predatory pricing by foreign firms. More recently, they have been used to protect domestic firms against any foreign competition.

Countervailing Duties A **countervailing duty** is a tariff imposed by one country designed to offset the effects of specific subsidies provided by foreign governments to their exporting firms. For example, if the German government provided subsidies to its firms that produce and export machine tools, the Canadian government might respond by imposing a countervailing duty—a tariff—on the imports of German machine tools designed to "level the playing field" between German and Canadian firms in that industry. Countervailing duties, which are commonly used by the U.S. government but much less so elsewhere, provide another case in which a trade-remedy law can become a covert method of protection.

There is no doubt that countervailing duties have sometimes been used to counteract the effects of foreign subsidies. Many governments complain, however, that countervailing duties are often used as thinly disguised protection. At the early stages of the development of countervailing duties, only subsidies whose prime effect was to distort trade were possible objects of countervailing duties. Even then, however, the existence of equivalent domestic subsidies was not taken into account when decisions were made to put countervailing duties on subsidized imports. Thus, the United States levies some countervailing duties against foreign goods even though the foreign subsidy is less than the domestic (U.S.) subsidy. This does not create a level playing field.

Over time, the type of subsidy that is subject to countervailing duties has evolved until almost any government program that affects industry now risks becoming the object of a countervailing duty. Because all governments, including most U.S. state governments, have programs that provide direct or indirect assistance to industry, the potential for the use of countervailing duties as thinly disguised trade barriers is enormous.

> **countervailing duty** A tariff imposed by one country designed to offset the effects of specific subsidies provided by foreign governments.

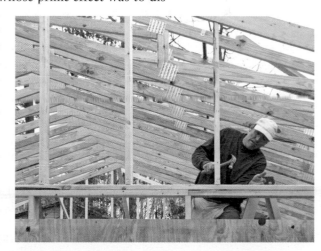

Softwood lumber (spruce, pine, and fir) is used extensively in North America for the framing of houses and small buildings. For many years, the United States levied countervailing duties on Canadian softwood lumber exports, alleging that Canadian provinces unfairly subsidized production. In 2006, the Canadian and U.S. governments reached an agreement to end the dispute.

> Countervailing duties can be used to offset the effects of foreign export subsidies, but often they are nothing more than thinly disguised protection.

The best-known example in Canada of a U.S. countervailing duty is the 27 percent duty imposed on U.S. imports of Canadian softwood lumber between 2001 and 2005. The U.S. government's claim was that Canadian provincial governments provided a subsidy to domestic lumber producers by charging artificially low *stumpage fees*—the fees paid by the companies to cut trees on Crown land. In 2006, the U.S. government agreed to eliminate the countervailing duty but only if restrictions were placed on Canadian lumber exports. Thus, a tariff was replaced by a combination of an export quota and an export tax.

34.3 Current Trade Policy

In the remainder of the chapter, we discuss trade policy in practice. We start with the many international agreements that govern current trade policies and then look in a little more detail at the NAFTA.

Before 1947, in the absence of any international agreement, any country was free to impose tariffs on its imports. However, when one country increased its tariffs, the action often triggered retaliatory actions by its trading partners. During the Great Depression in the 1930s, widespread increases in protection occurred as many countries sought to raise their employment and output by raising its tariffs. The end result was lowered efficiency, less trade, and a deeper economic decline. Since the end of the Second World War, much effort has been devoted to reducing tariff barriers, both on a multilateral and on a regional basis.

The GATT and the WTO

One of the most notable achievements of the post–Second World War era was the creation in 1947 of the General Agreement on Tariffs and Trade (GATT). The principle of the GATT was that each member country agreed not to make unilateral tariff increases. This prevented the outbreak of "tariff wars" in which countries raised tariffs to protect particular domestic industries and to retaliate against other countries' tariff increases. The GATT has since been replaced by the World Trade Organization (WTO), which continues the work of the GATT.

The Uruguay Round The Uruguay Round—the final round of trade agreements under the GATT—was completed in 1994 after years of negotiations. It reduced world tariffs by about 40 percent. A significant failure of these negotiations was the absence of an agreement to liberalize trade in agricultural goods. The European Union and Canada both resisted an agreement in this area. The EU's Common Agricultural Policy (CAP) provides general support for most of its agricultural products, many of which are exported. Canada, which has free trade in many agricultural commodities, was concerned about maintaining its "supply management" over a number of industries including poultry, eggs, and dairy products. These schemes restrict domestic production and push domestic prices well above world levels. The Canadian government made (and continues to make) such high domestic prices possible by imposing very high tariffs on the import of foreign products. In the case of imported milk and cheese, for example, the Canadian tariffs are *well over 200 percent*.

Despite the failure to achieve free trade in agricultural products, the Uruguay Round was generally viewed as a success. Perhaps its most significant achievement was the creation of the World Trade Organization (WTO) to replace the GATT. An important part of the WTO is its formal dispute-settlement mechanism. This mechanism allows countries to take cases of alleged trade violations—such as illegal subsidies or tariffs—to the WTO for a formal ruling, and obliges member countries to follow the ruling. The WTO's dispute-settlement mechanism is thus a significant step toward a "rules-based" global trading system.

The Doha Round Agriculture also plays a central role in the ongoing round of trade negotiations, which began in Doha, Qatar, in 2000. Many issues were discussed and negotiated over the next several years, ranging from competition policy to antidumping and from environmental policies to electronic commerce. But one of the most contentious issues is agriculture. The WTO member governments claim to be committed to reducing export subsidies and other forms of government support to agriculture. Movements in this direction will naturally cause political friction within the developed economies that currently protect and support their agricultural producers. A failure to reduce agricultural support in the developed countries, however, will increase the political frictions that already exist between developed and developing nations. For the many developing countries that have natural comparative advantages in agricultural products and that cannot afford to compete in a "subsidy war" with the developed countries, the liberalization of trade in agricultural products is crucial. They see the Doha round as central to their economic development.

International trade negotiations sometimes generate considerable grass-roots opposition. There is some opposition to the reduction of tariffs in developed countries and some controversy regarding the appropriate way to address the concerns of developing countries.

Opposition to the WTO Despite the WTO's successes in recent years, the organization has many critics. One common criticism is that the WTO's process of negotiating trade agreements pays insufficient attention to environmental and labour standards, especially as they exist in the developing countries. Another criticism is that the presence of the WTO does not prevent some rich and powerful countries from ruthlessly pursuing their own interests, often to the detriment of economic conditions in weaker countries. *Applying Economic Concepts 34-1* addresses some of the often-heard criticisms of the WTO and argues that, as imperfect as the institution may be, it holds out much promise for continued progress in trade liberalization.

For more information on the WTO, see its website at www. wto.org.

Regional Trade Agreements

Regional agreements seek to liberalize trade over a much smaller group of countries than the WTO membership. Three standard forms of regional trade-liberalizing agreements are *free trade areas, customs unions*, and *common markets*.

A **free trade area** (**FTA**) is the least comprehensive of the three. It allows for tariff-free trade among the member countries, but it leaves each member free to establish its own trade policy with respect to other countries. As a result, members are required to maintain customs points at their common borders to make sure that imports into the free trade area do not all enter through the member that is levying the lowest tariff on each item. They must also agree on *rules of origin* to establish when a good is made in a member country and hence is able to pass tariff-free across their borders, and when it

free trade area (FTA) An agreement among two or more countries to abolish tariffs on trade among themselves while each remains free to set its own tariffs against other countries.

APPLYING ECONOMIC CONCEPTS 34-1

Does the WTO Do More Harm Than Good?

There are many critics of the World Trade Organization. Extremists argue that all institutions supporting globalization should be abolished. Other critics admit that globalization is inevitable but say that the WTO is so faulty in providing a rules-based system that it does more harm than good.

Supporters of the WTO argue that it is the best hope for poor countries that would be most oppressed in a lawless world in which rich countries, particularly the United States and members of the European Union, could behave as they wanted. Rather than allowing the poorer countries to flounder in a lawless world, the WTO provides a rules-based regime and has a dispute-settlement function that has heard more than 300 cases. Even if the rich countries do exert undue power over the negotiations, at least the WTO meetings provide a forum for poor nations to speak out and broker alliances. The alternative—no voice in a no-rules system—would be much worse.

Critics often respond that while the existence of the dispute-settlement mechanism may be beneficial, the enforcement of those settlements is undermined by disparities in economic power. Nations with large economies can use trade sanctions against small nations, but the small nation that attempts the same often inflicts the most harm on its own economy. Supporters of the WTO agree that this *is* a major defect, but the dispute-settlement mechanism has accomplished much, and to discard it because of imperfect enforcement would be a great loss. What is needed is *reform*—with larger economies agreeing to graduated enforcement mechanisms, including stiffer penalties for themselves.

Critics also claim that the WTO is a failure because it does not permit the imposition of trade sanctions against countries that pollute their own environments or exploit their own workers. But the poorest countries, many of whom are strong WTO supporters, fear that advanced countries would use environmental and labour standards written into the body of trade agreements as disguised non-tariff barriers. To the poorer countries it would be "policy imperialism" to argue that they should be forced to accept the standards of environmental and labour protection that the rich countries can only now afford. Nonetheless, environmental and labour protections are being written into some new trade agreements, and it remains to be seen if they will work beneficially or harmfully—or not at all.

Critics also complain that the WTO is undemocratic. In response, supporters point out that it is representatives of sovereign nations, usually elected ones, who conduct the negotiations, and that any agreements must be ratified by respective national parliaments before they come into effect. It is unlikely that any organization able to achieve agreement among 155 member-country governments could be any more democratic while still being effective.

Finally, some critics claim that the WTO is simply a tool for those who advocate a doctrinaire form of laissez-faire capitalism. It is true that some WTO supporters believe that unfettered free markets can meet all social requirements. A far larger number of supporters, however, believe that the market system needs government involvement if it is to meet societal needs for social justice and growth. The vast majority of supporters agree that most, if not all, trade restrictions are harmful and that the WTO, with its mission of continued trade liberalization, can create significant benefits to rich and poor countries alike.

---

is imported from outside the FTA and hence is subject to tariffs when it crosses borders within the FTA. The three countries in North America formed a free-trade area when they created the NAFTA in 1994.

In recent years, Canada has signed bilateral free-trade agreements with Israel, Chile, Costa Rica, Peru, Colombia, and Jordan and is currently negotiating with Japan and the European Union. In 2012, Canada gained admission to the Trans-Pacific Partnership (TPP), a new proposed free-trade agreement between several Pacific-rim countries, including Australia, New Zealand, the United States, Chile, Singapore, Vietnam, and others. The details of the agreement are currently being negotiated. Canada's ongoing efforts to negotiate free-trade agreements with many countries reveal a desire on the part of the Canadian government to diversify Canada's pattern of trade. See *Applying Economic Concepts 34-2* for more on this important topic.

A **customs union** is a free trade area in which the member countries agree to establish a common trade policy with the rest of the world. Because they have a common trade policy,

customs union A group of countries that agree to have free trade among themselves and a common set of barriers against imports from the rest of the world.

the members need neither customs controls on goods moving among themselves nor rules of origin. Once a good has entered any member country it has met the common rules and regulations and paid the common tariff and so it may henceforth be treated the same as a good that is produced within the union. An example of a customs union is Mercosur, an agreement linking Argentina, Brazil, Paraguay, and Uruguay. A **common market** is a customs union that also has free movement of labour and capital among its members. The European Union is by far the most successful example of a common market.

common market A customs union with the added provision that labour and capital can move freely among the members.

Trade Creation and Trade Diversion

A major effect of regional trade liberalization is to alter the pattern of production and trade as countries reallocate their resources toward the production of goods in which they have a comparative advantage. Economists divide the effects on trade into two categories: *trade creation* and *trade diversion*. These concepts were first developed by Jacob Viner, a Canadian-born economist who taught at the University of Chicago and Princeton University in the first half of the twentieth century.

Trade creation occurs when producers in one member country find that they can export products to another member country that previously were produced there because of tariff protection. For example, when the North American Free Trade Agreement (NAFTA) eliminated most cross-border tariffs among Mexico, Canada, and the United States, some U.S. firms found that they could undersell their Canadian competitors in some product lines, and some Canadian firms found that they could undersell their U.S. competitors in other product lines. As a result, specialization occurred, and new international trade developed among the three countries.

trade creation A consequence of reduced trade barriers among a set of countries whereby trade within the group is increased and trade with the rest of the world remains roughly constant.

Trade creation represents efficient specialization according to comparative advantage.

Trade diversion occurs when exporters in one member country *replace* foreign exporters as suppliers to another member country. For example, trade diversion occurs when U.S. firms find that they can undersell competitors from the rest of the world in the Canadian market, not because they are the cheapest source of supply, but because their tariff-free prices under NAFTA are lower than the tariff-burdened prices of imports from other countries. This effect is a gain to U.S. firms and Canadian consumers of the product. U.S. firms get new business and therefore they clearly gain. Canadian consumers buy the product at a lower, tariff-free price from the U.S. producer than they used to pay to the third-country producer (with a tariff), and so they are also better off. But Canada as a whole is worse off as a result of the trade diversion. Canada is now buying the product from a U.S. producer at a higher price with no tariff. Before the agreement, it was buying from a third-country producer at a lower price (and collecting tariff revenue).

trade diversion A consequence of reduced trade barriers among a set of countries whereby trade within the group replaces trade that used to take place with countries outside the group.

From the global perspective, trade diversion represents an inefficient use of resources.

The main argument *against* regional trade agreements is that the costs of trade diversion may outweigh the benefits of trade creation. While recognizing this possibility, many economists believe that regional agreements, especially among only a few countries, are much easier to negotiate than multilateral agreements through the WTO. In addition, regional agreements may represent effective *incremental* progress in what is a very lengthy process of achieving global free trade.

APPLYING ECONOMIC CONCEPTS 34-2

The Transformation of Canada's International Trade

Look at Canada's location on a world map and you will immediately see why the vast majority of Canada's international trade has long been (and likely will always be) with the United States. In 2011, for example, trade with the United States accounted for 72 percent of Canadian merchandise exports and 61 percent of merchandise imports.*

Many economists argue that Canada would benefit by increasing the share of its total trade that occurs with countries other than the United States. With greater diversification in its trade, Canada would be less vulnerable to downturns in the U.S. economy. This concern increased during the 2008–2009 global recession, which hit the U.S. economy especially hard and from which the United States was still slowly recovering five years later. Other economists acknowledge the benefits of greater diversification but argue that the more important goal should be to increase the *overall volume* of Canadian trade. According to the theory of comparative advantage that we reviewed in Chapter 33, a greater volume of trade suggests greater gains from trade, with implications for growth in average material living standards.

Greater trade between Canada and the "emerging" markets of Asia, South America, and parts of Africa may help Canada achieve both outcomes—greater trade diversification and an expansion of overall trade flows.

Events in the United States

Canada's trade with the United States declined significantly during the 2008–2009 global recession.

_____
*A country's "merchandise" trade is the trade in goods, excluding the trade in services. In a typical year in Canada, roughly three-quarters of total trade is merchandise trade.

For more on Canada's export performance and some of the challenges faced by Canadian exporting firms, see *EDC Global Export Forecast*, published annually by Export Development Canada, www.edc.ca.

Merchandise exports to the United States fell from $370 billion in 2008 to $331 billion in 2011, while merchandise imports fell and then recovered to their 2008 level of $281 billion. But Canadian exports to the United States had been declining well before the recession. The collapse in the high-tech sector in 2000–2001, the heightened security concerns in the aftermath of the 2001 terrorist attacks in New York and Washington, and the dramatic appreciation of the Canadian dollar from 2004 through 2008 (driven mostly by rising commodity prices) all put immense strains on Canadian exports to the United States. For many Canadian exporting firms, the decade of the 2000s presented severe challenges.

How did Canada's exporters respond to these challenges? Unable to compete, thousands of businesses closed their doors, and others relocated to other countries. Many survivors, however, met the challenges through an extraordinary transformation. Faced with little or no growth in traditional markets, many Canadian exporters launched into riskier emerging markets and discovered their potential for growth. Canadian merchandise exports to the emerging markets grew from just 4 percent of total merchandise exports in 2000 to 11 percent by 2011. Although still a small share of Canada's total trade, Canadian trade with the emerging world accounted for the majority of the *growth* of total merchandise exports over this period. Having tasted success in these markets, there is good reason to expect Canadian firms to continue this expansion.

Canadian Trade Policy

The ongoing transformation in Canadian trade is also driven by changes in government policy. After the creation of the Canada–U.S. Free Trade Agreement in 1989, its expansion into NAFTA to include Mexico in 1994,

The North American Free Trade Agreement

The NAFTA dates from 1994 and is an extension of the 1989 Canada–U.S. Free Trade Agreement (FTA). It established a free trade area, as opposed to a customs union; each member country retains its own external trade policy, and rules of origin are needed to determine when a good is made within North America and thus allowed to move freely among the members.

National Treatment The fundamental principle that guides the NAFTA is that of *national treatment*. The principle of national treatment is that individual countries are free to establish any laws they want, with the sole proviso that these laws must not and the Canada–Chile free-trade agreement in 1997, Canadian trade negotiations virtually ceased for a decade. Adding to the inactivity was the glacial pace of discussions within WTO's Doha Round. As a result, Canada's trade pattern across various countries was relatively stable.

In 2007, however, Canadian trade negotiators began a flurry of activity. Between 2007 and 2011, five bilateral free-trade agreements were finalized by the Canadian government, and discussions on a number of others were initiated. Ongoing negotiations with the European Union, India, China, Japan, and the members of the new Trans-Pacific Partnership could potentially lead to enormous changes in Canada's trade opportunities over the near future.

Projections

Canada's trade landscape is likely to be quite different in just a few years. The accompanying figure shows the change in Canada's merchandise trade (exports plus imports) as a share of GDP with the United States, the combined emerging economies, and all other countries, since 2000. The actual increase in the relative importance of trade with the emerging economies between 2000 and 2011 is clear. Though not shown in the figure, the projections for the future are equally striking: Export Development Canada projects that if current trends continue, emerging markets will account for over 30 percent of Canada's total trade by 2025.

Greater trade with the emerging world will have the effect of increasing Canada's overall trade volumes and also of diversifying Canada's trade away from the United States. The first will lead to greater gains from trade; the second will reduce our dependence on the U.S. economy and increase our trade linkages with countries projected to have higher rates of future economic growth. Canada stands to gain on both fronts.

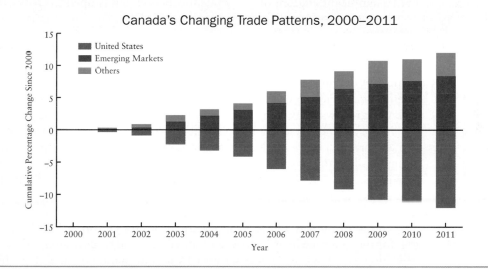

Canada's Changing Trade Patterns, 2000–2011

discriminate on the basis of nationality. For example, Canada can choose to have stringent laws against dumping pollutants in waterways or against the emission of noxious gases into the atmosphere. The principle of national treatment requires that the Canadian government enforce these laws equally on all firms located in Canada, independent of their ownership or nationality. It is against the NAFTA conditions to apply more stringent laws to foreign-owned firms than to domestic firms, or vice versa. Canada can also choose to impose strict product standards related to the chemical content of paint or the nutritional content of foods, but again the NAFTA condition requires that such laws be applied to products independent of where they are produced. For example, it would be against the NAFTA conditions to require a specific level of fuel efficiency on imported cars but not on those cars produced and sold in Canada.

The principle of national treatment allows each member country a maximum of policy independence while preventing national policies from being used as trade barriers. In the absence of national treatment, Canada could impose stringent environmental or product standards on the products of *foreign* firms only and thereby offer effective protection to its domestic firms who need only satisfy less stringent standards.

Other Major Provisions There are several other major provisions in the NAFTA.

1. All tariffs on trade between Canada, the United States, and Mexico were eliminated as of 2010.

2. The principle of national treatment (described above) applies to foreign investment once it enters a country, but each country can screen foreign investment before it enters.

3. Some restrictions on trade and investment are not eliminated by the agreement. In Canada's case, the main examples are supply-managed agricultural products and cultural industries such as magazine and book publishing.

4. Trade in most non-agricultural service industries is liberalized and subject to the principle of national treatment.

5. A significant amount of government procurement is open to cross-border bidding, though a large part is still exempt from NAFTA.

Dispute Settlement From Canada's point of view, by far the biggest setback in the negotiations for the Canada–U.S. FTA was the failure to obtain agreement on a common regime for countervailing and antidumping duties. In view of that failure, no significant attempt was made to deal with this issue in the subsequent NAFTA negotiations. The U.S. Congress was unwilling to abandon the unilateral use of these powerful weapons.

In the absence of such a multilateral regime, a NAFTA dispute-settlement mechanism was created. Under it, the justifications required for the levying of antidumping and countervailing duties are subject to review by a panel of Canadians, Americans, and Mexicans. This international review replaces appeal through the domestic courts. The panel has the power to suspend any duties until it is satisfied that the domestic laws have been correctly and fairly applied.

The establishment of the dispute-settlement mechanism in NAFTA was path breaking: for the first time in its history, the United States agreed to submit the administration of its domestic laws to *binding* scrutiny by an international panel that often contains a majority of foreigners.

Results The Canada–U.S. FTA aroused a great debate in Canada. Indeed, the Canadian federal election of 1988 was fought almost entirely on the issue of free trade. Supporters looked for major increases in the security of existing trade from U.S. protectionist attacks and for a growth of new trade. Detractors predicted a flight of firms to the United States, the loss of many Canadian jobs, and even the demise of Canada's political independence.

By and large, however, both the Canada–U.S. FTA and the NAFTA agreements worked out just about as expected by their supporters. Industry restructured in the direction of greater export orientation in all three countries, and trade creation occurred. The flow of trade among the three countries increased markedly, but especially so between Canada and the United States. As the theory of trade predicts, specialization

For information about the NAFTA, go to the website for the NAFTA Secretariat: www.nafta-sec-alena.org.

APPLYING ECONOMIC CONCEPTS 34-3

Canadian Wine: A Free-Trade Success Story

Before the Canada–U.S. FTA was signed in 1989, great fears were expressed over the fate of the Canadian wine industry, located mainly in Ontario and British Columbia. It was heavily tariff protected and, with a few notable exceptions, produced mainly cheap, low-quality products. Contrary to most people's expectations, rather than being decimated, the industry now produces a wide variety of high-quality products, some of which win international competitions.

The nature of the pre-FTA protection largely explains the dramatic turnaround of the Canadian wine industry once the FTA took effect. First, Canadian wine producers had been protected by high tariffs on imported wine but were at the same time required by law to produce wine by using only domestically grown grapes. The domestic grape growers, however, produced varieties of grapes not conducive to the production of high-quality wines, and with a captive domestic market, they had little incentive to change their behaviour. Thus, Canadian wine producers concentrated their efforts on "hiding" the attributes of poor-quality grapes rather than enhancing the attributes of high-quality grapes. The result was low-quality wine.

The second important aspect of the protection was that the high Canadian tariff was levied on a per unit rather than on an *ad valorem* basis. For example, the tariff was expressed as so many dollars per litre rather than as a specific percentage of the price. Charging a tariff by the litre gave most protection to the low-quality wines with low value per litre. The higher the per-litre value of the wine, the lower the percentage tariff protection. For example, a $5-per-litre tariff would have the following effects. A low-quality imported wine valued at $5 per

litre would have its price raised to $10, a 100 percent increase in price, whereas a higher-quality imported wine valued at $25 per litre would have its price increased to $30, only a 20 percent increase in price.

Responding to these incentives, the Canadian industry concentrated on producing low-quality wines. The market for these wines was protected by the nearly prohibitive tariffs on competing low-quality imports and by the high prices charged for high-quality imports. In addition, protection was provided by many hidden charges that the various provincial governments' liquor monopolies levied in order to protect local producers.

When the tariff was removed under the FTA, the incentives were to move up-market, producing much more value per hectare of land. Fortunately, much of the Canadian wine-growing land in the Okanagan Valley in B.C. and the Niagara Peninsula in Ontario is well suited for growing the grapes required for good wines. Within a very few years, and with some government assistance to grape growers to make the transition from low-quality to high-quality grapes, Canadian wines were competing effectively with imported products in the medium-quality range. B.C. and Ontario wines do not yet reach the quality of major French wines in the $50 to $70 (per bottle) range, but they compete very effectively in quality with wines in the $15 to $25 range and sometimes even higher up the quality scale.

The success of the wine industry is a good example of how tariffs can distort incentives and push an industry into a structure that makes it dependent on the tariff. Looking at the pre-FTA industry, very few people suspected that it would be able to survive, let alone become a world-class industry.

occurred in many areas, resulting in more U.S. imports of some product lines from Canada and more U.S. exports of other goods to Canada. In 1988, before the Canada–U.S. FTA took effect, Canada exported $85 billion in goods to the United States and imported $74 billion from the United States. By 2011, the value of Canada–U.S. trade had almost quadrupled—Canadian exports of goods to the United States had increased to $331 billion and imports from the United States had increased to $281 billion. (Note that these figures exclude trade in services; with services included, the increase in Canada–U.S. trade between 1988 and 2011 would be even larger.)[2]

---

[2] These data are in nominal dollars, which naturally grow over time along with real GDP and the price level. As a share of GDP, however, Canadian trade with the United States has also grown substantially. In 1988, exports and imports of goods (excluding services) with the United States were each roughly 13 percent of Canadian GDP; by 2011, they were each almost 18 percent of Canadian GDP.

It is hard to say how much trade diversion there has been and will be in the future. The greatest potential for trade diversion is with Mexico, which competes in the Canadian and U.S. markets with a large number of products produced in other low-wage countries. Southeast Asian exporters to the United States and Canada have been worried that Mexico would capture some of their markets by virtue of having tariff-free access denied to their goods. Most estimates predict, however, that trade creation will dominate over trade diversion.

Most transitional difficulties were initially felt in each country's import-competing industries, just as theory predicts. Such an agreement as the NAFTA brings its advantages by encouraging a movement of resources out of protected but inefficient import-competing industries, which decline, and into efficient export industries, which expand because they have better access to the markets of other member countries. Southern Ontario and parts of Quebec had difficulties as some traditional exports fell and labour and capital were shifting to sectors where trade was expanding. By the late 1990s, however, Southern Ontario was booming again and its most profitable sectors were those that exported to the United States.

There were also some pleasant surprises resulting from free trade. Two Canadian industries that many economists expected to suffer from the FTA and the NAFTA were winemaking and textiles. Yet both of these industries prospered as Canadian firms improved quality, productivity, and benefited from increased access to the huge U.S. market. *Applying Economic Concepts 34-3* discusses the success of the Canadian wine industry after the tariffs on wine were eliminated.

Finally, the dispute-settlement mechanism seems to have worked well. A large number of disputes have arisen and have been referred to panels. (Interested readers can read updated accounts of settled and ongoing disputes on the website for the Department of Foreign Affairs and International Trade at **www.international.gc.ca**.) Panel members have usually reacted as professionals rather than as nationals. Most cases have been decided on their merits; allegations that decisions were reached on national rather than professional grounds have been rare.

SUMMARY

34.1 Free Trade or Protection?   LO 1, 2

- The case for free trade is that world output of all products can be higher under free trade than when protectionism restricts regional specialization.
- Trade protection may be advocated to promote economic diversification or to provide protection for specific groups. The cost of such protection is lower average living standards.
- Protection can also be urged on the grounds that it may lead to higher living standards for the protectionist country than would a policy of free trade. Such a result might come about by using market power to influence the terms of trade or by developing a dynamic comparative advantage by allowing inexperienced or uneconomically small industries to become efficient enough to compete with foreign industries.
- Some invalid protectionist arguments are that (a) mutually advantageous trade is impossible because one trader's gain must always be the other's loss; (b) buying abroad sends our money abroad, while buying at home keeps our money at home; (c) our high-paid workers must be protected against the competition from low-paid foreign workers; and (d) imports are to be discouraged because they reduce national income and cause unemployment.

34.2 **Methods of Protection**   LO 3, 4

- A tariff raises the domestic price of the imported product and leads to a reduction in the level of imports. Domestic consumers lose and domestic producers gain. The overall effect of a tariff is a deadweight loss for the importing country.
- A quota (or voluntary export restriction) restricts the amount of imports and thus drives up the domestic price of the good. Domestic consumers lose and domestic

producers gain. The overall effect is a *larger* deadweight loss than with a tariff because, rather than the importing country collecting tariff revenue, foreign producers benefit from a higher price.
- Antidumping and countervailing duties, although providing legitimate restraints on unfair trading practices, are often used as serious barriers to trade.

34.3 **Current Trade Policy**   LO 5, 6

- The General Agreement on Tariffs and Trade (GATT), under which countries agreed to reduce trade barriers through multilateral negotiations and not to raise them unilaterally, has greatly reduced world tariffs since its inception in 1947.
- The World Trade Organization (WTO) was created in 1995 as the successor to GATT. It has 155 member countries and contains a formal dispute-settlement mechanism.
- Regional trade-liberalizing agreements, such as free trade areas and common markets, bring efficiency gains

through trade creation and efficiency losses through trade diversion.
- The North American Free Trade Agreement (NAFTA) is the world's largest and most successful free trade area, and the European Union is the world's largest and most successful common market.
- NAFTA is based on the principle of "national treatment." This allows Canada, the United States, and Mexico to implement whatever social, economic, or environmental policies they choose providing that such policies treat foreign and domestic firms (and their products) equally.

KEY CONCEPTS

Free trade and protection
Tariffs and import quotas
Voluntary export restrictions (VERs)
Countervailing and antidumping duties

The General Agreement on Tariffs and Trade (GATT)
The World Trade Organization (WTO)
Common markets, customs unions, and free-trade areas

Trade creation and trade diversion
Non-tariff barriers
The North American Free Trade Agreement (NAFTA)

STUDY EXERCISES

MyEconLab   Make the grade with MyEconLab: Study Exercises marked in red can be found on MyEconLab. You can practise them as often as you want, and most feature step-by-step guided instructions to help you find the right answer.

1. Fill in the blanks to make the following statements correct.

   a. The _____ argument provided the rationale for Canada's National Policy of 1876. A high tariff wall allowed many Canadian industries to develop where they may not have been able to compete otherwise.
   b. Advertisements that encourage us to "buy Canadian" are promoting a(n) _____ argument

   for protection. The reason is that money spent on imported goods must ultimately be spent on _____ goods and services anyway.
   c. Invalid arguments for protection usually come from a misunderstanding of the gains from _____ or from the misbelief that protection can increase total _____.

2. Fill in the blanks to make the following statements correct.

   a. A tariff imposed on the import of leather shoes will cause a(n) _____ in the domestic price. Total quantity of leather shoes sold in Canada will _____. Domestic (Canadian) production of leather shoes will _____ and the quantity of shoes imported will _____.

   b. The beneficiaries of the tariff described above are _____ because they receive a higher price for the same good and _____ because they receive tariff revenue. The parties that are clearly worse off are _____ because they now pay a higher price for the same good, and _____ because they sell less in the Canadian market.

   c. The overall effect of a tariff on the importing country is a(n) _____ in welfare. The tariff creates a(n) _____ loss for the economy.

   d. Suppose an import quota restricted the import of leather shoes into Canada to 20 000 pairs per year when the free trade imported amount was 40 000 pairs. The domestic price will _____, total quantity sold in Canada will _____, and domestic production will _____.

   e. The beneficiaries of the quota described above are _____ and _____ because they both receive a higher price in the Canadian market. The party that is clearly worse off is _____ because they are now paying a higher price.

   f. The overall effect of an import quota on the importing country is a(n) _____ in welfare. The quota imposes a(n) _____ loss for the economy.

3. Fill in the blanks to make the following statements correct.

   a. A regional trade agreement, such as the NAFTA, or a common market, such as the European Union, allows for _____, whereby trade within the group of member countries is increased.

   b. A regional trade agreement, such as the NAFTA, or a common market, such as the European Union, also results in _____, whereby trade within the group of member countries replaces trade previously done with other _____.

   c. The fundamental principle that guides the NAFTA is the principle of _____, which means that any member country can implement the policies of its choosing, as long as _____ and _____ firms are treated equally.

4. Canada produces steel domestically and also imports it from abroad. Assume that the world market for steel is competitive and that Canada is a small producer, unable to affect the world price. Since Canada imports steel, we know that in the absence of trade, the Canadian equilibrium price would exceed the world price.

   a. Draw a diagram showing the Canadian market for steel, with imports at the world price.

   b. Explain why the imposition of a tariff on imported steel will increase the price of steel in Canada.

   c. Who benefits and who is harmed by such a tariff? Show these effects in your diagram.

5. The diagram below shows the Canadian market for leather shoes, which we assume to be competitive. The world price is p_w. If the Canadian government imposes a tariff of t dollars per unit, the domestic price then rises to $p_w + t$

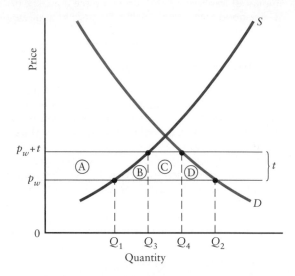

   a. What quantity of leather shoes is imported before the tariff is imposed? After the tariff?

   b. What is the effect of the tariff on the Canadian production of shoes? Which areas in the diagram show the increase in domestic producer surplus?

   c. Which areas in the diagram show the reduction in domestic consumer surplus as a result of the higher Canadian price?

   d. The Canadian government earns tariff revenue on the imported shoes. Which area in the diagram shows this tariff revenue?

   e. What is the overall effect of this tariff on the economy? Which area in the diagram shows the deadweight loss?

6. Use the diagram from Question 5 to analyze the effects of imposing an import quota instead of a tariff to protect domestic shoe producers. Draw the diagram as in Question 5 and answer the following questions.

   a. Explain why an import quota of Q_3Q_4 raises the domestic price to $p_w + t$.

   b. With import quotas, the Canadian government earns no tariff revenue. Who gets this money now?

   c. Is the import quota better or worse than the tariff for Canada as a whole? Explain.

7. Under pressure from the Canadian and U.S. governments in the early 1980s, Japanese automobile producers agreed to restrict their exports to the North American market. After the formal agreement ended,

the Japanese producers decided unilaterally to continue restricting their exports. Carefully review Figure 34-2 on page 857 and then answer the following questions.

a. Explain why the Japanese producers would voluntarily continue these restrictions.
b. Explain why an agreement to export only 100 000 cars to North America is better for the Japanese producers than a North American tariff that results in the same volume of Japanese exports.
c. Who is paying for these benefits to the Japanese producers?

8. Go to Statistics Canada's website: **www.statcan.gc.ca**. Search for "exports and imports," and answer the following questions related to imports and exports of *goods* (trade data for *services* are generally harder to obtain).

a. For the most recent year shown, what was the value of Canada's exports to the United States? To the European Union?
b. For the same year, what was the value of Canada's imports from the United States? From the European Union?
c. Compute what economists call the "volume of trade" (the sum of exports and imports) between Canada and the United States. How has the volume of trade grown over the past five years? Has trade grown faster than national income?

9. The table below shows the prices *in Canada* of cotton towels produced in the United States, Canada, and Malaysia. Assume that all cotton towels are identical.

Producing Country	Canadian Price ($) Without Tariff	Canadian Price ($) With 20% Tariff
Canada	4.75	4.75
United States	4.50	5.40
Malaysia	4.00	4.80

a. Suppose Canada imposes a 20 percent tariff on imported towels from any country. Assuming that Canadians purchase only the lowest-price towels, from which country will Canada buy its towels?
b. Now suppose Canada eliminates tariffs on towels from all countries. Which towels will Canada now buy?
c. Canada and the United States now negotiate a free-trade agreement that eliminates all tariffs between the two countries, but Canada maintains the 20 percent tariff on other countries. Which towels now get imported into Canada?
d. Which of the situations described above is called trade creation and which is called trade diversion?

10. In the past few years, trade between Canada and China has been growing quickly (though from a very low level). Many observers are concerned that Canadian

firms are not able to compete with Chinese ones and that Canada may therefore be harmed by trading more with China. Comment on the following points in relation to the above worries:

a. "Chinese are the most expensive cheap labour I have ever encountered." Statement by the owner of a Canadian firm that is moving back to Canada from China.
b. The theory of the gains from trade says that a high-productivity, high-wage country can gain from trading with a low-wage, low-productivity country.
c. Technological change is rapidly reducing labour costs as a proportion of total costs in many products; in many industries that use high-tech production methods this proportion is already well below 20 percent.

11. Import quotas and voluntary export restrictions are often used instead of tariffs.

a. What real difference, if any, is there among quotas, voluntary export restrictions (VERs), and tariffs?
b. Explain why lobbyists for some import-competing industries (such as cheese, milk, shoes) support import quotas while lobbyists for others (such as pizza manufacturers, soft drink manufacturers, retail stores) oppose them.
c. Would you expect labour unions to support or oppose import quotas? Why?

12. Consider a mythical country called Forestland, which exports a large amount of lumber to a nearby country called Houseland. The lumber industry in Houseland has convinced its federal government that it is being harmed by the low prices being charged by the lumber producers in Forestland. You are an advisor to the government in Forestland. Explain who gains and who loses from each of the following policies.

a. Houseland imposes a tariff on lumber imports from Forestland.
b. Forestland imposes a tax on each unit of lumber exported to Houseland.
c. Forestland agrees to restrict its exports of lumber to Houseland.
d. Which policy is likely to garner the most political support in Houseland? In Forestland?

13. Canada has recently imposed antidumping duties of up to 43 percent on hot-rolled steel imports from France, Russia, Slovakia, and Romania. The allegation is that these countries were dumping steel into the Canadian market.

a. Who benefits from such alleged dumping? Who is harmed?
b. Who benefits from the imposition of the antidumping duties? Who is harmed?
c. Is Canada as a whole made better off by the imposition of the duties? Explain.

Exchange Rates and the Balance of Payments

LEARNING OBJECTIVES (LO)

After studying this chapter you will be able to

1 list the components of Canada's balance of payments and explain why the balance of payments must always balance.

2 describe the demand for and supply of foreign exchange.

3 discuss various factors that cause fluctuations in exchange rates.

4 discuss why a current account deficit is not necessarily undesirable.

5 understand the theory of purchasing power parity (PPP) and its limitations.

6 explain how flexible exchange rates can dampen the effects of external shocks.

CANADIANS import products from other countries and take vacations abroad. For both reasons, they care about the exchange rate between the Canadian dollar and foreign currencies. When the Canadian dollar depreciates, it costs more to purchase imported products, and foreign vacations become more expensive. On the other hand, Canadian firms that export their products to other countries usually benefit from a depreciation of the Canadian dollar because foreigners are induced to buy more Canadian products. In some way or another, most Canadians are affected by changes in the exchange rate.

In this chapter we examine what determines the exchange rate, why it changes, and the effects these changes have on the economy. The discussion will bring together material on three topics studied elsewhere in this book: the theory of supply and demand (Chapter 3), monetary policy and inflation (Chapters 29 and 30), and international trade (Chapter 33).

We begin by examining a country's balance of payments—the record of transactions in goods, services, and assets with the rest of the world. After introducing terms, we see why the balance of payments is defined in such a way that it *always* balances.

35.1 The Balance of Payments

Statistics Canada documents transactions between Canada and the rest of the world. The record of such transactions is made in the **balance of payments accounts**. Each transaction, such as the exports or imports of goods, or the international purchase or sales of assets, is classified according to whether the transaction generates a *payment* or a *receipt* for Canada.

Table 35-1 shows the major items in the Canadian balance of payments accounts for 2011. Transactions that represent a receipt for Canada, such as the sale of a product or asset to foreigners, are recorded in the balance of payments accounts as a *credit* item. Transactions that represent a payment for Canada, such as the purchase of a product or asset from foreigners, are recorded as a *debit* item.

There are two main categories to the balance of payments: the *current account* and the *capital account*. We examine each account in turn.

balance of payments accounts A summary record of a country's transactions with the rest of the world, including the buying and selling of goods, services, and assets.

The Current Account

The **current account** records transactions arising from trade in goods and services. It also includes net investment income earned from foreign asset holdings. The current account is divided into two main sections.

The first section, called the **trade account**, records payments and receipts arising from the import and export of goods, such as computers and cars, and services, such as legal or architectural services. (Tourism constitutes a large part of the trade in services.) Canadian imports of goods and services require a payment to foreigners and thus are entered as debit items on the trade account; Canadian exports of goods and services generate a receipt to Canada and thus are recorded as credit items.

The second section, called the **capital-service account**, records the payments and receipts that represent income on assets. When a firm located in Canada, for example, pays dividends to foreign owners, the payments to foreigners are a debit item in Canada's balance of payments. In contrast, when Canadians earn income from their foreign-located investments, these receipts for Canada are recorded as credit items.

As shown in Table 35-1, Canadian exports of goods and services in 2011 were $534 billion, while imports of goods and services were slightly larger at $556 billion. The trade account therefore had a deficit of just over $22 billion—meaning that Canada purchased $22 billion more in goods and services from the rest of the world than it sold to the world. The capital-service account that year was also in deficit—Canadians paid $26 billion more to foreigners as investment income (plus transfers) than they received from foreigners. The overall current account balance in 2011 (the sum of the trade and capital-service accounts) had a deficit of $48.4 billion.

current account The part of the balance of payments accounts that records payments and receipts arising from trade in goods and services and from interest and dividends that are earned on assets owned in one country and invested in another.

trade account In the balance of payments, this account records the value of exports and imports of goods and services.

capital-service account In the balance of payments, this account records the payments and receipts that represent income on assets (such as interest and dividends).

The Capital Account

The **capital account** records international transactions in assets, including bonds, shares of companies, real estate, and factories. When a Canadian purchases a foreign asset, the transaction is treated just like the purchase of foreign goods. Since purchasing a foreign asset requires a payment from Canadians to foreigners, it is entered as a debit item in the Canadian capital account. Note that when Canadians purchase foreign assets, financial capital is leaving Canada and going abroad, and so this is called a *capital outflow*.

capital account The part of the balance of payments accounts that records payments and receipts arising from the purchase and sale of assets.

TABLE 35-1 Canadian Balance of Payments, 2011 (billions of dollars)

CURRENT ACCOUNT

Trade Account	
Merchandise exports	+458.2
Service exports	+75.3
Merchandise imports	−455.9
Service imports	−100.0
Trade balance	−22.4

Capital-Service Account	
Net investment income (including unilateral transfers)	−26.0
Current Account Balance	**−48.4**

CAPITAL ACCOUNT

Net change in Canadian investments abroad [capital outflow (−)]	−103.1
Net change in foreign investments in Canada [capital inflow (+)]	+167.0

Official Financing Account	
Changes in official international reserves [increases (−)]	−8.1
Capital Account Balance	**+55.8**
Statistical Discrepancy	**−7.4**
Balance of Payments	**0.0**

The overall balance of payments always balances, but the individual components do not have to. In 2011, Canada had an overall trade deficit (including trade in goods and services) of $22.4 billion. There was also a deficit of $26.0 billion on the capital-service account. There was thus a $48.4 billion deficit on the current account. There was a surplus on the capital account of $55.8 billion because the trading of assets internationally resulted in a net inflow of capital. The statistical discrepancy entry of −$7.4 billion compensates for the inability to measure some items accurately. The current account plus the capital account (plus the statistical discrepancy) is equal to the balance of payments—which is always zero.

(*Source:* Statistics Canada, www.statcan.gc.ca. Search for "balance of payments, 2011.")

When a foreigner purchases a Canadian asset, the transaction is treated just like the sale of Canadian goods. It generates a receipt for Canada and thus is entered as a credit item in the Canadian capital account. When Canadians sell assets to foreigners, financial capital is entering Canada from abroad, and so this is called a *capital inflow.*

As shown in Table 35-1, in 2011, Canadians increased their holdings of assets abroad by $103.1 billion, resulting in a capital outflow of that amount. At the same time, foreigners increased their holdings of assets in Canada by $167 billion, resulting in a capital inflow of that amount. Though not shown in the table, the capital account distinguishes between *direct investment* and *portfolio investment*. The former involves the purchase or sale of assets that alter the legal control of those assets, such as when a controlling interest of a company is purchased. The latter involves transactions in assets that do not alter the legal control of the assets, such as when a minority of a company's shares is purchased.

One part of the capital account shows the government's transactions in its official foreign-exchange reserves. This *official financing account* is included as part of the capital account because official reserves are *assets* rather than goods or services. If the government increases its reserves, it does so by purchasing foreign-currency assets, and this is recorded as a debit item in the official financing account. If the government instead reduces its reserves, it sells some foreign-currency assets, and this transaction would be recorded as a credit item in the official financing account. In 2011, the Government of Canada increased its official reserves by $8.1 billion.

In 2011, the overall capital account had a surplus of $55.8 billion, meaning that there was a net capital inflow of this amount to Canada from the rest of the world. In other words, foreign households, firms and governments increased their net holdings of Canadian assets by $55.8 billion in 2011.

The Balance of Payments Must Balance

The current account balance represents the difference between the payments and receipts from international transactions in goods and services. The capital account balance is the difference between payments and receipts from international transactions in assets. The balance of payments is the sum of current account and capital account balances. In any given period (usually a year) the *current account plus the capital account must equal zero*. In other words, the balance of payments is always equal to zero. In algebraic terms, we can write

$$\text{Balance of payments} = CA + KA = 0$$

where *CA* is the current account balance and *KA* is the capital account balance. Note that this is an *identity*—the accounting system used for the balance of payments defines transactions in such a way that $CA + KA = 0$. But this accounting system is based on some economic logic. Let's consider an example that illustrates the logical connection between the current and capital accounts.

Consider a year in which Canadian households, firms, and governments, taken together, purchase $100 billion in goods and services from the rest of the world. During the same year, Canadians sell $150 billion of goods and services to the rest of the world. Exports are $150 billion and imports are $100 billion, so Canada has a current account surplus of $50 billion, $CA = \$50$ billion. (We suppose for simplicity that the capital-service account is zero.) The meaning of this $50 billion surplus is that Canadians now have claims on foreigners equal to $50 billion—that is, foreigners owe Canadians $50 billion. What does Canada do with these claims?

Consider two possibilities.

1. Canadians purchase $50 billion more of goods and services from the rest of the world. In this case, Canada's imports rise to $150 billion and the current account is now in balance $(CA = 0)$. Since there have been no transactions in assets, the capital account is also in balance $(KA = 0)$. It is clear now that $CA + KA = 0$.

2. Canadians purchase $50 billion more of assets from foreigners—a capital outflow from Canada. They could purchase land, bonds, corporate shares, or factories. But whatever they purchase, the capital account will now be in deficit by $50 billion $(KA = -\$50$ billion$)$. In this case, the current account surplus of $50 billion is exactly offset by the capital account deficit of $50 billion. Once again we have $CA + KA = 0$.

Of course, Canadians could do a combination of these two options—buy some more imports and some assets as well, with a total value of $50 billion. In this case, we would still have $CA + KA = 0$.

Some readers may wonder why Canadians couldn't simply leave their purchases of goods and services unchanged *and* decide not to purchase any additional assets. For example, couldn't we have the *CA* surplus of $50 billion but not make any transactions in the capital account (so that $KA = 0$)? With such a *CA* surplus, however, Canadians are holding an "IOU" from foreigners of $50 billion which is an asset for Canada as a whole. That asset can be held in many forms (stocks, bonds, bank balances, etc.), any of which will appear in the balance of payments as a capital account deficit. Balance of payments accounting ensures that any *CA* balance is matched by an increase of some assets in the capital account so that $CA + KA = 0$.

> **Any surplus on the current account must be matched by an equal deficit on the capital account. A current account surplus thus implies a capital outflow. The balance of payments is always zero.**

Notice that the opposite situation is also possible and that the balance of payments again sums to zero. Suppose Canadians purchase $75 billion more in goods and services from the rest of the world than they sell—so Canada has a current account deficit of $75 billion, $CA = -\$75$ billion. (We continue to assume that the capital-service account is zero.) The rest of the world now has claims of this amount on Canadians, meaning that Canadians owe $75 billion to foreigners. Foreigners can either purchase more Canadian goods and services or more Canadian assets. If foreigners purchase $75 billion in additional Canadian goods and services, Canada's current account is balanced ($CA = 0$) and we again have $CA + KA = 0$. If foreigners choose instead to purchase $75 billion in Canadian assets, then Canada's capital account will be in surplus by $75 billion—a capital inflow. In this case, the current account will be in deficit ($CA = -\$75$billion) and the capital account will be in surplus ($KA = \$75$ billion), but again we see that $CA + KA = 0$.

For balance of payments statistics for many countries, see the IMF's website: www.imf.org.

Any deficit in the current account must be matched by an equal surplus in the capital account. A current-account deficit thus implies a capital inflow. The balance of payments is always zero.

Let's go back and review the actual numbers from Table 35-1. In 2011, Canada had a current account deficit of $48.4 billion. In order to purchase these net imports of goods and services, Canadian firms and households had to sell the same value (aside from the statistical discrepancy) of assets to foreigners in that year, so there was a capital inflow, or capital account surplus. The balance of payments, as always, was in balance. That the balance of payments always sums to zero is important. This result is not based on assumptions about behaviour or any other theoretical reasoning—it is an *accounting identity*. Many people nonetheless find balance of payments accounting confusing. *Applying Economic Concepts 35-1* discusses an individual student's balance of payments with the rest of the world and illustrates why an individual's balance of payments must always balance.

No Such Thing as a Balance of Payments Deficit!

Unless further qualified, the term "balance of payments deficit" does not make sense since the balance of payments must always balance. But such a term is nonetheless often used in the press and even by some economists. What does this mean? Most often the term is used carelessly—a balance of payments deficit is mentioned when what is actually meant is a current account deficit.

There are also occasions when people speak of a country as having a balance of payments deficit or surplus when they are actually referring to the balance of all accounts *excluding* the official financing account. In other words, they are referring to the combined balance on current and capital accounts, *excluding* the changes in the government's foreign-currency reserves. For example, consider a year in which the Government of Canada sells $5 billion of its foreign-currency reserves. This transaction is a credit item in the official financing account (part of Canada's capital account). It must be the case that *all other* items in the current and capital accounts *combined* sum to an overall deficit. In this case, some people might say that Canada's balance of payments "deficit" is being financed by the government's sale of foreign-currency reserves. But when we use the terms properly, we know that Canada's balance of payments, as always, is balanced.

APPLYING ECONOMIC CONCEPTS 35-1

A Student's Balance of Payments with the Rest of the World

Many students find a country's balance of payments confusing, especially the idea that the balance of payments *must always* balance. Why, they often ask, can't Canada export more goods and services to the world than it imports and at the same time have a net sale of assets to the rest of the world? The connection between the current-account transactions and the capital-account transactions is not always obvious.

Perhaps the easiest way to see this connection is to consider an individual's "balance of payments" with the rest of the world. Of course, most individuals would not normally compute their balance of payments, but by doing so we can recognize the everyday concepts involved and also see the necessary connection between any individual's "current account" and "capital account." The reason that Canada's balance of payments must always balance is exactly the same reason that an individual's balance of payments must always balance.

The table shows the balance of payments for Stefan, a university student. Stefan is fortunate in several respects. First, his parents are able to provide some of the funds needed to finance his education. Second, he has a summer job that pays well. Third, he was given some Canada Savings Bonds when he was born that provide him with some interest income every year.

Stefan's Balance of Payments

Current Account (Income and Expenditure)	
Labour income ("exports")	+$10 000
Purchase of goods and services ("imports")	−$17 000
Interest income	+$ 500
Transfers (from his parents)	+$10 000
Current Account Balance	+$3 500

Capital Account (Changes in Assets) (− denotes an increase in assets, or a "capital outflow")	
Purchase of mutual funds	−$1 500
Increase in savings account deposits	−$2 000
Capital Account Balance	−$3 500
BALANCE OF PAYMENTS	$0

The top part of the table shows Stefan's income and expenditures for a single year. This is his current account. The bottom part shows the *change* in Stefan's assets over the same year. This is his capital account. (Note that for Stefan as well as for any country, the capital account does not show the overall stock of assets—it only shows the *changes* in the stock of assets during the year.)

Let's begin with his current account. Stefan has a good summer job that earns him $10 000 after taxes. This $10 000 represents Stefan's "exports" to the rest of the world—he earns this income by selling his labour services to a tree-planting company. Over the year, however, he spends $17 000 on tuition, books, clothes, groceries, and other goods and services. These are Stefan's "imports" from the rest of the world. Stefan clearly has a "trade deficit" equal to $7000—he "imports" more than he "exports."

There are two other sources of income shown in Stefan's current account. First, he earns $500 in interest income. Second, his parents give him $10 000 to help pay for his education—a *transfer* in the terminology of balance of payments accounting. The interest income and transfer together make up Stefan's "capital-service account"—Stefan has a surplus of $10 500.

Stefan's overall current account shows a surplus of $3500. This means he receives $3500 more than he spends on goods and services. But where does this $3500 go?

Now let's consider Stefan's capital account, the bottom part of the table. The $3500 surplus on current account *must* end up as increases in Stefan's assets. He invests $1500 in a mutual fund and he also increases his savings-account deposits by $2000. In both cases he is purchasing assets—he buys units in a mutual fund and he also "buys" a bank deposit. Since Stefan must make a payment to purchase these assets, each appears as a debit item in his capital account. Stefan's capital account balance is a deficit of $3500; in other words, there is a "capital outflow" of $3500.

Finally, note that Stefan's current account and capital account *must* sum to zero. There is no way around this. Any surplus of income over expenditures (on current account) must show up as an increase in his assets (or a decrease in his debts) on his capital account. Conversely, any excess of expenditures over income must be financed by reducing his assets (or by increasing his debts). Stefan's balance of payments *must* balance.

What is true for Stefan is true for any individual and also true for any accounting unit you choose to consider. Saskatoon's balance of payments with the rest of the world must balance. Saskatchewan's balance of payments with the rest of the world must balance. Western Canada's balance of payments with the rest of the world must balance. And so must Canada's, and any other country's.

Strictly speaking, a balance of payments deficit or surplus cannot exist. When the terms are used, a "balance of payments deficit" probably refers to a situation in which the government is selling official foreign-currency reserves. A "balance of payments surplus" probably refers to a situation in which the government is buying official foreign-currency reserves. In both cases, as always, the balance of payments is actually in balance.

Summary

This brings us to the end of our discussion of the balance of payments. Keep in mind that this is just an exercise in accounting. Though at times you may find it difficult to keep the various credits and debits in the various accounts straight in your mind, remember that the structure of the accounting system is quite simple. Here is a brief review:

1. The current account shows all transactions in goods and services between Canada and the rest of the world (including investment income and transfers).

2. The capital account shows all transactions in assets between Canada and the rest of the world. Part of the capital account shows the change in the government's holding of foreign-currency reserves.

3. All transactions involving a payment from Canada appear as debit items. All transactions involving a receipt to Canada appear as credit items.

4. The balance of payments—the sum of the current account and the capital account—must, by definition, always be zero.

We now go on to explore how exchange rates are determined in the foreign-exchange market. We will see that a knowledge of the various categories in the balance of payments will help in our understanding of why changes in exchange rates occur.

| 35.2 The Foreign-Exchange Market

Money is vital in any sophisticated economy that relies on specialization and trade. Yet money as we know it is a *national* matter. If you live in Argentina, you earn pesos and spend pesos; if you operate a business in Austria, you borrow euros and pay your workers in euros. The currency of a country is acceptable within the border of that country, but usually it will not be accepted by firms and households in another country. Just try buying your next pair of jeans in Canada with British pounds sterling or Japanese yen.

Trade between countries normally requires the exchange of the currency of one country for that of another.

exchange rate The number of units of domestic currency required to purchase one unit of foreign currency.

The exchange of one currency for another is called a *foreign-exchange transaction*. The **exchange rate** is the rate at which one currency exchanges for another. In Canada's case, the exchange rate is the Canadian-dollar price of one unit of foreign currency. For example, in July 2012, the price of one U.S. dollar was 1.03 Canadian dollars. Thus, the Canada–U.S. exchange rate was 1.03.

Note that in the Canadian news media the exchange rate is usually expressed in the opposite way—as the number of U.S. dollars that it takes to buy one Canadian dollar. So instead of reporting that the Canadian–U.S. exchange rate in July 2012 was 1.03, the press would say that the Canadian dollar was "worth" 97 U.S. cents (1/1.03 = 0.97).

We can choose to define the Canada–U.S. exchange rate either way: as the Canadian-dollar price of one U.S. dollar (Cdn\$/U.S.\$) or as the U.S.-dollar price of one Canadian dollar (U.S.\$/Cdn\$). But we must choose one method and stick to it; otherwise, our discussions will quickly become very confusing. In this book we *always* define the exchange rate in the way Canadian economists usually do—as the Canadian-dollar price of one unit of foreign currency. This definition makes it clear that foreign currency, like any good or service, has a price expressed in Canadian dollars. In this case, the price has a special name—the exchange rate.

An **appreciation** of the Canadian dollar means that the Canadian dollar has become more valuable so that it takes fewer Canadian dollars to purchase one unit of foreign currency. For example, if the Canadian dollar appreciates against the U.S. dollar from 1.03 to 0.97, it takes 6 fewer Canadian cents to purchase one U.S. dollar. Thus, an appreciation of the Canadian dollar implies a *fall* in the exchange rate. Conversely, a **depreciation** of the Canadian dollar means that the Canadian dollar has become less valuable so that it takes more Canadian dollars to purchase one unit of foreign currency. Thus, a depreciation of the Canadian dollar means a *rise* in the exchange rate.

> An appreciation of the Canadian dollar is a fall in the exchange rate; a depreciation of the Canadian dollar is a rise in the exchange rate.

appreciation A fall in the exchange rate—the domestic currency has become more valuable so that it takes fewer units of domestic currency to purchase one unit of foreign currency.

depreciation A rise in the exchange rate—the domestic currency has become less valuable so that it takes more units of domestic currency to purchase one unit of foreign currency

We now go on to build a simple theory of the foreign-exchange market. This will allow us to analyze the determinants of the exchange rate. To keep things simple, we use an example involving trade between Canada and Europe, and thus we examine the determination of the exchange rate between the two currencies: the Canadian dollar and the euro. In this example, think of Europe as a shorthand for "the rest of the world" and the euro as a shorthand for "all other currencies."

> Because Canadian dollars are traded for euros in the foreign-exchange market, it follows that a demand for euros implies a supply of Canadian dollars and that a supply of euros implies a demand for Canadian dollars.

For this reason, a theory of the exchange rate between dollars and euros can deal *either* with the demand and supply of dollars *or* with the demand and supply of euros; both need not be considered. We will concentrate on the demand, supply, and price of euros. Thus, the market we will be considering (in general terms) is the

Trade between countries that use different currencies requires that currencies also be exchanged; this takes place in foreign-exchange markets where exchange rates—the price of one currency in terms of another—are determined.

foreign-exchange market—the "product" is foreign exchange (euros in our case) and the "price" is the exchange rate (the Canadian-dollar price of euros).

We develop our example in terms of the demand and supply analysis first encountered in Chapter 3. To do so, we need only recall that in the market for foreign exchange, transactions that generate a receipt for Canada in its balance of payments represent a *supply* of foreign exchange. Foreign exchange is being supplied by the foreigners who need Canadian funds to purchase Canadian goods or assets. Conversely, transactions that are a payment from Canada in the balance of payments represent a *demand* for foreign exchange. Foreign exchange is being demanded by the Canadians who are purchasing foreign goods or assets. In what follows we make the (realistic) assumption that the Bank of Canada makes no transactions in the foreign-exchange market. Later we discuss the role of central-bank transactions.

The Supply of Foreign Exchange

Whenever foreigners purchase Canadian goods, services, or assets, they supply foreign currency to the foreign-exchange market and demand, in return, Canadian dollars with which to pay for their purchases. Thus, the supply of foreign exchange (and the associated demand for Canadian dollars) arises from Canada's sales of goods, services, and assets to the rest of the world.

Canadian Exports One important source of supply of foreign exchange is foreigners who wish to buy Canadian-made goods and services. A French importer of lumber is such a purchaser; an Austrian couple planning a vacation in Canada is another; the Hungarian government seeking to buy Canadian engineering services is a third. All are sources of supply of foreign exchange, arising out of international trade. Each potential buyer wants to sell its own currency in exchange for Canadian dollars that it can then use to purchase Canadian goods and services.

Asset Sales: Capital Inflows A second source of supply of foreign exchange comes from foreigners who want to purchase Canadian assets, such as government or corporate bonds, real estate, or shares in a Canadian firm. To buy Canadian assets, holders of foreign currencies must first sell their foreign currency and buy Canadian dollars. As we saw earlier in the chapter, when Canadians sell assets to foreigners, we say there is a *capital inflow* to Canada.

Reserve Currency Firms, banks, and governments often accumulate and hold foreign-exchange reserves, just as individuals maintain savings accounts. These reserves may be in several different currencies. For example, the government of Poland may decide to increase its reserve holdings of Canadian dollars and reduce its reserve holdings of euros; if it does so, it will be a supplier of euros (and a demander of Canadian dollars) in foreign-exchange markets.

The Total Supply of Foreign Exchange The supply of foreign exchange (or the demand for Canadian dollars) is the sum of the supplies for all the purposes just discussed—for purchases of Canadian exports, for capital inflow to Canada, and for the purchase of Canadian dollars to add to currency reserves.

Furthermore, because people, firms, and governments in all countries purchase goods and assets from many other countries, the demand for any one currency will be the aggregate demand of individuals, firms, and governments in a number of different countries. Thus, the total supply of foreign exchange (or the demand for Canadian dollars) may include Germans who are offering euros, Japanese who are offering yen, Argentinians who are offering pesos, and so on. For simplicity, however, we go back to our two-country example and use only Canada and Europe.

The Supply Curve for Foreign Exchange The supply of foreign exchange on the foreign-exchange market is represented by a positively sloped curve, such as the one shown in Figure 35-1. This figure plots the Canadian-dollar price of euros (the exchange rate) on the vertical axis and the quantity of euros on the horizontal axis. Moving up the vertical axis, more dollars are needed to purchase one euro—the Canadian dollar is depreciating. Moving down the vertical axis, fewer dollars are needed to purchase one euro—the dollar is appreciating.

Why is the supply curve for foreign exchange positively sloped? Let's consider what happens when Europeans are buying Canadian exports. If the Canadian dollar is depreciating (moving up the vertical axis), the euro prices of the Canadian exports are falling and so Europeans will want to buy more. To make these additional purchases, they increase their supply of euros to the foreign-exchange market in order to acquire the Canadian dollars they need to pay for the Canadian products. In the opposite case, when the dollar appreciates (moving down the vertical axis), the euro price of Canadian exports rises. European consumers will buy fewer Canadian goods and thus supply less foreign exchange.[1]

FIGURE 35-1 The Foreign-Exchange Market

The demand for foreign exchange is negatively sloped, and the supply of foreign exchange is positively sloped, when plotted against the exchange rate, measured as the Canadian-dollar price of one unit of foreign currency. The demand for foreign exchange is given by the blue line D. It represents the sum of transactions on both current and capital accounts that require payments to foreigners. The supply of foreign exchange is given by the red line S. It represents the sum of transactions on both current and capital accounts that represent receipts from foreigners.

In this example, the equilibrium value of the exchange rate is 1.50—it takes 1.50 Canadian dollars to purchase one euro.

Similar considerations affect other sources of supply of foreign exchange. When the Canadian dollar depreciates (a higher exchange rate), Canadian securities and other assets become more attractive purchases, and the quantity purchased by foreigners will rise. With this rise, the amount of foreign exchange supplied to pay for the purchases will increase.

The supply curve for foreign exchange is positively sloped when it is plotted against the exchange rate; a depreciation of the Canadian dollar (a rise in the exchange rate) increases the quantity of foreign exchange supplied.

[1] We have assumed here that the foreign price elasticity of demand for Canadian exports is greater than 1, so that a price change leads to a proportionately larger change in quantity demanded. This is a common assumption in the analysis of international trade.

The Demand for Foreign Exchange

The demand for foreign exchange arises from all international transactions that represent a payment for Canada in our balance of payments. What sorts of international transactions generate a demand for foreign exchange (and a supply of Canadian dollars)? They are the same sort of transactions we just discussed, but this time they are moving in the opposite direction—Canadians, rather than foreigners, are doing the purchasing. Canadians seeking to purchase foreign products will be supplying Canadian dollars and demanding foreign exchange for this purpose. Canadians may also seek to purchase foreign assets. If they do, they will supply Canadian dollars and demand foreign exchange. Similarly, a country with reserves of Canadian dollars may decide to sell them in order to demand some other currency.

The Demand Curve for Foreign Exchange When the Canadian dollar depreciates against the euro, the Canadian-dollar price of European goods rises. Because it takes more dollars to buy the same European good at an unchanged euro price, Canadians will buy fewer of the now more expensive European goods. The amount of foreign exchange being demanded by Canadians in order to pay for imported European goods will fall.[2] In the opposite case, when the Canadian dollar appreciates, European goods become cheaper, more are sold, and more dollars are spent on them. Thus, more foreign exchange will be demanded to pay for the extra imports. This same argument applies in exactly the same way to the purchases of foreign assets. Figure 35-1 shows the demand curve for foreign exchange.

> The demand curve for foreign exchange is negatively sloped when it is plotted against the exchange rate; an appreciation of the Canadian dollar (a fall in the exchange rate) increases the quantity of foreign exchange demanded.

| 35.3 The Determination of Exchange Rates

flexible exchange rate An exchange rate that is left free to be determined by the forces of demand and supply on the free market, with no intervention by central banks.

fixed exchange rate An exchange rate that is maintained within a small range around its publicly stated par value by the intervention in the foreign-exchange market by a country's central bank.

The demand and supply curves in Figure 35-1 do not include official financing transactions (the demands for or supplies of foreign exchange by the Bank of Canada). To complete our analysis, we must incorporate the role of official financing transactions. We need to consider three important cases:

1. When the central bank makes no transactions in the foreign-exchange market, there is said to be a purely *floating* or **flexible exchange rate**.

2. When the central bank intervenes in the foreign-exchange market to "fix" or "peg" the exchange rate at a particular value, there is said to be a **fixed exchange rate** or *pegged exchange rate*.

---

[2] As long as the price elasticity of demand for imports is greater than 1, the fall in the volume of imports will exceed the rise in price, and hence fewer dollars will be spent on them. This condition (and the one in the previous footnote on page 881) is related to a famous long-standing issue in international economics, called the *Marshall-Lerner condition*. In what follows, we take the standard approach of assuming that both the price elasticity of demand for imports and the price elasticity of the demand for Canadian exports exceeds 1. This guarantees that the slopes of the curves are as shown in Figure 35-1.

3. Between these two "pure" systems is a variety of possible intermediate cases, including the *adjustable peg* and the *managed float*. In the adjustable peg system, central banks fix specific values for their exchange rates, but they explicitly recognize that circumstances may arise in which they will change that value. In a managed float, the central bank seeks to have some stabilizing influence on the exchange rate but does not try to fix it at some publicly announced value.

Most industrialized countries today operate a mostly flexible exchange rate. It is mostly market determined but the central bank sometimes intervenes to offset short-run fluctuations. The countries of the European Union (EU) had a system of fixed exchange rates (relative to one another's currencies) between 1979 and 1999. In 1999 most of the countries of the EU adopted a common currency—the euro (an important exception being the United Kingdom). Within what is now called the *euro zone*, the countries have no exchange rates for national currencies but the single common currency has a flexible exchange rate relative to countries outside the euro zone. The United States, Japan, the United Kingdom, Australia, and most other major industrialized countries have flexible exchange rates with relatively small amounts of foreign-exchange intervention by their central banks.

Canada alternated between a system of fixed exchange rates and flexible exchange rates (with limited intervention) throughout most of the period between the Second World War and 1970. In contrast, most other countries pegged their currencies to the U.S. dollar under the Bretton Woods system. Canada has had a flexible exchange rate since 1970. Later in the chapter we examine the issues involved in choosing between a flexible and fixed exchange-rate system. For now, let's explore how the various systems operate.

Flexible Exchange Rates

We begin with an exchange rate that is set in a freely competitive market, with no intervention by the central bank. Like any competitive price, the exchange rate fluctuates as the conditions of demand and supply change.

Suppose the current exchange rate is so high (say, e_1 in Figure 35-2) that the quantity of foreign exchange supplied exceeds the quantity demanded. There is thus an excess supply of foreign exchange (and an excess demand of Canadian dollars). This excess supply of foreign exchange, just as in our analysis in Chapter 3, will cause the price of foreign exchange (the exchange rate) to fall. As the exchange rate falls—an appreciation of the Canadian dollar—the euro price of Canadian goods rises, and this leads to a

FIGURE 35-2 Fixed and Flexible Exchanges Rates

In the absence of central-bank intervention, the exchange rate adjusts to clear the foreign-exchange market. The demand for and supply of foreign exchange are as in Figure 35-1 on page 881. If official financing is zero, there is a purely flexible exchange rate. It will adjust to equate the demand and supply of foreign exchange; this occurs at E with an exchange rate of e_0.

If the exchange rate is higher than that, say at e_1, the supply of foreign exchange will exceed the demand. The exchange rate will fall (the dollar will appreciate) until it reaches e_0, where balance is achieved at E. If the exchange rate is below e_0, say at e_2, the demand for foreign exchange will exceed the supply. The exchange rate will rise (the dollar will depreciate) until it reaches e_0, where balance is achieved at E.

In the case of a fixed exchange rate, the central bank uses its official financing transactions to meet the excess demands or supplies that arise at the fixed value of the exchange rate. For example, if it chooses to fix the exchange rate at e_1, there will be an excess supply of foreign exchange. The central bank will purchase foreign exchange (and sell dollars) to meet the excess supply and keep the exchange rate constant. Alternatively, if the central bank chooses to fix the exchange rate at e_2, there will be an excess demand for foreign exchange. The central bank will sell foreign exchange (and buy dollars) to meet the excess demand and keep the exchange rate constant.

reduction in the quantity of foreign exchange supplied. Also, as the exchange rate falls, the Canadian-dollar price of European goods falls, and this fall leads to an increase in the quantity of foreign exchange demanded. Thus, the excess supply of foreign exchange leads to a fall in the exchange rate, which in turn reduces the amount of excess supply. Where the two curves intersect, quantity demanded equals quantity supplied, and the exchange rate is at its equilibrium or market-clearing value.

What happens when the exchange rate is below its equilibrium value, such as at e_2 in Figure 35-2? The quantity of foreign exchange demanded will exceed the quantity supplied. With foreign exchange in excess demand, its price will naturally rise, and as it does the amount of excess demand will be reduced until equilibrium is re-established.

> A foreign-exchange market is like other competitive markets in that the forces of demand and supply lead to an equilibrium price at which quantity demanded equals quantity supplied.

Recall that we have been assuming that there is no official financing by the central bank. We now consider a system of fixed exchange rates in which official financing plays a central role in the analysis.

Fixed Exchange Rates

If the central bank chooses to fix the exchange rate at a particular value, its official financing transactions must offset any excess demand or supply of foreign exchange that arises at that exchange rate. These transactions are described in Figure 35-2.

The gold standard that operated for much of the nineteenth century and the early part of the twentieth century was a fixed exchange-rate system. The Bretton Woods system, established by international agreement in 1944 and operated until the early 1970s, was a fixed exchange-rate system that provided for circumstances under which exchange rates could be adjusted. It was thus an adjustable peg system; the International Monetary Fund (IMF) has its origins in the Bretton Woods system, and one of its principal tasks was approving and monitoring exchange-rate changes. The European Exchange Rate Mechanism (ERM), which existed from 1979 to 1999, was also a fixed exchange-rate system for the countries in the European Union; their exchange rates were fixed to one another but floated as a block against the U.S. dollar and other currencies. As mentioned earlier, this system of separate currencies with fixed exchange rates was replaced in 1999 when most of the countries of the EU adopted a common currency—the euro.

Applying Economic Concepts 35-2 examines how a fixed exchange-rate system operates. It shows why a central bank that chooses to fix its exchange rate must give up some control of its foreign-exchange reserves as occurred in Thailand in 1997 and is occurring in China today. We now go on to study the workings of a flexible exchange-rate system, the system used in Canada and most industrialized countries.

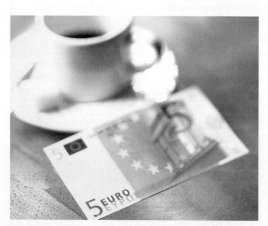

In 1999, 11 countries of the European Union adopted a common currency—the euro. By 2012, when 17 countries were in the euro zone, the price of one euro was 1.35 Canadian dollars.

Changes in Flexible Exchange Rates

What causes exchange rates to vary? The simplest answer to this question is changes in demand or supply in the foreign-exchange market. Anything that shifts the demand curve for foreign exchange to the right or the supply curve for foreign exchange to the left leads to a rise in the exchange rate—a depreciation of the Canadian dollar. Conversely, anything that shifts the demand curve for foreign exchange to the left or the supply curve for foreign exchange to the right leads to a fall in the exchange rate—an appreciation of the Canadian dollar. These points are nothing more than a restatement of the laws of supply and demand, applied now to the market for foreign exchange; they are illustrated in Figure 35-3.

For information on the European Central Bank, see its website: www.ecb.int.

What causes the shifts in demand and supply that lead to changes in exchange rates? There are many causes, some transitory and some persistent. Let's look at several of the most important ones.

A Rise in the World Price of Exports Suppose there is an increase in the world price of a major Canadian export, such as wheat, oil, copper, or nickel. For almost all of Canada's major exports, Canada's production is small relative to the world market and so no event in Canada is likely to cause a change in the world price. The higher world price, whether caused by an increase in world demand or by a reduction in supply from

FIGURE 35-3 Changes in a Flexible Exchange Rate

(i) Demand shifts

(ii) Supply shifts

An increase in the demand for foreign exchange or a decrease in the supply will cause the Canadian dollar to depreciate (the exchange rate to rise); a decrease in the demand or an increase in supply will cause the dollar to appreciate (the exchange rate to fall). The initial demand and supply curves are D_0 and S_0. Equilibrium is at E_0 with an exchange rate of e_0. An increase in the demand for foreign exchange from D_0 to D_1 in part (i), or a decrease in the supply of foreign exchange from S_0 to S_1 in part (ii), will cause the dollar to depreciate. In both parts, the new equilibrium is at E_1, and the dollar depreciation is shown by the rise in the exchange rate from e_0 to e_1. Conversely, a decrease in the demand for foreign exchange or an increase in the supply of foreign exchange will cause the dollar to appreciate and the equilibrium exchange rate to fall.

APPLYING ECONOMIC CONCEPTS 35-2

Managing Fixed Exchange Rates

This box provides some details on how a central bank operates a regime of fixed exchange rates. Though Canada has a flexible exchange rate (with very rare foreign-exchange intervention by the Bank of Canada), we will imagine a situation in which the Bank of Canada pegs the Canadian–U.S. exchange rate. The accompanying figure shows the *monthly* demand for and supply of foreign exchange (U.S. dollars).

Suppose the Bank of Canada fixed the exchange rate between the narrow limits of, say, C$0.95 to C$1.05 to the U.S. dollar. The Bank then stabilizes the exchange rate in the face of seasonal, cyclical, and other fluctuations in demand and supply, entering the market to prevent the rate from going outside the permitted band. At the price of $0.95, the Bank offers to buy any amount of U.S. dollars; at the price of $1.05, the Bank offers to sell any amount of U.S. dollars. When the Bank buys U.S. dollars, its foreign-exchange reserves rise; when it sells U.S. dollars, its foreign-exchange reserves fall.

We make the following observations:

1. If the demand curve cuts the supply curve in the range 0.95 to 1.05, as D_0 does in the accompanying figure, the Bank need not intervene in the market.

2. If the demand curve shifts to D_1, there is an excess demand for U.S. dollars that the Bank must satisfy. The Bank sells U.S. dollars from its reserves to the extent of Q_4Q_1 per month in order to prevent the exchange rate from rising above 1.05.

3. If the demand curve shifts to D_2, there is an excess supply of U.S. dollars that the Bank must satisfy. The Bank buys U.S. dollars to the extent of Q_2Q_3 per month in order to prevent the exchange rate from falling below 0.95.

If, on average, the demand and supply curves intersect in the range 0.95 to 1.05, the Bank's foreign-exchange reserves will be relatively stable, with the Bank buying U.S. dollars when the demand is abnormally low and selling them when the demand is abnormally high. Over a long period, however, the average level of reserves will be fairly stable.

If conditions change, the Bank's foreign-exchange reserves will rise or fall more or less continuously. For example, suppose the average level of demand becomes D_1, with fluctuations on either side of this level. The average drain on the Bank's foreign-exchange reserves will then be Q_4Q_1 *per month*. But this situation cannot continue indefinitely because the Bank has only a limited amount of foreign-exchange reserves. In this situation, there are two alternatives: the Bank can change the fixed exchange rate so that the band of permissible prices straddles the new equilibrium price, or government policy can try to shift the curves so that the intersection is in the band 0.95 to 1.05. To accomplish this goal, the government must restrict demand for foreign exchange: it can impose import quotas and foreign-travel restrictions, or it can seek to increase

larger producing countries, means that the world's consumers are prepared to offer more foreign currency per unit of these Canadian exports. The increase in the supply of foreign exchange occurs even if the volume of Canadian exports is unchanged; if Canadian exports increase in response to the higher world price, the supply of foreign exchange increases further. The increase in the supply of foreign exchange causes a reduction in the exchange rate—an appreciation of the Canadian dollar.

A Rise in the Foreign Price of Imports Suppose the euro price of European automobiles increases sharply. Suppose also that Canadian consumers have an elastic demand for European cars because they can easily switch to Canadian-made substitutes. Consequently, they spend fewer euros for European automobiles than they did before and hence demand less foreign exchange. The demand curve for foreign exchange shifts to the left, and the Canadian dollar will appreciate. If the demand for European cars were inelastic, total spending on them would rise, and the demand for foreign exchange would shift to the right, leading to a depreciation of the Canadian dollar. For many products, demand will be relatively inelastic in the short run and so the short-run effect the supply of U.S. dollars by encouraging Canadian exports.

Thailand in 1997 provides an example of an exchange rate fixed at a level that led to a persistent excess demand for foreign exchange. Thailand's central bank had fixed the value of its currency, the baht, to the U.S. dollar. When an excess demand for foreign currency developed in Thailand, the central bank began to deplete its stock of foreign-exchange reserves as it purchased the baht in an attempt to support its external value. By July of 1997, however, the central bank's stock of foreign-exchange reserves had been depleted to such an extent that it could no longer fix the exchange rate. With an excess demand for foreign exchange and a central bank that could no longer fix the exchange rate, depreciation was the natural result. The baht depreciated dramatically and Thailand then moved away from a fixed exchange-rate system.

For most of the past decade, China has operated an adjustable peg exchange-rate system for its currency, the yuan (sometimes called the renminbi). In 2005 the exchange rate was 8.3 yuan to the U.S. dollar but today it has appreciated to be about 6.2 yuan to the U.S. dollar. Throughout this period, the Chinese central bank has held the exchange rate above the free-market equilibrium level; in other words, the yuan has been undervalued relative to what would have been observed with a purely flexible exchange

rate. As a result, there has been a persistent excess supply of foreign currency offered in exchange for Chinese yuan (and thus an excess demand for the Chinese yuan). To reduce the amount of appreciation of the yuan, the Chinese central bank purchases foreign-exchange reserves every month. In recent years, these purchases have led to an enormous accumulation of foreign-exchange reserves in China.

of a rise in foreign prices will be a depreciation of the Canadian dollar. This is illustrated in part (i) of Figure 35-3.

> Exchange rates often respond to changes in the prices of major exports and imports. A rise in the world price of Canadian exports causes the Canadian dollar to appreciate. If demand for foreign products is inelastic, a rise in the price of Canadian imports causes the Canadian dollar to depreciate.

Changes in Overall Price Levels Suppose that instead of a change in the price of a specific product there is a change in *all* prices because of general inflation. We consider separate cases, each corresponding to a different pattern of Canadian inflation relative to foreign inflation.

Equal Inflation in Both Countries. Suppose inflation is running at 5 percent in both Canada and Europe. In this case, the euro prices of European goods and the dollar prices of Canadian goods both rise by 5 percent. At the *existing* exchange rate, the dollar prices of European goods and the euro prices of Canadian goods will each rise by 5 percent, and hence the relative prices of imports and domestically produced goods will be unchanged in both countries. Since there is no reason to expect a change in either country's demand for imports at the original exchange rate, the inflation in the two countries leaves the equilibrium exchange rate unchanged.

Inflation in Only One Country. What will happen if there is inflation in Canada while the price level remains stable in Europe? The dollar price of Canadian goods will rise, and they will become more expensive in Europe. This increase will cause the quantity of Canadian exports, and therefore the amount of foreign exchange supplied by European importers, to decrease. Thus, the supply curve for foreign exchange shifts to the left.

At the same time, European goods in Canada will have an unchanged Canadian-dollar price, while the price of Canadian goods sold in Canada will increase because of the inflation. Thus, European goods will be more attractive compared with Canadian goods (because they have become relatively cheaper), and thus more European goods will be bought in Canada. At any exchange rate, the amount of foreign exchange demanded to purchase imports will rise. Thus, the demand curve for foreign exchange shifts to the right.

Canadian inflation that is unmatched in Europe will therefore cause the supply curve for foreign exchange to shift to the left and the demand curve for foreign exchange to shift to the right. As a result, the equilibrium exchange rate *must* rise—there is a depreciation of the Canadian dollar relative to the euro.

Inflation at Unequal Rates. The two foregoing examples are, of course, just limiting cases of a more general situation in which the rate of inflation is different in the two countries. The arguments can readily be extended when we realize that it is the *relative* inflation in two countries that determines whether home goods or foreign goods look more or less attractive. If country A's inflation rate is higher than country B's, country A's exports are becoming relatively expensive in B's markets while imports from B are becoming relatively cheap in A's markets. This causes A's currency to depreciate relative to B's.

> Other things being equal, if Canada has higher inflation than other countries, the Canadian dollar will be depreciating relative to other currencies. If Canada has lower inflation than other countries, the Canadian dollar will be appreciating.

An increase in the world price of a major Canadian export, such as forestry products, generally leads to an appreciation of the Canadian dollar.

Capital Movements Flows of financial capital can exert strong influences on exchange rates. For example, an increased desire by Canadians to purchase European assets (a capital outflow from Canada) will shift the demand curve for foreign exchange to the right, and the dollar will depreciate. In contrast, a desire by foreigners to increase their holdings of Canadian assets will shift the supply curve for foreign currency to the right and cause the Canadian dollar to appreciate.

Short-Term Capital Movements. An important motive for short-term capital flows is a change in interest rates. International traders hold transaction balances just as do domestic traders. These balances are often lent out on a short-term basis rather than being left idle. Naturally, the holders of these balances will tend to lend them, other things being equal, in markets in which interest rates are highest. This is often referred to as the *carry trade*. If one country's short-term interest rate rises above the rates in other countries (say, because that country undertakes a contractionary monetary policy), there will tend to be a large inflow of short-term capital into that country in an effort to take advantage of the high rate. This inflow of financial capital will increase the demand for the domestic currency and cause it to appreciate. If the short-term interest rate should fall in one country (say, because of a monetary expansion in that country), there will tend to be a shift of financial capital away from that country, and its currency will tend to depreciate. We saw this basic relationship between interest rates, capital flows, and the exchange rate in Chapter 28 when we discussed the monetary transmission mechanism in an open economy.

> Changes in monetary policy lead to changes in interest rates and thus to international flows of financial capital. A contractionary monetary policy in Canada will lead to a rise in Canadian interest rates, a capital inflow, and an appreciation of the Canadian dollar. An expansionary monetary policy in Canada will lead to a reduction in Canadian interest rates, a capital outflow, and a depreciation of the Canadian dollar.

A second motive for short-term capital movements is speculation about the *future value* of a country's exchange rate. If foreigners expect the Canadian dollar to appreciate in the near future, they will be induced to buy assets that pay off in Canadian dollars, such as Canadian stocks or bonds; if they expect the Canadian dollar to depreciate in the near future, they will be reluctant to buy or to hold Canadian securities.

Long-Term Capital Movements. Long-term capital movements are largely influenced by long-term expectations about another country's profit opportunities and the long-run value of its currency. A French firm would be more willing to purchase a Canadian factory if it expected that the dollar profits would buy more euros in future years than the profits from investment in a French factory. This could happen if the Canadian firm earned greater profits than the French firm, with exchange rates remaining unchanged. It could also happen if the profits were the same but the French firm expected the Canadian dollar to appreciate relative to the euro.

Structural Changes

An economy can undergo structural changes that alter the equilibrium exchange rate. *Structural change* is an all-purpose term for a change in cost structures, the invention of new products, changes in preferences between products, or anything else that affects the pattern of comparative advantage. Consider two examples.

Suppose the reluctance of firms in one country to adopt technological innovations results in that country's products not improving as rapidly as those produced in other countries. Consumers' demand will shift slowly away from the first country's products and toward those of its foreign competitors. This shift will cause a gradual depreciation in the first country's currency because fewer people want to buy that country's goods and thus fewer people want to buy that country's currency. For this reason, a country with faster productivity growth than other countries tends to experience an appreciation of its currency.

A second example relates to the discovery of valuable mineral resources. Prominent examples are the development of natural gas in the Netherlands in the early 1960s, the development of North Sea oil in the United Kingdom in the 1970s, and the recent discovery of large diamond deposits in the Northwest Territories. If firms in one country make such a discovery and begin selling these resources to the rest of the world, the foreign purchasers must supply their foreign currency in order to purchase the currency of the exporting country. The result is an appreciation of the currency of the exporting country.

> Anything that leads to changes in the pattern of trade, such as changes in costs or changes in demand, will generally lead to changes in exchange rates.

The Volatility of Exchange Rates

We have discussed several variables that can lead to changes in the exchange rate, including changes in relative prices, changes in interest rates, and changes in the pattern of trade. Since these variables are changing at different times by different amounts and often in different directions, it should not be surprising that exchange rates are constantly changing. Indeed, exchange rates are one of the most volatile of all macro-economic variables. One reason for this volatility that we have not yet discussed is that foreign-exchange traders, when they are deciding whether to buy or sell foreign currency, respond to all sorts of "news" that they think will influence economic conditions, both currently and in the future. Since such news is constantly becoming available, the exchange rate is continuously changing as this new information leads traders to change their demand and supply decisions. *Applying Economic Concepts 35-3* discusses in more detail how news affects the volatility of exchange rates.

| 35.4 Three Policy Issues

This chapter has so far explained how the balance of payments accounts are constructed and how exchange rates are determined. It is now time to use this knowledge to explore some important policy issues. We examine three issues commonly discussed in the media. As we will see, these media discussions are not always as well informed as they could be. We pose the three policy issues as questions:

1. Is a current account deficit "bad" and a surplus "good"?

2. Is there a "correct" value for the Canadian dollar?

3. Should Canada fix its exchange rate with the U.S. dollar?

Current Account Deficits and Surpluses

Figure 35-4 shows the path of Canada's current account balance (as a percentage of GDP) since 1961. In most years, Canada has a significant trade surplus since it exports more goods and services to the world than it imports. But because it makes more investment payments (both interest and dividends) to foreigners than it receives from foreigners, it has a deficit on the capital-service portion of the current account. During most of the 1960–1995 period, Canada had an overall current account deficit of between 2 and 4 percent of GDP. From the late 1990s to 2007, however, Canada's trade surplus increased by more than the capital-service deficit, and the result was a significant

APPLYING ECONOMIC CONCEPTS 35-3

News and the Exchange Rate

Foreign-exchange markets are different from markets for consumer goods in that the vast bulk of trading takes place between professional foreign-exchange traders working for banks, mutual-fund companies, and pension funds. These traders do not meet one another face to face. Rather, they do their transactions over the telephone or the computer, and the other party to the transaction could be anywhere in the world. The structure of this market has one interesting implication: exchange rates respond to news. Let's see why this is and what this means.

Deals done by professional traders are all on a large scale, typically involving sums no smaller than $1 million and often very much larger. Each trader tends to specialize in trades between a small number of currencies, say the Canadian and the U.S. dollars, or the U.S. dollar and the Japanese yen. But the traders for all currencies for each bank sit close together in a trading room so they can hear what is going on in the other markets. When a big news event breaks, anywhere in the world, this will be shouted out simultaneously to all traders in the room.

Each trader is also faced with several computer screens and many buttons that connect him or her quickly by telephone to other traders. Speed of transaction can be very important if you are dealing with large amounts of money in a market that is continuously changing the prices quoted. The most recent price quotes from around the world appear on the screens. However, contracts are agreed over the telephone (and are recorded in case of a disagreement) and the paperwork follows within two days.

As exchange rates are closely related to expectations and to interest rates, the foreign-exchange traders have to keep an eye on all major news events affecting the economic environment. Since all the players in the foreign-exchange markets are professionals, they are well informed, not just about what has happened but also about forecasts of what is likely to happen. Accordingly, the exchange rate at any point in time reflects not just history but also current expectations of future events.

As soon as some future event comes to be expected—such as the central bank's plans to tighten monetary policy—it will be reflected in the current exchange rate. Events expected to happen soon will be given more weight than those events expected to happen in the more distant future. The fact that expectations of future events are incorporated quickly into the exchange rate has an interesting implication: the only component in today's news that will cause the exchange rate to change is what was *not expected* to happen. Economists attribute the unforecastable component of news to a random error. It is random in the sense that it has no detectable pattern and it is unrelated to the information available before it happened.

Some events are clearly unforecastable, like an earthquake or a head of state having a heart attack. Others are the production of economic statistics for which forecasts have generally been published. In the latter case it is the deviation of announced figures from their forecast value that tends to move exchange rates.

Exchange rates are therefore moved by news. And since much news is random and unpredictable, many changes in exchange rates will tend to be random. Some people, observing the volatility of exchange rates, conclude that foreign-exchange markets are inefficient. However, with well-informed professional traders who have forward-looking expectations, new information is rapidly transmitted into prices. The volatility of exchange rates, therefore, largely reflects the volatility of relevant, but unexpected, events around the world.

Current news events, the announcements made by public officials, and the expectation of future events play a large role in determining whether currency traders decide to buy or sell foreign exchange. The frequency and randomness of news releases partly explain why exchange rates tend to be so volatile.

turnaround in the current account balance. But with the arrival of the global recession in 2008, Canada's exports fell far more than its imports and the result was a return to current account deficits.

As we have learned, Canada's balance of payments are defined in such a way that they must always balance, so during the 1960–1995 period the current account

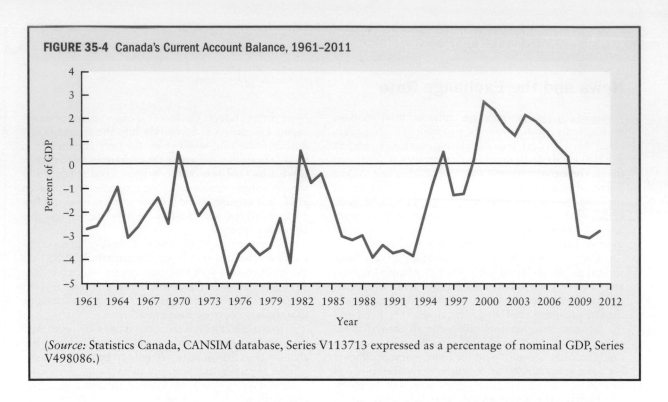

FIGURE 35-4 Canada's Current Account Balance, 1961–2011

(*Source:* Statistics Canada, CANSIM database, Series V113713 expressed as a percentage of nominal GDP, Series V498086.)

deficits were matched by capital account surpluses of the same size. During these years, Canada was selling more assets to the rest of the world—both bonds and equity—than it was buying from the rest of the world. Similarly, the current account surpluses from 1998 to 2007 were matched by capital account deficits, meaning that in recent years Canada was buying more assets from foreigners than we were selling to foreigners.

It is common for TV anchors to report negatively on an increase in the current account deficit and positively on its decline. But are current account deficits really a problem? Should we be celebrating Canada's current account surpluses when they occur? We address this issue in three parts.

Mercantilism Many people argue that a current account deficit is undesirable because it means that Canada is buying more goods and services from the world than it is selling to the world. Central to this view is the belief that exports are "good" and imports are "bad." We discussed this belief, and argued why it was incorrect, in Chapter 34 when we explored some of the invalid arguments for trade protection.

As a carryover from a long-discredited eighteenth-century doctrine called *mercantilism*, a current account surplus is sometimes called a "favourable balance," and a current account deficit is sometimes called an "unfavourable balance." Mercantilists, both ancient and modern, believe that a country's gains from trade arise only from having a "favourable" balance of trade—that is, by exporting more goods and services than it imports. But this belief misses the central point of comparative advantage that we explored in Chapter 33—that countries gain from trade because trade allows each country to specialize in the production of those products in which its opportunity costs are low. The gains from trade have *nothing* to do with whether there is a trade deficit or a trade surplus.

Lessons from History 35-1 discusses the doctrine of mercantilism. The lesson to be learned is that the gains from trade depend on the *volume* of trade (exports plus imports) rather than the *balance* of trade (exports minus imports). There is nothing inherently bad about having a current account deficit and nothing inherently good about having a current account surplus.

International Borrowing If Canada has a current account deficit, it also has a capital account surplus. It is a net seller of assets to the rest of the world. These assets are either bonds, in which case Canadians are borrowing from foreigners, or they are shares in firms (equities), in which case Canadians are selling their capital stock to foreigners.

It follows that the question "Should Canada have a current account deficit?" is the same as the question "Should Canadians be net sellers of assets to foreigners?" It is not immediately clear that the answer to this question should be no. It is true that by selling bonds to foreigners, Canadians increase their indebtedness to foreigners and will eventually have to redeem the bonds and pay interest. And by selling income-earning equities to foreigners, Canadians give up a stream of income that they would otherwise have. But, in both cases, they get a lump sum of funds that can be used for any type of consumption or investment. Is it obviously "better" to have a lower debt or a higher

---

LESSONS FROM HISTORY 35-1

Mercantilism, Then and Now

Media commentators, politicians, and much of the general public often appear to believe that a country should export more than it imports and thereby secure a current account surplus. They appear to believe that the benefits derived from international trade are measured by the size of that surplus.

This view is related to the *exploitation doctrine* of international trade: one country's surplus is another country's deficit. Hence, one country's gain, judged by its surplus, must be another country's loss, judged by its deficit.

People who hold such views today are echoing an ancient economic doctrine called *mercantilism*. The mercantilists were a group of economists who preceded Adam Smith. They judged the success of trade by the size of the trade balance. In many cases, this doctrine made sense in terms of their objective, which was to use international trade as a means of building up the political and military power of the state, rather than as a means of raising the living standards of its citizens. A current account surplus allowed the country (then and now) to acquire assets. (In those days, the assets took the form of gold. Today, they are mostly claims on the currencies of other countries.) These assets could then be used to pay armies, to purchase weapons from abroad, and to finance colonial expansions.

If the objective is to promote the welfare and living standards of ordinary citizens, however, the mercantilist focus on the balance of trade makes no sense. The principle of comparative advantage shows that average living standards are maximized by having individuals, regions, and countries specialize in the things they produce comparatively best and then trading to obtain the things they produce comparatively worst. With specialization, domestic consumers get access to products they want at the lowest possible prices, while domestic firms are able to sell their products at higher prices than would otherwise be possible. The more specialization takes place, the more trade occurs and thus the more average living standards increase.

For the country as a whole, therefore, the gains from trade are to be judged by the *volume* of trade rather than by the *balance* of trade. A situation in which there is a large volume of trade even though each country has a zero balance of trade is thus entirely satisfactory. Furthermore, a change in policy that results in an equal increase in both exports and imports will generate gains because it allows for specialization according to comparative advantage, even though it causes no change in either country's trade balance.

future income stream than to have a lump sum of funds right now? If it were obviously better, no family would ever borrow money to buy a house or a car, and no firm would ever borrow money to build a factory.

> A country that has a current account deficit is either borrowing from the rest of the world or selling some of its capital assets to the rest of the world. This is not necessarily undesirable.

To argue that it is undesirable for Canada to have a current account deficit is to argue that Canadians as a whole should not borrow from (or sell assets to) the rest of the world. But surely the wisdom of borrowing depends on *why* Canadians are borrowing. It is therefore important to know *why* there is a current account deficit.

Causes of Current Account Deficits There are several possible causes of a current account deficit. This can be seen most clearly by recalling some national-income accounting from Chapter 20. Recall that GDP is equal to the sum of actual consumption, investment, government purchases, and net exports,

$$GDP = C_a + I_a + G_a + NX_a$$

where the subscript "*a*" denotes *actual* expenditure rather than desired expenditure. Next, recall from Chapter 20 the difference between GDP and GNP where the latter is the total income that accrues to Canadian residents. GNP is equal to GDP plus the net investment income received from abroad, which we call R.

$$GNP = GDP + R = C_a + I_a + G_a + NX_a + R$$

Note that the current account balance is simply the trade balance, NX_a, plus the net investment income, R. We denote the actual current account balance CA_a. If CA_a is positive, there is a current account surplus; if CA_a is negative, there is a current account deficit. The equation now becomes

$$GNP = C_a + I_a + G_a + CA_a \tag{35-1}$$

Now consider how the income accruing to Canadian households (GNP) can be spent. There are only three ways to dispose of income. It can be consumed, saved, or paid in taxes. That is,

$$GNP = C_a + S_a + T_a \tag{35-2}$$

By equating Equations 35-1 and 35-2, and by omitting the "*a*" subscripts for simplicity, we derive an interesting relationship among national saving, investment, and the current account balance:

$$C + I + G + CA = C + S + T$$
$$\Rightarrow CA = S + (T - G) - I$$

This last equation says that the current account balance in any year is exactly equal to the excess of national saving, $S + (T - G)$, over domestic investment I. If Canadians (and their governments) decide to save more than is needed to finance the amount of domestic investment, where do the excess funds go? They are used to acquire foreign assets, and thus Canada has a current account surplus ($CA > 0$). In contrast, if Canadians do not save enough to finance the amount of domestic investment, the balance must be financed by foreign funds. Thus, Canada has a current account deficit ($CA < 0$). Finally, we can re-arrange this equation very slightly to get

$$CA = (S - I) + (T - G) \qquad (35\text{-}3)$$

which says that the current account balance is equal to the excess of private saving over investment plus the government budget surplus.

Equation 35-3 shows three separate reasons for any given increase in the current account deficit (a fall in CA). First, a reduction in private saving, other things being equal, will lead to a rise in the current account deficit. Second, a rise in domestic investment, other things being equal, will increase the current account deficit. Finally, other things being equal, a rise in the government's budget deficit (a smaller value of $T - G$) will raise the current account deficit. This third case is often referred to as a situation of *twin deficits*. That is, a rise in the government's budget deficit will also have the effect (if S and I remain constant) of increasing the current account deficit.

An increase in the level of investment, a decrease in the level of private saving, and an increase in the government's budget deficit are all possible causes of an increase in a country's current account deficit.

It makes little sense to discuss the desirability of a change in the current account deficit without first knowing the *cause* of the change. Knowing the cause is crucial to knowing whether the change in the current account deficit is undesirable. The following two examples illustrate this important point.

First, suppose business opportunities in Canada are very promising and, as a result, there is an increase in the level of private-sector investment. Most people would consider such an investment boom desirable because it would increase current output and employment and, by increasing the country's capital stock, it would also increase the level of potential output in the future. But as is clear from Equation 35-3, other things being equal, the effect of the rise in Canadian investment is an increase in the Canadian current account deficit. The current account deficit increases because, in the absence of increased domestic saving, the increase in domestic investment can only take place if it is financed by a capital inflow from other countries. This capital inflow represents a rise in Canada's current account deficit (or capital account surplus). In this case, however, it would be difficult to argue that the increase in Canada's current account deficit is undesirable as it simply reflects a boom in domestic business opportunities.

For a second example, suppose the domestic economy begins to slow and households and firms become pessimistic about the future. In such a situation, we expect households to increase their saving and firms to reduce their investment, thus increasing the value of $(S - I)$. As the economy slows we would also expect the government's net tax revenues to fall, thus decreasing the value of $(T - G)$. But it is possible that the first effect dominates the second effect, thus leading to an increase in the current account surplus. Is the increase in Canada's current account surplus desirable? Most people would probably agree that the onset of a recession as just described is surely undesirable, involving a loss of output and employment.

An increase in domestic investment, other things being equal, will lead to an increase in the current account deficit. But there is little that is undesirable about this situation.

A country's current account deficit can increase for a number of reasons. Whether the rise in the current account deficit is desirable depends on its underlying cause. A rise in the current account deficit may reflect a positive economic development; a decline in the current account deficit may reflect a negative economic development.

Is There a "Correct" Value for the Canadian Dollar?

From the summer of 1997 to the end of 1999, the external value of the Canadian dollar fell from about 72 to 65 U.S. cents. (The exchange rate increased from 1.39 to 1.54.) It was common to hear financial commentators discuss how the Canadian dollar was "undervalued." Retailers selling imported products and firms using imported supplies complained that the weak Canadian dollar was undermining their business. Opposite statements were heard between 2002 and 2008 when, as a result of high world prices for raw materials, the Canadian dollar appreciated enormously. At the time, some financial commentators argued that the Canadian dollar was "overvalued." Canadian firms in the tourist-oriented hospitality industry and those exporting manufactured products complained that the strong Canadian dollar was damaging their business. In both cases, the observers appeared to believe that there was some "correct" value for the Canadian dollar. Is there?

As we saw in the previous section, a country that chooses to use a flexible exchange rate has its exchange rate determined by competitive forces in the foreign-exchange market. In Canada, and other countries as well, fluctuations in exchange rates have many causes. Some changes may be good for Canada, such as a worldwide shortage of wheat that drives up the world price of wheat, a major Canadian export. Others may be bad for Canada, such as the discovery of new copper deposits in Chile that drives down the price of copper, also a major Canadian export. But the various supply and demand forces are coming together in the foreign-exchange market to determine the equilibrium value of the exchange rate. Changes in this value may reflect positive or negative events for Canada, but it is difficult to think of this equilibrium value as being either "too high" or "too low."

With a flexible exchange rate, the market determines the value of the exchange rate. With respect to the forces of demand and supply, the equilibrium exchange rate is the "correct" exchange rate.

Saying that the current equilibrium exchange rate is the "correct" rate in no way suggests that this "correct" rate is constant. Indeed, foreign-exchange markets are so large, with so many participants in so many countries, each responding to a slightly different set of events and expectations, that the equilibrium exchange rate is constantly changing. In other words, as various forces lead to frequent changes in the demand for and supply of the Canadian dollar in foreign-exchange markets, the "correct" value of the Canadian exchange rate is constantly changing.

Some economists accept that the current exchange rate, as determined by the foreign-exchange market, is indeed the correct rate, but they make a distinction between the current value of the exchange rate and its long-run value. These economists argue that, whereas various shocks may cause the exchange rate to rise or fall in the short run, there nonetheless exists some "fundamental" level to which it will eventually return. This brings us to the theory of *purchasing power parity*.

Purchasing Power Parity The theory of **purchasing power parity (PPP)** holds that, over the long term, the value of the exchange rate between two currencies depends on the two currencies' relative purchasing power. The theory holds that a currency will tend to have the same purchasing power when it is spent in its home country as it would have if it were converted to foreign exchange and spent in the foreign country. Another way to say the same thing is that the price of *identical baskets of goods* should be the same in the two countries when the price is expressed in the same currency. If we let P_C and P_E be the price levels in Canada and Europe, respectively, and let e be the Canadian-dollar price of euros (the exchange rate), then the theory of purchasing power parity predicts the following equality in the long run:

$$P_C = e \times P_E \qquad (35\text{-}4)$$

This equation simply says that if a basket of goods costs 1000 euros in Europe and the exchange rate is 1.3 (that is, 1.3 Canadian dollars per euro), then that same basket of goods should cost 1300 dollars in Canada ($1.3 \times 1000 = 1300$).

According to the theory of purchasing power parity, the exchange rate between two countries' currencies is determined by the relative price levels in the two countries.

The idea behind PPP is a simple one. Suppose that Equation 35-4 did *not* hold—specifically, suppose that P_C was greater than $e \times P_F$, so that Canadian-dollar prices in Canada exceeded the Canadian-dollar prices of the same goods in Europe. In this case, people would eventually increase their purchases of the cheaper European goods and reduce their purchases of the expensive Canadian goods. These actions would have the effect of depreciating the Canadian dollar (a rise in e); this depreciation would continue until the equality was re-established.

The *PPP exchange rate* is the value of the exchange rate that makes Equation 35-4 hold. That is, the PPP exchange rate (between the Canadian dollar and the euro) is defined to be

$$e^{PPP} \equiv P_C/P_E \qquad (35\text{-}5)$$

Note that the PPP exchange rate is itself not constant. If inflation is higher in Canada than in Europe, for example, P_C will be rising faster than P_E and so the PPP exchange rate will be rising. Conversely, if inflation is lower in Canada than in Europe, P_C will be rising more slowly than P_E and the PPP exchange rate will be falling.[3]

A Caveat About PPP Should we expect the *actual* exchange rate to equal the PPP exchange rate? The theory of purchasing power parity predicts that if the actual exchange rate (e) does not equal the PPP exchange rate (e^{PPP}), then demands and supplies of Canadian and European goods will change until the equality holds. Thus, the theory of PPP predicts that the actual exchange rate will eventually equal the PPP exchange rate.

---

[3] For a very readable review of the PPP theory and its empirical testing, see R. Lafrance and L. Schembri, "Purchasing Power Parity: Definitions, Measurement, and Interpretation," *Bank of Canada Review*, Autumn, 2002.

purchasing power parity (PPP) The theory that, over the long term, the exchange rate between two currencies adjusts to reflect relative price levels.

For The Economist's *Big Mac Index, which uses the idea of PPP, see its website:* www.economist.com.

Figure 35-5 shows the path of the actual Canadian–U.S. exchange rate and the PPP exchange rate since 1981. It is clear from the figure that there are long periods over which the actual exchange rate deviates significantly from the PPP exchange rate. Why is this the case? Is there something wrong with the theory of purchasing power parity?

Recall from Equation 35-4 that P_C and P_E were defined as the prices of *identical baskets of goods* in Canada and Europe, respectively. Given that the goods are the same, the argument that the prices should (eventually) be equated across the two countries is sensible—if the prices are not equated across the two countries, there would be an incentive to purchase in the cheaper country rather than in the more expensive country, and this would lead to changes in the exchange rate until Equation 35-4 *did* hold.

One problem, however, when we apply the theory of purchasing power parity to *national price indices,* such as the Consumer Price Index or the implicit GDP deflator, is that the two baskets of goods are typically *not* the same—for two reasons.

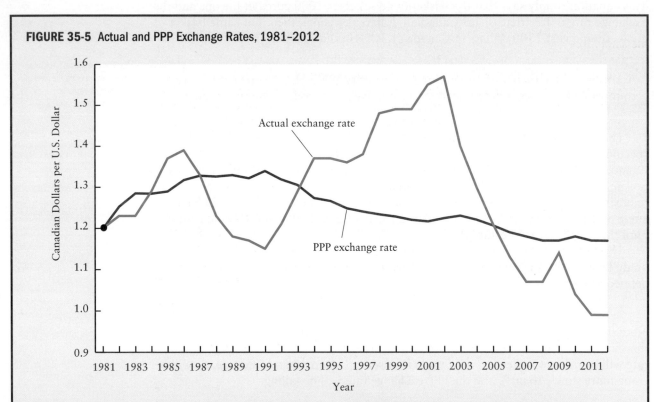

FIGURE 35-5 Actual and PPP Exchange Rates, 1981–2012

The actual exchange rate deviates from the PPP exchange rate for extended periods. The Canada–U.S. PPP exchange rate is the ratio of Canadian to U.S. price indices. This PPP exchange rate increased during the 1980s when Canadian inflation was above that in the United States; it declined over the next 20 years when Canadian inflation was lower than in the United States. The actual Canada–U.S. exchange rate has fluctuated more dramatically and shows little tendency to track the PPP exchange rate. (The PPP exchange rate is a ratio of two price indexes; it has been constructed to be equal to the actual exchange rate in 1981, the first year of the sample period.)

(*Source:* Canadian CPI is from the Bank of Canada, Series PCPISA, annual average. U.S. CPI is from U.S. Bureau of Labor Statistics: www.bls.gov. Exchange rate is from Statistics Canada, CANSIM database, Series V37432, annual average.)

Different Countries Produce Different Goods. Suppose we apply the theory of PPP to the Canada–Europe exchange rate and we use the GDP deflators from the two countries as the measures of prices. Recall from Chapter 20 that the GDP deflator is an index of prices of goods *produced within the country*. But Canada and Europe clearly produce very different goods. The price of forest products will have a large weight in the Canadian GDP deflator but less weight in the European GDP deflator; in contrast, the price of wine will have a much larger weight in the European GDP deflator than in the Canadian GDP deflator.

The implication of these differences for the theory of PPP is important. As long as changes in the *relative* prices of goods occur, such as a change in the price of forest products relative to wine, then P_C (the Canadian GDP deflator) will change relative to P_E (the European GDP deflator) *even though the prices of individual goods might be equated across the two countries.* Thus, differences in the structure of the price indices between two countries mean that using a PPP exchange rate computed on the basis of Equation 35-5 will be misleading. In other words, in the presence of changing relative prices, there is no reason to expect the actual exchange rate to equal the PPP exchange rate.

Non-Traded Goods Are Important. The previous discussion emphasized that the *baskets* of goods across two countries might differ even though the products in the baskets were the same. But even if Canada and Europe produced exactly the same range of goods, so that the various weights in the GDP deflators were the same, there is another reason why the basket of goods in Canada differs from the basket of goods in Europe. Many products in any country are *not traded internationally*, such as haircuts, restaurant meals, dry cleaning, car-repair and landscaping services, and tickets to theatres or sporting events. But, since such products cannot be traded across international boundaries, there is nothing that will force their prices to be equal across the two countries. If haircuts are more expensive in Paris than in Toronto (as they are), we do not expect people to shift their consumption of haircuts away from Paris toward Toronto, and thus we should not expect the actual exchange rate to move to make Equation 35-4 hold.

The conclusion of this discussion is that we must be very careful in selecting the price indices we use when we apply the theory of purchasing power parity. We know that countries have different patterns of production and thus have different structures to their national price indices. Thus, in the presence of changes in relative prices of various products, the national price indices can change in ways that will not lead to changes in the exchange rate. Similarly, the presence of non-traded goods implies that some differences in prices across countries will not lead to changes in the location of demand and thus changes in the exchange rate.

> Changes in relative prices and the presence of non-traded goods imply that purchasing power parity need not hold—not even in the long run.

Should Canada Have a Fixed Exchange Rate?

In recent years, some economists have suggested that Canada peg the value of its currency to the U.S. dollar. Advocates of a fixed Canadian exchange rate see this policy as a means of avoiding the significant fluctuations in the Canadian–U.S. dollar exchange rate that would otherwise occur—fluctuations such as the 10 percent depreciation that occurred between 1997 and 1999 and the 60 percent appreciation that occurred between 2002 and 2008. They argue that exchange-rate fluctuations generate uncertainty for importers and exporters and thus increase the costs associated with trade.

Others have gone further in suggesting that Canada actually abandon its currency altogether and simply adopt the U.S. dollar. They point to the European Union, which introduced the euro as its common currency in 1999. If a common currency is acceptable to most of Europe, why should Canada and the United States be any different?[4]

These are contentious suggestions that have attracted a great deal of public attention in recent years. We examine this issue by comparing the main benefits of flexible and fixed exchange rates. Whereas flexible exchange rates dampen the effects on output and employment from external shocks to the economy, fixed exchange rates reduce the uncertainty faced by importers and exporters.

Flexible Exchange Rates as "Shock Absorbers" For most of the years following the Second World War, Canada has used a flexible exchange rate. Even when most other major countries chose to peg the value of their currencies to the U.S. dollar (and to gold) under the Bretton Woods system, Canada usually chose a flexible exchange rate (there were a few short periods in which Canada fixed its exchange rate). For all of its history Canada's economy has been heavily reliant on the export of resource-based products, the prices of which are determined in world markets and are often highly variable from year to year. Changes in these prices constitute changes in Canada's terms of trade and, as we saw earlier in this chapter, changes in a country's terms of trade are an important reason why exchange rates are so variable.

That the exchange rate adjusts in response to shocks is actually the main advantage of a flexible (rather than fixed) exchange rate. A flexible exchange rate acts as a "shock absorber," dampening the effects on the country's output and employment from external shocks. To understand how this happens, consider a simple example.

Suppose a reduction in world demand leads to a reduction in the world prices of raw materials, which are major Canadian exports. When world demand for raw materials declines, there is a reduction in demand for Canadian exports and an accompanying reduction in demand for Canadian dollars (or a reduction in the supply of foreign exchange) in the foreign-exchange market. The effect on Canadian real GDP is shown in part (ii) of Figure 35-6 by the leftward shift of the AD curve. The effect in the foreign-exchange market is shown in part (i) by the leftward shift of the supply curve for foreign exchange. Consider the effect of this shock in two different situations. In the first, the Bank of Canada maintains a fixed exchange rate; in the second, the Bank of Canada allows the exchange rate to be freely determined by demand and supply.

If the Bank of Canada fixes the exchange rate at e_0, the reduction in the supply of foreign exchange from S_0 to S_1 leads to an excess demand for foreign currency. To keep the exchange rate fixed at e_0, the Bank must sell sufficient foreign-exchange reserves to satisfy the excess demand. But the negative shock to aggregate demand still occurs and thus output and employment in Canada fall, as shown in part (ii) of Figure 35-6. If this shock is large and persistent enough, Canadian wages will eventually fall and the AS curve will eventually shift downward, returning real GDP to the level of potential output. But the closing of the recessionary gap may be slow and painful.

If Canada instead has a flexible exchange rate, the reduction in the world prices of raw materials will lead to a reduction in the supply of foreign exchange and thus to a

---

[4] After over a decade of apparent success with the euro, by late 2012 Europe's adoption of a common currency was viewed by many economists as a failure. A major problem within the euro zone is the absence of independent monetary policies and flexible exchange rates between the various member countries. Individual countries within the euro zone therefore lack the macroeconomic "shock absorbers" discussed in this section.

FIGURE 35-6 Flexible Exchange Rates as a Shock Absorber

(i) Foreign-exchange market

(ii) AD and AS

Flexible exchange rates adjust to terms of trade shocks and thus dampen the effect on output and employment. The economy begins with the exchange rate equal to e_0 in part (i) and GDP equal to Y^* in part (ii). A reduction in the world's demand for Canadian exports causes a reduction in the supply of foreign exchange, shifting S_0 to S_1 in part (i).

With a fixed exchange rate, the Bank of Canada maintains the exchange rate at e_0, satisfying the excess demand for foreign exchange by selling its foreign-currency reserves. The reduction in the demand for Canada's exports is a negative aggregate demand shock. AD_0 shifts to the left to AD_1 in part (ii), causing GDP to fall to Y_1. The recessionary gap eventually pushes wages down, the AS curve shifts downward over time, and the economy moves along AD_1 to Y^*. The adjustment, however, may be very slow.

With a flexible exchange rate, the Bank of Canada allows the Canadian dollar to depreciate. The exchange rate rises to e_1 in part (i). The reduction in demand for Canadian exports still causes the AD curve to shift to the left in part (ii), but the shift is dampened by the depreciation of the dollar, which makes Canadian exports more attractive in world markets. The AD curve shifts only to AD_2 and so GDP falls only to Y_2. There is still a recession, but smaller than in the case with a fixed exchange rate.

depreciation of the Canadian dollar. The exchange rate will increase from e_0 to e_1. The AD curve will shift to the left, reducing Canada's GDP, just as in the fixed-exchange-rate case, but it will not shift as far. The sectors of the Canadian economy producing raw materials will still be in recession, for there has been a reduction in demand for these products. But the overall Canadian downturn will be dampened by the depreciation of the Canadian dollar. Other exporting sectors of the Canadian economy will actually *expand* as a result of the depreciation because their products are now less expensive in world markets. Thus, as shown in part (ii) of Figure 35-6, the leftward shift of the AD curve will not be as large as in the case of the fixed exchange rate. The overall result is that, with a flexible exchange rate, the decline in world demand for Canadian goods leads to a less severe Canadian recession than if Canada had a fixed exchange rate.

One of the advantages of flexible exchange rates is that, in response to shocks to the terms of trade, the exchange rate can act as a shock absorber, dampening the effects of the shock on output and employment.

The Asian Crisis of 1997–1998 provides an excellent example of how Canada's flexible exchange rate dampened the effects of a negative external shock. When the Asian countries of Malaysia, Indonesia, Thailand, and South Korea experienced their large recessions in 1997 and 1998, their demand for many raw materials declined sharply. As they are major users of raw materials, the effect was felt on world markets. The average prices of raw materials fell by roughly 30 percent from the summer of 1997 to the end of 1998. Many of these raw materials, of course, are important exports for Canada, and so the decline in their world prices implied a terms-of-trade deterioration for Canada.

Especially hard hit was British Columbia's forestry sector, in which output fell dramatically in many paper and lumber mills because of the lack of sales in Asia. As expected, there was also a significant depreciation of the Canadian dollar, just as described in Figure 35-6. But as the Canadian dollar depreciated, the Canadian manufacturing sector, concentrated mainly in Ontario and Quebec, was given a large boost. The 10 percent depreciation of the Canadian dollar meant that Canadian machinery, furniture, telecommunications equipment, and a whole range of other products were now more attractive in world markets. Thus, the boom in the Central Canadian manufacturing sector offset to some extent the significant recession that was going on in British Columbia. If Canada had had a fixed exchange rate, the 10 percent depreciation would not have occurred. But the initial shock from the Asian Crisis would still have taken place. The net result would have been lower output and higher unemployment than actually occurred.

A few years later, between 2002 and 2008, the opposite forces were at work, and once again Canada's flexible exchange rate acted as a shock absorber. Because of strong global economic growth, especially in China and India, world prices for energy and other raw materials increased significantly. This was a positive shock to Canadian aggregate demand, and the price increase caused an improvement in Canada's terms of trade and an appreciation of the Canadian dollar by more than 60 percent. During this period the energy and commodity-producing sectors of the Canadian economy were booming. At the same time, however, the appreciation of the Canadian dollar tended to reduce activity in the central Canadian manufacturing sector, thus dampening the overall effect of the positive shock on the Canadian economy.

Note that having a fixed exchange rate does not prevent a country from being subjected to shocks from the rest of the world. Some advocates of fixed exchange rates seem to think that by fixing the value of a country's currency, the country is shielding itself from undesirable fluctuations. But shocks to a country's terms of trade will always occur. As long as there are changes in the demand for and supply of various products around the world, there will also be changes in a country's terms of trade. What Figure 35-6 shows, however, is that by fixing the exchange rate and thus avoiding the fluctuations in the value of the currency, the effects of the shock merely show up as increased volatility in output and employment.

> A country will always experience shocks in its terms of trade. A flexible exchange rate absorbs some of the shock, reducing the effect on output and employment. A fixed exchange rate simply redistributes the effect of the shock—the exchange rate is smoother but output and employment are more volatile.

Trade, Transaction Costs, and Uncertainty Despite the benefits of international trade, there are costs involved in exporting and importing goods and services. The *transaction costs* of international trade involve the costs associated with converting one currency to another, as must be done either by the importer or by the exporter of the product that is traded. For example, if you have an import–export business in Canada and want to import some bicycles from Japan, you will probably have to purchase Japanese yen at a bank or foreign-exchange dealer and, with those yen, pay the Japanese seller for the bicycles. Even if the Japanese seller accepts Canadian dollars for the bicycles, and this often is the case, he will be required to convert those Canadian dollars into yen before he can use that money in Japan to pay his workers or pay for other costs of production.

> **The greater is the volume of trade between two countries, the higher are the aggregate transaction costs associated with international trade.**

Such transaction costs exist even if trade takes place between two countries with fixed exchange rates. For example, if the Bank of Canada pegged the value of the Canadian dollar to the U.S. dollar, any trade between the two countries would still require the costly conversion of one currency to the other. Thus, the existence of transaction costs cannot be used as an argument in favour of fixed exchange rates and against flexible exchange rates. As long as there are two currencies, the transaction costs must be borne by one party or the other. These transaction costs could be avoided only if the two countries shared a common currency.

Many economists believe, however, that the volatility of flexible exchange rates generates another type of cost for importers and exporters. Specifically, the unpredictability of the exchange rate leads to *uncertainty* about the profitability of any specific international transaction. Such uncertainty, given risk-averse firms, can be expected to lead to a smaller volume of international trade and thus to fewer benefits from such trade.

For example, suppose a Canadian appliance manufacturer enters into a contract to purchase a specified amount of steel from a Japanese producer for a specified yen price in one year's time. In this case, the Japanese producer bears no *foreign-exchange risk* because the price is specified in yen. But the Canadian appliance manufacturer bears considerable risk. If the yen depreciates relative to the dollar over the coming year, fewer Canadian dollars will be required to pay for the steel. But if the yen appreciates relative to the dollar over the coming year, more Canadian dollars will be required to pay for the steel. The Canadian buyer therefore faces a risk in terms of the Canadian-dollar cost of the steel. If the firm is *risk averse*, meaning simply that it would be prepared to pay a cost to avoid the risk, the presence of the risk may lead to fewer international transactions of this type. Perhaps to avoid the foreign-exchange risk, the Canadian buyer will decide instead to buy Canadian-made steel, even though it may be slightly more expensive or not quite the right type that is needed.

> **If the presence of foreign-exchange risk leads to less international trade, there will be a reduction in the gains from trade.**

Many of the people who advocate Canada's move to a fixed exchange rate point to the avoidance of this foreign-exchange risk as the main benefit. They argue that if the Canadian dollar were pegged in value to the U.S. dollar, both importers and exporters would face less uncertainty on the most important part of their trade—that between Canada and the United States. With the greater certainty, they argue, would come greater trade flows and thus an increase in the overall gains from trade.

But many economists disagree. While accepting the basic argument regarding the risks created by flexible (and volatile) exchange rates, they note that importers and exporters already have the means to avoid this uncertainty. In particular, traders can participate in *forward markets* in which they can buy or sell foreign exchange *in the future* at prices specified today. For example, the Canadian appliance manufacturer could enter into a contract to purchase the required amount of yen in one year's time at a price specified today. In this case, no matter what happened to the yen–dollar exchange rate in the intervening year, the uncertainty regarding the Canadian-dollar price of the steel would be entirely eliminated.

Limitations for Monetary Policy One final point should be noted about the choice between flexible and fixed exchange rates. If the Bank of Canada chooses to allow the exchange rate to fluctuate in response to shocks, it can focus its monetary policy on the control of inflation. In other words, it can adjust its monetary policy—sometimes tightening and other times loosening—to keep inflation close to the stated 2 percent target. But if the Bank chooses instead to fix the exchange rate, it is not *also* able to control inflation.

As we saw in Chapter 29, the Bank of Canada conducts its monetary policy by establishing a target for the overnight interest rate and maintaining that rate through its lending and borrowing activities with the commercial banks. If the Bank chooses to intervene in the foreign-exchange market to keep the exchange rate fixed—sometimes buying foreign exchange and other times selling it—these transactions will influence the Canadian money supply directly and thus influence Canadian interest rates. But these changes in interest rates may not be consistent with the Bank's policy objective of keeping inflation close to the 2 percent target.

> Efforts by the Bank of Canada to maintain a fixed exchange rate are likely to be inconsistent with its efforts to keep inflation close to the 2 percent target.

Summing Up So, should Canada give up its flexible exchange rate and instead peg the value of the Canadian dollar to the U.S. dollar? Advocates of this policy emphasize the foreign-exchange risk faced by importers, exporters, and investors, and the gains from increased trade that would result from a fixed exchange rate. Opponents to the policy emphasize the shock-absorption benefits from a flexible exchange rate.

This debate will surely continue, partly because it is difficult to quantify the costs and benefits of a flexible exchange rate. Economists on both sides of the debate understand and accept the logic of the arguments from the other side. But researchers have so far been unable to determine how much of a shock is absorbed by a flexible exchange rate, and thus to estimate how much more volatile output and employment would be with a fixed exchange rate. Similarly, it is very difficult to estimate just how much more trade would take place if the foreign-exchange risk faced by traders were eliminated by means of a fixed exchange rate. Without convincing empirical evidence supporting the move to a fixed exchange rate, however, the status quo will probably remain. It is probably safe to assume that Canada will continue to have a flexible exchange rate, at least for the next several years.

SUMMARY

35.1 The Balance of Payments

- Actual transactions among Canadian firms, households, and governments and those in the rest of the world are reported in the balance of payments accounts. In these accounts, any transaction that represents a receipt for Canada (Canadians sell goods or assets to foreigners) is recorded as a credit item. Any transaction that represents a payment from Canada (Canadians purchase goods or assets from foreigners) is recorded as a debit item.
- Categories in the balance of payments accounts are the trade account, the capital-service account, the current account (which is equal to the trade account plus the capital-service account), and the capital account (which includes the official financing account).
- If all transactions are recorded in the balance of payments, the sum of all credit items necessarily equals the sum of all debit items. Thus, the balance of payments must always balance.
- A country with a current account deficit must also have a capital inflow—a capital account surplus. A country with a current account surplus must also have a capital outflow—a capital account deficit.

35.2 The Foreign-Exchange Market

- The exchange rate between the Canadian dollar and some foreign currency is defined as the number of Canadian dollars required to purchase one unit of the foreign currency. A rise in the exchange rate is a depreciation of the Canadian dollar; a fall in the exchange rate is an appreciation of the Canadian dollar.
- The supply of foreign exchange (or the demand for Canadian dollars) arises from Canadian exports of goods and services, capital flows into Canada, and the desire of foreign banks, firms, and governments to use Canadian dollars as part of their reserves.
- The demand for foreign exchange (or the supply of Canadian dollars to purchase foreign currencies) arises from Canadian imports of goods and services, capital flows from Canada, and the desire of holders of Canadian dollars to decrease the size of their holdings.
- A depreciation of the Canadian dollar lowers the foreign price of Canadian exports and increases the amount of foreign exchange supplied (to purchase Canadian exports). Thus, the supply curve for foreign exchange is positively sloped when plotted against the exchange rate.
- A depreciation of the Canadian dollar raises the dollar price of imports from abroad and hence lowers the amount of foreign exchange demanded to purchase foreign goods. Thus, the demand curve for foreign exchange is negatively sloped when plotted against the exchange rate.

35.3 The Determination of Exchange Rates

- When the central bank does not intervene in the foreign exchange market, there is a purely flexible exchange rate. Under fixed exchange rates, the central bank intervenes in the foreign-exchange market to maintain the exchange rate at an announced value. To do this, the central bank must hold sufficient stocks of foreign-exchange reserves.
- Under a flexible, or floating, exchange rate, the exchange rate is determined by supply of and demand for the currency.
- The Canadian dollar will appreciate in foreign-exchange markets if there is an increase in the supply of foreign exchange (an increase in the demand for Canadian dollars) or if there is a reduction in the demand for foreign exchange (a reduction in the supply of Canadian dollars). The opposite changes will lead to a depreciation of the Canadian dollar.
- Changes in the exchange rate are caused by changes in such things as changes in world prices, the rate of inflation in different countries, capital flows, structural conditions, and expectations about the future exchange rate.

35.4 Three Policy Issues

- The view that current account deficits are undesirable is usually based on the mercantilist notion that exports are "good" and imports are "bad." But the gains from trade have nothing to do with the balance of trade—they depend on the volume of trade.
- From national income accounting, the current account balance is given by

$$CA = (S - I) + (T - G)$$

- An increase in investment, a decrease in saving, and an increase in the government budget deficit can each be the cause of a rise in the current account deficit.
- With a flexible exchange rate, supply and demand in the foreign-exchange market determine the "correct" value of the exchange rate. But this "correct" value is constantly changing as market conditions vary.
- The theory of purchasing power parity (PPP) predicts that exchange rates will adjust so that the purchasing power of a given currency is the same in different countries. That is, the prices of identical baskets of goods will be equated in different countries (when expressed in the same currency).
- If price indices from different countries are used as the basis for computing the PPP exchange rate, differences in the structure of price indices across countries, together with the presence of non-traded goods, can be responsible for persistent deviations of the actual exchange rate from this measure of the PPP exchange rate.
- An important benefit of a flexible exchange rate is that it acts as a shock absorber, dampening the effects on output and employment from shocks to a country's terms of trade.
- An important benefit of fixed exchange rates is that they reduce transaction costs and foreign-exchange risk faced by importers and exporters.

KEY CONCEPTS

Balance of payments
Current and capital accounts
Changes in official reserves
Foreign exchange and exchange rates
Appreciation and depreciation

Sources of the demand for and
 supply of foreign exchange
Fixed and flexible exchange rates
Mercantilism
Purchasing power parity

PPP exchange rate
Flexible exchange rates as shock
 absorbers
Foreign-exchange risk

STUDY EXERCISES

MyEconLab   Make the grade with MyEconLab: Study Exercises marked in red can be found on MyEconLab. You can practise them as often as you want, and most feature step-by-step guided instructions to help you find the right answer.

1. Fill in the blanks to make the following statements correct.

   a. If a wine shop in Alberta buys a case of wine from Chile, the transaction is recorded as a(n) _____ in the _____ account, which is a subsection of the _____ account.

   b. If a Canadian receives dividend payments from a firm in Britain, the transaction is recorded as a(n) _____ in the _____ account, which is a subsection of the _____ account.

   c. If a German pension-fund manager purchases a B.C. Hydro bond, the transaction is recorded as a(n) _____ in the _____ account. If a Canadian sells her ownership stake in a newspaper chain to an American, the transaction is recorded as a(n) _____ in the _____ account.

   d. The sum of the current account and the capital account is known as the _____ and must *always* equal _____.

2. Fill in the blanks to make the following statements correct.

   a. A depreciation of the Canadian dollar means that it takes _____ Canadian dollars to purchase one unit of foreign currency, and there has been a(n) _____ in the exchange rate. An appreciation of the Canadian dollar means that it takes _____ Canadian dollars to purchase one unit of foreign currency, and there has been a(n) _____ in the exchange rate.

b. Suppose a newscaster tells us that the Canadian dollar is valued at 89.6 U.S. cents. Using the definition from this chapter, we say the Canadian–U.S. exchange rate is _____, meaning that it takes _____ Canadian dollars to buy one U.S. dollar.

c. The exchange rate is determined at the intersection of the _____ curve for foreign exchange and the _____ curve for foreign exchange. An exchange rate above this level means an excess _____ foreign exchange, which is also an excess _____ Canadian dollars. The exchange rate will _____ and the Canadian dollar will _____.

d. If there is a rise in foreign GDP, and foreign demand for Canadian goods increases, there will be a(n) _____ in supply of foreign currency. The Canadian dollar will _____.

e. An increase in Canadian prices relative to foreign prices will cause a(n) _____ in the demand for foreign exchange, and a(n) _____ in the supply of foreign exchange. The exchange rate will _____ and the Canadian dollar will therefore _____.

3. Fill in the blanks to make the following statements correct.

a. If the exchange rate is determined by the equality of supply and demand for foreign exchange and the central bank makes no foreign-exchange transactions, we say there is a(n) _____ exchange rate.

b. If the central bank buys and sells foreign exchange in an effort to maintain the exchange rate at a specific value, we say we have a(n) _____ exchange rate.

c. If the central bank pegs the exchange rate above its free-market equilibrium level, there will be a(n) _____ foreign exchange and the central bank will _____ foreign currency.

d. If the central bank pegs the exchange rate below its free-market equilibrium level, there will be a(n) _____ foreign exchange and the central bank will _____ foreign currency.

4. The table below shows Scott's financial details for 2013. Answer the following questions about his "balance of payments."

Scott's Financial Details, 2013	
Income from lifeguarding	$2 500
Income from lawn mowing	3 500
Gift from grandparents	1 000
Interest from bank deposits	150
Expenditure on coffee and pastry	1 000
Expenditure on tuition	3 500
Purchase of mutual funds	1 200
Bank balance at end of year	3 500
Increase in bank balance during the year	1 450

a. What is Scott's "trade balance"? Explain.

b. What is Scott's overall current account balance? Explain.

c. What is Scott's capital account balance? Explain.

d. There is one (and only one) piece of information shown above that is not needed to compute Scott's balance of payments. What is it? Explain why it is not needed.

5. The diagram below shows the demand for foreign currency (the supply of Canadian dollars) and the supply of foreign currency (the demand for Canadian dollars). The equilibrium exchange rate is e^*. Assume that Canada has a purely flexible exchange rate.

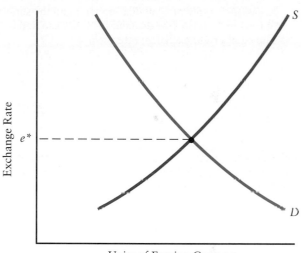

Units of Foreign Currency

a. Show in the diagram the effect of a general inflation in Canada (when there is no inflation in the rest of the world). Explain.

b. Show what happens to the exchange rate if there is a large increase in foreign demand for Canadian telecommunications equipment. Explain.

c. Show the effect of an increase in Canadian investors' demand for Japanese government bonds. Explain.

6. What is the probable effect of each of the following on the exchange rate of a country, other things being equal?

a. The quantity of oil imports is greatly decreased, but the expenditure on imported oil is higher because of price increases.

b. The country's inflation rate falls much lower than that of its trading partners.

c. Rising labour costs of the country's manufacturers lead to a worsening ability to compete in world markets.

d. The government greatly expands its gifts of food and machinery to developing countries.

e. A major boom occurs with rising employment.
f. The central bank raises interest rates sharply.
g. More domestic oil is discovered and developed.

7. Many commentators are perplexed when they observe a depreciation of the Canadian dollar but not a reduction in the Canadian current account deficit. Explain why there is not a precise relationship between the value of the dollar and the current account balance. Give one example of an event that would give rise to each of the following:

   a. Appreciation of the Canadian dollar and a fall in Canada's current account surplus
   b. Depreciation of the Canadian dollar and a fall in Canada's current account surplus

8. The diagram below shows the demand for foreign currency (the supply of Canadian dollars) and the supply of foreign currency (the demand for Canadian dollars). The equilibrium exchange rate is e^*.

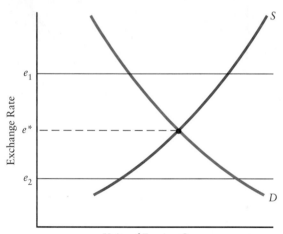

a. Suppose the Bank of Canada decides to fix the exchange rate at e_1. What must the Bank do to accomplish its goal? How do the Bank's actions show up in the balance of payments accounts?
b. In part (a), explain why some people would call this a "a balance of payments surplus" even though the balance of payments is in balance.
c. Now suppose the Bank of Canada decides to fix the exchange rate at e_2. What must the Bank do to accomplish this goal? How do the Bank's actions show up in the balance of payments accounts?
d. With the exchange rate fixed at e_2, explain why some people would call this a "balance of payments deficit" even though the balance of payments is in balance.

9. Suppose that Canadian real GDP is equal to potential output, the price level is stable, and the exchange rate is equal to e_0, its market-clearing value. There is then an upturn in the world demand for construction materials, especially lumber.

a. Draw a diagram of the foreign-exchange market. Assuming that Canada has a flexible exchange rate, show the likely effect on Canada's exchange rate of the increase in world demand for construction materials.
b. Explain the Bank of Canada's participation in the foreign-exchange market if Canada's exchange rate is fixed at e_0.
c. Now draw an *AD/AS* diagram for the Canadian economy. What is the likely effect of the shock on Canadian GDP under the conditions in part (a)?
d. On the same *AD/AS* diagram from part (c), show the effect of the shock on Canadian GDP under the conditions of part (b).
e. Explain how a flexible exchange rate acts as a shock absorber, insulating the economy from both positive and negative shocks.

10. Every few months, *The Economist* publishes its "Big Mac Index." Using the current exchange rates, it compares the U.S.-dollar price of Big Macs in several countries. It then concludes that countries in which the Big Mac is cheaper (in U.S. dollars) than in the United States have "undervalued" currencies. Similarly, countries with Big Macs more expensive than in the United States have "overvalued" currencies. The table below shows data from July 2012. (Data from **www.economist.com**.) It shows the domestic-currency prices of Big Macs in various countries. It also shows the exchange rate, expressed as the number of units of domestic currency needed to purchase one U.S. dollar.

Country	Domestic Currency Price	Exchange Rate	U.S. Dollar Price
Canada	$3.89 (Cdn.)	1.02	$___
Australia	$4.56 (Aus.)	0.97	$___
U.S.A.	$4.33	1.00	$___
Japan	320 yen	78.22	$___
Euro area	3.58 euros	0.83	$___
U.K.	2.69 pounds	0.65	$___

a. For each country, use the exchange rate provided to convert the domestic-currency price to the U.S.-dollar price. The price in terms of the currency for any country i is $P_i = e \times P_{U.S.}$.
b. By the logic used in *The Economist*, which currencies are overvalued and which are undervalued relative to the U.S. dollar?
c. Are Big Macs traded goods? If not, does this present a problem for *The Economist*? Explain.

  d. Which of the following goods do you think would be a better candidate for this exercise? Explain your choice.
  (i) cement
  (ii) diamonds
  (iii) fresh fruit
  (iv) computer RAM chips

11. A former Canadian prime minister once suggested that Canada should try to have balanced trade, industry by industry.

   a. Do you think this makes sense? Explain.
   b. How about the idea of balanced trade, country by country? Explain whether this makes sense.

12. In 2007, after the Canadian dollar had appreciated significantly over the previous few years, a letter to *The Globe and Mail* said that "the economy of this once wonderful country is in the sewer and the politicians keep on tinkering, not knowing how to fix it." The letter proposed a 20 percent depreciation of the Canadian dollar and argued that the immediate effects would be (among other things)

   • a dramatic rise in exports
   • a dramatic fall in imports
   • a large net inflow of new foreign investment

   a. What could the Bank of Canada do to generate a 20 percent depreciation of the Canadian dollar?
   b. Would the action necessary in part (a) be consistent with the Bank's stated commitment to keeping inflation close to the 2 percent target? Explain.
   c. However such a depreciation of the Canadian dollar might occur, is it possible to have the three effects claimed by the author of the letter? Explain.

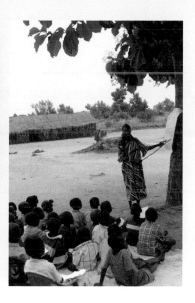

MyEconLab — Additional Chapter Online

The chapter **Challenges Facing the Developing Countries** can be found on the MyEconLab. www.myeconlab.com

Mathematical Notes

1. Because one cannot divide by zero, the ratio $\Delta Y / \Delta X$ cannot be evaluated when $\Delta X = 0$. However, as ΔX *approaches* zero, the ratio $\Delta Y / \Delta X$ increases without limit:

$$\lim_{\Delta X \to 0} \frac{\Delta Y}{\Delta X} = \infty$$

Therefore, we say that the slope of a vertical line (when $\Delta X = 0$ for any ΔY) is equal to infinity. (p. 46)

2. Many variables affect the quantity demanded. Using functional notation, the argument of the next several pages of the text can be anticipated. Let Q^D represent the quantity of a commodity demanded and

$$T, \overline{Y}, N, \hat{Y}, p, p_j$$

represent, respectively, tastes, average household income, population, income distribution, the commodity's own price, and the price of the jth other commodity.

The demand function is

$$Q^D = D(T, \overline{Y}, N, \hat{Y}, p, p_j), \qquad j = 1, 2, \ldots, n$$

The demand schedule or curve is given by

$$Q^D = d(p) \Big|_{T, \overline{Y}, N, \hat{Y}, p_j}$$

where the notation means that the variables to the right of the vertical line are held constant.

This function is correctly described as the demand function with respect to price, all other variables being held constant. This function, often written concisely as $Q^D = d(p)$, shifts in response to changes in other variables. Consider average income: if, as is usually hypothesized, $\partial Q^D / \partial \overline{Y} > 0$, then increases in average income shift $Q^D = d(p)$ rightward and decreases in average income shift $Q^D = d(p)$ leftward. Changes in other variables likewise shift this function in the direction implied by the relationship of that variable to the quantity demanded. (p. 56)

3. Quantity demanded is a simple and straightforward but frequently misunderstood concept in everyday use, but it has a clear mathematical meaning. It refers to the dependent variable in the demand function from note 2:

$$Q^D = D(T, \overline{Y}, N, \hat{Y}, p, p_j)$$

It takes on a specific value whenever a specific value is assigned to each of the independent variables. The value of Q^D changes whenever the value of any independent variable is changed. Q^D could change, for example, as a result of a change in any one price, in average income, in the distribution of income, in tastes, or in population. It could also change as a result of the net effect of changes in all of the independent variables occurring at once.

Some textbooks reserve the term *change in quantity demanded* for a movement along a demand curve, that is, a change in Q^D as a result *only* of a change in p. They then use other words for a change in Q^D caused by a change in the other variables in the demand function. This usage is potentially confusing because it gives the single variable Q^D more than one name.

Our usage, which corresponds to that in more advanced treatments, avoids this confusion. We call Q^D *quantity demanded* and refer to any change in Q^D as a *change in quantity demanded*. In this usage it is correct to say that a movement along a demand curve is a change in quantity demanded, but it is incorrect to say that a change in quantity demanded can occur *only because of* a movement along a demand curve (because Q^D can change for other reasons, for example, a *ceteris paribus* change in average household income). (p. 63)

4. Similar to the way we treated quantity demanded in note 2, let Q^S represent the quantity of a commodity supplied and

$$C, X, p, w_i$$

represent, respectively, producers' goals, technology, the product's price, and the price of the ith input.

The supply function is

$$Q^S = S(C, X, p, w_i), \qquad i = 1, 2, \ldots, m$$

The supply schedule or curve is given by

$$Q^S = s(p)\Big|_{C, X, w_j}$$

This is the supply function with respect to price, all other variables being held constant. This function, often written concisely as $Q^S = s(p)$, shifts in response to changes in other variables. (p. 64)

5. Equilibrium occurs where $Q^D = Q^S$. For *specified values of all other variables,* this requires that

$$d(p) = s(p) \qquad [5.1]$$

Equation 5.1 defines an equilibrium value of p; hence, although p is an *independent* or *exogenous* variable in each of the supply and demand functions, it is an *endogenous* variable in the economic model that imposes the equilibrium condition expressed in Equation 5.1. Price is endogenous because it is assumed to adjust to bring about equality between quantity demanded and quantity supplied. Equilibrium quantity, also an endogenous variable, is determined by substituting the equilibrium price into either $d(p)$ or $s(p)$.

Graphically, Equation 5.1 is satisfied only at the point where the demand and supply curves intersect. Thus, supply and demand curves are said to determine the equilibrium values of the endogenous variables, price and quantity. A shift in any of the independent variables held constant in the d and s functions will shift the demand or supply curves and lead to different equilibrium values for price and quantity. (p. 70)

6. The axis reversal arose in the following way. Alfred Marshall (1842–1924) theorized in terms of "demand price" and "supply price," which were the prices that would lead to a given quantity being demanded or supplied. Thus,

$$p^D = d(Q) \qquad [6.1]$$

$$p^S = s(Q) \qquad [6.2]$$

and the condition of equilibrium is

$$d(Q) = s(Q)$$

When graphing the behavioural relationships expressed in Equations 6.1 and 6.2, Marshall naturally put the independent variable, Q, on the horizontal axis.

Leon Walras (1834–1910), whose formulation of the working of a competitive market has become the accepted one, focused on quantity demanded and quantity supplied *at a given price.* Thus,

$$Q^D = d(p)$$

$$Q^S = s(p)$$

and the condition of equilibrium is

$$d(p) = s(p)$$

Walras did not use graphical representation. Had he done so, he would surely have placed p (his independent variable) on the horizontal axis.

Marshall's work influenced later generations of economists, in particular because he was the great popularizer of graphical analysis in economics. Today, we use his graphs, even for Walras's analysis. The axis reversal is thus one of those historical accidents that seem odd to people who did not live through the "perfectly natural" sequence of steps that produced it. (p. 71)

7. The definition in the text uses finite changes and is called *arc elasticity.* The parallel definition using derivatives is

$$\eta = \frac{dQ}{dp} \cdot \frac{p}{Q}$$

and is called *point elasticity.* Further discussion appears in the *Additional Topic* "Some Further Details About Demand Elasticity." (p. 85)

8. The propositions in the text are proved as follows. Letting *TE* stand for total expenditure, we can write

$$TE = p \cdot Q$$

It follows that the change in total expenditure is

$$dTE = Q \cdot dp + p \cdot dQ \qquad [8.1]$$

Multiplying and dividing both terms on the right-hand side of Equation 8.1 by $p \cdot Q$ yields

$$dTE = \left[\frac{dp}{p} + \frac{dQ}{Q} \right] \cdot (p \cdot Q)$$

Because dp and dQ are opposite in sign as we move along the demand curve, dTE will have the same sign as the term in brackets on the right-hand side that dominates—that is, on which percentage change is largest.

A second way of arranging Equation 8.1 is to divide both sides by dp to get

$$\frac{dTE}{dp} = Q + p \cdot \frac{dQ}{dp} \qquad [8.2]$$

From the definition of point elasticity in note 7, however,

$$Q \cdot \eta = p \cdot \frac{dQ}{dp} \qquad [8.3]$$

which we can substitute into Equation 8.1 to obtain

$$\frac{dTE}{dp} = Q + Q \cdot \eta = Q \cdot (1 + \eta) \qquad [8.4]$$

Because η is a negative number, the sign of the right-hand side of Equation 8.4 is negative if the absolute value of η exceeds unity (elastic demand) and positive if it is less than unity (inelastic demand).

Total expenditure is maximized when dTE/dp is equal to zero. As can be seen from Equation 8.4, this occurs when elasticity is equal to -1. (p. 89)

9. The distinction made between an incremental change and a marginal change is the distinction for the function $Y = Y(X)$ between $\Delta Y/\Delta X$ and the derivative dY/dX. The latter is the limit of the former as ΔX approaches zero. We shall meet this distinction repeatedly—in this chapter in reference to marginal and incremental *utility* and in later chapters with respect to such concepts as marginal and incremental *product, cost,* and *revenue.* Where Y is a function of more than one variable—for example, $Y = f(X,Z)$—the marginal relationship between Y and X is the partial derivative $\partial Y/\partial X$ rather than the total derivative dY/dX. (p. 125)

10. The hypothesis of diminishing marginal utility requires that we can measure utility of consumption by a function

$$U = U(X_1, X_2, \ldots, X_n)$$

where $X_1, \ldots, X_n$ are quantities of the n goods consumed by a household. It really embodies two utility hypotheses: first,

$$\partial U/\partial X_i > 0$$

which says that the consumer can get more utility by increasing consumption of the commodity; second,

$$\partial^2 U/\partial X_i^2 < 0$$

which says that the utility of *additional* consumption of some good declines as the amount of that good consumed increases. (p. 126)

11. Because the slope of the indifference curve is negative, it is the absolute value of the slope that declines as one moves downward to the right along the curve. The algebraic value, of course, increases. The phrase *diminishing marginal rate of substitution* thus refers to the absolute, not the algebraic, value of the slope. (p. 145)

12. The relationship between the slope of the budget line and relative prices can be seen as follows. In the two-good example with prices held constant, a change in expenditure (ΔE) is given by the equation

$$\Delta E = p_C \cdot \Delta C + p_F \cdot \Delta F \qquad [12.1]$$

Expenditure is constant for all combinations of F and C that lie on the same budget line. Thus, along such a line we have $\Delta E = 0$. This implies

$$p_C \cdot \Delta C + p_F \cdot \Delta F = 0 \qquad [12.2]$$

and thus

$$\Delta C/\Delta F = -p_F/p_C \qquad [12.3]$$

The ratio $\Delta C/\Delta F$ is the slope of the budget line. It is negative because, with a fixed budget, one must consume less C in order to consume more F. In other words, Equation 12.3 says that the negative of the slope of the budget line is the ratio of the absolute prices (i.e., the relative price). Although prices do not show directly in Figure 6A-3, they are implicit in the budget line: Its slope depends solely on the relative price, while its position, given a fixed money income, depends on the absolute prices of the two goods. (p. 147)

13. *Marginal product,* as defined in the text, is really *incremental* product. More advanced treatments distinguish between this notion and marginal product as the limit of the ratio as ΔL approaches

zero. Marginal product thus measures the rate at which total product is changing as one factor is varied and is the partial derivative of the total product with respect to the variable factor. In symbols,

$$MP = \frac{\partial TP}{\partial L}$$

(p. 164)

14. We have referred specifically both to diminishing *marginal* product and to diminishing *average* product. In most cases, eventually diminishing marginal product implies eventually diminishing average product. This is, however, not necessary, as the accompanying figure shows.

    In this case, marginal product diminishes after v units of the variable factor are employed. Because marginal product falls toward, but never quite reaches, a value of m, average product rises continually toward, but never quite reaches, the same value. (p. 166)

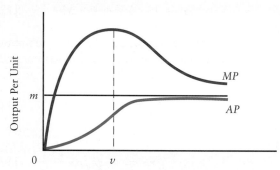

Units of the Variable Factor

15. Let Q be the quantity of output and L the quantity of the variable factor. In the short run,

$$TP = Q = f(L) \qquad [15.1]$$

We now define

$$AP = \frac{Q}{L} = \frac{f(L)}{L} \qquad [15.2]$$

$$MP = \frac{dQ}{dL} \qquad [15.3]$$

We are concerned with the relationship between AP and MP. Where average product is rising, at a maximum, or falling is determined by its derivative with respect to L:

$$\frac{d(Q/L)}{dL} = \frac{L \cdot (dQ/dL) - Q}{L^2} \qquad [15.4]$$

This may be rewritten

$$\frac{1}{L} \cdot \left[\frac{dQ}{dL} - \frac{Q}{L} \right] = \frac{1}{L} \cdot (MP - AP) \qquad [15.5]$$

Clearly, when MP is greater than AP, the expression in Equation 15.5 is positive and thus AP is rising. When MP is less than AP, AP is falling. When they are equal, AP is neither rising nor falling. (p. 166)

16. The text defines *incremental cost*. Strictly, marginal cost is the rate of change of total cost with respect to output, Q. Thus,

$$MC = \frac{dTC}{dQ}$$

From the definitions, $TC = TFC + TVC$. Fixed costs are not a function of output. Thus, we may write $TC = Z + f(Q)$, where $f(Q)$ is total variable costs and Z is a constant. From this we see that $MC = df(Q)/dQ$. MC is thus independent of the size of the fixed costs. (p. 167)

17. This point is easily seen if a little algebra is used:

$$AVC = \frac{TVC}{Q}$$

but note that $TVC = L \cdot w$ and $Q = AP \cdot L$, where L is the quantity of the variable factor used and w is its cost per unit. Therefore,

$$AVC = \frac{L \cdot w}{AP \cdot L} = \frac{w}{AP}$$

Because w is a constant, it follows that AVC and AP vary inversely with each other, and when AP is at its maximum value, AVC must be at its minimum value. (p. 170)

18. A little elementary calculus will prove the point:

$$MC = \frac{dTC}{dQ} = \frac{dTVC}{dQ} = \frac{d(L \cdot w)}{dQ}$$

If w does not vary with output,

$$MC = \frac{dL}{dQ} \cdot w$$

However, referring to note 15 (Equation 15.3), we see that

$$\frac{dL}{dQ} = \frac{1}{MP}$$

Thus,

$$MC = \frac{w}{MP}$$

Because w is fixed, MC varies negatively with MP. When MP is at a maximum, MC is at a minimum. (p. 170)

19. Strictly speaking, the marginal rate of substitution refers to the slope of the tangent to the isoquant at a particular point, whereas the calculations in Table 8A-1 refer to the average rate of substitution between two distinct points on the isoquant. Assume a production function

$$Q = Q(K,L) \qquad [19.1]$$

Isoquants are given by the function

$$K = I(L, \overline{Q}) \qquad [19.2]$$

derived from Equation 19.1 by expressing K as an explicit function of L and Q. A single isoquant relates to a particular level of output, $\overline{Q}$. Define Q_K and Q_L as an alternative, more compact notation for $\partial Q/\partial K$ and $\partial Q/\partial L$, the marginal products of capital and labour. Also, let Q_{KK} and Q_{LL} stand for $\partial^2 Q/\partial K^2$ and $\partial^2 Q/\partial L^2$, respectively. To obtain the slope of the isoquant, totally differentiate Equation 19.1 to obtain

$$dQ = Q_K.dK + Q_L \cdot dL$$

Then, because we are moving along a single isoquant, set $dQ = 0$ to obtain

$$\frac{dK}{dL} = -\frac{Q_L}{Q_K} = MRS$$

Diminishing marginal productivity implies $Q_{LL} < 0$ and $Q_{KK} < 0$, and hence, as we move down the isoquant of Figure 8A-1, Q_K is rising and Q_L is falling, so the absolute value of MRS is diminishing. This is called the *hypothesis of a diminishing marginal rate of substitution*. (p. 195)

20. Formally, the problem is to choose K and L in order to maximize

$$Q = Q(K, L)$$

subject to the constraint

$$p_K \cdot K + p_L \cdot L = C$$

To do this, form the Lagrangean,

$$\mathcal{L} = Q(K,L) - \lambda(p_K \cdot K + p_L \cdot L - C)$$

where λ is called the Lagrange multiplier.

The first-order conditions for this maximization problem are

$$Q_K = \lambda \cdot p_K \qquad [20.1]$$
$$Q_L = \lambda \cdot p_L \qquad [20.2]$$
$$p_K \cdot K + p_L \cdot L = C \qquad [20.3]$$

Dividing Equation 20.1 by Equation 20.2 yields

$$\frac{Q_K}{Q_L} = \frac{p_K}{p_L}$$

That is, the ratio of the marginal products, which is -1 times the MRS, is equal to the ratio of the factor prices, which is -1 times the slope of the isocost line. (p. 197)

21. Marginal revenue is mathematically the derivative of total revenue with respect to output, dTR/dQ. Incremental revenue is $\Delta TR/\Delta Q$. However, the term *marginal revenue* is used loosely to refer to both concepts. (p. 205)

22. For notes 22 through 24, it is helpful first to define some terms. Let

$$\pi_n = TR_n - TC_n$$

where π_n is the profit when Q_n units are sold.

If the firm is maximizing its profits by producing Q_n units, its profits must be at least as large as the profits at output zero.

That is,

$$\pi_n \geq \pi_0 \qquad [22.1]$$

This condition says that profits from producing must be greater than profits from not producing. Condition 22.1 can be rewritten as

$$TR_n - TVC_n - TFC_n$$
$$\geq TR_0 - TVC_0 - TFC_0 \qquad [22.2]$$

However, note that by definition

$$TR_0 = 0 \qquad [22.3]$$
$$TVC_0 = 0 \qquad [22.4]$$
$$TFC_n = TFC_0 = Z \qquad [22.5]$$

where Z is a constant. By substituting Equations 22.3, 22.4, and Equation 22.5 into Condition 22.2, we get

$$TR_n - TVC_n \geq 0$$

from which we obtain

$$TR_n \geq TVC_n$$

This proves Rule 1.

On a per-unit basis, it becomes

$$\frac{TR_n}{Q_n} \geq \frac{TVC_n}{Q_n} \qquad [22.6]$$

where Q_n is the number of units produced.

Because $TR_n = Q_n \times p_n$, where p_n is the price when n units are sold, Condition 22.6 may be rewritten as

$$p_n \geq AVC_n$$

(p. 207)

23. Using elementary calculus, we may prove Rule 2.

$$\pi_n = TR_n - TC_n$$

each of which is a function of output Q. To maximize π, it is necessary that

$$\frac{d\pi}{dQ} = 0 \qquad [23.1]$$

and that

$$\frac{d^2\pi}{dQ^2} < 0 \qquad [23.2]$$

From the definitions,

$$\frac{d\pi}{dQ} = \frac{dTR}{dQ} - \frac{dTC}{dQ} = MR - MC \quad [23.3]$$

From Equations 23.1 and 23.3, a necessary condition for attaining maximum π is $MR - MC = 0$, or $MR = MC$, as is required by Rule 2. (p. 208)

24. To prove that for a negatively sloped demand curve, marginal revenue is less than price, let $p = p(Q)$. Then

$$TR = p \cdot Q = p(Q) \cdot Q$$

$$MR = \frac{dTR}{dQ} = Q \cdot \frac{dp}{dQ} + p$$

For a negatively sloped demand curve, dp/dQ is negative, and thus MR is less than price for positive values of Q. (p. 229)

25. The equation for a downward-sloping straight-line demand curve with price on the vertical axis is

$$p = a - b \cdot Q$$

where a is the vertical intercept (when $Q=0$) and $-b$ is the slope of the demand curve. Total revenue is price times quantity:

$$TR = p \cdot Q = a \cdot Q - b \cdot Q^2$$

Marginal revenue is

$$MR = \frac{dTR}{dQ} = a - 2 \cdot b \cdot Q$$

Thus, the MR curve and the demand curve are both straight lines, they have the same vertical intercept (a), and the (absolute value of the) slope of the MR curve ($2b$) is twice that of the demand curve (b). (p. 230)

26. The marginal revenue produced by the factor involves two elements: first, the additional output that an extra unit of the factor produces and, second, the change in price of the product that the extra output causes. Let Q be output, R revenue, and L the number of units of the variable factor hired. The contribution to revenue of additional labour is $\partial R/\partial L$. This, in turn, depends on the contribution of the extra labour to output $\partial Q/\partial L$ (the marginal product of the factor) and $\partial R/\partial Q$ (the firm's marginal revenue from the extra output). Thus,

$$\frac{\partial R}{\partial L} = \frac{\partial Q}{\partial L} \cdot \frac{\partial R}{\partial Q}$$

We define the left-hand side as marginal revenue product, MRP. Thus,

$$MRP = MP \cdot MR$$

(p. 311)

27. The proposition that the marginal labour cost is above the average labour cost when the average is rising is essentially the same mathematical proposition proved in note 15. Nevertheless, let us do it again, using elementary calculus.

The quantity of labour supplied depends on the wage rate: $L^s = f(w)$. Total labour cost along the supply curve is $w \cdot L^s$. The average cost of labour is $(w \cdot L^s)/L^s = w$. The marginal cost of labour is

$$\frac{d(w \cdot L^s)}{dL^s} = w + L^s \cdot \frac{dw}{dL^s}$$

Rewrite this as

$$MC = AC + L^s \cdot \frac{dw}{dL^s}$$

As long as the supply curve slopes upward, $dw/dL^s > 0$; therefore, $MC > AC$. (p. 345)

28. In the text, we define MPC as an incremental ratio. For mathematical treatment, it is sometimes convenient to define all marginal concepts as derivatives: $MPC = dC/dY_D$, $MPS = dS/dY_D$, and so on. (p. 524)

29. The basic relationship is

$$Y_D = C + S$$

Dividing through by Y_D yields

$$\frac{Y_D}{Y_D} = \frac{C}{Y_D} + \frac{S}{Y_D}$$

and thus

$$1 = APC + APS$$

Next, take the first difference of the basic relationship to get

$$\Delta Y_D = \Delta C + \Delta S$$

Dividing through by ΔY_D gives

$$\frac{\Delta Y_D}{\Delta Y_D} = \frac{\Delta C}{\Delta Y_D} + \frac{\Delta S}{\Delta Y_D}$$

and thus

$$1 = MPC + MPS$$

(p. 525)

30. The total expenditure over all rounds is the sum of an infinite series. If we let A stand for autonomous expenditure and z for the marginal propensity to spend, the change in autonomous expenditure is ΔA in the first round, $z \cdot \Delta A$ in the second, $z^2 \cdot \Delta A$ in the third, and so on. This can be written as

$$\Delta A \cdot (1 + z + z^2 + \ldots + z^n)$$

If z is less than 1, the series in parentheses converges to $1/(1 - z)$ as n approaches infinity. The total change in expenditure is thus $\Delta A/(1 - z)$. In the example in the box, $z = 0.80$; therefore, the change in total expenditure is

$$\frac{\Delta A}{1 - z} = \frac{\Delta A}{0.2} = 5 \cdot \Delta A$$

(p. 538)

31. The "rule of 72" says that any sum growing at the rate of X percent per year will double in approximately $72/X$ years. For two sums growing at the rates of X percent and Y percent per year, the *difference* between the two sums will double in approximately $72/(X - Y)$ years. The rule of 72 is only an approximation, but at low annual rates of growth it is extremely accurate. (pp. 622, 634)

32. A simple example of a production function is $GDP = z(LK)^{\frac{1}{2}}$. This equation says that to find the amount of GDP produced, multiply the amount of labour by the amount of capital, take the square root, and multiply the result by the constant z. This production function has positive but diminishing marginal returns to either factor. This can be seen by evaluating the first and second partial derivatives and showing the first derivatives to be positive and the second derivatives to be negative.

For example,

$$\frac{\partial GDP}{\partial K} = \frac{z \cdot L^{1/2}}{2 \cdot K^{1/2}} > 0$$

and

$$\frac{\partial^2 GDP}{\partial K^2} = -\frac{z \cdot L^{1/2}}{4 \cdot K^{3/2}} < 0$$

(p. 644)

33. The production function $GDP = z(LK)^{1/2}$ displays constant returns to scale. To see this, multiply both L and K by the same constant, θ, and see that this multiplies the whole value of GDP by θ:

$$z(\theta L \cdot \theta K)^{1/2} = z(\theta^2 \cdot LK)^{1/2} = \theta z(LK)^{1/2} = \theta \cdot GDP$$

(p. 646)

34. This is easily proved. The banking system wants sufficient deposits (D) to establish the target ratio

(v) of deposits to reserves (R). This gives $R/D = v$. Any change in D of size ΔD has to be accompanied by a change in R of ΔR of sufficient size to restore v. Thus, $\Delta R/\Delta D = v$, so $\Delta D = \Delta R/v$ and $\Delta D/\Delta R = 1/v$. This can be shown also in terms of the deposits created by the sequence in Table 27-7. Let v be the reserve ratio and $e = 1 - v$ be the excess reserves per dollar of new deposits. If X dollars are initially deposited in the system, the successive rounds of new deposits will be $X, eX, e^2X, e^3X, \ldots$. The series

$$X + eX + e^2X + e^3X + \ldots$$
$$= X \cdot [1 + e + e^2 + e^3 + \ldots]$$

has a limit of $X \cdot \dfrac{1}{1 - e}$

$$= X \cdot \frac{1}{1 - (1 - v)} = \frac{X}{v}$$

This is the total new deposits created by an injection of $X of new reserves into the banking system. For example, when $v = 0.20$, an injection of $100 into the system will lead to an overall increase in deposits of $500. (p. 681)

35. Suppose that the public wants to hold a fraction, c, of deposits in cash, C. Now suppose that X dollars are injected into the system. Ultimately, this money will be held either as reserves by the banking system or as cash by the public. Thus, we have

$$\Delta C + \Delta R = X$$

From the banking system's reserve behaviour, we have $\Delta R = v \cdot \Delta D$, and from the public's cash behaviour, we have $\Delta C = c \cdot \Delta D$. Substituting into the above equation, we get the result that

$$\Delta D = \frac{X}{v + c}$$

From this we can also relate the change in reserves and the change in cash holdings to the initial injection:

$$\Delta R = \frac{v}{v + c} \cdot X$$
$$\Delta C = \frac{c}{v + c} \cdot X$$

For example, when $v = 0.20$ and $c = 0.05$, an injection of $100 will lead to an increase in reserves of $80, an increase in cash in the hands of the public of $20, and an increase in deposits of $400. (p. 682)

36. Let d be the government's debt-to-GDP ratio and let Δd be the annual change in d. The percentage change in d over the year is therefore $\Delta d/d$, which for small percentage changes is very closely approximated by

$$\Delta d/d = \Delta D/D - \Delta GDP/GDP$$

where ΔD is the budget deficit and is equal to $G - T + iD$. The second term is the percentage change in *nominal* GDP, which is approximately equal to $g + n$, where g is the growth rate of real GDP and π is the rate of inflation. We therefore rewrite the expression as

$$\Delta d/d = (G - T + iD)/D - (g + \pi)$$

Now, multiply both sides by d to get:

$$\Delta d = (G - T + iD)/GDP - (g + \pi)d$$

We can now let x be the primary budget deficit $(G - T)$ as a share of GDP. The equation then becomes

$$\Delta d = x + (i - \pi - g)d$$

Finally, note that the real interest rate on government bonds is $r = i - \pi$, and so our final equation becomes

$$\Delta d = x + (r - g)d$$

(p. 809)

Photo Credits

Timeline of Great Economists

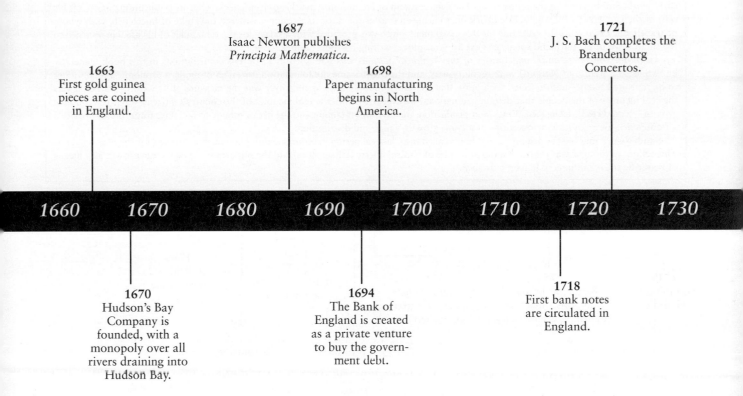

1663
First gold guinea
pieces are coined
in England.

1687
Isaac Newton publishes
Principia Mathematica.

1698
Paper manufacturing
begins in North
America.

1721
J. S. Bach completes the
Brandenburg
Concertos.

1660 1670 1680 1690 1700 1710 1720 1730

1670
Hudson's Bay
Company is
founded, with a
monopoly over all
rivers draining into
Hudson Bay.

1694
The Bank of
England is created
as a private venture
to buy the govern-
ment debt.

1718
First bank notes
are circulated in
England.

ADAM SMITH   *(1723–1790)*

Adam Smith was born in 1723 in the small Scottish town of Kirkcaldy. He is perhaps the single most influential figure in the development of modern economics, and even those who have never studied economics know of his most famous work, *The Wealth of Nations,* and are familiar with the terms *laissez-faire* and the *invisible hand,* both attributable to Smith. He described the workings of the capitalist market economy, the division of labour in production, the role of money, free trade, and the nature of economic growth. Even today, the breadth of his scholarship is considered astounding.

Smith was raised by his mother, as his father had died before his birth. His intellectual promise was discovered early, and at age 14 Smith was sent to study at Glasgow and then at Oxford. He returned to an appointment as professor of moral philosophy at University of Glasgow, where he became one of the leading philosophers of his day. He lectured on natural theology, ethics, jurisprudence, and political economy to students who travelled from as far away as Russia to hear his lectures.

In 1759, Smith published *The Theory of Moral Sentiments,* in which he attempted to identify the origins of moral judgment. In this early work, Smith writes of the motivation of self-interest and of the morality that keeps it in check. After its publication, Smith left his post at the University of Glasgow to embark on a European tour as the tutor to a young aristocrat, the Duke of Buccleuch, with whom he travelled for two years. In exchange for this assignment Smith was provided with a salary for the remainder of his life. He returned to the small town of his birth and spent the next 10 years alone, writing his most famous work.

An Inquiry into the Nature and Causes of the Wealth of Nations was published in 1776. His contributions in this book (generally known as *The Wealth of Nations*) were revolutionary, and the text became the foundation for much of modern economics. It continues to be reprinted today. Smith rejected the notion that a country's supply of gold and silver was the measure of its wealth—rather, it was the real incomes of the people that determined national wealth. Growth in the real incomes of the country's citizens—that is, economic growth—would result from specialization in production, the division of labour, and the use of money to facilitate trade. Smith provided a framework for analyzing the questions of income growth, value, and distribution.

Smith's work marked the beginning of what is called the Classical period in economic thought, which continued for the next 75 years. This school of thought was centred on the principles of natural liberty (laissez-faire) and the importance of economic growth as a means of bettering the conditions of human existence.

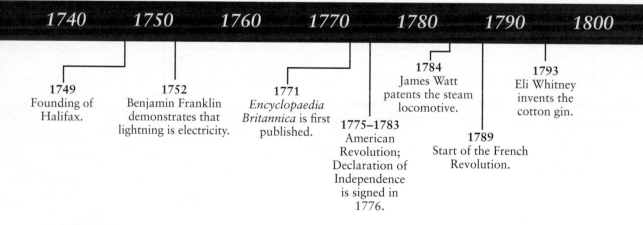

| 1740 | 1750 | 1760 | 1770 | 1780 | 1790 | 1800 |

1749
Founding of Halifax.

1752
Benjamin Franklin demonstrates that lightning is electricity.

1771
Encyclopaedia Britannica is first published.

1775–1783
American Revolution; Declaration of Independence is signed in 1776.

1784
James Watt patents the steam locomotive.

1789
Start of the French Revolution.

1793
Eli Whitney invents the cotton gin.

THOMAS MALTHUS   *(1766–1834)*

Thomas Malthus was born into a reasonably well-to-do English family. He was educated at Cambridge, and from 1805 until his death he held the first British professorship of political economy in the East India Company's college at Haileybury. In 1798 he published *An Essay on the Principle of Population as It Affects the Future Improvement of Society,* which was revised many times in subsequent years until finally he published *A Summary View of the Principle of Population* in 1830.

It is these essays on population for which Malthus is best known. His first proposition was that population, when unchecked, would increase in a geometric progression such that the population would double every 25 years. His second proposition was that the means of subsistence (i.e., the food supply) cannot possibly increase faster than in arithmetic progression (increasing by a given number of units every year). The result would be population growth eventually outstripping food production, and thus abject poverty and suffering for the majority of people in every society.

Malthus's population theory had tremendous intellectual influence at the time and became an integral part of the Classical theory of income distribution. However, it is no longer taken as a good description of current or past trends.

DAVID RICARDO   *(1772–1823)*

David Ricardo was born in London to parents who had emigrated from the Netherlands. Ricardo's father was very successful in money markets, and Ricardo himself was very wealthy before he was 30 by earning money on the stock exchange. He had little formal education, but after reading Adam Smith's *The Wealth of Nations* in 1799, he chose to divide his time between studying and writing about political economy and increasing his own personal wealth.

Ricardo's place in the history of economics was assured by his achievement in constructing an abstract model of how capitalism worked. He built an analytic "system" using deductive reasoning that characterizes economic theorizing to the present day. The three critical principles in Ricardo's system were (1) the theory of rent, (2) Thomas Malthus's population principle, and (3) the wages-fund doctrine. Ricardo published *The Principles of Political Economy and Taxation* in 1817, and the work dominated Classical economics for the following half-century.

Ricardo also contributed the concept of comparative advantage to the study of international trade. Ricardo's theories regarding the gains from trade had some influence on the repeal of the British Corn Laws in 1846—tariffs on the importation of grains into Great Britain—and the subsequent transformation of that country during the nineteenth century from a country of high tariffs to one of completely free trade.

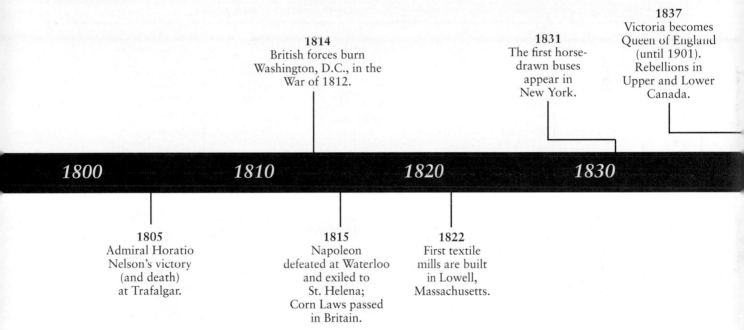

1837
Victoria becomes
Queen of England
(until 1901).
Rebellions in
Upper and Lower
Canada.

1831
The first horse-
drawn buses
appear in
New York.

1814
British forces burn
Washington, D.C., in the
War of 1812.

1800   **1810**   **1820**   **1830**

1805
Admiral Horatio
Nelson's victory
(and death)
at Trafalgar.

1815
Napoleon
defeated at Waterloo
and exiled to
St. Helena;
Corn Laws passed
in Britain.

1822
First textile
mills are built
in Lowell,
Massachusetts.

JOHN STUART MILL   *(1806–1873)*

John Stuart Mill, born in London, was the son of James Mill, a prominent British historian, economist, and philosopher. By age 12 he was acquainted with the major economics works of the day, and at 13 he was correcting the proofs of his father's book, *Elements of Political Economy*. J. S. Mill spent most of his life working at the East India Company—his extraordinarily prolific writing career was conducted entirely as an aside. In 1848 he published his *Principles of Political Economy*, which updated the principles found in Adam Smith's *The Wealth of Nations* and which remained the basic textbook for students of economics until the end of the nineteenth century. In *Principles*, Mill made an important contribution to the economics discipline by distinguishing between the economics of production and of distribution. He pointed out that economic laws had nothing to do with the distribution of wealth, which was a societal matter, but had everything to do with production.

Previous to Mill's *Principles* was his *System of Logic* (1843), which was the century's most influential text on logic and the theory of knowledge. His essays on ethics, contemporary culture, and freedom of speech, such as *Utilitarianism* and *On Liberty*, are still widely studied today.

KARL MARX *(1818–1883)*

Karl Marx was born in Trier, Germany (then part of Prussia), and studied law, history, and philosophy at the universities of Bonn, Berlin, and Jena. Marx travelled between Prussia, Paris, and Brussels, working at various jobs until finally settling in London in 1849, where he lived the remainder of his life. Most of his time was spent in the mainly unpaid pursuits of writing and studying economics in the library of the British Museum. Marx's contributions to economics are intricately bound to his views of history and society. *The Communist Manifesto* was published with Friedrich Engels in 1848, his *Critique of Political Economy* was published in 1859, and in 1867 the first volume of *Das Kapital* was completed. (The remaining volumes, edited by Engels, were published after Marx's death.)

For Marx, capitalism was a stage in an evolutionary process from a primitive agricultural economy toward an inevitable elimination of private property and the class structure. Marx's "labour theory of value," whereby the quantity of labour used in the manufacture of a product determined its value, held the central place in his economic thought. He believed that the worker provided "surplus value" to the capitalist. The capitalist would then use the profit arising from this surplus value to reinvest in plant and machinery. Through time, more would be spent for plant and machinery than for wages, which would lead to lower profits (since profits arose only from the surplus value from labour) and a resulting squeeze in the real income of workers. Marx believed that in the capitalists' effort to maintain profits in this unstable system, there would emerge a "reserve army of the unemployed." The resulting class conflict would become increasingly acute until revolution by the workers would overthrow capitalism.

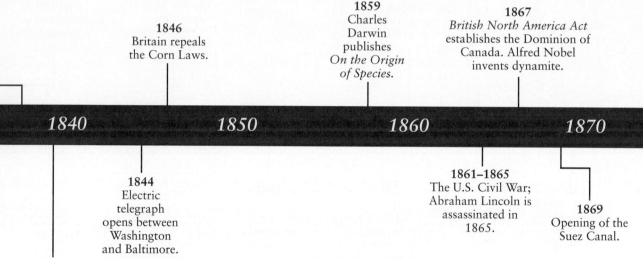

1846 Britain repeals the Corn Laws.

1859 Charles Darwin publishes *On the Origin of Species.*

1867 *British North America Act* establishes the Dominion of Canada. Alfred Nobel invents dynamite.

1840   **1850**   **1860**   **1870**

1844 Electric telegraph opens between Washington and Baltimore.

1861–1865 The U.S. Civil War; Abraham Lincoln is assassinated in 1865.

1869 Opening of the Suez Canal.

1840 *Act of Union* unites Upper and Lower Canada.

LEON WALRAS *(1834–1910)*

Leon Walras was born in France, the son of an economist. After being trained inauspiciously in engineering and performing poorly in mathematics, Walras spent some time pursuing other endeavours, such as novel writing and working for the railway. Eventually he promised his father he would study economics, and by 1870 he was given a professorship in economics in the Faculty of Law at the University of Lausanne in Switzerland. Once there, Walras began the feverish activity that eventually led to his important contributions to economic theory.

In the 1870s, Walras was one of three economists to put forward the marginal utility theory of value (simultaneously with William Stanley Jevons of England and Carl Menger of Austria). Further, he constructed a mathematical model of general equilibrium using a system of simultaneous equations that he used to argue that equilibrium prices and quantities are uniquely determined. Central to general equilibrium analysis is the notion that the prices and quantities of all commodities are determined simultaneously because the whole system is interdependent. Walras's most important work was *Elements of Pure Economics,* published in 1874. In addition to all of Walras's other accomplishments in economics (and despite his early poor performance in mathematics!), we today regard him as the founder of mathematical economics.

Leon Walras and Alfred Marshall are regarded by many economists as the two most important economic theorists who ever lived. Much of the framework of economic theory studied today is either Walrasian or Marshallian in character.

CARL MENGER   *(1840–1921)*

Carl Menger was born in Galicia (then part of Austria), and he came from a family of Austrian civil servants and army officers. After studying law in Prague and Vienna, he turned to economics and in 1871 published *Grundsatze der Volkswirtschaftslehre* (translated as *Principles of Economics*), for which he became famous. He held a professorship at the University of Vienna until 1903. Menger was the founder of a school of thought known as the "Austrian School," which effectively displaced the German historical method on the continent and which survives today as an alternative to mainstream Neoclassical economics.

Menger was one of three economists in the 1870s who independently put forward a theory of value based on marginal utility. Prior to what economists now call the "marginal revolution," value was thought to be derived solely from the inputs of labour and capital. Menger developed the marginal utility theory of value, in which the value of any good is determined by individuals' subjective evaluations of that good. According to Menger, a good has some value if it has the ability to satisfy some human want or desire, and *utility* is the capacity of the good to do so. Menger went on to develop the idea that the individual will maximize total utility at the point where the last unit of each good consumed provides equal utility—that is, where marginal utilities are equal.

Menger's emphasis on the marginal utility theory of value led him to focus on consumption rather than production as the determinant of price. Menger focused only on the demand for goods and largely ignored the supply. It would remain for Alfred Marshall and Leon Walras to combine demand and supply for a more complete picture of price determination.

1871
The Great Fire destroys much of Chicago.

1876
Alexander Graham Bell founds Bell Telephone Co.

1880
Thomas Edison invents the electric light bulb.

1885
The last spike is driven on the Canadian Pacific Railway. Louis Riel is hanged.

1870   *1875*   *1880*   *1885*

ALFRED MARSHALL   *(1842–1924)*

Alfred Marshall was born in Clapham, England, the son of a bank cashier, and was descended from a long line of clerics. Marshall's father, despite intense effort, was unable to steer the young Marshall into the church. Instead, Marshall followed his passion for mathematics at Cambridge and chose economics as a field of study after reading J. S. Mill's *Principles of Political Economy*. His career was then spent mainly at Cambridge, where he taught economics to John Maynard Keynes, Arthur Pigou, Joan Robinson, and countless other British theorists in the "Cambridge tradition." His *Principles of Economics,* published in 1890, replaced Mill's *Principles* as the dominant economics textbook of English-speaking universities.

Marshall institutionalized modern marginal analysis, the basic concepts of supply and demand, and perhaps most importantly the notion of economic equilibrium resulting from the interaction of supply and demand. He also pioneered partial equilibrium analysis—examining the forces of supply and demand in a particular market provided that all other influences can be excluded, *ceteris paribus.*

Although many of the ideas had been put forward by earlier writers, Marshall was able to synthesize the previous analyses of utility and cost and present a thorough and complete statement of the laws of demand and supply. Marshall refined and developed microeconomic theory to such a degree that much of what he wrote would be familiar to students of this textbook today.

It is also interesting to note that although Alfred Marshall and Leon Walras were simultaneously expanding the frontiers of economic theory, there was almost no communication between the two men. Though Marshall chose partial equilibrium analysis as the appropriate method for dealing with selected markets in a complex world, he did acknowledge the correctness of Walras's general equilibrium system. Walras, on the other hand, was adamant (and sometimes rude) in his opposition to the methods that Marshall was putting forward. History has shown that both the partial and the general equilibrium approaches to economic analysis are required for understanding the functioning of the economy.

THORSTEIN VEBLEN *(1857–1929)*

Thorstein Veblen was born on a farm in Wisconsin to Norwegian parents. He received his Ph.D. in philosophy from Yale University, after which he returned to his father's farm because he was unable to secure an academic position. For seven years he remained there, reading voraciously on economics and other social sciences. Eventually, he took academic positions at the University of Chicago, Stanford University, the University of Missouri, and the New School for Social Research (in New York). Veblen was the founder of "institutional economics," the only uniquely North American school of economic thought.

In 1899, Veblen published *The Theory of the Leisure Class,* in which he sought to apply Charles Darwin's evolutionism to the study of modern economic life. He examined problems in the social institutions of the day, and savagely criticized Classical and Neoclassical economic analysis. Although Veblen failed to shift the path of mainstream economic analysis, he did contribute the idea of the importance of long-run institutional studies as a useful complement to short-run price theory analysis. He also reminded the profession that economics is a *social* science, and not merely a branch of mathematics.

Veblen remains most famous today for his idea of "conspicuous consumption." He observed that some commodities were consumed not for their intrinsic qualities but because they carried snob appeal. He suggested that the more expensive such a commodity became, the greater might be its ability to confer status on its purchaser.

1896 First modern Olympic Games are held in Athens. Klondike Gold Rush begins.

1900 J. P. Morgan buys out Andrew Carnegie, forming the biggest business in the world, U.S. Steel.

1890   **1895**   **1900**   **1905**

1889 Gustave Eiffel designs the Eiffel Tower for the Paris World Exposition.

1898 Spanish-American War.

1903 The Wright Brothers' first successful flight.

VILFREDO PARETO *(1848–1923)*

Vilfredo Pareto was an Italian, born in Paris, and was trained to be an engineer. Though he actually practised as an engineer, he would later succeed Leon Walras to the Chair of Economics in the Faculty of Law at the University of Lausanne.

Pareto built on the system of general equilibrium that Walras had developed. In his *Cours d'économie politique* (1897) and his *Manuel d'économie politique* (1906), Pareto set forth the foundations of modern welfare economics. He showed that theories of consumer behaviour and exchange could be constructed on assumptions of ordinal utility, rather than cardinal utility, eliminating the need to compare one person's utility with another's. Using the indifference curve analysis developed by F. Y. Edgeworth, Pareto was able to demonstrate that total welfare could be increased by an exchange if one person could be made better off without anyone else becoming worse off. Pareto applied this analysis to consumption and exchange as well as to production. Pareto's contributions in this area are remembered in economists' references to *Pareto optimality* and *Pareto efficiency.*

JOSEPH SCHUMPETER   *(1883–1950)*

Joseph Schumpeter was born in Triesch, Moravia (now in the Czech Republic). He was a university professor and later a minister of finance in Austria. In 1932, he emigrated to the United States to avoid the rise to power of Adolf Hitler. He spent his remaining years at Harvard University.

Schumpeter, a pioneering theorist of innovation, emphasized the role of the entrepreneur in economic development. The existence of the entrepreneur meant continuous innovation and waves of adaptation to changing technology. He is best known for his theory of "creative destruction," where the prospect of monopoly profits provides owners the incentive to finance inventions and innovations. One monopoly can replace another with superior technology or a superior product, thereby circumventing the entry barriers of a monopolized industry. He criticized mainstream economists for emphasizing the static (allocative) efficiency of perfect competition—a market structure that would, if it could ever be achieved, retard technological change and economic growth.

Schumpeter's best known works are *The Theory of Economic Development* (1911), *Business Cycles* (1939), and *Capitalism, Socialism and Democracy* (1943).

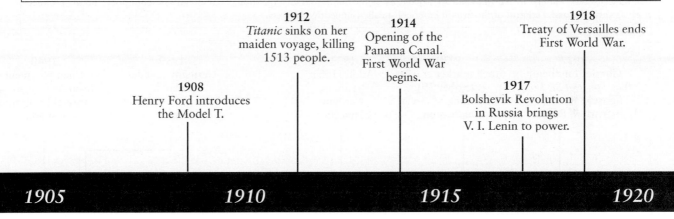

1908
Henry Ford introduces
the Model T.

1912
Titanic sinks on her
maiden voyage, killing
1513 people.

1914
Opening of the
Panama Canal.
First World War
begins.

1917
Bolshevik Revolution
in Russia brings
V. I. Lenin to power.

1918
Treaty of Versailles ends
First World War.

1905   1910   1915   1920

JOHN MAYNARD KEYNES   *(1883–1946)*

John Maynard Keynes was born in Cambridge, England. His parents were both intellectuals, and his father, John Neville Keynes, was a famous logician and writer on economic methodology. The young Keynes was educated at Eton and then at Kings College, Cambridge, where he was a student of Alfred Marshall and Arthur Pigou. His career included appointments to the Treasury in Britain during both world wars, a leading role in the establishment of the International Monetary Fund (through discussions at Bretton Woods, New Hampshire, in 1944), and editorship of the *Economic Journal* from 1911 to 1945, all in addition to his academic position at Kings College.

Keynes published extensively during his life, but his most influential work, *The General Theory of Employment, Interest, and Money,* appeared in 1936. This book was published in the midst of the Great Depression when the output of goods and services had fallen drastically, unemployment was intolerably high, and it had become clear to many that the market would not self-adjust to achieve potential output within an acceptable period of time. Fluctuations in economic activity were familiar at this point, but the failure of the economy to recover rapidly from this depression was unprecedented. Neoclassical economists held that during a downturn both wages and the interest rate would fall low enough to induce investment and employment and bring about a recovery. They believed that the persistent unemployment during the 1930s was caused by inflexible wages and they recommended that workers be convinced to accept wage cuts.

Keynes believed that this policy, though perhaps correct for a single industry, was not correct for the entire economy. Widespread wage cuts would reduce the consumption portion of aggregate demand, which would offset any increase in employment. Keynes argued that unemployment could be cured only by manipulating aggregate demand, whereby increased demand (through government expenditure) would increase the price level, reduce real wages, and thereby stimulate employment.

Keynes's views found acceptance after the publication of his *General Theory* and had a profound effect on government policy around the world, particularly in the 1940s, 1950s, and 1960s. As we know from this textbook, Keynes's name is associated with much of macroeconomics, from its basic theory to the Keynesian short-run aggregate supply curve and the Keynesian consumption function. His contributions to economics go well beyond what can be mentioned in a few paragraphs—in effect, he laid the foundations for modern macroeconomics.

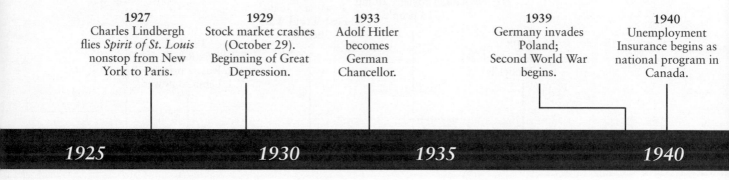

EDWARD CHAMBERLIN   *(1899–1967)*

Edward Chamberlin was born in La Conner, Washington, and received his Ph.D. from Harvard University in 1927. He became a full professor at Harvard in 1937 and stayed there until his retirement in 1966. He published *The Theory of Monopolistic Competition* in 1933.

Before Chamberlin's book (which appeared more or less simultaneously with Joan Robinson's *The Economics of Imperfect Competition*), the models of perfect competition and monopoly had been fairly well worked out. Though economists were aware of a middle ground between these two market structures and some analysis of duopoly (two sellers) had been presented, it was Chamberlin and Robinson who closely examined this problem of imperfect markets.

Chamberlin's main contribution was explaining the importance of product differentiation for firms in market structures between perfect competition and monopoly. Chamberlin saw that though there may be a large number of firms in the market (the competitive element), each firm created for itself a unique product or advantage that gave it some control over price (the monopoly element). Specifically, he identified items such as copyrights, trademarks, brand names, and location as monopoly elements behind a product. Though Alfred Marshall regarded price as the only variable in question, Chamberlin saw both price and the product itself as variables under control of the firm in monopolistically competitive markets.

1927
Charles Lindbergh flies *Spirit of St. Louis* nonstop from New York to Paris.

1929
Stock market crashes (October 29). Beginning of Great Depression.

1933
Adolf Hitler becomes German Chancellor.

1939
Germany invades Poland; Second World War begins.

1940
Unemployment Insurance begins as national program in Canada.

1925   1930   1935   1940

1922
The Soviet Union is formed; Joseph Stalin named Secretary General of the Communist Party.

FRIEDRICH AUGUST VON HAYEK   *(1899–1992)*

Friedrich von Hayek was born in Vienna and studied at the University of Vienna, where he was trained in the Austrian tradition of economics (a school of thought originating with Carl Menger). He held academic positions at the London School of Economics and the University of Chicago. He returned to Europe in 1962 to the University of Freiburg in what was then West Germany and the University of Salzburg in Austria. He was awarded the Nobel Prize in Economics in 1974.

Hayek contributed new ideas and theories in many different areas of economics, but he is perhaps best known for his general conception of economics as a "coordination problem." His observation of market economies suggested that the relative prices determined in free markets provided the signals that allowed the actions of all decision makers to mesh—even though there was no formal planning taking place to coordinate these actions. He emphasized this "spontaneous order" at work in the economy as the subject matter for economics. The role of knowledge and information in the market process became central to Hayek, an idea that has grown in importance to the economics profession over the years.

Hayek's theory of business cycles provided an example of the breakdown of this coordination. A monetary disturbance (e.g., an increase in the money supply) would distort the signals (relative prices) by artificially raising the return to certain types of economic activity. When the disturbance disappeared, the boom caused by these distorted signals would be followed by a slump. Although Hayek's business-cycle theory was eclipsed by the Keynesian revolution, his emphasis on economics as a coordination problem has had a major influence on contemporary economic thought.

Hayek was also prominent in advocating the virtues of free markets as contributing to human freedom in the broad sense as well as to economic efficiency in the narrow sense. His *The Road to Serfdom* (1944) sounded an alarm about the political and economic implications of the then-growing belief in the virtues of central planning. His *Constitution of Liberty* (1960) is a much deeper philosophical analysis of the forces, economic and otherwise, that contribute to the liberty of the individual.

MILTON FRIEDMAN   *(1912–2006)*

Milton Friedman completed graduate studies in economics at the University of Chicago and at Columbia University, where he received his Ph.D. in 1946. Most of Friedman's academic career was spent as a professor at the University of Chicago, and after retiring in 1977 he was a senior research fellow at the Hoover Institution at Stanford University. Friedman is best known as one of the leading proponents of Monetarism and for his belief in the power of free markets. His work greatly influenced modern macroeconomics.

Friedman made his first significant mark on the profession with the publication of *The Theory of the Consumption Function* in 1957. There he developed the permanent income hypothesis and argued that consumption depends on long-run average income rather than current disposable income, as it does in Keynesian analysis. This was an early example of a macroeconomic theory that emphasized the importance of forward-looking consumers. In 1963, he co-authored with Anna Schwartz his most influential book, *A Monetary History of the United States, 1867–1960,* where they presented evidence in support of the Monetarist view that changes in the supply of money can cause dramatic fluctuations in the level of economic activity. Although this view was seriously challenged by subsequent research, Friedman helped the profession to understand the power of and the limitations of monetary policy.

Capitalism and Freedom (1962) and *Free to Choose* (1980), the latter co-written with his wife, Rose Friedman, are part of Friedman's attempts to communicate his ideas about economics and, in particular, the power of the free market, to a mass audience of non-economists. Both books became international bestsellers, and these books, in addition to his writing for newspapers and magazines, made Milton Friedman one of the most famous modern economists. He was awarded the Nobel Prize in Economics in 1976.

1941
United States enters war after the attack on Pearl Harbor (December 7).

1944
Bretton Woods Conference. IMF and World Bank are created.

1945
United States drops atomic bomb on Japan; Second World War ends.

1949
Mao Tse-tung's communists gain control of China.

1957
Treaty of Rome establishes the European Common Market.

1940   *1945*   *1950*   *1955*

JOHN KENNETH GALBRAITH   *(1908–2006)*

John Kenneth Galbraith was born on a farm in southeastern Ontario, to a family of Scottish-Canadian farmers. He began his undergraduate education at the Ontario Agricultural College in Guelph in 1926, where he studied agricultural economics and animal husbandry. He moved to California to study at the University of California at Berkeley and completed a Ph.D. in agricultural economics in 1934. Galbraith was hired by Harvard University in 1934 and, aside from his government and diplomatic postings, remained on staff there until his death.

Galbraith was heavily influenced by the ideas of John Maynard Keynes, Thorstein Veblen, and the "institutional" school of economics. He rejected the technical and mathematical approach of Neoclassical economics. Instead he emphasized the interplay of economics, politics, culture, and tradition, a combination that does not lend itself well to mathematical modelling. He was much more of a "political economist" in the style of the nineteenth century than a theoretical economist of the late twentieth century.

His most famous book was *The Affluent Society* (1958), where he argued that the United States had become obsessed with overproducing consumer goods and instead should be making large public investments in highways, education, and other public services. His expression "private opulence and public squalor" became well known, and many would agree is even more relevant today than it was when he wrote the words more than 50 years ago. In a later book, *The New Industrial State* (1967), Galbraith argued that very few U.S. industries fit economists' model of perfect competition, and that the economy was dominated by large, powerful firms. In general, Galbraith continued to write about topics that he believed the economics profession had neglected—topics such as advertising, the separation of corporate ownership and management, oligopoly, and government and military spending.

Because of Galbraith's desire to focus on the interplay of economics, politics, and society, he was often criticized (or ignored) by mainstream economists. But he was undeterred. And while many economists disagreed with his approach and some of his political views, he was widely recognized as a gifted and insightful writer and speaker.

KENNETH ARROW *(b. 1921)*

Kenneth Arrow was born and educated in New York City. He began graduate work at Columbia University and received an M.A. in mathematics in 1941. Over the following 10 years, after Arrow had completed his Ph.D. course work, he served in the U.S. Army Air Corps during World War II and held various research jobs while searching for a dissertation topic. His dissertation, which earned him his Ph.D. from Columbia in 1951, subsequently became a classic in economics, *Social Choice and Individual Values* (1951). Kenneth Arrow is currently professor emeritus at Stanford University.

In his 1951 book, Arrow presented his "Impossibility Theorem," in which he shows that it is not possible to construct a set of voting rules for making public choices that is simultaneously democratic and efficient. This theorem led to decades of work by economists, philosophers, and political scientists in the field of social choice theory.

Arrow also made significant contributions in other areas of economics. In 1954 (with Gerard Debreu) he constructed a mathematical model of an economy with many individual, interrelated markets and proved the existence of a theoretical general market-clearing equilibrium. Arrow's work in the economics of uncertainty was also a major contribution. In *Essays in the Theory of Risk-Bearing* (1971), he introduced the concepts of moral hazard and adverse selection (among other ideas about risk), which we encounter in Chapter 16 of this book. Arrow was one of the first economists to develop the idea of "learning by doing," which has played an important role in modern theories of economic growth.

Arrow was awarded the Nobel Prize in 1972 (jointly with British economist John Hicks) and in 2004 was awarded the National Medal of Science, the United States' highest scientific honour.

1962 Cuban Missile Crisis (October).

1967 Canada celebrates its Centennial; Montreal hosts Expo '67.

1973 First OPEC oil shock.

1960 **1965** **1970** **1975**

1959 St. Lawrence Seaway officially opens.

1963 U.S. President John F. Kennedy assassinated.

1969 Neil Armstrong is first person to walk on the moon.

1975 Bill Gates and Paul Allen found Microsoft Corporation.

PAUL SAMUELSON *(1915–2009)*

Paul Samuelson was born in Gary, Indiana, the son of a drugstore owner. He received his PhD in economics in 1941 from Harvard University and spent his academic career at the Massachusetts Institute of Technology (MIT).

Samuelson is generally regarded as one of the greatest economic theorists of the twentieth century. While still a graduate student at Harvard, Samuelson wrote most of *Foundations of Economic Analysis* (1947), which was path-breaking at the time and used mathematical analysis and constrained optimization techniques to shed insight into economic behaviour. He systematized economic theory into a more rigorous mathematical discipline, which has had enormous effects on the way economics is studied today.

Though Samuelson made major contributions to many branches of economics, three are particularly notable. First, he showed how the central predictions of demand theory could be tested using the "revealed preferences" of consumers from observed market behaviour. Second, in international trade theory, he made important contributions in the analysis of the gains from trade and the effects of tariff protection on the distribution of income. Third, most familiar to readers of this book, he is credited with introducing the 45°-line model of short-run national income determination. This diagram, encountered throughout Chapters 21 and 22 of this book, has become the standard tool for teaching the Keynesian theory of national-income determination in the short run. Samuelson's work also provided valuable insights in other areas of economics, including government taxation and expenditure, capital theory, and theories of economic growth.

Samuelson was also well known for his famous introductory economics textbook, *Economics,* first published in 1948, which provided a systematic treatment of both micro- and macroeconomics in a way that had not been presented before. In general, he is credited with raising the level of scientific and mathematical analysis in economics. Samuelson was awarded the Nobel Prize in Economics in 1970, and was the first American scholar to receive this honour.

Index

Key terms and their page references are in boldface.

Common Abbreviations Used in the Text

Greek Letters	η	(eta)	Elasticity
	Δ	(delta)	Change in

Abbreviations

Microeconomics

ATC	Average Total Cost
AVC	Average Variable Cost
D	Demand
i	Interest Rate
LRAC	Long-Run Average Cost
MC	Marginal Cost
MP	Marginal Product
MR	Marginal Revenue
MRP	Marginal Revenue Product
S	Supply
TC	Total Cost
TR	Total Revenue

Macroeconomics

AD	Aggregate Demand
AS	Aggregate Supply
AE	(Desired) Aggregate Expenditure
C	Aggregate Consumption Expenditure
CPI	Consumer Price Index
G	Government Purchases
GDP	Gross Domestic Product
GNP	Gross National Product
I	Aggregate Investment Expenditure
i	Nominal Interest Rate
IM	Imports of Goods and Services
M_S, M_D	Money Supply/Money Demand
M1, M2, M2+	Measures of Money Supply
P	Price Level
r	Real Interest Rate
S	Private Saving
T	Government Tax Revenue (Net of Transfers)
U	Unemployment Rate
U^*	Natural Rate of Unemployment (NAIRU)
X	Exports of Goods and Services
X-IM or NX	Net Exports of Goods and Services
Y	Real GDP
Y^*	Potential GDP
Y_D	Disposable Income